INHIBITION

AND

LEARNING

Edited by

R. A. BOAKES and M. S. HALLIDAY
Laboratory of Experimental Psychology
University of Sussex,
Sussex, England

1972

ACADEMIC PRESS · LONDON · NEW YORK

ACADEMIC PRESS INC. (LONDON) LTD.
24/28 Oval Road,
London NW1

United States Edition published by
ACADEMIC PRESS INC.
111 Fifth Avenue
New York, New York 10003

Library of Congress Catalog Card Number: 79–185199
ISBN: 0 12 108050 1

PRINTED IN GREAT BRITAIN BY
COX & WYMAN LTD., LONDON, FAKENHAM AND READING

Contributors

A. AMSEL   Department of Psychology, The University of Texas at Austin, Mezes Hall 211, Austin, Texas 78712, U.S.A.

E. A. ASRATIAN   Institute of Higher Nervous Activity and Neurophysiology, U.S.S.R. Academy of Science, Moscow, G–17, Piatnotskaya 48, U.S.S.R.

I. BEALE   Dalhousie University, Halifax, Nova Scotia, Canada

M. E. BITTERMAN   Laboratory of Sensory Science, University of Hawaii, 1993 East–West Road, Honolulu, Hawaii 96822, U.S.A.

C. J. BRIMER   Department of Psychology, Dalhousie University, Halifax, Nova Scotia, Canada

R. A. BOAKES   Laboratory of Experimental Psychology, University of Sussex, Brighton, Sussex, England

A. DICKINSON   Laboratory of Experimental Psychology, University of Sussex, Brighton, Sussex, England

R. J. DOUGLAS   Department of Psychology, University of Washington, Seattle, Washington 98105, U.S.A.

E. GRASTYÁN   Institute of Psychology, University Medical School, Pecs, Hungary

M. S. HALLIDAY   Laboratory of Experimental Psychology, University of Sussex, Brighton, Sussex, England

E. HEARST   Department of Psychology, Indiana University, Bloomington, Indiana 47401, U.S.A.

W. K. HONIG   Department of Psychology, Dalhousie University, Halifax, Nova Scotia, Canada

R. L. ISAACSON   Department of Psychology, University of Florida, Gainesville, Florida 32601, U.S.A.

J. R. ISON   Department of Psychology, University of Rochester, College of Arts and Science, River Campus Station, Rochester, New York 14627, U.S.A.

J. KONORSKI   Department of Neurophysiology, Nencki Institute of Experimental Biology, 3 Pasteur Street, Warsaw 22, Poland

R. V. KRANE   Department of Psychology, University of Rochester, College of Arts and Science, River Campus Station, Rochester, New York 14627, U.S.A.

D. LANDER   Dalhousie University, Halifax, Nova Scotia, Canada

J. S. LITNER   Department of Psychology, Queen's University, Kingston, Ontario, Canada

E. M. MACPHAIL   Laboratory of Experimental Psychology, Universiy oft Sussex, Brighton, Sussex, England

P. MOLNAR   Institute of Physiology, University Medical School, Pecs, Hungary

D. MUIR   Dalhousie University, Halifax, Nova Scotia, Canada

R. A. RESCORLA   Department of Psychology, Yale University, 333 Cedar Street, New Haven, Connecticut 06510, U.S.A.

M. RICHELLE   Institut de Psychologie et des Scences de l'Education, Universitie de Liege, 32 Boulevard de la Constitution, Liege, Belgium

H. S. TERRACE   Department of Psychology, Columbia University, Schemerhorn Hall 360, New York, N.Y. 10027, U.S.A.

E. THOMAS   Department of Psychology, Bryn Mawr College, Bryn Mawr, Pa 19010, U.S.A.

A. M. UTTLEY   Laboratory of Experimental Psychology, University of Sussex, Brighton, Sussex, England

A. R. WAGNER   Department of Psychology, Yale University, 333 Cedar Street, New Haven, Connecticut 06510, U.S.A.

D. M. WARBARTON   Department of Psychology, University of Reading, Building 3, Earley Gate, Whiteknights, Reading, England

R. G. WEISMAN   Department of Psychology, Queen's University, Kingston, Ontario, Canada

Preface

The 1960's saw an increase in the frequency with which the term "inhibition" was used by Western psychologists involved in the study of animal behaviour. This revival of interest in the concept of inhibition arose independently within three rather separate areas of research. In physiological psychology, those working on the behavioural functions of brain mechanisms found that lesions in certain sub-cortical areas produced changes in an animal's behaviour that could best be described as a decrease in capacity to inhibit responding. Quite separately, workers studying operant discrimination learning devised techniques for obtaining inhibitory generalization gradients; interest developed in the origin of these gradients, in their relationship to behavioural contrast and peak shift, and in their implications for theories of discrimination learning. Finally a renewal of interest in classical conditioning among Western psychologists led to theoretical developments, based mainly on the results of research using compound stimuli, in which the concept of inhibition played a major role.

As there appeared to be a wide range of different uses of the term *inhibition* in these separate areas of research we felt that a great deal might be gained from a conference in which psychologists working in these different areas could exchange views, together with psychologists from Eastern Europe where the Pavlovian tradition of interest in inhibition has remained unbroken. There turned out to be an almost embarrassing degree of interest in this idea, with the result that a very large number of papers were presented at the conference, which took place in April 1971 at the University of Sussex.

The contents of this book are based on the proceedings of the conference and the origin of each chapter is a paper that was presented at that time. However, the number and range of conference contributions was much greater than those represented here, and in the task of selecting papers, made necessary for the preparation of a single volume, our choice was governed by the relevance of a paper to problems of inhibition. This has meant, unfortunately, that a number of excellent papers, which were on subjects related to topics discussed in this book but which were less directly related to inhibition, have been excluded.

The chapters have been somewhat arbitrarily divided into four approximately equal sections. These sections are artificial in that they do not define isolated groups of topics: many chapters would be equally appropriate in another section and most chapters make reference to work described in other sections. Nevertheless these sections do represent to some extent clusters of related interests. At the beginning of each section a brief introduction is given to the chapters within it.

Our thanks go to the contributors to this volume for their willing and prompt cooperation and to our colleagues in the Laboratory of Experimental Psychology at the University of Sussex who were never reluctant to provide valuable advice. The conference was made possible by grants from the Society for the Experimental Analysis of Behaviour and the British Council, by the help of Professor N. S. Sutherland who allowed us generous use of laboratory facilities, and by the hard work of Miss Monica Robinson and Miss Susan Ford. Finally we would like to thank our wives for their patient help during the preparation of this book.

JANUARY 1972   R. A. BOAKES
                                                M. S. HALLIDAY

Contents

CONTRIBUTORS v

PREFACE vii

A Inhibition and Instrumental Discrimination Learning

1 Some Persistent Problems in the Analysis of Conditioned Inhibition

E. HEARST

I. Introduction 5
II. The Definition of Conditioned Inhibition 6
III. The Measurement and Detection of Conditioned Inhibition . 11
IV. Problems in the Analysis of Inhibition 17
V. Concluding Comments 34
Acknowledgements 37
References 37

2 Stimulus and Response Reduction: Two Aspects of Inhibitory Control in Learning

W. K. HONIG, I. BEALE, P. SERAGANIAN, D. LANDER and D. MUIR

I. Introduction 41
II. Studies of Negative Gradients and the Peak Shift . . 44
III. Discrimination Performance with the Advance Procedure . 54
IV. General Discussion 64
V. Conclusions 69
Acknowledgements . . . . . ' 69
References 69

3 Discrimination Involving Response-Independent Reinforcement: Implications for Behavioural Contrast

M. S. HALLIDAY and R. A. BOAKES

I. Introduction 73
II. Experiment I: Discrimination Between VI and Free VI
Following Pretraining with Free Reinforcement . . 76

III. Experiment II: Successive Discrimination Between VI and
Free VI without Prior Training 81
IV. Experiment III: Choice Between VI and Free VI . . 86
V. Implications for a Theory of Contrast 92
VI. Conclusion 95
Acknowledgements 96
References 96

4 Conditioned Inhibition in Successive Discrimination Learning

H. S. TERRACE

I. Introduction 99
II. Inhibitory Stimulus Control 101
III. Inhibition as a Stimulus-produced Decrement in Responding 102
IV. Differences in Performance Following Discrimination Learning with and without Errors 105
V. "Active" vs. "Passive" Inhibition 111
VI. Measurement of Active Inhibition 111
VII. The Role of Active Inhibition in Discrimination Learning . 112
VIII. Conclusion 116
Acknowledgements 117
References 117

5 Inhibition in the Acquisition and Reversal of Simultaneous Discriminations

E. M. MACPHAIL

I. Introduction 121
II. Relative Approach Strength to S⁻ Following Acquisition or Reversal of a Simultaneous Discrimination . . . 126
III. Behavioural Contrast in Acquisition and Reversal of a Discrete Trial Simultaneous Discrimination 139
IV. Concluding Comments 150
Acknowledgements 150
References 150

6 Comparative Studies of the Role of Inhibition in Reversal Learning

M. E. BITTERMAN

I. Introduction 153
II. Experiment I: Reversal Learning in Pigeons Under Unitary Conditions 157
III. Experiment II: Reversal Learning in Pigeons Under Unitary Conditions (further data) 161

IV. Experiment III: Reversal Learning in Goldfish Under Unitary
       Conditions   163
V. Experiment IV: Reversal Learning in Goldfish Under Choice
       Conditions   167
VI. Summary and Conclusions   172
Acknowledgements   174
References   174

B Analogues of Pavlovian Inhibition in Instrumental Conditioning

7 Positive Induction in the Extinction of Differential Instrumental Conditioning

J. R. ISON and R. V. KRANE

I. Introduction   181
II. Experiment I: Effects of Trial Spacing During Extinction .   185
III. Experiment II: Inter-Stimulus Interval Effects . . .   188
IV. Experiment III: Effects of Overtraining   192
V. Experiment IV: Avoidance Responses and Goal-box Con-
       finement Time   194
VI. Discussion   197
VII. Conclusions   202
Acknowledgements   203
References   203

8 Disinhibition of an Operant Response

C. J. BRIMER

I. Introduction   205
II. Inhibitory Operations   209
III. Stimulus Parameters   212
IV. Response Inhibition and Disinhibition   218
V. Concluding Remarks   224
Acknowledgements   225
References   225

9 Temporal Regulation of Behaviour and Inhibition

M. RICHELLE

I. Introduction   229
II. Fixed-Interval vs. DRL Schedules: Intraspecific and Inter-
       specific Comparisons   233
III. Extinction in Temporally Regulated Behaviour: a Phenomenon
       of Generalized Inhibition?   237
IV. Concluding Remarks   248
References   249

10   The Role of Pavlovian Events in Avoidance Training

R. G. WEISMAN and J. S. LITNER

    I. Introduction   253

    II. Revised Two-process Theory   254

    III. Pavlovian Events in Discrete-trial Avoidance Learning   .   258

    IV. Avoidance Learning as an Instance of Positive Reinforcement 267

    Acknowledgements   269

    References   269

C   Inhibition and Classical Conditioning

11   Inhibition and Mediation in Classical and Instrumental Learning

A. AMSEL

    I. Introduction   275

    II. Mediation in Instrumental Learning   277

    III. Inhibition in Simple Classical Conditioning   .   .   .   290

    IV. Conclusion   294

    References   297

12   Inhibition in Pavlovian Conditioning: Application of a Theory

A. R. WAGNER and R. A. RESCORLA

    I. Introduction   301

    II. The Model   302

    III. Implications for Inhibition   306

    IV. Basic Data   310

    V. Additional Inhibitory Procedures Involving Nonreinforcement 314

    VI. Inhibitory Procedures Involving Reinforcement .   .   .   320

    VII. Repeated Nonreinforced Presentation of a Stimulus   .   .   325

    VIII. Conclusion   333

    References   334

Appendix: A Simple and Accurate Simulator of the Wagner and Rescorla Equations

A. M. UTTLEY

    I. Circuit Principles   338

    II. Technical Details   338

    III. A Typical Simulation   339

13   Some Ideas Concerning Physiological Mechanisms of so-called Internal Inhibition

J. KONORSKI

    I. Introduction   341

    II. Experimental Data on the Transformations of Excitatory into
        Inhibitory CRs, and Vice Versa   343
   III. A New Theory of Internal Inhibition   347
   IV. The Problem of Motor-act Inhibition   351
    V. Conclusion   353
   VI. Postscript   354
  References   356

14 Excitatory and Inhibitory Processes in Hypothalamic Conditioning

E. THOMAS

     I. Introduction   359
    II. Experiment I   363
   III. Experiment II   371
   IV. General Discussion   376
  Acknowledgements   379
  References   379

15 Genesis and Localization of Conditioned Inhibition

E. A. ASRATIAN

     I. Introduction   381
    II. Localization of Internal Inhibition   382
   III. Mechanism of Internal Inhibition   387
   IV. Conclusion   394
  References   395

D Physiological Mechanisms of Behavioural Inhibition

16 The Significance of Inhibition in Motivation and Reinforcement

P. MOLNÁR and E. GRASTYÁN

     I. Introduction   403
    II. Experiment I: Characteristics of the Locomotor Responses
        Elicited by Electrical Stimulation of the Upper Brain Stem   408
   III. Experiment II: A Dual, Motivating and Sleep-inducing Effect
       of Ipsiversive Stimulation   419
   IV. Experiment III: Behavioural and Electrical Accompaniments
       of the Restraint and Release of an Instrumental Approach
       Reaction   422
    V. Conclusions   425
  Acknowledgements   428
  References   428

17 The Cholinergic Control of Internal Inhibition
D. M. WARBURTON

I. Introduction 431
II. Acquisition of Single Alternation 433
III. Cholinergic Effects on Stable Baselines 442
IV. Ascending Reticular Pathways 449
V. Ascending Reticular Activation and Discrimination . . 459
VI. Concluding Remarks 457
Acknowledgements 457
References 458

18 Septal Damage and Response Output under Frustrative Non-reward
A. DICKINSON

I. Introduction 461
II. General Experimental Procedures and Results . . . 463
III. Septal Damage and Control of Response Output . . 463
IV. Theoretical Interpretations of Nonreward Persistence . . 469
V. Frustration Attenuation 473
VI. Frustration Potentiation 481
VII. Concluding Comments 489
Acknowledgements 493
References 493

19 Neural Systems of the Limbic Brain and Behavioural Inhibition
R. L. ISAACSON

I. Introduction 497
II. The Limbic System and Memory 498
III. Hippocampal-Hypothalamic Relationships 512
IV. Behavioural Evidence for an Ergotropic Balance Following Hippocampal Destruction 516
V. Evidence for a Trophotropic Balance After Amygdala Lesions 517
VI. The Ergotropic-Trophotropic Systems and Memory . . 520
VII. Conclusion 525
Acknowledgements 525
References 525

20 Pavlovian Conditioning and the Brain
R. J. DOUGLAS

I. Introduction 529
II. Internal Inhibition and Excitation 530
III. Hippocampal Lesions and Behaviour 531

IV. Behaviour Unaffected by Hippocampal Lesions . . . 538
V. Excitation and the Mediation of Reinforcement . . . 538
VI. Association Learning 539
VII. The Drug Parallel 541
VIII. Development 543
IX. The Model: Putting it all Together 544
X. The Nature of Internal Inhibition 549
Acknowledgements 550
References 550
AUTHOR INDEX 555
SUBJECT INDEX 565

A | Inhibition and Instrumental Discrimination Learning

A

All the chapters in this section are concerned with phenomena occurring in discrimination situations under free operant conditions and mainly deal with research in which pigeons are used as subjects. In Chapter 1 Hearst discusses the problems of defining a concept of inhibition in such a context, its relationship to other approaches to inhibition and its relevance to various "side-effects" of discrimination learning.

Among these side-effects is the occurrence of negative gradients when generalization is tested following certain forms of discrimination training. The problems involved in their description as *inhibitory gradients* are discussed in Chapter 2 by Honig and his co-authors. In this chapter they present the results of a number of experiments using a novel method, the "advance key" procedure, to investigate discrimination and generalization.

Another common side-effect of discrimination situations of this general kind is that of *behavioural contrast*. In a free-operant situation where responses in the presence of one stimulus are reinforced and in the presence of a second stimulus reinforcement is omitted, the decrease in response rate to the second stimulus is usually accompanied by an increase in rate to the first stimulus. This phenomenon is the subject of Chapter 3, in which Halliday and Boakes compare the common situation described here with the absence of contrast in situations in which responding to one stimulus is decreased by the introduction of free reinforcement.

In Chapter 4 Terrace reviews the evidence on these and other side-effects of discrimination learning, including that from studies in which a discrimination is learned without errors. He suggests that this evidence is best accounted for by postulating two kinds of inhibition, which he terms *active* and *passive*. In Chapter 5 the characteristics of successive discriminations are compared to those of simultaneous discriminations and reversed simultaneous discriminations by Macphail, who demonstrates that one can obtain behavioural contrast effects in a simultaneous discrimination.

The subject of the final chapter of this section is the serial reversal of a successive discrimination. Bitterman in Chapter 6 describes a number of experiments, involving fish as well as pigeons, and examines the question of whether improvement in learning found over a series of reversals can be explained in terms of changes in the inhibition of responding to the negative stimulus.

Some Persistent Problems in the Analysis of Conditioned Inhibition

ELIOT HEARST

Indiana University, Bloomington, Ind. U.S.A.

I. Introduction 5
II. The Definition of Conditioned Inhibition 6
III. The Measurement and Detection of Conditioned Inhibition . . 11
IV. Problems in the Analysis of Inhibition 17
  A. The "Reduced Excitation" Argument 17
  B. Specificity of Conditioned Inhibition 21
  C. Inattention, Inhibition, and Indifference 25
  D. Generalization Gradients and Conditioned Inhibition . . 30
V. Concluding Comments 34
Acknowledgements 37
References 37

I. Introduction

Western experimental psychologists are currently devoting increased attention to the phenomenon of conditioned inhibition, a topic that for more than fifty years has been a major research concern of their colleagues in Eastern Europe. It seems too early to tell whether this facilitation of interest in the West will be transient or sustained, and whether a pronounced rebound-from-suppression will occur such that an unexpectedly large amount of relevant work will appear within the next few years and thereby compensate for the past neglect. The main purpose of this chapter is to discuss some conceptual and methodological problems that I think need to be squarely faced, carefully analysed, and eventually resolved if the experimental study of conditioned inhibition is not to become suppressed once again.

The attempt here will be more in the direction of posing and (hopefully) clarifying some problems that need resolution than in presenting specific experimental results or in offering any final solutions. The concept of inhibition seems to me an essential one for understanding many aspects of animal and human learning, but I will try to give some of the arguments against the value of the concept as effectively as my own biases permit. I must confess in advance that the ratio of speculations to hard empirical facts will probably far exceed 1·00 in this paper. Such a lopsided ratio certainly

5

causes me some pain as an experimenter who mainly uses Skinner Boxes and an operant type of analysis in his own research, but I suppose that years of watching pigeons stick their necks out have inspired me to do the same.

Extensive reviews of prior research on conditioned inhibition and so-called inhibitory generalization are already available for classical conditioning (Rescorla, 1969a) and operant conditioning (Hearst *et al.*, 1970); see also Diamond *et. al.* (1963), Konorski (1967), and elsewhere in the present volume. Therefore, no vigorous attempt will be made to summarize the experimental basis for many of the statements in the following discussion. However, Hearst *et al.* (1970) have pointed out that conclusions about the presence of "inhibitory control" in a particular situation depend greatly on the individual experimenter's specific criteria for deciding when a stimulus is inhibitory. And there have been more than just one or two such definitions or criteria, frequently vague or implicit, used in past work. As a result, conclusions based on one type of definition have failed to satisfy or influence workers who employ a different set of criteria. Therefore, it seems worthwhile first to re-examine Hearst *et al.*'s tentative definition and to compare its features with some others that have previously been offered. After this is done, the reader may be in a better position to evaluate the strengths and weaknesses of the approach to be favoured in the later discussion, as well as of other approaches. Readers familiar with our previous monograph may wish to skip the next two sections of this chapter or, alternatively, to read them and wonder why it took us so many more words in 1970 to say essentially the same thing.

II. The Definition of Conditioned Inhibition

As a first step towards formulating a clearer set of criteria for defining inhibitory effects, Hearst *et al.* proposed that a distinction be maintained between (a) stimuli as multidimensional events and (b) particular elements, attributes, or dimensions of these events. Of course, this is by no means a novel distinction; see, for example, numerous discussions of the word "stimulus" in the history of psychology, and the recent reviews and evaluations of work on stimulus selection and integration in Garner (1970), Richardson (1971), and Trabasso and Bower (1968). Nevertheless, the distinction does seem to have been unwisely disregarded in several recent controversies over the concept of inhibition in operant conditioning.

An *inhibitory stimulus** was defined by Hearst *et al.* as a multidimensional environmental event that as a result of conditioning (in this case based on

*Henceforth, the term conditioned inhibitor (CI) will generally be used to refer to this kind of stimulus; likewise, the term conditioned excitor (CE) will refer to an excitatory stimulus. Note that Pavlov (1927, p. 68) used the label "conditioned inhibition" more specifically. He applied it to a particular type of training procedure rather than to a general category of learned behavioural effects.

some *negative* correlation between presentation of the stimulus and subsequent occurrences of another event or outcome, such as "reinforcement") develops the capacity to decrease performance below the level occurring when that stimulus is absent. Thus the definition includes both a decremental effect on behaviour and an establishing (associative) operation. The definition stresses the "relational" nature of CI, since the effectiveness of a presumed CI is dependent upon the context (situation and level of behaviour) in which it is presented. Analogously, an *excitatory stimulus** refers to an event that as a result of conditioning (in this case based on some *positive* correlation between the presentation of the stimulus and subsequent occurrences of another event or outcome) develops the capacity to increase performance above the level occurring when that stimulus is absent.

The additional terms *inhibitory dimensional control* and *excitatory dimensional control* were used by Hearst *et al.* to refer to empirical generalization gradients that are characterized by progressively stronger or weaker behaviour the further one moves away from an inhibitory or excitatory stimulus, respectively, along some dimension. To summarize, within this framework CEs and CIs are defined empirically in terms of the results of a presence vs. absence test involving a total stimulus event, whereas excitatory and inhibitory dimensional control are demonstrated by systematic changes in behaviour arising from variations in some dimension or aspect of a total stimulus which can itself be independently shown to be a CE or CI. The presence vs. absence test should tell us whether the (multidimensional) stimulus event produces learned excitatory or inhibitory effects, compared of course to other treatment groups included to control for various kinds of nonassociative effects. The generalization test *can* reveal which specific elements or features of the total stimulus controlled the subject's behaviour during original learning or, stated more cognitively, which elements or features were encoded as attributes of the learned material in the representation of the total stimulus event in the subject's memory.

According to this set of definitions, there is no inevitable relationship between measures of facilitation or suppression obtained by presentation vs. removal of the total stimulus and measures of gradient slope obtained by varying a given dimension or element of that stimulus. A specific stimulus may qualify as a CI even when (a) no generalization tests have been performed; see the numerous classic experimental studies of conditioned inhibition described in Hearst *et al.* (1970), Konorski (1967), Pavlov (1927), and Rescorla (1969a), very few of which included generalization tests in their investigations; or (b) obtained gradients along some dimension of that stimulus are flat. In the latter case the experimenter may, for example, have varied a stimulus aspect unnoticed by subjects during original

*See footnote opposite.

learning. Additional empirical work would obviously be required in that situation to determine the effective aspect or aspects or the CI (i.e. what is frequently called the 'functional stimulus').

Furthermore, the mere observation of an incremental gradient around a training stimulus would not demonstrate that the stimulus was a CI. This point is by no means accepted by everyone, however, since workers often employ demonstrations of an incremental gradient around S⁻* as sufficient evidence that S⁻ exerts an inhibitory function. Our earlier monograph criticized the general logic behind such an inference: for example, we argued that an incremental gradient could conceivably arise if various dimensional values were differentially excitatory and the training stimulus was relatively less excitatory or even neutral (i.e. its presentation would have little or no effect on performance). Later in this chapter we will mention some procedures that seem to produce this type of result. Arguments and conclusions similar to ours were also presented by Bloomfield (1969), who (somewhat too strongly, in my opinion) maintained that "the curvature, or otherwise, of the S⁻ gradients . . . has nothing to do with the question of whether inhibition is present or not", and by Wilton and Godbout (1970), who stated that "the obtaining of a gradient around S⁻ on a dimension orthogonal to S⁺ does not allow us to distinguish between the operation of excitation reduction at S⁻ and inhibition at S⁻; it allows us only to say that S⁻ controls responding".

Several details and implications of our above definition of an inhibitory stimulus ought to be spelled out so that it can be more easily evaluated. First, the definition is confined to stimuli that develop inhibitory properties as a *result of conditioning*. Therefore, CIs ought to produce relatively durable effects when compared to the usually transient and weak effects of, say, novel or habituated stimuli. "Nonassociative" effects of the latter kind are excluded from our definition, but they do provide valuable control baselines against which to evaluate presumed CIs. Although Pavlov (1927) did attach the label "external inhibition" or "unconditioned inhibition" to the decremental effect of a novel stimulus on responding, he attributed the effect to the "intervention of an excitatory process, in most cases in the form of an investigatory reflex, and this has only a secondary inhibiting or disinhibiting effect upon the conditioned reflexes". However, in the same passage he proposed that differential (internal) inhibition, which is close in meaning to the term CI as used by Rescorla and the present writer, "is

*The conventional abbreviations CS⁺ and CS⁻ will be used to refer respectively to positive (correlated with reinforcement) and negative (correlated with no reinforcement) stimuli in classical conditioning, and S⁺ and S⁻ to refer to their operant counterparts. In discussions and examples of CE and CI, I will assume that the phenomena described for classical conditioning have clear analogues in operant conditioning, and vice-versa, unless otherwise stated.

brought about by a primary development of an inhibitory process" (1927, p. 130). Apparently Pavlov also preferred to apply the term "inhibition" to effects that involve conditioning.

Second, only those decrements produced by *discrete external stimuli* fall within the category of inhibitory effects, as Rescorla and the present writer have defined them. Although other experimenters might classify as inhibitory such phenomena as the gradual decline of responding during continued extinction of a free-operant response, or the progressive impairment of performance that occurs during a long and fatiguing task, we currently limit our usage of the term to the effects of the presentation of specific external stimuli. Hearst *et al.* (1970) referred to the problems that arise when various other phenomena are included in the category of CI; however, we did not preclude the likely possibility that the category will eventually have to be broadened to include at least some of them.

Third, for inhibitory control to be convincingly inferred, all the conditions responsible for the initiation and maintenance of baseline performance (e.g. reinforcement schedule, drive level, amount of reinforcement, presence of S^+) must be held constant and then a *stimulus presented* which leads to a decrease in performance. As Thomas (Chapter 14) similarly observed, the potential for performing the response is still presumed to be present when inhibition is inferred. Decremental effects due to changes in the initiating or maintaining variables themselves (e.g. complete removal of reinforcement, decreases in the frequency or amount of reinforcement, lowered drive, withdrawal or variation of S^+) seem more parsimoniously described in terms of manipulations of only one type of factor (excitatory). Thus the mere observation of a behavioural decrement would not necessarily mean that inhibitory effects are involved. Consequently, our definition differs from ones of the kind employed in this volume (Chapter 8) by Brimer (he applied the term "inhibitory" to any procedure that "produces a decrease in the baseline response rate"). We find such a definition too general to be very useful.

Criteria similar to ours seem to characterize traditional definitions of inhibition, in physiology as well as psychology. Like Thomas (Chapter 14) and despite the obvious dangers, we consider it a definite advantage to conceptualize behavioural inhibition in a way that corresponds as closely as possible to its physiological usage. For example, the physiologist Brunton (1883, quoted in Diamond *et al.*, 1963) stated: "By inhibition we mean the arrest of the functions of a structure or organ, by the action upon it of another, while its power to execute those functions is still retained, and can be manifested as soon as the restraining power is removed. It is thus distinguished from paralysis, in which the function is abolished and not merely restrained." No neurophysiologist would infer the action of inhibition if he merely reduced the intensity of an eliciting stimulus, or removed it completely, and then observed a decrease in neural firing rates. Typically, inhibition is inferred from a decremental effect produced by the addition of some new stimulation, while the original conditions are maintained.

Fourth, conditioned inhibition develops from a training procedure that involves some *negative relationship* between the presentation of an external stimulus and subsequent occurrences of another event or outcome. A reinforcement theorist might prefer to say that the stimulus is somehow associated with a decline in the probability of a Pavlovian US or an operant primary or secondary reinforcer.* Therefore, explicit counterconditioning with a different US (e.g. pairing a stimulus with shock after pairing it with food) could not create a CI, as the term is used here. Such pairing with a different US would merely involve an additional kind of excitatory conditioning, since it is based on a positive relationship between the presentation of the stimulus and the occurrence of a US. By the same token, a stimulus that signalled punishment of an operant response could not be labelled a CI.

Our statement that CI training involves some negative relationship between a stimulus and the occurrences of another event seems to be the most controversial aspect of the proposed definition, and therefore the one most likely to be revised, although the statement does appear quite compatible with Pavlov's and Konorski's general views. In contrast, Wagner and Rescorla (Chapter 12) list certain *reinforcement* operations (e.g. reductions in US magnitude) as potentially "inhibitory", although they concede that cues associated with these operations have not yet been convincingly demonstrated to be CIs by standard assays for conditioned inhibition. Other contributors to this volume (e.g., Halliday and Boakes, Chapter 3) consider stimuli associated with such reinforcement procedures as DRL, DRO (omission training), and response-independent reward schedules as possible candidates for CI, since subjects (in order to obtain reinforcement on DRL and DRO at least) must withhold a specific prepotent response. Although stimuli associated with DRL and DRO procedures do produce low rates of the specific CR recorded by the experimenter, subjects that learn the appropriate contingency still obtain numerous reinforcements during that stimulus, but presumably for some other incompletely-specified

---

*At present, only fragmentary evidence is available comparing the specific associative operations that may or may not establish CI [e.g. simple extinction of behaviour to an excitatory stimulus, discriminative conditioning (Pavlov's differential inhibition), signal for US termination, backward conditioning, extinction below zero, Rescorla's "explicitly-unpaired" signal, a signal for a mere decline in US frequency, etc.]. This important question will not be covered in much detail here. Readers are referred to Rescorla's excellent review and analysis (1969a) of work on the problem in Pavlovian conditioning, and to the extensive treatment of relevant issues and methodology offered by Wagner and Rescorla in the present volume.

response or chain of responses. Consequently, the stimulus develops or regains its positive relationship with a US or operant reinforcer and may well reveal itself to be excitatory via assays for CE or CI, provided of course that the withheld CR is not used as the performance index. Assays of this kind certainly ought to be performed to check the value of the present approach. To reiterate, our definition stresses the outcomes with which the *stimulus* is associated, rather than the consequences produced by particular *responses* during the stimulus (cf. Estes, 1969).

Additional reasons why our definition of CI explicitly includes the provision of a negative relationship between the stimulus and probability of reinforcement should become apparent in subsequent sections of this chapter (Section IV B). If the reader thinks he detects a distinct Tolmanian tinge to the present approach, I would not argue with him. Latent attitudes often manifest themselves in performance.

Fifth, even though CI always refers to a decrease in some behavioural effect, it *may be occasionally measured as an increase in response output*. For example, by establishing a positive relationship between a CS and an aversive US, an experimenter can produce a "conditioned emotional response", which is usually measured in terms of the suppressive effect of this CS+ on operant behaviour (the bigger the emotional effect of CS+, the fewer the operant responses). The CS+ thus qualifies as a conditioned excitor because its positive relationship with the US endows it with the power to elicit the "emotional" effect. Consequently, CI in this situation would most clearly be demonstrated if presentation of an additional stimulus in combination with CS+ were to decrease the suppression of operant behaviour (i.e. more responses are made), compared of course to the effects of the same stimulus on CS+ responding in various non-associative treatment groups. See Rescorla (1969b) for an illustrative discussion of such conditioned inhibition of a conditioned emotional response.

Whatever reservations the reader (or the writer) may have about all the above features of the definition of CI, they at least seem to be specific enough that the value of each can eventually be determined. Personally, the writer considers them as tentative guides to his research and conceptualization, rather than as statements to be defended to the death.

III. The Measurement and Detection of Conditioned Inhibition

A basic point to remember in studying CI is that an appreciable level of behaviour, usually produced by some reinforcement operation, must be established in order to enable detection of inhibitory effects. That is, an above-zero level of responding obviously has to be present to detect the response decrements caused by presentation of a CI or to observe the systematic changes in behaviour that characterize inhibitory dimensional control. In the latter case, if values far from the value of the presumed CI themselves produce zero responding, there is no way to measure less responding at the CI itself; see, for example, the interpretive problems arising from such floor effects in generalization gradients obtained by Johnson and Anderson (1970), Terrace (1966a), Terrace (Chapter 4) and Weisman and Palmer (1969).

However, the technical problem of ensuring an above-zero baseline seems a relatively easy one to handle (see Hearst *et al.*, 1970; Rescorla, 1969a, and the various assays for CI summarized later in this section), compared to the problem of selecting and justifying appropriate control treatments to assess the role of prior learning or "association" in any obtained decrements. That is, establishment of some associative neutral or zero point seems crucial to an approach that posits a fundamental distinction between excitation and inhibition as *learned* effects acting in opposite directions. We must know the extent to which the stimulus in question would affect baseline responding even if it had never been specifically associated with either the delivery or nondelivery of reinforcement. But since no stimulus that catches the subject's attention is likely to prove behaviourally neutral, in the sense that it will have absolutely no effect on responding, our zero point or zone of neutrality will have to be established empirically and will almost certainly vary as a function of stimulus and task parameters.

The choice of control treatments to be used in demarcating such a neutral "zone" obviously depends to a certain degree on one's theoretical biases. However, any appropriate treatment would presumably hold constant as many of the details of original training as possible (e.g. number and rate of stimulus presentations, overall density and patterning of reinforcements, etc.). Along these lines Rescorla (1967) and Hearst *et al.* (1970) listed and evaluated several treatments that seem reasonable as standards against which to measure the learned effects of CEs and CIs. Some of these are as follows:

(1) a *novel-stimulus* group, which never receives presentations of the stimulus prior to the test sessions for CE or CI. Thus associations could not have been established between the stimulus and USs, operant reinforcers, responses, or general situational cues. Any incremental or decremental effect the stimulus produces during testing in this group would have to depend on factors extraneous to the specific conditioning procedure administered to other subjects. Such a group has often been used in the past to assess "external inhibition" or simple generalization decrement (Brown and Jenkins, 1967; Pavlov, 1927, p. 77).

(2) a *habituated-stimulus* group, which receives the same number of stimulus presentations during "training" as the CE or CI groups, but without any USs or operant reinforcers available in the situation. Thus, as in

(1), associations could not have been formed between the stimulus and the delivery or nondelivery of reinforcement. Any effects the stimulus produces during testing in this group might be attributed to mere familiarity or experience with the stimulus. Because groups given this kind of pretraining often exhibit a retardation of normal learning when the stimulus is subsequently converted into an S^+, some workers have suggested that unreinforced pre-exposures produce "latent inhibition"—an interpretation which has been challenged in several recent papers. More about this point later.

(3) an *uncorrelated-stimulus* group, which receives the same number of stimulus presentations during training as the CE and CI groups, as well as the same number of reinforcement and extinction periods. For this group, however, the stimulus presentations are out of phase with the periods of reinforcement and nonreinforcement. Therefore, associative learning could not possibly develop, one can argue, because the probability of reinforcement is approximately equal in the presence and absence of the stimulus. This type of group was recommended by Rescorla (1967) as the proper control procedure for evaluating the outcome of Pavlovian conditioning. He contended that one of the advantages of his approach, which stresses CS–US contingencies rather than CS–US pairings, lies in its potentiality for generating a manipulable continuum with a tentative zero point (the behaviour of groups treated with this "truly random control") from which both increases and decreases in behaviour can be evaluated.

In Rescorla's experimental work (1969b) the above three treatments yielded stimuli that had only minor effects during summation tests for CE or CI, whereas stimuli explicitly paired or unpaired with the (aversive) US produced relatively strong facilitatory or suppressive effects respectively. Therefore, so long as the specific stimuli selected for study are not extremely salient or intense (and of course most experimenters choose their CSs so they are not), there is some empirical basis for believing that stimuli presented after any of the three treatments will prove rather ineffective. However, the generality of Rescorla's results for other situations and baselines remains uncertain. Since each of the three treatments is interesting in its own right and has certain advantages and disadvantages for drawing conclusions about the associative nature of CE and CI (see Estes, 1969 especially pp. 180–181; Hearst *et al.*, 1970; Kremer and Kamin 1971; Rescorla, 1967; and Seligman, 1969, for additional evaluations), the best and certainly the safest strategy would appear to be one that includes and compares within a given experiment as many as possible of the different treatments. Other comparison groups, for example, pretreatments involving so-called "extradimensional" discrimination training, in which subjects do receive correlated reinforcement and extinction but with stimuli orthogonal to the final test stimuli (Hearst, 1971; Honig, 1969) may also prove valuable in isolating the main factors responsible for the learned effects we have called CE and CI.

Once such experimental and control groups have been selected and exposed to their particular treatments, there are a variety of testing techniques or assays that may then be used to permit a decision about whether a particular stimulus is excitatory or inhibitory. Here is a list of such assays:

(1) *Combined cues.* Our basic definition of a conditioned inhibitor, in terms of its learned capacity to reduce some behavioural effect below the level occurring in its absence, implies what Rescorla has called a "summation" test—which is virtually the same as what Hearst *et al.* preferred to label a "combined-cue" test. The stimulus being tested for CI is combined for the first time with some specific S^+, or is presented in a general situation (e.g. ongoing free-operant behaviour) that is already known to evoke an appreciable amount of behaviour. To qualify as CI, (a) the presentation of the stimulus would have to significantly reduce the normal level of responding, (b) the presentation of the stimulus would have to produce a much larger decremental effect than the same stimulus in the various (nonassociative) comparison groups, and (c) the subsequent removal of the stimulus would have to lead to a partial or full restoration of baseline behaviour.

In my opinion, the combined-cue test is the fundamental way of determining whether a stimulus is a CI, and Rescorla (1969a) seems to agree since he says it "is perhaps the most direct method of measuring inhibition". Of course, it also corresponds to one of Pavlov's basic techniques for detecting CI. However, an indication of CI from this type of assay is apparently insufficient evidence for concluding that a stimulus is inhibitory since, aside from the possible development of CI, there may be alternative explanations for the occurrence of (a) to (c) above. For example, Rescorla (1969a) suggested that "shifts in attention" could also create such a result: prior association of a stimulus with nonreinforcement may cause the subject to attend so strongly to it that attention to S^+s normally maintaining the response is decreased, and consequently overall responding declines. Some potential ways of evaluating this and other alternative explanations will be considered in a later section of this chapter.

Decremental effects of a stimulus upon continuous eating or drinking behaviour may also be a sensitive index of appetitive CI. Or, if primary reinforcements like food or water are frequently but briefly available, subjects may approach and consume fewer reinforcements when such a CI is present than when it is absent. This technique is a variant of the combined-cue test: consummatory behaviour rather than experimentally-conditioned behaviour provides the baseline against which decrements are to be measured. A similar procedure is one occasionally employed in classical conditioning, when the inhibitory effects of a CI are assayed by presenting it simultaneously with the US and measuring its decremental effect on the UR. Rescorla (1969a) and Konorski (1967) provide some discussion of work done with this general method. Thomas' ingenious "threshold-probe technique" (Chapter 14) seems a welcome variant of the combined-cue assay.

(2) *Transfer or new learning.* The retarding (or facilitating) effects of CIs may be measured by attempting to convert them into S^+s (or S^-s). For example, the presumed CI may be made an S^+ for some behaviour; if the stimulus is inhibitory, subjects should be retarded in their acquisition of appropriate responding to it, compared to non-associative comparison groups. Hearst *et al.* (1970) labelled this and some similar methods "resistance-to-reinforcement" procedures. On the other hand, conversion of the presumed CI into the S^- of a discrimination should lead to quicker disappearance of responding during S^- than would occur in the various comparison groups. We will discuss this general method again later, but summaries of research with it may be found in Hearst *et al.* (1970), Rescorla (1969a), and Wagner and Rescorla (Chapter 12).

(3) *Choice or preference.* Subjects may be given a choice between responding to the presumed CI and responding to a stimulus assumed to be or previously demonstrated to be relatively neutral. An appetitive CI ought to be selected significantly less often than the neutral stimulus (Hearst *et al.*, 1970). On the other hand, an appetitive CE should be selected significantly more often than the neutral stimulus.

(4) *Secondary reinforcement.* An appetitive CI, for example, ought to acquire the properties of a positive secondary reinforcer with relatively great difficulty (e.g. when later paired with food delivery). Unlike the transfer or choice assays mentioned in (2) and (3) above, the CI would be tested by briefly presenting it after a response and measuring its power to strengthen prior behaviour, rather than by presenting it independently of behaviour and measuring its power to evoke responding. As an index of CI, this method seems more indirect than any so far mentioned.

(5) *Stimulus-termination.* The "escape-from-S^-" test of Terrace (1971, and this volume, Chapter 4) and the "advance procedure" of Honig *et al.* (Chapter 2), in which the subject can perform an operant response that controls the duration of particular stimuli, seem to be hybrids of methods (3) and (4) above. Although somewhat indirect as assays of CI as defined in the present chapter, they may prove very useful in future studies of phenomena relevant to the topic of inhibition.

(6) *"Symptoms" or by-products of inhibitory control.* There are a variety of related behavioural effects that investigators sometimes offer as evidence that "inhibition" is operating in a particular situation. Several studies have examined correlations among measures of these different effects, but strong

conclusions about the relationship of any of them to the phenomenon of CI appear premature. Research is badly needed comparing results from methods (1) and (2) above, which seem the most direct ways of isolating and quantifying CI, with qualitative and quantitative measures of phenomena like (a) behavioural contrast and Pavlovian induction; (b) peak shift in studies of stimulus generalization following training with S^+ and S^- that lie on the same dimension; (c) stimulus-produced frustration evaluated, say, by emotional or aggressive behaviour occurring in the stimulus; (d) spontaneous recovery; (e) the susceptibility of behaviour in the stimulus to disinhibition—note that Skinner (1938, pp. 97–102) admitted that his arguments denying the need for a general concept of inhibition would be seriously threatened if disinhibition could be reliably demonstrated in an operant situation: he was unsuccessful in attempts to produce such an effect during operant extinction by tossing his subjects in the air or turning on a light, but Brimer (1970, and this volume, Ch. 8) has recently presented convincing evidence of disinhibition in a variety of operant situations; (f) stress-induced breakdowns in appetitive discrimination performance (Bloomfield, 1969); and (g) the recovery of suppressed behaviour as a result of the administration of certain drugs. The interested reader can consult Bloomfield (1969), Hearst *et al.* (1970), Rescorla (1969a), Terrace (1966b), and Wilton and Godbout (1970) for discussions of possibilities of this kind.

One of the main goals of the remainder of the present article is to suggest ways in which experimenters might interpret inconsistent outcomes about CI from assays like the above, particularly (1) and (2). What, for example, could we conclude if one type of assay yielded clear evidence of CI but the other yielded none (or even evidence of CE)? We will make a plea that, in the future, experimenters systematically and regularly compare results from a variety of different assays following a given set of associative or non-associative treatments. Such constant comparison should prove useful in refining and evaluating the concept of CI and in assessing the general role of inhibition in learning.

The rest of this chapter also represents an attempt to come to grips with some interesting problems that were either completely evaded or glibly dismissed in our earlier monograph and in the above introductory material. For example, attention will be devoted to the following questions: Is *inhibition merely reduced excitation*? Those who deny the need for a concept of inhibition often argue that since it is invariably measured as a decrease in some excitatory effect, the concept can be eliminated completely and an analysis of all effects accomplished in terms of positive and negative changes in only one factor (excitatory). In my opinion, this controversy is more than just a "semantic quibble". *Should the definition of inhibition restrict it specifically to situations involving a particular US or operant reinforcer or response?* At the beginning of his review Rescorla (1969a) carefully limited Pavlovian CI to situations in which the same US controls both excitation and inhibition. This criterion may be unduly restrictive, especially since evidence suggests that CIs which produce decremental effects in one situation may often have similar effects in situations that involve different USs and responses. Furthermore, CIs may produce predictable and reciprocal effects when tested across appetitive–aversive boundaries. *How can we distinguish progressive changes in "attention" to a stimulus from its development as a CI?* Shifts in the attention-getting capacity or salience of a particular stimulus often provide an alternative explanation of effects that an experimenter would like to attribute to the development of CI. For example, the retardation of positive conditioning that may occur when a formerly negative stimulus is converted into an S^+ could mean either that some active suppression of behaviour during the stimulus was involved or that, as a result of prior experience with the stimulus, the subject no longer attended strongly to it. Another related question is whether "indifference" to a stimulus is empirically synonymous with "inattention" to it. I suppose not and will speculate about possible tests for distinguishing the two. *Of what direct value is the study of generalization gradients (dimensional control) for the analysis of CI?* Since our earlier monograph concentrated on this question, the discussion of it here will be rather limited. However, some recent data will be described in support of our argument that an incremental gradient around S^- does not necessarily imply CI.

IV. Problems in the Analysis of Inhibition

A. The "Reduced Excitation" Argument

One of the major reasons for the negative attitude of many American behaviourists towards the concept of inhibition stems from Skinner's (1938) strongly-expressed opinion that use of this general concept, besides implying a dubious neurological analogy, violates the canon of parsimony.* For example, he argued that

> "the term inhibition has been loosely used to designate any decline in reflex strength or the resulting diminished state ... The property of the mere direction of the change does not establish a useful class of data" ... [when contrasted with excitation] "inhibition refers to *any low state of strength* or the process of reaching it. We do not need the term because we do not need its opposite. Excitation and inhibition refer to what is here seen to be a

---

*Skinner (1938, pp. 232–233) also made several rather specific criticisms of Pavlov's experiments on conditioned inhibition, but recently Brown and Jenkins (1967) and also Jenkins (1965) offered a defence of Pavlov's technique and an experiment of their own which seems to serve as an effective answer to Skinner's criticisms.

c

continuum of degrees of reflex strength and we have no need to designate its two extremes" (1938, pp. 17–18, italics mine).

Like Skinner, there are many investigators who would maintain that virtually every one of the effects we have described as inhibitory could be more simply interpreted as mere reductions in a single factor (excitatory). If I can play the devil's advocate for a moment, such critics would begin their argument with the observation that procedures for establishing so-called CIs are always superimposed on some prevailing level of excitation—which is certainly true. All that these procedures basically achieve, the critics would continue, is the reduction or neutralization of excitatory generalization to the specific stimuli we later call CIs.

Suppose that the novel combination of S^+ (light) and S^- (tone) produces much less responding than occurs to (a) the light alone, and to (b) the combination of the S^+ (light) and a novel or habituated or previously uncorrelated tone. Such evidence of CI from a combined-cue assay would be attributed by these critics to the fact that behaviour originally conditioned to the light S^+ or to general situational cues would normally generalize somewhat to the tone. The association of the tone with nonreinforcement during its establishment as an S^- merely reduces such excitatory generalization in comparison to the amount of generalization that still occurs in the three kinds of comparison treatment. All that remains, they would conclude, are varying degrees of response strength to the tone and there is no need to posit any inhibitory factor in describing the results.

Or, suppose that the critics are confronted with evidence of CI from Rescorla's retardation-of-learning test (where, for example, the normal rate of acquisition of behaviour to a tone S^+ is greatly impaired by pretraining in which the tone was correlated in some way with nonreinforcement). In this case they might contend that pretraining (which necessarily takes place in the context of reinforcement since USs or operant reinforcers occur in the absence of S^-) merely reduces excitatory generalization from non-tone periods to the tone itself. Therefore, they would say, later acquisition of a response to the tone S^+ is impaired relative to the various comparison treatments, which have not had an equivalent reduction of excitatory generalization from non-tone periods.

One can certainly advocate and convincingly defend this point of view, namely that we should be as parsimonious as possible and therefore limit ourselves to statements about varying degrees of primary and generalized response strength and the ways and means of increasing or decreasing such strength. Presumably, this approach could be extended to handle all results that other workers prefer to interpret in terms of CI. However, I find the "excitation-only" approach unappealing, partly because it ignores physiological, anatomical, and biochemical data suggesting that both excitatory and inhibitory processes are involved in nervous-system action and can be meaningfully and usefully separated, but mainly because the behavioural separation of CE and CI seems to have great heuristic value. If we restrict ourselves to descriptions only in terms of a continuum of observable response strength to particular stimuli, it seems to me that we are likely to overlook possibly profound differences in the properties of various stimuli, all of which produce an extremely low or zero level of responding. That is, the various stimuli appear merely to have no excitatory power; "all that is observed is that the (CI) is now ineffective in evoking the response, as it was prior to conditioning" (Skinner, 1938, p. 96).

A conceptual framework that includes both excitatory and inhibitory effects seems to encourage a deeper experimental and theoretical analysis of the reasons why a stimulus may be ineffective, which is probably a very important problem for psychologists to study. Assays of the kind described above for detecting CI, plus other behavioural measures, can help us to determine whether the absence of response to a stimulus means, among other possibilities, that the subject (a) has simply not learned the appropriate response to the stimulus in operant conditioning, or has not learned that the US follows the CS in classical conditioning; (b) fails to attend to the stimulus, perhaps because of some physiological deficit or as a result of prior habituation to it; (c) has merely stopped making the response to the stimulus (reduced excitation due perhaps to simple extinction or forgetting); the response may have previously occurred to the stimulus because of actual reinforcement of the response during the stimulus or generalization from reinforcement of the response in the absence of the stimulus. Although the subject no longer responds to the stimulus (treats it as essentially a neutral or irrelevant event) it may still be noticed (such a general possibility seems similar to the alternative interpretation of extinction that Pavlov labelled the "passive disappearance of a positive CR"); or (d) has developed a rather specific form of ("active") competing or antagonistic behaviour during the stimulus. Also, (e) some general emotional or motivational state (e.g. "pessimism" or "relief") could have become conditioned to the stimulus, and this state might indirectly suppress behaviour.

These alternatives are admittedly rather vague and intuitively based at present. With some justification, empirically-minded colleagues will contend that distinguishing among them is hardly worth a serious attempt. But as Rescorla (1967) pointed out for classical conditioning, Western psychologists often view learning as either excitatory or absent and as a result they fail to search for differences in the properties of stimuli that do not themselves evoke much responding. In my opinion Rescorla has made a great contribution in his attempt to reverse this trend. If we consider the ever increasing number of papers appearing on inhibitory learning in the last few years, and the variety of reasons responsible for the conference that produced the present volume, it is clear that Rescorla's argument has turned out to be a fruitful and influential one.

In a later section of this chapter an attempt will be made to differentiate more precisely among the alternatives (a) to (e) through the use of specific experimental procedures. For example, only alternatives (d) or (e) would seem to predict an appreciable *decline* in ongoing behaviour when the ineffective stimulus is tested for CI via a combined-cue test. All the others ought to result in little or no decremental effect.

One of the interesting aspects of Terrace's comparison (1966b) of discriminations learned with and without errors lies in the fact that S^-s produced by either procedure evoke virtually no responding from subjects by the end of training, and yet other specific measures do reveal consistent and provocative differences in the properties of the two stimuli. An analysis in terms of mere observable levels of keypecking (degrees of excitation) occurring during the two S^-s at the end of training would have concealed some important differences in their properties. The reader will recognize the similarity between my comments on the value of a deeper analysis of "not-responding" and Jenkins' discussion (1965) of failures-to-respond in terms of different subclasses of movement patterns. More empirical work is badly needed categorizing and recording specific behaviours of a subject when it is not performing the CR, e.g. during S^-, (cf. Smith and Malott, 1971; Terrace, Chapter 4).

Along these lines, there may be at least one other potential way to avoid explicit use of a concept of inhibition in interpreting most of the phenomena discussed in this chapter. An alternative view would attribute such effects to the acquisition of some consistent but experimentally-unspecified response in the presence of the "CI"; this response merely interferes with the experimentally-measured behaviour and thereby decreases its output. According to this point of view, no active restraint of the measured behaviour is ever involved, but simply competition or conflict between two rather specific learned responses (cf. Migler and Millenson, 1969). Such an account is obviously based on principles similar to those underlying so-called interference theories of extinction. Explanations of this kind, while intuitively reasonable, inevitably suffer from the difficulty of specifying and measuring the interfering response. However, explanations that are phrased in terms of inhibition or restraint of behaviour are not free of analogous difficulties, since inhibition is often conceptualized as a *response tendency* opposed to excitation!

Research designed to determine the generality of inhibitory effects with respect to the original US, reinforcer, or response, and across appetitive and aversive boundaries, might cast considerable light on the above possibilities. In my opinion, some but by no means all of the decrements produced by CIs can be attributed to the development of specific motor responses that compete with or are antagonistic to the measured CR. In addition to this specific source of response reduction, CIs probably also evoke more general expectancies or emotional states that mediate CR decrement. This point is related to a second main problem in the analysis and definition of CI, to be discussed now.

B. SPECIFICITY OF CONDITIONED INHIBITION

Our definition of CI did not necessarily restrict its action to a particular US or response. Similarly, Pavlov seemed to assume that CIs would have rather non-specific effects. Experiments from his laboratory (Pavlov, 1927, pp. 76–77) were said to demonstrate that inhibition established originally with a particular reflex will exert its influence upon "all other conditioned reflexes whether homogeneous [same US] or heterogeneous [different US]". However, he and his colleagues apparently employed the same response (salivation) in all these experiments, although sometimes it was elicited by food (alimentary conditioning) and sometimes by acid (defensive conditioning). But another investigator, Rodnick (1937), did obtain evidence for transfer of CI based on one aversive reflex (shock—GSR) to another (air puff—eye-blink).

These suggestive findings, as well as many others summarized by Rescorla and Solomon (1967), lead one to infer that Pavlovian appetitive or aversive CS⁻s, acting via the mediation of correlated central states, ought to have rather general inhibiting effects on appetitive or aversive instrumental behaviour respectively. This was also Rescorla and Solomon's conclusion. Therefore, it is surprising that Rescorla (1969a) was so careful, at least in his introductory remarks, to restrict the definition of CI to situations in which the same US was used to establish both excitation and inhibition. Rescorla appears to have included this restriction for at least two reasons, one of which involves the differentiation of CI from certain attentional effects—a discussion of which will be delayed until later.

The other reason was to rule out explicit counterconditioning with another US as an establishing operation for CI. If, for example, a stimulus previously paired with shock were combined with an appetitive S^+, it would probably reduce the normally-occurring behaviour to S^+. However, many experimenters would not care to include such a decremental effect within the category of CI. Fortunately, our above definition precludes such a possibility, since it restricts CI to learned effects resulting from some negative correlation between a stimulus and subsequent occurrences of another event. This definition seems to conform in spirit to the one employed by Pavlov and Konorski who, besides defining CI in terms of a correlation with no-US, also did not place strict limitations on the US employed in training vs. testing.

At the end of his review, Rescorla (1969a) suggested a reformulation of his original definition of CI "in terms of the operation of arranging a negative CS–US contingency and the outcome of a particular change in behaviour". This reformulation automatically rules out explicit counterconditioning with another US (i.e. a positive contingency) as an operation for establishing CI. However, would Rescorla still insist that the same US be involved in the positive- and negative-contingency procedures that establish CE and CI respectively? Removal of such a restriction would seem welcome since it might, for one thing, encourage more research on the generality of CIs within and across appetitive–aversive boundaries. Rescorla and Solomon (1967) proposed that appetitive CS⁻s may have the general property of reducing ongoing behaviour maintained by other appetitive USs and enhancing instrumental responses reinforced by the avoidance of any type of aversive US. See also Bolles and Grossen (1970), Konorski (1967), Noah (1969), and Overmier and Bull (1970) for other results, occasionally inconsistent, on this kind of reciprocal relation between appetitive and aversive effects. In other words, the decremental actions of a CI may be specific to *either* appetitive or aversive behaviour, but fairly general within each category.

Closely related to the question of whether the term CI should be limited only to phenomena involving particular USs or drives is the question of restrictions as to specific response systems. Once again, Rescorla (1969a) limits his definition:

> "the conditioned inhibitor should be specific to the behaviour controlled by the excitor; the discussion is concerned only with stimuli which inhibit specifically the responses generated by excitatory conditioning with a particular US, not with stimuli that suppress all behaviour ... one would not expect a general decrement in all the organism's responses from a conditioned inhibitor any more than one would expect a general increment in all responses from performing excitatory conditioning with a particular US."

In my opinion, this restriction should be omitted from the definition of CI. The question of the transferability of a CI to responses other than those involved in original conditioning ought probably to be preserved as an important empirical question, particularly when operant responses are involved. Although one can only agree with Rescorla's expectation that CEs and CIs will not uniformly facilitate or suppress *all* the responses of an organism—doubt has already been expressed above as to the transferability of such facilitation or suppression across appetitive–aversive categories—evidence from operant experiments, for example, some of the studies reviewed in Bolles and Grossen (1970) and Trapold and Overmier (1971) do suggest effects of a more general nature than Rescorla implied.

Research on the transferability of CIs seems valuable for reasons other than mere curiosity about the generality of CI. In our earlier monograph we argued that such studies may help us to understand the mechanisms through which a CI exerts its effects. For example, would an S^- demonstrated to be a CI via keypecking for food in pigeons also decrease measures of pressing a treadle, or shuttling across a chamber, or positioning the head some distance from the key, when one of the latter responses is required for food reinforcement in the same subjects? If a CI were to prove very general in its suppressive effects, one might prefer to attribute most of its action to the mediation of an emotional or motivational state elicited by the CI, e.g. "pessimism" evoked by a signal that "food won't come" (Rescorla and Solomon, 1967), and not to a direct effect on the strength of a specific operant CR or to interference from particular (competing) behaviours occurring during the CI. As mentioned earlier, it would also be very valuable to actually observe the subjects during original training of the CI and to see whether any specific "competing responses" do consistently emerge. If so, the above transfer phase could be designed to involve reinforcement of a response that is very similar to the observed competing response. The "interference" explanation would then predict, if anything, a facilitation of such behaviour when the CI is presented, whereas the "central state" interpretation would predict a reduction (cf. Overmier et al., 1971).

Outcomes indicating rather general effects of a CI would obviously be consistent with Pavlov's views on the nature of inhibition and with Rescorla and Solomon's implicit and explicit suggestions concerning possible mechanisms through which Pavlovian CS^+s and CS^-s act to increase or reduce operant behaviour—see Thomas' comments on "general inhibition" in neurophysiological studies (this volume, Chapter 14) and Stein et al.'s (1971) ethological analysis of conditioned suppression as the result of a "general state that reduced the rate of all ongoing behavioural movements". Strangely enough for someone who characteristically avoids the postulation of mediating organismic states, Skinner (1938) proposed a similar alternative. He argued that a so-called CI may depress the strength of a new reflex not only because of a conditioned change in the strength of a particular reflex but also through the mediation of an emotional state bound up with nonreinforcement.

"A failure to reinforce has two effects: a change in reflex strength through conditioning and an emotional state. In 'conditioned inhibition' the transfer should be due to the former, but an indication of transfer may in reality be based on the latter." (1938, p. 234.)

Transfer tests for CE and CI with other USs, operant reinforcers, and responses may help to separate these two important alternatives.

If, on the other hand, the suppressive action of a CI proved to be rather specific to the original situation and response, a more limited and presumably more peripheralistic conception of the underlying mechanisms for CI would seem required. Explanations based on the establishment of specific competing or antagonistic behaviours during CI would gain support, and would appear to offer the most objective and parsimonious account of the results—see Wendt (1936) and Terrace, this volume, Chapter 4.

The relevance of such transfer studies for evaluating the "reduced excitation" argument outlined in the immediately preceding section of this chapter seems worth specific mention. If a CI has decremental effects upon a great variety of different behaviours, mere reduction in the (excitatory) strength of a particular response would be insufficient to explain its action. Furthermore, if a CI developed via classical conditioning with food reinforcement were, for example, to decrease measures of leverpressing in rats on appetitive procedures but increase measures of leverpressing on shock-avoidance procedures—as might be expected from some findings reported in Rescorla and Solomon (1967) and Bolles and Grossen (1970)—how could an argument in terms of mere "reduced excitation", or in terms of specific competing or antagonistic behaviour occurring in the stimulus, handle both positive and negative effects on the same response? In these eventualities, postulation of some mediating emotional or motivational state would appear inevitable.

Therefore, studies of the trans-situationality of CIs, although rare up to now, seem potentially helpful in evaluating the contention that CI can best be interpreted as mere reduced excitation of a particular response*. To the extent that a CI transfers its suppressive effects to other USs and response classes, this simple explanation seems to be weakened. On the other hand, the results of studies like that of Brown and Jenkins (1967)—which was certainly an important and well-conceived experiment—do not strike me as providing a very strong argument for the value of inhibition as a theoretical

---

*Convincing evidence of disinhibition in operant conditioning, such as that provided by Brimer in this volume (Chapter 8), is also extremely hard for single-process (excitation) interpretations to handle, as Skinner himself noted (1938). If only changes in a single process are involved, why should an extraneous stimulus reduce a specific response under one set of conditions (external inhibition) and facilitate the same response under another set (disinhibition)? A solid answer to this question might represent a breakthrough in the general analysis of behavioural inhibition.

concept. In the Brown–Jenkins study a tone was made a signal for nonrein-forcement of discriminated pecking on the left side of a split key. In a later test, the tone also reduced discriminated pecking on the right side of the key. This result could be simply interpreted in terms of the prior conditioning of "reduced keypecking" to the tone; no postulation of CI seems necessary. However, the reduced-keypecking explanation could not easily be applied if the tone were found to suppress a variety of other operant appetitive behaviours.

Let us return now to Rescorla's second reason for limiting CI to a specific US and response. He argued (Rescorla, 1969a, pp. 82 and 85) that stimuli producing decremental effects on many different responses and in many different situations are most likely to bring about these effects through shifts in the attention of the subject.

"The treatment designed to make S_1 an inhibitor may lead the organism to attend to S_1 to the detriment of attention to S_0 [a known excitor of response] ... Presumably, if this is the case, S_1 would disrupt the normal response to S_0 largely without regard to the nature of the response it controlled or what US generated that response ... If the effect of S_1 in modifying S_0's reaction depends heavily upon the nature of that reaction, then S_1 is primarily a conditioned inhibitor rather than a stimulus controlling shifts in attention."

However, as suggested earlier, CIs may turn out to have rather general effects on behaviour even when shifts in attention are controlled (see also the next section of this chapter). Such widespread effects could result from the elicitation by the CI of some mediating emotional state and have nothing very much to do with attention shifts. Apparently both Rescorla (1969a) and Skinner (1938; but see Jenkins, 1965), want to rule out transfer by such mediation from consideration as CI, but it seems premature for anyone to take a rigid position on the matter. As Skinner (1938, p. 233) said: "There is little or no distinction to be drawn between inhibition and one kind of emotion." Probably the most conservative and practical plan is to press on regardless and let research with a variety of appetitive and aversive tests for CI decide among these various alternatives.

C. INATTENTION, INHIBITION AND INDIFFERENCE

A variety of specific assays for detecting CI have been employed or suggested in the past and summarized above, but very few experimenters have carefully compared the outcomes of several of these assays. The determination of a profile of scores on such assays is admittedly a very time-consuming task, since a group design would probably be required; how could individual subjects provide easily interpreted data from several different kinds of tests? However, despite the technical problems, such comparisons of outcomes seem essential to determine whether presumed CIs do in fact produce a consistent pattern of results on various assays that investigators accept as intuitively reasonable ways of measuring CI. As we shall see, comparisons of this kind could also enable assessment of various alternative explanations for the decrements we have labelled CI.

A profile of scores on such assays is unlikely always to reveal a consistent and easily interpreted constellation of outcomes. For now, I would like to discuss some implications of only a few potential patterns of results. The discussion will stress comparison of only two of the tests, combined-cues and new-learning (cf. the very similar analysis of Wagner and Rescorla, this volume, Chapter 12).

Although especially hard-nosed readers are likely to be aghast at the mere thought of it, and may not be able to read much further without a pause for their favourite pacifier, I have found it useful to organize analysis of "failures-to-respond" into three general and somewhat loosely-defined kinds of phenomena: inattention, inhibition, and indifference. I will return to these three general categories later, after an attempt to develop the distinctions among them through the use of several examples.

Let us first consider the possibility that a presumed CI satisfies a combined-cue test for conditioned inhibition. Rescorla (1969a) has noted that such an effect might not necessarily involve so-called CI, but rather arise from *increased* relative attention to the stimulus in question. To evaluate this alternative explanation Rescorla recommended, among other strategies, the use of a retardation-of-learning test to supplement data from the combined-cue test. By pairing the stimulus with reinforcement, it would be converted into an S^+. If the stimulus exerted its decremental effect in the combined-cue test mainly by "attracting attention", subjects for which it now serves as an S^+ ought to show facilitated rather than retarded acquisition of appropriate behaviour in its presence, compared to the various nonassociative treatments. The basic assumption here is, of course, the reasonable one that conditioning will proceed faster for subjects which initially attend relatively strongly to a training stimulus. (Research on orientation or investigatory reflexes would tend to support this assumption.) If, on the other hand, the stimulus is mainly a CI, acquisition of behaviour during S^+ ought to be retarded. Thus, comparison of the outcomes of a combined-cue test and a new-learning test should often enable a tentative choice between explanations based on increased salience or attention and those based on the development of CI.

Consider next the possibility that a presumed CI satisfies a retardation-of-learning test for conditioned inhibition. This isolated finding could also be interpreted in at least two ways, as a result of *reduced* attention to the stimulus or of the development of CI: learning to respond to S^+ could have been retarded either because subjects attended relatively little to the stimulus, or because the stimulus actually controlled a tendency that opposed excitatory conditioning. Results from a procedure that is frequently described as producing "latent inhibition" are very relevant in this connection; mere pre-exposures to a particular stimulus, in the absence of any other experimentally programmed events like reinforcement, hinder its later establishment as an S^+, compared to the same stimulus in non-pre-exposed subjects. Unlike most of the phenomena discussed previously in this chapter, the comparison of interest here is not between (a) a group that has received pretraining in which the stimulus is negatively correlated with reinforcement and (b) various nonassociative comparison groups. Rather, the comparison is between two of the nonassociative groups themselves (the novel-stimulus and habituated-stimulus treatments). Consequently, retardations of learning obtained within the latent-inhibition paradigm may arise from a different source than CI. In fact, latent inhibition would automatically be excluded from our strict definition of CI, since no negative correlation between the stimulus and USs or operant reinforcers was arranged during "training" prior to retardation-of-learning tests.

However, it would be somewhat cavalier to eliminate the latent-inhibition effect from consideration merely because it does not conform to all provisions of our favourite definition. Investigators of this phenomenon (e.g. Lubow, 1965) have often suggested that some kind of *learned* (inhibitory) response which is antagonistic to the to-be-acquired response may develop during the pre-exposure period, although this response is never precisely specified. Besides this hypothesis, investigators have also seriously considered the possibility that attention to the stimulus weakens during pre-exposure; subjects "habituate" to the stimulus. Both these alternative explanations would predict slower learning in the pre-exposed group than in a group for which the stimulus is novel.

One strategy for distinguishing between these two alternatives seems to follow naturally from Rescorla's and our discussions of empirical tests for separating attention vs. inhibition explanations of CI. That is, a combined-cue test could be arranged for a stimulus that has demonstrated so-called latent inhibition via a retardation-of-learning test. If such a stimulus appreciably reduces performance when combined with a well-established S^+, support would accrue for the notion that some consistent "response" or "expectancy" did develop to the stimulus during pre-exposure, and this response or expectancy subsequently played a major role in blocking acquisition of the to-be-conditioned response. However, if pre-exposures have merely reduced attention to the stimulus, it should have little or no effect in a combined-cue test.

Another valuable way of testing these two explanations of latent inhibition would be to compare the relative rapidity with which a pre-exposed stimulus can be converted into either an S^+ or S^-, compared to the same stimulus in non-pre-exposed subjects. If, for example, repeated pre-exposures of a tone were to retard learning of a subsequent discrimination between tone and silence, regardless of whether the tone served as S^+ or S^- in that discrimination, then the attention-decrement hypothesis would receive strong support. On the other hand, if such pre-exposure facilitated learning of the discrimination in which the tone was S^-, but retarded learning of the discrimination in which it was S^+, the hypothesis that some kind of inhibitory learning had been involved would receive support.

Carl Halgren recently conceived such a strategy and is now completing a doctoral dissertation at Indiana University along these lines. Unknown to him, however, there were two prominent researchers who, together with their colleagues, had independently devised the same general strategy. They published their results while he was still in the midst of running his study. Wagner and Rescorla's findings are summarized in their chapter in this volume and also in Reiss and Wagner (1971) and Rescorla (1971). These experiments revealed that nonreinforced pre-exposures of a stimulus retarded subsequent conditioning of *either* excitation or inhibition to the stimulus. Moreover, the pre-exposed stimulus was relatively ineffective in a combined-cue test. Therefore, "latent inhibition" is apparently a misnomer. The phenomenon seems best attributed to reduced attention, or to a decline in "stimulus salience", rather than to some form of inhibitory learning; note also Lubow and Moore's (1959) failure to identify a mediating peripheral response in their studies of latent inhibition.

Unlike Rescorla and Wagner, Halgren used an operant appetitive discrimination task. Nevertheless, he analogously found that stimulus pre-exposure retards subsequent discrimination learning regardless of whether the pre-exposed stimulus serves as S^+ or S^- (the absence of the stimulus was S^- or S^+ respectively in his two main groups).

As a third example, consider the possibility that after administering some new experimental treatment to a stimulus an investigator obtains no effect of the stimulus when it is first presented in combination with a well-conditioned S^+. If he knew from past experience that such a combined-cue assay is ordinarily sensitive enough to detect CI, he would probably conclude that the new treatment produced a stimulus which is not a CI. But does the ineffectiveness of the stimulus during the combined-cue test mean that (a) the organism merely failed to attend to it; or (b) the organism definitely noticed the stimulus but was indifferent to it? Quite conceivably, a subject may still attend to a stimulus, or to a particular feature of the stimulus, even though he performs equivalently in its presence and absence (cf. Estes, 1969; Farthing and Hearst, 1970; Mackintosh, 1969; Peterson and Premack, 1971). As Estes suggested in such cases, special tests with a different type of performance measure may be required to reveal what the subject has actually learned about the stimulus.

Alternatives (a) and (b) might be separated, for example, by a test in which the ineffective stimulus is converted into an S^+. If failure-to-attend was mainly the reason for the lack of effect in the combined-cue test, transformation of the stimulus into an S^+ ought to be retarded compared to the usual (novel-stimulus) controls. On the other hand, if subjects were merely indifferent to the stimulus there should be little or no retardation of excitatory conditioning to S^+. Generalization gradients obtained along various dimensions of the ineffective stimulus might also provide valuable supplementary data indicating whether and how strongly subjects still attended to it (cf. Estes, 1969).

A tentative summary of inferences that seem reasonable from the above specific sets of empirical outcomes is as follows: if the organism is "indifferent" to a particular stimulus, the stimulus should produce no significant decremental effect in either the combined-cue or new-learning tests; since the stimulus may still be attended to, it could even facilitate learning of new behaviour under certain circumstances. If some treatment decreases the salience or attention-getting capacity of the stimulus, it should be comparatively hard to convert into either an S^+ or S^-, but should show no significant effect in a combined-cue test. If the treatment somehow increases the attention of the organism to the stimulus, it may have a decremental effect in a combined-cue test, but, if anything, a facilitatory effect when the stimulus is converted into either an S^+ or S^-. Finally, if the stimulus is inhibitory, it should exert a clear decremental effect in both the combined-cue and conversion-into-S^+ tests, and perhaps a facilitatory effect if it is made the S^- of some subsequent discrimination.

Unfortunately, there are a variety of other outcomes which are not at all simple to interpret. Furthermore, the most appropriate comparison treatment for evaluating each possible outcome is sometimes not immediately obvious. The different kinds of effects may interact with each other to yield results that are hard to interpret. However, constant comparisons of these and other assays for CI should eventually permit a strong decision about the scope and value of a concept of inhibition in learning. Such comparisons should also help to determine whether under certain conditions organisms may justifiably be said to be "indifferent" to particular stimuli to which they attend, and under other conditions to be "inattentive" to the same stimuli. Obviously, any evaluation of all these possibilities ought to remain extremely conservative until the various assays have been more extensively studied and compared.

D. Generalization Gradients and Conditioned Inhibition

In our previous monograph we argued that the rather common practice of using the shape and slope of generalization gradients to infer the "inhibitory function of a stimulus" is a dubious procedure. Gradients along specific dimensions of a stimulus may be flat (or even peaked at the value associated with extinction: see Davis, 1971) and yet the stimulus itself may qualify as a CI, according to the type of definition offered by Pavlov, Konorski, Rescorla, and Hearst *et al.* As an experimental example of this possibility, let us review the results of Lyons (1969a; 1969b). He found that, compared to "single-stimulus" controls and to pigeons that had learned "with errors", the S$^-$ (vertical line) of an errorless discrimination produced the greatest suppression of responding when combined with S$^+$ (green). Thus, the errorless S$^-$ met the main criteria for a CI, according to the approach favoured in this chapter. However, when the tilt of the line was systematically varied on its usual (black) background, very irregular and unreliable gradients were obtained. On the basis of the response-suppressing power of the errorless S$^-$, Lyons concluded that errorless training does not produce a neutral S$^-$, a conclusion that contradicts the one made by Terrace (1966a) on the basis of the flat generalization gradients he obtained along a dimension of S$^-$ after discrimination learning without errors.

Because Lyons used a novel method of producing errorless learning (response prevention), the relevance of his results for Terrace's analysis remains somewhat unclear. However, Daniel Johnson (personal communication, 1971) has similarly observed large decrements in responding when an errorless S$^-$ (line-tilt or wavelength) is combined with an S$^+$ (wavelength or line-tilt respectively), but following discrimination learning established by Terrace's *fading* procedure (see also Hearst *et al.*, 1970). Therefore, all the available evidence from combined-cue assays indicates that an errorless S$^-$ qualifies as a CI, although generalization gradients around such an S$^-$ have never revealed an incremental gradient.

It seems clear that the occurrence of an irregular or flat gradient along some dimension of a stimulus implies nothing, in and of itself, about the possible inhibitory function of that stimulus. The stimulus could also be excitatory or neutral. Some experimentally-established baseline of absolute responding appears necessary as a standard against which to measure any learned decrements produced by the stimulus. Combined-cue or new-learning tests apparently provide reasonable ways of accomplishing this goal.

Most investigators seem to grant our argument that mere evidence of a

flat gradient along a single dimension of a stimulus permits no solid conclusions about whether that stimulus is a CI. However, as an alternative to
combined-cue or new-learning tests, several investigators have suggested
variation of other dimensions of the presumed inhibitory stimulus. If
variation of some dimension does yield an incremental gradient around S⁻
then, the argument would go, one could in fact conclude that the stimulus
was inhibitory (see Terrace, 1966a). However, the logical inferences that

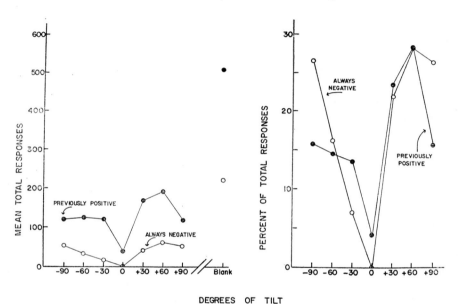

DEGREES OF TILT

Fig. 1. Gradients of absolute generalization (mean total responses) and relative generalization (mean per cent of total responses to lines) for the Always Negative and Previously
Positive subjects. For both groups the S⁻ during discrimination training just prior to the
generalization test was a vertical line (0°). The mean total responses to the blank stimulus
(S⁺) are given on the extreme right of the absolute gradient.

one can justifiably draw about CI from the finding of such an incremental
gradient are not clear. My opinion is that no strong conclusions about
whether a stimulus is inhibitory can be inferred from that sort of information. Independent assays of the capacity of the stimulus to reduce some
behavioural effect seem also required. The verbal argument in favour of
this view has already been summarized above (and more extensively in
Hearst *et al.*, 1970). Therefore, the following discussion will be restricted
to some of the experimental bases for this belief, which are admittedly
rather meagre at present.

The gradients displayed in Fig. 1 (from Zentall *et al.*, 1971) provide an example for consideration. The gradients for the group labelled "Previously Positive" were obtained from pigeons ($n = 3$) for which a black vertical line ($0°$) on an otherwise white response key had initially served as the S^+ in a successive Go; No go discrimination (S^- was the blank white key). After mastery of that discrimination, the S^+ and S^- were interchanged and this new discrimination remained in force until mastery. Then each subject received a standard generalization test in extinction along the line-tilt dimension. The group gradient, and the gradients of each of the three individual subjects, all showed a minimum at the vertical line.

Another group ($n = 4$) mastered only the second discrimination and then was tested for generalization in exactly the same way as the first group. For the second group, of course, the vertical line had been "Always Negative". Generalization data for this group are shown in the other gradients of Fig. 1. Keep in mind that the generalization test followed mastery of the same discrimination for all seven birds in the experiment.

Every individual bird in the experiment displayed a minimum at S^-. This simple result is the one of most relevance for our general argument, to be pursued shortly. However, the reader will also note that the mean absolute gradient of the Always Negative birds was distinctly flatter than for the Previously Positive group. On the other hand, the mean relative gradient of the Always Negative group was, if anything, somewhat steeper than that of the other group. What can we conclude about the inhibitory function of S^- from the generalization gradients of the two groups?

If we make a decision about this question merely on the basis of the shape and slope of the gradients, as has been done often in the past, we could presumably conclude that (a) the S^- in each group was inhibitory (because both gradients had a minimum at S^-); (b) the Always Negative S^- was less inhibitory than the Previously Positive S^-—because the absolute gradient of the latter group was steeper (see Terrace, 1966a, who used absolute gradients for a decision of this kind); and (c) the Previously Positive S^- was, if anything, less inhibitory than the Always Negative S^-—because the relative gradient of the latter group was somewhat steeper. Conclusion (b) might be criticized because of the small number of responses (floor effect) in the Always Negative group. Unfortunately, low response levels are not unusual for generalization tests conducted in extinction along some dimension of S^-. As suggested earlier in this chapter and in Hearst et al. (1970), investigators probably ought to concern themselves more with the measurement artifacts created by such floor effects than they have in the past.

In any event, the major problem still remains of deciding whether S^- is inhibitory in both groups of Fig. 1. I cannot see how the shape and slope of the gradients themselves provide any clear answer to that question. Conclusion (a), one often accepted in recent research, seems dubious because we have no baseline from which to measure the learned capacity of each S⁻ to reduce responding. Zero responses occurred to S⁻ during testing in the Always Negative group, and this observation might reasonably lead us to suspect that presentation of S⁻ in that group would greatly suppress ongoing behaviour if a combined-cue test were arranged. However, the higher response level to S⁻ in the Previously Positive group could mean that the stimulus in that group was simply less inhibitory than S⁻ in the other group, or that it was neutral or even excitatory. For example, presentation of a vertical line in the Always Negative group might greatly suppress ongoing behaviour to some auditory or visual S⁺, whereas presentation of the S⁻ in the Previously Positive group might have relatively little effect or even a facilitative effect. We appear to need data from independently-arranged combined-cue tests of this kind to evaluate all these possibilities.

As a matter of fact, results bearing on these alternatives have been recently obtained by my colleague at Indiana University, S. L. Guth, in a series of unpublished studies that involve discrete-trial operant procedures with rats. Under a variety of conditions (e.g. wide variations in the duration of discrimination training), he has found that an S⁻ (tone) which was previously an S⁺ for barpressing does not reduce (and sometimes increases) barpressing when combined for the first time with a strong S⁺ (light), whereas an Always-Negative S⁻ (the same tone) does reduce barpressing to the light S⁺ (cf. Thomas' analogous findings and interpretations in his Experiment 1, this volume, Chapter 14). It would be valuable to examine auditory generalization data in such an experiment, to see how gradient measures correlate with combined-cue assays, but Guth did not determine gradients around S⁻ in this work.

The use of a retardation-of-learning test to determine whether S⁻ is inhibitory in the two groups of Fig. 1 would probably also yield results contradicting conclusion (a) that the S⁻ in both groups is inhibitory. An S⁻ that was formerly an S⁺ might prove quite easy to convert into an S⁺. Konorski notes in his contribution to this volume that an Always Negative CS⁻ strongly resists transformation into an excitatory CS, whereas a Previously Positive CS⁻ is very quickly transformed. Once again, the mere occurrence of an incremental gradient around S⁻ seems insufficient evidence for concluding that S⁻ is inhibitory.

No one has performed the major task of carefully comparing properties of gradients along dimensions of a presumed CI with various independent indices of CI, such as those obtainable from combined-cue or new-learning assays. The above criticism of the logic of inferring CI from incremental gradients was based on scattered experimental results from quite different experimental situations, stimuli and species (pigeons, Zentall et al; rats, Guth; cats, Thomas; dogs, Konorski). Other evidence supporting our

D

point of view is also rather indirect or tenuous. For example, in this volume
Wagner and Rescorla review data indicating that simple extinction of an
excitatory stimulus, in the absence of reinforcement at other stimuli, does
not generate CI; however, Honig (1961) obtained U-shaped gradients
around such a stimulus. Wagner and Rescorla also conclude that mere
stimulus pre-exposure in the absence of reinforcement does not produce CI,
but Siegel (1969) obtained incremental gradients around such a stimulus.
Until someone performs an extensive series of studies, with many inter-ex-
periment differences controlled and with comparisons made among several
measures of stimulus generalization and CI, my argument that incremental
gradients do not necessarily demonstrate the presence of CI remains more a
distinct logical possibility than a statement backed by strong empirical
evidence. Possibly, serious discrepancies between these two types of
measures will not arise often enough to fret about. But I think experimental
work along these lines is needed and will prove important for clarifying many
phenomena of CI and stimulus generalization.

Perhaps my argument concerning the ambiguity of the relationship
between generalization gradients and conditioned inhibition boils down
to the one offered by Skinner (1938, p. 233), who remarked that "it is only
when the differentiating component has the status of a stimulus that inhibitory power is assigned to it. When it is a single property or a change in a
property, the analogy with true inhibition is less compelling." Hopefully,
Freudian wish-fulfilment does not account for my interpreting this comment to mean that Skinner was particularly sceptical about inferring inhibition from manipulations of specific dimensions or aspects of a total stimulus
event. Although it would be hard to specify exactly when a "component
has the status of a stimulus" (see also Skinner, 1938, p. 169, footnote 1),
he did seem to believe that the only defensible way of introducing the
concept of inhibition into a behavioural analysis was to use it in reference
to decremental effects produced by the presentation of a "total" stimulus.

V. Concluding Comments

According to the approach favoured in this chapter, the term "conditioned
inhibitor" (CI) refers to a stimulus that, as a result of some prior association with a decrease in the probability of reinforcement, has acquired the
power to restrain or prevent a behavioural effect that would otherwise occur.
A variety of specific assays for detecting and measuring CI were briefly
reviewed, but the combined-cue and new-learning techniques proposed
and used by Pavlov, Konorski, and Rescorla were emphasized as the most
promising and direct. All procedures for assessing CI seem to require the
establishment of a point of associative neutrality, some empirically-deter-
mined baseline against which to measure excitatory (facilitative) and inhibi-

tory (suppressive) effects. Several "nonassociative" treatments were listed as reasonable procedures for establishing such a baseline, but no strong position favouring any one of them was taken in this chapter. In fact, our recommendation was that as many as possible of these different treatment groups be incorporated within any given experiment. In that way, a variety of alternative explanations for ensuing stimulus-produced effects may simultaneously be evaluated.

Along with the utilization of a greater variety of assays and "control" treatments, more research on the generality (trans-situationality) of the effects of CIs across different USs, response systems, and appetitive or aversive drives appears needed to permit eventual decisions about the usefulness of the concept of inhibition in behaviour and about the mechanisms of action of presumed CIs. Can they be said merely to "reduce excitation", or do they function actively by evoking specific competing or antagonistic behaviour from the subject? Another important possibility involves the elicitation by the CI of some emotional or motivational state, like "pessimism" or "relief", which then mediates the suppressive effects of the CI on performance. In connection with these possibilities we noted that empirical work is badly needed categorizing and recording specific behaviours of a subject when it is not performing the CR.

We also suggested how extensive comparisons of the outcomes of various assays for CI could help to differentiate among absences-of-response to a familiar stimulus that occur because of (a) failure to notice the stimulus (inattention); (b) prior learning that the stimulus is irrelevant in that behavioural situation, although the subject may still notice the stimulus (indifference); or (c) some active restraint of behaviour or some general negative expectancy that has developed during the stimulus (inhibition). The use of the shape and slope of generalization gradients for inferring the "inhibitory function" of a stimulus was criticized as generally yielding inconclusive results; experimental examples exist in which (a) flat gradients have been found along dimensions of an S^- that was independently demonstrated to be CI by a combined-cue test; and (b) incremental gradients have been found around an S^- that indirect evidence suggests would fail to demonstrate CI by either a combined-cue or retardation-of-learning test.

For many years Konorski has been experimenting and theorizing on these and similar problems. However, until the appearance of Rescorla's paper (1967), experimental psychologists in the West had tended to neglect the study and analysis of stimuli that themselves evoke little or no behaviour. Neutral, weakly inhibitory, and strongly inhibitory stimuli, when presented in isolation, would obviously all yield approximately zero levels of behaviour. Therefore, unless an experimenter designed his studies with the explicit goal of differentiating among such stimuli by means of special detection techniques, he would hardly have very much reason to suspect that conditioned inhibition is an important and pervasive phenomenon. There seems little question that subjects can learn correlations between stimuli, responses, and the absence or lowered probability of reinforcing events—just as they can learn correlations between stimuli, responses, and the presentation or increased probability of reinforcing events. If the reader doubts whether anyone could possibly disagree with that statement, then he might ask himself why prevalent theories of learning emphasize so strongly the excitatory half of the picture (e.g. learning is a result of "*reinforced* practice").

Since all behavioural situations outside the laboratory involve a succession of discrete stimuli, some attended to and some not, some overtly responded to and some not, it would seem that psychologists who aspire to a comprehensive analysis of behaviour should pursue and study the reasons for the nonappearance of certain responses in the observable stream of behaviour, as well as the reasons for the appearance of (more easily specified) overt CRs. As Rescorla (1969b) remarked, "it no longer makes sense to treat conditioned inhibition as the weak sister of excitation". According to Pavlov, Konorski, Rescorla, and the approach of the present writer, inhibition certainly *does* refer to something more than "any low state of strength" of response (Skinner, 1938, p. 17). The mere absence of response to an isolated stimulus may occur for reasons other than CI.

An interesting prospect involves the possibility that important differences may be discovered between the general properties of CEs and CIs. Although the conditions of their separate establishment may appear symmetrical (e.g., positive contingency vs. negative contingency), future experiments may reveal systematic differences in their growth parameters, rates of decay as a function of time since original training, sensitivity to changes in stimulus intensity, learning rates as related to the developmental level or age of the subject, latency of effects, and susceptibility to disruption by novel external stimuli, interfering events, specific brain lesions, or drugs. Pavlov (1927, p. 66) thought that "inhibition is in every respect more labile [unstable] than excitation" (see also Gerbrandt, 1965), but few experiments performed outside of Eastern Europe have actually investigated such potentially important possibilities in any great detail. Therefore, along with the study of CI in its own right, I hope that the future brings more research designed to compare the properties of conditioned excitation with those of conditioned inhibition. If consistent and substantial differences do emerge between the two it will be hard to maintain, as do many Western psychologists, that only a single process (excitation) is needed in the analysis of behaviour.

Acknowledgements

The research connected with this article has been supported by National Institute of Mental Health Grants MH-12120 and MH-19300 at the University of Missouri and Indiana University respectively. Stanley Franklin, Dexter Gormley, Minnie Koresko, Carol B. Mills, Leigh Shallenberger, and Sharron Taus provided valuable advice and assistance. I also thank numerous colleagues and students who carefully read and constructively criticized an earlier version of this chapter.

References

Bloomfield, T. M. (1969). Behavioural contrast and the peak shift. In: R. M. Gilbert and N. S. Sutherland (Eds.), *Animal Discrimination Learning*. Academic Press, London, pp. 215–241.

Bolles, R. C. and Grossen, N. E. (1970). The noncontingent manipulation of inventive motivation. In: J. H. Reynierse (Ed.), *Current Issues in Animal Learning*. University of Nebraska Press, Lincoln, pp. 143–174.

Brimer, C. J. (1970). Disinhibition of an operant response. *Learning and Motivation*, **1**, 346–371.

Brown, P. L. and Jenkins, H. M. (1967). Conditioned inhibition and excitation in operant discrimination learning. *Journal of Experimental Psychology*, **75**, 255–266.

Davis, J. M. (1971). Testing for inhibitory stimulus control with S⁻ superimposed on S⁺. *Journal of the Experimental Analysis of Behavior*, **15**, 365–369.

Diamond, S., Balvin, R. S. and Diamond, F. R. (1963). *Inhibition and Choice*. Harper and Row, New York.

Estes, W. K. (1969). New perspectives on some old issues in association theory. In: N. J. Mackintosh and W. K. Honig (Eds.), *Fundamental Issues in Associative Learning*. Dalhousie University Press, Halifax, pp. 162–189.

Farthing, G. W. and Hearst, E. (1970). Attention in the pigeon: Testing with compounds or elements. *Learning and Motivation*, **1**, 65–78.

Garner, W. R. (1970). The stimulus in information processing. *American Psychologist*, **25**, 350–358.

Gerbrandt, L. K. (1965). Neural systems of response release and control. *Psychological Bulletin*, **64**, 113–123.

Hearst, E. (1971). Differential transfer of excitatory vs. inhibitory pretraining to intradimensional discrimination learning in pigeons. *Journal of Comparative and Physiological Psychology*, **75**, 206–215.

Hearst, E., Besley, S. and Farthing, G. W. (1970). Inhibition and the stimulus control of operant behaviour. *Journal of the Experimental Analysis of Behavior*, **14**, 373–409.

Honig, W. K. (1961). Generalization of extinction on the spectral continuum. *Psychological Record*, **11**, 269–278.

Honig, W. K. (1969). Attentional factors governing the slope of the generalization gradient. In: R. M. Gilbert and N. S. Sutherland (Eds.), *Animal Discrimination Learning*. Academic Press, London, pp. 35–62.

Jenkins, H. M. (1965). Generalization gradients and the concept of inhibition. In D. Mostofsky (Ed.), *Stimulus Generalization*. Stanford University Press, Palo Alto, pp. 55–61.

Johnson, D. F. and Anderson, W. H. (1970). Generalization gradients around Sᐃ following errorless discrimination learning. *Psychonomic Science*, **21**, 298–300.

Konorski, J. (1967). *Integrative Activity of the Brain*. University of Chicago Press, Chicago.

Kremer, E. F. and Kamin, L. J. (1971). The truly random control procedure: associative or nonassociative effects in rats. *Journal of Comparative and Physiological Psychology*, **74**, 203–210.

Lubow, R. E. (1965). Latent inhibition: Effects of frequency of nonreinforced pre-exposure of the CS. *Journal of Comparative and Physiological Psychology*, **60**, 454–457.

Lubow, R. E. and Moore, A. U. (1959). Latent inhibition: The effect of non-reinforced pre-exposure to the conditional stimulus. *Journal of Comparative and Physiological Psychology*, **52**, 415–419.

Lyons, J. (1969a). Stimulus generalization along the dimension of S$^+$ as a function of discrimination learning with and without error. *Journal of Experimental Psychology*, **81**, 95–100.

Lyons, J. (1969b). Stimulus generalization as a function of discrimination learning with and without errors. *Science*, **163**, 490–491.

Mackintosh, N. J. (1969). Epilogue: Issues and problems in associative learning. In: N. J. Mackintosh and W. K. Honig (Eds.), *Fundamental Issues in Associative Learning*. Dalhousie University Press, Halifax, pp. 190–203.

Migler, B. and Millenson, J. R. (1969). Analysis of response rates during stimulus generalization. *Journal of the Experimental Analysis of Behavior*, **12**, 81–87.

Noah, J. C. (1969). *The effects of appetitive and aversive Pavlovian conditioned stimuli on free-operant avoidance*. Unpublished doctoral dissertation, University of Missouri, Columbia, pp. 1–70.

Overmier, J. B. and Bull, J. A. (1970). Influences of appetitive Pavlovian conditioning upon avoidance behavior. In: J. H. Reynierse (Ed.), *Current Issues in Animal Learning*. University of Nebraska Press, Lincoln, pp. 117–141.

Overmier, J. B., Bull, J. A. and Pack, K. (1971). On instrumental response interaction as explaining the influences of Pavlovian CS$^+$s upon avoidance behaviour. *Learning and Motivation*, **2**, 103–112.

Pavlov, I. P. (1927). *Conditioned Reflexes*. Oxford University Press, London.

Peterson, J. and Premack, D. (1971). A method for mapping stimulus distance into reinforcement value. *Learning and Motivation*, **2**, 40–48.

Reiss, S. and Wagner, A. R. (1971). CS habituation produces a "Latent Inhibition Effect" but no active conditioned inhibition. *Learning and Motivation*, **2**, (in press).

Rescorla, R. A. (1967). Pavlovian conditioning and its proper control procedures. *Psychological Review*, **74**, 71–80.

Rescorla, R. A. (1969a). Pavlovian conditioned inhibition. *Psychological Bulletin*, **72**, 77–94.

Rescorla, R. A. (1969b). Conditioned inhibition of fear. In: N. J. Mackintosh and W. K. Honig (Eds.), *Fundamental Issues in Associative Learning*. Dalhousie University Press, Halifax, pp. 65–89.

Rescorla, R. A. (1971). Summation and retardation tests of latent inhibition. *Journal of Comparative and Physiological Psychology*, **75**, 77–81.

Rescorla, R. A. and Solomon, R. L. (1967). Two-process learning theory: Relationships between Pavlovian conditioning and instrumental learning. *Psychological Review*, **74**, 151–182.

Richardson, J. (1971). Cue effectiveness and abstraction in paired-associate learning. *Psychological Bulletin*, **75**, 73–91.

Rodnick, E. H. (1937). Does the interval of delay of conditioned responses possess inhibitory properties? *Journal of Experimental Psychology*, **20**, 507–527.

Seligman, M. E. P. (1969). Control group and conditioning: a comment on operationism. *Psychological Review*, **76**, 484–491.

Siegel, S. (1969). Generalization of latent inhibition. *Journal of Comparative and Physiological Psychology*, **69**, 157–159.

Skinner, B. F. (1938). *The Behavior of Organisms*. D. Appleton-Century Co., New York.

Smith, S. G. and Malott, R. M. (1971). An analysis of the nonmatching components of the stimulus matching paradigm. *Psychonomic Science*, **23**, 73–75.

Stein, N., Hoffman, H. S. and Stitt, C. (1971). Collateral behavior of the pigeon during conditioned suppression of key pecking. *Journal of the Experimental Analysis of Behavior*, **15**, 83–93.

Terrace, H. S. (1966a). Discrimination learning and inhibition. *Science*, **154**, 1677–1680.

Terrace, H. S. (1966b). Stimulus control. In W. K. Honig (Ed.), *Operant Behavior: Areas of Research and Application*. Appleton-Century-Crofts, New York, pp. 271–344.

Terrace, H. S. (1971). Escape from S⁻. *Learning and Motivation*, **2**, 148–163.

Trabasso, T. and Bower, G. H. (1968). *Attention in Learning: Theory and Research*. John Wiley and Sons, New York.

Trapold, M. A. and Overmier, J. B. (1971). The second learning process in instrumental learning. In: A. H. Black and W. F. Prokasy (Eds.), *Classical Conditioning II*. Appleton-Century-Crofts (in press).

Weisman, R. G. and Palmer, J. A. (1969). Factors influencing inhibitory stimulus control: discrimination training and prior nondifferential reinforcement. *Journal of the Experimental Analysis of Behavior*, **12**, 229–237.

Wendt, G. R. (1936). An interpretation of inhibition of conditioned reflexes as competition between reaction systems. *Psychological Review*, **43**, 258–281.

Wilton, R. N. and Godbout, R. C. (1970). Stimulus control in discrimination learning. *British Journal of Psychology*, **61**, 109–114.

Zentall, T., Collins, N. and Hearst, E. (1971). Generalization gradients around a formerly positive S⁻. *Psychonomic Science*, **22**, 257–259.

2 | Stimulus and Response Reduction: Two Aspects of Inhibitory Control in Learning

W. K. HONIG, I. BEALE, P. SERAGANIAN,
D. LANDER and D. MUIR

Dalhousie University, Halifax, Nova Scotia, Canada

I. Introduction 41
  A. The "Advance Procedure" 43
II. Studies of Negative Gradients and the Peak Shift 44
  A. Inhibitory Gradients Obtained with the Advance Procedure . 44
  B. Peak Shift After Training with the Advance Procedure . . 47
  C. Negative Gradients Following Advance Training and Multiple
    Training 50
III. Discrimination Performance with the Advance Procedure . . 54
  A. Introduction of the Advance Contingency in a Conceptual Task . 54
  B. Shifting Between Concurrent and Multiple Schedules . . 58
  C. Transfer of the Advance Procedure 60
  D. What Maintains the Advance Response? 61
IV. General Discussion 64
  A. S⁻ Reduction and Inhibition 66
  B. The Nature of the Advance Response 66
  C. Applications and Extensions of the Advance Procedure . . 67
V. Conclusions 69
Acknowledgements 69
References 69

I. Introduction

In most experiments on discrimination learning, the experimenter has exclusive control over the presentation of the discriminative stimuli. He designs a programme to present some stimuli which are positively correlated with reinforcement and others which are negatively correlated with reinforcement, and then observes a reduction of the rate, probability, or magnitude of the response of interest when the negative stimuli are presented. Current theoretical analyses of conditioned inhibition and inhibitory stimulus control (Hearst, Chapter 1, this volume; Hearst *et al.*, 1970; Jenkins, 1965; Rescorla, 1969; Terrace, Chapter 4, this volume) are all formulated with this experimental background in mind. An inhibitory stimulus is seen as the cause of a reduction of the response "below the level occurring when that stimulus is absent" (Hearst, Chapter 1). Thus, the theoretical treatment of inhibition is largely determined by a unidirectional cause-and-effect relationship between stimuli and responses. This kind of relationship has been the general focus of interest in research on and theoretical treatments of animal learning.

In this chapter, we will describe a procedure in which the experimenter shares the control of the discriminative stimuli with the subject. The time, or duration of such stimuli, which has to this point been almost exclusively an independent variable, becomes an important dependent variable, since it is determined in part by the subject's behaviour. We will see that the time is reduced if the stimulus is associated with extinction or a relatively poor schedule of reinforcement. A reduction in rate in the presence of the negative stimulus can still, of course, occur, but it is neither implied nor excluded by a reduction in the duration of S⁻.

None of the current definitions or analyses of inhibitory control deal with the possibility of a reduction in stimulus time, although, as Terrace points out in this volume, escape from S⁻ can be observed following the kind of discrimination training procedures which will produce inhibitory phenomena. Indeed, the definition of inhibition in terms of rate or probability of responding assumes a predetermined duration or rate of presentation of the inhibitory stimulus. Therefore, the observation that the duration of S⁻ is reduced when it is under the subject's control will not fall within the current categories of inhibitory phenomena. If the current definitions are accepted, the reader may consider our contribution to be irrelevant to the principal topic of this book. On the other hand, we hope to show that many of our findings with time as a dependent variable are parallel to those which give evidence for inhibitory processes as observed with rate or probability of response. The management of stimulus duration represents an adjustment to environmental contingencies that is at least as appropriate as the differentiation of rates of responding.

Procedures in which the subject controls the duration of the discriminative stimuli are not, of course, entirely new. When concurrent operants are simultaneously available, the subject, in choosing one, removes himself to some extent from the other. Herrnstein (1961) found that pigeons apportion their responses to two keys in the same ratio as the rates of reinforcements available on the two keys. While he interpreted the results in terms of differential rates of responding applied to the two keys over a constant time, one can achieve the same outcome by assuming, as do Baum and Rachlin (1969), that the subject responded at a constant rate but divided the time between the two keys according to the appropriate ratio. The latter authors investigated this possibility. In their procedure, the pigeon divided his time between two sections of an experimental chamber, which were differentially associated with two reinforcement schedules. Aside from standing in the appropriate half of the chamber, no explicit response was required for delivery of reinforcement. Baum and Rachlin showed that pigeons would divide their time according to the ratio observed by Herrnstein. With the use of a two-key pigeon chamber, Honig (1962) found that pigeons acquired a hue discrimination more rapidly and with fewer errors when the stimuli were simultaneously presented, rather than successively. He interpreted this result in terms of a differential distribution of time spent pecking to the two keys (see also Honig, 1967). He suggested that the pigeon could reduce errors if S$^-$ acted as a cue to shift responding to S$^+$. When S$^+$ was removed from the situation after training, the pigeons still pecked at S$^-$ at a considerable rate.

One problem with this kind of procedure is that when two or more discriminative stimuli are present simultaneously, their durations are formally the same, and their effective durations (in terms of controlling responding) cannot be determined precisely. For this reason, concurrent schedules with an explicit change-over (CO) response, originally developed by Findley (1958), have become very useful. With this procedure, only one stimulus is present at a time, its duration can be measured, and subjects can choose between discriminative stimuli which have no fixed location, such as tones. In his review of such concurrent schedules, Catania (1966) again reaches the general conclusion that total responses are "apportioned" between stimuli in the same ratio as the frequency of reinforcements available in the concurrent schedules. Although rate of responding is not explicitly reported in much of the work reviewed by Catania, he gives the general impression that the subjects apportion the time between stimuli, and respond at a constant rate. This impression is strengthened by a subsequent experiment by Brownstein and Pliskoff (1968) which showed that pigeons will apportion the time spent in each component of a CO concurrent schedule in the usual way, even when the food is delivered on a time-based schedule within each component, without the requirement of any specific appetitive response.

A. THE "ADVANCE PROCEDURE"

A method that will be called the advance procedure was developed independently by Ivan Beale and A. S. W. Winton, and by Peter Seraganian and W. K. Honig, for carrying out the research that will be described below. This method is clearly related to the CO concurrent procedure, in that two responses are studied: the appetitive behaviour procuring primary reinforcement, and the "advance" response which controls the duration of the discriminative stimuli. If the subject (a pigeon in our case) makes an advance response, he terminates the current stimulus, and presents the next one in a preprogrammed series. When the stimuli are randomly ordered, the next is unpredictable. In the concurrent procedure, the stimuli are ordered in strict alternation; thus the outcome of each CO response is predictable for the subject. In the Honig–Seraganian version of the advance procedure, the duration of each stimulus is limited, and the next is presented automatically when the time expires, while in concurrent schedules, the stimuli are generally not changed independently of the CO response. For our purposes, the concurrent procedure can be considered as one instance of a class of possible advance procedures, an instance in which only two stimuli are presented, in which they alternate, and in which their duration is regulated exclusively by the advance response.

When subjects are run with an advance procedure, two primary dependent measures are obtained: the *time* (T) for which each stimulus (or class of stimuli) is presented, and the *number of responses* (R) emitted in the presence of that stimulus. The *rate of responding* (r) is obtained by dividing the total responses in each stimulus by the time spent in it (R/T). The absolute values of these dependent measures vary widely from study to study, depending on particular experimental conditions. To facilitate comparisons, we will frequently provide discrimination ratios (DR's) in this report. The DR for time, DR(T), is the proportion of the total time that the pigeon spends in the positive stimulus (or set of positive stimuli); the DR for total responses, DR(R), is the proportion of the total responses that are emitted in the presence of that stimulus, and the DR for rate, DR(r), is the rate of responding to the positive stimulus divided by the sum of the rates to the positive and negative stimuli. In experiments involving multiple schedules or extended trials, S^+ and S^- are usually presented for equal lengths of time, so that DR(T) is ·50 and DR(R) and DR(r) are necessarily equal. When S^+ and S^- are not presented for equal lengths of time in a multiple schedule, this difference is corrected in advance of calculating discrimination ratios.

II. Studies of Negative Gradients and the Peak Shift

A. Inhibitory Gradients Obtained with the Advance Procedure

Beale and Winton (1970) studied negative gradients following discrimination training in which S^+ was a blue key and S^- was a vertical black line on a blue background. The general training strategy was the same as that used to obtain incremental or "inhibitory" gradients when S^+ is orthogonal to the stimulus on which the gradient is obtained (Hearst, 1969; Honig, *et al.*, 1963; Jenkins and Harrison, 1962; Weisman and Palmer, 1969; see also the review of Hearst *et al.*, 1970). Their experiment differed from the usual procedure by providing discrimination training with a concurrent schedule, and giving the generalization test with an advance procedure in which the subject determined the length of time each stimulus was presented. In the more traditional work on negative gradients, a multiple schedule (usually with time-out periods between components) is used for training, and the test stimuli are all presented by the experimenter for each length of time.

1. *Method*

After preliminary training, the six pigeons used in this study were exposed to equal concurrent reinforcement schedules associated with a black cross and a black circle on a white surround. An advance key to the right of the main key was illuminated and operative. Each response to this key alternated the concurrent schedules, and prevented reinforcement for 1·5 sec (i.e. initiated an "advance delay" for 1·5 sec). The purpose of this phase was to familiarize the subjects with the operation of the advance key.

In concurrent discrimination training, a blue light on the main key was associated with a VI 5 min reinforcement schedule, while a black vertical line on the blue key (S⁻) was associated with extinction. Each response to the advance key alternated these conditions. Each pigeon was run until 90 to 95% of the total responses were emitted in the presence of S⁺, i.e. until DR(R) reached ·90.

In the two sessions after criterion was reached, each bird received two generalization tests in extinction. In each case, six different line orientations were presented on the main key according to five random sequences. In the *multiple* test, the advance key was covered, and each stimulus was presented for 1 min at a time. In the *advance* test (called the concurrent test in the published report), the advance key was available, and each response to it effected a stimulus change advancing the test programme to the next stimulus. Each subject completed an integral number of sequences so that each stimulus value was presented an equal number of times. Three subjects were given the multiple test first, and three the advance test first.

2. *Results*

The manner in which the subjects met the discrimination criterion is summarized in Table I which presents DR(T), DR(R) and DR(r) for each bird. While each subject met the criterion in terms of total responses, this was accomplished by a combination of a differential distribution of time between components and differential response rates. No bird met the criterion in terms of DR(T) or DR(r) alone, although the option to do so was of course available.

The results of the generalization tests are presented in Fig. 1. Clear incremental gradients were obtained with time or total responses as response measures. The gradient based on rate is very shallow. A clear minimum of

TABLE I

Discrimination ratios based on the last training session

Birds	From Beale and Winton (1970)		
	DR(R)	DR(T)	DR(r)
S1	91	84	67
S2	96	90	75
S3	95	84	77
S4	91	82	68
S5	92	82	72
S6	95	74	86
Mean	93	83	74

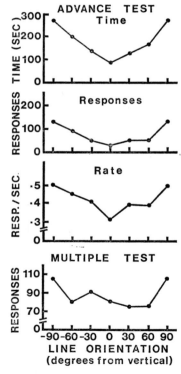

FIG. 1. Mean generalization gradients obtained with the advance test and the multiple test by Beale and Winton (1970). Data based on total responses, stimulus duration, and response rate are shown.

responding at S⁻ was shown only by two of the five birds (see Beale and Winton, 1970, for individual data). The gradient obtained from the multiple test is of course based on rate. It is quite similar to that obtained from the rate measure of the advance test data. The data from individual subjects are extremely irregular.

Since Beale and Winton did not present S^+ in the course of testing, DR's are not available from their tests. But the sensitivity of the response measures can be assessed by comparing test values obtained from S^- and from values furthest from S^- on the gradient ($\pm$ 90°). These DR's are as follows:

advance test: DR(R) = ·82; DR(T) = ·75; DR(r) = ·59
multiple test: DR(r) = ·53

These measures are ordered in the same way as those taken from the end of training, although they are of course somewhat lower, since two values from the gradient are used in the comparison, rather than S^+ and S^-. The incremental form of the total response gradient is clearly due primarily to differences in time and not differences in rate.

3. *Discussion*

Incremental gradients have been obtained with the advance procedure which are similar to those obtained on the dimension of line orientation with traditional "multiple test" methods (Honig *et al.*, 1963). With duration as a dependent variable, a finding has been obtained which is parallel to the direct evidence for inhibition, when such data are provided by differential response rates around S^- (Hearst *et al.*, 1970; Jenkins, 1965). If we wish to provide further justification of duration as an indicator of inhibitory stimulus control, it will be helpful to use the same measure to demonstrate other phenomena which are associated with inhibitory processes. One such phenomenon is the peak shift, which follows discrimination training between two stimuli on the same dimension. Rate of responding to S^+ is less than that to one or more stimuli that are further removed from S^-. Perhaps the same result can be obtained with stimulus duration as a dependent measure.

B. Peak Shift After Training with the Advance Procedure

While peak shift following discrimination training has been demonstrated along a number of visual dimensions, including line orientation (Bloomfield, 1967), the phenomenon has been obtained only after training with multiple schedules and not with concurrent schedules. Honig (1962) failed to obtain it when he trained pigeons with the simultaneous discrimination referred to above, although other subjects run with a multiple schedule provided peak shift data comparable to those of Hanson (1959). Winton and Beale (1971) have studied peak shift following concurrent training when the generalization gradient was carried out with the advance procedure.

1. *Method*

The first part of their study involved non-differential training with a tilted line either present or absent on a blue background. Since no stimulus control on the dimension of line orientation was subsequently observed, this phase, which is described in the published report, will be omitted here. In the discrimination phase, responding to the advance key alternated a VI 2 min with a VI 10 min schedule. For three birds, the former was associated with a line tilted 60° from the vertical, and the latter with a line tilted at 30°; for two subjects this relationship was reversed. In order to facilitate control by line orientation, the brightnesses of the stimuli were varied irregularly during the first 33 discrimination sessions, but were then equated. Two different VI schedules were used (rather than VI and extinction) in order to maintain some responding to the less favourable stimulus. This would facilitate detection of a negative peak shift, i.e. less responding to a value further removed from S^+ on the test dimension than is S^-.

Each bird reached criterion when the relative number of responses matched the relative rates of reinforcement; that is, when DR(R) reached ·84. A generalization test was then carried out with seven stimuli ordered in four different sequences. The advance contingency was in effect, and each bird was allowed to complete an integral number of sequences in the course of about 30 min. Another test was given after each subject completed sixty training sessions. One subject that did not reach criterion in time for the first test was tested only after sixty sessions.

2. *Results*

The data from the first post-discrimination test given to each subject are seen in Fig. 2. Since both S^+ and S^- were presented in the test, DR's can

TABLE II

Discrimination ratios based on the first post-discrimination test
of Winton and Beale

Subject	DR(R)	DR(T)	DR(r)
B1	·88	·85	·58
B2	·78	·73	·58
B3	·83	·80	·61
B4	·90	·77	·66
B5	·84	·72	·61
Mean	·85	·77	·61

be assessed from the test data. These ratios are presented in Table II. The relationships among discrimination measures observed by Beale and Winton are confirmed in this study. The mean DR(R) is ·85, corresponding closely to the DR of ·84 required to meet criterion. DR(T) is ·77, and DR(r) is much below this at ·61. It should be noted that it was again a combination of differential stimulus durations and response rates that produced the criterion performance. Corresponding to the discrimination ratios, we may note that the gradient slopes are less when based on the rate measure than on the other two measures.

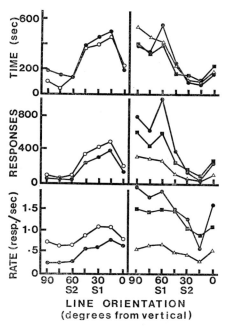

FIG. 2. Generalization gradients obtained with the advance procedure by Winton and Beale (1971). The first post-discrimination test is shown for each subject. Data based on total responses, stimulus duration, and rate are shown. The data are presented separately for subjects with 30° as S1 and with 60° as S1.

Both positive and negative peak shift can be observed with at least one measure for each subject on the first post-discrimination test. Positive peak shift is defined here simply as an instance of greater responsiveness to at least one of the two values lying "beyond" S1, and negative peak shift is similarly defined as an instance of less responsiveness to one or both of the values lying "beyond" S 2. Four of the five subjects showed positive peak shift in terms of total responses and time, while only two subjects showed

E

positive peak shift in terms of response rate. Oddly enough, one of these was the subject (B1) that did not show peak shift in terms of R or T. The subjects generally showed negative peak shifts, with a few exceptions. However, as Winton and Beale point out, the stimuli at which negative peak shift can be observed are also further from S^+ than is S^-, and responding to these may be less simply because of greater generalization decrement at these values. To demonstrate negative peak shift unequivocally, one needs an "upturn" in the gradient at some point beyond S^-. This upturn can in fact be seen for the subjects that show the best evidence of negative peak shift.

3. *Discussion*

The occurrence of positive peak shift is often taken to suggest the operation of inhibitory control at and around the negative stimulus. Negative peak shift with an "upturn" in the gradient leads to a similar conclusion. It is of particular interest that these phenomena could be observed for four of the five subjects in each case in terms of the time that they spent in the presence of various stimuli on the test dimension. This finding confirms the evidence for inhibitory stimulus control from the duration gradients obtained by Beale and Winton. The evidence of positive peak shift in terms of the rate measure was less striking than that based on total responses and duration. Some peak shift may be expected in terms of the rate measure simply because reliable differences in rate did develop in the course of training, and Thomas (1962) showed that even with only partial attainment of a multiple schedule discrimination, a moderate amount of peak or area shift will result. It would have been of interest if Winton and Beale had given a test with fixed stimulus periods (as they did in their earlier study) to determine whether peak shift in terms of rate occurs under those more constrained conditions.

C. Negative Gradients Following Advance Training and Multiple Training

In the two studies by Beale and Winton, all birds were trained with a concurrent, or advance, procedure. The test data reflect the skills acquired in that procedure, of keeping the duration of S^- relatively short in comparison to the duration of S^+. Rate differences in testing were much less marked than differences in stimulus duration. It is of interest to determine whether birds who have been trained with the traditional multiple schedule will control stimulus duration in the same way, or whether their behaviour in testing will primarily reflect the differences in response rate that are acquired in the course of multiple discrimination training. Beale *et al.* (in press) have recently completed a study in which two different groups of pigeons received advance training and multiple training and were then given generalization tests.

1. *Method*

For both groups of four birds, a vertical line alternated with a blank blue key during training. For seven sessions, responding to both stimuli was reinforced on a VI 1 min schedule until 30 reinforcements were collected. During the first four of these sessions, the advance key was illuminated, and the birds could switch back and forth (in regular alternation) between the discriminative stimuli. During the last three sessions, the advance key was not illuminated, and the stimuli alternated every minute. Beginning with the eighth session, the schedule associated with the vertical line was changed to extinction. For the multiple schedule group, the advance key was inoperative, and the stimuli with their associated reinforcement schedules alternated every minute. The advance group could alternate the stimulus and the associated reinforcement schedule by pecking at the advance key. Each period ended automatically after 60 sec if no advance response was made. A training session was run until 30 reinforcements were collected. After nine discrimination sessions, a generalization test on the dimension of line orientation was administered to both groups. The advance key was operative, and the general procedure was the same as that used by Beale and Winton, save that a maximum stimulus duration of 60 sec was allowed.

After the test, the training conditions were reversed for the two groups after one or two additional sessions: the advance contingency was made available to the multiple schedule group, and was removed for the other group. After twelve further training sessions, a second test was given to each group. The four subjects currently being run with the advance procedure were then given a third generalization test for a positive (decremental) gradient with various spectral values in the absence of the vertical line. The advance procedure was in effect. The spectral values were 501 nm (the blue training value), 538 nm, 555 nm, 576 nm and 606 nm. Only the first and third tests will be considered here.

2. *Results*

This study provides an opportunity to compare the acquisition of stimulus control during advance and multiple procedures. However, a consideration of the training data will be left to the next section of this chapter, where they can be grouped together with training data from other experiments. Normalized data from the first generalization test are seen in Figs. 3 and 4 in terms of time and response rate. While there was a good deal of variability among birds, those subjects trained with the advance procedure provided much better negative gradients. They produced an incremental gradient of stimulus duration, while that from the multiple schedule birds was essentially flat. Rate differences among test stimuli are also more pronounced for the advance group, although one or two multiple schedule birds provide an incremental gradient.

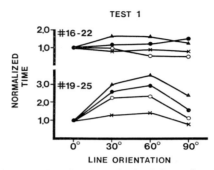

Fig. 3. Gradients of stimulus duration obtained from the advance group (Subjects 19–25) and the multiple group (Subjects 16–22) by Beale, Lander and Honig (in press). The gradients have been "folded" by averaging values for line orientations which differ to the same degree from S⁻, and normalized, by expressing test values as proportions of the S⁻ value (0°).

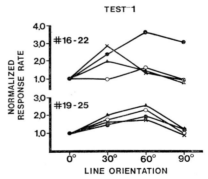

Fig. 4. Gradients of response rate obtained from the advance group (Subjects 19–25) and the multiple group (Subjects 16–22) by Beale, Lander and Honig (in press). The gradients have been "folded" and normalized as in Fig. 3.

The data from the test with spectral values indicate clear decremental gradients for each subject in terms of time and response rate (Fig. 5). In order to make the slopes comparable, the data were normalized for each subject by setting the value obtained at 501 nm (S⁺) at 1·00 and expressing the remaining values as decimal fractions. The gradients for time and rate of responding are quite similar, although the latter is slightly steeper.

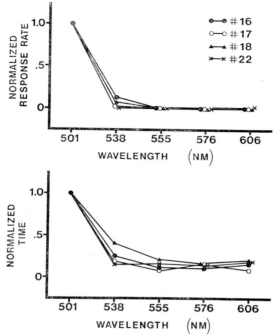

Fig. 5. Positive gradients on the dimension of spectral value obtained by Beale, Lander and Honig after training four pigeons with the advance procedure. Normalized data are presented for stimulus duration and for response rate. The spectral value used for S+ was 501 nm.

3. Discussion

Discrimination training with the advance (or concurrent) procedure appears necessary to produce incremental gradients of stimulus duration. The multiple schedule group was familiarized with the operation of the advance key before differential training began, but this was not sufficient. It is unlikely that these birds failed to use the advance key in testing because S⁻ was insufficiently "negative" for them; they developed a reasonable discrimination performance (DR(r) was about ·80 at the end of the first phase of training), and they acquired appropriate use of the advance key very quickly when they were switched to the advance procedure after the first test. It may not, of course, be necessary for birds to have advance key training with the same stimuli that are then incorporated into the generalization test. Data on the "transfer" of advance responding between different specific discriminations will be presented later in this chapter. From these data one would gather that if birds were trained with the advance procedure in, let us say, an auditory discrimination, and the procedure were then made available after multiple training on a visual problem, they would then produce incremental gradients on an appropriate visual dimension.

The failure to obtain a negative gradient in terms of response rate from the advance group is to be expected from the results of Beale and Winton. It is somewhat surprising that the multiple group did not provide better evidence of inhibitory control in terms of the rate measure. Perhaps the rate difference (with a mean DR of about ·80) was not large enough at the end of training. Since the stimuli were alternated regularly (to make training comparable to the advance procedure), stimulus control over responding may in part have come under control of the sequence of stimuli, rather than under the stimuli themselves.

The positive gradients obtained at the end of the experiment are of particular interest because they show that appropriate advance responding is not restricted to the negative stimulus and stimuli similar to it. The various spectral values are presumably orthogonal to the dimension of line orientation, so that responding would not have been determined by a differential similarity between S^- and specific test stimuli. The subjects could apparently "appreciate" the presence of S^+ by staying in the presence of that stimulus much longer than the others. There is some question whether the gradient is really ordered, or whether all test stimuli other than S^+ were treated similarly by the subjects. We should note that the first stimulus interval, from 501 to 538 nm, is a very large one for the pigeon, and responding is greatly reduced at the latter value. Furthermore, response rate as a measure results in a gradient that is no more orderly than that based on time. The former measure normally produces a very orderly gradient when the test stimuli are not too different from S^+.

III. Discrimination Performance with the Advance Procedure

This section provides a summary of recent work from our laboratory in which the advance procedure was used in discrimination training. The main questions of concern to us are these: (1) What is the effect of introducing the advance procedure in the course of discrimination training, especially in terms of the various indices of stimulus control? (2) Can advance responding provide a general indicator of stimulus control that is independent of rate differences? (3) What conditions maintain and govern the advance response itself? These questions are by no means fully answered in this chapter, but at least some data relevant to each one are available.

A. INTRODUCTION OF THE ADVANCE CONTINGENCY IN A CONCEPTUAL TASK

The advance procedure was first used by Honig and Seraganian (1971) as a response to frustration engendered by poor discrimination performance in a conceptual task. In a procedure based on the methods of Herrnstein and Loveland (1964) and described in detail by Siegel and Honig (1970), pigeons are successively presented with a large number of positive and negative instances of the concept of "human being" displayed in a naturalistic setting. Discrimination performance tended to stabilize at a DR of ·65–·70, which reflected a tendency to respond during negative periods (rather than a failure of responding to positive instances). We were interested in determining whether this failure to suppress responding in S^+ was due to a "true" failure to discriminate between instances, or whether it was an aspect of our procedure that could be circumvented by providing the subject with an opportunity to terminate a negative trial and to move on to the next trial in a randomly ordered sequence.

1. Method

Subjects pecked at 2 in × 2 in plexiglass panel as the response key, which was transilluminated with coloured pictures projected by a Kodak Carousel projector. Each of the 40 daily trials lasted 90 sec and was followed by a blackout of 10 sec. Positive slides were associated with a VI 62·5 sec reinforcement schedule; negative slides, with extinction. During advance sessions, a small round white advance key was illuminated next to the main response panel. A single peck had the immediate effect of advancing the slide projector and initiating the next trial. Each advance response resulted in an advance delay of reinforcement of 2 sec. If the subject had not advanced out of the immediately preceding trial, a trial could be terminated by the first advance response. If the pigeon had advanced into a given trial, advance responses were ineffective for the first 5 sec of that trial. If the pigeon did not make an advance response, the trial was terminated after 90 sec and was followed by the usual 10-sec inter-trial interval.

Seven birds were run in the first study. For three of them, the advance contingency was removed (by darkening the advance key and making it ineffective) and then reintroduced, in order to replicate the effects of introducing that contingency.

2. Results

When the advance key was made available, most birds began to peck at it spontaneously. Only one or two were given a special procedure to strengthen the advance response. The advance key was lit at the beginning of the session while the main panel was dark, and the advance response was required to initiate the session. This procedure was dropped as soon as "regular" advance responding appeared. For each bird, the number of effective advance responses increased markedly from zero or a few responses during one session to 20 or more (out of a possible 40) in the next. The latter is designated as the first "effective advance session" for each bird, and data are presented with temporal reference to it.

The advance performance can be assessed in terms of the amount of time for which S^+ and S^- periods are presented during a session; the maximum in each case is 1800 sec. This measure will be used here because a DR based on time can easily be obtained from it. The number of positive and negative periods terminated in a given session are also of interest, but will not be presented here. Suffice it to say that typically a subject advances out of most or all of the S^- periods, and out of about half of the positive periods or fewer; some subjects advance out of very few positive periods. The latency of advancing out of negative periods is generally quite short; the subject does not peck for a while at the main key and then, failing to obtain reinforcement, switches to the advance key. An analysis comparing the latencies of terminating positive and negative trials (ignoring non-terminated trials) showed that the median latencies of terminating negative trials were much shorter.

The mean time spent in the presence of positive and negative stimuli during the first six effective advance sessions is shown in Fig. 6 (upper). There was practically no overlap of the distributions, and no bird ever spent more time in S^+ than in S^-. The DR(T)'s based on these data are as follows: Session 1: ·68; Session 2: ·76; Session 3: ·80; Session 4: ·84; Session 5: ·80; Session 6: ·78.

The mean DR's based on total responses and response rate are shown in Fig. 6 (lower). Before the first effective advance session, the DR had reached the usual ·70 value, and showed little sign of improving. As soon as the advance contingency "took hold", DR(R) increased markedly; this was observed for all animals. DR(r), on the other hand, stayed the same as before. Thus, while instances of S^- were presented, the bird pecked at them at the same relative rate as in the absence of the advance contingency, but the birds did improve their performance by terminating S^- periods and thus reducing the time in the presence of those stimuli.

When the advance contingency was withdrawn, the discrimination ratio declined, although that transition is not presented here. The decline is, however, evident from the replication data, which are plotted as open symbols in Fig. 6. The baseline of the discrimination is somewhat higher for the replication, due to additional training received on the discrimination problem, but it is lower than the performance with the advance procedure previously in effect. When the advance key was made available for the second time, all birds used it in the first session on which it was introduced. The data are marred by poor performances on the second advance day, but otherwise they are similar to those described above.

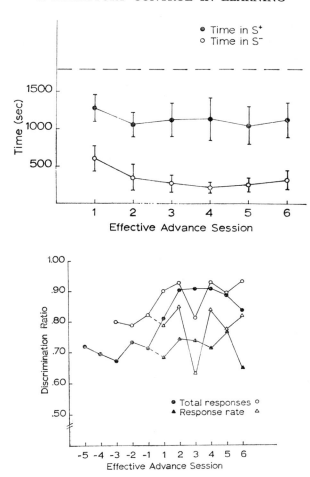

FIG. 6. *Upper*: time spent in the presence of S+ and S− by seven birds run on the advance procedure. One standard deviation to either side of the mean is indicated by the vertical lines. The dashed line indicates the maximum duration of each stimulus. *Lower*: discrimination ratios of total responses and rate before and after the advance procedure took effect. Filled symbols represent data from seven birds when the procedure was first introduced; open symbols represent data from three subjects with whom the procedure was replicated. (From Honig and Seraganian, 1971.)

3. *Discussion*

The results show quite clearly that pigeons, given the opportunity to terminate stimuli in a complex discrimination, will spend much more time in positive than with negative instances. It is unlikely that these results are artefactual. While we have not run birds in which the advance key was illuminated but initially ineffective, the observed extinction of advance responding (see below) indicates that the greater number of advance responses in S⁻ periods is not because a lower response rate to the main panel provides a greater opportunity for competing behaviour. Advance key responding may in the long run be maintained by the fact that appropriate advance responses do improve the overall rate of reinforcement. But it is unlikely that this factor alone can explain our results. First of all, advance responding will have this effect only if it is differentially applied to S⁺ and S⁻ periods; indiscriminate advance responding will not lead to any net gain in the rate of reinforcement. Thus, this explanation of our results already implies the kind of discrimination that we actually observed. Secondly, the very rapid and accurate development of advance responding suggests that it was the consequences of the response in terms of stimulus changes rather than some net long-term improvement in reinforcement density, that strengthened and maintained the behaviour.

B. SHIFTING BETWEEN CONCURRENT AND MULTIPLE SCHEDULES

The study by Beale, Lander and Honig described in the previous section affords a comparison of the discrimination performance with and without the advance contingency from the outset of training. Both of their groups—the multiple schedule group and the advance group—were switched to the opposite training procedure after the first generalization test for negative stimulus control. The advance procedure involved alternating stimuli that were limited to 60 sec on each presentation.

1. *Results*

The training data are described in Fig. 7, from which a number of salient points emerge. The group run first with the advance procedure does better

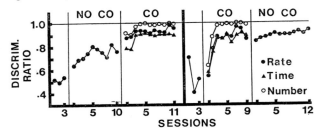

FIG. 7. Mean indices of discrimination performance from birds run on the advance procedure (CO) and on the multiple procedure (No go) by Beale, Lander and Honig. Data from the group given the multiple procedure first are shown to the left of centre, and those from the group given the advance procedure first are shown to the right. The procedures were switched at the break in the curves. Where the multiple procedure is in effect, only one curve is shown, since DR(R) and DR(r) are the same under this condition, while there are three curves shown where the advance procedure is in effect. Data from the last three sessions before discrimination training began are also shown.

than the multiple schedule group on all measures from the outset of training, including response rate (DR(r)). Furthermore, with the advance procedure, improvement is very rapid in terms of total responses, and approaches a DR of 1·00 even in the third session of training, although pretraining involved seven sessions of equal reinforcement with the two stimuli in question. As soon as the advance contingency was introduced for the multiple schedule birds, their performance in terms of total responses also reached almost 100% accuracy. The discrimination of the other group, for whom the advance contingency was withdrawn, was somewhat impaired, although it tended to recover to some extent in the course of further training.

2. Discussion

The effects of shifting between multiple and concurrent schedules are very similar to those of introducing and withdrawing the advance contingency. It may be worth considering the determinants of the improved performance during the advance procedure. Total responses result from the application of a local rate of responding for a given time, and the differences between discrimination performance with and without the advance contingency in effect could be due entirely to differences in the relative duration of S⁻ under the two procedures. In such a case, DR(r) would be the same under advance and multiple procedures, while DR(R) (and, obviously, DR(T)) would differ. The data from the study by Honig and Seraganian support that impression. However, it is also possible that the local rate will change as a function of the duration of S⁻. In successive discrimination training, it is often observed that responding is suppressed at the beginning of an extended S⁻ period, but "breaks through" towards the end. If this is the case, then DR(r) will not be the same under multiple and advance procedures; if local rate increases during S⁻, DR(r) will be lower during multiple training. The data from Beale, Lander and Honig support this notion; during the first phase of discrimination training, DR(r) from the advance group was consistently higher than from the multiple group. Following the switch of conditions, a similar difference is seen, although it is not as great.*

It appears, therefore, that the pigeons switched out of S⁻ while responding to that stimulus was relatively low. Perhaps S⁻ is "most negative" shortly after its onset, and is most likely to induce both suppression of appetitive responding and behaviour leading to its termination. Perhaps responding to S⁻ was reinforced towards the end of its presentation in the multiple

*Since DR(r) is based on a ratio of rates, differences in this index can reflect different rates to S⁺ as well as to S⁻. The data collected by Beale et al. (in press) indicate that differences in DR(r) between groups can be largely attributed to differences in rate to S⁻, and that changes in the DR(r) within groups likewise reflect increases or decreases in response rate to S⁻, not S⁺.

schedule by the appearance of S^+. Whatever the reason may be for the relationship between S^- duration and response rate, it would be useful to sort it out experimentally. A multiple schedule group could be yoked to an advance group so that it receives the same temporal pattern of positive and negative stimuli, but has no control over terminating them. It would also be possible, although technically more challenging, to record the duration of S^- periods with an advance group, and then to obtain data on response rates during the comparable portions of S^- intervals presented to a multiple group.

C. Transfer of the Advance Procedure

Peter Seraganian has studied transfer of the advance response between independent discriminations. His one subject was initially trained on a "bird concept", for which the presence of one or more birds in a picture provided the positive feature. This subject demonstrated the usual improvement in performance on this problem when the advance contingency was introduced. DR(R) was over ·90, while DR(T) varied between ·68 and ·78. A simple blue-green discrimination was introduced for one session while the advance key was unlit; otherwise the training parameters were the same. During this session, the pigeon achieved a DR of ·58. For the next two sessions, the advance key was lit and effective. The subject used it immediately, terminating all 20 S^- periods and only one S^+ period in each session. DR(R) rose to 1·00, while DR(T) reached ·89.

Seraganian then introduced a much harder auditory discrimination between a white noise of 88 db as S^+ and the ambient noise level in the box as S^-. The advance contingency was in effect during all sessions; however, due to a programming error, the advance into the next period was delayed by 5 sec after an effective advance response for the first 13 sessions. During the first three sessions, the subject showed little evidence of discrimination, and did not make a single response to the advance key. Beginning with the fourth session, the discrimination improved, and the advance contingency was used to good effect. During the last five sessions with this procedure, the median DR(R) was ·89, the median DR(T) was ·70, and the median DR(r) was ·78. The subject terminated a median 16 S^- periods, but never more than one S^+ period, in a session. On the fourteenth session, the programming error was corrected, and four sessions were run in which effective advance responses produced the next stimulus immediately. DR(R), DR(T) and DR(r) increased to ·96, ·84 and ·87, respectively, by the fourth session.

These findings indicate that if the advance procedure is mastered in the course of performing one discrimination, it can be transferred to another, partly learned discrimination. Furthermore, it may assist in the attainment of a difficult discrimination when the contingency is present from the start of training. We cannot demonstrate that the application of the advance response to the later problems was facilitated by its acquisition in the first problem, unless we run appropriate control procedures. Subjects should be exposed to the advance contingency on the later problems without the benefit of advance training on the first problem. It is, however, unlikely that Seraganian's pigeon would have performed as well on the blue-green discrimination without prior training. The fact that he terminated every S⁻ period right from the start suggests that the appropriate performance of the advance response was being transferred, not acquired. It is notable that the same bird failed to make any advance responses on the auditory problem until he had some experience with the discriminative stimuli and their contingencies.

D. WHAT MAINTAINS THE ADVANCE RESPONSE?

To this point, we have treated the advance response as one way in which an organism can adjust the stimuli in its environment in accordance with the contingencies with which they are associated. Yet the response is also a bit of instrumental behaviour, and as such it is under the control of stimuli, subject to motivating conditions, and sensitive to its consequences. The manner in which it is governed by current stimuli has been elucidated, in part, by the previous sections of this chapter. Clearly, it is likely to occur in the presence of S⁻ and stimuli similar to S⁻ and in the presence of stimuli that differ from S⁺ (cf. the decremental gradient of Beale *et al.*, in press), and unlikely to occur in the presence of S⁺ and stimuli similar to S⁺.

We know much less about the government of the advance response by its consequences. A bit of preliminary research has been done on the conditions necessary to maintain advance responding, but a systematic attack on this problem has not been carried out. Seraganian, using the "bird concept" described in the previous section, showed that if the advance contingency is discontinued, but the advance key is lit, the advance response will extinguish. At first the number of advance responses increased, but this was no doubt due to the fact that S⁻ was on for a much longer time, since it could not be terminated by the advance response. Eventually the behaviour declined.

An effective advance response in S⁻ always produces the stimuli associated with the next programmed trial. In the work described so far, this generally involves the termination of S⁻ and the presentation of S⁺, except that advance responding will be followed by an S⁻ period on half the trials if they are presented in random order. The negative reinforcement of terminating S⁻ and the positive reinforcement of producing S⁺ are therefore confounded. A proper analysis involves the kinds of problems that are encountered in the study of escape from S⁻ (Rilling *et al.*, 1969; Terrace, 1971(b); see also Terrace, Chapter 4). It is very difficult to initiate S⁺ without terminating S⁻. It is easier to terminate S⁻ without initiating S⁺, but this procedure involves the progression from one condition of no reinforcement (S⁻) to another (the inter-trial interval).

Darwin Muir has investigated the effects of terminating S⁻ without the production of S⁺ with two pigeons, both of which had previous experience with the advance contingency. The birds were trained with a blue key as S⁺ and with a white vertical bar superimposed on the blue key as S⁻. In the absence of an advance response, each trial lasted 60 sec and was followed by a 10-sec blackout. On this multiple schedule, the trials alternated in a regular fashion. An advance response resulted in an immediate stimulus change from S⁻ to S⁺ or vice versa, a 2-sec delay of reinforcement, and a 5-sec blackout of the advance key. Each session was run until 30 reinforcements were collected on a VI 1 min schedule. Muir used regular alternation of S⁺ and S⁻ in order to provide continuous reinforcement of the advance responding in S⁻, rather than the partial reinforcement (and possibly partial punishment) of that response in a randomly alternating sequence of trials, where two or three S⁻ periods may be programmed in succession. This strict alternation will also discourage responding in S⁺, since such behaviour can never be reinforced by the appearance of S⁺. Table III provides data from the last three of eight regular sessions of this nature, at which time the discrimination and the advance responding had stabilized at very good levels. In this table, the level of advance responding is indicated as the ratio of S⁻ periods terminated to the number of periods presented.

Beginning with the ninth session, a response to the advance key terminated the stimulus that was being displayed at the time, and introduced a time-out for the duration of the current trial. Data are presented for the 15 sessions for which this procedure was in effect. During Sessions 10 and 11, a programming error (or equipment failure) resulted in equal reinforcement in S⁺ and S⁻. On Session 12, differential reinforcement was reinstated. This aberration resulted in a reduction of discrimination performance in terms of all three ratios. The number of advance responses decreased in Session 11 for both birds. For Subject 25, advance responding recovered as the discrimination was re-established (cf. DR(r)), and DR(T) returned briefly to a level of ·85. After this, the advance responding gradually declined until very few advance responses were made, and DR(T) reached ·50, while DR(R) and DR(r) remained at a very high level. Subject 19 showed less recovery of the advance responding, and DR(T) never really recovered from its drop on Session 11.

On Session 24, the initial conditions were reinstated, and both birds recovered appropriate responding to the advance key, with a concomitant rise in DR(T)—Subject 19 on the first session, and Subject 25 on the second.

TABLE III

Advance responding and discrimination ratios with and without immediate presentation of S$^+$ following the advance response[a]

Session	Proportion of S$^-$ Periods Terminated		DR(R)		DR(T)		DR(r)	
	S19	S25	S19	S25	S19	S25	S19	S25
6	40/45	41/41	·99	·99	·91	·92	·92	·93
7	36/36	32/32	·98	·99	·91	·90	·85	·93
8	27/37	34/34	1·00	·99	·93	·91	·96	·93
9	25/28	32/32	·99	·99	·78	·91	·97	·90
10	21/25	30/30	·94	·99	·74	·90	·85	·94
11	5/18	18/22	·70	·79	·55	·68	·65	·63
12	19/30	15/32	·74	·85	·66	·58	·59	·81
13	9/31	8/30	·91	·96	·53	·52	·90	·95
14	12/31	29/32	·97	·98	·56	·84	·98	·91
15	12/32	25/31	·97	·99	·55	·75	·97	·96
16	14/32	24/32	·95	·98	·58	·67	·94	·96
17	17/32	15/32	·98	·98	·62	·56	·96	·98
18	9/35	5/31	·97	·99	·54	·53	·97	·99
19	13/32	15/32	·99	·99	·58	·59	·98	·98
20	10/32	5/32	·99	·99	·54	·50	·98	·99
21	19/32	3/33	·97	·98	·61	·50	·96	·98
22	15/31	4/31	·97	·98	·60	·51	·95	·98
23	12/33	4/32	·98	·98	·56	·50	·97	·98
24	37/37	5/33	·98	·99	·93	·51	·79	·99
25	34/34	35/36	·99	·99	·94	·81	·84	·96
26	32/32	31/31	·99	·99	·95	·91	·81	·94
27	35/35	32/32	·98	·99	·94	·92	·79	·88

[a] During Sessions 6, 7 and 8, each advance response in S$^-$ terminated the negative trial and initiated a positive trial. During Sessions 9–23, advance responses terminated the negative stimulus and initiated time out until the scheduled end of the trial. During Sessions 24, 25, 26 and 27, the initial conditions were reinstated. (For details, see text.)

1. Discussion

During the sessions in which advance responding merely terminated the discriminative stimulus, neither subject ever made an advance response in S$^+$, so the consideration of these results need not be clouded by the question whether advance responses were punished by a termination of S$^+$ and therefore declined in number. The decline seems to have been due to the omission of the events that reinforce the advance behaviour. Termination of S$^-$

is not sufficient to maintain the behaviour, except possibly at a low level. It appears that the presentation of S^+ is required.

Experiments of this nature, which examine the reinforcing or aversive properties of discriminative stimuli, are always hard to interpret. The time out, which followed the termination of S^- was associated with lack of reinforcement to the same extent as S^-. Thus, the net gain of terminating S^- may be very small, although the work of Rilling *et al.* (1969) and Terrace (1971b) indicates that such behaviour is maintained. Secondly, the appearance of S^+ is accompanied by the increased proximity of the next reinforcement on the VI schedule. Advance responding may have declined because it was no longer accompanied by a net gain in reinforcement density. We have argued above that the rapid acquisition and transfer of advance behaviour puts such an interpretation in doubt; and here, again, we should note that advance responding recovered very quickly when the appearance of S^+ was made contingent upon it. None the less, it would be useful to develop research paradigms in which the appearance of S^+ and the reduction of time to the next reinforcement are unconfounded.

Whatever the outcome of such experiments, it does seem that a relative gain in the "desirability" of the stimulus situation is necessary to initiate and maintain advance behaviour. When equal reinforcement schedules are associated with the discriminative stimuli, advance responding appears to diminish. Admittedly, this circumstance was generated in Muir's study by accident, and needs to be studied independently of the other manipulations that he carried out. Furthermore, before a difference in primary reinforcement contingencies is detected, advance responding does not occur, as Seraganian showed. It is, of course, true that if equal concurrent reinforcement schedules are in effect, subjects will generally switch between their associated stimuli. (Beale *et al.* (in press) have shown this in the pretraining phases of their experiments described above.) But this switching tends to drop out if the reinforcement programme associated with each stimulus is interrupted while the other stimulus is presented. In other words, the switching will occur only if it produces a gain in overall reinforcement density.

IV. General Discussion

A. S^- REDUCTION AND INHIBITION

The research reviewed in this chapter provides ample evidence that pigeons, when provided with control over the duration of discriminative stimuli, will manage their duration in such a way as to reflect their differential correlation with reinforcement. The duration of S^- is reduced in relation to that of S^+ and that of values differing from S^- on a stimulus dimension orthogonal to the difference between S^+ and S^-. Since inhibitory processes are normally identified and analysed in terms of a reduction of responding in the presence of S^-, our results may be considered outside the range of inhibitory phenomena. However, if we simply accept the duration of S^- as a dependent variable, then our results do meet some of the criteria of conditioned inhibition suggested by Hearst in this volume, by Hearst et al. (1970), and by Rescorla (1969). First, the reduction of S^- is in all probability due to the association between that stimulus and lack of reinforcement, or a relatively unfavourable schedule. In the studies by Beale and Winton, and Beale et al. (in press), S^+ and S^- were equally associated with reinforcement in advance of discrimination training, while Winton and Beale failed to show any generalization decrement between S1 (the original training value) and S2 (the value later associated with a poor reinforcement schedule) in the first generalization test. In studies on concept attainment, pigeons generalize broadly between displays containing S^+ and those which do not, unless discrimination training is carried out. While there are values which the subject will terminate after training simply because they differ sufficiently from S^+, as shown by the positive gradient obtained by Beale et al. (in press) this possible explanation of S^- reduction was obviated in most or all of the present studies.

Second, the reduction of S^- was produced by the presentation of a discrete external stimulus, namely S^- itself (or a similar value). While the reinforcement of the response terminating S^- may have been the appearance of S^+ or a relative gain in reinforcement density, the response is caused by the appearance of S^-. Similarly, when response rates are reduced in the presence of S^-, this reduction may be "maintained" by an avoidance of frustration, or some similar process, but the immediate cause of the reduction is the presence of S^-.

Third, we have been able to distinguish between S^- as an inhibitory stimulus, in that its duration is reduced relative to S^+, and inhibitory dimensional control in the form of incremental generalization gradients (cf. Hearst et al., 1970). Finally, we have at least in some cases, observed the reduction of S^- while all other major aspects of the procedure remained unchanged, particularly when the advance contingency was introduced in the Honig–Seraganian procedure. What we have not done—and this appears to be a critical test of inhibitory function both for Hearst and for Rescorla—is to run a combined-cue or "summation" test. In such a test, the subject would terminate a combination of S^- and an independently trained S^+ more readily than he would terminate S^+ alone (cf. Hearst, this volume, Chapter 1). Since our studies were not explicitly designed to test the termination of S^- as an inhibitory phenomenon, we may perhaps be forgiven for having failed to meet this rather stringent criterion.

F

B. The Nature of the Advance Response

We have seen that the reduction of S⁻ frequently accompanies a reduction in rate of responding when S⁻ is present. The termination of S⁻ is of course due to an *increase* in the strength of the advance response (in terms of a reduced latency or increased probability of that behaviour). To what extent are these two changes in responding related? We may ask this question with reference to some of the "by-products" of discrimination learning that involves "active" inhibition, as they are described by Terrace, Chapter 4 (see also Terrace, 1971a). Perhaps the termination of S⁻ is merely one such "by-product". Birds that make errors display a lot of "emotional" behaviour in S⁻, which presumably competes with pecking, but is not under the control of any consequences that can be clearly identified. We doubt very much that striking the advance key comes into this category, but we have not conclusively shown that such responding will remain at a low level when it has no consequences. However, Rilling *et al.* (1969) and Terrace (1971b) have run appropriate "displacement" control groups in their studies of escape from S⁻, and obtained very little responding to the escape key.

The reduction of unreinforced appetitive responding may be due to an escape from, or "reduction" of, the presence of S⁻ by turning away from it. Perhaps the formalized advance response merely provides an explicit form of such behaviour, much as the changeover response in a concurrent schedule is a formalized version of the shifts between S⁺ and S⁻ when they are simultaneously presented. At this time, our results do not indicate that advance responding will be maintained by the termination of S⁻, but, as indicated above, Muir's findings are not entirely conclusive. One problem is that in this study, the termination of S⁻ put the organism into a blackout which was associated with extinction, while for Terrace (1971b) and Rilling *et al.* (1969), the escape response, while interrupting S⁻, did not alter a number of other visual stimuli which were equally associated with reinforcement and extinction.

Finally, it is possible that the emission of behaviour that competes with appetitive responding also precludes the frustration or whatever negative state results from having responded in vain. It would be hard to demonstrate such an outcome, and even harder to show that the advance response is controlled by it. On the other hand, it has probably not been shown that escape from S⁻ is simply maintained by the escape from that stimulus as such and not by the escape from responding to it. To do this, one would have to design an experiment showing escape from an S⁻ that is negatively correlated with non-contingent or "free" reinforcement. Indeed, the failure of Terrace to obtain escape from S⁻ when the discriminative control was acquired without errors lends support to the suggestion that terminating it is maintained by the fact that the subject can circumvent unreinforced behaviour. On the other hand, we think it unlikely that advance responding would not be maintained in a discrimination problem in which the subject made no errors, or very few. Since most of our experiments involved relatively difficult problems (or a schedule discrimination), the advance procedure has almost always enabled the subject to avoid making errors. Indeed, the initial motivation for some of us (Honig and Seraganian, 1971) in this research was to develop a procedure with this effect. But there is no reason at this time to believe that the subject would fail to utilize the advance contingency even in a very easy discrimination that could otherwise be performed with DR's approaching 1·00. It would be interesting to determine whether the termination of S$^-$ is *sufficient* to maintain advance responding in a difficult discrimination in which the subject makes errors, but not in any easy discrimination in which he does not. Such an experiment has never been run.

In short, it would seem that the reduction of responsiveness in the presence of S$^-$ and the reduction of S$^-$ duration by the subject cannot be understood in terms of a common set of processes which lead at the same time to a suppression of the appetitive response and the "activation" of the advance response. It is very likely that the latter must be understood in terms of the reinforcing appearance of S$^+$. In other words, the advance response is a bit of discriminative behaviour which is differentially emitted in the presence of stimuli that are differentially correlated with reinforcement. The positive gradient of stimulus duration obtained by Beale, Lander and Honig (in press) supports this interpretation. It is very unlikely that the advance response in the presence of new stimuli differing from S$^+$ can be explained as "displaced" keypecking, as escape from S$^-$, as the avoidance of unreinforced responses, etc. (Indeed, the subjects made very few "errors" to the test stimuli.) It can be explained much more readily as a response that is highly probable when it is likely to lead to a "net gain" in the positive associative value of the discriminative stimulus, i.e. in a change from a stimulus that is different from S$^+$, to S$^+$ itself, but very improbable when no such gain is possible.

C. APPLICATIONS AND EXTENSIONS OF THE ADVANCE PROCEDURE

If we simply view advance responding as a bit of appropriate discriminative behaviour, which results in the "management" of stimulus durations, we are in a position to ask a number of interesting questions to which it would be relevant. It may elucidate the differences in difficulty between certain "standard" discriminative situations. It is well known that for pigeons, at least, visual discriminations are relatively easy, provided that the stimuli are not too similar, while auditory discriminations are generally difficult. One is led to believe that the pigeon hears poorly, or is "insensitive" to auditory cues. Perhaps the pigeon's problem is simply that he cannot turn away from a negative tone that fills his chamber, while he can turn away from a localized key that is illuminated by S^-. Since the advance response terminates either kind of S^- equally effectively, we may find that visual and auditory discriminations are not very different when stimulus duration is the dependent variable.

A sensitive measure like the duration of S^- may also be helpful in analysing some subtle phenomena associated with discriminative control. The weaker of two redundant negative stimuli, or the one introduced second in training, often fails to acquire the capacity to reduce responsiveness. It is "overshadowed" or "blocked" by the stronger, or first-presented, of the redundant stimuli. Explanations of these phenomena are often couched in terms of attentional mechanisms (cf. Honig, 1970; Sutherland and Mackintosh, 1971). If the subject fails to attend to the redundant stimulus, a test involving the advance procedure should fail to produce a reduction in "overshadowed" or "blocked" stimuli, just as standard tests of stimulus control fail to detect a marked reduction in responsiveness to them. But if the phenomena in question result from the failure of such negative stimuli to develop the capacity to suppress or inhibit responding, the subjects may be able to demonstrate some learning about their negative correlation with reinforcement by spending relatively less time in their presence.

The "management" of stimulus durations could be investigated with methods that differ from the contingency associated with terminating discriminative stimuli. One could permit the pigeon to extend, rather than terminate, the current stimulus and thus retard, rather than advance, the discrimination programme. Such a "retardation" response should occur predominantly in S^+, and not in S^-. The recent work of Baum and Rachlin (1969) suggests that pigeons will extend responding in S^+. But as far as we know, no one has ever run a discrimination programme in which stimuli are automatically terminated, but their termination can be over-ridden by the subject. Such a procedure would involve the problem that the consequence of a retardation response is not as obvious to the subject as the effect of the advance response, since the stimulus remains the same instead of changing when the response is made. However, it would be possible to add a "clock" during the stimulus periods which resets whenever the retardation response occurs. It has been suggested by Anger (1963) that free-operant avoidance behaviour is supported by a mechanism of this sort— that the subject "resets" conditioned aversive temporal stimuli that are differentially associated with shock as a function of the time elapsed since the last avoidance response.

V. Conclusions

The foregoing discussion has emphasized two main points which we believe to be supported by the empirical work reported in this chapter. First, a procedure which provides the subject with partial control over duration of discriminative stimuli, can be used to demonstrate the inhibitory function of stimuli negatively correlated with reinforcement if stimulus duration is the dependent variable. This measure appears to be more sensitive than the traditional reduction of responsiveness in the presence of S^-. While the advance contingency provides findings that meet some of the current criteria of inhibitory phenomena, the advance response itself is not related in any obvious way to the reduction of responding to S^-. It can best be described as a response that is differentially emitted in the presence of S^- and S^+, and maintained by the termination of the former and/or the appearance of the latter. Second, we suggest that the advance procedure is one of a class of possible procedures which could be used to study the way in which animals can "manage" aspects of their environment other than the procuring of reinforcers or the avoidance of aversive stimuli. The management of stimuli may well be useful in reflecting what the organism has learned about the contingencies inherent in his situation. Since the specific responses which manage the stimuli can be applied to a number of different discriminations, such procedures may permit the investigation of problems which cannot be attacked with the more traditional techniques of controlling and measuring responsiveness in the presence of the discriminative stimuli themselves.

Acknowledgements

Much of the research was supported by grant APT–102 from the National Research Council of Canada and by the Faculty of Graduate Studies, Dalhousie University. The paper was written while W. K. Honig was at the University of Cambridge in the Sub-Department of Animal Behaviour, and a Visiting Fellow at St John's College. Ivan Beale was on leave from the University of Auckland.

References

Anger, D. (1963). The role of temporal discriminations in the reinforcement of Sidman avoidance behavior. *Journal of the Experimental Analysis of Behavior*, **6**, 477–506.

Baum, W. M. and Rachlin, H. C. (1969). Choice as time allocation. *Journal of the Experimental Analysis of Behavior*, **12**, 861–874.

Beale, I. L. and Winton, A. S. W. (1970). Inhibitory control in concurrent schedules. *Journal of the Experimental Analysis of Behavior*, **14**, 133–137.

Beale, I. L., Lander, D. G. and Honig, W. K. (in press). Inhibition in a successive discrimination allowing choice.

Bloomfield, T. M. (1967). A peak shift on a line tilt continuum. *Journal of the Experimental Analysis of Behavior*, **10**, 361–366.

Brownstein, A. J. and Pliskoff, S. S. (1968). Some effects of relative reinforcement rate and changeover delay in response-independent concurrent schedules of reinforcement. *Journal of the Experimental Analysis of Behavior*, **11**, 683–688.

Catania, A. C. (1966). Concurrent operants. In: W. K. Honig (Ed.), *Operant Behavior: Areas of Research and Application*. New York: Appleton-Century-Crofts, pp. 213–270.

Findley, J. D. (1958). Preference and switching under concurrent scheduling. *Journal of the Experimental Analysis of Behavior*, **1**, 123–144.

Hanson, H. M. (1959). Effects of discrimination training on stimulus generalization. *Journal of Experimental Psychology*, **58**, 321–334.

Hearst, E. (1969). Excitation, inhibition, and discrimination learning. In: N. J. Mackintosh and W. K. Honig (Eds.), *Fundamental Issues in Associative Learning* Halifax, Canada: Dalhousie University Press, pp. 1–41.

Hearst, E., Besley, Serena and Farthing, G. W. (1970). Inhibition and the stimulus control of operant behavior. *Journal of the Experimental Analysis of Behavior*, **14**, 373–409.

Herrnstein, R. J. (1961). Relative and absolute strength of response as a function of frequency of reinforcement. *Journal of the Experimental Analysis of Behavior*, **4**, 267–272.

Herrnstein, R. J. and Loveland, D. H. (1964). Complex visual concept in the pigeon. *Science*, **146**, 549–551.

Honig, W. K. (1962). Prediction of preference, transposition, and transposition-reversal from the generalization gradient. *Journal of Experimental Psychology*, **64**, 239–248.

Honig, W. K. (1967). Prediction of preference, transposition, and transposition reversal from the generalization gradient. In: G. A. Kimble (Ed.), *Foundations of Conditioning and Learning*. New York: Appleton-Century-Crofts, pp. 354–382.

Honig, W. K. (1970). Attention and the modulation of stimulus control. In: D. Mostofsky (Ed.), *Attention: Contemporary Studies and Analyses*. New York: Appleton-Century-Crofts, pp. 193–238.

Honig, W. K. and Seraganian, P. (1971). Discrimination performance on a conceptual task with stimulus period duration controlled by the subject. Paper presented at meetings of the Canadian Psychological Association, St John's, Newfoundland.

Honig, W. K., Boneau, C. A., Burstein, K. R. and Pennypacker, H. S. (1963). Positive and negative generalization gradients obtained after equivalent training conditions. *Journal of Comparative and Physiological Psychology*, **56**, 111–116.

Jenkins, H. M. (1965). Generalization gradients and the concept of inhibition. In: D. Mostofsky (Ed.), *Stimulus Generalization*. Palo Alto: Stanford University Press, pp. 55–61.

Jenkins, H. M. and Harrison, R. H. (1962). Generalization gradients of inhibition following auditory discrimination learning. *Journal of the Experimental Analysis of Behavior*, **5**, 435–441.

Rescorla, R. A. (1969). Pavlovian conditioned inhibition. *Psychological Bulletin*, **72**, 77–94.

Rilling, M., Askew, H. R., Ahlskog, J. E. and Kramer, T. J. (1969). Aversive properties of the negative stimulus in a successive discrimination. *Journal of the Experimental Analysis of Behavior*, **12**, 917–932.

Siegel, R. K. and Honig, W. K. (1970). Pigeon concept formation: Successive and simultaneous acquisition. *Journal of the Experimental Analysis of Behavior*, **13**, 385–390.

Sutherland, N. S. and Mackintosh, N. J. (1971). *Mechanisms of Animal Discrimination Learning.* London: Academic Press.

Terrace, H. S. (1966). Stimulus control. In: W. K. Honig (Ed.), *Operant Behavior: Areas of Research and Application.* New York: Appleton-Century-Crofts, pp. 271–344.

Terrace, H. S. (1971a). By-products of discrimination learning. In: G. Bower and J. T. Spence (Eds.), *The Psychology of Learning and Motivation, Vol. 15.* New York: Academic Press.

Terrace, H. S. (1971b). Escape from S⁻. *Learning and Motivation*, **2**, 148–163.

Thomas, D. R. (1962). The effects of drive and discrimination training on stimulus generalization. *Journal of Experimental Psychology*, **64**, 24–28.

Weisman, R. G. and Palmer, J. A. (1969). Factors influencing inhibitory stimulus control: discrimination training and prior non-differential reinforcement. *Journal of the Experimental Analysis of Behavior*, **12**, 229–237.

Winton, A. S. W. and Beale, I. L. (1971). Peak shift in concurrent schedules. *Journal of the Experimental Analysis of Behavior*, **15**, 73–81.

Discrimination Involving Response-Independent Reinforcement: Implications for Behavioural Contrast

M. S. HALLIDAY and R. A. BOAKES

University of Sussex, Brighton, Sussex, England

I. Introduction 73
II. Experiment I: Discrimination Between VI and Free VI Following
Pretraining with Free Reinforcement 76
III. Experiment II: Successive Discrimination Between VI and Free VI
without Prior Training 81
IV. Experiment III: Choice Between VI and Free VI 86
V. Implications for a Theory of Contrast 92
VI. Conclusion 95
Acknowledgements 96
References 96

I. Introduction

When experimental extinction is introduced into a situation in which an instrumental response has been maintained by reinforcement two separable changes are involved: the removal of the previous contingency between responding and reinforcement, and the removal of reinforcement from the situation. It is impossible to remove reinforcement while leaving contingencies unchanged, but it is possible to investigate the effects of removing the contingency alone by making reinforcement independent of responding, but keeping its frequency of occurrence constant. There is still no satisfactory account of what is involved when responding decreases during extinction, and it seems to us that it may well be necessary to understand the relative roles of these two aspects of extinction as a step towards such an account. For example, if there were little difference between the two procedures, this would strongly support accounts that stress response contingencies (Wagner and Rescorla, Chapter 12, this volume), as opposed to those in which the effects of nonreward are emphasized (e.g. Amsel, Chapter 11, this volume). The form and implications of such comparisons will, we hope, become clear in the course of this paper.

Response-independent schedules of reinforcement have attracted surprisingly little attention. Skinner (1938) presents the results of a study in which, following the establishment of barpressing on a FI schedule, reinforcement was presented at the same regular intervals, but was made independent of the rat's behaviour. A fairly rapid decline in responding was observed, reaching an asymptotic level which appeared to be higher than that typically obtained in extinction. To explain this terminal level of responding Skinner appealed to the principle of superstitious reinforcement, suggesting that occasional chance contiguities between a response and subsequent reinforcement might be sufficient to maintain a low response rate.

Most later studies of response-independent reinforcement have concentrated on the problem of superstition. Thus, Herrnstein (1966) presents results from a single pigeon and stresses the relatively small decrease in response rate, (about 50%) obtained following a change from fixed interval training to prolonged training on a response-independent fixed interval schedule. This result appears to be atypical since response rates usually show a much more rapid drop with the introduction of response-independent reinforcement (e.g. Edwards, *et al.*, 1968). A comparison by Zeiler (1968) between fixed interval and variable-interval schedules of response-independent reinforcement suggests that superstitious maintenance of responding is much more pronounced with fixed-interval schedules. This suggestion seems eminently reasonable, since a scallop pattern of responding, established by FI training, will ensure a high correlation in time between responses and reinforcements when the response-independent condition is introduced.

In this paper Zeiler introduced the terminology "fixed-time" (FT) and "variable-time" (VT) to describe response-independent schedules. Though it is convenient to avoid continual repetition of the mouthful "response-independent", we have not found Zeiler's alternative very satisfactory on either mnemonic or logical grounds. Since the terms FT and VT have not yet been widely used, we would like to recommend the use of "Free" for "response-independent". Thus, for the rest of this paper "Free VI" should be read as "response-independent variable-interval schedule of reinforcement.

While none of the above four papers made any direct comparison between free schedules and extinction, this has been done in two more recent studies. Neuringer (1969) showed that after only three reinforced responses the number of keypecks made by pigeons on a subsequent Free VI 30 sec schedule was very much greater than the number produced by a control group in extinction. A more detailed comparison was made by Rescorla and Skucy (1969) using rats as subjects. In their Expt I barpressing was first established on a response-contingent VI schedule and then either free reinforcement or delayed reinforcement on the same variable-interval schedule, or extinction was introduced. There was a surprising degree of similarity in the initial effects of the three procedures. Responding decreased somewhat more rapidly under extinction conditions, but the major difference was in the higher asymptotic level of responding under the Free VI and delayed reinforcement conditions. Further experiments suggested that this terminal level of responding was partly due to the maintenance of general activity in the neighbourhood of the bar and partly to food acting as a discriminative stimulus for responding. There was no evidence to support Skinner's suggestion that superstitious reinforcement maintained this final low level.

The properties of free reinforcement schedules investigated in this chapter are concerned with the problem of behavioural contrast. In the standard procedure for obtaining this phenomenon a pigeon is first trained to peck a key on a VI schedule when either stimulus S_1 or stimulus S_2 is displayed on the key. Once a stable level of responding has been reached, reinforcement is omitted in the presence of S_2. The normal consequence is a decrease in responding to S_2 and an increase, the contrast effect, in the rate of responding to S_1.

In the analysis of behavioural contrast different workers have put very different emphases on the two aspects of extinction. One kind of account (e.g. Reynolds, 1961) has stressed removal of reinforcement as the critical variable, claiming that contrast occurs in the S_1 component whenever the reinforcement density in the S_2 component is low, relative to that in S_1. The major alternative approach (e.g. Terrace, 1968) is one where the important aspect of extinction—at least as far as behavioural contrast is concerned—is the change of response contingency leading to decreased responding. From this second approach contrast would also be expected in a situation where the change in the S_2 component was to a schedule, which altered response contingencies so as to produce a decrease in responding, but maintained the previously established reinforcement density.

Two examples of this kind of situation have been reported. One is the introduction of a DRL schedule in the S_2 component, whereby only responses that follow a pause of at least t sec from the preceding response are reinforced (Terrace, 1968; Weisman, 1969). The second example is provided by the introduction of a DRO schedule in the S_2 component, such that the reinforcer is presented when t sec have elapsed since the last response (Weisman, 1970a). In both cases the value of the schedule parameter, t, can be continuously adjusted so that the average rate of reinforcement remains the same as that in the VI schedule that is maintained in the S_1 component. When this is done behavioural contrast occurs in both situations; this result is, of course, not expected from the account that stresses relative rates of reinforcement.

Though both DRL and DRO schedules in general lead to a decrease in responding, they do so by imposing new response contingencies. In both cases there is effectively a negative correlation between responding and reinforcement: in both schedules—given a minimal rate of responding with a DRL—more responding is accompanied by less reinforcement. This is not comparable to extinction conditions. To understand the way in which the introduction of extinction in a multiple schedule results in contrast, we need to know what the effects are of eliminating any contingency between responses and reinforcements; namely those of introducing a free reinforcement schedule.

It seemed to us, as also to Weisman (1970b), that the introduction of free reinforcement schedules might provide an exception to Terrace's (1968) generalization that procedures which lead to a decline in response rate in one component of a multiple schedule produce behavioural contrast in the other component, together with either peak-shift or inhibitory gradient effects.

In each experiment the subjects were naïve, adult homing pigeons maintained throughout at 80% of their *ad libitum* body weights.

II. Experiment I: Discrimination Between VI and Free VI Following Pretraining with Free Reinforcement

The general procedure used in this and the following experiment closely followed the standard one for behavioural contrast studies which has been described above. Following baseline training on a variable interval schedule in both S_1 and S_2 components, a discrimination phase was introduced in which the reinforcement schedule associated with S_1 remained unchanged for all subjects, while the schedule associated with S_2 changed to free reinforcement on the same variable interval schedule for some subjects and to extinction for the remainder. Since both previous evidence and a personal communication from Weisman suggested that free reinforcement in this situation might lead to a very slow and irregular decline in responding, Expt I included some pretraining and selection of subjects designed to avoid this. A more detailed account of this experiment may be found in Halliday and Boakes (1971).

1. *Method*

Six subjects were run in the first part of the experiment and then this was replicated with a further six subjects. The apparatus was a standard pigeon chamber with a single response key that could be trans-illuminated by an in-line projector. This provided either uniform white or blue illumination of the key or the projection of a 5 mm × 15mm white rectangle at various orientations. The intensities of the stimuli could be varied by dropping resistors.

In the pretraining phase that followed autoshaping the key was blue and responding was first maintained on a variable-interval schedule. In the first two sessions the mean interval of the schedule was progressively increased to 1 min and then maintained at this value for a further six sessions. A final six sessions were then given with a Free VI one min schedule. Each pretraining session consisted of 20 components of 90-sec duration, separated by a 3-sec interval when the chamber was dark and responses ineffective.

For each subject the rate of responding during the final two Free VI sessions was expressed as a percentage of the response rate for the final two VI sessions. Within each group of six subjects the two with the highest percentages were discarded from the experiment at this point. The remaining eight subjects were given nondifferential training, in which responses to either the white (S_1) or the 50° rectangle (S_2) were reinforced on VI 1 min. The two stimuli occurred with equal frequency in semi-random order and each session contained 24 90-sec components. This training was continued for a minimum of 16 sessions or until response rates had stabilized. One subject still showed considerable variability after 27 sessions and was then dropped from the experiment.

In the discrimination phase the only change was either to withhold reinforcement in the presence of S_2 (3 subjects: *mult* VI 1 min EXT) or associate a free variable-interval schedule with S_2 (4 subjects: *mult* VI 1 min Free VI 1 min). Subjects in the two conditions were matched on the basis of their performance in the pretraining phase. After ten sessions of discrimination training each subject was given a generalization test in extinction for two successive sessions. The six stimuli in the test were S_1 and rectangles at 10, 30, 50, 70, and 90 degrees to the vertical. Each session contained 24 90-sec stimulus presentations in blocks of six, such that each block contained each of the stimuli in randomized order.

2. Results

The main results were straightforward: all three Extinction subjects showed a behavioural contrast effect, none of the four Free VI subjects showed any sign of contrast. Response rates for the final five sessions of non-differential training and the ten sessions of discrimination training for the Free VI subjects are shown in Fig. 1. As the response rates to S_2 declined in the discrimination phase, rates to S_1 also declined initially, but at a slower rate. With two subjects S_1 rates returned to the baseline values, shown by a broken line in Fig. 1, by the tenth session of discrimination.

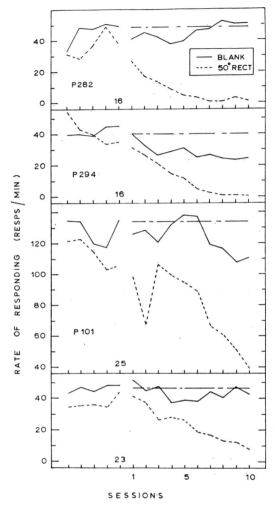

FIG. 1. Rates of responding in the final five sessions of nondifferential training and the ten sessions of discrimination training between VI 1 min and Free VI 1 min in Expt I (from Halliday and Boakes, 1971).

The corresponding results for the Extinction subjects are shown in Fig. 2. A behavioural contrast effect is seen for each bird, in that with the decline of responding to S_2, response rates to S_1 increase and remain above the baselines.

Changes in responding to S_2 are compared for the two conditions in Fig. 3, where each point represents the response rate to S_2 as a percentage

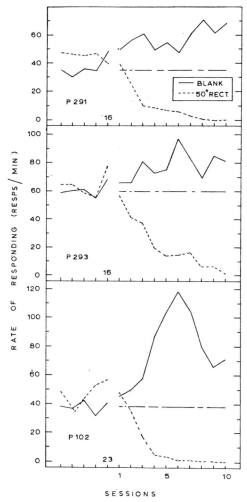

Fig. 2. Rates of responding in the final five sessions of nondifferential training and the ten sessions of discrimination training between VI 1 min and Extinction in Expt I (from Halliday and Boakes, 1971).

of the median rate to this stimulus in the final five sessions of nondifferential training. It can be seen that there is no clear difference between the rate of decline under Free VI conditions (solid lines) and that under Extinction conditions (dashed lines).

The results of the generalization tests were inconclusive, as only one subject in the Extinction group gave an inhibitory gradient and the remaining subjects showed no systematic changes in responding as a function of the orientation of the rectangle. Thus this experiment throws no light on the question of whether Free VI and Extinction procedures differ in their effects on inhibitory gradients.

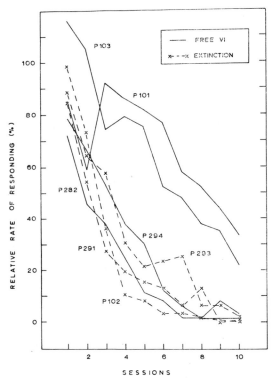

FIG. 3. Relative rates of responding to S_2 during discrimination phase in Expt I. Rates of responding are shown as a percentage of prior rates to this stimulus in the final five sessions of nondifferential training (from Halliday and Boakes, 1971).

3. Discussion

This experiment indicates that a decrease in responding in S_2 resulting from the introduction of a Free VI schedule in that component does not produce behavioural contrast in S_1. The reduction in response rate for Free VI subjects was in some cases as rapid as that shown by Extinction subjects and hence the absence of contrast cannot be due to a slower decline of response rates to S_2 with the Free VI schedule. Nor is it likely that weak contrast effects may have occurred which the present procedure was too insensitive to detect, since the changes in response rate in S_1 shown by the Free VI subjects were all in the direction of rate reduction.

III. Experiment II: Successive Discrimination Between VI and Free VI without Prior Training

Since some aspects of the results of Expt I may have been influenced by the particular pretraining and selection procedures employed, it seemed important to find out what happened when these were omitted. Apart from the absence of a pretraining phase, the method used in this experiment was identical to that used in Expt I.

1. *Method*

Eight subjects were trained in the apparatus used in Expt I. Following magazine training and autoshaping there were two sessions in which responses to the white key (S_1) and the 50° rectangle (S_2) were reinforced on a variable interval schedule whose mean interval was progressively increased to 1 min. For the following 18 sessions nondifferential training was given on a *mult* VI 1 min VI 1 min schedule whose conditions were identical to those in Expt 1. One subject still showed considerable variability at the end of this phase and was therefore discarded from the experiment.

In the initial discrimination phase the conditions for four birds were *mult* VI 1 min Free VI 1 min and for the remaining three *mult* VI 1 min EXT. The parameters for this phase were again identical to those in the discrimination phase of Expt I. Each subject received a total of 24 sessions in this phase, with the exception of one subject P122, in the Extinction group. On the tenth session a programming error occurred with this bird, such that S_2 was associated with Free VI, and the subject was discarded at this point.

2. *Results*

The most marked difference between the results of this experiment and those of Expt I was in the rate at which responding by the Free VI subjects declined in the S_2 component. For example, for the Free VI subjects in this experiment, the median rate of responding over Discrimination Sessions 8–10 was 51% of the response rate to S_2 in the final five sessions of baseline training, whereas in Expt I the comparable figure for Free VI subjects was 20%. There was no overlap on this measure between the two groups (Mann–Whitney, $p < 0.05$). This difference can be seen in Fig. 4, where for each group of subjects in both Expts I and II the median rate of responding to S_2 is shown as a percentage of the baseline rate. The rates for the Free VI group in Expt II decrease at a rate comparable to other subjects for the first 4–5 sessions, but thereafter the decline becomes much slower and irregular. There were no obvious differences between the Extinction subjects in the two experiments.

G

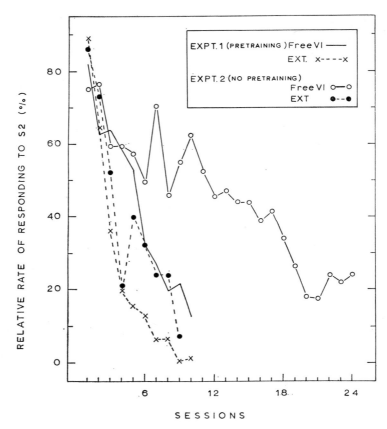

Fig. 4. Median relative rates of responding to S_2 for each group in Expts I and II during the discrimination phase. For each subject rates were calculated as a percentage of prior rates to this stimulus, as in Fig. 3.

The irregularity and slow decline of S_2 responding shown by the Free VI subjects is clearly seen in the individual data presented in Fig. 5. For two subjects, P114 and P133, differences in response rates to S_1 and S_2 become marked only after 18 sessions of discrimination training. Looking now at the rates to S_1, the evidence on contrast as seen in Fig. 5 is less clear than in Expt I: for two subjects rates are in general below the baseline level during the discrimination phase, while for the other two these rates are above this level. Of the last two birds P133 appears to show a contrast effect. However, there are two factors that suggest that the rise in S_1 rates for this subject in Discrimination Sessions 3–14 probably does not reflect a behavioural contrast effect: first, there is little indication of discrimination

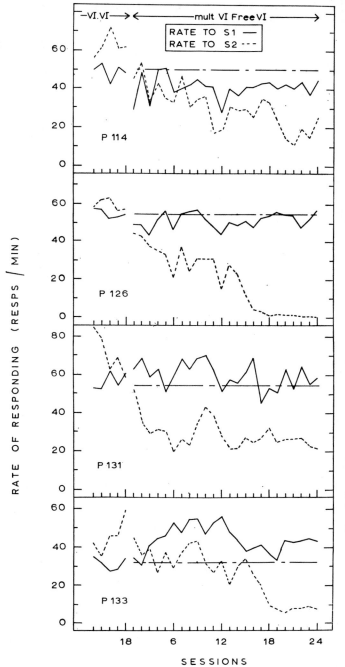

FIG. 5. Rates of responding for the Free VI subjects in Expt II in the final five sessions of nondifferential training and the 24 sessions of discrimination training.

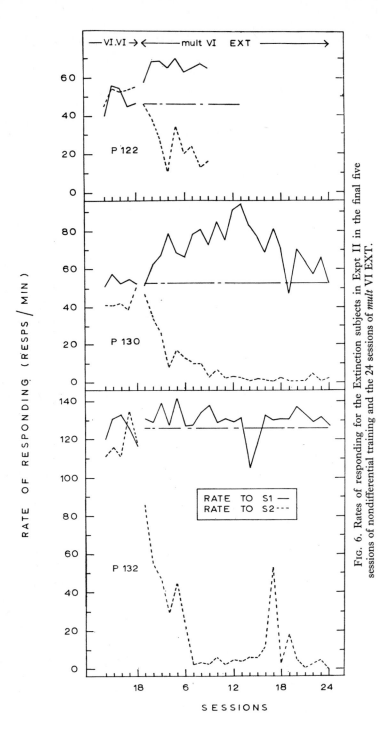

FIG. 6. Rates of responding for the Extinction subjects in Expt II in the final five sessions of nondifferential training and the 24 sessions of *mult* VI EXT.

during this period, and, second, the S_1 rates are little higher than the prior rates to S_2.

The equivalent results for Extinction subjects are shown in Fig. 6. As in Expt I all three subjects showed behavioural contrast, even where, as for P132, prior response rates were already unusually high and comparable to those of a Free VI subject, P101, in Expt 1.

3. *Discussion*

These results do not alter the conclusions suggested by Expt I concerning the absence of behavioural contrast during discrimination between response contingent and response independent reinforcement. In the first experiment it was possible that the imbalance of pretraining conditions might have exaggerated contrast effects in the Extinction subjects and masked possible contrast in the Free VI subjects. This possibility is not supported by the present results. There was no evidence that omission of the pretraining phase affected responding by Extinction subjects in either the S_1 or S_2 components. Furthermore, for the Free VI subjects, although the decline in S_2 responding was slower, there was no general rise in responding in the S_1 component.

When, as in this last case, a discrimination develops very slowly, it becomes difficult to detect unambiguous contrast effects, since changes in S_1 responding have to be compared with a baseline level established many sessions earlier. Thus, since long-term fluctuations in response rate occur with prolonged variable interval training, the data for individual subjects become increasingly unreliable. One can therefore probably only refer to averaged group data, and not just point to two or three representative subjects, in answering the question: does contrast occur when S_2 responding is reduced by a free reinforcement schedule, in the absence of pretraining? The results of Expt II strongly suggest that contrast does not occur, but they do not, of course, prove the null hypothesis.

The relatively slow development of discrimination in the Free VI group in this experiment is difficult to interpret. An unfortunate feature of the baseline behaviour (which was only noticed after the experiment had ended) was that all four subjects assigned to theFree VI conditions were, by chance, responding more rapidly in the S_2 component than in the S_1 component during the last few baseline sessions. In contrast, the comparable subjects in Expt I responded more slowly during the S_2 component, at least during the last two baseline sessions. This difference between the two experiments makes it difficult to say with confidence that the slower decline of S_2 responding under Free VI in Expt II was a consequence of the omission of the pretraining and selection procedures used in Expt I. However the differences in baseline rates of responding were, in general, small and were typically unstable and we are inclined to the view that the major factor was probably that of prior exposure to a free reinforcement schedule.

IV. Experiment III: Choice Between VI and Free VI

The results of Expts I and II are compatible with an account of contrast based on relative rates of reinforcement, as are also the data obtained in the final phase of Expt II. However, as we have seen, a simple version of such an account, one based only on reinforcement densities in the S_1 and S_2 components during the discrimination, cannot handle results obtained from studies using DRL and DRO schedules (Terrace, 1968; Weisman, 1969; Weisman, 1970a). These studies entail at least a re-formulation of this account, one form of which is: contrast occurs in the S_1 component when the situation in the S_2 component "worsens" (Bloomfield, 1969).

The claim that a change from A to B represents a worsening of the situation for the animal implies that, given the choice, it will prefer A to B. In order to accommodate the results of the first two experiments the relativity account outlined above must therefore predict that pigeons are either indifferent between a VI and a Free VI schedule of equal frequency, or else prefer Free VI. The present experiment was designed to test this prediction by using a concurrent chain procedure to measure preferences between such schedules. Since it was felt that differences in rates of responding during Free VI might well affect preferences, a group of birds was included for which the Free VI schedule was associated with an unilluminated response key, since this was expected to elicit very few responses. Subjects were first trained on the second link of the chain (*mult* VI Free VI), and only when performance had stabilized on this schedule was the initial concurrent link of the chain introduced. Training was so arranged that at no time was the stimulus to be associated with Free VI present during response-contingent reinforcement.

1. *Method*

Eight subjects were initially used in a counterbalanced design, but the behaviour of one was so erratic in the early stages of the experiment that testing was discontinued. The apparatus was a standard pigeon chamber with two response keys spaced 120 mm apart and at an equal distance from the midline of the front panel. Each response key could be trans-illuminated by an in-line projector, which provided either uniform red or green illumination of the key, or the projection of a white diagonal cross or a white horizontal wavy line on a black background. The colours were associated with VI or Free VI in the second link of the chain; the patterns were present only in the first link of the chain.

Following magazine training an auto-shaping procedure was used in which each subject received noncontingent reinforcement in the presence of one colour and contingent reinforcement when pecking the other. On "contingent" trials the first response to the key terminated the trial and produced immediate reinforcement; when no response occurred, reinforcement was presented after 5 sec. On "noncontingent" trials responses were recorded, but had no programmed consequences, and reinforcement always occurred 5 sec after the start of the trial. During inter-trial intervals, lasting 30 sec, the house light and both keylights were extinguished. A total of 40 trials occurred in each session. On contingent trials the response key was green for four subjects and red for the other three subjects. On noncontingent trials the other colour was present on one key for the three subjects in the Coloured Key group, but for the four subjects in the Dark Key group neither key was illuminated. The type of trial and the position of the illuminated key were varied according to independent Gellerman sequences.

The second phase of the procedure consisted of a transition from the auto-shaping situation to a multiple schedule. This began when each subject had responded during a session and then had received a further three sessions of auto-shaping. Over a period of four sessions the inter-trial interval was reduced to 5 sec and the length of a trial was progressively increased from a fixed duration of 5 sec to a variable duration, mean 60 sec. Contingent and noncontingent trials occurred with equal frequency and all trials ended with reinforcement. The conditions at the end of the transition (*mult* VI 1 min Free VI 1 min with components of variable duration) were maintained for seven sessions or until response rates were stable.

The concurrent chain procedure was then introduced by starting trials with the simultaneous presentation of the two patterns. A single peck at either stimulus terminated the first link of the chain and resulted in the presentation of one of the second link stimuli on that key. For four birds (counter-balanced across conditions) responses to the cross in the first link of the chain resulted in the presentation of the Free VI stimulus, while responses to the wavy line produced the VI stimulus; for the remaining birds the relationships were reversed. Four sessions were given with CRF in the first link of the chain; the schedule on this link was then increased to VI 30 sec and remained at this value throughout the remainder of the experiment. The experimental procedure at this stage is illustrated in Fig. 7.

Training was continued until performance stabilized on all response measures. Since all subjects showed a preference for the stimulus associated with the VI schedule, the value of the noncontingent schedule was reduced to Free VI 30 sec and training was once again continued until response rates stabilized. One bird (P7) failed to reverse its preference even at this value and was therefore given a further 12 sessions with the noncontingent schedule reduced to Free VI 15 sec. In the final stage of the experiment the Free VI schedule reverted to 60 sec (equal to the VI schedule) and training was once again continued until rates stabilized.

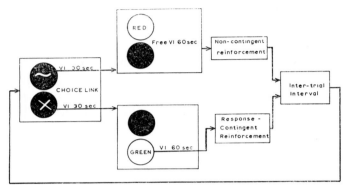

Fig. 7. Diagram of the conditions used for the concurrent chain procedure used in Expt III.

2. Results

At no stage did the shape of the stimulus in the first link of the chain or its colour in the second link have any systematic effect on the results; the subjects will therefore be treated as two groups, one with a dark key (N = 4) and one with a coloured key (N = 3) associated with Free VI.

Auto-shaping resulted in responding to the VI key in both groups and to the Free VI key in the coloured key group. Very few responses were made to the dark key at this or any subsequent stage of training; responding to the dark key never rose above 10% of that to the lighted key, and during most sessions was only 1–2% of the rate on the VI key. The dark key procedure was therefore effective in virtually eliminating responding during the Free VI.

In the coloured key group responding to the Free VI stimulus decreased in the period before the introduction of the concurrent chain; in two birds it fell to zero and in one (P7) to 30–35% of the VI rate. During the four sessions with CRF on the first link of the chain there was a tendency for the VI rate to increase in all subjects; most subjects showed large latencies during the first link of the chain, often taking a minute or more before making a response. Delay in making a response in the first link of the chain was highly correlated with the percentage increase in the VI rate in the second link of the chain ($\tau = \cdot62$, $p = \cdot025$). The subjects in the coloured key group also increased their rate in the Free VI during these sessions to about 50% of the VI rate.

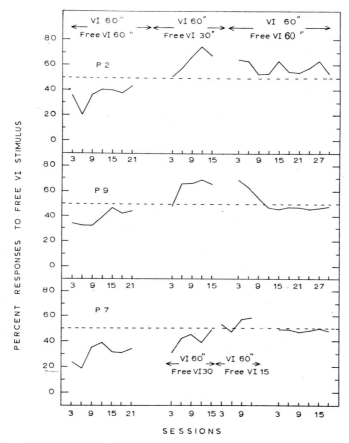

FIG. 8. Responses to the first link stimulus associated with Free VI made by the Coloured Key subjects in Expt III as percentages of the total responses in the first link of the concurrent chain. Calculated over blocks of three sessions.

Performance in the first link for the remainder of the experiment is shown for each subject in the Coloured Key group in Fig. 8, and in the Dark Key group in Fig. 9. These figures show relative preference for the Free VI stimulus and each point represents the percentage of total first link responses made to this stimulus over a block of three sessions. When initially the mean intervals of the second link schedules are both 1 min, this measure is less than 50% for all subjects. In both groups most subjects eventually stabilize at about 40%. With the decrease in the mean inter-reinforcement interval of the Free VI schedule to 30 sec, six subjects reversed their preference and came to respond more to the stimulus

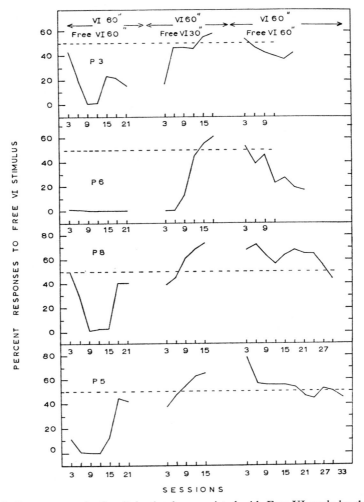

FIG. 9. Responses to the first link stimulus associated with Free VI made by the Dark Key subjects in Expt III as percentages of the total responses in the first link of the concurrent chain. Calculated over blocks of three sessions.

associated with free reinforcement. The remaining subject, P7, did not show such a preference, which only appeared when the inter-reinforcement interval was further reduced to 15 sec. When, in the final phase of the experiment, the mean inter-reinforcement interval of the Free VI schedule was again 1 min, preference for the Free VI stimulus was reduced in all subjects. However only two subjects, P3 and P6, showed a clearly renewed preference for the VI stimulus and two subjects, P2 and P8, continued to show some preference for the Free VI stimulus.

The median number of responses in the first link and the median rates of responding in the second link in the final five sessions of each phase of the concurrent chain procedure are given in Table I. Except for response rates to the Free VI stimulus in the second link of the chain, there are no significant differences between the results for the Dark Key and Coloured Key groups. The apparent changes in second-link response rates, following changes in the Free VI schedule, were not significant.

TABLE I

	Median Responses in First Link		Median Rate in Second Link	
Dark Key group	VI Stimulus	Free VI Stimulus	VI Stimulus	Free VI Stimulus
VI = 60 sec				
Free VI = 60 sec	266·0	64·0	55·0	·9
VI = 60 sec				
Free VI = 30 sec	165·0	202·0	53·8	2·7
VI = 60 sec				
Free VI = 60 sec	222·0	124·0	57·5	·6
Coloured Key group				
VI = 60 sec				
Free VI = 60 sec	260·0	138·0	69·1	43·2
VI = 60 sec				
Free VI = 30 sec	220·0	301·0	92·2	36·4
VI = 60 sec				
Free VI = 60 sec	243·0	223·0	95·0	7·0

3. *Discussion*

These results indicate that, when a concurrent chain procedure is used to measure preferences, pigeons prefer a VI 1 min schedule to a Free VI 1 min schedule. It might be argued that this procedure is inappropriate for the measurement of preferences where free reinforcement schedules are involved, because of interactions between behaviour in the two links of the chain. This does not seem likely for a number of reasons.

(a) In the Coloured Key group there was significantly more responding in the second link under the Free VI schedule than there was in the Dark Key group; if the rate on the choice key in the first link was strongly influenced by the rate in the second link, the Dark Key group should have maintained a greater preference for the VI than the Coloured Key group. However, this preference was not maintained. (b) Unlike most concurrent chain experiments, the position of the key associated with the two schedules was randomly changed from trial to trial; thus position was an irrelevant cue and this should tend to reduce the tendency for the rate in the choice link to be governed by that in the second link. (c) Changes in reinforcement rate in the Free VI schedule produced considerable and systematic changes in preference in the first link of the chain, yet these changes in preference were not accompanied by similar changes in rate of responding in the second link. (d) As a further check correlations were carried out for each bird between its rate of responding on the choice key and its rate on the second link schedule associated with that key (same key); these correlations were compared with similar correlations of rate on the choice key and rate in the other second link schedule (different key). These correlations were largely positive with a mean value of 0·12, but there was no tendency for the "same key" correlations to be higher than the "different key" ones. Thus the overall positive correlation presumably only reflects daily changes in activity affecting all rate measures to some degree.

There is a possible conflict between these results and those of Neuringer (1969) who used a concurrent chain procedure to measure preferences between FI and Free FI schedules. Over a range of intervals he failed to find a preference for FI schedules over Free FI schedules under conditions very similar to those in Expt III. Apart from the use of fixed-interval schedules and differences in initial training, the only other obvious difference from our conditions was that the mean first-link duration was longer, 90 sec as opposed to 30 sec in Expt III. There is evidence (Fantino, 1969) that relative rate measures tend towards 50% as the first link is increased in length, but it is not clear whether this is sufficient to explain the discrepancy. Alternatively pigeons may prefer VI to Free VI, but not FI to Free FI.

V. Implications for a Theory of Contrast

Among the major results that a theory of contrast is required to explain are the following:

1. contrast occurs in the paradigm situation where the complete omission of reinforcement in the S_2 component leads to a decrease in responding;
2. contrast occurs when responding in the S_2 component is reduced by the introduction of a DRL or a DRO schedule which maintains the average density of reinforcement in that schedule (Weisman, 1969; Weisman, 1970a);
3. contrast occurs in a multiple schedule with a VI 1 min in the S_1

component and a VI 5 min in the S_2 component, if in the prior baseline training condition responding to both stimuli had been reinforced on a VI 1 min schedule, but does *not* occur if in baseline training responding had been reinforced on a VI 5 min schedule (Terrace, 1968);

4. contrast occurs if reinforcement is maintained in the S_2 component but punishment of responding is introduced (Terrace, 1968);

5. contrast does *not* occur in a discrimination in which reinforcement is absent in the S_2 component where the discrimination has been learned without errors (Terrace, Chapter 4);

6. contrast does *not* occur in a discrimination where a reduction in S_2 responding follows the introduction of free reinforcers, as shown by the present results from Expts I and II.

This last item makes it clear that a reduction of responding in the S_2 component is not a sufficient condition for the occurrence of contrast. Items 2, 3, 4 and 5 show that the occurrence of contrast is not solely determined by the relative density of reinforcement in the components of the multiple schedule during the discrimination. The suggestion that contrast follows an increase within the S_2 component in "the correlation in time of responding and non-reinforcement" (Weisman, 1970b) does not appear to work, since a transition from a variable-interval schedule to a free variable-interval schedule represents such an increase. Finally there is the possibility that the critical factor is a "worsening" of conditions in the S_2 component (Bloomfield, 1969). In order to explain Item 2, this possibility depends on the untested assumption that subjects prefer variable-interval schedules to both DRO and DRL schedules with equated reinforcement densities. Furthermore this proposed relationship between preference and contrast is questioned by the results of Expt III above, where a variable-interval schedule was preferred to a free variable-interval schedule.

Thus none of these four suggestions appears to account for all six of the items listed above. It may well be that there is no single critical factor that will allow one to predict *a priori* whether or not behavioural contrast will occur in some novel situation. Given this possibility we wish to propose an approach to the phenomenon which we will term a "response inhibition rebound" hypothesis and which follows very closely the account given by Terrace in Chapter 4, and also resembles Pavlov's (1927) account of positive induction.

This hypothesis is based on the assumption that certain operations, which may not be definable in terms of a common element, lead to the establishment of an inhibitory process, which may possibly be characterized as the learning of an antagonistic response (Konorski, Chapter 13; Terrace, Chapter 4). The operations include the omission of reinforcement, the introduction of schedules in which the withholding of responses is differentially reinforced (as in DRL and DRO schedules) and, following work suggesting a close connection between the effects of nonreward and of punishment (Wagner, 1966), the punishment of responses as in contingent shock studies (Brethower and Reynolds, 1962). This inhibitory process does not become established in an error-less discrimination or when responding is reduced by the presentation of free reinforcers since in these conditions the animal is not required to withhold responding. The existence of this process can normally be inferred from its effect in suppressing responses and from the occurrence of the various common by-products of discrimination learning discussed by Terrace (Chapter 4). Under certain conditions the process may be present, but a particular effect diminished or nonexistent: for example, we would take Dickenson's results (Chapter 18) to indicate that certain lesions reduce the effect of inhibition on the emission of responses.

Behavioural contrast can be taken to be one indicator of such a process. We would suggest that in any situation where at least one stimulus is associated with the inhibition of a particular response, as outlined above, then a "rebound" effect occurs when another stimulus, in whose presence that response is an appropriate one, is presented, so that the response is made with extra vigour. This account is tentative, vague and, inevitably we believe, makes reference to processes which are not operationally definable. However, together with the assumption that response decrements produced by free reinforcement do not result in inhibition, it does suggest the following specific predictions:

1. The response-specific aspect of the account implies that behavioural contrast should not occur when the change in the S_2 component is (a) from free reinforcement to no reinforcement, given that responding has ceased before the transition, or (b) from the reinforcement of some response other than that maintained in the S_1 component to the extinction of that response;
2. the effect of response-independent shock in the S_2 component should be similar to that of response-independent reinforcement, in that a decrement in S_2 responding should occur without a contrast effect in the S_1 component.
3. since we believe that disinhibitory effects indicate whether a response decrement was produced by an inhibitory process, such effects would not be expected where a decrement is produced by free reinforcement in a situation where such effects could be obtained following decrements in responding produced by the omission of reinforcement, by punishment or by DRL or DRO schedules (Brimer, Chapter 8).

Finally we would like to note that behavioural contrast may be a pheno-menon that is highly specific with respect to the species and to the response that is investigated. Westbrook (1971) has found that when pigeons are used in a situation in which a barpress is the operant, the development of a discrimination is not accompanied by an increase in response rate in the S_1 component. If anything, rate of barpressing is reduced in the S_1 component when reinforcement is withheld in the S_2 component. This may mean that behavioural contrast, as typically studied in situations where pigeons peck at a key, is an idiosyncratic phenomenon, possibly because of the close relationship between pecking and the unconditioned response elicited by grain, as suggested by auto-shaping studies (Brown and Jenkins, 1968). Alternatively this result may imply that the kind of interaction between behaviours in the components of a discrimination is determined by the form of antagonistic response produced by the inhibitory process.

VI. Conclusion

In this chapter we have described the development of a successive dis-crimination in a free-operant situation between a response-dependent reinforcement schedule and a response-independent schedule with the same reinforcement density. In Expt I, where a pretraining procedure was in-cluded, subjects learned the discrimination almost as rapidly as those in an otherwise comparable situation in which reinforcement was omitted during the S_2 component. In Expt II, where no pretraining was included, the dis-crimination between VI and Free VI schedules was learned more slowly. In neither of the experiments was there evidence that the decrement in S_2 responding produced by the introduction of free reinforcement was accompanied by an increase in S_1 responding.

The absence of a behavioural contrast effect in this situation, when put together with the results of a number of related studies, creates difficulties for most theories of behavioural contrast. An exception is a theory that appeals to preferences between schedules, but to explain the present results such a theory must predict that pigeons prefer a Free VI schedule to the equivalent response-dependent schedule, or at least are indifferent between them. The results from Expt III, where this prediction was tested, suggested the contrary, in that a preference for the response-dependent schedule was found.

In view of the absence of an account of behavioural contrast that con-sistently handles the various results, we have outlined a "response inhibi-tion rebound" theory which makes certain predictions that do not appear to follow from other approaches. Whatever the success of this theory in hand-ling what appears to be a very intractable phenomenon, we would like to suggest that one assumption it contains is particularly important. This is that the response decrements produced by free reinforcement do not involve an inhibitory process of the same kind as decrements produced by extinction. A recurring problem, which was frequently raised during the conference discussions, is that of distinguishing between response decrements *per se* and the existence of an inhibitory process. The study of the properties of free reinforcement may provide an example of response decrements occurring without inhibition, which could help to clarify this distinction and hence to increase our understanding of inhibition.

Acknowledgements

This research was supported in part by the S.R.C. and M.R.C. We are very grateful for the help of Miss R. Ismail, Miss H. Neville, T. J. Lobstein and R. Ottley.

References

Bloomfield, T. M. (1969). Behavioural contrast and the peak shift. In: Gilbert, R. M. and Sutherland, N. S. (Eds.) *Animal Discrimination Learning*. London: Academic Press.

Brethower, D. M. and Reynolds, G. S. (1962). A facilitative effect of punishment on unpunished behavior. *Journal of the Experimental Analysis of Behavior*, **5**, 191–199.

Brown, P. L. and Jenkins, H. M. (1968). Autoshaping of the pigeon's key-peck. *Journal of the Experimental Analysis of Behavior*, **11**, 1–8.

Edwards, D. D., West, J. R. and Jackson, V. (1968). The role of contingencies in the control of behavior. *Psychonomic Science*, **10**, 39–40.

Fantino, E. (1969). Choice and rate of reinforcement. *Journal of the Experimental Analysis of Behavior*, **12**, 723–730.

Grusec, T. (1968). The peak-shift in stimulus generalization: equivalent effect of errors and non-contingent shock. *Journal of the Experimental Analysis of Behavior*, **11**, 239–250.

Halliday, M. S. and Boakes, R. A. (1971). Behavioural contrast and response-independent reinforcement. *Journal of the Experimental Analysis of Behavior*, **16**, 429–434.

Hearst, E., Besley, S. and Farthing, G. W. (1970). Inhibition and the stimulus control of operant behavior. *Journal of the Experimental Analysis of Behavior*, **3** (Pt. 2), 373–409.

Herrnstein, R. J. (1966). Superstition: a corollary of the principles of operant conditioning. In: W. K. Honig (Ed.) *Operant Behavior*. New York: Appleton-Century-Crofts.

Neuringer, A. J. (1969). Delayed reinforcement versus reinforcement after a fixed interval. *Journal of the Experimental Analysis of Behavior*, **12**, 375–384.

Pavlov, I. P. (1927). *Conditioned Reflexes*. London: Oxford University Press.

Rescorla, R. A. (1969). Pavlovian conditioned inhibition. *Psychological Bulletin*, **72**, 77–94.

Rescorla, R. A. and Skucy, J. C. (1969). Effect of response-independent reinforcers during extinction. *Journal of Comparative and Physiological Psychology*, **67**, 712–726

Reynolds, G. S. (1961). Behavioral contrast. *Journal of the Experimental Analysis of Behavior*, **4**, 57–71.

Skinner, B. F. (1938). *The Behavior of Organisms*. New York: Appleton-Century-Crofts.

Terrace, H. S. (1968). Discrimination learning, the peak shift and behavioral contrast. *Journal of the Experimental Analysis of Behavior*, **11**, 727–741.

Wagner, A. R. (1966). Frustration and punishment. In: R. H. Haber (Ed.) *Research on Motivation*. New York: Holt, Rinehart and Winston, pp. 229–239.

Weisman, R. G. (1969). Some determinants of inhibitory stimulus control. *Journal of the Experimental Analysis of Behavior*, **12**, 443–450.

Weisman, R. G. (1970a). Factors influencing inhibitory stimulus control: differential reinforcement of other behavior during discrimination training. *Journal of the Experimental Analysis of Behavior*, **14**, 87–92.

Weisman, R. G. (1970b). Determinants of inhibitory stimulus control. In: Reynierse, J. H. (Ed.) *Current Issues in Animal Learning*. Lincoln: University of Nebraska.

Westbrook, F. (1971). The transfer of discriminative control. Unpublished D.Phil. thesis, University of Sussex.

Zeiler, M. D. (1968). Fixed and variable schedules of response-independent reinforcement. *Journal of the Experimental Analysis of Behavior*, **11**, 405–414.

H

maintain continuous contact. In a successive discrimination, for example, a human subject might be required to hold on to a joystick throughout each S^+ and S^- trial. On S^+ trials the correct response is pulling the joystick towards the subject. By definition, no reinforcement is available in S^- but the subject is required to hold on to the joystick in a neutral position. In the neutral position the joystick cannot be moved away from the subject. However, attempts by the subject to push the joystick in a direction opposite to the direction of the response required in S^+ can be recorded by means of a strain gauge connected to the base of the joystick. In this manner the modified joystick allows the experimenter to record responding to S^- that is antagonistic to the response to S^+.

Electromyographic recording might provide an alternative procedure for detecting antagonistic responses. A human subject, for example, might be required to move his forefinger laterally in order to interrupt a beam of light during each presentation of S^+. During S^- he would be required to hold his finger still. By means of electrodes attached to the forearm, the experimenter might be able to record any tendency of the subject to move his finger in the opposite direction (to the right). One advantage of this procedure is that it would allow the experimenter to record the antagonistic responses in situations in which the subject was not in constant contact with the response manipulandum.

VII. The Role of Active Inhibition in Discrimination Learning

A means of measuring active inhibition directly would not only allow us to verify that this phenomenon exists but it would also allow us to study its time course and to relate active inhibition to some of the other by-products of discrimination learning described above. On the basis of our current knowledge of such by-products it appears reasonable to speculate that active inhibition is a sufficient condition for the occurrence of conditioned inhibition as measured by either the gradient or summation method. Indeed, as we will argue later, one important reason for measuring active inhibition is that neither the gradient nor the summation methods may be able to distinguish between active and passive inhibition. Without a means of measuring active inhibition, one of the important stages of the development of a discrimination may go unnoticed.

The evidence we have considered earlier suggests the following account of what takes place during the acquisition of a discrimination with errors:

1. Nonreinforced keypecks to S^- result in frustration. Accordingly, one can observe such emotional responses as wing-flapping, striking the key, turning away from the key and so on (cf. Fig. 2), in the presence of S^-.

2. Responses incompatible with keypecking are strengthened, presumably by the avoidance of frustration which would have occurred had a keypeck been emitted.

3. S^- functions as an aversive stimulus. That is to say, a new response can be conditioned whose sole consequence is the temporary removal of S^- (Terrace, 1971b). This escape response presumably functions to reduce the frequency of emotional responses evoked by S^-.

4. Inhibitory stimulus control with respect to S^- is established. Given that S^+ and S^- are from orthogonal continua, a post-discrimination generalization gradient obtained along the S^- continuum would yield a gradient with a minimum at S^- (Jenkins and Harrison, 1962; Terrace, 1966b).

5. If S^+ and S^- were from the same stimulus continuum, a peak-shift would be obtained on a post-discrimination generalization test (Hanson, 1959).

6. The rate of responding to S^+ would increase above its baseline value (Reynolds, 1961; Terrace, 1963a). Similarly, in a trial procedure, the latency of the response to S^+ would decrease below its baseline level (Jenkins, 1961; Terrace, 1963a). This increase in the strength of the response to S^+ is presumed to be an after-effect of conditioned inhibition which occurred during S^-.

None of the above by-products of discrimination learning occur following discrimination learning without errors (Terrace, 1971a). In view of this generalization one might well ask why it is necessary to appeal to active inhibition as a precursor of other by-products of discrimination learning? Why not instead simply attempt to relate the various by-products described above to the occurrence of errors? There are at least two reasons why this cannot be done. The first, and less significant, of these reasons is that many of the above by-products of discrimination learning have been observed in experiments in which the concept of an error (i.e. a nonreinforced response to S^-) seems irrelevant. Consider, for example, the following discriminations in which S_1 and S_2 are paired with the schedules of reinforcement shown in Table I.

TABLE I

S_1		S_2	Abbreviation
Schedule:	Variable interval 1′	Variable interval 5′	*mult* VI 1′ VI 5′
	Variable interval 1′	Differential reinforcement of low rate 8″	*mult* VI 1′ DRL 8″
	Variable interval 1′	Variable interval 1′ + shock	*mult* VI 1′ VI 1′ + shock

ɪ

Behavioural contrast and the peak shift have been observed following discrimination training on each of the above schedules (Terrace, 1968; Guttman, 1959; Weisman, 1969). Inhibitory stimulus control has been observed following discrimination on *mult* VI 1′ VI 5′ and *mult* VI DRL training (Weisman, 1969). While one could conceivably stretch the concept of an error to handle nonreinforced responses on a DRL schedule, it becomes more difficult, if not impossible, to do so in the case of VI 5′ and VI 1′+ shock schedules of reinforcement. Thus in schedules such as *mult* VI 1′ VI 5′, *mult* VI DRL and *mult* VI 1 VI′ 1′+shock it is not clear how one could appeal to the occurrence of errors as a contributing factor to the occurrence of behavioural contrast, the peak-shift, inhibitory stimulus control or of other by-products of discrimination learning.

The second problem that arises when one attempts to relate by-products of discrimination learning to the occurrence of errors is the absence of any systematic relationship between the magnitude of such by-products and the number of errors. Consider, for example, the nature of the relationship that one would expect to obtain if behavioural contrast was related to the occurrence of errors during the formation of a discrimination. In the extreme case, contrast does not occur following discrimination learning without errors and it does occur following discrimination learning with errors. However, this author's attempts, in greater than a hundred cases, to predict the magnitude of the increase in the rate of responding to S^+ from the number of errors that occurred during discrimination learning failed to reveal a systematic relationship between the amount of contrast and the number of errors. A doubling of the rate of responding to S^+ appeared just as likely to occur when a subject made a few hundred errors as when he made a few thousand errors. A similar problem arises when one attempts to relate the magnitude of a peak-shift or the slope of an inhibitory gradient to the number of errors that occurred during discrimination learning.

One possible explanation for the lack of a simple relationship between error frequency and such by-products of discrimination learning as contrast, the peak-shift and inhibitory stimulus control is that the subjects in these experiments may show individual differences in frustration tolerance. Nonreinforcement may produce different degrees of frustration in different subjects. This in turn may produce different amounts of active inhibition. If one assumes that the degree of active inhibition one observes is proportional to the amount of frustration that results from nonreinforcement (rather than to the number of errors that occur during discrimination learning) it may yet prove possible to find a systematic relationship between active inhibition and various other by-products of discrimination learning.

According to this formulation the degree of active inhibition (a presumed direct measure of frustration) that develops during the acquisition of a discrimination should allow one to predict the magnitude of behavioural contrast as well as of other by-products of discrimination learning. It should also be noted that, once responding to S^- decreases, frustration resulting from nonreinforcement also decreases. This in turn decreases the tendency to make responses during S^- that are specifically incompatible with the response to S^+. Thus as frustration decreases so does active inhibition. As noted earlier, the gradual diminution of active inhibition does not mean that responding to the manipulandum increases. It rather appears that antagonistic responding is replaced by a wide variety of behaviours which bear no special relationship to the response to S^+.

At this stage in our understanding of how active inhibition is superseded by passive inhibition it is impossible to provide a detailed account of this process. It does however seem reasonable to pursue certain important implications of the shift from active to passive inhibition. One such implication brings us a step closer to specifying the nature of active inhibition. A central property of active inhibition appears to be its dependence upon the prior occurrence of frustration. It is also the absence of frustration that distinguishes active from passive inhibition. In this sense it appears that the phenomenon of active inhibition is an unstated *sine qua non* of the concept of conditioned inhibition. Were passive inhibition all that could be observed in instances of reductions in the frequency of a conditioned response it would appear doubtful that the concept of conditioned inhibition would command much interest among students of conditioned behaviour. As many psychologists have noted, one could quite satisfactorily account for such reductions in response frequency by appeal to a reduction in excitation. On the other hand, it does not appear helpful to appeal to a reduction in the level of excitation in accounting for reductions in the frequency of a conditioned response that results from the establishment of one or many specific new responses that are incompatible with the original response. These responses, which have been established without recourse to any external reinforcer, appear to have been strengthened by the avoidance of frustration.

One problem with a definition of active inhibition that is based upon frustration is that frustration remains an unmeasurable entity. It may appear, therefore, that the logic of using frustration as a basis for defining active inhibition has all of the advantages, noted by Bertrand Russell, of theft after honest toil. If our analysis of active inhibition were to stop at this point it would be hard to shake off the criticism that active inhibition has been defined by appeal to an entity to which we have assigned the very characteristics we are trying to explain. It should be recalled, however, that our analysis of active inhibition also attempted to specify this phenomenon (and indirectly frustration) via two types of empirical observations. One is the direct measurement of antagonistic responses. If this proves feasible one would, at the very least, be able to point to responses that are incompatible with the response to S_2 that have been established without any explicit experimenter-delivered reinforcement. The second empirical basis of the concept of active inhibition has already been demonstrated. This is the phenomenon of escape from S^- behaviour. One is led to the conclusion, albeit by a process of elimination, that the reinforcement for such escape behaviour is the elimination of a stimulus rendered aversive by the frustration it has occasioned. If, as postulated earlier, escape from S^- behaviour, along with other by-products of discrimination learning are shown to depend upon the degree to which antagonistic responses have been established at the beginning of discrimination learning the theory that frustration is necessary for the development of active inhibition would have been shown to rest on firm ground.

A second important implication of the distinction between active and passive inhibition has to do with what is measured by the gradient and summation measures that have been preferred as measures of conditioned inhibition. Consider, for example, the Brown and Jenkins experiment. While the tone may initially exert its effect of occasioning nonresponding because of the development of active inhibition, it seems reasonable to assume that the tone continues to exert the same effect after active inhibition gives way to passive inhibition. Inhibitory stimulus control may also result from situations where either active or passive inhibition is present. Indeed, the persistence of inhibitory stimulus control with continued discrimination training (cf. Farthing and Hearst, 1968; Selekman, 1970), long after other by-products of discrimination learning have dropped out, suggests that gradients of inhibition may be obtained in the absence of active inhibition.

VIII. Conclusion

After many years of unanswered criticisms, recent theoretical analyses and experiments have secured the status of conditioned inhibition as an important factor in our understanding of discrimination learning. While many questions concerning the domain and boundary conditions of conditioned inhibition remain to be answered, it seems clear that conditioned inhibition is a concrete phenomenon that can no longer be dismissed as the result of a generalization decrement or a reduction in excitation.

One important aspect of conditioned inhibition that has yet to receive systematic attention is the topography of behaviour that occurs in the presence of S^- during the formation of a successive discrimination. Specifically, what is the relationship of the topographies of the responses which replace the conditioned response to the topography of the conditioned response? It was postulated that there were two distinct varieties of behaviour that replaced the conditioned response as the strength of the conditioned response weakened. Initially, responses *antagonistic* to the response to S^+ occurred in the presence of S^-. Examples of this behaviour would include turning away from S^-, pulling back from S^- and so on. The strength of such responses were presumed to increase because they did not produce frustration (as was the case when a nonreinforced conditioned response occurred). The establishment of behaviour antagonistic to the conditioned response which is strengthened by the omission of frustration was referred to as "active inhibition". Active inhibition is eventually superceded by a second type of nonresponding referred to as "passive inhibition". During this stage of training, frustration resulting from nonreinforced responses of the same topography as the conditioned response no longer occurs. This is true because the conditioned response has been replaced by responses antagonistic to it. Examples of passive inhibition would include exploring the experimental chamber, roosting (in the case of pigeons), periods of low activity, and so on.

A comparison of characteristics of discrimination performance following discrimination learning with and without errors led to the conclusion that active inhibition was absent following discrimination learning without errors. Since frustration resulting from nonreinforced responding is absent in the case of discrimination learning without errors, it appears that only passive inhibition occurs in the presence of S^- in this type of discrimination learning. While this hypothesis has yet to be confirmed empirically, some recently developed techniques for measuring active inhibition directly should reveal whether active inhibition is indeed absent both following discrimination learning without errors and in other situations in which a stimulus-correlated reduction in the frequency of a response would not be expected to produce frustration.

Acknowledgements

The research described in this paper has been supported in part by grants from the National Institute of Health (HD 00930) and by the National Science Foundation (GB 8111X1).

References

Amsel, A. (1958). The role of frustrative non-reward in noncontinuous reward situations. *Psychological Bulletin*, **55**, 102–119.
Amsel, A. (1962). Frustrative non-reward in partial reinforcement and discrimination learning; some recent history and a theoretical extension. *Psychological Review*, **69**, 306–328.

Bernheim, J. W. (1968). Comment. *Psychonomic Science*, **11**, 327.

Brown, P. L. and Jenkins, H. M. (1967). Conditioned inhibition and excitation in operant discrimination learning. *Journal of Experimental Psychology*, **75**, 255–266.

Farthing, G. W. and Hearst, E. (1968). Generalization gradients of inhibition after different amounts of training. *Journal of the Experimental Analysis of Behavior*, **11**, 743–752.

Ferster, C. B. and Skinner, B. F. (1957). *Schedules of Reinforcement*. New York: Appleton–Century–Crofts.

Grusec, T. (1968). The peak-shift in stimulus generalization: Equivalent effects of errors and non-contingent shock. *Journal of the Experimental Analysis of Behavior*, **11**, 39–49.

Guttman, N. (1959). Generalization gradients around stimuli associated with different reinforcement schedules. *Journal of Experimental Psychology*, **58**, 335–340.

Guttman, N. and Kalish, H. I. (1956). Discriminability and stimulus generalization. *Journal of Experimental Psychology*, **51**, 79–88.

Hanson, H. M. (1959). Effects of discrimination training on stimulus generalization. *Journal of Experimental Psychology*, **58**, 321–334.

Hearst, E., Besley, S. and Farthing, W. G. (1970). Inhibition and the stimulus control of operant behavior. *Journal of the Experimental Analysis of Behavior*, (supplement), **14**, 373–409.

Honig, W. K., Boneau, C. A., Burstein, K. R. and Pennypacker, H. S. (1963). Positive and negative generalization gradients obtained after equivalent training conditions. *Journal of Comparative Physiological Psychology*, **56**, 111–116.

Hull, C. L. (1950). Simple qualitative discrimination learning. *Psychological Review*, **57**, 303–313.

Jenkins, H. M. (1961). The effect of discrimination training on extinction. *Journal of Experimental Psychology*, **61**, 111–121.

Jenkins, H. M. (1965). Generalization gradients and the concept of inhibition. In: D. I. Mostofsky (Ed.) *Stimulus Generalization*. Stanford: Stanford University Press.

Jenkins, H. M. and Harrison, R. H. (1962). Generalization gradients of inhibition following auditory discrimination learning. *Journal of the Experimental Analysis of Behavior*, **5**, 435–441.

Loucks, R. B. (1933). An appraisal of Pavlov's systematization of behavior from the experimental standpoint. *Journal of Comparative Psychology*, **15**, 1–47.

Lyons, J. (1969). Stimulus generalization as a function of discrimination learning with and without errors. *Science*, **163**, 490–491.

Pavlov, I. P. (1927). *Conditioned Reflexes*. London: Oxford University Press, (tr. G. V. Anrep).

Premack, D. (1969). On some boundary conditions of contrast. In: J. Tapp (Ed.) *Reinforcement and Behavior*. New York: Academic Press.

Rescorla, R. A. (1969). Pavlovian conditioned inhibition. *Psychological Bulletin*, **72**, 77–94.

Reynolds, G. S. (1961). Behavioral contrast. *Journal of the Experimental Analysis of Behavior*, **4**, 57–71.

Selekman, W. (1970). Gradients of preference and post-discrimination gradients along the wave-length continuum following training to a white light. Unpublished doctoral dissertation, Columbia University.

Skinner, B. F. (1938). *The Behavior of Organisms; an Experimental Analysis*. New York: Appleton–Century.

Spence, K. W. (1936). The nature of discrimination learning in animals. *Psychological Review*, **43**, 427–449.

Terrace, H. S. (1963a). Discrimination learning with and without errors. *Journal of the Experimental Analysis of Behavior*, **6**, 1–27.

Terrace, H. S. (1963b). Errorless transfer of a discrimination across two contin ua. *Journal of the Experimental Analysis of Behavior*, **6**, 223–232.

Terrace, H. S. (1964). Wavelength generalization after discrimination learning with and without errors. *Science*, **144**, 78–80.

Terrace, H. S. (1966a). Stimulus Control. In: W. K. Honig (Ed.), *Operant Behavior: Areas of Research and Application*. New York: Appleton-Century-Crofts.

Terrace, H. S. (1966b). Discrimination learning and inhibition. *Science*, **154**, 1677–1680.

Terrace, H. S. (1968). Discrimination learning, the peak-shift, and behavioral contrast. *Journal of the Experimental Analysis of Behavior*, **11**, 727–741.

Terrace, H. S. (1971a). By-products of discrimination learning. In: Bower, G. and Spence, J. (Eds.), *The Psychology of Learning and Motivation, Volume* 5. New York: Academic Press.

Terrace, H. S. (1971b). Escape from S⁻. *Learning and Motivation*, **2**, 148–163.

Weisman, R. G. (1969). Some determinants of inhibitory stimulus control. *Journal of the Experimental Analysis of Behavior*, **12**, 443–450.

Wilkie, D. M. (in press). Variable-time reinforcement in multiple and concurrent schedules. *Journal of the Experimental Analysis of Behavior*.

5 | Inhibition in the Acquisition and Reversal of Simultaneous Discriminations

E. M. MACPHAIL

University of Sussex, Brighton, Sussex, England

I. Introduction	121
II. Relative Approach Strength to S⁻ Following Acquisition or Reversal	
of a Simultaneous Discrimination	126
A. Experiment I	126
B. Experiment II	129
C. Experiment III	131
III. Behavioural Contrast in Acquisition and Reversal of a Discrete Trial	
Simultaneous Discrimination	139
A. Experiment IV	139
IV. Concluding Comments	150
Acknowledgements	150
References	150

I. Introduction

Acquisition of either a simultaneous or a successive discrimination is conventionally preceded by a period of pretraining that creates in subjects a tendency to approach both stimuli. The essence of acquiring a successive discrimination is the reduction of the tendency to approach S⁻, whereas the essence of mastery of a simultaneous discrimination lies in establishing an adequate difference between the tendencies to approach the two stimuli. The simultaneous task could, therefore, be acquired by increasing the tendency to approach S⁺ or by reducing the tendency to approach S⁻, or by altering the approach tendencies to both stimuli appropriately. Spence's (1937) account of transposition learning in animals assumes that in the course of simultaneous acquisition the approach tendency to S⁺ does increase, and that the tendency to approach S⁻ decreases (as a consequence of the growth of inhibition). Spence's notions have recently been used to account for the shapes of the generalization gradients obtained following successive training (e.g. Hearst, 1969), but it is still not clear that his analysis is appropriate for the simultaneous situation; for example, Bloomfield (1969) writes that "what simultaneous and errorless discriminations have in common, and what differentiates them both from ordinary successive discrimination training, is the absence of inhibition". This paper concerns the nature of the changes that occur in the animal's tendency to approach S⁻ during simultaneous acquisition, and the work reported in it was originally prompted by an analysis of some behavioural changes seen in pigeons following brain lesions.

The first relevant finding from physiological work is that certain lesions result in a disruption of performance of successive discriminations, without any corresponding disturbance of simultaneous discrimination acquisition; this result has been found in mammals (e.g. Kimble, 1963; Swanson and Isaacson, 1967), and, in a recent experiment, in pigeons (Macphail, 1971). In the latter experiment, subjects were trained post-operatively to respond to a key that could be illuminated with red or green light, reinforcement being available in the presence of both stimuli on a VI 60 sec schedule. When rates had stabilized, discrimination training commenced; subjects experienced 12 days of training in which responses to the red key were no longer reinforced. It was found that the lesioned subjects were, relative to appropriate control subjects, impaired in their ability to withhold responses in the presence of the red key. Following successive discrimination training, the same birds acquired a simultaneous position discrimination, using a conventional discrete trials procedure, and it was found that the lesioned birds had no deficit in its acquisition. An implication of this lesion-induced dissociation between simultaneous and successive discriminations is that the latter involve some mechanism which is not necessary for the performance of the former. Many analyses of these and other similar results obtained from lesioned animals suggest that the subjects suffer from the disruption of an inhibitory process (e.g. Kimble 1968; Douglas, Chapter 20); applied to the simultaneous situation, the argument might be either that animals do not significantly reduce their approach tendency to S⁻ during acquisition, or that the approach tendency is reduced, but not by the same inhibitory process that is used in successive acquisition.

A second dissociation obtained by physiological techniques is between the acquisition and reversal of simultaneous discriminations. The subjects in the Macphail (1971) experiment, having acquired the simultaneous position discrimination, were then required to perform a series of six reversals of the discrimination, one per day, each to the same criterion (15 successive correct choices). Lesioned birds were, relative to controls, severely impaired over the series of reversals. Similar results have been found in earlier mammalian studies (Douglas, Chapter 20). The basic deficit of lesioned subjects lies in their abnormal perseveration to the former S⁺. It is clear that in reversal learning, some reduction in approach strength to S⁻ is a prerequisite of successful performance, since otherwise the new S⁺ will not be sampled. A plausible account of these lesion-induced dissociations is, therefore, that in both successive discriminations and reversal of simultaneous discriminations, approach strength to S⁻ is reduced by the same process, whereas in simultaneous acquisition, approach strength to S⁻ is either not reduced, or is reduced by some different process (which is not disrupted by the brain lesions in question).

There is also evidence available from studies using only intact subjects to support the view that simultaneous acquisition involves different mechanisms from those involved in successive discrimination and reversal performance.

The first two relevant experiments used operant versions of the conventional simultaneous discrimination situation. Honig (1962) compared generalization gradients following simultaneous and successive acquisition of a colour discrimination by pigeons. Peak shift was observed following successive training, but not following simultaneous training. It should be pointed out that Honig's simultaneous situation was in fact a concurrent schedule, S⁺ being correlated with a VI 60 sec reinforcement schedule, and S⁻ with extinction. Honig's suggestion was that in this situation, subjects came to regard S⁻ as a cue to switch to S⁺.

Support for Honig's suggestion is provided by Beale and Winton (1970), who employed a concurrent schedule of the type originated by Findley (1958). In their experiment, which is fully described in Honig's contribution to this book (Chapter 2), pigeons were given a choice between a main key, on which a *mult* VI EXT schedule was in force, and a changeover key which, when pecked, alternated the component on the main key. Subsequent generalization tests showed that varying the S⁻ of the multiple schedule systematically altered the latency to peck the changeover key, but did not affect the absolute rate of responding on the main key when no changeover key was available. It appears, therefore, that in this situation, subjects saw S⁻ as a cue to peck the changeover key, and not as an inhibitory stimulus in any conventional sense. Following standard successive Go; No go discriminations, rates to S⁻ in generalization tests do vary with distance from the original S⁻ (e.g. Hearst, 1969); it may be presumed, therefore, that the nonappearance of inhibitory gradients in the absence of the changeover key was due to the availability of that key in acquisition.

Each of the above experiments suggests important differences between the standard successive Go; No go procedure, and procedures in which a choice between two alternative stimuli is available to subjects, and in each case it seems probable that the difference lies in the subjects' response to S⁻.

There are two experiments using intact animals that suggest a difference between the processes involved in acquisition and reversal of simultaneous discriminations. The first was carried out by Clayton (1966), who showed that acquisition of a T^- maze problem by rats was, if anything, faster with long inter-trial intervals whereas reversal of the discrimination was impaired, the nature of this impairment apparently being a longer perseveration to the original S^+. This result, although it implies a difference between the mechanisms involved, yields little information on the possible nature of that difference.

An experiment that suggested differential modes of response to S^- in acquisition and reversal was carried out in this laboratory (Macphail 1970); the experiment showed that pigeons given three serial reversals of a red–green discrimination each day found the second of each day's reversals (R2s) less difficult (in terms of trials to criterion) than either first reversals (R1s) or third reversals (R3s). R1s were regarded as being analogous to conventional acquisition as, due to the occurrence of overnight "forgetting" (Mackintosh *et al.*, 1968), birds showed no preference for either stimulus at the beginning of R1s. Analysis of error patterns showed that the relative ease of R2s was due to the fact that birds performing R2s were less likely to make an error following a run of correct choices than were birds performing R1s or R3s. It was argued that this result was due to the operation of two factors: first, birds performing R1s did not learn to avoid S^- (owing to the absence of a run of initial errors), and so, after a sequence of correct choices, had to choose between a stimulus that was accumulating approach strength and a stimulus that was neutral rather than (as at a comparable point in R2s or R3s) inhibitory; second, birds performing R3s had, after their initial error run, learned to avoid both stimuli, and so switched control to irrelevant features (in this case, primarily to position).

It appears, therefore, that data collected from a number of different situations can be accounted for on the assumption that the strength of approach to S^- is not reduced in simultaneous acquisition in the same way that it is during reversal learning or successive discrimination. The obvious way to check this proposal would seem to be, to compare the strength of approach to S^-, presented in isolation, following simultaneous acquisition training with the corresponding strength following either successive training or reversal training. Now data of this sort for the successive case was collected by Honig, during the generalization testing phase of his 1962 experiment. What emerged was that response strength to S^- following simultaneous training was significantly higher than following successive training, and it seems to have been primarily this fact that led Honig to conclude that "genuine extinction" did not develop to S^- in the simultaneous situation. The result can, however, be explained on the assumption that the same inhibitory process operates in both situations, but is involved less in the simultaneous situation; in fact, this is a reasonable suggestion, as more than seven times as many responses to S⁻ were made in the successive, as opposed to the simultaneous, case. It can be seen that the problem of establishing comparable criteria for the mastery of the two types of discrimination is virtually insurmountable, and for this reason, the experiments reported here were designed to compare responses to S⁻ following simultaneous acquisition of a discrimination with those following reversal of the discrimination. Before describing the experiments, one further theoretical assumption will be made clear.

It has been argued so far that approach strength to S⁻ in acquisition of simultaneous discriminations is probably either not reduced or reduced by some process that is not involved in reversal learning or successive discriminations. Although some necessary controls are lacking, it seems to be the case that in both Honig's experiment and that of Beale and Winton, approach strength to S⁻ was reduced during the course of acquisition. The probability is, therefore, that, if the proposed account is tenable, response strength to S⁻ is reduced during simultaneous acquisition, by some alternative process. What might such an alternative process be? An obvious possibility is that a competing response involving approach to S⁺ is formed; there are a number of strategies that might give rise to such response competition—subjects might, for example, learn Honig's rule of attaching to S⁻ the response of switching to S⁺ or they might, like Siegel's (1969) rats, learn (in a discrimination where position is irrelevant) to approach the left, unless black, say, is there, in which case, approach the right. It will be assumed that the establishment of such competing responses will be less effective in reducing response strength where no alternative is in fact available than will the generation of response inhibition during successive acquisition and reversal learning. Such an assumption is implicit in Honig's discussion, and is intuitively reasonable. The rationale underlying Expts I, II and III was, then, that pigeons should, following the acquisition of a simultaneous discrimination, respond more readily to S⁻, when presented in isolation, than following reversal of the discrimination. Approach strengths to S⁺ following the two procedures were also measured, to ensure that the results were not contaminated by large changes in overall approach strength between acquisition and reversal.

Expts I, II and III were not independent, but various versions of an identical approach to the problem; the results of all three experiments were similar in important respects, and will be reported in detail for Expt III only. In each of these experiments subjects were trained and overtrained on either acquisition alone, or acquisition and reversal of a simultaneous discrimination. On the day after completion of that stage, birds were given a series of trials under extinction conditions, where either S⁻ or S⁺ (but not both) was available on each trial. It was anticipated that the ratio of responses on S⁻ to those on S⁺ would be higher after acquisition than after reversal. On the next day, birds were run in the same conditions, except that responses to S⁺ were rewarded; in other words, birds now learned a successive discrimination with the same cue positive as in the preceding acquisition or reversal training. It was anticipated that there would be more transfer to the successive condition in birds that had experienced reversal.

II. Relative Approach Strength to S⁻ Following Acquisition or Reversal of a Simultaneous Discrimination

A. Experiment I

Expt I examined the response of birds to S⁻ of a red–green discrimination, having performed acquisition with green positive, or acquisition with red positive and reversal with green positive; in each case, S⁻ in the successive tests was red. Prior to original acquisition of this discrimination, birds were trained on a position discrimination, the point of this procedure being to reduce the possibility of extinction during reversal learning.

In this experiment, as in the following two, a number of techniques were used to ensure that sufficient extinction responding occurred to allow meaningful comparisons between the groups. Firstly, extensive pretraining was given, and the final day of this pretraining was run under partially reinforced conditions. Secondly, a certain amount of overtraining was given following mastery of the discrimination or its reversal, and, thirdly, there was a response requirement of five pecks to terminate each choice trial.

1. Method

a. Subjects. Eight experimentally naïve pigeons were used. They were housed in individual cages with water freely available, and maintained at 80% of their *ad lib.* feeding weights throughout the experiment.

b. Apparatus. Animals were tested in a pigeon chamber ($30 \times 30 \times 30$ cm) placed in a dark sound-attenuated cubicle, which contained three response keys, each 2 cm in diameter. The centre key was mounted directly above a grain feeder at a height of 20 cm above the floor. The remaining two keys were mounted on either side of the centre key at the same level. The keys were 8 cm apart, centre to centre. The centre key could be illuminated from behind by white light; the side keys could each be illuminated by red or green light. A houselight located in the roof of the chamber was continuously illuminated and white noise was also provided throughout.

The control of the sequence of events in the chamber, and the collection of data were carried out on-line by the Elliot 4130 computer installed in the laboratory. Programmes were written in the Experiment Control Language developed in this laboratory (Francis and Sutherland, 1969).

c. Pretraining. Subjects were pretrained to respond to all three keys by the use of an auto-shaping procedure. On each trial, one key was illuminated for 8 sec or until the bird had pecked it the number of times required by the current criterion. Each response to an illuminated key resulted in a clearly audible click from a relay mounted on the back of the front wall of the chamber; responses to keys that were not illuminated had no programmed consequences. At key offset, the hopper was activated for 4 sec, and this was followed by an inter-trial interval of variable duration, having an average of 40 sec. Where a subject did not make any responses on a given trial, the same key was illuminated on the subsequent trial. The centre key was illuminated on the first trial of each day, and thereafter on every third noncorrection trial, the intervening two noncorrection trials being distributed between the side keys according to a Gellermann sequence; the side key illuminated was alternatively red and green. The response requirement criterion was set at one at the beginning of each day's session, and raised in steps of two to a maximum of five each time a subject achieved criterion on ten successive trials. Training continued on this schedule until a subject had achieved a run of ten successive noncorrection trials with criterion set at five; there was a maximum of 60 trials each day. On the day following completion of the run of ten 5-response trials, subjects underwent the final phase of pretraining; trials in this phase were organized in precisely the same way, except that 50% of the trials were not reinforced, on a random basis. Birds typically performed this phase perfectly, emitting 90 responses over the 30 trials required (i.e. 10 at criterion 1, 30 at 3, and 50 at 5).

d. Simultaneous acquisition and reversal training. Each trial commenced with the illumination of the centre key. A peck to this key extinguished it and illuminated the two side keys, one of which was red, one green. The colour of the side keys was varied according to a Gellermann sequence, there being no more than three successive trials on which the same colour appeared on a given key. Responses to the side keys resulted in audible clicks; when one key had been pecked five times, the side keys were extinguished, and, if the key in question was correct for the discrimination, the food hopper was activated for 4 sec. The next trial was initiated 14 sec after the response requirement had been met. Responses to keys that were not illuminated had no scheduled consequences, and were not recorded. Training continued until ten successive correct choices had been made, and was completed in a single session.

e. Discrimination overtraining. In overtraining, subjects were given, on one day, 40 trials which were conducted in the same way as they were in discrimination training.

f. Successive extinction test. Each trial commenced with the illumination of the centre key; a response to this key extinguished it, and illuminated the side keys, which were now both the same colour, the order of colours being determined by a Gellermann sequence. The side keys remained on for 4 sec, and responses made during that time to either key were counted, and resulted in auditory feedback. The succeeding trial began 10 sec after the side lights had been extinguished, and testing, which was completed in one session, continued until a bird failed to peck the centre key within 10 min of its illumination.

g. Successive acquisition. Conditions were similar to those obtaining in the extinction test, with two major modifications: first, if a bird failed to peck the centre key within 8 sec of its onset, the key was nevertheless extinguished, and the side keys were illuminated; second, when S^+ was on the side keys, the trial invariably ended with 4-sec food reinforcement, either as soon as the bird had responded five times, or, when it failed to do so, after 8 sec. Trials on which S^- was displayed were identical to those of the extinction test. Training, which was completed in one session, continued until the bird, over 20 successive trials, responded five times on all positive trials, and made no responses on any negative trials.

h. Experimental design. The eight birds completed all stages of pretraining and on the following day acquired a position discrimination, with the right key correct; they were then assigned at random to either of two groups. Group AQ performed, on successive days, a colour discrimination (with green as S^+), overtraining with green positive, the extinction test, and successive acquisition with green positive. Group REV performed a colour discrimination with red positive, overtraining of that discrimination, a colour discrimination reversal, with green now positive, followed by overtraining, extinction, and successive acquisition with green positive.

2. Results and Discussions

As stated earlier, only a summary of the results of the first two experiments will be presented. Groups AQ and REV did not differ significantly in trials to criterion on either the position discrimination, or the acquisition of the colour discrimination, although acquisition with red positive was a somewhat simpler task than with green positive; similarly, acquisition with green positive was not significantly easier than reversal with green positive.

The original hypothesis received no support from the extinction and successive acquisition tests; there were no significant differences between the groups in absolute numbers of extinction responses to either S^+ or S^-, nor in ratios of negative to total extinction responses (which ranged from 3 to 17% in Group AQ, and from 7 to 32% in Group REV). In successive acquisition, Group AQ in fact made significantly fewer responses to the negative key (p < ·05, 2-tailed t test), although the groups did not differ significantly in trials to criterion on that task.

These results indicate that the nonreversed birds are, if anything, more efficient at withholding responses in the presence of S⁻. A similar conclusion may be drawn from the overtraining performance, where the mean number of errors made by group REV subjects was 3·5, as opposed to a mean of 0·5 for Group AQ subjects; the difference between these means was significant at the ·01 level. It will be recalled that the argument presented in Macphail (1970) was precisely that reversed subjects should be relatively more efficient at avoiding S⁻ following a series of correct choices. Thus the pattern of these errors also tends to disconfirm the original hypothesis.

These results were in an unexpected direction, and it seemed possible, if unlikely, that they were due to the somewhat unusual procedure of having trained subjects on a position discrimination prior to original acquisition of the colour discrimination; accordingly the experiment was re-run without the introduction of the position discrimination.

B. Experiment II

1. Method

The procedures and design of this experiment were identical to those of Expt I, except that colour discrimination was performed on the day following pretraining, and no position discrimination training was given. As in Expt I, there were two groups, Group AQ ($N = 4$), given acquisition only, and Group REV ($N = 4$), given acquisition and reversal training.

2. Results and Discussion

The overall pattern of results was identical to that found in Expt I, except that, in this experiment, there were no significant differences between the groups in either error scores in successive acquisition, or error scores in overtraining. In the extinction test of this experiment, responses to the negative stimulus ranged from 4 to 21% of total extinction responses (for Group AQ), and from 5 to 22% for Group REV.

It seemed possible that the results of this experiment and of Expt I might reflect a breakdown of discrimination in extinction conditions that might, for example, nullify a superior discrimination in the REV Groups at the end of training. Accordingly, the first ten extinction trials, five of which showed red on the side keys, and five green, were analysed for the individual subjects of both experiments. The results of this analysis are shown on Table I; unfortunately, trial by trial data was lost for one subject in Group AQ of Expt II.

K

TABLE I

Experiments I and II: first ten trials of extinction

	Positive (green) Trials			Negative (red) Trials			
	Left key Responses	Right key Responses	Total (G)	Left key Responses	Right key Responses	Total (R)	$\frac{R}{R+G} \times 100$
EXPERIMENT I							
Group AQ Subjects							
1832	0	43	43	18	0	18	29·5
1834	21	7	28	3	5	8	22·2
1838	50	0	50	0	21	21	29·6
1841	43	6	49	1	3	4	7·5
Means			42·5			12·8	22·2
Group REV Subjects							
1828	7	39	46	9	5	14	23·3
1833	8	19	27	9	1	10	27·0
1837	18	27	45	14	1	15	25·0
1839	37	16	53	22	19	41	43·6
Means			42·8			20·0	29·7
EXPERIMENT II							
Group AQ Subjects							
1845	30	0	30	0	4	4	11·8
1847	0	31	31	13	0	13	29·5
1850	50	2	52	3	4	7	11·9
Means			37·7			8·0	17·7
Group REV Subjects							
1830	24	8	32	7	0	7	17·9
1835	57	0	57	2	0	2	3·4
1843	7	41	48	19	0	19	28·4
1877	5	41	46	9	8	17	27·0
Means			45·8			11·3	19·2

Once again, it can be seen that no significant differences between the groups emerged in terms of responses to S^- relative to those to S^+.

One important observation arises from this analysis, and it concerns the performance of Birds 1832, 1838, 1845, and 1847 of the AQ Groups. Each of these birds, over these initial ten trials, invariably responded on one side key when the side keys were green, and on the other, when the side keys were red. This is the behaviour that would be generated if the birds had adopted the following hypothesis: go (e.g.) left unless left is red, in which case go right. Performance of this kind was noted in rats by Siegel (1969) where, it should be pointed out, the animals were in a maze in which the positive and negative stimuli were not simultaneously visible. In other words, it appears to be the case that these birds did adopt a strategy which would enable solution of the simultaneous discrimination without any reduction in approach strength to S^- in isolation; moreover, there is reason to suppose that birds are more likely to adopt such a strategy in acquisition rather than reversal, as four of the seven AQ birds for whom data was available performed in this way, whereas none of the eight REV birds did so. It can be seen, however, that even these AQ birds, over the first ten trials, made more than twice as many responses to the green as to the red stimulus, and in fact over all extinction trials, made approximately five times as many.

The results of Expt II are clearly in close agreement with those of Expt I, and so indicate that the position discrimination introduced in that experiment had little effect on the birds' subsequent performance. It is quite clear that these experiments provide no support whatever for the proposal that birds should show less approach strength to S^- presented in isolation following reversal than following acquisition of a simultaneous discrimination. In fact, the trend is in the opposite direction. The final experiment of this series was run to ensure the generality of these findings. In this third experiment, the dimension used for discrimination training was position; one reason for choosing position is that, although it has been shown that position reversal, as opposed to acquisition, is affected by hyperstriatal lesions, a similar selective deficit in colour reversal has not yet been demonstrated in birds.

C. EXPERIMENT III.

One important question left unanswered by Expts I and II is whether the low rates of response to S^- following simultaneous acquisition necessarily imply that response strength to negative stimuli is reduced during discrimination to a level below that established in pretraining. That reversal does involve a reduction may be inferred from the data shown on Table I. Responses to S^- following reversal are clearly much lower than those to S^+ following acquisition; it could be, however, that acquisition involves only the selective growth of approach strength to S^+, with no corresponding change in approach strength to S^-. A pretraining only control group was introduced in this experiment to measure resistance to extinction in the absence of any discrimination experience.

1. *Method*

a. Subjects and apparatus. Twelve experimentally naïve pigeons were used. Details of their maintenance, and of the apparatus used, are identical to those described in Expt I.

b. Pretraining. The pretraining procedure was identical to that used in Expts I and II, except that the side keys were, when illuminated, invariably red.

c. Acquisition and reversal: training and overtraining. The procedures used here were again identical to those of the previous experiments, except that, as in pretraining, red was the only colour used on the side keys; choices were made, that is, between two illuminated side keys, each of which was red.

d. Successive extinction and acquisition. Trials were again organized in these tests as they were in Expts I and II, except that, where in those experiments both side keys would have been green (the positive stimulus), in this experiment only the right (positive) key was illuminated (with red light), and where both keys would have been red, only the left (negative) key was illuminated. Responses to an illuminated key obtained feedback clicks; responses to an unlit key had no programmed consequences.

e. Experimental design. All subjects completed the pretraining procedures. Groups AQ and REV ($N = 4$ in each case) then underwent the same sets of procedures as the corresponding groups in Expts I and II; for Group AQ, the positive key in acquisition was the right key, and for Group REV the positive key in acquisition was the left key. Group PT birds ($N = 4$) were transferred to the extinction test on the day following completion of pretraining.

2. *Results and Discussion*

Table II summarizes the performance of the two groups that underwent discrimination training. There were no significant differences between the

TABLE II

	Experiment III: Position Discrimination							
	Acquisition				Reversal			
	Trials to Criterion		Over training Errors		Trials to Criterion		Over training Errors	
Group	Mean	S.D.	Mean	S.D.	Mean	S.D.	Mean	S.D.
AQ	20·0	3·1	0·8	1·3				
REV	14·5	4·7	0·0	0·0	28·8	5·3	2·0	1·2

groups in acquisition of the discrimination; Group REV trials to criterion on reversal were, however, significantly higher than those of Group AQ in acquisition (p < ·05). That is, in this experiment, reversal of the discrimination was significantly more difficult than its original acquisition; there were, however, no significant differences between these two groups in overtraining errors.

The results obtained from the three groups in the successive tests are summarized in Table III. Comparison of Groups AQ and REV reveals only

TABLE III

	Experiment III: Successive Tests							
	Extinction					Acquisition		
	Positive (Right key) Responses		Negative (Left key) Responses		Errors		Trials to Criterion	
Group	Mean	S.D.	Mean	S.D.	Mean	S.D.	Mean	S.D.
AQ	211·3	47·5	24·5	16·0	15·0	12·5	47·8	18·0
REV	106·5	9·7	29·5	15·9	16·3	9·0	49·3	9·5
PT	21·5	11·3	34·0	7·8				

one significant difference between them, which is that Group REV subjects made significantly fewer responses to S^+ in the extinction test (p < ·01). The proportion of the total responses made on the negative key ranged from 5 to 20% in Group AQ, and from 1 to 35% in Group REV.

To establish whether the device of illuminating only one side key had been successful in its purpose of providing effectively only one available stimulus, responses to the side key that was not illuminated were recorded in both successive situations. It was found that no such responses were made by any subject in the extinction test; two birds (one from Group AQ and one from Group REV) responded to an unlit key in the acquisition test. One of these birds made only one response, and the other, four, all to the positive key on trials on which the negative key was illuminated. It is clear, therefore, that this technique was satisfactory.

Comparison of Groups AQ and PT indicates that, whereas responses to S^+ are greatly enhanced by discrimination training, there is no significant difference between the groups in total responses to the negative (left) key in extinction. In other words, there is by this measure no evidence that acquisition training reduces response strength to S^- from its level prior to discrimination training. However, analysis of the data obtained over the first ten extinction trials leads to a different conclusion: Table IV presents

TABLE IV

Experiment III: First ten Trials of Extinction

	Positive (Right key) Responses	Negative (Left key) Responses	$\dfrac{\text{Neg}}{\text{Neg} + \text{Pos}} \times 100$
Group AQ			
Subjects			
1856	62	7	10·1
1860	34	0	0·0
1863	46	0	0·0
1875	75	1	1·3
Means	54·5	2·0	2·9
Group REV			
Subjects			
1857	41	5	10·9
1862	54	31	36·5
1865	35	15	30·0
1869	48	18	27·3
Means	44·5	17·3	26·2
Group PT			
Subjects			
1851	0	16	100·0
1859	21	24	53·3
1861	16	22	57·9
1872	14	35	71·4
Means	12·8	24·3	70·7

the individual data for those trials for Groups AQ, REV and PT. From this table it can be seen that the mean number of responses made to the left (negative) key following pretraining alone was 24·3, whereas the corresponding number following acquisition training was 2·0, and, following reversal, 17·3. It may therefore be concluded that acquisition does involve a marked reduction of response strength on the negative key, and that this is obscured in the total extinction scores by two factors: first, subjects that have learned the discrimination show considerably more resistance to extinction, and second, the discrimination tends to break down as extinction proceeds.

Table IV also shows no overlap between the numbers of extinction responses on the positive key of Groups AQ and PT, the mean number in Group AQ being more than four times that of Group PT. This too is a striking finding: it indicates that the discrimination training, consisting of choices (mostly rewarded) between the two keys markedly increased response strength to S$^+$ at the start of extinction, as compared to that established at the end of pretraining. It should be pointed out that pretraining conditions were more similar to those of extinction than were the discrimination conditions, in that only one key was available in extinction; it will be recalled, also, that pretraining ended with one day's training on which only 50% of trials were reinforced. Therefore the acquisition training of this experiment had the effect of both increasing response rate on S^+ over the first five trials of extinction by a factor of more than four, and decreasing the corresponding rate on S^- by a factor of more than 12. The unavoidable conclusion would seem to be that subjects in Group AQ learned a great deal about the significance, as regards reinforcement, of both S^+ and S^-.

3. *General Discussion of Experiments I, II and III.*

The results of all three experiments are in general agreement on important points, and provide no support for the proposal that reversed subjects are more likely to withhold responses to S^- presented in isolation than subjects having performed only the acquisition of the discrimination. The trend, in fact, has been in the opposite direction. For example, although the differences in question rarely achieved statistical significance, the three main phases of each experiment each provided evidence to suggest that more inhibition was generated in the acquisition only groups. In the discrimination and reversal training phase, mean Group REV overtraining error scores following reversal were invariably higher than those of Group AQ following acquisition; it will be recalled that Macphail (1970) suggested that the accuracy with which a simultaneous discrimination is maintained following its acquisition is in part, at least, a function of the amount of inhibition generated on the negative stimulus. In the extinction test phase, analysis of the first ten trial data showed, in all three experiments, that mean S^- response scores were lower in Group AQ than in Group REV subjects, both in absolute terms and relative to total responses over the ten trials. Finally, in the successive acquisition phase, mean scores (both of errors and trials to criterion) were lower in Group AQ than Group REV, in all these experiments.

A consideration of the significance of these results should emphasise the extinction test data, for two reasons; first, it is clear that, at this stage, Macphail's (1970) proposal concerning the role of inhibition in maintaining the accuracy of discriminations is still speculative. Second, although one may conclude that Group AQ subjects showed at least as much transfer to the successive acquisition situation as did Group REV birds, there were no data to show how much, if any, transfer either group displayed. It would, in fact, not be a simple matter to obtain a control group that could be used to demonstrate that such an effect was due to differences established prior to successive discrimination training in response to S^-, as opposed to S^+. For example, in Expt III, the obvious control group for Group AQ

(Group PT) showed large differences from Group AQ in approach strength to both S^- and S^+ prior to the point at which acquisition training might have been commenced, so that any difference in transfer found in successive acquisition in Group AQ relative to Group PT could have been ascribed to prior differences in approach strength to either stimulus.

The two basic findings of the extinction tests were as follows: first, rates of response in the presence of S^- were, relative to those in the presence of S^+, at least as low in subjects given acquisition alone as in those that had experienced reversal; second, subjects that had experienced acquisition alone, like subjects that experienced reversal, showed a reduction in response strength to S^- as a consequence of discrimination training. The problem now, therefore, is to reconcile these facts to the arguments presented in the Introduction.*

It might be argued that, although the same inhibitory process is involved in both acquisition and reversal, it is significantly less necessary for efficient performance in acquisition as the original response strength on S^- is small, relative to that on S^- at the start of a reversal: the generality of this argument must, of course, depend on pretraining conditions. It is not, however, possible to decide whether a greater reduction in approach strength was required by the AQ or the REV Groups in these experiments; for example, in Table IV it can be seen that mean negative responses over the first ten trials were 24·3 following pretraining alone, and 2·0, following acquisition training; mean positive responses following acquisition alone were 54·5, and, following reversal, negative responses were 17·3 (it should be noted that the S^+ extinction scores of Group AQ are not in fact the ideal control, as they were made to the right key, whereas Group REV extinction negative responses were to the left key). Thus the absolute drop in response is larger in Group REV, whereas the relative drop is larger in Group AQ; there does not seem to be any clear sense in which one measure is more valid than the other.

A second possibility is that, although normal subjects do reduce approach

---

*An objection that might be raised to the validity of the extinction data obtained from REV Groups is that their response rates to S^- may be artificially high owing to overnight "forgetting," a phenomenon known to occur during serial reversal performance (see, for example, Bitterman, Chapter 6). This presents no serious difficulty, for two reasons; first, there is obviously very little overnight forgetting by REV Groups, as indicated by their very low level of errors during overtraining. Although REV Group subjects did indeed tend to make more errors than the AQ Group birds, this difference reached significance on only one occasion, and it is reasonable to expect that, had a further day's overtraining been given (so giving a measure of overnight forgetting following overtraining of a discrimination) virtually no errors would have occurred in either group. Second, as the first ten trials data of Group AQ in Expt III emphasize, the important feature of these experiments was, not the high rates of response to S^- in extinction by the REV Group subjects, but the low rates exhibited by the AQ Groups.

strength to S$^-$ in simultaneous acquisition, brain-lesioned animals do not; but this proposal does not account for the distinction between simultaneous and successive acquisition suggested by the behavioural studies of Honig (1962) and Beale and Winton (1970). Moreover, it is hard to see that reduction of approach strength on S$^-$ would not (as implied by this suggestion) facilitate acquisition.

Finally, possible alternative inhibitory processes must be considered; it was argued in the Introduction that the most plausible way in which approach strength to S$^-$ might be reduced in the course of simultaneous acquisition would be by competing responses, generated by such strategies as: peck the other key when (say) green appears, or, peck left unless the key is red, etc. It was (and is) assumed that the establishment of such competing responses would be less effective in obtaining response reduction when only S$^-$ was available than would the generation of inhibition in the course of reversal and successive acquisition. It is implicit in the argument that this latter process is in some sense more directly opposed to approach responding. Is it possible that there may be alternative inhibitory processes, each of which is equally directly opposed to approach? Terrace's contribution to this conference argues that this is indeed the case; there appears to be a real difference between active and passive inhibition, each of which successfully obtains an absence of responding to S$^-$ alone. Successive acquisition with errors involves active inhibition; as brain lesion studies imply that reversal and conventional successive inhibition involve the same inhibitory mechanism, it is reasonable to assume that reversal too must involve active inhibition. The question is, therefore, could simultaneous acquisition involve passive inhibition, as is the case in errorless successive discriminations? Comparison of the situations reveals a good measure of agreement between them: for example, Terrace (1964, 1966a) has shown that pigeons, after acquisition of an errorless discrimination, show neither peak shift nor U-shaped inhibitory gradients; in the experiments described in the Introduction, Honig (1962) and Beale and Winton (1970) failed to obtain, respectively, peak shift and U-shaped inhibitory gradients following acquisition of discriminations, in the concurrent situation. Similarly, just as certain brain lesions may disrupt successive discriminations and reversals of simultaneous discriminations, without affecting the acquisition of simultaneous discriminations, so certain drugs have been shown to disrupt errorful, but not errorless, discriminations (Terrace, 1963).

A further feature of errorless discrimination learning is the absence of behavioural contrast in S$^+$ components; that this may be the case in simultaneous acquisition also is suggested by both Honig's (1962) and Beale and Winton's (1970) data. Honig noted that the rate of response to S$^+$ in the simultaneous situation was much lower than in his successive discrimination (although it did seem to be rather higher, to judge from rates shown in generalization testing, than in single-stimulus traning); Beale and Winton found a slight increase in absolute response rate to S^+ in only two of their six subjects during discrimination training.

Catania (1966) has, on the other hand, made out a strong case for the occurrence of behavioural contrast during discrimination performance in concurrent schedules. In the first place, he has shown that the overall rate of response in the VI component of a *conc* VI EXT schedule is higher than during the corresponding component of a *conc* VI VI schedule. Now, provided there is, as in Catania's experiments, a change over delay (COD), subjects respond very rarely to S^- during *conc* VI EXT schedules, so that, of course, more time is available for responding to S^+. Catania argues, however, that although this is the case, time spent responding is not the critical variable. In support of this view, he reports an experiment in which birds were run on a concurrent schedule in which one key was on a conventional VI schedule of reinforcement, and the other key was illuminated only when reinforcement was programmed (a stimulus-correlated VI schedule). The effect of this procedure was to reduce the response rate on the stimulus-correlated VI key to a low level, and so to increase the time available on the VI key. The overall rate of response to the VI key nevertheless remained essentially identical to that seen in the conventional *conc* VI VI procedure, and considerably lower than that seen in the *conc* VI EXT situation. In other words, it appears that, provided the rate of reinforcement in the alternative key remains constant, subjects "spread out" the number of responses appropriate to the reinforcement schedule in operation over the time available; where more time is available, but relative reinforcement frequency is unchanged, absolute rates of response (per unit time spent responding on the key) fall, so that the overall rate over the session remains constant.

The force of Catania's argument is weakened, however, by a recent study of Silberberg and Fantino (1970). These authors made a detailed analysis of the fine grain of responding in concurrent schedules, and showed that, where VI schedules are in force on both keys, the overall rate on each key is a composite of two distinct rates, one, a rapid bursting during the COD, and the other, a slower, steady rate during the post-COD interval. This analysis has considerable relevance to Catania's data; for example, it can be seen that, where one key is pecked on fewer occasions (as in the stimulus-correlated VI case), relatively few rapid COD bursts should occur on the other key, so that the overall rate on that key would fall, even if no change had occurred in either of the two types of responding (i.e. during or after CODs). The same argument, of course applies to the *conc* VI EXT case; but in fact there are virtually no responses to S^- in *conc* VI EXT schedules (one effect of the COD being, in fact, to punish such responses), so that essentially no COD bursts will occur. The possible effects of the absence of bursts are problematical; clearly, the steady rate of response maintained on the VI key in a *conc* VI EXT schedule is higher than that maintained in the *conc* VI Stimulus-Correlated VI situation, but whether this is due to the removal of reinforcement in one component of the former situation (in which case it might be regarded as a contrast-like phenomenon), or to an inhibitory effect of bursts on the steady rate in the latter situation cannot be satisfactorily determined. As eliminating the COD in a *conc* VI EXT schedule frequently results in persistent "superstitious" responding to S⁻, it would clearly be difficult, in the normal concurrent situation, to obtain estimates of behavioural contrast that are not contaminated in some way by the problems associated with changeovers.

III. Behavioural Contrast in Acquisition and Reversal of a Discrete Trial Simultaneous Discrimination

The final experiment to be reported here investigates the occurrence of behavioural contrast during discrimination in a situation which is close to a conventional discrete trial choice procedure and does not permit switches to S⁺ following selection of S⁻, but does allow measurements of rate to S⁺. Animals were given both acquisition and reversal training to enable comparisons to be made between changes in rate that might occur in each—for example, a small increase in rate to S⁺ during acquisition would not rule out the notion that passive inhibition was primarily involved in simultaneous acquisition, if a much larger increase in rate was seen in reversal.

A. EXPERIMENT IV

The basic design of this experiment was as follows: birds were pretrained to respond on an FI 5 sec schedule to the side keys of a 3-key discrimination apparatus, each side key being individually illuminated at irregular intervals to show either a red light or a grid. A discrimination was then introduced, in which responses to S⁺ obtained reinforcements on an FI 5 sec schedule, while responses to S⁻ terminated the trial immediately. Increases in rate to S⁺, relative to that established in baseline training, would, if they occurred, be regarded as being analogous to the occurrence of behavioural contrast in successive discrimination training. A pilot experiment showed that subjects undergoing successive discriminations using a discrete trial procedure with an FI 5 sec schedule on a single key did indeed show marked increases in rate to S⁺ on the introduction of a discrimination.

The subjects in this experiment were barbary doves; these were used as it was thought that reducing the genetic variability between subjects might significantly reduce their behavioural variability (which, as regards behavioural contrast, can be embarrassingly large—see Macphail, 1971).

1. *Method*

a. Subjects. Five barbary doves (*streptopelia risoria*) served as subjects. They were maintained at 80% of their *ad lib*. feeding weights throughout the experiment.

b. Apparatus. The apparatus differed from that used in the first three experiments in only one important respect: behind each side key was an in-line projector which could project either red light or a grid of black lines, oriented at 40°, on a white background.

c. Pretraining. Subjects were initially trained, by the use of an autoshaping procedure, to peck the centre key. When pecking reliably, a programme that combined autoshaping with fixed interval training was introduced. Each trial commenced with the illumination of the centre key; a peck on this key extinguished it, and illuminated one of the side keys with either the grid or red light. The first response to the illuminated side key that occurred after 5 sec of its onset extinguished it and gave access to grain in the hopper for 4 sec. Where a bird failed to peck between the end of the 5th and 10th sec since side key illumination, the side key was extinguished and food delivered automatically. All pecks to an illuminated side key resulted in a clearly audible feedback click. The side key stimulus was alternately red light or the grid, and the order of sides was determined by the use of a Gellermann sequence, so that no more than three trials in succession were on the same side (except that, when a free reinforcement had been delivered, the same key was illuminated on the next trial). The inter-trial interval ranged from 8 to 37 sec, and was varied irregularly, with an average interval of 20 sec. There were 60 trials a day, and pretraining continued until the subject was responding reliably on all trials, so that no free reinforcements were being delivered, and rates of response were relatively steady over a ten-day period.

d. Acquisition and reversal training. Each trial commenced with the illumination of the centre key; a peck to this key extinguished it and illuminated both side keys, one, with red light, the other, with the grid. Responses to S^+ (which was, in acquisition, the grid for three subjects, and red for the other two) were reinforced on an FI 5 sec schedule, and responses to S^- terminated the trial immediately, each side key being extinguished. Both side keys were illuminated until either reinforcement was delivered, or S^- was pecked; it was therefore possible for a subject to peck S^+ several times (within 5 sec of illumination onset) and then to peck S^-, and terminate the trial without reinforcement. The inter-trial interval, as in pretraining, averaged 20 sec, and the side on which S^+ appeared was varied according to a Gellermann sequence. Responses to S^+ only resulted in feedback clicks. There were 60 trials per day, and acquisition and reversal continued until 50 or more reinforcements had been obtained for four consecutive days (there were no free reinforcements during training). Where a bird failed to peck the centre key within 15 min of its illumination at the start of a trial, training ended for the day, and 60 trials were given the following day, in the usual way.

2. *Results*

Throughout pretraining, acquisition, and reversal, the latency from side key illumination to the first response to a side key was recorded on each trial. In pretraining and positive training trials (i.e. trials that terminated in reinforcement), the number of responses emitted in the first 5 sec of side key illumination was recorded, again for each trial. In calculating rates of response on positive trials, the latency to the first response was excluded from the time available for responding, so that a running rate measure was obtained.

Fig. 1 summarizes the data of principal importance, showing the mean rates of response to each stimulus during the last five days of pretraining, and to S^+ during acquisition and reversal; the S^+ points were plotted for all days on which at least five correct choices were made.* It is clear that response rate does increase on the introduction of the discrimination; in all five cases, the rate on S^+ is higher than on any of the last five days' pre-training on the corresponding stimulus on at least one of the first two days of discrimination training. It can also be seen that this rate tends to drop as training proceeds: for four of the five subjects, the mean S^+ rate on either Day 1 or Day 2 of acquisition was higher than the corresponding rate on either of the last two days of acquisition training.

Precisely the same pattern of rate changes is seen during reversal: in four of the five cases, there is no overlap between the higher of the S^+ rates on the first two days of reversal and any of the rates recorded on that

---

*On two occasions, birds stopped responding before completing 60 trials, having obtained more than 50 reinforcements on the previous day. One bird (S18) stopped after 31 consecutive correct trials, and the other (S95), after 51 trials, of which 45 were correct. No reason for their stopping was apparent, and those days were counted as satisfying the 50 out of 60 correct criterion. As is shown on the figure, birds also failed, on a number of occasions, to complete 60 trials at the presolution stage. During acquisition, however, all birds obtained at least five reinforcements on each day's training, so that all acquisition days are represented on Fig. 1. Four of the five birds (excepting only S94) failed to obtain five reinforcements on the first day of reversal training, completing from 15 to 45 trials, with 0 to 3 reinforcements; as averaging rates obtained from less than five trials is not likely to produce reliable data, their performance on those days has been omitted from Fig. 1.

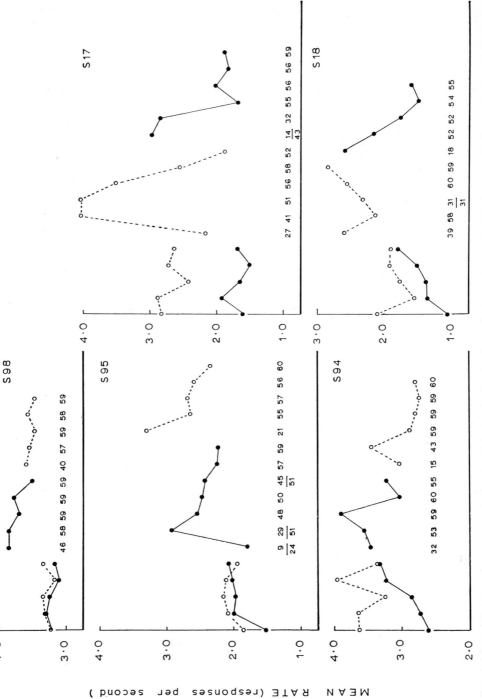

Fig. 1. Mean daily rates of response to both stimuli during the last five days of pre-training, and to S⁺ during acquisition and reversal. Also shown are the number of S⁺ trials during acquisition and reversal, along with the number of trials completed, where this was less than 60. ●——● Grid S⁺;

stimulus in pretraining, and in all five cases, that rate is higher than either of the S^+ rates recorded on the last two days of reversal training.

Mean latencies, which ranged from 0·8 to 2·3 sec during pretraining, were inversely related to the rate changes in acquisition and reversal training, but were somewhat less orderly, and showed more overlap with pretraining latencies. The mean latency on whichever of the first two days of acquisition training had the higher rate was lower, in all five cases, than the median mean latency for response to the corresponding stimulus over the last five days of pretraining; for four of the five birds, that same latency was lower than either of those recorded over the last two days of acquisition training. During reversal, the same trends were found: the mean latency on whichever of the first two days of reversal yielded the higher rate was lower, in four of the five cases, than the median mean latency over the last five days pretraining, and in three cases, that latency was lower than either of those recorded during the last two days of reversal training.

The rates reported were of course averaged irrespective of the side on which the stimulus was displayed; it is possible that the rise in rate may have been an artifact brought about by subjects that, throughout pretraining, pecked faster whenever the stimulus was on, say, the left, and pecked at the same rate during discrimination training, but chose S^+ more often when it appeared on the left than when displayed on the right. This possibility was tested by a further analysis of pretraining performance which obtained, for each stimulus, mean rates for the left-and right-hand keys. Owing to a programming error, this analysis was only possible for three of the birds. This analysis gave ten mean rates for each stimulus over the last five days pretraining, five for left-hand trials, and five for right-hand trials. For all three subjects, the mean rate (averaged over sides) on one of the first two days of both acquisition and reversal was higher than any of the ten mean rates recorded for the corresponding stimulus in pretraining. It is clear, therefore, that these are genuine increases in response rate, irrespective of the side of presentation of S^+.

Finally, it can be seen from Fig. 1 that the amount of contrast seen (relative to baseline rates) does not differ significantly between acquisition and reversal; the contrast magnitude in reversal tends, if anything, to be somewhat less than in acquisition.

In summary, the results are as follows: in the early stages of the acquisition or reversal of a simultaneous discrimination, birds tend to choose more rapidly than in pretraining (despite the fact that effectively no choice is required in pretraining), and to respond at a higher rate on the key. Once the discrimination is mastered, S^+ rates tend to fall to approximately their baseline values.

3. *Discussion*

As the behavioural situation used in this experiment is novel, attention will be drawn to some of its essential features. First, it is clearly very close to the conventional discrete trial simultaneous situation, using a non-correction procedure; incorrect choices immediately terminate a trial, and correct responses preceding the response that obtains food reward result in feedback clicks that are in themselves sufficient to indicate that a correct choice has been made. As might be expected, trials on which subjects switched from S^+ to S^- were extremely rare; four of the five birds never switched keys during a trial, and the fifth bird did so on only three occasions.

The rates of response are relatively high, rising as they do to mean rates of over four responses a second; similar rates were obtained from pigeons in a pilot experiment using a successive discrete trials situation with an FI 5 sec schedule. It must be emphasized that these rates are averaged over the duration of a burst only—and should not therefore be compared to rates obtained in, for example, free operant situations, where periods of non-responding occur intermittently.

An immediate question is whether these rate changes are in fact instances of behavioural contrast; in a strict sense, they are not, in that the rate increases to S^+ are not contrasted to opposite changes in rate to S^-. However, in the absence of any alternative account of the changes seen, it is most parsimonious at this stage to assume that the increases do have a similar causation to conventional behavioural contrast. Changes in rate to S^- could, of course, have been assessed had the negative key also been on an FI 5 sec schedule (where the final peck would merely have terminated the trial without reinforcement). The reason for not using such a situation in this experiment was that feedback as to the correctness or otherwise of a choice would be delayed by 5 sec, so distinguishing it in an important respect from conventional discrete trial choice situations. Whether rate decreases to S^- should be regarded as necessary for the demonstration of contrast in this case is dubious; with a decreasing probability of choice of S^-, the overall rate of response to S^- over the session would clearly decrease, and it can be argued that this is precisely what happens in successive operant discriminations—that, as discrimination proceeds, the animal chooses to respond less and less often to S^-, while responding at the same rate in individual bursts (e.g. Blough 1963). As a parallel argument can be applied to rate increases in S^+ in conventional successive discriminations, an interesting outcome of the present experiment (and of the pilot experiment) is that, if the S^+ rate changes are instances of contrast, then contrast can occur in terms of changes in the absolute rates of response within bursts (whether this is in fact the case in conventional operant successive discriminations is, of course, an open question).

The occurrence of contrast during acquisition, and the fact that the amount of contrast seen is comparable to that found in reversal, indicates (in so far as contrast is a reliable index), that simultaneous discrimination acquisition involves "active inhibition", and so cannot be distinguished on that score from successive discrimination or simultaneous reversals. The fact that the contrast effects diminish rapidly on solution of the discrimination suggests a possible account of the Beale and Winton (1970) and Honig (1962) results; Terrace (1966b) has shown that contrast and peak shift tend to go together, and that, for example, following the disappearance of contrast after prolonged successive discrimination training, the peak shift is also found to be absent. There may therefore have been transient contrast effects at an early stage in both Honig's and Beale and Winton's experiments, and had generalization tests been instituted at that stage, the peak shift (in Honig's experiment) and U-shaped inhibitory gradients (Beale and Winton) might have been obtained. The rapid decline in rates also indicates that further investigations of contrast in the conventional concurrent situation should examine acquisition as well as asymptotic response rates.

At this stage it is appropriate to recapitulate the results of the series of experiments described in this paper, and to consider their further implications. The first three experiments clearly indicated that pigeons do learn to withhold responses to S⁻ in the course of acquiring a simultaneous discrimination; the fourth experiment showed that behavioural contrast, which is widely believed to be a by-product of the generation of active inhibition, does occur during simultaneous discrimination acquisition. The general conclusion that may be drawn, therefore, is that simultaneous and successive acquisition do employ the same inhibitory mechanism; it was argued above that data obtained from earlier experiments using concurrent schedules could be reconciled with this finding, but difficulties remain concerning two other phenomena whose earlier interpretation supposed that inhibition was not involved in simultaneous acquisition.

Lesion-induced dissociations between simultaneous and successive acquisition, and between simultaneous acquisition and reversal, present a serious problem now that there is no good reason to believe that any major difference exists, in terms of the mechanisms involved, between these situations. It seems likely that future analyses of the deficits induced by brain damage should rely on more detailed accounts of the growth and decline of excitation and inhibition in the behavioural situations employed. These experiments suggest that the deficits may not be explained by appealing to the notion that some gross behavioural process, such as inhibition, has

L

been disrupted; it becomes necessary to look for some more subtle aspect of the presumably large number of separable effects of reinforcement or nonreinforcement that may critically distinguish the situations in which dissociations have been obtained. The implication is clear: to understand the effects of brain lesions, psychologists must first better understand the behaviour of intact animals.

The proposed explanation of the performance of pigeons undergoing three reversals each day could be modified in a number of ways: one alternative is that the basic tenet of the account, namely, that subjects performing R1s do not learn to inhibit responses to S⁻, is valid, but that precisely this fact distinguishes R1s from conventional acquisition. This suggestion becomes plausible on the assumption that birds with experience of serial reversals come to expect nonreward as much as reward at the outset of R1s, and so experience less frustration on nonreinforced trials in R1s than do subjects whose initial expectation of reward is relatively high, as in conventional acquisition (and in R2s and R3s). Such an account, combined with the notion that frustration is critically involved in the generation of inhibition, enables the results of the Macphail (1970) experiment to be reconciled with those presented here.

4. *Alternative Interpretations of Behavioural Contrast in a Simultaneous Discrimination*

The pattern of results obtained in Expt IV would seem to militate against two possible accounts of behavioural contrast. The first is a modification of Jenkins' (1961) explanation of decreased latencies to S⁺ found in a discrete trial successive discrimination; Jenkins' proposal was that, as discrimination developed, latencies to S⁻ increased, so that latencies to S⁺ were now shorter than S⁻ latencies. In this way, short latencies were differentially reinforced, so that subjects formed a spurious discrimination between short and long latencies, and consequently decreased S⁺ latencies. The same argument can, of course, be applied to rate changes in the conventional operant successive discrimination. In this experiment, however, there were no rate changes to S⁻, as only one response to S⁻ was possible. There does not seem any sense in which a discrimination could be formed between a single response and a burst of responses so that an increase of response rate within the burst would occur.

A second account of the genesis of behavioural contrast is that it is the result of response suppression in the presence of S⁻. Applied to this situation, the proposal might be that, on approximately 50% of trials, subjects look first at S⁻, suppress responding to it, and look for S⁺, which is then pecked. This account is clearly unsatisfactory, as latencies decrease when discrimination is introduced, and tend to rise as contrast falls. On positive trials, that is, it seems that response suppression (if it occurs) is correlated with a drop in contrast. An alternative proposal might be that, on trials where S$^-$ is chosen, subjects withhold, or attempt to withhold, responses to that stimulus. Surprisingly, there was little evidence for increased latencies to S$^-$ during acquisition or reversal of the discrimination; most latency changes were very small (one or two tenths of a second), and not systematic in any obvious way. In place of any attempt to summarize the negative trial latency data, a detailed account of the performance of one bird (S17), that showed a large contrast effect in both acquisition and reversal, will be presented. This bird showed (as did three of the other birds) a marked position tendency at the outset of both acquisition and reversal. On Day 1 of acquisition, this subject chose the right-hand key on 51 out of 60 trials (24 S$^+$, and 27; S$^-$): S$^+$ was red, and the median of the mean latencies to red on the right-hand key during the last five days' pretraining was 1·7 sec, the corresponding latency for the grid stimulus being 2·2 sec. On Day 1, considering right-hand choices only, the mean latency for S$^+$ (red) trials was 2·1 sec, and, for S$^-$, 3·4 sec. There was, in other words, evidence that latencies to both stimuli had risen. It will be noted that, for this bird, response rate fell on Day 1. On Day 2, mean S$^+$ latency fell to 1·5 sec (that is, below the pretraining median), and S$^-$ fell to 3·1 sec (still above the pretraining median of 2·2 sec). In other words, S$^+$ latencies over these two days did vary inversely with rate of response, and the long S$^-$ latencies of Day 1 indicate that increased S$^-$ latencies are not in themselves sufficient to cause contrast. Data from Day 1 of reversal of this subject indicate that increased S$^-$ latencies are not necessary prerequisites of contrast. On this occasion, all 14 choices of S$^+$ (the grid) were to the right-hand key, as were 22 of the 29 S$^-$ trials. The mean S$^+$ latency was 1·8 sec (the corresponding pretraining median being 2·2 sec), and the mean S$^-$ latency was 1·6 sec (corresponding pretraining latency, 1·7 sec). That is, both latencies fell as compared to pretraining latencies, and the S$^-$ latency was in fact shorter than the S$^+$ latency, although this is probably not a consequence of the discrimination, as the pretraining latencies to that stimulus were also shorter. It can be seen from Fig. 1 that on Day 1 of reversal, S$^+$ rate was well above the corresponding pretraining rate, as well as the terminal S$^+$ rate of acquisition training. It is also interesting to note that on Day 1 of reversal, there was no indication of a solution in terms of choices (all S$^+$ choices being to the right-hand key).

The discussion so far has indicated that contrast may occur without any distinction being made between S$^+$ and S$^-$ in terms of latencies or choices, and without a separation of S$^+$ and S$^-$ rates. It also appears, from the eventual decline of S$^+$ rates, that the mere presentation of S$^-$ is not sufficient to sustain contrast; what is necessary is that S$^-$ should be selected on a sizeable proportion of trials. One possibility is that an effect of the nonreward following an S^- choice is the generation of frustration, which, in turn, energizes responding on the succeeding trial. To assess the validity of this account, a sequential analysis was carried out in the following way: for each day's training, mean rates to S^+ on a given side on trials immediately following trials on which S^- had been selected were compared to mean S^+ rates on the other trials where S^+ had been on that side (giving a maximum of two comparisons each day for each bird). Of the 39 available comparisons for acquisition, 24 showed a faster rate to S^+ on trials immediately following errors; 19 of the 37 comparisons obtained in reversal similarly showed a faster rate on trials following errors. Neither of these comparisons approaches statistical significance ($p > 0.1$, one-tailed binomial test, for the acquisition data). Many of these comparisons were obtained on days on which only one or two S^+ trials immediately following errors occurred; in case using such small samples may have obscured a real trend, the analysis was carried out again, considering only data from days that met the following requirements: first, that at least five S^+ trials immediately following errors occurred on one side, and second, that at least five other S^+ trials occurred on that side. This analysis also failed to find any significant differences between rates on trials immediately following errors and rates on other trials. The sequential data do not, therefore, support the view that the rate increases seen in this experiment were, in any simple sense, the immediate consequence of the frustration occasioned by nonreward. It may be added that, in any case, the differences seen between mean rates immediately following errors, and rates on the other trials, were generally very small compared to the large increases seen relative to prediscrimination baseline rates.

There remain two further possible accounts of the results which will be discussed here. The first proposes that nonreward induced frustration is conditioned to the situation, and that the drive-like properties of conditioned frustration galvanize ongoing activity; the second proposes that S^+ rates increase as a result of what might be called "elation" at achieving a solution of the discrimination—that, in other words, S^+ trials become more attractive in contrast to S^-. The first proposal encounters a difficulty with the fact that the occurrence of errors, although, perhaps, a necessary condition of contrast, is not a sufficient condition. For example, although S17 made 33 errors on Day 1 of acquisition, S^+ rates on that day fell, in comparison to pretraining rates. The second proposal faces the objection that contrast can occur prior to any indication, in latency or choice data, that the discrimination has been solved. In each case, somewhat unsatisfactory *ad hoc* assumptions, which preserve the proposed account, may be made. The conditioned frustration hypothesis can explain the failure of S^+ rate to increase in every case at the outset of a discrimination as due to the fact that, at this early stage, there may be a tendency to extinguish altogether, and that this tendency, with its accompanying decreased latencies and rates, is not always counteracted by the additional drive attending responding. The elation hypothesis may assume that attempted solutions (e.g. the adoption of a position habit) are as effective as the correct solution; this proposal also has difficulty with S17's Day 1 data; where, despite the adoption of a position habit, rates fell. In this case, it could be argued that the position habit did not represent a confident solution attempt as much as a systematic mode of response in a stressful situation.

It can now be seen that the main stumbling block for each of these accounts is the occasional nonappearance of contrast at an early stage of discrimination training. In each case, it seems necessary to appeal to some notion such as the animals' assumption that the situation is indeed a discrimination, and not an extinction situation, or one in which the rate of reinforcement has been arbitrarily reduced. In other words, contrast may be said to occur only where an animal responds to a situation as though it is a discrimination capable of solution. In the absence of any rules for determining whether or not an animal is so responding, such an account is, regrettably, circular; but it can be seen that one implication is that, where an animal's previous experience is such as to make it more likely that it should attempt to discriminate, it should be more likely that contrast will occur. Some evidence to support this view was obtained in subsequent work with four of the birds used in Expt IV. These birds were each given six further reversals, using the same criterion, with identical stimuli and training procedures. It is a reasonable assumption that serial reversal training should indeed increase the likelihood of subjects' attempting to discriminate following the occurrence of errors at the start of a reversal. An interesting finding was that, in all 24 reversals, the S^+ rate on Day 1 was higher than both the S^+ rate on the final day's training of the previous discrimination having the same S^+, and the S^+ rate on the final day's training of the immediately preceding discrimination (having the other stimulus as S^+). Contrast, that is, invariably appears early in training in subjects with previous experience of discrimination acquisition and reversal.

The gradual disappearance of contrast can, similarly, be accommodated by each hypothesis; in the absence of trials on which nonreward occurs, conditioned frustration should extinguish, and S^+ trials will no longer be contrasted to S^- trials. There now seems little real difference between these accounts: each supposes that some consequence of the aversive nature of nonrewarded trials carries over to succeeding trials, and increases the vigour of responding in those trials, through increasing either the total drive present, or the attractiveness of S^+ trials. None of the data of the present experiment is relevant to a decision between the two alternatives which will, therefore, not be discussed further.

IV. Concluding Comments

The experiments reported in this paper, although using intact subjects, were carried out primarily as a consequence of previous work with brain-lesioned subjects. Their aim was to confirm a widely-held hypothesis concerning the nature of the deficit brought about by certain types of brain lesion, namely, that the lesioned animals were impaired in their ability to generate inhibition. All of the experimental results were in total disagreement with the predictions that had been derived from this hypothesis, and it was argued that a satisfactory analysis of such deficits must wait upon a deeper understanding of the behaviour of intact subjects. The rationale underlying this work is, then, that there is a reciprocal interaction between physiological psychology and, for want of a better term, purely behavioural psychology, and that this interaction should be of benefit to both disciplines. Results obtained by physiological psychologists will frequently pose important questions for behavioural theorists; similarly, certain proposals of such theorists should be amenable to tests using physiological techniques. The immediate conclusion of the work reported here is that inhibition is generated during acquisition of simultaneous discriminations; it is a measure of the comparative neglect of the area by purely behavioural psychologists that such a demonstration was not available before now.

Acknowledgements

This work was supported by a grant from the U.K. Medical Research Council. I am grateful to Mr Brian Humphreys for his assistance in the conduct of these experiments.

Computing facilities at the University of Sussex were made available by a grant from the U.K. Science Research Council.

References

Beale, I. L. and Winton, A. S. W. (1970). Inhibitory stimulus control in concurrent schedules. *Journal of the Experimental Analysis of Behavior*, **14,** 133–137.
Bloomfield, T. M. (1969). Behavioural contrast and the peak shift. In: R. M. Gilbert and N. S. Sutherland (Eds.), *Animal Discrimination Learning*. London: Academic Press, pp. 215–241.
Blough, D. S. (1963). Interresponse time as a function of continuous variables: a new method and some data. *Journal of the Experimental Analysis of Behavior*, **6,** 237–246.
Catania, A. C. (1966). Concurrent operants. In: W. K. Honig (Ed.), *Operant Behavior: Areas of Research and Application*. New York: Appleton–Century- pp. 213–270.

Clayton, K. N. (1966). T-maze acquisition and reversal as a function of inter-trial interval. *Journal of Comparative and Physiological Psychology*, **62**, 409–414.

Findley, J. D. (1958). Preference and switching under concurrent scheduling. *Journal of the Experimental Analysis of Behavior*, **5**, 123–144.

Francis, J. G. F. and Sutherland, N. S. (1969). A system for controlling animal experiments on-line. In N. Moray (Ed.), *On-Line Computing for Psychology*. Sheffield: University of Sheffield, pp. 43–56.

Hearst, E. (1969). Excitation, inhibition, and discrimination learning. In: N. J. Mackintosh and W. K. Honig (Eds.), *Fundamental Issues in Associative Learning*. Halifax: Dalhousie University Press, pp. 1–41.

Honig, W. K. (1962). Prediction of preference, transposition, and transposition-reversal from the generalization gradient. *Journal of Experimental Psychology*, **64**, 239–248.

Jenkins, H. M. (1961). The effect of discrimination training on extinction. *Journal of Experimental Psychology*, **61**, 111–121.

Kimble, D. P. (1963). The effects of bilateral hippocampal lesions in rats. *Journal of Comparative and Physiological Psychology*, **56**, 273–283.

Kimble, D. P. (1968). Hippocampus and internal inhibition. *Psychological Bulletin*, **70**, 285–295.

Mackintosh, N. J., McGonigle, B., Holgate, V. and Vanderver, V. (1968). Factors underlying improvement in serial reversal learning. *Canadian Journal of Psychology*, **22**, 85–95.

Macphail, E. M. (1970). Serial reversal performance in pigeons: role of inhibition. *Learning and Motivation*, **1**, 401–410.

Macphail, E. M. (1971). Hyperstriatial lesions in pigeons: effects on response inhibition, behavioral contrast, and reversal learning. *Journal of Comparative and Physiological Psychology*, **75**, 500–507.

Siegel, S. (1969). Discrimination overtraining and shift behavior. In: R. M. Gilbert and N. S. Sutherland (Eds.), *Animal Discrimination Learning*. New York: Academic Press, pp. 187–213.

Silberberg, A. and Fantino, E. (1970). Choice, rate of reinforcement, and the changeover delay. *Journal of the Experimental Analysis of Behavior*, **13**, 187–197.

Spence, K. W. (1937). The differential response in animals to stimuli varying within a single dimension. *Psychological Review*, **44**, 430–444.

Swanson, A. M. and Isaacson, R. L. (1967). Hippocampal ablation and performance during withdrawal of reinforcement. *Journal of Comparative and Physiological Psychology*, **64**, 30–35.

Terrace, H. S. (1963). Errorless discrimination learning in the pigeon: effects of chlorpromazine and imipramine. *Science*, **140**, 318–319.

Terrace, H. S. (1964). Wavelength generalization after discrimination training with and without error. *Science*, **144**, 78–80.

Terrace, H. S. (1966a). Discrimination learning and inhibition. *Science*, **154**, 1677–1680.

Terrace, H. S. (1966b). Behavioral contrast and the peak shift: effects of extended discrimination training. *Journal of the Experimental Analysis of Behavior*, 613–617.

6 | Comparative Studies of the Role of Inhibition in Reversal Learning

M. E. BITTERMAN

University of South Florida, Tampa, Florida, U.S.A.

I. Introduction	. . . .	153
II. Experiment I: Reversal Learning in Pigeons Under Unitary Conditions	. . . .	157
III. Experiment II: Reversal Learning in Pigeons Under Unitary Conditions (further data)	. . . .	161
IV. Experiment III: Reversal Learning in Goldfish Under Unitary Conditions	. . . .	163
V. Experiment IV: Reversal Learning in Goldfish Under Choice Conditions	. . . .	167
VI. Summary and Conclusions .	. . . .	172
Acknowledgements .	. . . .	174
References	. . . .	174

I. Introduction

Progressive improvement in the reversal performance of mammals, birds and reptiles has been demonstrated repeatedly in choice situations. The procedure in those experiments is to present two stimuli, A and B, on each trial, and first to reward the animal for choosing A but not B (Reversal 0). After a preference for A has been developed, B rather than A is rewarded until the preference has been reversed (Reversal 1), whereupon A is rewarded once more (Reversal 2), and so forth. The animal is trained in each problem either for a fixed number of trials or until it has achieved some specified criterion of performance, but in both cases the results are the same: the difficulty of reversal (measured either in terms of errors made in a fixed number of trials, or in terms of trials or errors to the criterion) declines progressively as training continues. Several different although not necessarily incompatible explanations of this phenomenon have been proposed.

How may training in A + B — be expected to influence performance in B + A —? Clearly, the reversal of sign should produce some negative

153

transfer—to the extent that the animal comes to B + A — with a pre-ference for A, the task should be a difficult one—and poor performance in Reversal 1 as compared with Reversal 0 confirms that expectation. There may, however, be sources of positive transfer as well. It is conceivable, certainly, that training in A + B — should contribute positively to per-formance in B + A — for the same reason that it contributes positively to performance in problems involving different stimuli (C + D —)—that is, because the performance of the animal in part reflects its adjust-ment to certain important features of the training situation that remain the same from problem to problem. Poor performance in Reversal 1 as com-pared with Reversal 0 does not rule out the possibility of positive transfer, but may mean only that the negative transfer exceeds the positive. It follows from this analysis that progressive improvement in habit reversal may be due either to decreasing negative transfer, or to positive transfer, or to both.

Evidence of decreasing negative transfer is provided by the fact that the number of errors made at the very outset of each reversal often declines from reversal to reversal. For example, in an experiment with rats trained in a series of daily position reversals, the probability of error on Trial 1 was 0·78 for Reversals 1–10, but only 0·57 for Reversals 31–40 (Bitterman et al., 1958). In an experiment with pigeons trained in a series of two-day colour reversals, the probability of error on Trial 1 fell progressively from 1·0 to 0·5 (Gonzalez et al., 1967). These results, which suggest that the preferences established in successive reversals tend increasingly to be lost in the intervals between reversals, may be explained in terms of inter-ference-produced forgetting (Behrend et al., 1970).

Evidence that improvement in reversal may be due in part to positive transfer comes from an experiment with chimpanzees by Schusterman (1964), who found that training in a series of criterion reversals with a single pair of stimulus-objects would improve performance in a sub-sequent series of discriminative problems with new objects selected for each problem. Positive transfer is indicated also by the finding that the learning curves for consecutive reversals sometimes improve in slope as well as in point of origin (Mackintosh et al., 1968), and by the finding in a variety of experiments that reversal performance may become even better with continued training than performance in the original problem (Bullock and Bitterman, 1962; Schusterman, 1964; Holmes and Bitterman, 1966).

One source of positive transfer was suggested early by Krechevsky (1932), who thought that his rats might have learned in the course of reversal training to base their choices on the consequences of immediately preceding choices. Much the same idea was expressed more concretely by

Hull (1952) in terms of the discrimination of stimulus-trace compounds. Since the animal is rewarded for choosing A in the presence of the traces either of A and reinforcement (when it has chosen A on the preceding trial) or of B and frustration (when it has chosen B on the preceding trial), choice of A becomes connected to each of those trace-compounds, while choice of B becomes connected in the same way to traces of B and reinforcement, and of A and frustration. Although visual traces are notoriously short-lived, it seems reasonable to suppose that some such mechanism may operate, at least in spatial problems, when practice is massed. Experiments on probability learning have, in fact, shown a spontaneous tendency in a variety of animals to respond in terms of the position of the rewarded alternative on the immediately preceding trial—either reward-following or its opposite, negative recency (Overall and Brown, 1959; Wilson et al., 1964; Kirk and Bitterman, 1965). In a spatial reversal experiment with rats, Stretch et al., (1964) found better performance with an inter-trial interval of 0 sec as compared with 12 min, although North (1950) earlier had found very little difference in the performance of rats trained with an inter-trial interval of 1 min as compared with 12 min. The results suggest that even 1 min may be too long for the carry-over of discriminable proprioceptive traces, and that another explanation must be sought for any positive transfer which occurs with longer inter-trial intervals. It should be noted that the trace-compounding interpretation also fails to account for Schusterman's finding of positive transfer from reversal training to discriminative training with other stimuli, which may point to the development in chimpanzees of a more generalized "win-stay, lose-shift" strategy.

Another explanation of positive transfer is that of Mackintosh (1969), who has suggested that progressive improvement in reversal may be due to progressive strengthening of attention to the relevant stimuli (which remain the same, of course, despite frequent change of sign). This attentional interpretation implies that the effects of reversal training should be specific to the stimulus-dimension employed, and some evidence of specificity is provided by the finding of Mackintosh and Little (1969) that reversal performance in pigeons, either with position or with colour as the relevant dimension, is better after 20 reversals with the same dimension relevant than after 20 reversals with both dimensions relevant by turns (one in odd- and the second in even-numbered problems). Other evidence directly contradicts Mackintosh's explanation on the conventional assumption that attention to one set of stimuli can be increased only at the expense of attention to other sets (Wyckoff, 1952; Zeaman and House, 1963; Sutherland, 1964; Lovejoy, 1966): The performance of pigeons trained in a series of reversals with position and colour relevant by turns (when one dimension is relevant the other is irrelevant) improves concurrently in both dimensions (Schade and Bitterman, 1966), and their asymptotic colour performance is no poorer than that of control animals trained only in colour reversals (Gonzalez and Bitterman, 1968).

The problem of interpretation is complicated by the fact that the results of reversal experiments are not the same for all animals. Warren (1966) found evidence in rhesus monkeys of positive transfer from reversal training to discriminative training with other stimuli, just as Schusterman (1964) had in chimpanzees, but he did not find the same effect in cats. Reversal experiments with fishes for the most part have failed entirely to show progressive improvement (Bitterman *et al.*, 1958; Warren, 1960; Behrend *et al.*, 1965), although some positive results have been reported. In an experiment with African mouthbreeders trained to discriminate between horizontal and vertical stripes, the learning curves for successive reversals were found to improve in slope but not in point of origin—that is, there was some sort of positive transfer, but no evidence of declining negative transfer (Wodinsky and Bitterman, 1957). African mouthbreeders trained in a series of daily position reversals with an inter-trial interval of 2 sec also have shown some improvement (Setterington and Bishop, 1967), which perhaps may be explained in terms of trace-discrimination, since improvement failed to appear in a subsequent experiment under like conditions with the inter-trial interval increased to 10 sec (Behrend and Bitterman, 1967). The only other evidence of improvement in fishes comes from an experiment with two Oscars and may reflect nothing more than improvement in the adjustment of the animals to the training situation, which was so poor to begin with, apparently, that they required more than 40 sessions to reach criterion in the original problem (Squier, 1969). The various explanations of improvement which have thus far been proposed are not, of course, mutually exclusive, and the results of comparative studies suggest, in fact, that improvement is produced by a variety of mechanisms, not all of which operate in all animals under all conditions.

Although progressive improvement in habit reversal has been studied widely in choice situations, little is known about the course of reversal learning in what elsewhere I have called *unitary* situations—that is, situations in which the stimuli to be discriminated are presented singly, rather than together, and the tendency of the animal to respond to each of them is measured in terms of time or rate (Bitterman, 1966). While performance in choice situations is jointly determined by the properties of the two stimuli presented on each trial, unitary situations permit separate assessments of those properties and thus promise a more detailed picture of reversal learning. The unitary experiment now to be reported does, in fact, provide some information about the mechanism of improvement in pigeons which could not have been anticipated from the results of the older choice experiments or the theoretical accounts of them: If, in accordance with a long tradition, the increasing readiness to respond to a stimulus which develops on reinforced trials is described as *excitation* and the increasing reluctance to respond which develops on nonreinforced trials is described as *inhibition*, then it may be said that the changes underlying improvement in pigeons are not excitatory but almost entirely inhibitory in character.

II. Experiment I: Reversal Learning in Pigeons Under Unitary Conditions

Pigeons were trained in a series of unitary red-green reversals (Woodard *et al.*, 1971). There was little experience at the outset of the experiment on which to base its design and some reason even to doubt that progressive improvement would appear. Reversal training of rats in a choice situation already had shown a close relationship between choices made on free trials and latency of response to the separate alternatives on forced trials (Davenport, 1959), but unitary experiments by North (1962) with rats and by Clark (1967) with pigeons had failed to yield any substantial evidence of improvement. Khavari and Heise (1967) had found some indication of improvement in rats under unitary conditions but had provided only scant information as to its course and extent. We began, therefore, with a discrete-trials procedure which had given fairly rapid unitary discrimination in previous experiments on amount and probability of reward (Graf *et al.*, 1964), and, finding good discrimination on the second day of training, went on to a two-day reversal procedure patterned after that of an earlier choice experiment with pigeons (Gonzalez *et al.*, 1967). As the results were being analysed, a paper by Beale (1970) appeared which reported some quite similar results obtained under free-operant conditions.

1. *Method*

The subjects were eight White Carneaux cocks, all experimentally naïve, which were maintained on a 24-hr feeding schedule at 80% of their *ad lib.* weights. They were trained in ventilated picnic chests. Centred on one wall of the animal's compartment in each chest was a single pigeon key, and below it was the aperture of a grain feeder. All events of the experiment were programmed automatically, and response-times were recorded on tape.

In the first stage of the experiment, the pigeons were trained in 40 discrete trials per day to peck at a white key for 3 sec of access to grain as reward. The key was dark and the aperture of the feeder illuminated with white light when the grain was presented. In the 30-sec intervals between trials, the enclosure was darkened almost completely, and each interval-response was penalized by resetting of the interval timer. At first, a single peck at the white key was sufficient to produce the reinforcements, but then the number of pecks required gradually was increased to 20. When FR-20 responding had stabilized,the colour of the key was changed to red on half the trials and green on the remaining trials of each day, in Geller-mann orders, with response to each colour reinforced as before. After 15 days of this nondifferentially reinforced pretraining with the two colours, discriminative training was begun.

In the original problem (R_0), red was positive (S^+) and green was negative (S^-). The twentieth response to S^+ (whenever it occurred—there was no time-limit on positive trials) turned off S^+ and initiated a reinforcement-cycle, which was followed by an inter-trial interval. The twentieth response to S^- (if it occurred) stopped the timing counter but had no other effect: S^- stayed on for 30 sec whether or not the animal responded, and if the ratio was not completed in that time a score of 30 sec was recorded. As in pretraining, there were 40 trials per day, 20 with each of the two colours in Gellermann orders, and the inter-trial interval was 30 sec.

The second problem, which was the first reversal (R_1), began on the third day of discriminative training—now green was positive and red was negative. The third problem, which was the second reversal (R_2), began on the fifth day of discriminative training, and so forth, through R_{18}, by which time asymptotic performance had been achieved. It should be clear, then, that the first day (Day 1) of each of these two-day problems except R_0 was a reversal day in the sense that the positive stimulus of the previous day now was negative and the negative stimulus of the previous day now was positive, while the second day (Day 2) of each problem was a nonreversal day in the sense that the positive and negative stimuli of the previous day continued to have the same values. Whether the first stimulus of each day was red or green, positive or negative, was balanced over days by the use of Gellermann orders.

2. Results

The performance of the animals in R_0, their early reversal performance (Reversals 1–2 pooled), and their asymptotic reversal performance (Reversals 11–18 pooled) are plotted in Fig. 1 in terms of the mean natural logarithm of time per trial (10 sec = 2·30; 30 sec = 3·40) for response to each stimulus in successive five-trial blocks. The asymptotic region of the data was selected by inspection of the learning curves for consecutive reversals. That the animals were indeed at asymptote in Reversals 11–18 is evidenced by the results of an analysis of variance which showed no significant effect of Reversals and no significant interaction of Reversals with any of the other main variables.

The curves for R_0 demonstrate the effectiveness of the training procedure. The animals responded differentially in the later trials of Day 1, and they made some further progress in discrimination on Day 2. Since the pre-training had established a strong tendency to respond to both stimuli, the

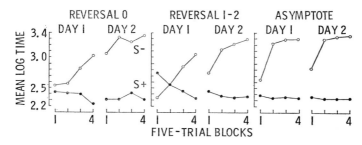

FIG. 1. The performance of the pigeons at various stages of training (R_0, R_{1-2}, and R_{11-18}) in Expt I.

only substantial change in performance produced by differential reinforcement was a decrease in readiness to respond to S^-.

The curves for Reversals 1–2, show marked negative transfer. At the outset of Day 1, the animals responded more rapidly to S^- (the positive stimulus of the preceding problem) than to S^+, but a substantial reversal of preference was accomplished at the end of Day 1. Although there was somewhat poorer retention from Day 1 to Day 2 in these early reversals than in R_0, discrimination was as good in the later trials of Day 2 as it was at the end of R_0.

Comparison of the curves for the early reversals with the asymptotic curves shows that there was substantial improvement in performance as reversal training continued, especially on Day 1. The improvement can be traced to two changes, both having to do with inhibition, if we use that term to designate a reluctance to respond produced by nonreinforcement. One of the changes is a *decline over reversals in the stability of inhibition.* Early in training, the animals came to each reversal with a considerable reluctance to respond to S^+ (the negative stimulus of the preceding problem); at asymptote, that reluctance was all but lost, and they responded much more readily to S^+ at the outset of each reversal. The second change is an *increase over reversals in the rate of inhibitory development within sessions.* No such changes were evident in excitation, a term used to designate a readiness to respond produced by reinforcement. The elevation of the asymptotic S⁻ curve on the first block of Day 1 trials might be mistaken for a decline in the stability of excitation, but it is only an artifact of the blocking of trials, because (as Fig. 2 shows) the rate of increase in time of response to S⁻ was very high at asymptote.

In comparison with performance in the original problem, the asymptotic performance was in one respect inferior and in another respect superior. Performance on the early trials of Day 2 was poorer at asymptote than in R_0 because of decreased inhibitory carryover. Day 1 performance was better at asymptote in that inhibition developed more rapidly. It seems, then, that the difference between asymptotic performance and performance in R_0 can be explained in the same terms as the difference between asymptotic performance and performance in the early reversals.

A trial-by-trial plot of the asymptotic performance is shown in Fig. 2. At the outset of each day, the animals would respond promptly to both

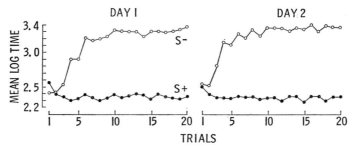

FIG. 2. The asymptotic (R_{11-18}) performance of the pigeons in Expt I.

stimuli, and then in the course of a few trials stop responding almost entirely to the negative. In the interval between sessions, the effects of the differential reinforcement tended largely to be lost, although not altogether. Statistical analysis shows that there was better discrimination on non-reversal days than on reversal days; the S⁺ curves did not differ significantly but the reluctance of the animals to respond to S⁻ was greater on Day 2 than on Day 1.

3. *Discussion*

The present results together with those of a free-operant experiment on pigeons recently reported by Beale (1970) provide clear evidence of progressive improvement in reversal under unitary conditions. Like the results obtained in choice experiments, the unitary results suggest that improvement is due in part to a decline in negative transfer and in part to positive transfer, but they go beyond the choice results in their suggestion that both components of improvement are primarily inhibitory in character. It should be noted that Beale did find some indication of a change in "the rate of acquisition of responding" to S^+, but it was small by comparison with two inhibitory changes that were observed—"an increase" between reversals "in the recovery of responding" to the S^- of the previous reversal, which I here call *decreased inhibitory carryover*, and "an increase in the rate of extinction of responding" to S^-, which I speak of here as an *increase in the rate of inhibitory development* (p. 351). The behaviour of rats in a unitary experiment by Khavari and Heise (1967) was very much like that of the pigeons, at least with respect to the relative importance of inhibition in discrimination and to its temporal instability. The "rat begins each new session with an approximately equal tendency to respond to the two stimuli", Khavari and Heise reported. "The tendency to respond to S^- then gradually weakens due to nonreinforcement, followed between sessions by a surprisingly rapid 'spontaneous recovery' of the response to the previously extinguished stimulus" (p. 272). The speed of forced runs to one or the other side of a T-maze in Davenport's (1959) study of spatial reversal learning in rats also showed decreasing inhibitory carryover and increasing rate of inhibitory development.

If the mechanisms of improvement in unitary and choice situations are indeed the same, the unitary results suggest that the decline in negative transfer which contributes to improvement in choice situations is due primarily to a decline in the stability of inhibition, an idea which seems perfectly reasonable. The phenomena of spontaneous recovery and disinhibition long ago indicated that inhibition is more susceptible to interference than is excitation. The idea that the evidence of positive transfer found in choice experiments, even with pigeons and rats alone, might be due almost entirely to increase in the rate of inhibitory development would be more likely to encounter resistance. An alternative view is that there are mechanisms of positive transfer which operate in choice but not in unitary situations, or at least in such uncomplicated ones as we have been considering here (Mackintosh and Mackintosh, 1964).

III. Experiment II: Reversal Learning in Pigeons Under Unitary Conditions (further data)

Both in Beale's experiment and in the one I have just reported, the pigeons came to Reversal 0 with very strong tendencies to respond to both stimuli which were developed in the course of extensive pretraining, and the possibility should be considered that the existence of such tendencies at the outset of discriminative training was responsible for the fact that the changes subsequently observed were primarily inhibitory. For evidence on this point, a second experiment was planned (in collaboration with W. T. Woodard and Jennifer Davis) which was to be a replica of the first with the exception that the discriminative training was to be preceded by a long period of random 50% reinforcement for response to each of the stimuli. Animals given such pretraining come to the discriminative training without reversal experience but with a cumulative frequency of reinforced and unreinforced responding to the two stimuli comparable to that afforded by reversal training. As it happened, the performance of the animals in R_0 and in the first two days of R_1 was so poor that two more days of training in R_1 were given, and there were four days of training as well in each subsequent reversal. Another departure from the original experimental plan was necessitated by the fact that White Carneaux pigeons were in short supply, and homing pigeons therefore were used, as they had been also in Beale's experiment.

1. *Method*

The subjects were nine experimentally naïve homing pigeons maintained at 80% of their *ad lib.* weights on a 24-hr feeding schedule. The apparatus was the same as that used in the first experiment, and the pretraining also was the same, with one important exception: after ratioresponding to the two colours had stabilized under conditions of consistent reinforcement, there were 20 training sessions of 40 trials, 20 with each colour, in which the probability of reinforcement for response to each colour was 0·5. The sequence of colours as well as the sequence of reinforced and nonreinforced trials with each colour followed Gellermann's rules. On nonreinforced trials, the procedure was the same as in the subsequent discriminative training; that is, the stimulus stayed on for 30 sec independently of the animal's response to it.

The discriminative training was the same as in the first experiment, except that four instead of two days of training were given in R_1 and each subsequent reversal. At this writing, the data of five reversals are available, the experiment being still in progress.

2. *Results and Discussion*

In Fig. 3, the performance of the animals on the first and second days of R_0, R_1, and R_5 is plotted in terms of mean log time of response to each stimulus on each block of five trials. By comparison with Expt I, R_0-performance was poor and R_1-performance even worse, but there was rapid improvement in the course of further training, and R_5-performance was not substantially inferior to that of the first experiment despite the fact that the effects of four rather than only two days of training now were to be overcome in each reversal. The pattern of improvement, furthermore, was exactly that of the first experiment—decline in inhibitory carryover and increase in the rate of inhibitory development. Trial-by-trial plots of response to S⁻ in R_5 have much the same character as the asymptotic curves for S⁻ shown in Fig. 2—the animals respond promptly to S⁻ at the start of each session and then soon stop responding to it—although the Day 1 plot for S⁺ still shows substantial carryover of inhibition from the preceding problem.

It is not clear whether the difference in the early performance of the animals in Expt II as compared with Expt I should be attributed to the

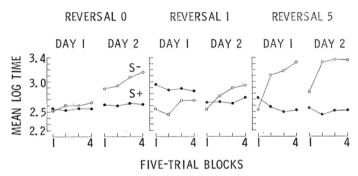

FIG. 3. The performance of the pigeons at various stages of training (R_0, R_1, and R_5) in Expt II.

difference in subjects, or to the retarding influence of prolonged partial reinforcement in the pretraining, or to both. The new results do, however, provide further indication of the generality of the earlier findings with respect to the pattern of improvement in pigeons trained under unitary conditions. Here, again, the principal changes were in the temporal stability of inhibition and in the rate of inhibitory development. The fact that both changes could be observed after prolonged nondifferential training with partial reinforcement suggests that they are produced by reversal training and are not due simply to the cumulative effects of the large number of reinforced and unreinforced trials with the two stimuli which occur in the course of reversal training.

IV. Experiment III: Reversal Learning in Goldfish Under Unitary Conditions

The results of Expt I led also to some experiments with goldfish, the first of which was of the same design (Woodward *et al.*, 1971). Our purpose was simply to extend the study of reversal learning in goldfish to unitary situations. On the assumption that the mechanisms of improvement are the same in unitary as in choice situations, there was considerable doubt as to whether improvement would be found, but we hoped nevertheless that the separate measures of responsiveness to S^+ and S^- obtainable in a unitary experiment might provide some further insight into the fish's adjustment to reversal training and perhaps put the results for pigeons in better perspective.

1. *Method*

The subjects were 13 4-in goldfish maintained under standard laboratory conditions on a 24-hr feeding schedule. They were trained in enclosures of black Plexiglas to which they were carried in their individual 2-gal living tanks. The experimental situation was different in one important respect from that used previously. Instead of striking at an illuminated target in one location and being rewarded with a worm discharged from a feeder at another location, the animals struck at an illuminated Plexiglas nipple through which liquid food (a mixture of Biorell and cornstarch cooked in water) could be delivered with a Davis pump (Holmes and Bitterman, 1969). Again, all the events of the experiment were programmed automatically, and response-times were printed on tape.

In the first stage of the experiment, the animals were trained in 40 discrete trials per day to strike at the nipple, which was illuminated with white light. The first response initiated a 10-sec reinforcement cycle, at the start of which a drop of the liquid food was delivered through the nipple, and another drop thereafter upon each contact of the animal with the nipple for the remainder of the cycle, during which the nipple continued to be illuminated. In the 30-sec inter-trial interval, the chamber was dark, and each response to the nipple was penalized by the resetting of the interval timer. The number of contacts with the nipple required to initiate a reinforcement-cycle then gradually was increased to ten—less than for the pigeons because the response seemed somewhat more difficult for goldfish than pecking for pigeons. When ratio-responding had stabilized, the colour of the nipple was changed to red on half the trials and green on the remaining trials of each day, and response to both colours was reinforced as before (the nipple being illuminated with white light during the reinforcement-cycle). Discriminative training was begun after 15–20 days of this nondifferentially reinforced pretraining with the two colours, and the procedure was exactly the same as in the first experiment with pigeons, except that each animal had 24 instead of only 18 reversals because asymptotic performance was achieved less rapidly by the goldfish.

2. *Results*

The performance of the goldfish in R_0, their early reversal performance (Reversals 1–2 pooled), and their asymptotic reversal performance (Reversals 17–24) are plotted in Fig. 4. The asymptotic region of the data was selected by inspection of the learning curves for consecutive reversals, and the judgement was confirmed by analysis of variance.

The curves for R_0 demonstrate the effectiveness of the training procedure. The goldfish began to discriminate on Day 1 and made further progress on Day 2. Again the only substantial change in performance was

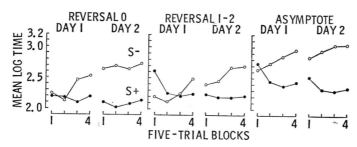

FIG. 4. The performance of the goldfish at various stages of training (R_0, R_{1-2}, and R_{17-24}) in Expt III.

an increase in reluctance to respond to S⁻, since the animals came to R_0 with a strong tendency to respond to both stimuli. The curves for the early reversals show marked negative transfer, but some reversal of preference is evident by the end of Day 1 and the reversal is completed on Day 2.

Comparison of the curves for the early reversals with the asymptotic curves suggests that there was substantial improvement in performance as reversal training continued, and the impression is confirmed by statistical analysis, but the basis of improvement seems to be different than in the pigeons. The goldfish showed moderate decrement over reversals in the temporal stability both of excitation and of inhibition, instead of inhibition alone. There is some question, however, as to whether these small changes in retention made any substantial contribution to the improvement, because the difference between reversal (Day 1) and nonreversal (Day 2) performance did not decline over reversals (the interaction of Stimuli × Days × Reversals, significant for the pigeons, was negligible for the goldfish). Furthermore, the goldfish showed no change over reversals in the rate of discrimination (the interaction of Stimuli × Trials × Reversals, significant for the pigeons, was negligible for the goldfish). Instead of the increased rate of inhibitory development evident in the performance of the pigeons, the goldfish showed what might be thought of as an accumulation of inhibition, response both to S⁺ and to S⁻ becoming progressively slower (change over reversals in time of response to both stimuli combined, negligible for the pigeons, was highly significant for the goldfish). The improvement over reversals in the performance of the goldfish was due

largely to the fact that the over-all increase in S⁻ times was much greater
than the increase in S⁺ times.

The asymptotic Day 1 performance of the goldfish was better also than
the Day 1 performance in R_0. The difference was due largely to the
temporal stability of inhibition at asymptote, which meant that there was
some speeding over trials of response to S⁺ as well as a slowing of response
to S⁻. In R_0, the animals began on Day 1 with a strong tendency to respond
to both stimuli, and the only change over trials was a slowing of response
to S⁻. The rate of inhibitory development was not appreciably greater at
asymptote than in R_0. Comparison of Day 2 performance at asymptote and
in R_0 again gives evidence in goldfish of decreased temporal stability both
of excitation and of inhibition at asymptote. The symmetry of the effect can
be seen more clearly in the trial-by-trial plot of asymptotic performance
which is shown in Fig. 5. The difference between these curves and those
for the pigeons is striking. At asymptote, the pigeons began each day with
prompt response to both stimuli and then soon stopped responding to S⁻;
the only indication of retention over the inter-session interval was that the
slowing of response to S⁻ was somewhat more precipitous on Day 2. The
goldfish, by contrast, continued to show good retention both of excitation

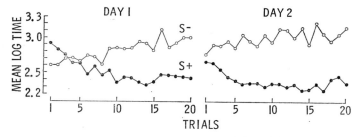

Fig. 5. The asymptotic performance (R_{17-24}) of the goldfish in Expt III.

and of inhibition; discrimination at asymptote was the product both of
a slowing of response to S⁻ and a speeding of response to S⁺.

3. Discussion

Experiments with fishes in choice situations have failed for the most part
to produce any clear evidence of progressive improvement like that found
in higher animals. For example, in a two-day, red-green reversal experiment very similar in design to the present one, pigeons showed improvement but goldfish did not (Gonzalez et al., 1967). In view of this history,
the most striking feature of the present results for the goldfish is the very

fact of progressive improvement. One explanation of the difference between the present results and the previous ones might be that there are mechanisms of improvement which operate in unitary but not in choice situations. It is perhaps worth mentioning in this connection that some indication of progressive improvement was shown by a single African mouthbreeder in a free-operant reversal experiment by Deterline (1960), but there was some reason to believe that the animal simply had learned to respond to stimulus-change. The present results cannot be explained in the same way because the stimuli were presented in Gellermann orders with 30-sec inter-trial intervals in darkness separating the presentations. Another explanation of the difference between the present results and previous ones might be that the instrumental technique used here for the first time in a reversal experiment is more powerful than techniques used earlier because of the close spatial contiguity of stimulus, response, and reward. We know from choice experiments with pigeons that an analogous departure from the conventional keypecking technique yields much improved reversal performance; if, instead of pecking a key illuminated with one of the colours to be discriminated, the pigeons are required to insert the head into the aperture of a grain-feeder illuminated with one of the colours, the slope of the reversal function is steepened appreciably (Gonzalez *et al.*, 1966).

The fact that goldfish show improvement does not mean, of course, that the mechanisms of improvement are the same as in pigeons, and the present results suggest that they may, in fact, be different in certain important respects. Such a conclusion cannot, however, rest on the outcome of a single experiment. The pattern of improvement shown by pigeons in unitary experiments is very much the same under a variety of conditions, but the generality of our results for goldfish remains to be determined. It is conceivable, for example, that the principal change in the performance of the goldfish and the change to which the improvement in their performance seemed primarily to be due—what has been referred to as the accumulation of inhibition over reversals—occurred only because the animals came to R_0 after many days of reinforcement for response to both stimuli. An experiment which did not begin with extensive pre-training might not show such a change and little, if any, improvement. It might be useful also in subsequent work to give more training per reversal in the hope of increasing the extent of improvement and thus facilitating the analysis of its course.

V. Experiment IV: Reversal Learning in Goldfish Under Choice Conditions

The evidence of progressive improvement in goldfish under unitary con ditions which I have just reported led to a series of experiments (in collaboration with F. Engelhardt) designed to determine whether goldfish trained by the same instrumental technique would show improvement under choice conditions. If improvement were found in these experiments, the explanation of the unitary results on the assumption that different mechanisms operate in unitary situations would lose force. I shall report here, not the entire series of experiments, but only some sample data which demonstrate improvement and tell something about the role of inhibition in that improvement.

1. *Method*

The apparatus used in our previous choice experiments with fishes has been illustrated in a number of papers (Bitterman, 1965; Behrend *et al.*, 1965). Each animal was trained in its individual 2-gal living tank. At one end of the tank, two Plexiglas targets which could be illuminated with coloured lights were introduced. At the other end of the tank was a feeding place, also suitably illuminated, at which the live *Tubifex* worms used as reinforcement were introduced by a feeder. For the present purposes, that situation was altered in two ways. Plexiglas nipples through which liquid food could be delivered were substituted for the targets; like the targets, they could be illuminated with coloured lights and will be referred to as the "stimulus-nipples". The worm-feeder was removed, and at the other end of the tank (in the old feeding area) a third Plexiglas nipple was installed. It will be referred to as the "centre key".

The subjects were 10 4-in goldfish maintained under standard conditions on a 24-hr feeding schedule. They were pretrained to feed from any of the three nipples when it was illuminated with white light, then to hit the white centre key to turn on one or the other of the stimulus-nipples (also white) from which food could be taken. After one further session in which the illuminated stimulus-nipples were red on some trials and green on others (both colours reinforced), discriminative training was begun.

There were 40 trials per day with an inter-trial interval of 6 sec. The chamber was dark in the inter-trial interval. Each trial began with the illumination of the centre key with white light. Response to the centre key turned off the centre-key light and illuminated the stimulus-nipples, one with red and the other with green light, the positions of the two colours being varied from trial to trial in accordance with Gellermann orders. Correct choice turned off both coloured lights and initiated a 6-sec reinforcement cycle during which the correct nipple was illuminated with white light and delivered food to the animal—a drop of liquid food was delivered when the correct choice was made, and another drop thereafter upon each contact of the animal with the nipple for the remainder of the cycle. For one group of five goldfish (TO), an incorrect choice produced a time-out in darkness. The duration of the time-out was controlled by a 10-sec timer which was reset by any response during the time-out period. After the time-out, the centre key was illuminated; response to the centre key turned on the correct stimulus-nipple alone (guidance), and response to it initiated a reinforcement cycle. A second group of five animals (S⁻ in TO) was treated like the first, except that the negative stimulus remained on during the entire time-out period. In Reversal 0, red was reinforced; in R_1, green; and so forth for 24 reversals, with two days of training in each.

2. *Results*

In Fig. 6, the performance of the two groups is plotted in terms of mean errors per reversal. Analysis of variance shows the decline in errors over

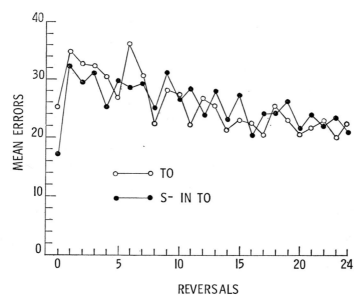

FIG. 6. The general course of improvement in the reversal performance of goldfish in Expt IV.

reversals to be statistically significant—every one of the ten goldfish gave clear evidence of improvement. The difference between the two groups was, however, negligible, and they therefore were combined in subsequent treatments.

In Fig. 7, the within-reversals performance of the combined groups is plotted in terms of mean errors per block of ten trials for the first, third, and sixth blocks of four reversals. The results for Day 1 are reminiscent of those for African mouthbreeders reported by Wodinsky and Bitterman (1957) in that the curves seem to differ primarily in slope rather than in point of origin, although analysis of variance, which shows the effects both of Reversals and of Trials to be significant, does not yield a significant

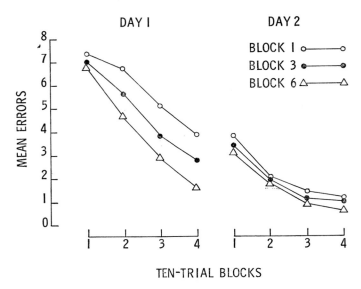

FIG. 7. The performance of the goldfish at various stages of training (the first, third, and sixth blocks of four reversals) in Expt IV.

interaction. Some evidence of decreased retention with continued reversal training is suggested by a comparison of performance on the last block of Day 1 trials and the first block of Day 2 trials. Even at asymptote, however, Day 1 performance continued to give evidence of substantial negative transfer, the mean number of errors in the first block of trials remaining considerably above the R_0 (chance) level.

3. Discussion

Again with respect to the results of this experiment it may be said that the fact of improvement is their most striking feature. In the choice situation used here, goldfish showed improvement in reversal which seems to have much in common with that found in higher animals. Since the problem was a visual one, an interpretation in terms of spatial reward-following is ruled out; since the procedure was fully automated, participation of the experimenter in the outcome cannot be suspected; since there was extensive pretraining and performance in R_0 was rather good, the improvement cannot be attributed simply to improved general adjustment to the experimental conditions; since the number of animals was substantial and the decline in errors highly significant, the improvement must be taken as more than an accidental fluctuation in performance.

Why improvement should occur under the conditions used here and not under the rather similar conditions of previous experiments is worth considering. The use of liquid food (rather than worms or pellets) as reward does not account for the difference. When the stimulus-nipples serve only as targets and the centre key is used as a feeder (each trial begins with illumination of the stimulus-nipples, and correct choice illuminates the centre key from which the fish takes food), there is no improvement. Nor does the spatial contiguity of reward with stimulus and response account for the difference. When the centre key is eliminated entirely (each trial begins with illumination of the stimulus-nipples, and correct choice is rewarded with food at the nipple), there is no improvement. It is conceivable that the use of a centre key as a prelude to choice is the important factor, and that the addition of a centre key to the situation used in earlier experiments also would produce improvement. It seems now, in any event, that results which once could be thought to indicate a rather fundamental difference in the learning of fishes and higher animals are the product only of some relatively trivial situational factors. An historical parallel called to mind is the early conclusion that rats are form-blind, which was found to be incorrect when Lashley invented the jumping apparatus. The comparative psychologist must remain keenly aware of such developments. The null hypothesis never can be accepted with confidence.

Mackintosh (1969) already has argued on the basis of the fragmentary evidence of improvement in fishes obtained in earlier experiments that there is no need to assume a qualitative difference between the learning of fishes and the learning of higher animals. In his view, fishes simply show *less* improvement than do higher animals because their attention to the relevant stimuli is not strengthened as much in the course of reversal training. It is important, however, to distinguish between the probability of obtaining improvement in reversal experiments and the magnitude of the improvement which is obtained. For one thing, it is clear now that we can find improvement in goldfish whenever we like. Furthermore, the magnitude of that improvement can be substantial—the decline in errors pictured in Fig. 6 is of the same order of magnitude, for example, as that found in a parallel experiment with pigeons (Gonzalez *et al.*, 1967)— although a comparison of animals in terms of the magnitude of improvement has very little meaning. Animals of the same species, trained with the same stimuli, will show much more marked improvement under one set of conditions than another (Gonzalez *et al.*, 1966). We find now that a centre key makes the difference between substantial improvement and no improvement at all in goldfish.

Of special interest here perhaps is the finding in this experiment that performance was unaffected by the "S⁻ in TO" procedure which greatly increased the animal's unreinforced experience with S⁻ and punished response to S⁻ by postponing its termination. The performance of rats in a unitary experiment by Khavari and Heise (1967) was markedly facilitated by a similar method. It is possible that the choice measure is less sensitive to the effects of such procedures. It also is possible that differential experience with S⁻ is less important for goldfish than for rats because, as the unitary results indicate, discrimination in goldfish is a more symmetrical process, continuing to reflect increases in readiness to respond to S⁺ as well as increases in reluctance to respond to S⁻.

As has been noted in relation to the results of Expt III, the fact that goldfish show improvement in reversal does not mean that the mechanisms of improvement are the same in goldfish as in other animals, however much we may be led by considerations of parsimony to favour such a conclusion. The present results have much in common with those obtained in choice experiments with pigeons, but there are differences, such as the persistence in goldfish of the marked negative transfer evident on the early trials of Day 1, and the unitary results show even more striking differences between the two animals. Required now are some parametric experiments, both unitary and choice, with a variety of animals designed to explore the generality of these differences and to isolate whatever factors in improvement may be specific to method or to species.

VI. Summary and Conclusions

In the first two of four experiments which are reported here, reversal learning in pigeons was studied under unitary conditions—that is, under conditions in which the stimuli to be discriminated are presented separately and the readiness of the animal to respond to each of them is measured. The results of these experiments together with those reported in a recent paper by Beale (1970) demonstrate that progressive improvement occurs in pigeons under unitary as well as under choice conditions and suggest that inhibition—defined simply as a reluctance to respond which develops on nonreinforced trials—plays a central role in the improvement.

At the outset of training, inhibition is temporally stable, at least to the extent that the reluctance to respond which is developed in one experimental session persists in the 24-hr interval between sessions; with continued training, however, the temporal stability of inhibition declines, and at asymptote there is little in the behaviour of pigeons to indicate whether a given stimulus was positive or negative in the preceding session, both stimuli being responded to readily on the early trials. In two-day reversal training (with positive and negative stimuli reversed every two days), this decline in the temporal stability of inhibition tends to improve performance on reversal days and to impair performance on nonreversal days. Another change in the course of reversal training is an increase in the rate at which inhibition develops within sessions. This change tends to improve performance both on reversal and on nonreversal days. Performance on reversal days, relatively poor to begin with, becomes better, then, on both accounts, while performance on nonreversal days changes relatively little, the decline in the temporal stability of inhibition being offset by the greater rate of inhibitory development.

Analysis of the progressive improvement in habit reversal which is found in choice situations has suggested that it may be traced both to decreasing negative transfer (attributed to proactive interference) and to positive transfer (variously explained). On the assumption that the mechanisms of improvement are the same in unitary and choice situations, the present results suggest that decline in negative transfer is due to decline in the temporal stability of inhibition, an hypothesis compatible with the conception of proactive interference on the old Pavlovian assumption that inhibition is particularly susceptible to interference. The present results point also to increased rate of inhibitory development as the main source of positive transfer, although current explanations of positive transfer in choice situations do not prepare us for such a conclusion.

In the third of the four experiments which are reported here, reversal learning in goldfish was studied under unitary conditions in much the same way as in the first experiment with pigeons. Clear evidence of improvement was found, although the underlying changes were rather different in goldfish than in pigeons. The goldfish showed some decline over reversals in the temporal stability both of inhibition and of excitation—defined as a readiness to respond generated on reinforced trials—but the change primarily responsible for the improvement was an increase over reversals in reluctance to respond to both stimuli which was more marked for the negative stimulus than for the positive. Since progressive improvement had been rather difficult to find in previous choice experiments with fishes of a variety of species, the results of the third experiment pointed either (1) to the operation of different mechanisms in unitary and choice situation or (2) to the inadequacy of the techniques employed in the previous work. In the fourth experiment which is reported here, reversal learning in goldfish was studied with the same new consummatory technique as was employed in the third experiment, and marked improvement appeared. The results gave some indication of greater retention-decrement in the later as compared with the earlier reversals, but decline in negative transfer did not appear to play an important part in the improvement.

Further experiments will be necessary to clarify the relation between the patterns of improvement which occur in unitary and choice situations and to assess the generality of the differences in pattern of improvement shown by pigeons and goldfish under the conditions studied here. The present results suggest that unitary experiments, which permit the separate measurement of excitatory and inhibitory changes, will contribute much to the understanding of improvement in choice situations. They also point to certain differences between the reversal learning of pigeons and goldfish in which inhibitory processes seem to play a central role.

Acknowledgements

I am indebted to my colleague, Dr. William T. Woodard, who collaborated in much of this work, which was supported by Grant MH17736 from the United States Public Health Service.

References

Beale, I. L. (1970). The effects of amount of training per reversal on successive reversals of a color discrimination. *Journal of the Experimental Analysis of Behavior*, **14**, 345–352.

Behrend, E. R. and Bitterman, M. E. (1967). Further experiments on habit reversal in the fish. *Psychonomic Science*, **8**, 363–364.

Behrend, E. R., Domesick, V. B. and Bitterman, M. E. (1965). Habit reversal in the fish. *Journal of Comparative and Physiological Psychology*, **60**, 407–411.

Behrend, E. R., Powers, A. S. and Bitterman, M. E. (1970). Interference and forgetting in bird and fish. *Science*, **167**, 389–390.

Bitterman, M. E. (1965). Phyletic differences in learning. *American Psychologist*, **20**, 396–410.

Bitterman, M. E. (1966). Animal learning. In: J. B. Sidowski (Ed.), *Experimental Methods and Instrumentation in Psychology*. McGraw-Hill, New York, pp. 451–484.

Bitterman, M. E., Wodinsky, J. and Candland, D. K. (1958). Some comparative psychology. *American Journal of Psychology*, **71**, 94–110.

Bullock, D. H. and Bitterman, M. E. (1962). Habit reversal in the pigeon. *Journal of Comparative and Physiological Psychology*, **55**, 958–962.

Clark, F. C. (1967). Operant discrimination, neutralization, and reversal with variations in S^d exposure. *Psychological Reports*, **20**, 79–98.

Davenport, J. W. (1959). Choice behavior and differential response strength in discrimination reversal learning. *Journal of Comparative and Physiological Psychology*, **52**, 349–352.

Deterline, W. A. (1960). Operant discrimination reversals: Comparative data. *Journal of the Experimental Analysis of Behavior*, **3**, 247–253.

Gonzalez, R. C. and Bitterman, M. E. (1968). Two-dimensional discriminative learning in the pigeon. *Journal of Comparative and Physiological Psychology*, **65**, 427–432.

Gonzalez, R. C., Berger, B. D. and Bitterman, M. E. (1966). A further comparison of keypecking with an ingestive technique for the study of discriminative learning in pigeons. *American Journal of Psychology*, **79**, 217–225.

Gonzalez, R. C., Behrend, E. R. and Bitterman, M. E. (1967). Reversal learning and forgetting in bird and fish. *Science*, **158**, 519–521.

Graf, V., Bullock, D. H. and Bitterman, M. E. (1964). Further experiments on probability-matching in the pigeon. *Journal of the Experimental Analysis of Behavior*, **7**, 151–157.

Holmes, N. K. and Bitterman, M. E. (1969). Measurement of consummatory behavior in the fish. *Journal of the Experimental Analysis of Behavior*, **12**, 39–41.

Holmes, P. A. and Bitterman, M. E. (1966). Spatial and visual habit reversal in the turtle. *Journal of Comparative and Physiological Psychology*, **62**, 328–331.

Hull, C. L. (1952). *A Behavior System*. Yale University Press, New Haven, pp. 114–116.

Khavari, K. A. and Heise, G. A. (1967). Analysis of discrimination reversal in the rat. *Psychonomic Science*, **9**, 271–272.

Kirk, K. L. and Bitterman, M. E. (1965). Probability-learning by the turtle. *Science*, **148**, 1484–1485.

Krechevsky, I. (1932). Antagonistic visual discrimination habits in the white rat. *Journal of Comparative Psychology*, **14**, 263–277.

Lovejoy, E. P. (1966). An analysis of the overlearning reversal effect. *Psychological Review*, **73**, 87–103.

Mackintosh, N. J. (1969). Comparative studies of reversal and probability learning: Rats, birds, and fish. In: R. M. Gilbert and N. S. Sutherland (Eds.), *Animal Discrimination Learning*. Academic Press, London, pp. 137–162.

Mackintosh, N. J. and Little, L. (1969). Selective attention and response strategies as factors in serial reversal learning. *Canadian Journal of Psychology*, **23**, 335–346.

Mackintosh, N. J. and Mackintosh, J. (1964). Performance of *Octopus* over a series of reversals of a simultaneous discrimination. *Animal Behavior*, **12**, 321–324.

Mackintosh, N. J., McGonigle, B., Holgate, V. and Vanderver, V. (1968). Factors underlying improvement in serial reversal learning. *Canadian Journal of Psychology*, **22**, 85–95.

North, A. J. (1950). Improvement in successive discrimination reversals. *Journal of Comparative and Physiological Psychology*, **43**, 442–460.

North, A. J. (1962). Discrimination reversal learning in a runway situation. *Journal of Comparative and Physiological Psychology*, **55**, 550–554.

Overall, J. E. and Brown, W. L. (1959). A comparison of the decision-behavior of rats and human subjects. *American Journal of Psychology*, **72**, 258–261.

Schade, A. F. and Bitterman, M. E. (1966). Improvement in habit reversal as related to dimensional set. *Journal of Comparative and Physiological Psychology*, **62**, 43–48.

Schusterman, R. J. (1964). Successive discrimination-reversal training and multiple discrimination training in one-trial learning by chimpanzees. *Journal of Comparative and Physiological Psychology*, **58**, 153–156.

Setterington, R. G. and Bishop, H. E. (1967). Habit reversal improvement in the fish. *Psychonomic Science*, **7**, 41–42.

Stretch, R. G. A., McGonigle, B. and Morton, A. (1964). Serial position-reversal learning in the rat: Trials/problem and the intertrial interval. *Journal of Comparative and Physiological Psychology*, **57**, 461–463.

Squier, L. H. (1969). Reversal learning improvement in the fish *Astronotus ocellatus* (Oscar). *Psychonomic Science*, **14**, 143–144.

Sutherland, N. S. (1964). The learning of discriminations by animals. *Endeavour*, **23**, 148–152.

Warren, J. M. (1960). Reversal learning by paradise fish (*Macropodus opercularis*). *Journal of Comparative and Physiological Psychology*, **53**, 376–378.

Warren, J. M. (1966). Reversal learning and the formation of learning sets by cats and rhesus monkeys. *Journal of Comparative and Physiological Psychology*, **61**, 421–428.

Wilson, W. A., Oscar, M. and Bitterman, M. E. (1964). Probability-learning in the monkey. *The Quarterly Journal of Experimental Psychology*, **16**, 163–165.

Wodinsky, J. and Bitterman, M. E. (1957). Discrimination-reversal in the fish. *American Journal of Psychology*, **70**, 569–576.

Woodard, W. T., Schoel, W. M. and Bitterman, M. E. (1971). Reversal learning with singly-presented stimuli in pigeons and goldfish. *Journal of Comparative and Physiological Psychology*, **76**, 460–461.

Wyckoff, L. B. (1952). The role of observing responses in discrimination learning. *Psychological Review*, **59**, 431–442.

Zeaman, D. and House, B. J. (1963). The role of attention in retardate discrimination learning. In: N. R. Ellis (Ed.), *Handbook of Mental Deficiency: Psychological Theory and Research*. McGraw-Hill, New York, pp. 159–223.

B | Analogues of Pavlovian Inhibition in Instrumental Conditioning

B

The chapters in this section are, like those in Section **A**, concerned with the role of inhibition in instrumental learning situations. However, they are more directly related to the Pavlovian concept of inhibition, and how ideas drawn from classical conditioning may be applied to instrumental learning. The work described involves a variety of experimental situations and in most cases the subjects of the experiments are rats.

In Chapter 7 Ison and Krane discuss the Pavlovian concepts of *positive* and *negative* induction and the analogies between these concepts and contrast effects observed in various instrumental learning situations. In particular they report results investigating such effects found in the extinction of responding in rats where there has been differential reinforcement of responding in two different runways. They conclude that the similarities between the various forms of inductive effects probably do not reflect a common underlying process.

Another central Pavlovian concept is that of *disinhibition*, and in Chapter 8 Brimer shows that disinhibition can readily be found in instrumental situations where the rate of responding has been reduced from a high level to a low one by any of a variety of procedures, including satiation; disinhibition is not found, however, in cases where the rate of responding has been low throughout.

Pavlov also emphasized the importance of *inhibition of delay* and Richelle, in Chapter 10, discusses the role of inhibition in delayed responding in instrumental situations, particularly in DRL and FI schedules, arguing that the temporal regulation of such behaviour can best be understood in terms of inhibition.

In the final chapter of this section Weisman and Litner discuss the role played by the termination of the warning signal in avoidance behaviour and present evidence that the inhibition of fear plays a central role in the reinforcement of avoidance behaviour.

7

Positive Induction in the Extinction of Differential Instrumental Conditioning

J. R. ISON and R. V. KRANE

University of Rochester, College of Arts and Sciences,
River Campus Station, Rochester, New York, U.S.A.

I. Introduction	. . . .	181
II. Experiment I:	Effects of Trial Spacing During Extinction . .	185
III. Experiment II:	Inter-Stimulus Interval Effects	188
IV. Experiment III:	Effects of Overtraining	192
V. Experiment IV:	Avoidance Responses and Goal-box Confinement Time	194
VI. Discussion	. . . .	197
VII. Conclusions	. . . .	202
Acknowledgements	. . . .	203
References	. . . .	203

I. Introduction

In discrimination learning the standard operations of reinforcement and nonreinforcement which are correlated with the positive and negative discriminanda sometimes produce anomalous reciprocal effects whereby reinforcement to the one (S$^+$) might suppress a subsequent reaction to the other (S$^-$) or, conversely, nonreinforcement to S$^-$ might enhance a subsequent reaction to S$^+$. These phenomena were first noted by Pavlov (1927) under some rather special conditions of discriminative classical conditioning and were called, respectively, "negative" and "positive induction". Negative induction was observed if after the completion of differential conditioning an attempt was made to convert an inhibitory CS− into an excitatory CS+ by pairing it with reinforcement. This conversion progressed rapidly if the stimulus was presented on consecutive occasions but was greatly retarded if the old CS+ (still reinforced) was presented prior to each reinforced trial with the old CS−; it was suggested that presentations of the excitatory CS+ intensified the inhibitory state associated with the old CS−. Positive induction was observed during the maintenance of a discrimination if the response to CS+ followed a trial to CS− by an unusually short inter-trial interval. On such trials the amplitude of the CR was abnormally high and here it was suggested that the presentation of the inhibitory CS— intensified the excitatory state associated with the CS+.

A second source of demonstrations of reciprocal effects of reinforcement and nonreinforcement is found in the procedures of discriminative operant conditioning in which different stimuli are associated with differentially dense reinforcement schedules. In particular transitions from the less dense to the more dense schedule are marked by an unusually high rate of responding, whereas contrary transitions are marked by an unusually low rate of responding (e.g. Bernheim and Williams, 1967). In addition, a separate phase differential procedure, in which multiple schedules are imposed only following the attainment of a stable rate on the S^+ schedule, results in an enhancement of the response rate associated with that schedule when the multiple schedules are imposed (see Terrace, Chapter 4, this volume). The reciprocal effects seen in operant conditioning are called "positive contrast" and "negative contrast", though this difference in labels is not to imply that the phenomena are necessarily any different from those obtained in Pavlovian conditioning. Rather the operant language follows the lead of Skinner (1938) who reserved "induction" for the phenomenon called "generalization" in the Pavlovian context and, thus, required a different label to denote this reciprocal effect; so the terms "positive contrast" and "negative contrast" within operant language were first applied to the Pavlovian phenomena, there being at that time no comparable operant data. Although the change in terminology may have the advantage of eschewing the Pavlovian interpretation, an interpretation borrowed, with some modification, from the reflex physiology of Sherrington, it unfortunately suggests that the effect may be dependent on some discriminative "comparison" of the differential schedules. Such a suggestion was evidently not intended in the choice of "contrast" to describe the phenomenon because Skinner proposed that Pavlovian positive induction, at least, might be attributed to a subtle effect of differentially reinforcing a compound CS made up of a transition from CS— to CS+ (Skinner, 1938).

Finally, a third experimental tradition in which reciprocal effects between S^+ and S^- have been demonstrated is that of differential instrumental conditioning, a procedure in which the discriminanda, typically runways, are presented separately and an approach in one is reinforced whereas an approach in the other is not reinforced, or is reinforced but with a less favoured stimulus. In the acquisition or maintenance of differential instrumental conditioning positive induction effects have never been observed, although a negative induction effect (or, variously, a "simultaneous negative contrast effect", a "concurrent depression effect") is a standard occurrence (e.g. Bower, 1961; Ludvigson and Gay, 1967; Ison et al., 1969). However, other effects are noted following acquisition if the old S^+ is no longer correlated with reinforcement or if the old S⁻ is no longer correlated with nonreinforcement. Senf and Miller (1967) demonstrated that the extinction of the reaction to the old S⁺ was retarded if presentations of S⁻ preceded each trial to the now nonreinforced old S⁺ (positive induction). Leonard *et al.* (1968) replicated this and also observed that acquisition of the reaction to the old S⁻ was retarded if that stimulus alternated with presentations of S⁻ (negative induction). In positive induction the occurrence of the nonreinforced S⁻ enhances the excitatory strength associated with the old S⁺ (or, perhaps, attenuates its developing inhibitory state) whereas in negative induction the occurrence of the reinforced S⁺ enhances the inhibitory strength associated with the old S⁻ (or, perhaps, attenuates its developing excitatory state).

Thus in each of these three general experimental paradigms for exploring discriminative performance induction (or contrast) effects may be obtained, and the effects are both positive (an enhancement of the reaction to S⁺) and negative (a reduction of the reaction to S⁻). Effects may be obtained during the acquisition and maintenance of the discrimination or in a subsequent stage of transformations from excitation to inhibition, or the reverse. And all of the phenomena may be described as reflecting a reciprocal or inverse outcome of reinforcement or nonreinforcement, an outcome in which a positive or negative effect on one of the discriminanda is accompanied by the opposite effect on the complementary discriminandum.

There are two potentially important consequences of these demonstrations, one concerned with the contribution of induction phenomena to the results of a variety of complex discrimination learning experiments and the other concerned with the implications of induction phenomena for discrimination learning theory. If induction phenomena were to occur over a wide range of experimental conditions then it may be argued that the effect of any particular variable on discrimination learning is produced indirectly because of a primary effect on the strength of induction. This argument can most plausibly be presented in the context of a possible account of the overlearning-reversal phenomenon, which is that overtraining on the initial discrimination results in a subsequent rapid learning of the reverse discrimination compared to reversal learning immediately on the attainment of criterion performance (Reid, 1953). First, it is clear that the induction processes of the sort demonstrated by Senf and Miller (1967) and by Leonard *et al.* (1968) must necessarily impede reversal learning because extinction of the reaction to the former S⁺ and acquisition of the reaction to the former S⁻ would be retarded by, respectively, positive and negative induction. Second, Pavlov (1927) reported that induction of the sort demonstrated in Pavlovian conditioning is eliminated by overtraining. With an assumption that the two sources of induction are tapping the same phenomenon and that, therefore, induction in differential instrumental conditioning similarly is reduced by overtraining on the initial discrimination, then the "overlearning-reversal phenomenon" may be examined as a special case of an "overlearning-induction phenomenon". The overlearning condition may produce the subsequent rapid reversal learning not because it produces some process which facilitates reversal but because it attenuates a process which impedes reversal. Similar arguments may be advanced for such other phenomena as "learning-how-to-learn", the effects of successive reversals, and so on.

It is evident that the value of this empirical extension of induction processes depends critically on the boundary conditions for their occurrence. The theoretical significance of induction processes similarly depends on the range of conditions under which induction may be obtained as well as the extent to which the various demonstrations of induction may be asserted to tap the same basic process, rather than sample a variety of different effects which resemble each other only superficially. If induction should be some unitary process which occurs as a ubiquitous consequence of all sorts of discrimination procedures then it follows that theoretical treatment of discrimination must accord that unitary process a cardinal status. Contrarily if the various demonstrations yield but superficially similar phenomena, and if their occurrence is restricted to rather special sets of conditions then theories should treat them as local secondary events to be described by other primary principles. These are serious considerations, for it cannot be denied that induction is a paradoxical phenomenon when viewed from the standpoint of conditioning-extinction theories of discrimination learning (e.g. Spence, 1936). Such theories have their empirical basis in the many and varied demonstrations that reinforcement facilitates and nonreinforcement degrades the behaviours which immediately precede them (the Law of Effect) and that these changes are accompanied by similar but less extensive changes in related behaviours in the presence of related stimuli (the Law of Generalization). Each of the varieties of induction suggests, contrarily, that reinforcement and nonreinforcement have reciprocal rather than similar effects on the responses to the two discriminations, for, e.g. reinforcement of one stimulus degrades the response to the other whereas nonreinforcement of that stimulus facilitates the response to the first.

Induction may be interpreted as showing that discrimination learning is *sui generis* and not to be accounted for by a simple concatenation of reinforcement contingencies and generalization. On the other hand, the results of analytic study of the phenomena may suggest straightforward extensions of traditional theory sufficient for their provision.

Most of our work is concerned with positive induction in the extinction of differential instrumental conditioning (extinction PI), an emphasis determined by a more general interest in reversal learning. In the research to be described three problems were investigated. The first was whether induction could be detected in the usual context of differential instrumental conditioning, a context which most typically includes relatively spaced trials. The second was that of determining the most favourable conditions for extinction PI, with the particular theme being whether these most favourable conditions might be the same as those for Pavlovian acquisition PI. The third was an attempt to arrive at a more molecular description of the effect of extinction PI on performance.

II. Experiment I: Effects of Trial Spacing During Extinction

In the first experiment (Ison and Krane, 1969) we looked for evidence of extinction PI following a broad range of acquisition trials (12–150) at the relatively long inter-trial interval (ITI) which seems characteristic of work in this area. The use of a wide range of trials seemed appropriate because Pavlovian induction is dependent on the amount of training given prior to the test (Pavlov, 1927) and, if induction should not be found, we needed to be sure that this negative outcome did not result because of an unfortunate choice of acquisition parameters. As an additional safeguard, with the same intent we included an extra set of groups run at an intermediate number of trials under identical conditions except for their having a very short ITI in extinction. The subjects in this and the following experiments were male albino rats usually obtained from the Holtzman Company, Madison, Wisconsin, about 100 days old.

The apparatus used in this experiment was two parallel alleyways, each 36 in long, one painted black and the other off-white. Each could be attached to a grey startbox. Photocells attached to the door and to the alleyways at distances of 12 in and 24 in from the start door permitted measurement of start time and running time. The animals were run whilst under 23-hr water deprivation and received ·2 cc water at the end of the positive alley, nothing at the end of the negative alley. In the main part of the experiment the subjects (N= 48) were assigned to four main groups differing in numbers of acquisition trials prior to extinction: 12, 30, 66, or 150 trials, half to each stimulus. Six trials per day were given with an ITI of about 10 min. Following acquisition half of the subjects within each group (the "control" subset) received 18 nonreinforced trials in the former positive alley (S^{+-}) at a rate of three per day for six days. The remaining half of each group (the "induction" subset) received 18 nonreinforced trials in the former positive alley interspersed with 18 nonreinforced trials in the former negative alley (S^{--}), at a rate of six trials per day. Two patterns of daily trials were used (ABBAAB or BAABBA) with an ITI for

the induction groups of 5 min. The control groups received their trials to
S^{+-} at the ITI specified in the pattern used by the induction groups. In
the secondary part of this experiment the subjects (N = 20) were treated
in acquisition exactly like the groups given 66 trials above. In extinction,
however, trials were given at a rate of nine S^{+-} trials per day and the ITI
in the induction subgroup was set at 30 sec rather than 5 min. The same
patterns of trials used in the main part of the experiment were imposed on
the induction subgroup so that trials to the former positive stimulus could
follow either a like trial or a trial to the former negative stimulus.

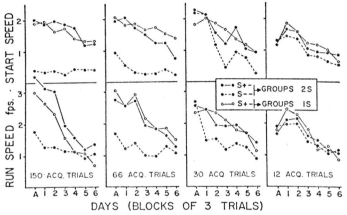

Fig. 1. Mean start and run speeds to the former S^+ and the former S^- on the terminal
acquisition day and the six days of extinction for the induction groups receiving both
stimuli in extinction (2S) and the control groups receiving only trials to S^+ (1S) (from
Ison and Krane, 1969).

The outcome in extinction for the main portion of this experiment is
given in Fig. 1 which depicts start and run speeds to the former positive
stimulus (S^{+-}) and to the former negative stimulus (S^{--}) on the terminal
day of acquisition and throughout extinction. The induction subgroups are
designated as "Groups 2S" and the control groups as "Groups 1S",
describing thereby the number of stimuli encountered in extinction. The
most obvious and important finding in these data is the failure to detect
any advantage in speed scores to the former positive alley produced by the
inclusion of trials to the negative stimulus. In fact, under these conditions
of relatively widely-spaced trials, exposure to S^{--} had no effect at all on
speeds to S^{+-} (in the analysis of variance all comparisons which included
induction vs. control conditions yielded F ratios approximating 1·0). The
extinction data for the groups given massed extinction trials is presented
in Fig. 2 in which trials to S^{+-} which followed trials to S^{--} are separated
out (in column A) from trials to S^{+-} which followed like trials to S^{+-}. In

general these data offered some evidence for extinction PI because the group received both S^{+-} and S^{--} in extinction tended to run faster than the control group which received trials only to S^{+-}. Statistical analysis of these data revealed that within the induction group trials to S^{+-} were faster if the preceding trials was to S^{--} rather than to S^{+-} (p < ·005) and that the induction group ran to S^{+-} faster than did the control group (p < ·001), at least on those trials in the induction group which followed exposures to S^{--}.

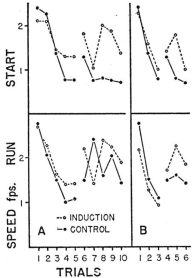

Fig. 2. Mean start and run speeds to the former S^+ in extinction. Column A depicts trials which followed S^-, column B trials which followed S^+. The control points depicted are those on comparable trial numbers (from Ison and Krane, 1969).

Of some further interest to induction processes are analyses of acquisition data in which trials to both S^+ and S^- were examined for the effect of the preceding trial being a reinforcement on S^+ or a nonreinforcement on S^-. Overall the effect of having a reinforcement on Trail N was to increase response speed on Trial N+1 (or, expressed otherwise, the effect of having a nonreinforcement on Trial N was to depress response speed on Trial N+1, there being no way to assess independently whether S^+ was increasing subsequent speeds, S^- decreasing subsequent speeds, or whether both effects were present).

Leonard et al. (1968) also observed that speeds were greater following reinforcement rather than following nonreinforcement on the preceding trial, in the same kind of spaced trial acquisition procedure.

The failure to obtain extinction PI with spaced trials in the main part of this experiment limits the empirical significance of induction for it seems unlikely that induction processes play a role in determining the outcome of discrimination learning and reversal experiments so long as those experiments are conducted with reasonably spaced trials. The outcome of the acquisition phase of the experiment is equally limiting for induction explanation of acquisition phenomena in differential instrumental conditioning because with spaced trials reinforcement produces a facilitatory after-effect (or nonreinforcement produces a depressive after-effect); the after-effects are similar in direction to the direct effect of reinforcement and nonreinforcement rather than, as is the defining characteristic of induction processes, in the opposite direction.

Although these data limit the empirical applicability of extinction PI they do not suggest that extinction PI is a different phenomenon from Pavlovian PI. Indeed one might conclude the contrary for it is reported similarly that Pavlovian PI is restricted to very short inter-trial intervals and that at long intervals the reciprocal induction effects merge into and are replaced by after effects of the same sort that were observed here during acquisition. The next two experiments were more directly concerned with the relationship between Pavlovian PI and extinction PI.

III. Experiment II: Inter-Stimulus Interval Effects

In this experiment (Krane and Ison, 1971) we made a finer analysis of the way in which ITI might affect extinction PI. Although the first experiment yielded one point of possible correspondence between extinction PI and Pavlovian PI, a closer examination of "massed" and "spaced" trial spacings suggests a source of confounding which may make this correspondence illusory. In the Pavlovian experiments the critical ITI is that between CS^+ and the preceding CS^-, and other ITIs, between, for example, successive CS^+ trials are not evidently important. But in the usual massed extinction trials all ITIs are short; it may be that the important temporal interval was not that between S^{+-} and the preceding S^{--} but, rather, that between successive trials to S^{+-}. In this experiment, therefore, these two transitions were manipulated separately. The experimental design involved three sets of groups which differed only in the temporal spacing of trials to S^{+-} (at 1, 4 or 10 min). Within each set one group, the control, received an unbroken string of trials to S^{+-} and the other, the induction group, received a trial to S^{--} just 30 sec before each exposure to S^{+-}. If the critical transition is that between S^{+-} and the preceding S^{--}, then all induction groups should yield extinction PI. Contrarily, if the critical transition is that between successive trials to S^{+-} then extinction PI should occur only in the set of groups given massed trials to S^{+-}.

The subjects were 108 naïve rats from the population used in Expt I, and the apparatus was the same. The animals were run at 23-hr food deprivation and were given five 45 mg Noyes food pellets in S^+ and were detained for 15 sec in the empty goal box of S^- (and S^{+-}). On the first four days of acquisition subjects received five S^+ trials and five S^- trials on each day in a quasi-random order. These trials were presented at various ITIs so that the intervals between different trials varied from 30 sec to about 7 min. This procedure was adopted to provide the animals with experience of trial transitions at various ITIs prior to the imposition of special control procedures on the fifth through the tenth days of acquisition. To eliminate stimulus generalization decrements in extinction due to the presence of unusual ITIs or stimulus sequences, each of the subjects was assigned to one of six groups, all of which received the six sequences of trials to be used in extinction. The groups differed in the order in which

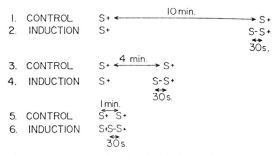

Fig. 3. Temporal arrangement of stimuli on induction and control conditions employed in acquisition and extinction, showing just two trials to S^+ and the position of the interposed S^- (from Krane and Ison, 1971).

the sequences were presented. These six stimulus patterns are given in Fig. 3 which shows two successive trials, the interposition of S^- in each induction condition, and the various ITIs. On these control days six trials to S^+ were given and in the induction conditions an S^- was given prior to each of the last five S^+ trials. Animals not given the interposed S^- received a run of five S^- trials at the end of each day. On the final (eleventh) acquisition day all subjects received a ten trial quasi-random pattern of S^+ and S^- trials with various ITIs, thereby concluding 61 S^+ and 55 S^- trials. In extinction, which followed on the next four days, the subjects were randomly assigned to one of these sets of groups receiving 1-min, 4-min, or 10-min intervals between presentations of the now nonreinforced S^+ (S^{+-}). Within each of these sets half received 20 trials to S^{+-} alone (Control condition) and half received a trial to S^{--} immediately before each S^{+-} (Induction condition). Thus each induction group received the same 30-sec interval between S^{--} and the following S^{+-}. Extinction was given at five trials to S^{+-} on each of four days.

Mean start and running speeds to S^{+-} on each trial of extinction are given in Fig. 4 which organizes the factorial design so as to show the effect of ITI in the Control condition (on the left) against the effect of ITI in the Induction condition (on the right). It is evident that in the Control condition massing the trials reduced extinction speeds, and the three groups extinguished in orderly fashion with the 10 min group exhibiting the most response strength and the 1 min group the least. This effect was not present

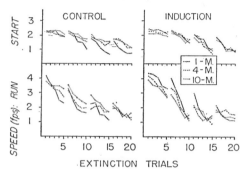

FIG. 4. Mean start and run speeds to two former S^+ in extinction as a function of ITI, control groups at left, induction groups at right (from Krane and Ison, 1971).

in the Induction condition where, indeed, the groups showed some signs of a reverse ordering. Analyses of variance supported the graphic indication that the effect of ITI was different in Control and Induction conditions ($p < \cdot025$), that in the Control condition the 1 min group had less response strength than did the 10 min group ($p < \cdot05$), but in the Induction condition the groups were not different. A direct comparison of Induction vs. Control procedures at each ITI is presented in Fig. 5 which depicts the mean difference between comparable groups divided by the standard error of the mean as estimated from the analysis of variance (i.e. $(I-C)\ \sigma_M$). Clearly the inclusion of the S^{--} trial increased relative speeds in the 1-min groups (that is, an extinction PI effect) but decreased relative speeds in the 10-min groups (showing, thereby, an inhibitory after effect of nonreinforcement on S^{--}).

Some further data of interest were obtained in the acquisition phase which indicated that the negative stimulus uniformly depressed speeds to the subsequent positive stimulus ($p < \cdot01$), an effect that did not depend on the ITI between S^+ trials. Thus in the acquisition of differential conditioning under both massed trial (this experiment) and spaced trial (Expt I) procedures nonreinforcement produces an inhibitory after-effect rather than an facilitatory induction effect.

The major empirical outcome of this experiment is clear. The effect of massed extinction training in the Control condition is to reduce extinction speeds, an effect not found in the Induction condition. A failure to find the effect of ITI in the Induction groups is in one way not surprising for, of course, each Induction group had an equal 30-sec ITI between S^{+-} and the preceding S^{--}. But the result of this was not to commonly lower

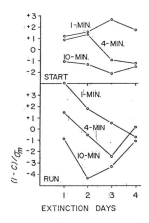

FIG. 5. Difference scores on start and run measures between induction and control conditions at each of the three ITIs, divided by the standard error of the mean (from Krane and Ison, 1971).

response speed as would be expected if the 30-sec interval between S^{+-} and S^{--} were simply an additional point on the ITI dimension which varied from 10 min down to 1 min between successive trials to S^{+-}. The insertion of S^{--} eliminated the ITI effect not by depressing speeds in the conditions which had, otherwise, spaced trials, but by increasing speeds in the conditions which had massed transitions between exposures to S^{+-}. The effect of the interposed S^{--} was to functionally space out the S^{+-} trials, to reduce the inhibitory after effect of one S^{+-} on its successor.

Thus we conclude that one necessary condition for producing extinction PI is short rather than long intervals between successive nonreinforced trials to the former positive stimulus, for if there are long temporal intervals between these stimuli then the insertion of the negative stimulus just before the positive stimulus provides an inhibitory after effect. This variable does not appear to be important in the determination of Pavlovian PI and, thus, these data are initial evidence for the conclusion that the two demonstrations of "positive induction" reveal the operation of fundamentally different processes. The next experiment adds further weight to this conclusion.

IV. Experiment III: Effects of Overtraining

In Pavlovian work induction is a transient phenomenon which appears when the discrimination has just become evident in performance and goes away with overtraining. In this experiment (Krane and Ison, 1970a) we focused on the relationship between overtraining and positive induction in the context of differential instrumental conditioning. Given the outcome of the prior experiment we were not unprepared for a finding that extinction PI might not share the relationship obtained in Pavlovian work. This expectation was strengthened by our growing belief that extinction PI may be a "control group phenomenon", that is, that the induction group does better only in relation to a control group that has some particularly aversive condition present in extinction. In Expt II this condition was the massing of extinction trials; in Expt III we thought that overtraining might play a similar role for it has been demonstrated that overtraining in differential conditioning enhances the effects of nonreinforcement in subsequent extinction (Birch et al., 1960).

The subjects were 28 male albino rats, 20 obtained from the same population used previously and eight obtained from Carworth Laboratories, Kingston, New York. The apparatus consisted of two parallel alleys, one white and one black, 80 in long, $3\frac{1}{2}$ in wide, and 4 in high. A system of photocells and Hunter Klockounters provided three 6-in speed measures, as start (first 6 in), run (centre 6 in) and goal (last 6 in) as well as an overall speed measure (over 78 in). On rewarded trials the 23-hr food deprived subjects received five 45 mg food pellets and on nonrewarded trials they were detained in the empty goalbox for 15 sec. Two sets of animals received either 50 trials (Groups 50, a total of 30 trials to S^+ and 20 trials to S^-) or 160 trials (Groups 160, a total of 85 trials to S^+ and 75 trials to S^-). On the two days prior to the terminal acquisition day all subjects were exposed, in counterbalanced order, to the stimulus arrays to be encountered in extinction which were, namely, 15 trials to S^+ in succession or 15 trials to S^+ with each S^+ preceded by S^-. On these days a 1-min ITI was maintained between successive trials to S^+. In extinction half of each group was assigned to the Induction condition and half the Control condition. On each of the two days of extinction animals in the Induction condition received 30 trials, with S^{+-} alternated with S^{--}, and those in the control condition received but the 15 S^{+-} trials.

Figure 6 depicts mean start speeds to S^{+-} for each of the four groups on each extinction trial (the start and total measures were most sensitive to the induction manipulation and yielded identical effects; run and goal speeds yielded similar but smaller differences). It is evident that the extinction conditions had the opposite effects on animals given but

50 trials compared to those given 160 trials; for Groups 160 the Induction subgroup had the greater resistance to extinction whereas for Groups 50 the Control subgroup had the greater resistance to extinction. Analyses of variance provided a significant interaction between extinction condition and number of acquisition trials (p < ·005), and, subsequently, confirmed the graphic indication that at 160 trials Induction was higher than Control (p < ·001) whereas at 50 trials the reverse obtained (p < ·02).

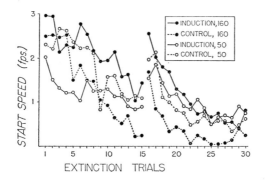

FIG. 6. Mean start speeds to the former S^+ in extinction for the induction groups and the control groups having had previously 50 or 160 acquisition trials (from Krane and Ison, 1970a).

Thus, if animals received overtraining then extinction PI was obtained, whereas if extinction followed immediately after the attainment of discrimination performance then S^{--} had an inhibitory after effect on the subsequent S^{--}. It is important to note that this interaction obtained in the absence of any apparent differences in the "negativity" of S^{--}. On both extinction days the two induction groups responded more rapidly to S^{+-} than to S^{--}, and their speeds to S^{--} were not different. These data, showing that overtraining on the original discrimination was necessary in order for extinction PI, establish a second significant difference between this sort of induction and the Pavlovian demonstrations of induction for these Pavlovian phenomena were found only in the absence of overtraining. The observation that in the Control condition overtraining reduced the resistance to extinction of the approach to S^{+-} corroborates the earlier data of Birch et al. (1960) and of Wieland (reported in Birch, 1961). There is a provocative similarity between the results of Expts II and III; in both cases the imposed variable, massed trials in Expt II and overtraining in Expt III, had its deleterious effect on the behaviour of the groups on the Control condition and the effect was absent or reversed in the behaviour of groups receiving the Induction condition. This consequence

o

of the interpolated negative stimulus is seen again in the following experiment.

V. Experiment IV: Avoidance Responses and Goal-box Confinement Time

In Expt III it was noted that extinction PI appeared to be accompanied by a sharp reduction in the number of avoidance responses made in extinction. However no systematic count of these was available and the major purpose of the present experiment was to examine avoidance behaviours in extinction. Two replications were run which differed in the duration of confinement in the empty goal box on nonreinforced trials, providing, thereby, another manipulation of the aversiveness of extinction conditions.

The apparatus and general procedures were the same as those in the prior experiment. All animals $(N = 24)$ received a total of 95 massed acquisition trials (55 to S^+ and 40 to S^-), with five trials to each stimulus on Day 1, ten trials to each on Day 2, then, on Days 3 and 4, 15 consecutive trials to S^+ alone (Control condition) and 15 trials to S^+ alternated with 15 to S^- (Induction condition), and on Day 5, a return to 10 S^+ and 10 S^- trials in quasi-random order. Massed extinction trials with a 1-min ITI between successive trials to S^{+-} followed on Days 6 and 7, at a rate of 15 trials to S^{+-} per day. In extinction half of the subjects were assigned to the usual S^{+-} Control condition and half to the usual alternated S^{+-} and S^{--} Induction condition. The experimental conditions of Replications 1 and 2 differed only in that the first set had a goal detention time of 15 sec in S^- or S^{+-} and the second set a detention time of two or three sec. The reinforcement in S^+ was ten 45 mg food pellets. In addition to the four speed measures of the prior experiment a record was kept of the frequency of avoidance responses and their locus in the runway during extinction. An avoidance response was defined as a turn of 180 deg from the goal after the start door was opened and before the final photocell had been broken.

Figure 7 depicts the mean of median speeds in blocks of three trials for each of the four speed measures, and Fig. 8 the mean number of avoidance responses per trial. The outcome of Replication 1 is on the left of each figure, that of Replication 2 on the right. In general in Replication 1 the induction group responded with higher speeds in extinction than did the control group, a difference that seemed most pronounced on the start measure and least pronounced on the goal measure; these differences were significant on start and total measures but not on run and goal measures. In Replication 2 the effects appear to be reduced and there was a reversal of the relative standing of the groups on run and goal measures; however in Replication 2 none of the speed differences reached traditional levels of significance although on start and run measures the differences came close

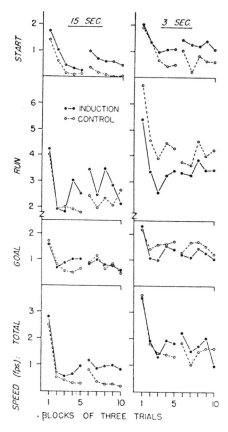

Fig. 7. Median speeds to the former S⁺ in extinction for the induction groups and the control groups, the 15-sec detention groups at left, the 3-sec detention groups at right (from Krane and Ison, 1970b).

to these values (for start, p = ·066 and for run the difference in the opposite direction had p = ·094). The data on the number of avoidance responses in extinction gave more appreciable differences in favour of the induction groups. In Replication 1 there was no overlap between the frequency distributions of the two groups (U = 0, p < ·001), and the distributions in Replication 2 were reliably disparate (U = 5·5, p < ·03). It is interesting that in both replications avoidance reactions tended to occur in the initial portions of the runway. In Replication 1 of the 162 avoidance reactions to S^{+-} in induction and control groups combined 119 occurred in the first half of the runway and 79 occurred before the animal had entered 6 in into the runway. Of the 59 avoidance responses observed in Replication 2 the comparable numbers were 38 and 21.

Direct comparisons of the two replications must be made with some

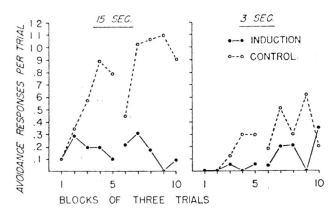

Fig. 8. Mean number of avoidance responses per trial to the former S^+ in extinction for the induction groups and control groups, the 15-sec detention groups at left, the 3-sec detention groups at right (from Krane and Ison, 1970b).

caution as the animals were run at different times. However some of the differences were very large and striking. In speeds there was very little overlap between the extinction scores with the animals in the short goal box detention time conditions running much faster. In avoidance responses there was no overlap between the two control groups, and the animals with the 3-sec goal box detention made fewer avoidance reactions than those with the 15-sec goal box detention (a mean of 21·8 vs. a mean of 7·5); in the two induction groups the difference was much smaller (5·5 vs. 2·7), and there was considerable overlap between the two distributions (U = 10, p = ·12). These data on avoidance reactions suggest, again, that the deleterious effect of a condition which increases the aversiveness of non-reinforcement, goal box detention time in this experiment, has a reduced effect in induction groups compared with its effect in control groups.

The similarities between the outcomes of the two replications are several. In both the facilitatory effects of the interposed S^{--} were most pronounced in the initial section of the runway and the induction procedure had an appreciable effect on reducing the number of avoidance responses which occurred in extinction. Both outcomes agreed in placing the primary locus of avoidance responses in the first sections of the runway, with about 50% occurring immediately on the presentation of the nonreinforced stimulus. It may be that the major effect of the induction procedure is to reduce the occurrence of avoidance reactions to S^{+-} and, because these avoidance reactions are otherwise most likely to occur at the presentation of S^{+-}, then extinction PI is most pronounced in speed measures collected at the beginning of the runway.

VI. Discussion

The several empirical outcomes of these experiments may be briefly summarized. First, extinction PI occurs with massed but not spaced extinction trials (Expt I). Second, the focus of massing must be on successive trials to the former positive stimulus; with only massed trials from the negative to the former positive stimulus and spaced trials between successive former positive stimuli, then an inhibitory after effect rather than induction occurs (Expt II). Third, extinction PI depends on overtraining on the initial discrimination, and if overtraining is not given then the interposed negative stimulus produces an inhibitory after-effect rather than extinction PI (Expt III). Fourth, extinction PI is greater with a long detention time on nonreinforced trials, and fifth, a major effect of the interposed negative stimuli is to reduce the number of avoidance responses to the former positive stimulus (Expt IV).

These outcomes make it unlikely that extinction PI in differential instrumental conditioning is the same phenomenon as PI in differential Pavlovian conditioning, although there are some superficial similarities between them. Thus, Pavlovian positive induction is indexed by a greater response strength to the positive stimulus if it is preceded by a negative stimulus; it is dependent on short inter-trial intervals; and with larger inter-trial intervals it is replaced by an inhibitory after-effect. But instrumental extinction PI should more properly be regarded as demonstrating that the interposed negative stimulus prevents a response decrement on the positive stimulus caused, in the control group, by the prior nonreinforcement of that stimulus. The negative stimulus has a disinhibitory effect rather than, as seems reasonable in Pavlovian conditioning, a direct excitatory effect. Extinction PI appears in those conditions which accentuate the suppressive outcome of nonreinforcement: massed extinction trials, overtraining, and long nonreinforcement detention times. It seems proper to conclude that extinction PI depends on the absence of decremental processes occurring in the control group rather than in processes directly and positively occurring in the experimental group. The short inter-trial intervals that are important in extinction PI are those between successive presentations of the former positive stimulus in the control group, and not, as in Pavlovian induction, those between the negative stimulus and the positive stimulus. The long inter-trial intervals which produce an inhibitory after-effect are again between successive presentations of the former positive stimulus and not, as in Pavlovian induction, those between the negative stimulus and the positive stimulus. And finally, overtraining is necessary for the demonstration of extinction PI but eliminates Pavlovian PI. These considerations force the conclusion that the phenomena are basically different and must be accounted for by different sorts of theoretical processes.

A word must be said about the relationship between these findings and the demonstrations of contrast in operant conditioning. There are a number of correspondences between Pavlovian induction and certain forms of operant contrast that suggest that these two phenomena may be manifestations of a single set of theoretical processes. In particular Terrace (1966) has shown that contrast declines with overtraining and Reynolds and Catania (1961) have shown that contrast is a function of the temporal transition from the negative to the positive discriminanda. Other writers have argued that positive contrast is a direct excitatory effect stemming from the emotional drive-enhancing properties of nonreinforcement (e.g. Scull *et al.*, 1970). Again these shared empirical characteristics which imply that Pavlovian and operant phenomena are the same, argue that instrumental extinction PI and the operant phenomenon are different. But there are perhaps other forms of operant contrast. For example, Staddon (1967) has investigated a contrast effect that results from the omission of reinforcement on multiple or tandem FIFI schedules, Wilton and Gay (1969) demonstrated a contrast-like effect that occurs to a stimulus that regularly precedes a stimulus that is associated with extinction, Nevin and Shettleworth (1966) have observed a labile but permanent contrast effect and so on. Although all of these phenomena seem alike in demonstrating a facilitatory effect on nonreinforcement and/or a depressive effect of reinforcement, the tenor of the present set of experiments suggest that this resemblance may be entirely superficial for the phenomena may be determined by quite different variables.

Given that the various phenomena are not reflecting some common unitary "induction process", a conclusion that, *prima facie*, demonstrations of contrast invalidate the traditional assumptions that discriminative performance results from a fairly simple concatenation of conditioning and extinction processes is clearly premature. If there is no single explanation that covers all instances of induction there should be no single theoretical argument that depends for its vigour on the "ubiquity" of induction phenomena. It may be that some instances of induction devolve very simply from a conditioning-extinction analysis as Skinner (1938) hinted, and Staddon (1967) demonstrated. Other explanations may take different forms, relying perhaps on emotional consequences of nonreinforcement to supplement the basic conditioning-extinction account (e.g. Scull *et al.*, 1970; Terrace, Chapter 4). Although some forms of induction may remain intractable from the standpoint of the conditioning-extinction model such a strong conclusion does not now appear to be appropriate, nor will it be appropriate until the various phenomena and their antecedents are catalogued much better than they are at present.

The explanatory approach to extinction PI depends on the interpretation to be made of the relative difference in response strength between the control group and the induction group: should this difference be seen as due to a positive facilitatory process present in the induction group whereby its performance is enhanced, or conversely, as due to a negative inhibitory process present only in the control group whereby its performance is lowered? As previously described, the several outcomes of our research seem more appropriate to the second of these possibilities. It certainly does not seem at all reasonable to attribute the extinction effect to an emotionally-based motivational enhancement of the reaction to S^{+-} by prior nonreinforcement of the response to S^{--}. If this were the case then there would be no reason to expect any difference in extinction PI resulting from differences in the trial distributions of successive exposure to S^{+-}, as was found in Expt II. Nor would it be anticipated that extinction PI depends on prior overtraining as was found in Expt III, for direct assessment of emotional reactions to nonreinforcement in the presence of the negative stimulus reveals that they are present around the stage of initial learning and then disappear with overtraining (Amsel and Ward, 1965). In fact the behaviour of the groups trained for a small number of trials in Expt IV suggest that emotional reactions to nonreinforcement on S^{--} were present in those groups and were responsible for the poorer performance of the small trials induction group compared to its control group. It seems likely, then, that extinction PI in differential conditioning should be regarded as an effect that appears only when the emotional reaction to nonreinforcement on S^- has been minimized, rather than as an effect that depends on the integrity of such reactions. So we assume then, in the hypotheses which follow, that extinction PI results because of a depressing effect on control group performance which is reduced by the occurrence of the interposed formerly negative stimulus.

The least complicated explanation is that the control group suffers a greater stimulus generalization decrement on going into extinction than does the induction group. Thus, it could be argued, in the acquisition of differential conditioning the animal encounters an intermixed series of trials consisting of exposures to both stimuli. This intermixing continues into extinction for the induction group but not for the control group and, therefore, the control group may be expected to undergo a greater stimulus change and a greater stimulus generalization decrement. This explanation was suggested by Leonard *et al*. (1968) in their study of positive and negative induction in differential conditioning. But in our experiments we were careful to expose the animals to the variety of stimulus conditions during acquisition which could be subsequently encountered in extinction, so it is difficult to argue that the control procedure of presenting an unbroken series of trials to the formerly positive stimulus imposed on unfamiliar stimulus sequence. Nor is it clear how the stimulus change account could be brought to bear on the various interactions observed, for the interposed S^{--} enhances response speeds to S^{+-} in some conditions, but reduces speeds to S^{+-} in other conditions. For these reasons this simple account of extinction PI is rejected as unprofitable and attention turned to more complicated analyses of the behaviour of the various control groups.

The outcomes of the last three experiments show that extinction PI is most likely to occur in experimental conditions which severely depress control group performance. In Expt II it was found that massing extinction trials reduced control speeds; in Expt III that overtraining on the initial discrimination reduced control group speeds, and in Expt IV that long confinement times in the empty goal box reduced control group speeds: in the several induction groups these relationships were reduced in size or actually reversed in sign. The decrements obtained in the control groups seem readily understood as the conditions under which they occur are all those which increase the aversiveness of nonreinforcement and the accumulation of the effects of that aversiveness across trials. It need only be assumed that: first, the emotional consequences of nonreinforcement are enhanced by overtraining and by increased confinement time; second, these consequences accumulate from trial to trial, if the trials are close together in time; and third, that the behavioural effect of the emotional consequences is to elicit avoidance tendencies which interfere with instrumental approach behaviours.

In the account of the extinction PI effect we may suppose that the occurrence of the old negative stimulus between successive presentations of the former positive stimulus might either decrease the emotional consequence of nonreinforcement or prevent its accumulation from one trial to the next. It is conceivable that the effect of the interpolated negative stimulus could reduce the effectiveness of nonreinforcement through a process described by Wagner and Rescorla (Chapter 12, this volume). It may be assumed that the inhibitory effect of nonreinforcement is a positive function of the excitatory processes prevailing at that time, and that these processes are determined by the presented stimulus plus the traces of stimuli that have been presented just recently. In the case of control groups given massed trials to the former positive stimulus both the presented stimulus and the traces of prior stimuli would all be associated with excitation, and their excitatory sum would be then relatively large. In the case of induction groups, contrarily, the stimulus compound present at the time of nonreinforcement would consist of the (excitatory) positive stimulus and the trace of the (inhibitory) negative stimulus. Thus, as the resulting sum of excitation would be relatively smaller, so would the inhibitory effect of nonreinforcement be reduced in the induction group.

A second suggestion is that the interpolated negative stimulus prevents the accumulation of the emotional consequences of nonreinforcement across successive trials to the formerly positive stimulus, and, in effect, turns a massed sequence of trials into a functionally spaced sequence. The necessity for extinction PI of giving massed trials to S^{+-} is explained because if the trials were spaced then the emotional consequences of nonreinforcement would have dissipated in the control group, and the interposition of S^{--} could have no further facilitative effect.

Indeed we may suppose that although the interposition of S^{--} can disrupt the accumulation of emotionality across successive trials to S^{+-}, the occurrence of nonreinforcement of S^{--} may itself have emotional consequences and in the absence of overtraining (Expt III), or in the absence of accumulated emotionality in spaced trial control groups (Expt II), this depressing effect may outweigh any facilitatory effect of the interposed S^{--}. Thus under conditions where accumulated emotional reactions are minimal—with spaced trials, small numbers of training trials, short detention periods, and, certainly, during the acquisition and maintenance of discrimination learning—then the facilitatory effect can only be minimal and the inhibitory effect of nonreinforcement prevails.

In thinking about how a negative stimulus might come to prevent the accumulation of the emotional consequences of nonreinforcement across trials to the formerly positive stimulus, it seems important that the subject has had considerable experience with nonreinforcement on that stimulus. We may suppose that as a result of this experience the animal learns reactions which effectively reduce the emotional consequences of nonreinforcement, reactions which are associated with the negative stimulus during acquisition. But, if these reactions are also elicited by the negative stimulus during extinction then their effects of reducing the emotional consequences of nonreinforcement must prevent the accumulation of emotional effects across trials. As was shown in Expt II, the presentation of S^{--} between two massed trials to S^{+-} would have the functional effect achieved otherwise by the imposition of long-time intervals between successive occurrences of S^{+-}.

In the context of differential instrumental conditioning these "defensive" reactions learned to the negative stimulus are entirely hypothetical, and are put forward here only because if there were reactions having such characteristics then our various findings about extinction PI would appropriately follow. But in other discrimination situations such reactions are not hypothetical but observable; thus Dickinson (Chapter 18, this volume) showed that rats will learn an operant response which removes the negative stimulus and Terrace (Chapter 4) proposed a mechanism by which such responses may be learned, a mechanism which seems to be compatible with the way we suppose that these responses might produce extinction PI. With these techniques it should be possible to directly discover whether defensive reactions elicited by the negative stimulus play the role in producing induction that we at present can only hypothesize.

VII. Conclusions

In our work on extinction PI we have been concerned primarily with the problem of whether induction is a necessary and ubiquitous consequence of discrimination learning, and whether extinction PI is the same phenomenon as other forms of induction (and behavioural contrast). We conclude that extinction PI is a local restricted phenomenon which, in particular, does not occur given moderate trial spacings. From an empirical standpoint this is a useful finding for it means that most phenomena of complex discrimination reversal and transfer experiments are not confounded by induction processes, because these phenomena appear not to be dependent on the presence of very brief inter-trial intervals. The second problem was approached by asking whether the experimental conditions which are favourable for the appearance of extinction PI are the same as those involved in Pavlovian PI. The answer is that they are not. Extinction PI depends on having short temporal intervals between successive trials to the formerly reinforced discriminandum and additionally demands some prior overtraining of the discrimination. Contrarily, Pavlovian PI depends only on there being short intervals between the positive stimulus and the preceding negative stimulus and its magnitude declines with overtraining. We conclude, thus, that these two demonstrations of induction reflect the operation of different theoretical processes. From a theoretical standpoint one may then argue that the various diverse demonstrations of "induction" should not be used to argue in favour of a drastic overhaul of discrimination theory in which, say, induction (in the Pavlovian sense) replaces generalization (again in the Pavlovian sense) as a central theoretical commitment. Instead the theoretical problem is to account for the various examples of the reciprocal effects of reinforcement and nonreinforcement, and the various conditions under which they appear, in terms of a theory in which the Laws of Reinforcement and Generalization provide the basic explanatory machinery.

Our present approach to this is suggested by the demonstrations that extinction PI occurs under those conditions which accentuate the aversive properties of extinction. Under these conditions of massed extinction trials, prior overtraining, and long detention times, performance in the control group suffers a precipitous decline, and it seems most reasonable to argue that extinction PI is a process that prevents this decline rather than a process which directly increases the strength of the response to the formerly positive stimulus. It is here that the theoretical similarities and differences between extinction PI and behavioural contrast are most apparent. As Terrace points out in Chapter 4, the aversiveness of non-reinforcement is also involved in the production of behavioural contrast; but this is correlated with the negative stimulus during acquisition of the discriminated operant, and appears to result in a direct enhancement of the response to the positive stimulus. Behavioural contrast appears to be produced by a temporary emotional after-effect of nonreinforcement on the negative stimulus which motivates performance in the presence of the positive stimulus. Contrarily we suggest that extinction PI occurs after the attainment of a terminal stage of discrimination learning in which the animal has learned to respond to the negative stimulus in such a way as to minimize its emotional consequences. We propose this as the mechanism by which the interposed negative stimulus partially separates the effects of nonreinforcement on one trial to the positive stimulus from the reaction to that stimulus on its subsequent presentation.

Acknowledgements

The research reported here was supported by NSF Research Grant GB 14814 and USPH Training Grant, MH 10825, and preparation of the manuscript by an NIMH Special Research Fellowship to J.R.I., MH 47502.

References

Amsel, A. and Ward, J. S. (1965). Frustration and persistence: Resistance to discrimination following prior experience with the discriminanda. *Psychological Monographs*, **79** (4, whole No. 597).

Bernheim, J. W. and Williams, D. R. (1967). Time-dependent contrast effects in a multiple schedule of food reinforcement. *Journal of the Experimental Analysis of Behavior*, **10**, 243–249.

Birch, D. (1961). A motivational interpretation of extinction. M. R. Jones (Ed.), *Nebraska Symposium on Motivation*, Lincoln, Nebraska: University of Nebraska Press, pp. 179–197.

Birch, D., Ison, J. R. and Sperling, S. E. (1960). Reversal learning under single stimulus presentation. *Journal of Experimental Psychology*, **60**, 36–40.

Bower, G. H. (1961). A contrast effect in differential conditioning. *Journal of Experimental Psychology*, **62**, 196–199.

Ison, J. R. and Krane, R. V. (1969). Induction in differential instrumental conditioning. *Journal of Experimental Psychology*, **80**, 183–185.

Ison, J. R., Glass, D. H. and Daly, H. D. (1969). Reward magnitude changes following differential conditioning and partial reinforcement. *Journal of Experimental Psychology*, **81**, 81–88.

Krane, R. V. and Ison, J. R. (1970a). Positive induction in differential instrumental conditioning: Effect of extended acquisition training. *Journal of Comparative and Physiological Psychology*, **73**, 334–340.

Krane, R. V. and Ison, J. R. (1970b). Positive induction at different points of the performance chain. *Psychonomic Science*, **21**, 37–39.

Krane, R. V. and Ison, J. R. (1971). Positive induction in differential instrumental conditioning: Effect of the inter-stimulus interval. *Journal of Comparative and Physiological Psychology*, **75**, 129–135.

Leonard, D. W., Weimer, J. and Albin, R. (1968). An examination of Pavlovian induction phenomena in differential instrumental conditioning. *Psychonomic Science*, **12**, 89–90.

Ludvigson, H. W. and Gay, R. A. (1967). An investigation of conditions determining contrast effects in differential reward conditioning. *Journal of Experimental Psychology*, **75**, 37–42.

Nevin, J. A. and Shettleworth, S. J. (1966). An analysis of contrast effects in multiple schedules. *Journal of the Experimental Analysis of Behavior*, **9**, 305–315.

Pavlov, I. P. (1927). *Conditioned Reflexes*. London: Oxford University Press.

Reid, L. S. (1953). The development of noncontinuity behavior through continuity learning. *Journal of Experimental Psychology*, **46**, 107–112.

Reynolds, G. S. and Catania, A. C. (1961). Behavioral contrast with fixed interval and low rate reinforcement. *Journal of the Experimental Analysis of Behavior*, **4**, 387–391.

Scull, J., Davies, K. and Amsel, A. (1970). Behavioral contrast and frustration effect in multiple and mixed fixed-interval schedules in the rat. *Journal of Comparative and Physiological Psychology*, **71**, 478–483.

Senf, G. M. and Miller, N. E. (1967). Evidence for Pavlovian induction in discrimination learning. *Journal of Comparative and Physiological Psychology*, **64**, 121–127.

Skinner, B. F. (1938). *The Behavior of Organisms*. New York: Appleton-Century-Crofts.

Spence, K. W. (1936). The nature of discrimination learning in animals. *Psychological Review*, **43**, 427–449.

Staddon, J. E. R. (1967). Attention and temporal discrimination: factors controlling responding under a cyclic-interval schedule. *Journal of the Experimental Analysis of Behavior*, **10**, 349–359.

Terrace, H. S. (1966). Behavior contrast and the peak shift: Effects of extended discrimination training. *Journal of the Experimental Analysis of Behavior*, **9**, 613–617.

Wilton, R. N. and Gay, R. A. (1969). Behavioral contrast in one component of a multiple schedule as a function of the reinforcement conditions operating in the following component. *Journal of the Experimental Analysis of Behavior*, **12**, 239–246.

8 | Disinhibition of an Operant Response

Dalhousie University, Halifax, Nova Scotia, Canada

I. Introduction	. . . .	205
II. Inhibitory Operations	. . . .	209
III. Stimulus Parameters .	. . . .	212
A. Stimulus Intensity	. . . .	212
B. Stimulus Novelty .	. . . .	213
C. External Inhibition and Disinhibition	. . . .	216
IV. Response Inhibition and Disinhibition .	. . . . .	218
A. Study A	. . . .	220
B. Study B	. . . .	222
V. Concluding Remarks .	. . . .	224
Acknowledgements .	. . . .	225
References	. . . .	225

I. Introduction

The phenomenon of disinhibition is inextricably connected with the classical work on conditioned reflexes carried out by Ivan P. Pavlov (1927). Pavlov first observed the fact, coined the name of "disinhibition", and in his published works referred to the phenomenon repeatedly. Disinhibition was one of the cornerstones on which Pavlov erected his neurophysiological theory of behaviour. According to Pavlov, disinhibition was not a rare, artificially-contrived laboratory phenomenon "but a striking reality of which we are freshly convinced every day" (Pavlov, 1928, p. 150).

At this time, we wish to give only a brief description of Pavlov's work. Additional references to Pavlov's findings will be found in later sections of the paper which deal with specific topics we have investigated in our own laboratory.

In the typical Pavlovian example of disinhibition a conditioned response (CR) is first elaborated and then extinguished until the subject no longer responds. At this stage if the conditioned stimulus (CS) is presented accompanied by an "extra stimulus", the CR again manifests itself. The extra stimulus is the disinhibitor—the reappearance of the CR is the phenomenon of disinhibition. From the examples given by Pavlov, a number of facts emerge. First, it is clear that a variety of different types of stimuli can act as disinhibitors to restore at least partially an extinguished conditioned response. Thus Pavlov at one time suggested that "Every unusual stimulus from the external world may be . . . a disinhibiting agent" (Pavlov, 1928, p. 149). Second, the restorative effect is typically of a temporary nature. In an example cited by Pavlov (1927, p. 84), the odour of camphor lost its disinhibitory effect after one application. Third, the extra stimulus need not still be present at the time of testing. Although Pavlov points out that the after effects of stimulation involved in disinhibition "can last from some seconds to some days" (Pavlov, 1928, p. 231), it would appear that in most cases the after effect is in the order of minutes. Perhaps the most intriguing fact about disinhibitory stimuli is that when these extra stimuli are presented in conjunction with the CS for an unextinguished or intact CR they have an inhibiting effect. This apparent paradox—that the same stimulus, which impedes an intact CR, facilitates an extinguished CR—was resolved by Pavlov as follows:

> . . . if you, having to do with an inhibitory process in the nervous system, join to this inhibited stimulus some new extra agent, the inhibited stimulus now manifests its own effect. This fact may be understood thus: the new extra agent inhibits the inhibition and as a result there is a freeing of the previously inhibited action, i.e. a positive effect. . . . This is the phenomenon of inhibition of inhibition. (Pavlov, 1928, p. 109.)

Thus, the extra stimulus in some basic sense always inhibits. When it inhibits inhibition, the phenomenon of disinhibition is observed.

From this interpretation, it is clear that inhibition is a basic concept in Pavlovian theory. According to Pavlov, experimental extinction depends on the accumulation of "internal inhibition". During extinction the CR is not destroyed or exhausted but is counteracted by the build up of an inhibitory process. For Pavlov the idea of an active process of inhibition was supported by three facts. First, a discriminative stimulus which had been extinguished ("conditioned inhibitor") was capable of suppressing any CR with which it had not previously been associated. Second, there was "spontaneous recovery" of an extinguished CR, which occurred simply as a function of the passage of time. Third, and most important, was the demonstration of disinhibition, where an extinguished CR was temporarily restored through the action of an extraneous stimulus. Thus fundamental to Pavlovian theory was the postulation of not one, but two active processes—excitation and inhibition.

While Pavlov frequently demonstrated the occurrence of disinhibition, he did not do any rigorous experimental work on the parameters which control the effect. Instead the disinhibition concept was rapidly incorporated into Pavlovian neurophysiological theory and used to explain other phenomena rather than serving as a focus of investigation in its own right. Similarly, while a number of North American investigators have published reports demonstrating a disinhibition effect (e.g. Gagné, 1941; Horns and Heron, 1940; Hunter, 1935; Razran, 1939; Switzer, 1933; Wenger, 1936; Winnick and Hunt, 1951; Yamaguchi and Ladioray, 1962), the phenomenon has appeared fragile and resistant to parametric investigation. This could be due to the nature of the testing situations that have been employed. In classical conditioning there is the possibility that the CS and the disinhibiting stimulus may interact so as to obscure the effects of the extra stimulus. Most of the early American studies that attempted to investigate the disinhibition phenomenon used the GSR as the response (e.g. Switzer, 1933; Wenger, 1936; Hovland, 1937). The problem that this involves is that almost any "extraneous" stimulus will, in and of itself, produce a GSR. With a discrete trial instrumental response (e.g. Gagné, 1941; Winnick and Hunt, 1951; Yamaguchi and Ladioray, 1962) such as is employed in runway studies, the handling of the subject between trials, and the distraction of the experimenter's presence during trials, does not augur well for a sensitive test of the effects of extraneous stimuli. On the other hand, the operant leverpressing procedure appears to be ideal in this respect, for the subject may be tested in a rigorously controlled and isolated environment. Although Skinner (1936), in an early investigation employing this type of operant response, reported a "failure to obtain disinhibition",* recent research (Brimer and Kamin, 1963; Flanagan and Webb, 1964; Singh and Wickens, 1968; Brimer, 1970a, b; Brimer and Wickson, 1971) has clearly demonstrated that disinhibition may be readily studied in the leverpress situation.

Disinhibition may be defined as the temporary reappearance of a suppressed or inhibited conditioned response due to the presentation of an extraneous stimulus. Thus, there are the obvious variables involved, namely, the extraneous (or disinhibiting) stimulus and the inhibition (or suppression) of the conditioned response. With the leverpress operant serving as the conditioned response we have adopted a standardized

*It is possible to object to Skinner's failure to show disinhibition both on the grounds that the majority of the tests involved inappropriate stimuli (e.g. pricking the tail of the subject or tossing the subject into the air), and that no criterion for extinction was adopted. However, an increase in response rate occurred in some animals when a light stimulus was used. Skinner interpreted these increases as due to facilitation of an otherwise "accidentally" depressed extinction curve. But such an interpretation is irrefutable because if there is a temporary increase in response rate, then for Skinner the extinction curve preceding this increase will always appear to be depressed. In any event, when Horns and Heron (1940) subsequently replicated Skinner's attempt, but employed a more rigorous extinction criterion and more appropriate disinhibiting stimuli, the results clearly indicated the occurrence of disinhibition.

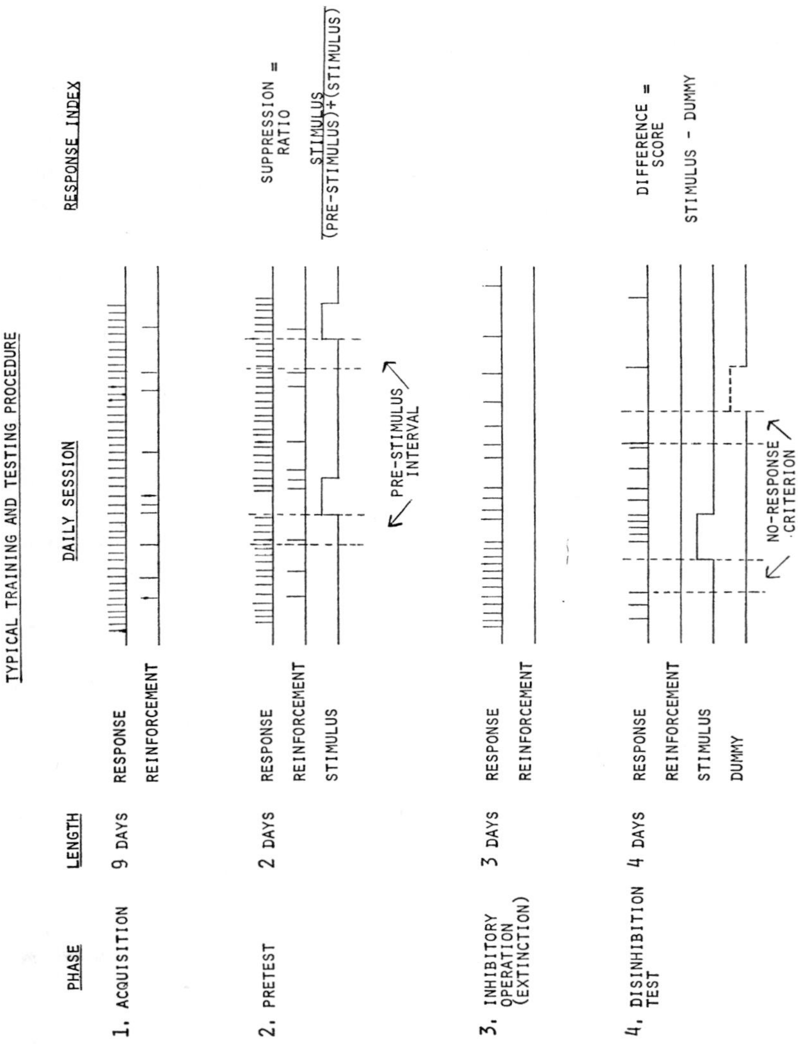

Fig. 1. Outline of typical training and testing procedure.

procedure to investigate these two variables. An outline of the procedure is presented in Fig. 1.

(1) Initially the male hooded rats are reduced to 75% of *ad lib*. weight and trained to leverpress for food in the Skinner box. Subjects are then given a series of 1-hr daily training sessions with a VI 2·5 min reinforcement schedule. Typically, acquisition training is continued for eight daily sessions.

(2) On each of the last two days of acquisition training the stimulus, which is later to serve as the disinhibitor, is presented twice during each session as a pretest. The effect of the stimulus is assessed by means of a suppression ratio the same as that employed by Kamin (1965). With such a ratio, a value of ·50 indicates no effect of the stimulus on response rate, while diminishing values indicate progressively greater response suppression with a lower limit of ·00 signifying complete suppression.

(3) Following acquisition training, some type of inhibitory operation, most frequently extinction, is introduced in order to suppress responding. In this context "inhibitory" is empirically defined as any operation that produces an observable decrement in responding. Typically there are three days of inhibition training prior to testing.

(4) During test sessions the inhibitory operation remains in effect but one stimulus and one dummy presentation is programmed to occur on each test day. The order of presentation is counter-balanced both between subjects in each experimental group and from day to day within each subject. In order to assure that the baseline response rate is at a comparably low level during the test, both the stimulus and dummy presentations are contingent on a 3-min no-response criterion. A test then consists of presenting the extraneous stimulus for three minutes immediately following the 3-min no-response criterion. The index of disinhibition is provided by the difference in responding during the stimulus and dummy intervals which occurred on the same test day. Normally testing is carried out for four days.

Employing this general procedure, we observe that during acquisition the stimulus suppresses responding on initial presentation but this inhibitory effect quickly washes out so that reliable suppression is never in evidence, at least with auditory stimuli, after the second pretest trial. On the other hand, the same stimulus presented during the test phase facilitates responding, i.e. produces a disinhibition effect. To the degree that a low baseline response rate can be maintained throughout the test phase, the disinhibition effect is found to persist over repeated test trials.

II. Inhibitory Operations

We can summarize the results of a large number of studies by stating that the disinhibition effect appears to be a highly general phenomenon. In one study (Brimer, 1970a) a $2 \times 2 \times 2$ factorial design was employed to investigate different inhibitory operations, stimulus modalities, and stimulus durations by means of the standard training and testing procedure outlined earlier. The inhibitory operation was either experimental extinction of the leverpressing response, or food satiation. The extraneous stimulus was either 80 db white noise or house illumination of approximately 22 cdm². The stimulus duration was either $1\frac{1}{2}$ sec or 3 min, although

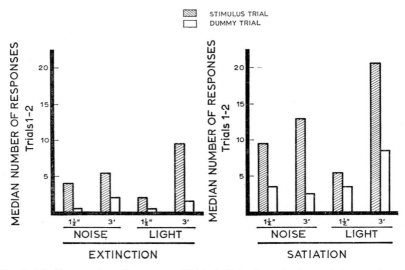

FIG. 2. Median number of responses (Trials 1–2) during stimulus and dummy intervals for the eight experimental conditions.

the test measure always consisted of the number of responses in the 3-min interval following stimulus onset. The results of the disinhibition test are summarized in Fig. 2, which presents the median number of responses for each type of presentation for the eight experimental conditions. It is obvious that disinhibition occurred, as demonstrated by the consistent tendency for more responses to occur during the stimulus, than during the dummy interval. For present purposes the important point is that the response rate was higher during the stimulus than during the dummy interval for a significantly greater than chance proportion of the subjects in both the extinction (26/32) and satiation conditions (24/32).

Following the completion of the above experiment, further studies have been carried out employing different stimuli and inhibitory operations. In one of these experiments leverpressing was inhibited by punishing each response with a brief electric shock. The basic procedure was the same as that previously outlined, except that there were no inhibition training days separate from the testing days. The punishment contingency suppressed leverpressing so rapidly that each subject could receive both stimulus and dummy presentations on the first day of punishment. The test results are presented in the left panel of Fig. 3. All eight animals had a higher response

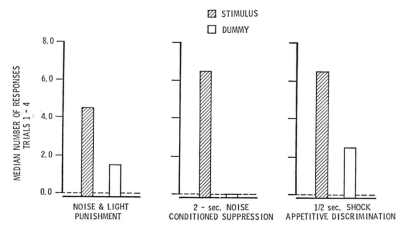

FIG. 3. Median number of responses (Trials 1–4) during stimulus and dummy intervals for the three different experimental conditions. The nature of the extraneous stimulus and the type of inhibitory operation are identified at the base of each panel. The punishment procedure employed the standard 3-min interval for each stimulus and dummy presentation. However, the test intervals lasted only 2 min in the conditioned suppression procedure and were of 1-min duration in the discrimination condition.

rate during the stimulus (simultaneous presentation of noise and light) than during the dummy interval.

In another experiment (Brimer and Wickson, 1971), subjects were tested for disinhibition when responding was inhibited by a standard conditioned suppression procedure. The CS was an overhead light of 3-min duration, the US was a $\frac{1}{2}$-sec 1·0 mA shock delivered at the termination of the CS. Following three initial conditioned suppression (inhibition) training days, disinhibition testing was introduced. On disinhibition trials, a 2-sec 70 db noise was presented repeatedly during the final two minutes of the CS interval. As before, stimulus and dummy presentations were alternated between and within subjects. The results for the four test trials appear in the middle panel of Fig. 3. The rate of responding was significantly higher during the stimulus than during the dummy period.

Finally, we have investigated the effect of introducing brief electric shocks during the S⁻ interval of an appetitive discrimination task (Brimer and Wickson, 1971). Disinhibition testing was carried out in the same way as before except that test trials of 1 min duration were employed. In order to receive a trial the subject had to meet a 60-sec no-response criterion within the first two minutes of an S⁻ interval. As before, there was one stimulus and one dummy presentation on each test day. The results for the disinhibition test are presented on the right-hand panel of Fig. 3. Once again, we observe that animals respond at a significantly higher rate during the stimulus than during the dummy interval.

In summary, it has been shown that disinhibition occurs with six different inhibitory operations: unsignalled shock,* extinction, food satiation, punishment, conditioned suppression and discrimination training. As described later in this chapter, we have also observed disinhibition with DRL training as has been reported recently by Contrucci *et al.* (1971). Finally, we might note that a number of other investigators have found a disinhibition effect during the early segment of a fixed interval reinforcement schedule (Flanagan and Webb, 1964; Hinrichs, 1968; Singh and Wickens, 1968).† Thus the obvious conclusion to be drawn from all of these experiments is, simply, that disinhibition will occur under a wide variety of inhibitory operations.

III. Stimulus Parameters

From the description of the preceding experiments, it is clear that disinhibition will also occur with stimuli of different modalities (light, noise, or shock) and different durations ($1\frac{1}{2}$ sec; 1, 2, and 3 min). Furthermore, continuous or intermittent presentation of the stimulus or stimulus after effects are sufficient to produce the disinhibition effect. Thus, like Pavlov, we find that a variety of stimuli may serve as effective disinhibitors. Three specific stimulus parameters that have been investigated are described below.

A. STIMULUS INTENSITY

In reference to the intensity of stimuli which can act as effective disinhibitors, Pavlov has suggested that "dis-inhibition is manifest only under certain conditions, viz.: if the disinhibiting agent is of average strength (not very strong and not too weak)" (Pavlov, 1928, p. 211). Thus it seems clear that Pavlov suggests that the function relating the intensity of the extra

---

*The evidence for a disinhibition effect when the response rate has been suppressed by unsignalled electric shock is reported in Brimer and Kamin (1963).

†Unlike the three studies cited above, Wolach and Ferraro (1969) have reported a failure to obtain any response facilitation during the early segment of a fixed interval cycle. Although the possible reasons for this failure are unclear at the present time it may be due in part to the relatively short stimulus durations that Wolach and Ferraro employed.

stimulus to the magnitude of the disinhibition effect is an inverted U shape. This corresponds with Pavlov's views on the effects of conditioned stimulus intensity since he believed that "too strong" a CS produced the "paradoxical" effect of poorer conditioning (Pavlov, 1927, pp. 271–272).

In our study of stimulus intensity, there were four independent experimental groups (13 subjects per group) tested with noise stimuli of 45, 65, 80, and 100 db. The training and testing procedure was identical to that outlined earlier. The inhibitory operation was experimental extinction.

The median suppression ratios for the four noise groups on the first pretest trial were: ·44, ·45, ·43, and ·33 for the 45, 65, 80, and 100 db intensity conditions respectively. Although there appears to be a tendency for the 100 db noise to produce the most suppression, due to the considerable variability that existed within each of the four groups, no significant differences were found between the different intensities for either Trial 1 or Trials 1 to 4. Considering the four groups collectively, a significantly above chance proportion of the subjects (41/52) had ratios below ·50 on the first pretest trial but this was no longer true by the second trial.

Over disinhibition trials 1 to 4 a significantly greater than chance proportion of the subjects (44·5/52) responded more during the stimulus than during the dummy intervals. The median difference scores for the first disinhibition test trial were 1·0, 2·0, 1·0 and 4·0 for the groups ordered in terms of increasing noise intensity. Again, although the data may suggest some slight tendency for difference scores to increase with stimulus intensity, the differences among groups are not significant for either trial 1 or trials 1 to 4.

Thus it appears that both inhibition and disinhibition are relatively insensitive to noise intensity. These results are in marked contrast to the CER situation which is very sensitive to far smaller variations in CS (noise) intensity (Kamin and Schaub, 1963; Kamin and Brimer, 1963). Such a discrepancy between the effects of stimulus intensity on conditioning and on disinhibition is in opposition to Pavlovian theory and encourages speculation that the stimulus plays very different roles in the two phenomena. Finally, there is no indication in the data of an inverted U-shaped function relating stimulus intensity to disinhibition, as Pavlov had suggested.

B. STIMULUS NOVELTY

In the course of investigating different stimulus conditions we have conducted four experiments (employing a total of 128 animals) under the standardized procedure in which subjects receive three days of extinction training prior to four days of disinhibition testing.

Figure 4 presents the mean response rates for the stimulus and dummy intervals for the four test trials. As the figure indicates, there is a progressive decline in the response rates so that the level of responding during both the stimulus and dummy intervals is significantly lower on Trial 4 than Trial 1.* Thus the disinhibition effect—measured by the

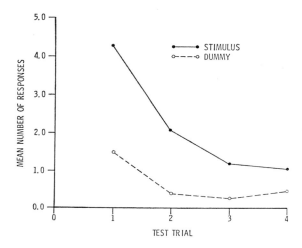

FIG. 4. Mean number of responses during stimulus and dummy intervals for subjects tested under extinction, as a function of test trial.

difference between stimulus and dummy response rates—diminishes with repeated trials. The question that this raises is whether this diminution is to be attributed to increasing familiarity with the stimulus, or to the progressive weakening of the basic tendency to perform the leverpressing response. In order to investigate this question, different independent groups of rats were differentially exposed to the light or noise stimulus during the pretest phase of acquisition training prior to the introduction of extinction and disinhibition testing (Brimer, 1970b). The results of this experiment revealed that varying the number of pretest trials did not differentially affect the magnitude of disinhibition. This, in turn, suggests that the lessening amount of disinhibition observed with repeated test trials is attributable to the progressive weakening of the basic tendency to leverpress.

It is possible to argue that the failure to find any effect of stimulus familiarity in this last experiment was due to a lack of transfer between acquisition and extinction conditions or to the fact that the pre-exposure

*Although the present comparison is based on pooled data, similar decreases in stimulus and dummy responding were obtained in each of the four separate experiments. Within each experiment the stimulus and dummy decrements were statistically reliable.

occurred several days prior to the test. In order to overcome these objections it would be necessary to carry out repeated disinhibition tests while the base-line (dummy) response rate remained relatively stable. In order to accomplish this, subjects were trained and tested for disinhibition under a differential reinforcement of low rate (DRL) schedule. The ten subjects were first given 40 magazine training trials followed by 80 CRF trials. On the following day all animals were introduced to the DRL schedule which required a minimum inter-response interval of 120 seconds. This schedule remained in effect throughout the subsequent eight 1-hr daily training sessions and ten disinhibition test days.* On each test day the extraneous stimulus, a 3-min light of approximately 22 cdm² intensity, was presented once to each subject at one of two fixed times, either 26 or 51 min after the start of the session. At the alternate test time there was a dummy presentation. Fig. 5 presents the results of the disinhibition test in blocks of two

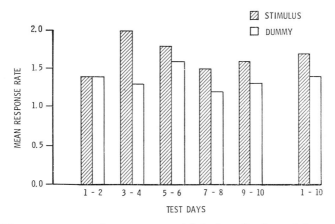

FIG. 5. Mean response rate (responses per min) during stimulus and dummy intervals as a function of blocks of two test days.

trials. As the figure indicates, there is no consistent tendency for the magnitude of the disinhibition effect to dissipate with repeated test trials. Subjects have significantly higher stimulus than dummy response rates over the ten test days.†

Viewed collectively, the results of the preceding two experiments present compelling evidence to suggest that stimulus familiarity is relatively

*By the start of disinhibition testing the response rates were significantly lower than they had been on the first day of DRL training. Thus, the low response rates displayed at the start of disinhibition testing may be said to reflect the outcome of an "inhibitory operation" as we have empirically defined this term.

†Actually, the two-tailed level of probability is between ·06 and ·05.

unimportant in the disinhibition phenomenon. This, as we note below, stands in sharp contrast to external inhibition.

C. EXTERNAL INHIBITION AND DISINHIBITION

Pavlov repeatedly points out that effective disinhibitors are "stimuli belonging to the group of mild external inhibitors" (Pavlov, 1927, p. 82). Elsewhere, Pavlov mentions that disinhibition may be produced by "any additional agent of average strength which provokes the orienting reaction (looking, listening, etc.) of the animal" (Pavlov, 1928, pp. 230–231). Like Pavlov, we have observed that the stimuli which disinhibit an extinguished response, inhibit the nonsuppressed response. Over the course of our investigations, we have run nine different groups of animals (varying in size from 8 to 13 subjects per group) all of which have received an identical training programme except for the type of extraneous stimulus that was employed. The different stimuli were the offset of 3-min noise or light, the onset of 3-min noise of different intensities, and $1\frac{1}{2}$-sec noise or light. At the end of the VI acquisition phase, the subjects received four pretest trials followed by three days of extinction training and four disinhibition test trials. To compare the relationship between inhibitory and disinhibitory effects a median suppression score was calculated for each group for the first pretest trial along with a disinhibition difference score for the first test trial. Fig. 6 plots the results. It is clear that the extraneous stimuli which, when presented during pretest inhibited responding, had just the opposite effect when they were presented during extinction. Therefore, the effects of the extraneous stimulus on leverpressing rate cannot be attributed to any direct property of the stimulus which simply interferes with, or facilitates, lever-pressing behaviour as Skinner (1936) at one time suggested.

In reference to the specific results depicted in Fig. 6, the different groups fall into three clusters. The onset and offset of light along with the 100 db noise tend to produce the greatest suppression on pretest and the most response facilitation during disinhibition testing. At the other end of the continuum the offset of noise and the $1\frac{1}{2}$-sec light tend to produce neither effect. The remaining groups fall between these two extremes. Although it might be possible to interpret the order of the groups in terms of a heterogeneous intensity dimension, the important point seems to be that there is a monotonic relationship between the inhibitory and disinhibitory capacity of the different stimuli.

The observation that an extraneous stimulus presented during reinforced training suppresses responding might be attributed to the fact that a novel or unexpected stimulus elicits "orienting" or "investigatory" reactions which are incompatible with the conditioned response. Such orienting reactions are known to extinguish rapidly, and this is consistent with the fact that with the noise stimulus significant interference has only been observed on initial stimulus presentation. On the other hand the same stimulus will facilitate responding when the response rate is suppressed and it is hardly possible to attribute this effect to incompatible orienting reactions. To what we might attribute this facilitating effect is simply unknown at the present time.

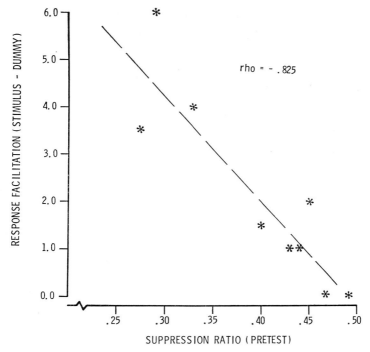

FIG. 6. Response facilitation on the first disinhibition test trial plotted against suppression ratio on the first pretest trial. Each point represents the median score on the two measures for an independent group of subjects.

Although there is an empirical relationship between the inhibiting and disinhibiting effects of different stimuli, this correspondence need not argue for any central similarity between the two phenomena. Indeed, as pointed out above, although the inhibition effect is very short-lived, disinhibition may persist for as long as ten trials providing the baseline response rate does not become too inhibited.* In the present state of our knowledge the

*It might be argued that the pretest and testing procedures employed in our standard experimental design are not completely comparable. On the one hand the stimulus is presented only once a day during disinhibition testing and is assessed against a dummy presentation. On the other hand more massed trials are employed during pretest without

most reasonable conclusion is simply that the relative effectiveness of a potential disinhibitor can be predicted by its inhibiting effects on an intact conditioned response. Thus we end up agreeing with Pavlov that an effective disinhibitor belongs to the class of stimuli known as external inhibitors. We disagree with Pavlov, however, that only "mild" external inhibitors can produce disinhibition. Rather, all of our evidence suggests a monotonic relationship; the stronger the external inhibitor the more pronounced will be the disinhibition effect. Finally, we note that novelty seems to play a far more important role in external inhibition than it does in the case of disinhibition.

IV. Response Inhibition and Disinhibition

In our experiments we have observed the disinhibition effect under seven different types of inhibitory operations: unsignalled shock, extinction, food satiation, punishment, conditioned suppression, discrimination conditioning and DRL training. It is possible to ask what properties a response must have in order for it to be disinhibited. For Pavlov, the simple answer was that the response had to be suppressed through the operation of a hypothetical cortical process called internal inhibition. In Pavlovian theory, there are four major procedures which produce internal inhibition, and thus make it possible for disinhibition to occur. These are: extinction, differentiation, conditioned inhibition, and inhibition of delay. Each of these procedures involves some type of extinction.* Thus, according to

*It might be argued that in delayed conditioning reinforcement continues in effect. However, this can be countered by pointing out that temporal intervals can act as CS's. Thus, in the case of delayed conditioning there would be two stimulus complexes, loosely designated as the early action of the stimulus (which is never reinforced) and the later action of the stimulus (which is always reinforced). Exactly where the dividing line falls is, of course, a moot question.

---

any counterbalancing for the order of the stimulus and dummy (prestimulus) presentations. Furthermore, all animals have had an earlier history of leverpressing in the Skinner box when they are tested for disinhibition. However, subjects have not had a history of *not* leverpressing in the chamber when they are pretested. To rectify these discrepancies, 15 experimental animals were given eight days pre-exposure to the Skinner box prior to acquisition training. After leverpress training and three days of VI practice, pretesting was begun. One 3-min stimulus (80 db noise) and one dummy presentation was programmed to occur on each 1-hr daily pretest session. The order of stimulus and dummy presentations were counterbalanced within and between days. An analysis of the pretest results revealed that the experimental animals were not significantly different from a control group of 15 subjects who had not received any pre-exposure to the Skinner box. A significantly above chance proportion of the animals (12/15 in each group) had lower stimulus than dummy suppression scores on the initial pretest trial. However, there were no significant differences between stimulus and dummy scores on any of the seven subsequent pretest days.

Thus it seems clear that external inhibition is much shorter-lived than disinhibition even when the training and testing procedures are made as similar as possible.

Pavlov, the suppressed state of the conditioned response that comes about through nonreinforcement can be disinhibited by the presentation of an appropriate external stimulus. However, the results of our work would suggest that the disinhibition phenomenon is even more general than Pavlov suggested. Because Pavlov did not employ shock to inhibit responding, it is impossible to know whether or not he would have predicted a disinhibition effect when shock is employed to suppress responding. However, it does seem clear that Pavlovian theory would not have predicted that disinhibition would occur when responding was reduced by satiating the animals with food, without any experimental extinction.

If Pavlovian theory is not sufficient to encompass all of the findings, the question arises as to what all of our different "inhibitory" operations might have in common. The obvious answer is that each reduces the baseline response rate to a very low level. It will be remembered that our standardized procedure guaranteed that the response rate would be low during the test, since a stimulus presentation was contingent on a 3-min no-response criterion. Thus it is possible that the disinhibition effect may be a simple consequence of testing when the response rate is at a very low level. It could be suggested that the opposed effects of extraneous stimuli depend exclusively on the current response rate: if the response rate is high, the stimulus produces a decrement in responding; but if the response rate is low, a response increment occurs. If such a view is correct, it should be possible to produce a so-called "disinhibition effect" without employing any inhibitory operation. We have carried out a number of studies to investigate this possibility, the critical findings of which can be summarized as follows.

(1) In the first experiment (Brimer, 1970a), it was observed that following a partial reinforcement schedule the response rate had to be reduced to a critical low range of values in order for disinhibition to occur. Not until the response rate was as low as two responses per minute was the disinhibition effect in evidence.

(2) In a series of related studies (Brimer, 1970a), the extraneous stimulus was presented during the early acquisition of the leverpress response. After a single reinforcement the response rate was slightly (but not significantly) greater than two responses per minute. However, in spite of this low level of responding, the extraneous stimulus failed to elicit any sign of a disinhibition effect.

On the basis of these findings, it appeared that a low response rate, by itself, was not a sufficient condition for disinhibition. However, in a subsequent study where the original training was with a continuous rather than an intermittent, reinforcement schedule (Brimer, 1970b), it was discovered that the response rate had to be reduced to a far lower level—less than $\frac{1}{2}$ response per min—in order for disinhibition to be observed. Thus the failure to find a disinhibition effect during the early acquisition of the leverpress response could be attributed to the fact that the response rate was not at a sufficiently low level. Consequently, we have recently carried out two further studies in an attempt to provide a more definitive answer to the original question. In both studies a two-lever chamber was employed where one lever was reinforced during both preliminary training and disinhibition testing. In the first study the responses on the alternate lever were initially reinforced and then extinguished to a very low level. In the second study reinforcement was never available on the alternative lever; instead, the "operant rate" was utilized in order to obtain a comparably low level of responding. The details of the procedures and findings are described below.

A. Study A

In the initial training phase, the 14 animals of Study A received an equal number of reinforcements on each of the two levers. Over a period of 20 days, the reinforcement schedule was gradually increased from CRF to VI 2·5 min. Following this preliminary training one of the two levers was placed on an extinction programme while the other continued to produce

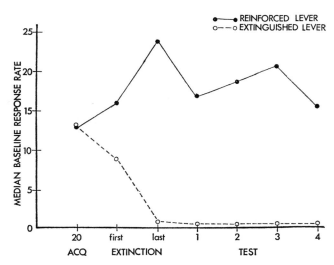

Fig. 7. Median baseline rate (responses per min) for the two levers on the last day of acquisition (ACQ-20), the first and last day of extinction training, and each of the four test days. The rate is based on the total number of responses emitted during each 2-hr daily session.

reinforcement according to the standard VI schedule. Extinction training was continued until the subject met a criterion of two consecutive days during which a minimum of two 3-min no-response intervals occurred on the extinguished lever. Once this criterion was obtained, testing was carried out in the usual manner. There was one stimulus and one dummy presentation on each of the four consecutive 2-hr daily test sessions. The extraneous stimulus was 80 db white noise presented for three consecutive minutes following a 3-min no-response interval on the extinguished lever.

Figure 7 depicts the rate of responding on each of the two levers during different phases of the experiment. It is obvious that the subjects were responding equally often on the two manipulanda at the end of the initial training phase. Furthermore, the extinction programme reduced responding on the nonreinforced lever to a rate of approximately ½ response per min.

The results of the disinhibition test are presented in Fig. 8. Looking first at the reinforced lever we find a significant decrement in responding

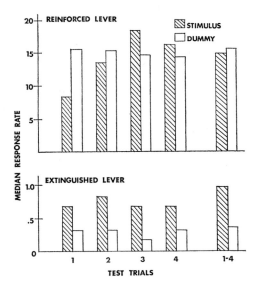

FIG. 8. Median response rate (responses per min) occurring on the reinforced and extinguished lever during stimulus and dummy intervals as a function of test trial.

on initial stimulus presentation, although none of the subsequent differences are reliable. In reference to the extinguished lever, it should be noted that the dummy response rate is maintained at a very low level—something less than $\frac{1}{2}$ response per min—over the course of the entire four test days. Under these conditions there is a tendency for more responding to occur during the stimulus than during the dummy intervals on each test day. This disinhibition effect is statistically reliable for the scores pooled over the four test trials.

The results of the present study duplicate a number of our earlier observations. When the response rate is high the stimulus suppresses responding, but when it is low, just the opposite reaction occurs. Furthermore, there is a tendency on the first test trial for suppression (on the reinforced lever) to be related to the magnitude of disinhibition (on the extinguished lever) although this correlation (*rho* $= -\cdot373$) failed to reach a statistically significant level. The present results also confirm our earlier conclusion that external inhibition is a far more transient effect than is the disinhibition phenomenon. Finally, it is of some importance that external inhibition and disinhibition may be simultaneously observed in the same animal in the two-lever situation. This finding would appear to rule out effectively a number of otherwise plausible interpretations that might be offered to explain the opposite effects of extraneous stimulation which were observed during separate pretest and test sessions in earlier experiments.

B. Study B

In the second study the basic idea was to test for disinhibition when the operant rate on the nonreinforced lever was at a level as low as that observed on the extinguished lever of the previous experiment, but where responding previously had not been at a substantially higher level. The training sequence was as follows: initially only one lever was available in the Skinner box and the 12 subjects received either three or four days of acquisition training on this lever with the standard VI 2·5 food reinforcement schedule. At this stage, the second lever was introduced. Responses on this new lever had no effect but reinforcement continued to be available, as before, on the original manipulandum. After a total of six days of acquisition training, testing was carried out in an identical fashion to that employed in the previous study.

Figure 9 depicts the baseline response rate for the acquisition and test days. It is clear that the operant rate was at the requisite $\frac{1}{2}$ response per min level by the start of the test sessions.

The main test results are presented in Fig. 10 along with relevant comparison data from Study A. In reference to the reinforced lever we find that the initial presentation of noise suppresses responding in the present study ($p < \cdot07$) much as it did in the previous study. Although not shown in the figure, there were no effects of stimulus presentation on the operant

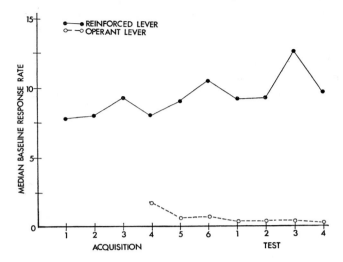

FIG. 9. Median baseline rate (responses per min) for the two levers on acquisition and test days. The rate is based on the number of responses emitted during each 2-hr daily session.

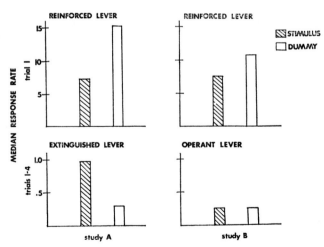

FIG. 10. Median response rate (responses per min) occurring on the reinforced and operant levers in Study B (right-hand panel) along with comparison data for reinforced and extinguished levers in Study A (left-hand panel). Rates are for the first trial for the reinforced lever and for the four pooled test trials for the nonreinforced lever.

lever after the first test trial. There may be some suggestion that the magnitude of the external inhibition is greater in Study A than B, but neither the stimulus nor the dummy response rates differed in the two studies.

Of course the critical data concerns the stimulus and dummy response rates on the nonreinforced lever. It is obvious from the figure that the stimulus in the current study had no effect on the operant rate. There is a significantly lower stimulus rate on the operant lever in Study B, in contrast to the extinguished lever of Study A, although the dummy rates in the two studies do not differ.

Thus, it appears that we have finally obtained a definitive answer to the question of whether or not a low response rate is a sufficient condition to produce disinhibition. On the basis of all of the evidence, the conclusion seems inescapable that the response rate first has to be reduced from a high to a low level before disinhibition will occur.

V. Concluding Remarks

The experiments which we have described in the previous sections make clear a number of empirical facts about the effects of extraneous stimulation during the acquisition and extinction of an operant response. The only serious attempt to develop a theory to account for such effects has been Pavlov's. However, Konorski (1948) has clearly documented how Pavlov's attempt to explain disinhibition in terms of cortical dynamics was unsuccessful. But if we are to reject Pavlovian theory the question arises as to whether there is any psychological theory which can explain the facts that we have amassed about the effects of extraneous stimulation. Although we have wrestled with this question for some time we have yet to come up with any satisfactory answer. The main stumbling block for any theoretical effort is the paradox to which Pavlov first called attention, namely, the fact that the same stimulus will produce exactly opposite effects at different stages of training. Furthermore, our results suggest the added complication that the inhibition of the conditioned response is a necessary, but not sufficient, condition for disinhibition to occur. It appears that the response not only has to be inhibited, but it must be suppressed to a critical low level. Thus, the irreducible empirical minimum derivable from our experiments seems to be this: disinhibition will be manifested only when a response which was once at a higher level of probability has been reduced to some critical lower level of probability.

In two recent review articles concerned with inhibitory conditioning with discrete external stimuli (Rescorla, 1969; Hearst et al., 1970) the possible use of disinhibition as an index of inhibition is acknowledged. However, the idea is rejected largely on the basis that it involves two additional assumptions, namely, "that conditioned inhibition is less stable than excitation and that conditioned excitation persists through conditioned-inhibition treatment" (Rescorla, 1969).

In regard to the first assumption it obviously must be true that when disinhibition occurs inhibition is more vulnerable to disruption than excitation. However, our data clearly suggest that this occurs only within some restricted range of values. Thus we would conclude that disinhibition implies *only* that there is a stage of inhibitory training when inhibition is less stable than excitation.

In regard to the second assumption, we would agree with Rescorla that the phenomenon of disinhibition implies that there is potential excitation that persists in the presence of an inhibitory operation. But we would argue along with Pavlov (1927) and Skinner (1936) that it is this aspect of disinhibition that provides one of the most compelling reasons for postulating a concept such as inhibition, for it is just under these circumstances that response decrements *cannot* be attributed to a simple loss of excitation. It is precisely the fact that an extinguished CR can be disinhibited that implies that extinction is not due to loss of excitation, but must be due to the excitation being overlaid by a new (inhibitory) process. Consequently, we would suggest that disinhibition provides the most appropriate measure for detecting the presence of inhibition. However, it should be remembered that the evidence from all of our studies to date indicates that *any* operation which suppresses responding to the requisite low level may, in turn, be disinhibited. Thus, in terms of a disinhibition criterion, it seems clear that the concept of inhibition has to be very broadly defined.

Acknowledgements

The research programme reported in this paper was supported in part by Grant APA–105 to the author from the National Research Council of Canada. The author wishes to express his appreciation to David Boyle, Bob Sainsbury, Jon Little, Susan Wickson for their assistance with the research.

References

Brimer, C. J. (1970a). Disinhibition of an operant response. *Learning and Motivation*, **1,** 346–372.

Brimer, C. J. (1970b). Inhibition and disinhibition of an operant response as a function of the amount and type of prior training. *Psychonomic Science*, **21,** 191–192.

Brimer, C. J. and Kamin, L. J. (1963). Disinhibition, habituation, sensitization, and the conditioned emotional response. *Journal of Comparative and Physiological Psychology*, **56,** 508–516.

Brimer, C. J. and Wickson, Susan (1971). Shock frequency, disinhibition, and conditioned suppression. *Learning and Motivation*, **2**, 124–137.

Contrucci, J. J., Hothersall, D. and Wickens, D. D. (1971). The effects of a novel stimulus introduced into a DRL schedule at two temporal placements. *Psychonomic Science*, **23**, 97–99.

Flanagan, B. and Webb, W. B. (1964). Disinhibition and external inhibition in fixed interval operant conditioning. *Psychonomic Science*, **1**, 123–124.

Gagné, R. M. (1941). External inhibition and disinhibition in a conditioned operant response. *Journal of Experimental Psychology*, **29**, 104–116.

Hearst, E., Besley, S. and Farthing, G. W. (1970). Inhibition and the stimulus control of operant behavior. *Journal of the Experimental Analysis of Behavior*, **14**, 373–409.

Hinrichs, J. V. (1968). Disinhibition of delay in fixed-interval instrumental conditioning. *Psychonomic Science*, **12**, 313–314.

Horns, H. L. and Heron, W. T. (1940). A study of disinhibition in the white rat. *Journal of Comparative Psychology*, **30**, 97–102.

Hovland, C. I. (1937). The generalization of conditioned responses. *Journal of Experimental Psychology*, **21**, 47–62.

Hunter, W. S. (1935). The disinhibition of experimental extinction in the white rat. *Science*, **81**, 77–78.

Kamin, L. J. (1965). Temporal and intensity characteristics of the conditioned stimulus. In: W. F. Prokasy (Ed.), *Classical Conditioning*. New York: Appleton–Century–Crofts.

Kamin, L. J. and Brimer, C. J. (1963). The effects of intensity of conditioned and unconditioned stimuli on a conditioned emotional response. *Canadian Journal of Psychology*, **17**, 194–198.

Kamin, L. J. and Schaub, R. E. (1963). Effects of conditioned stimulus intensity on the conditioned emotional response. *Journal of Comparative and Physiological Psychology*, **56**, 502–507.

Konorski, J. (1948). *Conditioned Reflexes and Neuron Organization*. New York: Cambridge University Press.

Pavlov, I. P. (1927). *Conditioned Reflexes*. Trans. by G. V. Anrep, New York: Dover.

Pavlov, I. P. (1928). *Lectures on Conditioned Reflexes*. Trans. by W. H. Gantt. New York: International Publishers.

Razran, G. H. (1939). Decremental and incremental effects of distracting stimuli upon the salivary CRs of 24 adult human subjects. *Journal of Experimental Psychology*, **24**, 647–652.

Rescorla, R. A. (1969). Pavlovian conditioned inhibition. *Psychological Bulletin*, **72**, 77–94.

Singh, D. and Wickens, D. D. (1968). Disinhibition in instrumental conditioning. *Journal of Comparative and Physiological Psychology*, **66**, 557–559.

Skinner, B. F. (1936). A failure to obtain "disinhibition". *Journal of Genetic Psychology*, **14**, 127–135.

Switzer, S. A. (1933). Disinhibition of the conditioned galvanic skin response. *Journal of Genetic Psychology*, **9**, 77–100.

Wenger, M. A. (1936). External inhibition and disinhibition produced by duplicate stimuli. *American Journal of Psychology*, **48**, 446–456.

Winnick, W. A. and Hunt, J. McV. (1951). The effect of an extra stimulus upon strength of response during acquisition and extinction. *Journal of Experimental Psychology*, **41**, 205–215.

Wolach, A. H. and Ferraro, D. P. (1969). A failure to obtain disinhibition in fixed-interval operant conditioning. *Psychonomic Science*, **15**, 47–48.

Yamaguchi, H. I. and Ladioray, G. I. (1962). Disinhibition as a function of extinction trials and stimulus intensity. *Journal of Comparative and Physiological Psychology*, **55**, 572–577.

9 | Temporal Regulation of Behaviour and Inhibition

M. RICHELLE

University of Liège, Liège, Belgium

I. Introduction	229
II. Fixed-Interval vs. DRL Schedules: Intraspecific and Interspecific Comparisons	233
A. FI and DRL Performance in Cats	233
B. From Cats to Mice: FI vs. DRL Performance	235
III. Extinction in Temporally Regulated Behaviour: a Phenomenon of Generalized Inhibition?	237
A. Cats: FI Schedules	237
B. Cats: DRL Schedules	238
C. Pigeons: Discrimination Between Visual Stimuli of Different Duration	244
IV. Concluding Remarks	248
References	249

I. Introduction

Little attention has been given so far to one important aspect of inhibition in the Pavlovian conceptual framework, namely *inhibition of delay*. The present contribution is an attempt to formulate several hypotheses by using this concept in the analysis of certain types of operant behaviour which have been generally treated, until now, in a purely descriptive manner.

Several classical procedures in operant conditioning involve some kind of control of the organism's behaviour by duration. The most familiar examples are Fixed-Interval and DRL schedules, and a variety of time discrimination schedules in which the subject is trained to respond differentially according to the different durations of some stimuli. We shall refer to the behaviour observed in these situations, including less classical varieties such as Harzem's Progressive Interval schedules (Harzem, 1969), by the general expression: *temporal regulations of behaviour*. The use of a common label does not imply, of course, common underlying mechanisms; it simply points to a class of contingencies in which temporal parameters are explicitly defined as essential factors in the control of behaviour.

Recently, several authors have attempted to discuss some general features of the behaviour so controlled (Richelle, 1968; Harzem, 1969; Kramer and Rilling, 1970). Whether or not the concept of inhibition appears useful in accounting for some of these features depends, of course, on the definition one wishes to adopt for that term. Inhibition refers to a variety of mechanisms, from the most rigorously described to the loosely hypothesized, in neurophysiology and psychology.*

In the latter field, a number of experimeters have discarded the concept of inhibition as lacking logical necessity and factual support, despite the wide use made of it by Pavlovian explanatory models. Those who dispensed with inhibition were not primarily concerned with temporal regulations but mainly with discriminative behaviour. In this domain, recent experimental and theoretical efforts have contributed to the renewal of interest in inhibition, and have led to more refined and better founded definitions (Terrace, 1966a, 1966b, 1968, 1969; Rescorla, 1969; Staddon, 1969; Hearst et al., 1970). These obviously form the background to many of the chapters in this book. As they refer specifically to inhibitory stimulus control, they do not necessarily apply to temporal regulations; duration, of course, is not a stimulus in the usual meaning of that term. A brief comparison of the conceptual and methodological problems raised by the notion of *inhibition* in the context of temporally regulated behaviour on the one hand, and of conditioned stimulus control on the other hand, therefore seems appropriate.

It can be argued that temporally regulated behaviour implies some process by which a response is not simply absent for a given delay, but is withheld during that delay. Some sort of inhibitory control would be at work whenever responses are distributed according to temporal constraints. This notion is not new: it is directly borrowed from Pavlov's interpretation of the phenomena of conditioned reactions to time, trace conditioned reflexes and delayed conditioned reactions (Pavlov, 1927). Pavlov thought it necessary to name this process *inhibition of delay*, as mentioned above. For him, it was not basically different from other types of internal inhibition (extinction and conditioned inhibition), though the conditions under which it originated were clearly distinct, and though it possessed some specific characteristics. Pavlov insisted among other things on the great individual variations and on the important part of the history of conditioning in the rate of formation of delayed reflexes. Delayed and trace conditioning offered him an especially appropriate context to demonstrate that inhibition was an active process (and not simply an absence of responding), by using the test of disinhibition. As Hearst points out in Chapter 1,

*For a recent thoughtful comment on the present status of inhibition in neurophysiology, see Schlag (1971).

"Skinner admitted that his argument, denying the need for a general concept of inhibition, would be seriously threatened if disinhibition could be reliably demonstrated in an operant situation." After his own failure to produce facts contradictory to his view, very few systematic attempts have been made to test disinhibition in operant behaviour, until recent work by Brimer, summarized in another chapter of this book. It is surprising that this problem was not approached long ago by using temporally defined schedules, such as Fixed-Interval or DRL schedules, since it was known that corresponding procedures in Pavlovian conditioning offered the best opportunity to show disinhibition effects. Recent studies by Flanagan and Webb (1964), by Singh and Wickens (1968), and by Hinrichs (1968) provide clear evidence for disinhibition in Fixed-Interval schedules. Similar effects were obtained by Contrucci *et al.* (1971) in DRL schedules with rats. Occasional observations made in our laboratory on cats under FI 5 min schedules are on the same lines. By watching the animals at the time the external test stimulus was presented, it appeared that one reason why disinhibition is not always reflected by an operant response is the fact that the orienting reflex to the stimulus is a response competing to a certain extent with the operant response. The ease with which Pavlov obtained disinhibition was probably due to the autonomic nature of the salivary response, and its greater independence from the neuromuscular system involved in the orienting reflex. Visceral reactions put under operant control by Miller and his co-workers (Miller, 1969) might provide a good way to test disinhibition of operant behaviour in conditions more comparable to those of Pavlov's experiments from the point of view of neurophysiological organization.

The concept of inhibition as applied to temporally regulated operant behaviour is close to the definition of inhibition as a "certain type of decrease in response output from a stable high level of responding"—a definition proposed in the frame of operant conditioning by Farthing and Hearst (1968). The qualification of the initial rate as *stable* and *high* (both terms are obviously lacking in precision), does not, however, seem necessary in temporal regulations: the initial rate in a DRL or an FI may be moderate and not stable at all. Moreover, the definition lacks one important specification as far as inhibition of delay is concerned: the decrease in response output is strictly related to the passage of time, rather than to certain properties of a given stimulus.

The relation between this inhibitory mechanism and time measuring mechanisms (temporal discrimination, time estimation or whatever you may call it) is a matter for further inquiry. We would not suggest that time measuring mechanisms are reducible to inhibition. But it might be plausible to make the hypothesis that time measuring mechanisms require, in order to exert their regulatory control on operant behaviour, the functioning of inhibitory mechanisms. Psychophysiological studies show that temporally regulated behaviour is generally impaired after lesions of cerebral centres to which inhibitory control of motor functions is usually attributed (Lejeune, 1971b).

If we accept the classical arguments given by Pavlov for respondent conditioning, and the few findings mentioned above on disinhibition in Fixed-Interval schedules, the experimental evidence in favour of this hypothesis is, at present, very scarce. This is, partly, because people have not usually attempted to analyse their data with the inhibition hypothesis in mind, as Kramer and Rilling (1970) have noted in their discussion of DRL schedules. On the other hand, authors who are currently rehabilitating inhibition, like Rescorla and Hearst, deliberately limit their concern to "those decrements produced by *discrete external stimuli*" (see Hearst, Chapter 1). Consequently, the favoured techniques to detect and measure inhibition are precisely those which are irrelevant to the study of the phenomenon in temporally regulated behaviour. You cannot superimpose time as a stimulus on some ongoing behaviour, conditioned or consummatory, you cannot manipulate combined cues, nor submit your subject to tests of transfer, choice or secondary reinforcement. The procedures available to the experimeter are among those classified by Hearst under the sixth and last heading of a list in which the sequence of items seems hierarchically ordered. This heading reads "*symptoms or by-products of inhibitory control*", and covers, in bulk, together with the important disinhibition effect, behavioural contrast and Pavlovian induction, peak shift in studies of intradimensional stimulus generalization, stimulus aversiveness and stress-induced breakdowns. We agree with Hearst that present knowledge does not allow strong conclusions about the relationship of any of these effects to the phenomenon of conditioned inhibition (though we would make an exception for disinhibition, discussed above), and that more research is badly needed in this area in order to substantiate hypotheses. As far as temporally regulated behaviour is concerned, these aspects should be considered, at least for heuristic purposes, as central rather than secondary (or "by-product") means to detect and measure inhibition.

We would suggest, for example, in agreement with Kramer and Rilling, that one should look for aversive properties of DRL schedules, and, we would add, of temporally defined schedules in general, when the time constraints fall beyond certain limits in a given species or individual. What is needed here is ingenious experimentation, that would lead to unequivocal quantitative data.

We are not ready to submit a coherent series of experimental results that would demonstrate the necessity of a concept of inhibition, so defined, to account for acquired temporal regulation of behaviour. All we want to do, for the present, is to bring together a few observations made in the course of various studies* carried out in our laboratory on different species and on different schedules involving temporal regulations. These observations might help us in formulating further hypotheses amenable to experimental verification. They are, most of the time, in agreement with Pavlov's description of inhibition of delay and some of its by-products.

II. Fixed-interval vs. DRL Schedules: Intraspecific and Inter-specific Comparisons

A. FI and DRL Performance in Cats

Fixed-interval schedules generate a familiar pattern of responding characterized by a pause after reinforcement. In cats, for intervals of 2, 5, 8 or 10 min, pausing usually extends over half of the delay or longer, i.e. up to 5 min or so (Richelle, 1967; Lejeune, 1971a). We call this pausing a *spontaneous* temporal regulation of behaviour, because it is not required by the contingencies as a condition for reinforcement. Subjects of the same species under DRL schedules show great difficulties in spacing their responses with delays greater than 1 or 2 min. This was verified repeatedly with various modalities of DRL: the classical one-lever procedure with and without limited hold; the two-lever procedure in which the subject starts the delay by a response on lever B in the limited hold after the critical delay has elapsed (Macar, 1971a, 1971b); the one-lever procedure in which the subject starts the delay by pushing the lever down and is reinforced if it releases it after a given time.

Why is the animal able to pause spontaneously for 5 min or so when it is not required, and *not* able to pause for 120 sec when this is the condition for reinforcement? It is, of course, not satisfying to answer that it is because the contingencies are different. We must specify the critical difference and account for the difference observed in behaviour.

One hypothesis is that the inhibitory mechanisms at work in DRL behaviour have an effectiveness limited to much shorter time-spans than in FI, because there is no compensation in a high output at the end of each delay. In FI, the pause is, as a rule, followed by a burst of responses. In DRL, the subject usually emits only one or two responses after pausing. In well-trained organisms, the IRT distribution shows a mode around the reinforced value, and a second mode corresponding to the class of the shortest IRTs. It has been observed in rats that most of these short IRTs are due to extra responses emitted right after the reinforced

*The hypotheses underlying these studies are not exclusively related to the problem of inhibition. They were summarized in Richelle (1968).

response, before the reinforcement is consumed. Results obtained by Macar with cats in a two-lever situation confirm this observation. The function of these responses might be compensatory. The interpretation suggested here would lead one to relate the phenomenon under discussion with the phenomenon of induction (behavioural contrast) on the one hand, and on the other hand, with a conception of temporal regulations as involving alternating phases of tension and relaxation.

Several lines of research are in progress to substantiate the empirical arguments in favour (or in disfavour) of this hypothesis.

1. If the hypothesis is correct, subjects should adjust to longer delays, or should perform better at a given delay when they are required to emit a given number of responses during the hold of a DRL. In an exploratory study, three cats were trained to emit 20 responses during the 25-sec limited hold in a DRL 40 sec. The experimental cage was equipped with two levers. The animal started the delay by pressing lever A; then the 20th response emitted on lever B between the 40th and the 65th second after pressing on A was reinforced with milk. The subjects had been exposed previously to DRL schedules using the two-lever procedure but without the FR contingency (i.e. one response during the limited hold of 10 sec provided the reinforcement). Requiring 20 responses instead of one resulted in an improved performance, in terms of proportion of reinforcements, of modal IRTs, and of stability. The procedure was not effective in eliminating a by-product of temporal regulations to be discussed below, i.e. generalized inhibition (see Section III).

2. Compensation for inhibition might possibly be achieved either by an output of responses of the same topography as the operant response, or by any kind of motor behaviour. If so, *collateral behaviour* (sometimes called mediating behaviour) would have nothing to do with the time measuring proper; its effects on the quality of temporal regulation would be accounted for by its aspecific compensatory function. This is currently being submitted to experimental test by systematically manipulating immobility and motor activity in temporal schedules.

In a preliminary study of four rats, part of the floor of a Skinnerbox was converted into an actometric platform, providing for continuous measurement of activity (or nonactivity). Leverpressing was reinforced when it occurred after the animal had spent a predetermined period of time (10 or 15 sec) immobile on the actometric platform. Operant immobility time (OIT) reached the required delay in 6 to 25 % of the cases (average value), depending on the individual. Their distribution, however, did not give clear evidence for a temporal regulation, i.e. there was no mode around the reinforced value. This is not conclusive, since the experiment extended over 10 to 44 sessions (again depending on the individual), much too short a period for obtaining good stabilization in temporal schedules of a more classical type. This first exploratory experiment was interrupted in order to introduce technical improvements: in particular, it seemed important to restrict the animal-activity progressively by changing the criterion of the actometer in the course of the sessions, as the conditioning progressed.

B. FROM CATS TO MICE: FI vs. DRL PERFORMANCE

The contrast between performances in FI and in DRL is particularly sharp in mice. Maurissen, in our laboratory, has conditioned albino mice on FI schedules, with intervals up to 4 min, using dry food as a reinforcer (Maurissen, 1970). He obtained the usual pattern of responding with distributions of responses close to those obtained with cats and rats. The index of curvature (Fry et al., 1960) for delays of 2 to 4 min was between 0·60 and 0·70 (using a subdivision of the interval into eight equal periods, the maximum value of the index being 0·875). These values are similar to those obtained in cats and rats (for values obtained in cats, see Richelle, 1969; Lejeune, 1971a). Maurissen failed to condition animals of the same species and strain on DRL 30 sec. After more than 60 daily sessions of 90 min, the subjects did not adjust to the delay, the IRT distribution showing no evidence of a temporal regulation comparable to that usually obtained in cats or rats.

Figure 1 shows IRT distributions of four individual subjects on the

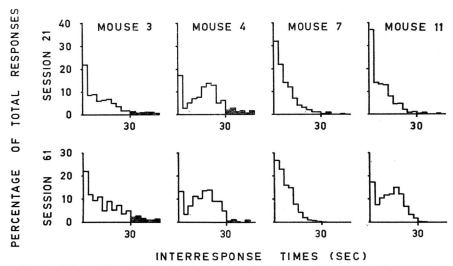

FIG. 1. Mice—DRL 30 sec. Relative frequencies of IRTs. The size of class-interval is 3 sec. Shaded areas indicate reinforced IRTs. The last class includes IRT's equal to or greater than 46 sec.

21st and the 61st sessions under DRL 30-sec schedule. In none of these do we find the mode of responses around the reinforced value, classically obtained in rats, cats, monkeys and humans, for similar and even longer delays (Conrad et al., 1958; Laties et al., 1965; Malott and Cumming, 1966; Ferraro et al., 1965; Hodos et al., 1962; Weiss et al., 1966; Macar, 1971a; Bruner and Revusky, 1961).

It did not matter whether the delay contingency was introduced abruptly from the start of conditioning or progressively increased by small steps to the final 30-sec value.

Table I gives comparative results obtained with animals trained from the start on DRL 30 sec and with animals trained on delays progressively lengthened from 5 to 30 sec. Each group was exposed to 66 daily sessions of 60 min each.

TABLE I

Progressive vs. abrupt DRL 30 sec in mice

| | Procedure | | | | | |
| | Abrupt | | | Progressive | | |
Subject N^r	16	17	18	19	20	21
Modal IRT (seconds)	17	17	26	17	17	⩽ 3
Number of Responses per hour	182	188	128	163	189	338

Mice seemed unable to adjust to delays longer than 15 or 20 sec in DRL. These negative results might not be enough to conclude that mouse behaviour cannot be controlled by DRL contingencies, but supposing that they are not due to some artefact, they raise an interesting problem as to the factors responsible for such a limitation. Actually, similar limitations were observed in one of the few laboratory species submitted to DRL schedules. As noted by Kramer and Rilling (1969), "pigeons perform poorly on DRL 20 second or longer under normal deprivation conditions" (Reynolds, 1964a, 1964b; Holz and Azrin, 1963; Holz et al., 1963; Kramer and Rilling, 1969). In a study extending over 250 sessions of $2\frac{1}{2}$ hr, Staddon (1965) failed to obtain satisfactory adjustment to the 30-sec delay (taking rats' performance as a reference). Some of his results have been redrawn in Fig. 2, for comparison with Maurissen's results in mice. The median IRT is plotted against the DRL value. The diagonal across the graph indicates the matching function. The left graph is for mice trained on

DRL 30 by progressively increasing the delay. There were about ten 1-hr sessions on each delay, except for the last 30-sec delay, on which there were 20 sessions. The graph on the right side of the figure is for pigeons—three individual subjects trained by Staddon, and results from Wilson and Keller (1953) included for comparison.

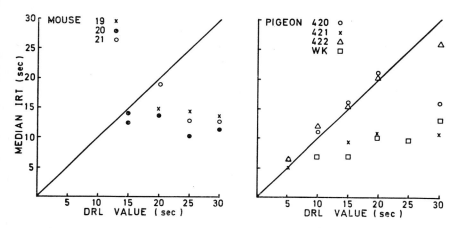

FIG. 2. Mice and pigeons: DRL performance. Comparison of results of mice and pigeons for different delays. See text (after Maurissen, 1970 and Staddon, 1965).

The comparison proposed in Fig. 2 is only indicative, as subjects were not run under exactly the same conditions in both studies. Differences in number and length of sessions might be important. However, it suggests in both species a difficulty in spacing responding by delays of 30 sec, a difficulty that is not encountered in rats, cats, monkeys or humans. If cross-species comparisons lead one to recognize characteristic limitations in some species, it would appear important to look for an explanation in the ethological description of the species and/or in the level of differentiation on the phylogenetic scale.

III. Extinction in Temporally Regulated Behaviour: A Phenomenon of Generalized Inhibition?

A. Cats: FI Schedules

In a study on FI performance in cats, Lejeune (1971a) in our laboratory, planned to condition the subjects on delays of 2, 5, 10 and 15 min successively. Daily sessions lasted 1 hr. The reinforcement was milk; the quantity delivered per reinforcement was proportional to the delay (1·2 cc for FI 2; 3 cc for FI 5; 7·5 cc for FI 10; 10 cc for FI 15). Two of the four animals, numbered 22 and 23, showed, in FI 5 min, a deterioration of performance resulting in progressive extinction. This process began after 30 sessions on FI 5 in one cat, after 50 in the other (about 30 sessions on FI 2 had taken place before sessions on FI 5). Figs. 3 and 4 show cumulative curves illustrating the process.

Nothing similar was observed in the two other subjects, which were conditioned with delays up to 10 or 15 min. Figure 5 shows typical cumulative curves from cat 25 on delays increasing from 2 to 15 min.

As the two subjects showing extinction were females, interference by variables related to sexual cycles is not excluded, a hypothesis that would require further verification with larger groups of subjects. If the extinction cannot be accounted for by some interfering variable, it might finally be considered as a generalization of the inhibition involved in the temporal contingencies. This generalization of inhibition would occur beyond some critical value of the delay (possibly different for different individuals in the same species according to variations in individual history or constitution). We never observed it in cats, males or females, for a 2-min delay used over a period of ten years in a number of experiments.

Referring to the inhibition hypothesis suggested in Section I above to account for the differences between FI and DRL performances, one would expect extinction (by generalized inhibition) more frequently and for shorter delays in DRL than in FI schedules. Observations on animals trained in DRL support this argument.

B. Cats: DRL Schedules

Using the two-lever procedure, Macar (1971b) conditioned three cats, on DRL-LH. Cats 30 (male) and 32 (female) were trained on DRL 60 sec LH 10 sec; cat 35 (female) on DRL 40 sec LH 10 sec. Daily sessions lasted 2 hr. The performance stabilized after 17 sessions for cats 30 and 35, after 40 sessions for cat 32.

Figure 6 shows the IRT distribution obtained by that time. The behaviour remained stable for twenty sessions or so. Then it deteriorated, progressively in cats 30 and 32, abruptly in cat 35, giving place to complete extinction (see Fig. 7).

These alterations of conditioned behaviour were accompanied by modifications in the general behaviour of the animals both in the experimental cage and in their living-cage. Cats 30 and 35 lay down in the experimental cage and remained somnolent during the whole session; they sometimes did not consume the milk offered to them. Though they ate and drank normally in their living quarters, they ran away when one attempted to touch or catch them, shuddered at slight noises and bristled up when an unfamiliar human approached. These behaviours contrast with the quiet-

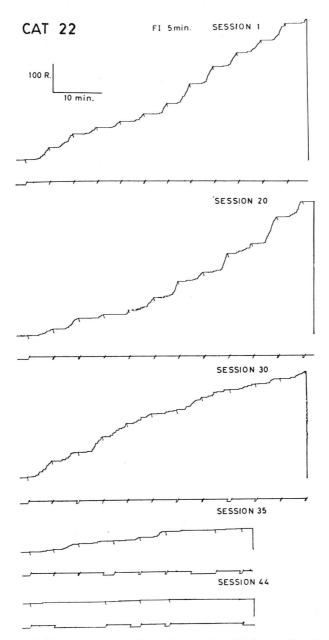

FIG. 3. Cats—fixed interval schedule. Extinction in a FI 5 min. Cumulative curves showing different stages of the deterioration of performance (after Lejeune, 1971a).

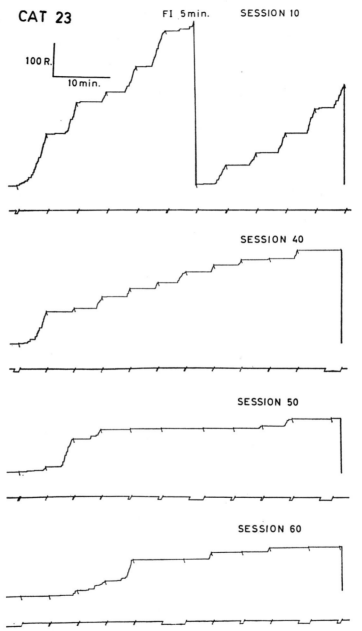

Fɪɢ. 4. Cats—fixed interval schedule. Extinction in a FI 5 min. Cumulative curves showing different stages of deterioration of performance (after Lejeune, 1971a).

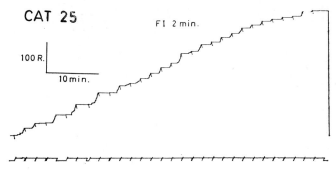

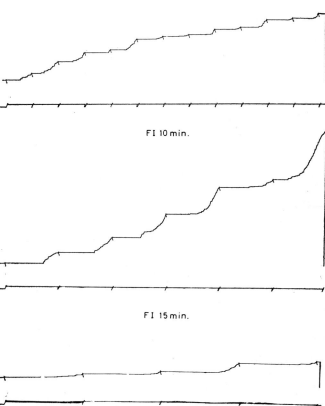

FIG. 5. Cats—fixed interval schedule. Typical cumulative curves showing a well-regulated performance under various delays from 2 to 15 min.

R

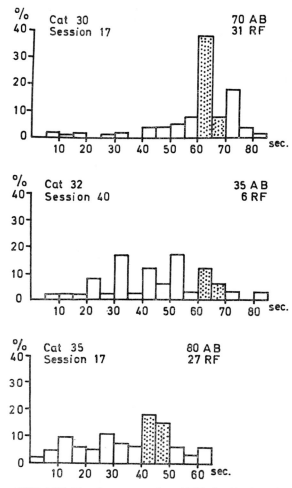

Fig. 6. Cats—DRL-LH. Two-lever procedure. IRT distributions for individual subjects for a session typical of stabilized performance. Abscissa: IRT, between response on lever A, starting the delay, and response on lever B. Ordinate: percentage of responses on B computed on the total number of responses on B following a response on A. Dotted area: reinforced responses, emitted during the LH. Cats 30 and 32: DRL 60 sec LH 10; cat 35: DRL 40 sec LH 10 (after Macar, 1971b).

ness of these animals prior to the extinction phase. In cat 32, normally more excited than the other two, the extinction of operant responses went together with increased agitation, not only in the experimental situation: the animal became difficult to approach and handle. These observations are typically similar to those made by Pavlov in his description of experimental neuroses.

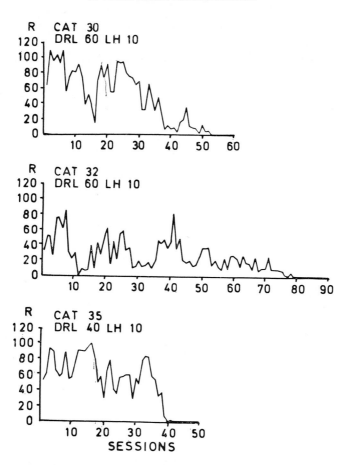

FIG. 7. Cats—DRL-LH. Two-lever procedure. Extinction of conditioned behaviour after prolonged exposure to the contingencies. Abscissa: successive sessions of the experiment; ordinate; number of sequences. *Response on lever A—Response on lever B* (after Macar, 1971b).

Macar has tried several procedures to reinstate the normal performance of her animals. Changing the amount of milk per reinforcement or changing the degree of food deprivation remained without effect. The limited hold was increased to 30 sec (instead of ten) during five sessions, when extinction was not yet complete. No improvement was observed. Novel auditory and visual stimuli were presented in the experimental situation, with the aim of provoking disinhibition. Cats 30 and 32 resumed responding eventually for a whole session the first time this manœuvre was used. But the effect disappeared with repetition.

Macar resorted to "experimental rest" used by most experimenters as an attempt to "cure" experimental neuroses. A ten days' rest had no effect in cat 32. In cat 30, after one month's rest, conditioned behaviour reappeared, but extinguished again within three sessions. In cat 35, a ten weeks' interruption resulted in spontaneous recovery, all the by-products of extinction having receded altogether.

Finally, the three cats were exposed to an FR schedule using only one lever. The experimenter failed to recondition cat 35 on this schedule. Cats 30 and 32 were easily trained, the FR being progressively increased from 1 to 60 responses, within 10 to 15 sessions. A stable FR 60 performance was maintained for 12 sessions. All the symptoms mentioned above disappeared. The DRL 60 LH 10 schedule was then substituted for the FR. The subjects responded, at a rate largely modified by the FR pattern, but the temporal regulation progressively reappeared. The experiment was interrupted for practical reasons after four sessions on DRL, so that nothing can be concluded as to the long-term effect of the FR schedule.

These cases carefully analysed by Macar are only examples of a frequently observed phenomenon. Extinction in DRL occurred in the majority of our cats in all experiments using delays of 40 sec or more, including an attempt, already mentioned, to compensate for inhibitory effects by requiring 20 responses instead of one during the limited hold. It will be remembered that no such extinction was observed in FI 2 min.

C. PIGEONS: DISCRIMINATION BETWEEN VISUAL STIMULI OF DIFFERENT DURATION

Turning to another species and to another type of temporal regulation, let us now consider some data obtained on pigeons in an experiment on time discrimination.

It has been suggested that spaced responding as obtained under DRL schedules, might not reflect an organism's capacity to discriminate duration, the performance involving other mechanisms than time estimation proper (such as motor inhibitory mechanisms mentioned above). Studies in which behaviour is put under discriminative control of some stimulus duration show that pigeons can discriminate durations of external events better than they can space their motor responses (Reynolds and Catania, 1962; Stubbs, 1968). Reynolds and Catania demonstrated that a visual stimulus of 30 sec could be discriminated from a 27-sec stimulus. Therefore the failure to adjust to DRL 30 sec is not due to the pigeon's inability to estimate a 30-sec interval of time.

The question remains, however, whether a task involving the discrimination of durations of external stimuli implies some inhibitory mechanism not at work in other types of discrimination. A decisive test, to satisfy

Hearst's and Rescorla's main requirements, would be to design an experiment in which one could test the inhibitory value of some stimulus as a function of its duration in a time discrimination task. To our knowledge, no such experiment has been performed until now. Again, we are left with cruder indices of possible inhibition from "by-products", such as generalized inhibition.

The results to be reported here are concerned with this problem. They are drawn from an experiment in progress in collaboration with Mantanus and Tefnin.

Two pigeons were exposed, in an operant conditioning apparatus, to the following terminal contingencies. At irregular intervals, averaging 1·5 stimulus presentation per minute, a yellow light, located at the top of the cage, was on for a predetermined duration; this duration was 10 sec when the signal was an S^+ and 5 sec when the signal was an S^-. (The final value of S^- was reached by progressive steps from an initial value of 0·1 sec. Details about the training procedure may be left out for our present purpose.) As soon as an S^+ or an S^- was on, the response-key was transilluminated in green, and it remained so for the whole duration of the signal plus 3 sec. During the 3 sec following an S^+, a single response was reinforced by access to the food magazine (6 sec) and switched off the green light. A response on the green-key after S^- was not reinforced, but it switched off the green light. Responses in S^+ or in S^- switched off the yellow signal and the green light behind the response key. Responses emitted between signals were recorded but were without effect. Daily sessions lasted four hrs.

This schedule was not intended to measure the discriminative threshold of pigeons for duration of visual stimuli, but at the selected value of S^+ and S^-, control by the longest duration was unequivocal. The percentage of responses to S^- remained between 0 and 10. Details of the discrimination itself will not be presented here.

In long sessions under this schedule, the two birds showed long and repeated pauses in responding, sometimes extending over half an hour and more. We made the hypothesis that this phenomenon was related to the temporal constraints of the schedule; the pigeons were required to attend to the signals until they were switched off and then react (or not react) according to their duration. Other things being equal, would the pauses occur with the same frequency and length when S^- was no longer presented? All S^- stimuli were eliminated, but the 10-sec S^+ signals remained. A response in the 3 sec following the end of the signal, while the key remained illuminated with green light, was reinforced. Thus, the number of signals providing the conditions for reinforcement was unchanged, and their distribution in time was exactly the same. The animal's task was simply to peck on the green key when the yellow light was off. Results of this procedure are shown in Figs. 8 and 9, in comparison with results of the time discrimination in two series of sessions, one before, one after the sessions without S⁻. Data summarized in these figures were averaged from ten 4-hr sessions in each series. Long pauses were clearly more frequent in the discrimination session, than in the session without S⁻, as can be seen from the cumulative frequency curves in Fig. 8. In Fig. 9 the sessions were divided into 5-min periods, and the percentage of responses after S⁺ computed for each period. The middle row-sessions (without S⁻) show a much higher percentage of responding than in the discrimination sessions (upper row: before; bottom row: after).

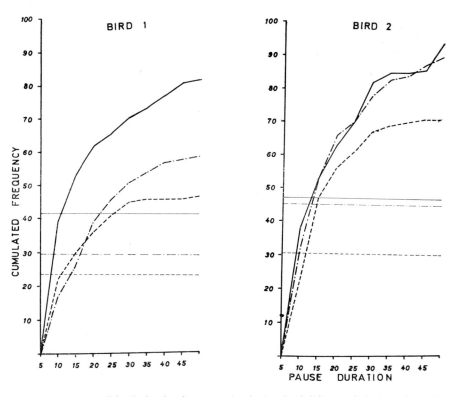

FIG. 8. Pigeons. Discrimination between visual stimuli of different durations. Cumulative frequency of pauses of different durations (from 5 min to 45 min and more). Ordinate: cumulated frequency (absolute numbers); abscissa: pause duration, in min. Solid line: average results from a first series of ten sessions of discrimination between S⁺ (10 sec) and S⁻ (5 sec); dotted line: averaged results from ten sessions without S⁻; broken line: averaged results from ten sessions of discrimination run after the session without S⁻. Horizontal lines indicate the mean number of pauses in the three conditions.

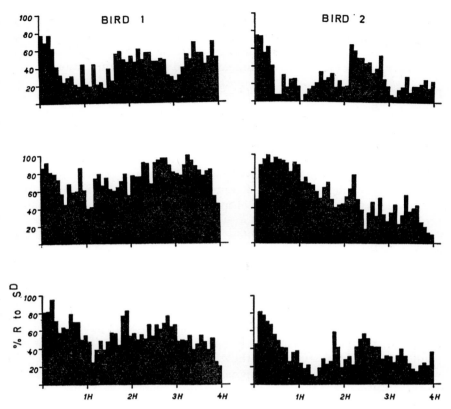

FIG. 9. Pigeons. Discrimination between visual stimuli of different durations. Percentage of responses to S^+ in successive periods of 5 min over 4 hr sessions. Upper row: discrimination sessions prior to S^+ only sessions. Middle row: S^+ only sessions. Lower row: discrimination sessions following S^+ only sessions.

It will be observed that replication of the discrimination task after the sessions without S^- reinstates the initial pattern both in terms of frequency of long pauses and in terms of percentage of responses to S^+. The similarity is particularly striking in bird two.

It can be concluded that the *nonresponding* to S^+ was not exclusively due to the spacing of S^+ presentations. The changes observed after elimination of S^- indicate that it had something to do with the discrimination involved in the original situation. The next step, of course, is to find out whether the critical factor was *discrimination*, or, specifically, *time discrimination*, or, eventually both. This is currently being investigated by exposing the same subjects to similar contingencies, except for the fact that S^+ and S^- no longer differ in duration but in colour.

Preliminary results indicate that part of the generalized inhibition effect observed in this situation is a by-product of the time discrimination as such. Further controls are required to obtain a refined measure of the respective effects of colour discrimination and time discrimination.

IV. Concluding Remarks

The observations presented and discussed above agree in attracting our attention to aspects of behaviour under temporally defined schedules generally neglected by experimenters. This neglect might be due to reasons completely unrelated to the intrinsic interest of the phenomena. For one thing, cross-species generalizations about the behaviour pattern generated by a given schedule are still often accepted uncritically, not to say dogmatically, and lead to underestimations of species differences. On the other hand, extinction of conditioned behaviour, when not deliberately intended by the experimenter, is generally considered as an undesirable mishap in the course of an experiment, and sometimes as a challenge to the control that the schedule is designed to exert on the organism.

We think that these "undesirable" effects, in the present cases, are worthy of attention in their own right. By trying to bring together systematically a few observations collected in various species and under various contingencies, we feel encouraged to formulate a few hypotheses and to design appropriate experiments in order to test them. The following points might help to summarize these hypotheses.

(a) Comparisons between temporal regulations of acquired behaviour under different schedules in a given species suggest that they involve some inhibitory process, varying in degree according to the contingencies.

(b) Pausing, spacing one's own responses and attending to the duration of some exteroceptive signal require this inhibitory process, which is conceived of as an *active process* and not simply as an *absence of responses*, and as a process that, beyond a certain point, must be compensated for in some way. (Of relevance here are general questions concerning the nature of induction or behavioural contrast, the possible aversiveness of contingencies involving inhibition, etc.

(c) Intraspecific and interspecific long-term studies on various schedules differing in many respects but involving some kind of temporal regulation show, under some circumstances, phenomena of extinction, that a number of arguments would lead to consider as *generalized inhibition*. This would be a typical by-product of temporal regulations when the contingencies make no provision for appropriate compensation of inhibition.

On the basis of these hypotheses, we would agree with Pavlov, Konorski, Rescorla and Hearst in considering inhibition as something more than "any low state of strength" of response or some mirror-image of excitation.

Despite the methodological difficulties to be encountered in designing decisive experiments, temporally regulated behaviour provides a privileged context for analysing inhibition as what it probably is, a regulatory mechanism central to the organization of behaviour conceived as a serially ordered chain of events.

References

Bruner, A. and Revusky, S. H. (1961). Collateral behaviour in humans. *Journal of the Experimental Analysis of Behavior*, **4**, 349–350.

Conrad, D. G., Sidman, M. and Herrnstein, R. J. (1958). The effect of deprivation upon temporally spaced responding. *Journal of the Experimental Analysis of Behavior*, **1**, 59–65.

Contrucci, J. J., Hothersall, D. and Wickens, D. D. (1971). The effect of a novel stimulus introduced into a DRL schedule at two temporal placements. *Psychonomic Science*, **23**, 97–99.

Farthing, G. W. and Hearst, E. (1968). Generalization gradients of inhibition after different amounts of training. *Journal of the Experimental Analysis of Behavior*, **11**, 743–752.

Ferraro, D. P., Schoenfeld, W. N. and Snapper, A. S. (1965). Sequential response effects in the white rat during conditioning and extinction on a DRL schedule. *Journal of the Experimental Analysis of Behavior*, **11**, 743–752.

Flanagan, B. and Webb, W. B. (1964). Disinhibition and external inhibition in fixed interval operant conditioning. *Psychonomic Science*, **1**, 123–124.

Fry, W., Kelleher, R. T. and Cook, L. (1960). A mathematical index of performance on fixed interval schedules of reinforcement. *Journal of the Experimental Analysis of Behavior*, **3**, 193–199.

Harzem, P. (1969). Temporal Discrimination. In: Gilbert, R. M. and Sutherland, N. S. (Eds.) *Animal Discrimination Learning*. London: Academic Press.

Hearst, E., Besley, S. and Farthing, G. W. (1970). Inhibition and the stimulus control of operant behavior, *Journal of the Experimental Analysis of Behavior*, suppl. to Vol. **14**, 373–409.

Hinrichs, J. V. (1968). Disinhibition of delay in fixed interval instrumental conditioning. *Psychonomic Science*, **12**, 313–314.

Hodos, W., Ross, G. S. and Brady, J. V. (1962). Complex response patterns during temporally spaced responding. *Journal of the Experimental Analysis of Behavior*, **5**, 473–479.

Holz, W. C. and Azrin, N. H. (1963). A comparison of several procedures for eliminating behavior. *Journal of the Experimental Analysis of Behavior*, **6**, 399–406.

Holz, W. C., Azrin, N. H. and Ulrich, R. E. (1963). Punishment of temporally spaced responding. *Journal of the Experimental Analysis of Behavior*, **6**, 281–290.

Kramer, T. J. and Rilling, M. (1969). Effects of timeout on spaced responding in pigeons. *Journal of the Experimental Analysis of Behavior*, **12**, 283–288.

Kramer, T. J. and Rilling, G. M. (1970). Differential reinforcement of low-rates: a selective critique. *Psychological Bulletin*, **74**, 225–254.

Laties, V. C., Weiss, B., Clark, R. L. and Reynolds, M. D. (1965). Overt "mediating" behavior during temporally spaced responding. *Journal of the Experimental Analysis of Behavior*, **8**, 107–116.

Lejeune, H. (1971a). Note sur les régulations temporelles acquises en programme à intervalle fixe chez le chat. *Revue du Comportement Animal*, **5**, 123–129.

Lejeune, H. (1971b). Lésions thalamiques medianes et régulation temporelle acquise en programme à intervalle fixe chez le rat albinos. *Physiology and Behavior*, **7**, 575–582.

Macar, F. (1971a). Addition d'une horloge externe dans un programme de conditionnement au temps chez le chat. *Journal de Psychologie Normale et Pathologique*, 89–100.

Macar, F. (1971b). Névrose expérimentale dans un programme de renforcement des débits de réponses lents chez le chat. *Journal de Psychologie Normale et Pathologique*, 191–205.

Malott, R. W. and Cumming, W. W. (1966). Concurrent schedules of inter-response time reinforcement: Probability of reinforcement and the lower bounds of the reinforced interresponse time intervals. *Journal of the Experimental Analysis of Behavior*, **9**, 317–326.

Maurissen, J. (1970). Régulations temporelles acquises en programme FI et DRL chez la souris. Unpublished thesis, University of Liège.

Miller, N. E. (1969). Learning of visceral and glandular responses. *Science*, **163**, 434–445.

Pavlov, I. P. (1927). *Conditioned Reflexes*. London: Oxford University Press.

Rescorla, R. A. (1969). Pavlovian conditioned inhibition. *Psychological Bulletin*, **72**, 77–94.

Reynolds, G. S. (1964a). Accurate and rapid reconditioning of spaced responding. *Journal of the Experimental Analysis of Behavior*, **7**, 273–276 (a).

Reynolds, G. S. (1964b). Temporally spaced responding in pigeons: Development and effects of deprivation and extinction. *Journal of the Experimental Analysis of Behavior*, **7**, 415–421 (b).

Reynolds, G. S. and Catania, A. L. (1962). Temporal discrimination in pigeons. *Science*, **135**, 314–315.

Richelle, M. (1967). Contribution à l'analyse des régulations temporelles du comportement à l'aide des techniques du conditionnement operant. In: Chauvin, R. et Médioni, J. (Eds.), *La Distribution Temporelle des Activités Animalés et Humaines*, Paris: Masson.

Richelle, M. (1968). Notions modernes de rythmes biologiques et régulations temporelles acquises. In: Ajuriaguerra, J. (Ed.), *Cycles Biologiques et Psychiatrie*, Geneva: Georg and Paris: Masson, pp. 233–255.

Richelle, M. (1969). Combined action of Diazepam and d-Amphetamine on Fixed-Interval performance in cats. *Journal of the Experimental Analysis of Behavior*, **12**, 989–998.

Schlag, J. (1971). Les concepts d'excitation et d'inhibition dans la physiologie des centres nerveux supérieurs. Lecture given at the Belgian Medical Academy. *Bulletin de l'Académie de Médecine* (in Press).

Singh, D. and Wickens, D. D. (1968). Disinhibition in instrumental conditioning. *Journal of Comparative and Physiological Psychology*, **66**, 557–559.

Staddon, J. E. R. (1965). Some properties of spaced responding in pigeons. *Journal of Experimental Analysis of Behavior*, **8**, 19–28.

Staddon, J. E. R. (1969). Inhibition and the operant. *Journal of the Experimental Analysis of Behavior*, **12**, 481–487.

Stubbs, A. (1968). The discrimination of stimulus duration by pigeons. *Journal of the Experimental Analysis of Behavior*, **11**, 223–238.

Terrace, H. S. (1966a). Stimulus Control. In: Honig, W. H. (Ed.), *Operant Behavior: Areas of Research and Applications*. New York: Appleton–Century–Crofts, pp. 271–344.

Terrace, H. S. (1966b). Discrimination learning and inhibition. *Science*, **154**, 1677–1680.

Terrace, H. S. (1968). Discrimination learning, the peak shift and behavioral contrast. *Journal of the Experimental Analysis of Behavior*, **11**, 727–741.

Terrace, H. S. (1969). Aversive properties of S⁻. Paper presented at the International Congress of Psychology, London, 1969.

Weiss, B., Laties, V. C., Siegel, L. and Goldstein, D. A. (1966). A computer analysis of serial interactions in spaced responding. *Journal of the Experimental Analysis of Behavior*, **9**, 619–626.

Wilson, M. P. and Keller, F. S. (1953). On the selective reinforcement of spaced responding. *Journal of Comparative and Physiological Psychology*, **46**, 190–193.

The Role of Pavlovian Events in Avoidance Training

10

R. G. WEISMAN and J. S. LITNER

Queen's University at Kingston, Ontario, Canada

I. Introduction 253
II. Revised Two-process Theory 254
  A. Pavlovian Conditioned Inhibition of Fear in Rats . . . 254
  B. Pavlovian Inhibitors of Fear Function as Positive Reinforcers . 256
III. Pavlovian Events in Discrete-trial Avoidance Learning . . . 258
  A. The Warning and Safety Signals in One-way Shuttle Avoidance Training as Pavlovian Events 258
  B. The Warning and Safety Signals in Discrete-trial Wheelturn Avoidance Training as Pavlovian Events 261
  C. Pavlovian Excitation of Fear by the Warning Signal . . . 263
  D. The Safety Signal in Discrete-trial Avoidance Training as a Conditioned Positive Reinforcer 265
IV. Avoidance Learning as an Instance of Positive Reinforcement . . 267
Acknowledgements 269
References 269

I. Introduction

Avoidance behaviour creates problems for most learning theories. Since the successful avoidant response prevents the occurrence of the putative reinforcer, it is difficult to understand how such behaviour could be maintained. Yet, it is known that such responses can be highly resistant to extinction. Two-process theory (Rescorla and Solomon, 1967) was developed to account for the reinforcement of avoidance behaviour. What we shall call traditional two-process theory states that early in the course of avoidance training pairing of the warning signal (WS) with an aversive stimulus results in Pavlovian conditioning of fear of the WS. Later in training avoidance responses are reinforced by escape from conditioned fear elicited by the WS. Inference of the strength of fear elicited by the WS from the strength of the avoidance response often provided the chief support for the explicit prediction of correlation between the two. Independent measurement of such fear has failed to yield correspondence of the sort required by traditional two-process theory. Kamin *et al.* (1963)

trained rats to various criteria of avoidance response acquisition, then tested the fear-eliciting properties of the WS by superimposing it on food-reinforced leverpressing. They found that conditioned suppression did not vary monotonically with continued avoidance training. Instead, conditioned fear of the WS first increased, then later declined as acquisition continued. In a similar study, Linden (1969), first suppressed food-reinforced lever-pressing with a tone paired with shock, then administered avoidance training with the Pavlovian CS as the WS for avoidance. When rats were returned to the leverpress task, suppression by the tone was greatly attenuated. If the reduction of Pavlovian conditioned fear by termination of the WS were the reinforcer of avoidance behaviour, as traditional two-process theory insists, conditioned suppression by the WS should have been increased systematically in both studies.

II. Revised Two-process Theory

The purpose of the present chapter is to describe a series of experiments that suggest an alternate or revised two-process theory of avoidance behaviour. Our experiments are based on a procedure developed by Rescorla and LoLordo (1965). These authors trained dogs to shuttle to avoid shock on a Sidman avoidance schedule, then subjected the dogs to Pavlovian fear conditioning in which one tone (CS+) signalled shock and second tone (CS−) signalled the nonoccurrence of shock. Tone presentations, both CS+ and CS−, were later superimposed on the Sidman avoidance task. The Pavlovian excitor of fear, CS+, elicited a marked increase in the rate of responding, while the Pavlovian inhibitor of fear, CS−, elicited a reduction in responding to almost zero.

A. PAVLOVIAN CONDITIONED INHIBITION OF FEAR IN RATS

In our successful replication (Weisman and Litner, 1969) of the Rescorla and LoLordo experiment we used rats as subjects. In our experiments we used, and continue to use, a wheelturn manipulandum in an operant chamber because pilot work assured us that the task yields a high rate (30–60 responses per min) of responding and a low rate of shock (less than 20 shocks per hr) in over 75% of the naïve rats trained with a Sidman avoidance schedule having a response-shock interval of 20 sec and a shock-shock interval of 5 sec. During Pavlovian conditioning, conducted in a separate chamber, we presented a tone that signalled shock in Group CS+, signalled the absence of shock in Group CS−, or was presented at random with respect to shock (Group TRC). We also included a Group No CS that was never confined in the Pavlovian conditioning chamber.

Mean response rates during successive 5-sec periods prior to, during (T), and following tone presentations across the avoidance test session are shown in Fig. 1. Presentation of the tone in Group CS+ reliably elicited an increase in the rate of responding; in Group CS— the tone elicited a reliable decrease in responding. In Groups TRC and No CS the tone had no measurable effect on responding. Thus, as in the Rescorla and LoLordo experiment, CS+ was a Pavlovian excitor of fear and CS— was a Pavlovian

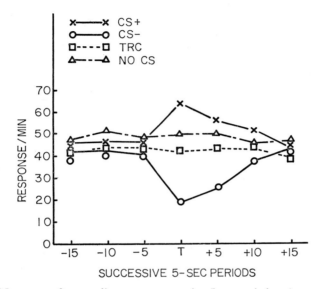

FIG. 1. Mean rate of responding across successive 5-sec periods prior to, during (T), and after tone presentation in a Sidman avoidance test session. Testing followed independent Pavlovian fear conditioning.

inhibitor of fear. In Rescorla and LoLordo's experiments, and in the present work, inhibitors of fear decrease the rate of free operant avoidance responding. The rate of responding changes in a direction consistent with intuitive notions about inhibition and with at least one recent definition of an inhibitory stimulus. An inhibitory stimulus, according to Hearst (Chapter 1) decreases the strength of ongoing behaviour below the level occurring when the stimulus is absent. Hearst's definition seems to ignore those instances in which Pavlovian excitatory stimuli elicit decreased responding. For example, a stimulus correlated with shock decreases the strength of food-reinforced operant responding and a conditioned inhibitory stimulus will restore response strength to at least the former level. Definitions that result in classification of conditioned suppression as an example of inhibition strike us as unfortunate and confusing. We prefer to define a Pavlovian inhibitory stimulus as an event correlated with the absence of the unconditioned stimulus which elicits behavioural changes opposed to those elicited by the conditioned excitor. Rescorla (1969) provides an extensive review of the measurement procedures used to assess the strength of an inhibitory stimulus.

Our revision of the two-process explanation of avoidance behaviour retains the assumption that the observed effects of Pavlovian stimuli on operant behaviour are not themselves mediators of other behaviour but are instead reliable indices of central nervous system emotional states (Rescorla and Solomon, 1967). More accurately what is measured is the interaction of the emotional state with an ongoing reinforcement schedule.

B. PAVLOVIAN INHIBITORS OF FEAR FUNCTION AS CONDITIONED POSITIVE REINFORCERS

A revised two-process model of the reinforcement of avoidance behaviour, advocated to one degree or another by a number of investigators, suggests that Pavlovian inhibition of fear produced by the avoidance response provides the reinforcement mechanism in avoidance learning. Those who advocate the revised model have noted that feedback stimuli, or safety signals, produced by the avoidance response, like CS— in Pavlovian fear conditioning, regularly precede a period free from shock. The model states that stimuli produced by responding in avoidance situations acquire the functional properties of Pavlovian inhibitory stimuli. It is important to note that acquisition is said to occur because of a forward relationship between the safety signal (SS) and the next shock and not because of a backward relationship between these stimuli and the previous shock or the previous response. The second critical statement of the model is that Pavlovian inhibitory stimuli, at least in a context of aversive stimuli, function as powerful conditioned reinforcers. Moreover, the reinforcement function of Pavlovian inhibitors of fear is independent of the situation in which the Pavlovian conditioning occurred. Thus a reinforcer for ongoing behaviour can acquire an inhibitory function either by explicit Pavlovian conditioning or during Pavlovian conditioning implicit in avoidance training itself.

Rescorla (1968) observed preference for responding on a panel that produced a stimulus established as a CS— through prior Pavlovian fear conditioning. Responses to either of two panels were effective in a Sidman avoidance schedule, but only responses to the preferred panel produced CS—. Conditioned reinforcement is known to affect preference, but its most powerful effect is said to be on the rate of responding. We modified both the distribution and rate of Sidman avoidance responding by arranging a contingency between an independently established Pavlovian inhibitor of fear and Sidman wheelturn avoidance responding (Weisman and Litner,

1969). Rats from Groups CS—, TRC, and No CS shown in Fig. 1 served
as subjects. Schedules, modified from Ferster and Skinner (1957), were
devised for the reinforcement of Sidman avoidance responding already
occurring at a substantial rate. During four avoidance sessions, administered after a baseline session, on each occasion that a rat emitted at least
ten responses in a 5-sec interval the tone was presented during the succeeding 5-sec interval. This differential reinforcement of high rate (DRH)
schedule required a momentary rate of at least 120 responses per minute
to produce the tone. The tone was omitted from two DRH-extinction
sessions. The contingency was then reversed; if a subject emitted zero or
one response in a 5-sec interval, then the tone was presented during the
succeeding 5-sec interval. During these sessions responding at a low
momentary rate, 12 or fewer responses per minute (DRL), was reinforced.
Finally two sessions of DRL-extinction, without the tone, were administered.

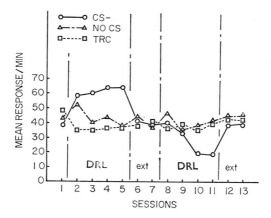

Fig. 2. Responding during baseline, DRM, DRM-extinction, DRL, and DRL-
extinction sessions.

Figure 2 presents response-rate functions for each group. Responding
was reliably increased by the DRH schedule, and reliably decreased by
the DRL schedule only in Group CS—. Response rates of Groups TRC
and No CS were relatively unchanged by either reinforcement contingency.
The obvious conclusion suggested by these data is that the tone functioned
as a reinforcer only for subjects with prior and independent Pavlovian
conditioning sessions in which the tone signalled shock-free periods.
Demonstration of a reinforcement function for a Pavlovian inhibitory
stimulus is in line with the notion that centrally mediated emotional states
are controlled by a Pavlovian process (Rescorla and Solomon, 1967). It is

s

difficult to understand how theories that posit only direct inhibition of operant responding could make sense of the reinforcement function of a Pavlovian conditioned inhibitor.

III. Pavlovian Events in Discrete-trial Avoidance Learning

Pavlovian fear conditioning, of one sort or another, is widely assumed to be an implicit function of avoidance training. Revised two-process theory, for example, has based its inferences concerning the acquisition of eliciting and reinforcing effects by the SS on the results of experiments designed to examine the products of Pavlovian inhibitory fear conditioning. We all know that avoidance behaviour is an instance of operant conditioning. What we sometimes forget is that any Pavlovian conditioning paradigm implicit in avoidance training must therefore differ in parametric detail from the usual experimenter-controlled Pavlovian paradigms. Virtually all Pavlovian fear-conditioning experiments hold the duration and distribution of CS+, CS−, and shock constant. Implicit conditioning of excitation to the WS and inhibition to the SS may well be influenced by systematic variation in the duration and distribution of the WS, SS, and shock produced by responding over the course of avoidance training. These considerations led us to construct an experimental procedure for extracting the Pavlovian events from avoidance training. The experiments presented here follow, in outline, our previous work (Weisman and Litner, 1969). However, in the present experiments discrete-trial avoidance training, or a yoked sequence of response-independent Pavlovian conditioned stimuli and shocks was substituted for the usual Pavlovian conditioning paradigms. We continued to use assessment procedures already developed to identify Pavlovian eliciting and operant conditioned reinforcing stimuli; only the form of conditioning under assessment changed.

A. THE WARNING AND SAFETY SIGNALS IN ONE-WAY SHUTTLE AVOIDANCE TRAINING AS PAVLOVIAN EVENTS

One of the earlier, and seemingly simpler, procedures for conducting discrete-trial avoidance training required the subject to respond to the WS by shuttling to the opposite compartment of a runway. In our variant of this often-used procedure, the partition separating the two compartments of the runway opened simultaneously with the onset of a tone, the WS. If the rat failed to run into the opposite chamber during the 5 sec after WS onset, then brief electric shocks (·5 sec at ·75 ma) were delivered at 2-sec intervals until the shuttle response was emitted. After a response the partition was lowered and the WS terminated. Following an inter-trial interval of 2·5–3·5 min (mean = 3·0 min) the rat was placed, by hand, back into the start compartment, and 10 sec later the next trial began. Training ceased when response latencies of under 5 sec were obtained on nine of ten consecutive trials.

This would appear to be the situation in which traditional two-process theory is most at home. Presumably, the WS acquires a fear eliciting function and the shuttle-avoidance response is reinforced by the termination of the WS. The possibility of an active role, as a fear inhibitor and positive reinforcer, for the safety signal in one-way shuttle avoidance has been either ignored or discounted (Bolles, 1970). The purpose of our experiment was to assess the acquisition of Pavlovian excitatory and inhibitory functions by the WS and SS respectively. We were especially interested in effects of the sequence of stimuli generated by the runway avoidance technique. Accordingly, yoked (Y) subjects were each presented with an identical sequence of stimuli as their counterparts acquiring the avoidance response, but without any noticeable opportunity to modify the duration or intensity of the stimuli. In Groups SS and SS-Y, immediately after the partition was lowered, an overhead signal lamp was illuminated for 5 sec. In Groups TRC and TRC-Y, 5-sec presentation of the light occurred at random with respect to WS offset. Presentation of the light was omitted in Groups No SS and No SS-Y. Thirty-six adult female hooded rats, equally divided among the groups, served as subjects. Prior to the experiment proper, each rat had four sessions of Sidman avoidance training. During testing, 20 5-sec presentations of the tone and light occurred during a Sidman avoidance session laid on after shuttle-avoidance training or yoked Pavlovian fear conditioning.

Rates of responding during successive 5-sec periods prior to, during (S), and after presentation of WS and SS to the yoked Pavlovian conditioning groups are shown in Fig. 3. Results for equivalent groups with prior one-way shuttle response training are shown in Fig. 4. The upper panels show results for Groups SS-Y and SS, the middle panels for Groups TRC-Y and TRC, and the lower panels present data from Groups No SS-Y and No SS. The first thing to notice in comparing Figs. 3 and 4 is that the effects of WS and SS do not differ reliably between avoidant and yoked subjects. We interpret this to mean that the sequence of stimuli resulting from avoidance training, and not the avoidance response itself, is the major determinant of the observed results. Comparison among the yoked groups revealed that light was an effective inhibitor of fear only in Group SS-Y where it had previously served as a signal for the nonoccurrence of shock; the light did not reduce responding in either Group TRC-Y or Group No SS-Y. A similar conclusion can, of course, be drawn from results obtained from the avoidant rats (Fig. 4).

The acquisition of the eliciting function of a Pavlovian conditioned inhibitor of fear by the SS is consistent with prediction from revised two-process theory. The inhibitory effect of the SS in one-way shuttle avoidance is not in line with Bolles' (1970) assertion that avoidance response acquisition in this situation might be too rapid for Pavlovian inhibition to occur.

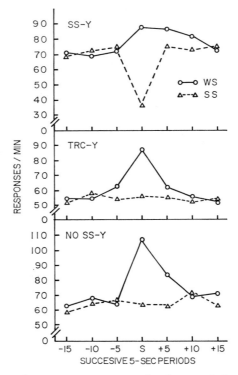

FIG. 3. Mean rates of response across successive 5-sec periods prior to, during (S), and after stimulus presentation in a Sidman avoidance test session. Testing followed conditioning yoked to discrete-trial shuttle avoidance training.

In our own laboratory (Weisman and Litner, 1971) acquisition of inhibition by CS—, even at an optimal inter-trial interval, required more trials than we administered in the present study. We are led to the conclusion that present in the sequence of stimuli resultant in avoidance training is a powerful, but as yet unanalysed, determinant of the inhibitory process.

The excitatory effect of the WS is also shown in Figs 3 and 4. The WS was not uniformly effective as an excitor of fear. The WS elevated response rates only slightly in Groups SS and SS-Y, but had a more pronounced and typical excitatory effect in the other groups. Interpretation of this finding is somewhat complex, but will be set out in a later section of the chapter.

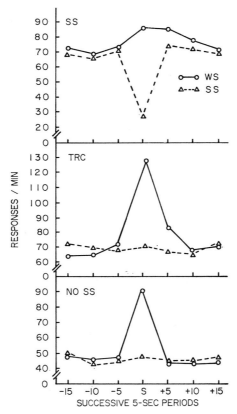

FIG. 4. Mean rates of responding across successive 5-sec periods prior to, during (S), and after stimulus presentation in a Sidman avoidance test session. Testing followed discrete-trial shuttle avoidance training.

B. THE WARNING AND SAFETY SIGNALS IN DISCRETE-TRIAL WHEELTURN AVOIDANCE TRAINING AS PAVLOVIAN EVENTS

Acquisition of leverpress and wheelturn avoidance behaviour by rats is said (Meyer *et al.*, 1960) to require many more shocks, and pose greater difficulties for the experimenter, than acquisition of one-way shuttle avoidance responding. Bolles (1970) sought to account for wide variation in the level of difficulty of several avoidance responses in terms of their similarity to the species-specific defence reactions elicited by shock. The question we sought to answer with the present experiment was whether the difference in the apparent level of difficulty between shuttle and wheelturn responses reflected a difference in reinforcement mechanism. If the revised two-process theory is to be of any general interest it must account for the reinforcement of a wide variety of avoidance responses and not just the simplest or the most difficult cases.

We chose to examine the acquisition of the wheelturn response in a discrete-trial paradigm simply because we have had more experience with this response than with leverpress avoidance responding. The procedure was similar to that of the shuttle response study, but physical identity between the response acquired during discrete-trial training and the response emitted during testing forced some important modifications in experimental design. Avoidance training was administered in three 50-trial sessions with the same WS, SS, and shock parameters as in the prior study. Yoked subjects received an identical sequence of stimuli in a separate Pavlovian conditioning chamber. Only the yoked subjects had prior Sidman avoidance training and subsequent testing on the avoidance baseline. Prior to discrete-trial training the avoidant subjects were experimentally naïve. Five avoidant subjects and their yoked counterparts were discarded from the experiment for failure to reach a criterion of 70% shock-free trials in the final session. The criterion was included because a high density of shock produced considerable variability in response rate among yoked subjects. The remaining 48 adult hooded female rats were apportioned equally to Groups SS, SS-Y, TRC, TRC-Y, No SS and No SS-Y as in the prior study.

The results of testing during a Sidman avoidance session are shown in Fig. 5. Responding was reliably disrupted by the light only when it had previously served as a safety signal, Group SS-Y. The light had no noticeable effect on avoidance responding when it was presented at random during prior yoked Pavlovian fear conditioning, Group TRC-Y, or when it was omitted from prior conditioning sessions, Group No SS-Y. In spite of the many procedural differences between this experiment and the shuttle-avoidance work, the SS became a Pavlovian inhibitor of fear in the course of training in both experiments. Of course, revised two-process theory states that this is necessary if avoidance behaviour is to be reinforced.

The excitatory effect of presenting the WS is also displayed in Fig. 5. Reliable excitation was obtained in Groups TRC-Y and No SS-Y. Responding in Group SS-Y was not affected by presentation of the WS. These findings are consistent with those of the prior study except that excitation, even in Groups TRC-Y and No SS-Y was not as marked in the present work.

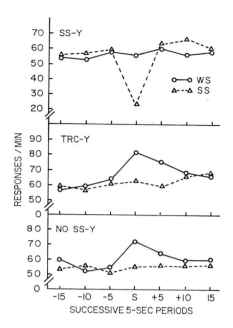

FIG. 5. Mean rates of responding across successive 5-sec periods prior to, during (S), and after stimulus presentation in a Sidman avoidance test session. Testing followed conditioning yoked to discrete-trial wheelturn avoidance training.

C. PAVLOVIAN EXCITATION OF FEAR ELICITED BY THE WARNING SIGNAL

The effects of WS presentation during testing in the present experiments appear to pose difficulties for both traditional and revised two-process theories. On the one hand, near absence of elicited fear of the WS among the SS groups illustrates once again that fear of the WS and avoidance performance need not be correlated. On the other hand, fear of the WS observed in the remaining groups suggests that without an explicit SS avoidance behaviour might still require termination of a conditioned excitor of fear.

Actually, interpretation of these results requires presentation of some relevant facts omitted until now. Namely, the acquisition of shuttle and wheelturn avoidance responses in the present experiments, like the acquisition of a number of other avoidance responses (Bolles, 1970; Bolles and Popp, 1964; Bower et al., 1965), was reliably accelerated by presentation of a response-produced safety signal. In the first experiment, Group SS reached a criterion of nine shuttle-avoidance responses in ten consecutive trials more rapidly than the other groups. In the second experiment,

Group SS made a greater number of wheelturn avoidance responses than the other groups. An important consequence of accelerated acquisition was a decrease in the number of WS-shock pairings early in training, and an increase in the number of runs of consecutive WS presentations without shock later in training. Perhaps, as in experiments by Kamin *et al.* (1963) and Linden (1969), fear of the WS extinguished in the course of avoidance training in Groups SS and SS-Y. This explanation implies that the WS in Group SS originally elicited conditioned fear which later extinguished, and that if training continued, fear of the WS would have extinguished in the other groups as well.

To replicate and extend our wheelturn avoidance study we administered Sidman avoidance test sessions at three successive stages of learning to eight additional rats trained under conditions like those in effect for Group SS-Y. Training occurred in 25-trial sessions and testing followed the first, third, and fifth yoked Pavlovian conditioning sessions. The results of each test are shown in the three panels of Fig. 6. The proportion of trials on which shock occurred, shown in the right-hand corner of each panel of Fig. 6, decreased markedly from the first to the fifth conditioning session. Fear of the WS was maximal after the first conditioning session and decreased after the third and fifth conditioning sessions. The SS disrupted avoidance behaviour after only a single 25-trial conditioning session and continued to inhibit fear in later test sessions. In the first test session, upper panel of Fig. 6, SS offset elicited a marked increase in responding. Offset of the SS elicited less fear in the next test session, middle panel of Fig. 6, and had no observable excitatory effect in the final test session, lower panel of Fig. 6. This biphasic effect of the SS is not observed in the terminal test performance, Figs 4 and 5, of subjects of yoked Pavlovian fear conditioning. In fact, biphasic effects of CS+ and CS− were not observed with typical explicit Pavlovian paradigms (Weisman and Litner, 1969; 1971). Also, the yoked paradigm generates Pavlovian inhibition more rapidly than explicit conditioning.

The argument that avoidance responses are reinforced by the termination of a fear eliciting stimulus, the traditional two-process position, is again demonstrated to be incorrect. The details are even more embarrassing; fear of the WS and the "efficiency" of avoidance responding are clearly negatively correlated in Fig. 6. The results of a number of related experiments, each based on a different avoidance procedure can be projected. The major parameter in each experiment could be the number of consecutive avoidance responses preceding the test session. Measurable inhibition of fear by the SS should be obtained prior to, or concomitant with, increases in the strength of the avoidance response as in Fig. 6. On the other hand, fear of the WS should decrease with increases in the number of consecutive avoidance responses emitted prior to test.

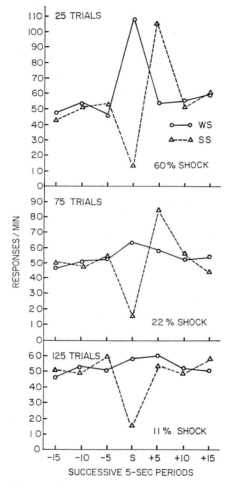

FIG. 6. Mean rates of responding across successive 5-sec periods prior to, during (S), and after stimulus presentation in Sidman avoidance test sessions. Testing followed 25, 75, and 125 trials of conditioning yoked to discrete-trial wheelturn avoidance training.

D. THE SAFETY SIGNAL IN DISCRETE-TRIAL AVOIDANCE TRAINING AS A CONDITIONED POSITIVE REINFORCER

Experiments reported in the present chapter show that the SS can become a powerful conditioned inhibitor of fear. In previous research (Weisman and Litner, 1969), already discussed in detail, we found that a conditioned inhibitor of fear was also a conditioned positive reinforcer. Revised two-process theory demands than an SS established as an inhibitor of fear in the course of avoidance training function as a conditioned positive reinforcer.

We examined the reinforcing properties of the SS in two highly similar experiments. The subjects of these experiments were chosen haphazardly from avoidant rats of the one-way shuttle and wheelturn experiments: four rats from each avoidance group were selected for each experiment. The one-way shuttle response experiment yielded subjects with prior Sidman avoidance training, but the wheelturn response experiment did not provide this benefit. It was necessary to administer 4–6 sessions of Sidman avoidance training to these subjects prior to the experiment proper. Then, a DRH schedule of conditioned reinforcement was superimposed on free-operant avoidance in a series of four Sidman avoidance sessions. This meant that increases in the rate of responding to ten or more responses in 5 sec, a momentary rate of 120 responses per min, produced 5-sec illumination of an overhead signal lamp. Additional sessions run without the light provided extinction data. The light had, of course, previously

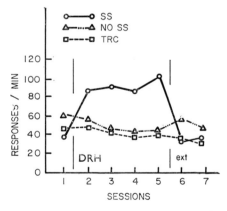

FIG. 7. Responding during baseline, DRH, and DRH-extinction sessions for rats with prior discrete-trial shuttle avoidance training.

served as a safety signal in Group SS in each experiment and therefore had demonstrated inhibitory properties (see Figs. 3–6). The light had no prior history as an SS, or a CS−, for the remaining subjects in each experiment.

The rate of responding during baseline, DRH-reinforcement, and DRH-extinction sessions is shown for prior shuttle avoidant and wheelturn avoidant rats in Figs. 7 and 8 respectively. In each experiment, DRH scheduling of the light had a sizeable and reliable positive reinforcement effect on the rate of responding only in Group SS. The light was not an effective conditioned reinforcer in Groups TRC or No SS where it had no previous history as a safety signal in discrete-trial avoidance training.

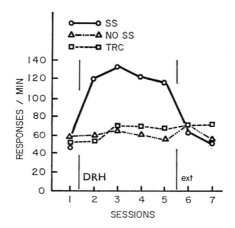

FIG. 8. Responding during baseline, DRH, and DRH-extinction sessions for rats with prior discrete-trial wheelturn avoidance training.

IV. Avoidance Learning as an Instance of Positive Reinforcement

Both Pavlovian fear conditioning and discrete-trial avoidance learning yield stimuli that inhibit fear. Indeed, the one-way shuttle task appears to yield Pavlovian inhibitory conditioning more rapidly than any of the standard Pavlovian differential conditioning paradigms. It is at least as important that the SS, no less than an independently established Pavlovian inhibitor of fear, CS—, is an effective conditioned reinforcer. Together these facts allow us to reconstruct the sequence of critical events in the reinforcement of avoidance behaviour. (a) Shocks presented in a given situation produce a conditioned motivational state. Pavlovian conditioned fear may, or may not reach its zenith in the presence of some explicit WS. It really does not matter. All that is required is that the situation becomes aversive through conditioning. It is clear that the situation in which avoidance training is administered does become aversive; Sidman (1962) and Verhave (1962) found animals respond to produce time out from an avoidance schedule. (b) It is also necessary that some stimulus comes to reliably signal the non-occurrence of shock, or at least a relatively longer time period free from shock than other stimuli (Weisman and Litner, 1971). Such stimuli become conditioned inhibitors of fear as in the present experiments. (c) Finally, some particular class of responses is scheduled to produce the Pavlovian inhibitor in a situation where the emotional or motivational state already described prevails. The result of this positive reinforcement contingency is an increase in the response strength of the class of behaviour labelled "avoidant". Classifying avoidance behaviour as an instance of positive reinforcement does not imply that the avoidance situation is not aversive or that fear is altogether absent during maintained avoidance responding. There is considerable evidence, some of it quite recent (Baron and Trenholme, 1971), to show that subjects will respond to remove situational or background cues correlated with an avoidance schedule.

Wagner and Rescorla (Chapter 12) implicate excitation conditioned to background cues, rather than generalization from CS+, as a critical determinant of Pavlovian inhibition by CS−. In the present context, this explanation states that all of the stimuli present, and not just the WS, gain in Pavlovian excitatory strength on each occasion that shock is delivered. Thus, the SS is presented in compound with excitatory background cues and fear present at SS onset is inhibited.

A weakness common to the elegant Wagner-Rescorla model and our revised two-process account of avoidance behaviour is the technical problem involved in assessing the effects of Pavlovian conditioning to background cues. Both positions appear to predict residual fear to background stimuli at a time when the WS no longer elicits fear. Perhaps greater resistance to extinction accrues to background stimuli because of increased intermittency of pairing with shock. On the other hand, the inhibition of fear may be even more independent of its excitation than we first supposed.

Traditional two-process theorists (Mowrer, 1947) and experimental analysts of behaviour (Herrnstein and Hineline, 1966) alike catalogue avoidance training procedures as instances of negative reinforcement. That is, avoidance responding is said to be reinforced by the termination of aversive stimuli or by a reduction in their density. Two-process theorists suggest conditioned fear as the source of aversive stimulation, while some "operant conditioners" now appear to favour a shock-density reduction notion. Some avoidance training procedures schedule both WS termination and reduced shock density. Other procedures schedule only a reduction in shock density (Herrnstein and Hineline, 1966; Bolles, 1970). Sometimes, as we shall see, neither event is a scheduled consequence of behaviour.

An interesting result of the present analysis of the reinforcement of avoidance behaviour is the rather trivial role escape from the WS and shock avoidance *per se* assume in the explanation. Powerful positive reinforcement effects can be obtained even when the class of responses producing the conditioned inhibitor has no discernible effect on shock density. For example, the rate of avoidance responding can be reduced by scheduling differential reinforcement of low rate by CS— (Weisman and Litner, 1969). Also, rats will acquire a leverpress response that is correlated with the nonoccurrence of shock even when responding has no effect on overall shock density (Hineline, 1970). We view the free operant schedules developed by Sidman (1953) and by Hineline (1970) as further instances of positive reinforcement by a response-produced SS. Rescorla (1967) has already suggested that a feedback stimulus produced by responses emitted in a Sidman avoidance schedule may become a conditioned inhibitor of fear. The reinforcer in Hineline's schedule may have a similar origin. Experiments designed to examine inhibitory and reinforcing functions of response-feedback stimuli in free responding and yoked subjects of Sidman and Hineline schedules could obviously provide support for our inferences.

It seems appropriate to ask whether there is any useful sense in continuing to describe the behaviour we have studied as avoidant? Reconstruction of the critical events in avoidance training by revised two-process theory classified avoidance learning as an instance of positive reinforcement. Often positive reinforcement is dependent on deprivation-induced motivational states; the avoidance case is unusual in that positive conditioned reinforcement is dependent on a Pavlovian-induced conditioned emotional state. The defining property shared by all positive reinforcers is the common effect of their onset, when scheduled as a consequence of behaviour. The motivational conditions under which the reinforcement effect is obtained is simply not a part of the shared functional definition.

Acknowledgements

This research was supported by Ontario Mental Health Foundation Grant No. 189. The authors gratefully acknowledge the technical assistance and critical advice rendered by Michael di Franco. The second author held tenure as a National Research Council Post-Graduate Fellow during the present work.

References

Azrin, N. H. and Holz, W. C. (1966). Punishment. In: W. K. Honig (Ed.), *Operant Behavior: Areas of Research and Application*. New York: Appleton–Century–Crofts.

Baron, A. and Trenholme, Irene A. (1971). Response-dependent and response-independent time out from an avoidance schedule. *Journal of the Experimental Analysis of Behavior*, **16**, 123–131.

Bolles, R. C. (1970). Species-specific defense reactions and avoidance learning. *Psychological Review*, **77**, 32–48.

Bolles, R. C. and Popp, R. J., Jr. (1964). Parameters affecting the acquisition of Sidman avoidance. *Journal of the Experimental Analysis of Behavior*, **7**, 315–321.

Bower, G., Starr, R. and Lazarovitz, L. (1965). Amount of response-produced change in the CS and avoidance learning. *Journal of Comparative and Physiological Psychology*, **59**, 13–17.

Estes, W. K. and Skinner, B. F. (1941). Some quantitative properties of anxiety. *Journal of Experimental Psychology*, **29**, 390–400.

Ferster, C. B. and Skinner, B. F. (1957). *Schedules of Reinforcement*. New York: Appleton–Century–Crofts.

Herrnstein, R. J. and Hineline, P. N. (1966). Negative reinforcement as shock-frequency reduction. *Journal of the Experimental Analysis of Behavior*, **9**, 421–430.

Hineline, P. N. (1970). Negative reinforcement without shock reduction. *Journal of the Experimental Analysis of Behavior*, **14**, 259–268.

Kamin, L. J., Brimer, C. J. and Black, A. H. (1963). Conditioned suppression as a monitor of fear of the CS in the course of avoidance training. *Journal of Comparative and Physiological Psychology*, **56**, 497–501.

Linden, D. R. (1969). Attenuation and reestablishment of the CER by discriminated avoidance conditioning in rats. *Journal of Comparative and Physiological Psychology*, **69**, 573–578.

Meyer, D. R., Cho, C. and Wesemann, A. F. (1960). On problems of conditioning discriminated leverpress avoidance responses. *Psychological Review*, **67**, 224–228.

Mowrer, O. H. (1947). On the dual nature of learning – a re-interpretation of "conditioning" and "problem-solving". *Harvard Educational Review*, **17**, 102–148.

Rescorla, R. A. (1967). Inhibition of delay in Pavlovian fear conditioning. *Journal of Comparative and Physiological Psychology*, **64**, 114–120.

Rescorla, R. A. (1968). Pavlovian conditioned fear in Sidman avoidance learning. *Journal of Comparative and Physiological Psychology*, **65**, 55–60.

Rescorla, R. A. (1969). Establishment of a positive reinforcer through contrast with shock. *Journal of Comparative and Physiological Psychology*, **67**, 260–263.

Rescorla, R. A. and LoLordo, V. M. (1965). Inhibition of avoidance behavior. *Journal of Comparative and Physiological Psychology*, **59**, 406–412.

Rescorla, R. A. and Solomon, R. L. (1967). Two-process learning theory. Relationships between Pavlovian conditioning and instrumental learning. *Psychological Review*, **74**, 151–182.

Sidman, M. (1953). Two temporal parameters of the maintenance of avoidance conditioning by the white rat. *Journal of Comparative and Physiological Psychology*, **46**, 253–261.

Sidman, M. (1962). Reduction of shock frequency as reinforcement for avoidance behavior. *Journal of the Experimental Analysis of Behavior*, **5**, 247–257.

Verhave, T. (1962). The functional properties of a time out from an avoidance schedule. *Journal of the Experimental Analysis of Behavior*, **5**, 391–422.

Weisman, R. G. and Litner, J. S. (1969). Positive conditioned reinforcement of Sidman avoidance behavior in rats. *Journal of Comparative and Physiological Psychology*, **68**, 597–603.

Weisman, R. G. and Litner, J. S. (1971). Role of the intertrial interval in Pavlovian differential conditioning of fear in rats. *Journal of Comparative and Physiological Psychology*, **74**, 211–218.

C | Inhibition and Classical Conditioning

C

In this section the focus of interest is on the concept of inhibition in classical conditioning and the nature and localization of the processes involved. However, in the first chapter of the section Amsel discusses the role of frustrative nonreward in producing response decrements in instrumental learning. He argues that such decreases in responding can best be explained in terms of competing excitatory tendencies, and, in particular, that a variety of results showing transfer of persistence in responding during extinction from one experimental situation to another cannot be explained in terms of inhibitory control. Amsel therefore suggests that inhibition may in fact only occur in the simplest forms of classical conditioning.

In Chapter 12 Wagner and Rescorla propose a formalized theory of classical conditioning in which inhibition plays a central role; they show how their theory predicts the development of inhibition in a variety of types of situation and present evidence supporting the theory; they also show that their theory predicts the development of inhibition even in situations where reinforcement is present and that experimental evidence appears to support these predictions.

Like Amsel, Konorski in Chapter 13 suggests that the phenomena which Pavlov and others have taken to be evidence for conditioned inhibition may not be the result of the development of specifically inhibitory connections. He suggests instead that all learning is excitatory and that inhibitory effects arise from innate reciprocally inhibitory connections between brain structures representing different types of unconditioned stimuli.

Thomas, in Chapter 14, makes a plea for more concordance between the behavioural and neurophysiological uses of the term inhibition. He describes experiments using exteroceptive conditioned stimuli and hypothalamic stimulation as the unconditioned stimulus; in these experiments he was able to measure the effects of excitatory and inhibitory conditioned stimuli on responsivity to hypothalamic stimulation. Such an approach, based on standard neurophysiological models may offer a new way of looking at the basic processes involved in inhibitory learning.

T

The account of the localization and mechanism of internal inhibition presented by Asratian in Chapter 15 is firmly within the Pavlovian tradition; however, Asratian differs from Pavlov in suggesting that internal inhibition is localized, not at the centre for the conditioned stimulus, but in intermediate links of the conditioned reflex arc.

Inhibition and Mediation in Classical, Pavlovian and Instrumental Conditioning

ABRAM AMSEL

University of Texas at Austin, Austin, Texas, U.S.A.

I. Introduction 275
II. Mediation in Instrumental Learning 277
III. Inhibition in Simple Classical Conditioning 290
IV. Conclusion 294
Acknowledgements 297
References 297

I. Introduction

About twenty years ago (Amsel, 1951), I suggested that a concept of frustrative inhibition (r_F) might be added as a third factor to Hull's two factor theory of inhibition. Since that time I often have felt that the concept of inhibition, as it applies to the understanding of instrumental behaviour, is imprecise and perhaps misleading. In a rather obscure footnote in a paper written ten years ago (Amsel, 1962), I ventured such an opinion in these words: "It is questionable that 'inhibition' is the appropriate and correct term to use in regard to response decrement related to frustrative non-reward. Better terms would be 'interference' or 'competition', since frustrative inhibition cannot be regarded as directly affecting the excitatory tendency out of which it grows. It [frustrative inhibition] is rather a new excitatory tendency which competes with the older one." Despite the footnote, the phrases "frustrative inhibition" and "the inhibitory (aversive) properties of nonreward" were used throughout the article in which the footnote appeared, and like many others I have continued to use these terms up to the present time. It is obviously difficult to keep from doing so.

To say that a concept of inhibition is not required in an account of instrumental response decrement and suppression might seem like a semantic quibble. Brown and Jenkins (1967), acknowledging that most investigators are dissatisfied with the implied analogy between neural inhibition and the response decrements encountered in the conditioning of the whole organism, have taken the reasonable position that identification of inhibitory stimulus control no more rests on a physiological analogue than does identification of excitatory stimulus control. In order to make my position seem something more than a quibble, I want first to present some of the recent thinking and research in our laboratory that have influenced my view. After that I will look at the classical-instrumental distinction, if not in an entirely new way, then at least in a somewhat different way than before. My purpose will be to show that the concepts of inhibition and of inhibitory control can only be applied meaningfully to the explanation of the simplest kind of associative learning, that is to say to learning that involves only direct unmediated connections; that the usual Thorndikian experiment and even, in some cases, the usual Pavlovian one, are much too complex mediationally to be regarded as appropriate experimental arrangements for the study of inhibitory control. Put another way, I am going to urge that the concepts of inhibition and inhibitory control be de-emphasized and that greater emphasis be placed on the role of mediation in response decrement and response persistence as studied in Pavlovian and Thorndikian experiments.

My view in this respect is different from Skinner's (1938), who a long time ago held that an explanation of response-strength reduction in terms of the weakening of excitation was possible without invoking a concept of inhibition. My position is that the true weakening of an excitatory tendency does indeed require inhibitory mechanisms for its explanation, but that suppressing the expression of one excitatory tendency by other counteractive excitatory factors does not so require. The consideration that overrides all others for me is that to talk about inhibition in Thorndikian, and perhaps in Pavlovian, reactions leads one to take too simplistic a view of the role of nonreinforcement and other aversive events in instrumental responding. To regard response decrement and suppression as events mediated by counteractive excitatory tendencies opens up a wider range of phenomena for observation and quickly dispels any idea that extinction and discrimination, say, are simple phenomena based on simple inhibitory control. In the context of these kinds of considerations, I would like to present a few out of many experimental results from our laboratory which I maintain could not have derived from a straight inhibitory position on nonreinforcement of instrumental or operant responses. These results seem to me to require that the effects of nonreinforcement be conceptualized in terms of more complex mediational mechanisms. Some of these experiments have been presented before in other contexts; some are recent and unpublished; but all have to do in one way or another with what have been called partial reinforcement (persistence) effects, as well as with other apparently mediated extinction effects. I will try to defend the position that, in whatever kinds of learning these persistence effects are demonstrable, the concept of inhibition cannot be applied very usefully.

II. Mediation in Instrumental Learning

For several years we have been working with a theory of instrumental reward learning in which the position is taken that persistence to a goal reflects learning to respond to cues of anticipated frustration (e.g. Amsel, 1958, 1962, 1967; Amsel et al., 1966; Amsel and Ward, 1965; Spence, 1960). The background for this theory, as it applies to the PRE, is a series of experiments beginning in the early 1950s, by many people in many laboratories, which have shown that frustrative nonreward can be regarded as influencing behaviour in at least three ways: (a) through nonspecific emotional-motivational effects which result in sharp increases in the vigour of ongoing behaviour: the FE as measured in a double runway, (b) through characteristic feedback stimuli from primary frustration which come to be associated with and control the direction of immediately following behaviour, and (c) through the directive properties of stimulus feedback from anticipatory (secondary) frustration. The four-stage frustration hypothesis of the PRE which emerged out of the findings of these early experiments is a classical-conditioning model, and it says, in effect, that in partial reward training stimuli arising out of conditioned frustration become instrumentally counterconditioned to goal-approach behaviour after first disrupting that behaviour.

The theory divides partial reinforcement acquisition (acquisition of approach to $S+$) into four stages, and describes the formation of a connection between s_F and the response of approaching a goal (R_{APP}). It depends on the primary frustrative reaction (R_F) to nonreward (NR), the formation of a learned anticipatory form of frustration (r_F) through classical conditioning, and the counterconditioning of the feedback stimulus (s_F) from avoidance to approach. *This theory conceptualizes how a disruptive process based on nonreward emerges in partial reinforcement acquisition and produces conflict in Stage 3, and how the disruption recedes in Stage 4 with the concomitant strengthening of the connection between s_F and R_{APP}.* This disruptive process does not occur in ordinary CRF training, and so there is no counterconditioning and extinction is rapid after CRF.

A general theory of persistence that I first proposed four years ago (Amsel, 1972) subsumes the frustration interpretation of the PRE as a special case. It is more general in the sense that persistence is held to result from the counterconditioning to ongoing behaviour of stimuli other than the specific frustration-produced stimuli called for in the theory of the partial reinforcement effect. According to this more general view, persistence develops in responding whenever an organism learns to approach, or to maintain a response, actively or passively, in the face of any kind of stimulus which arouses a competing-disruptive response. In

STAGES	FRUSTRATION THEORY OF THE PRE	MORE GENERAL THEORY OF PERSISTENCE
1.	$S^{\pm} \longrightarrow r_R \longrightarrow s_R \longrightarrow R_{APP}$	$S_o \longrightarrow R_o$
2.	$S^{\pm} \longrightarrow r_R \longrightarrow s_R \longrightarrow R_{APP}[NR] \longrightarrow R_F$	
3.	$S^{\pm} \Big\langle \begin{array}{l} r_R \longrightarrow s_R \longrightarrow R_{APP} \\ \qquad\qquad \updownarrow \text{ CONFLICT} \\ r_F \longrightarrow s_F \longrightarrow R_{AVD} \end{array}$	$\boxed{\begin{array}{l} S_o \\ (S_x) \end{array}} \Big\langle \begin{array}{l} R_o \\ R_x \end{array}$
4.	$S^{\pm} \Big\langle \begin{array}{l} r_R \longrightarrow s_R \longrightarrow R_{APP} \\ r_F \longrightarrow s_F \longrightarrow R_{AVD} \end{array}$	$\boxed{\begin{array}{l} S_o \\ (S_x) \end{array}} \Big\langle \begin{array}{l} R_o \\ R_x \end{array}$

FIG. 1. The specific frustration theory of persistence and a more general theory of persistence that subsumes frustration theory as a special case (from Amsel, 1972).

terms of a stimulus-response schema, what I have just proposed in its special and general forms is schematized in the left- and right-hand portions, respectively, of Fig. 1.

According to this schema, when S_x is introduced into a situation, S_o, an interfering response (R_x) is at first evoked, but as instrumental counterconditioning of S_x to R_o occurs, the original ongoing response (R_o) becomes more dominant, and, in the process, the $S_o \rightarrow R_o$ tendency has become more resistant to disruption by stimuli of the class, S_x. I am certainly not prepared to give an exhaustive list of members of the class, S_x; but, generally speaking, S_x can be regarded as stimuli to whose disruptive effects organisms are said to habituate. I have suggested that the s_F of the frustration theory of the PRE is simply one of these kinds of stimuli, which emerges out of a special chain of circumstances in partial reinforcement acquisition, elicits responses that disrupt ongoing behaviour, and is finally instrumentally counterconditioned to that behaviour, increasing the resistance of the goal-approach behaviour to disruption by s_F (and perhaps also by other members of the class of stimuli, S_x). The experiments I will now describe have had to do more with the special frustration conception than with the general one.

We have been greatly influenced in our work by an experiment performed some time ago, independently, and published at about the same time, by Theios (1962) and Jenkins (1962). Since the Theios experiment was published shortly before the Jenkins, I will call this the Theios–Jenkins experiment. Theios, using a runway apparatus and rats as subjects, and Jenkins, working with pigeons in a discrete-trial Skinner box, demonstrated that persistence acquired in partial-reward acquisition carries through a block of continuous rewards, interpolated between acquisition and extinction. This was an important finding because it contra-indicated a discrimination hypothesis as a necessary part of the explanation of the PRE, and provided an experimental model for studying persistence in terms of long-lasting—even permanent—mediational mechanisms.

Several published and as yet unpublished experiments from our laboratory have extended the limits of the basic Theios–Jenkins result, both in between-subjects and within-subject experiments, but I can only describe a few of these here, and I will ask you to consider whether or not a concept of simple inhibitory control can handle these findings, or would even have suggested doing the experiments. Figure 2 shows the results of an experiment conducted by Rashotte and Surridge (1969). In this experiment, there was one trial every *three* days, and it was run according to the Theios–Jenkins sequence; a CRF phase was interpolated between acquisition and extinction of a running response, measured over five, one-foot segments of a runway.

This experiment and an earlier one (Donin *et al.*, 1967) extend the findings of Theios and Jenkins. First of all, the experiment is conducted with a very large inter-trial interval making it even more unlikely that discriminating the transition from acquisition to extinction can account for the results. Secondly, the finding is extended to include, not only partial reward, but also partial delay of reward, a condition in which every acquisition trial ends in reward. It seems not unreasonable, then, to think that in the case of training involving widely spaced rewards and non-rewards, persistent behaviour may be mediated by some internal process that has characteristics beyond what is implied by simple inhibitory control.

We have been dealing so far with persistence, developed and measured in the same physical situation. However, an instrumental counterconditioning view of persistence, as we have so far employed the term, implies that a connection of some kind is formed in acquisition between an initially disruptive internal stimulus and some ongoing behaviour. If this mediational control is powerful, the counterconditioned response might be evoked not only in the physical situation in which the connection was formed, as in the usual PRE experiment or the Theios–Jenkins experiment, but in any situation in which the internal mediator comes into play. An

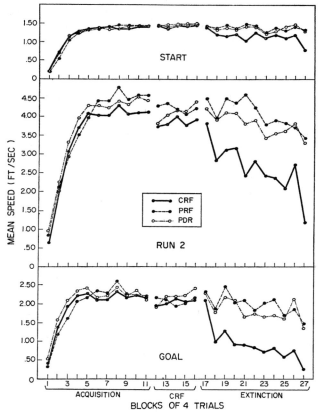

FIG. 2. Relative persistence (resistance to extinction) after partial reward and partial delay of reward even after interpolation, between acquisition and extinction, of a block of continuously rewarded trials for all groups; and even though the experiment was run at one trial every three days (data from Rashotte and Surridge, 1969).

experiment, which I have referred to many times, performed a few years ago by Robert Ross, is a case in point. Figure 3 is an outline of the experiment. Again, you can see in it features of the Theios–Jenkins experiment; but there are also important additional features, which I should point out. First of all, the preliminary learning phase involves not one but three different responses, each different from the response continuously reinforced in Phase 2 and extinguished in Phase 3. Running and jumping (across a short gap) in Phase 1 were meant to be compatible with the Phase 2–Phase 3 response, while climbing is clearly incompatible. If under a PRF schedule in Phase 1 subjects learn to make the required response to cues from anticipated frustration, these responses may emerge in Phase-3 extinction in a different situation, under different motivational conditions—in fact, under circumstances in which there is no history of persistence training.

I will not give detailed results for this experiment but summarize them and their implications. Ross's results, like the earlier work of Theios and Jenkins, and the later ones from our laboratory, demonstrated that persistence acquired in partial reward acquisition survives a block of continuous reinforcement to affect extinction. In addition, however, Ross demonstrated that persistence acquired in one situation can have effects in a somewhat different situation; that persistence can transfer to different responses and different motivational conditions from those existing when it was developed. Reactions to anticipated frustration learned when hungry in a black box emerge when the subject is anticipating frustration, when

PHASES OF EXPERIMENT	(1) PRELIMINARY LEARNING	(2) ACQUISITION RUNNING RESPONSE	(3) EXTINCTION RUNNING RESPONSE
APPARATUS	(A) SHORT, BLACK WIDE BOX	(B) LONG, WHITE NARROW RUNWAY	(B)
MOTIVATION	HUNGER	THIRST	THIRST
EXPERIMENTAL CONDITIONS	RUNNING CONTINUOUS (RC) PARTIAL (RP) JUMPING CONTINUOUS (JC) PARTIAL (JP) CLIMBING CONTINUOUS (CC) PARTIAL (CP)	RUNNING CONTINUOUS REWARD	RUNNING CONTINUOUS NONREWARD

FIG. 3. Design of the Ross experiment (after Amsel, 1967). The variables (partial vs. continuous; nature of the response) are introduced in Phase 1. All subjects run under identical conditions in Phases 2 and 3. Motivation is changed from Phase 1 to Phases 2–3, as are stimulus characteristics of the apparatus.

thirsty, in a long, high, white runway, even though there had been no persistence training in that runway. It might be said that in this experiment the rat "regresses" in the Phase-3 extinction to the response acquired under PRF in Phase 1. Several (11 out of 13) of the partial climbing animals actually climbed in the long, high, white runway in extinction, and because climbing disrupted running behaviour quickly, there was the appearance, in a comparison of the two climbing groups, of a reversed PRE. These findings can be taken as again pointing up the importance of mediational control, relative to external stimulus control, in the emergence of the partial reward persistence effect in extinction. Even more, however, they make it difficult to account (in stimulus-response terms, at any rate) for the emergence of the Phase-1 responses in extinction without a counter-conditioning interpretation. Simple passive habituation to the disruptive effects of frustration in acquisition would not account for the emergence of the climbing response in Phase-3 extinction. To invoke a concept of inhibition operating in extinction is even less helpful.

Another experimental example of how persistence effects transfer and seem to depend on counterconditioning is again a derivative of the Theios-Jenkins and the Ross experiments. We had been engaged in a series of within-subject experiments (Amsel *et al.*, 1966) in which animals trained to run for CRF in one stimulus alley and to PRF in a different stimulus alley extinguished as though they had been under PRF conditions in both. This suggested transfer of the PRE. We thought it would be interesting to find a within-subject experimental situation in which animals would learn *idiosyncratic response rituals* under partial-reward-like disruptive conditions to one stimulus (S_1), while learning to respond under CRF conditions to another discriminative stimulus (S_2). If our view of how persistence is mediated is tenable, these response rituals learned to S_1 should emerge to the other stimulus (S_2) when the continuously rewarded response to that stimulus (S_2) is extinguished. A few years ago, Michael Rashotte and I struck upon a within-subject experiment of this sort. It is based on Logan's conception of correlated reinforcement (Logan, 1961) and particularly on the procedure he terms *discontinuously negatively correlated reinforcement* (DNC). A DNC condition in an alley is one in which the rat must run slowly to be rewarded (somewhat like the Skinnerian DRL schedule). In our case the application of this procedure meant that the subject had to take 5 sec or longer to traverse the alley to find food in the goal box. If he ran faster he found no food. In these experiments each rat runs in two 5-ft alleys, one black and the other white. In the black alley, the DNC condition obtains; in the white alley the subject runs under uncorrelated CRF. Speeds are taken over five 1-ft segments. The data for each trial can be plotted, speed against segment of the alley, to provide a speed profile of the rat's performance.

We have performed a series of experiments (e.g. Rashotte and Amsel, 1968; Amsel and Rashotte, 1969) which do seem to show quite clearly that, when subjects are run under CRF in one discriminative-stimulus alley and under DNC conditions to another stimulus, most animals do, in fact, learn idiosyncratic response rituals to the DNC stimulus at the same time as they perform in a quite normal fashion to the stimulus signalling uncorrelated continuous reinforcement. This can be seen very clearly in Fig. 4, which shows the acquisition response profiles over five 1-ft segments

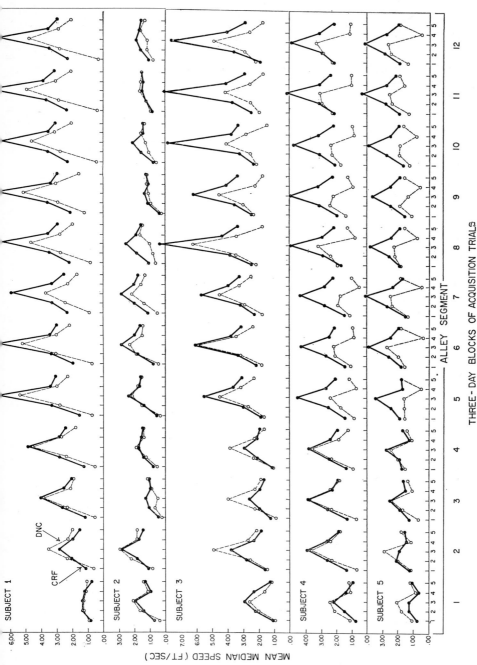

FIG. 4. Profiles of acquisition running speed over a five-segment alley for each of five subjects running under both DNC and CRF conditions.

of the alley for five rats. Remember, a response profile plots for each subject, over individual trials (or a small block of trials), its speed over each of the five successive 1-ft segments of our DNC runway. Each horizontal panel plots the acquisition speed data for a single rat in the DNC and CRF alleys. Note that, in general, CRF profiles are describable as inverted Vs, while the DNC profiles are, by the end of training, quite idiosyncratic and ritualized. (In more old-fashioned terms, these profiles may be described as goal gradients.) Different rats learn to respond slowly in different ways under DNC conditions; that is to say, different rats take time differently in the segments of the runway. *They do not learn to inhibit responding; rather they learn to respond quite actively but in different ways.*

In a series of experiments of this sort we have been successful in demonstrating that the DNC pattern does, in fact, emerge in the extinction of responding to the CRF stimulus. The DNC pattern emerges most clearly when in a successive-phase design responding to the CRF stimulus undergoes extinction while responding to the DNC stimulus does not, as in the design shown in Fig. 5, which, as you can see, is in broad outline the same as the Ross experiment.

	Phase 1	*Phase 2*	*Phase 3*
Group A	S_1 DNC	S_2 CRF	S_2 EXT
Group B	S_1 PRF	S_2 CRF	S_2 EXT
Group C	S_1 CRF	S_2 CRF	S_2 EXT

FIG. 5. Design of successive phase DNC experiment.

This experiment, and others subsequent to the first, included a yoked PRF/CRF control. The yoked condition is one in which for every subject in the DNC/CRF condition, a subject in the PRF/CRF condition gets the same percentage of reward under PRF conditions, and in the same positions in the sequence of trials, as its DNC mate earns by running slowly.

An indication that the pattern of responding learned to the DNC stimulus in acquisition emerges in the extinction of responding to the continuously reinforced stimulus can be seen in Fig. 6. Shown here are the data for five DNC/CRF subjects and their five PRF/CRF yoked controls over the three phases of the experiment.

The remarkable thing about these data is that a response ritual emerges in extinction to a stimulus which did not evoke that ritual before. It seems clear that this pattern of behaviour emerges because something happens in extinction which calls forth an association that was formed in acquisition

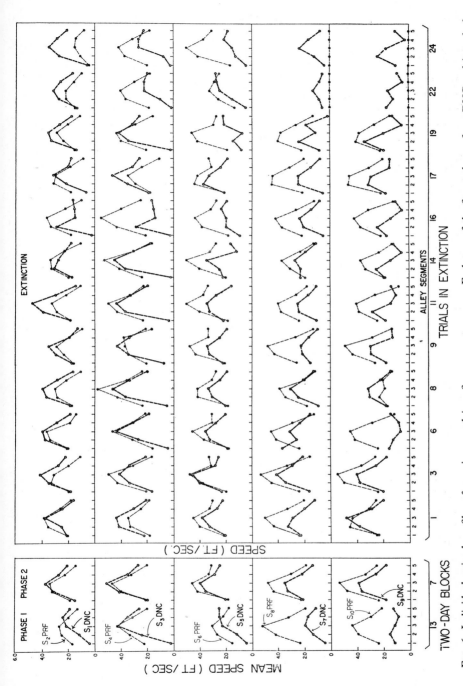

FIG. 6. Individual animal profiles of running speed in a five-segment runway. Each row of the figure shows, for a DNC and its yoked PRF control, profiles over the three phases of the experiment. (See text for explanation; data from Rashotte and Amsel, 1968.)

in relation to a different stimulus. The mechanism, in learning-theory terms, is mediated or secondary stimulus generalization. We think this series of experiments is a powerful demonstration of how countercondi-tioning and mediation control persistence effects in extinction. They do not support a position based on direct (S⁻) inhibitory control. The concept of inhibitory control is not broad enough to include the emergence of a response in extinction which seems unrelated to what the animal learned in just-prior acquisition to that stimulus. An animal may persist by doing something to cues signalling frustration, punishment, or other disruptive events that he has learned much earlier in life in a situation not at all similar to the current one. Another way of putting it is that to persist is, in a sense, to regress. What this comes down to is that, in frustration-theory terms, a frustration-regression hypothesis is supported if frustration

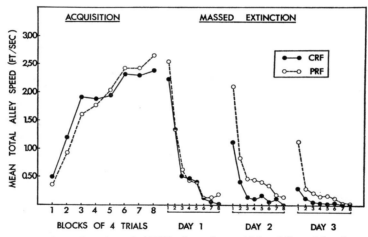

Fɪɢ. 7. Data from Amsel *et al.* (1971). Spaced acquisition followed by three massed extinctions.

means anticipatory (conditioned) frustration (r_F). Perhaps frustration-aggression, the kind of thing Azrin and others have been studying with nonreinforcement and electric shock punishment, applies only to primary (unconditioned) frustration (R_F) or pain (R_P). In any event a concept of inhibitory control based on nonreinforcement or punishment would not seem to account for any of these data.

And now I would ask how a concept of inhibitory control would be applied to the extinction phenomena in the following recent experiments.

The first of these experiments (Amsel *et al.*, 1971) involved the sequence of phases and results shown in Figs. 7 and 8; spaced acquisition under

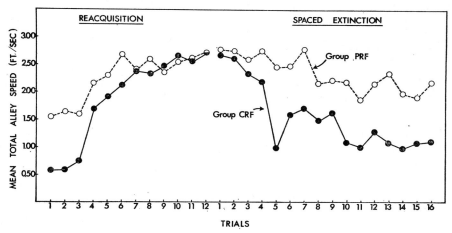

FIG. 8. Data from Amsel *et al.* (1971). Spaced reacquisition under CRF conditions followed by spaced extinction.

CRF or PRF conditions followed by massed extinctions, "vacation", spaced reacquisition under CRF conditions and spaced extinction. As you can see, the first massed extinction revealed no differential effect of PRF or CRF training; but as events progressed it became clear that what had been manipulated in the original spaced acquisition left some permanent differential effect on behaviour. There were long-term effects on performance that could not have been appreciated or understood by observing simply the first massed extinction. What had been learned in Phase 1 was sustained through successive massed extinctions, "vacation" and spaced reacquisition to affect quite strongly the final spaced extinction.

The second of the recent experimental results (based on work with Wong and McCuller) has to do with persistence built by virtue of training with fixed ratio schedules. The experimental outline is shown in Fig. 9. We have been able to show (Fig. 10) that training rats on an FR 10 in a box greatly enhances persistence in a runway; and that this persistence is further augmented by increasing the FR requirement from 10 to 120.

Can we account for the different extinction patterns in the runway on the basis of differences in inhibitory control? If so, how? It seems to us that what we must refer to is some persistence built in the FR training schedules that transfers to extinction in runways. External stimulus control, excitatory or inhibitory, cannot account for these findings—mainly because the external situation in which the persistence develops is so greatly different from that in which it is tested. Obviously, the mere shaping of a rat to perform on an FR 10 schedule makes it more generally persistent in performing a no-longer-reinforcing response.

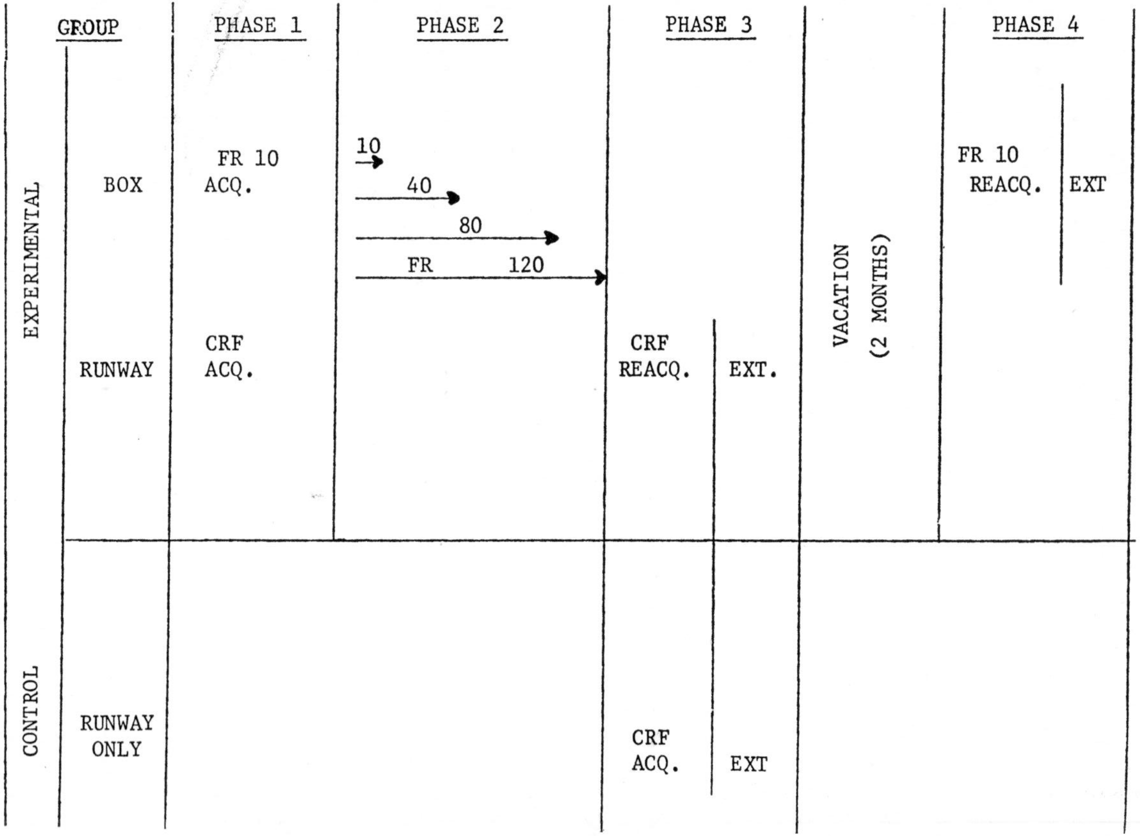

Fig. 9. Design of ratio-runway experiment.

Another recent experiment, by Traupmann and Wong (1971), has addressed itself to an issue raised in an experiment by Sutherland *et al.* (1965), which involves, essentially, the reverse of the Theios–Jenkins experiment. Sutherland *et al.*, have shown that when CRF training precedes PRF training, resistance to subsequent extinction is reduced relative to appropriate control groups. The question raised by Traupmann and Wong is whether this finding will hold generally over a wider range of values of amount of prior CRF and PRF training. The answer is, as usual, that things are more complex than they seemed at first. The study they ran involved 16 or 64 CRF trials followed by 0, 4, or 32 PRF trials, then

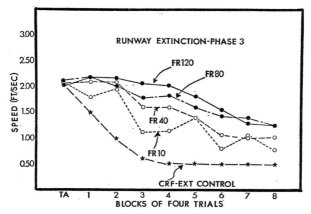

FIG. 10. Extinction in a runway following various levels of ratio responding in a lever-box. (TA = terminal acquisition level.)

extinction. What I am going to show you are the data from the two groups run 16 or 64 CRF followed by 32 PRF trials and extinction. The other four groups show rapid extinction and add nothing to the picture I present as Fig. 11.

Relative to terminal acquisition the groups are about equally persistent early in extinction but the 16-CRF group is more persistent towards the end of the extinction phase. This ties in with a notion I have entertained before (Amsel, 1967) that a specific intensity of s_F is counter-conditioned in PRF, training and that this specific intensity has a bearing on extinction performance. The argument goes like this: In the 64-CRF group, subjects start with a high intensity of R_F when switched to PRF, and only a high intensity of S_F gets counterconditioned to approach. In the 16-CRF group, subjects start PRF training with a lower intensity of R_F and during PRF training various levels of frustration are counterconditioned to

υ

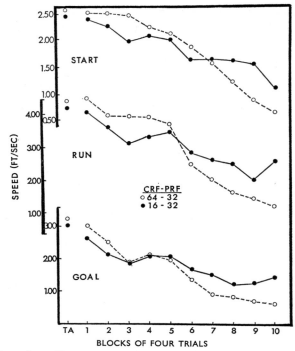

Fig. 11. Data from Traupmann and Wong (1971) showing patterns of persistent responding in extinction as a function of CRF-PRF training.

approach. In extinction the 64-CRF subjects persist as long as s_F intensity is high, but have no tendency to approach to lower intensities; the 16-CRF subjects persist longer because they have been conditioned to approach in the presence of both weak and strong s_F.

We have seen these same kinds of data in another recent experiment of this kind and the finding seems firm. Forgive me if I replay the record and ask again whether a concept of simple inhibition is of any use in explaining such a phenomenon.

III. Inhibition in Simple Classical Conditioning

If, as I have claimed, a concept of simple inhibition or inhibitory control has no important application in the study of instrumental (Thorndikian, operant) reactions, how does it apply—or does it apply?—in the study of behaviour more generally? I think perhaps it does apply, but only in the case of the simplest associative connections, the kind that presumably involve no mediation beyond the simple connection itself.

I have felt for some time that there is such a level of simple classical conditioning and that it is different from what many people now call Pavlovian conditioning. An examination of a book titled *Classical Conditioning* edited by Prokasy (1965) makes it apparent, at least to me, that this kind of split can begin to be detected between those who study the conditioning of short latency responses like the eye-blink in humans (Ross, 1965) and the nictitating membrane and eye-blink of the rabbit (Gormezano, 1965), on the one hand, and those who work with a more traditional Pavlovian preparation, on the other. The latter group tends also to work with responses of longer latency, and very often the split is reflected in arguments about CS-US interval duration. For reasonable levels of conditioning to occur in systems such as the eyelid and nictitating membrane it is usually necessary to employ very short CS-US intervals (the optimal intervals tend to run from about ·2 to ·5 sec). But in even some of the later adaptations of the Pavlovian procedures (e.g. Ost and Lauer, 1965) as well as in the neo-Pavlovian work on the CER (e.g. Kamin, 1965) and Pavlovian fear conditioning by R. L. Solomon and some of his more recent students (e.g. Overmeir, 1967; Rescorla, 1967; Rescorla and Solomon, 1967), conditioning (or conditioned suppression in Kamin's case) is readily observable at very much larger CS-US intervals.

This kind of difference in findings has led to statements such as the following: ". . . there is little in these data to suggest that conditioning is difficult with intervals longer than a second or two" (Ost and Lauer, 1965). "The assertion—and it has been made—that 'classical conditioning cannot occur' with CS-US intervals greater than a few seconds is clearly incorrect. Perhaps the most surprising fact is that, *in the light of Pavlovian data,* such an assertion was ever made" (Kamin, 1965, italics added). Statements such as these suggest that eyelid conditioning procedures have been atypical, if not actually inferior, situations in which to view classical conditioning.

But another argument can also be made—that there is a kind of true classical conditioning which identifies a relatively narrow range of conditions abstracted from the broader Pavlovian experimental paradigm, and that it is at this level that CS-US interval is a critical factor. I am here also suggesting that it may only be at this level that genuine inhibitory effects are important. Rescorla and Solomon (1967) have recently struggled with the identification of what they call ". . . a pure case of Pavlovian conditioning". Possibly classical, as opposed to Pavlovian conditioning, in the sense of the distinction I have been implying, can be studied in relatively pure form only within restricted limits of the CS-US interval. A corollary to this view would be that in the Pavlovian procedures "conditioning" is possible with relatively long CS-US intervals because the CS-CR or the CR-US intervals can be bridged by intermediary mechanisms which are in the nature of the simpler conditioned expectancies formed in classical conditioning. And it is my position that these intermediary mechanisms make a concept of inhibition in Pavlovian and instrumental learning superfluous or at most of limited importance.

Many years ago Hebb (1956) made a related point and long before that Schlosberg (1937) did. Hebb said, "Classical conditioning is identified in two ways: (A) it is the procedure of Pavlov, and (B) it is the procedure in which the CR is irrelevant to occurrence of the US or reinforcement. Instrumental conditioning, on the other hand, is obtained by a procedure in which the CR determines whether the US, or reinforcement, will occur or not." He pointed out that salivary secretion is instrumental by definition B because the dog must not only reach out for and seize the food in Pavlov's procedure but also secrete saliva if the food is to be positively reinforcing. After showing how the same considerations apply to "acid in mouth" as US and to pupillary contraction and eyeblink to a puff of air on the cornea, Hebb concluded that classical conditioning, by definition B, is "not what was worked on in the classical period and is not Pavlovian". He ended by saying that when we say "classical" perhaps we mean "involuntary"; Kimble (1964) has said the same thing. By involuntary, what I would mean is "without a mediating expectancy".

In one of his last major articles Spence (1966) summarized and interpreted a series of experiments from his laboratory and elsewhere having to do with cognitive and drive factors in eyelid conditioning. In this paper, he sought to integrate findings from a series of experiments in eyelid conditioning in which a "masking" procedure had been employed. In the masking situation, the conditioning of the eye-blink response is imbedded in a larger set of experimental manipulations designed to reduce the influence of cognitive (expectancy) factors and particularly to minimize awareness of the transition from acquisition to extinction. Under these masking conditionings, Spence and his students have found that extinction following continuous reinforcement is very greatly retarded and very much like the rate found in experiments with lower animals; and that under the masking conditions the partial reinforcement extinction effect is absent in humans as it often is in animal experiments on classical aversive conditioning (see Spence, 1966; Wagner et al., 1967a for several references).

A simple extension of the reasoning provided by Spence in this article (I hasten to say an extension he would not necessarily have made) also takes us to the point of proposing that there is a level of "pure" classical conditioning—a kind of conditioning American psychologists have always been working towards, as reflected by their preoccupation with a distinction between voluntary and involuntary factors—a kind of conditioning that involves fewer and simpler factors than those involved in Pavlovian procedures. Such a level of conditioning is likely not attained completely even with the masking procedure. A related possibility is that the mechanisms that are a part of this presumed simplest level of conditioning are of a different order than those involved in the Pavlovian procedures. At the simplest (involuntary) level expectancies are formed *but do not already operate*. At the Pavlovian and Thorndikian levels these expectancies operate to control behaviour, positively and negatively. But whether expectancies are positive or negative they are excitatory states. If inhibition operates it is in the reduction in strength of the expectancies in pure classical conditioning; it is, in this sense, a factor in Pavlovian or Thorndikian (operant) cases only indirectly. And, in this sense, inhibition affects both positive and negative expectancies.

Clearly Pavlov's work was what Hilgard and Marquis (1940) referred to when they used the word "classical" to represent Pavlovian as against Thorndikian procedures, and the chapter on Pavlov in Hilgard and Bower's (1966) recent revision is titled "Pavlov's Classical Conditioning". In this sense Pavlov's is, of course, the classical procedure. Nevertheless, it is possible to argue that while Pavlovian procedures provide the paradigm for the temporal sequence of stimuli and responses defining classical conditioning, they are much more complex than the paradigm requires. The distinction made by Tolman (1937), Hilgard and Marquis (1940) and others required a classical-conditioning procedure different and more simply reflexive, in a sense, than Pavlov's—more like eye-blink conditioning, and still more like Spence's later procedures in which, despite the short interstimulus interval, he masked the experimental conditions to reduce the level of awareness of contingencies in human eyelid conditioning.

I am now suggesting that it may be reasonable to take the position that at the simplest level of conditioning we are dealing only with the *formation of expectancies*; that the usual Pavlovian conditioning procedures are complex enough to already involve these expectancies as mediators; and that Pavlovian conditioned responses (not classically conditioned responses) are preparatory responses of the kind described by Hebb (1956), and more recently by Perkins (1968), as necessary for the food US in classical, appetitive Pavlovian conditioning to be reinforcing.

Arguing in this way, a preparatory response in a Pavlovian experiment is already a kind of low-level instrumental response controlled by an underlying and conceptually simpler conditioned expectancy. The expectancy is not directly observable, but the preparatory response may be quite observable, as when a dog salivates before a food US (Hebb, 1956; Perkins, 1968) or learns to position itself so as to modify the noxious consequences of a US (Wagner *et al.*, 1967b). If it could be shown that the phenomena described as partial reinforcement acquisition and extinction effects

(Spence, 1966), and inductive-contrast effects (Amsel, 1971) are not observable in the most basic associative conditioning but only occur in behaviour mediated by expectancy and/or preparatory responding, such a demonstration might lead to a distinction of some importance in our understanding of the simpler forms of associative learning. It seems logical to assert that the most primary kind of associative learning cannot already involve learned mediating responses of any kind. At the same time, it is reasonable to suppose that this most elemental associative conditioning gives rise to the operation of classically conditioned expectancy which is necessary for the appearance of a variety of acquisition and extinction effects in partially reinforced Pavlovian preparatory responding and Thorndikian instrumental learning. Similarly, we may find that inductive phenomena, of the kind that Pavlov described, are mediated by conditioned expectancies, and that these phenomena do not occur in the simplest associative conditioning, but are dependent, in the Thorndikian case and in the Pavlovian case, on the more central conditioned expectancy itself.

While I would join Hebb (1956) and the others in proposing that many, if not most, of the phenomena of Pavlovian conditioning are phenomena of instrumental learning, I differ from them in that I believe (a) that this congruity is based on the fact of mediation in both cases, and (b) that the concepts of Pavlovian conditioning may be more appropriate to a purer and simpler form of associative learning. The recent manifestation of strong interest in the standard techniques of the Pavlovian procedures for laboratory investigation seem to have as their main purpose an attempt to validate the facts of Pavlovian conditioning. According to the present view they cannot be regarded as reflecting the simplicity required by the classical conditioning paradigm. The term "associative shifting" in Thorndike's (1911) distinction between associative shifting and trial-and-error learning is close to the concept of unmediated classical conditioning that would be acceptable in the present context, as would Tolman's description of "substitute-stimulus" learning as a case in which "the second stimulus object is made by the experimenter simply to follow the first without any activity or intervention on the part of the experimental individual. As a result, the latter develops an expectation that the second stimulus object is going to follow the first" (Tolman, 1937).

IV. Conclusion

The argument can be summarized as follows: It may be of some heuristic value to distinguish among three levels of complexity in simple learning—pure unmediated (classical) conditioning, Pavlovian (preparatory) conditioning, and Thorndikian (instrumental) conditioning. Further, and particularly in light of the important work from Miller's laboratory in the last few years on instrumental conditioning of autonomic responses and even the salivary response (see, e.g. Miller and Carmona, 1967), I expect that we may find it difficult in the foreseeable future to think of the simplest conditioning (of expectancy) except as a model for some hypothetical mediator, as, for example, in the case of the fractional anticipatory reactions in the theories of Hull, Spence, Mowrer, and Logan, and in my own work. More direct indicants of this simplest kind of conditioning may have to await some further advances in neurophysiology. We may be able to approach a behavioural examination of basic conditioning only when we study highly reflexive responses of short latency and duration—perhaps in certain animal preparations and in responses like the human eye-blink under conditions of more or less complete removal of cognitive involvement.

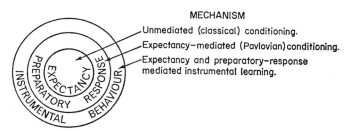

MECHANISM
Unmediated (classical) conditioning.
Expectancy-mediated (Pavlovian) conditioning.
Expectancy and preparatory-response mediated instrumental learning.

Fig. 12.

What we have then is a view of simple learning that can be schematized, in terms of the "centrality" or degree of mediation in the learning, as the three concentric circles shown in Fig. 12.

It seems clear that according to such a model Pavlovian preparatory conditioning would require the more central expectancy core for its expression. It is not so clear whether instrumental learning requires the preparatory Pavlovian responses, or whether there can be short-circuiting of the causal chain, with instrumental learning proceeding at times only on the basis of the simpler conditioned expectancies.

Another way of putting this last possibility suggested by one of my students, Thomas McCuller, is as shown in Fig. 13. In terms of required mediation, the sets Pavlovian conditioning (P) and instrumental conditioning (I) fall completely within the set of simplest conditioned expectancies (E), but I and P are, perhaps, only partially overlapping sets.

In the light of such a distinction, I would now be willing to maintain that the assertion with which I opened my remarks—that a simple concept of inhibition is only indirectly involved in an account of instrumental response suppression—may be worth serious consideration. A concept of inhibition might apply at the simplest associative levels; but, in Pavlovian and operant-instrumental learning, expectancies conditioned at the simplest level, such as conditioned fear or conditioned frustration, are already the controlling factors. Both are excitatory tendencies, and we deal with competition between them. In Mowrer's (1960) terms, conditioned relief might produce approach and so be said to "inhibit" avoidance produced by conditioned fear. But we do not ordinarily think of relief as an inhibitor, except in Rescorla's (1969) sense of a competitive suppressive factor, a concept of inhibition which I am here rejecting.

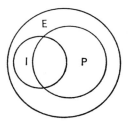

Fig. 13.

So the proposition I am asking you to consider is that a concept of inhibition is not aptly applied either to (a) Pavlovian conditioning in which temporal intervals are long enough to allow mediation to operate, or (b) instrumental-operant kinds of learning. While it would take a separate paper to document the case completely or even adequately, behavioural studies have uncovered a number and variety of paradoxical effects, particularly related to extinction and discrimination learning, for which explanations in terms of a simple inhibitory concept would be inadequate. In the case of extinction we have to deal with partial reinforcement effects, faster extinction after larger numbers or magnitude of reward, and sub-zero extinction (extinction below the initial "operant" level), to give a few examples. In the case of discrimination learning there is the over-learning reversal effect, which seems to be demonstrable only when reward is large; and there are the "by-products" of discrimination that Terrace and others have spoken of—peak shift, behavioural contrast, and its Pavlovian counterpart, induction. I have discussed many of these paradoxical phenomena recently within the context of frustration theory (Amsel, 1967, 1971) and in relation to a more general theory of persistence (Amsel, 1972). I am guessing that none of these phenomena can be observed at the simplest levels of associative learning. Aversive events, be they shocks or nonrewards, produce competing *excitatory* tendencies; avoidance is not inhibition. Disruptive events, be they novel stimuli, or stimuli out of their usual context, exercise their suppressive effects through earlier learned associations, not in a simple inhibitive manner. Neither aversive nor disruptive events act directly on the strength of another associative connection. Perhaps at the level of the simplest unmediated associations, if we can find ways to study them, we will discover true, unmediated inhibitory effects.

Acknowledgements

All of the experimental work from our laboratory described here, the preparation of this paper, and attendance at the Conference in Sussex have been supported by research and travel grants from the National Science Foundation.

References

Amsel, A. (1951). A three-factor theory of inhibition: An addition to Hull's two-factor theory. Paper delivered at Southern Soc. for Phil. and Psychol. Meetings, Roanoke, 1951.

Amsel, A. (1958). The role of frustrative nonreward in noncontinuous reward situations. *Psychological Bulletin*, **55**, 102–119.

Amsel, A. (1962). Frustrative nonreward in partial reinforcement and discrimination learning: Some recent history and a theoretical extension. *Psychological Review*, **69**, 306–328.

Amsel, A. (1967). Partial reinforcement effects on vigor and persistence: Advances in frustration theory derived from a variety of within-subjects experiments. In: K. W. Spence and J. T. Spence (Eds.), *The Psychology of Learning and Motivation*. Vol. I. New York: Academic Press, pp. 1–65.

Amsel, A. (1971). Positive induction, behavioral contrast, and generalization of inhibition in discrimination learning. In: H. H. Kendler and J. T. Spence (Eds.), *Essays in Neobehaviorism: A Memorial Volume for Kenneth W. Spence*. New York: Appleton–Century–Crofts, pp. 217–236.

Amsel, A. (1972). Behavioral habituation, counterconditioning, and a general theory of persistence. In: A. H. Black and W. F. Prokasy (Eds.), *Classical Conditioning II: Current Research and Theory*. New York: Appleton–Century–Crofts.

Amsel, A. and Rashotte, M. E. (1969). Transfer of experimenter-imposed slow-response patterns to the extinction of a continuously rewarded response. *Journal of Comparative and Physiological Psychology*, **69**, 185–189.

Amsel, A. and Ward, J. S. (1965). Frustration and persistence: Resistance to discrimination following prior experience with the discriminanda. *Psychological Monographs*, **79**, No. 4 (whole No. 597).

Amsel, A., Rashotte, M. E. and MacKinnon, J. R. (1966). Partial reinforcement effects within subject and between subjects. *Psychological Monographs*, **80**, No. 20 (whole No. 628).

Amsel, A., Wong, P. T. P. and Traupmann, K. L. (1971). Short-term and long-term factors in extinction and durable persistence. *Journal of Experimental Psychology* (in Press).

Brown, P. L. and Jenkins, H. M. (1967). Conditioned inhibition and excitation in operant discrimination learning. *Journal of Experimental Psychology*, **75**, 255–266.

Donin, Janet A., Surridge, C. T. and Amsel, A. (1967). Extinction following partial delay of reward with immediate continuous reward interpolated, at 24-hour intervals. *Journal of Experimental Psychology*, **74**, 50–53.

Gormezano, I. (1965). Yoked comparisons of classical and instrumental conditioning of the eyelid response; and an addendum on "voluntary responders". In: W. F. Prokasy (Eds.), *Classical Conditioning*. New York: Appleton–Century–Crofts, pp. 48–70.

Hebb, D. O. (1956). The distinction between "classical" and "instrumental", *Canadian Journal of Psychology*, **10**, 165–166.

Hilgard, E. R. and Bower, G. H. (1966). *Theories of Learning*. New York: Appleton–Century–Crofts.

Hilgard, E. R. and Marquis, D. G. (1940). *Conditioning and Learning*. New York: Appleton–Century.

Jenkins, H. M. (1962). Resistance to extinction when partial reinforcement is followed by regular reinforcement. *Journal of Experimental Psychology*, **64**, 441–450.

Kamin, L. (1965). Temporal and intensity characteristics of the conditioned stimulus. In W. F. Prokasy (Ed.), *Classical Conditioning*. New York: Appleton–Century–Crofts, pp. 118–147.

Kimble, G. A. (1964). Comments on Professor Grant's paper. In: A. W. Melton (Ed.), *Categories of Human Learning*. New York: Academic Press, pp. 32–45.

Logan, F. A. (1961). *Incentive*. New Haven: Yale University Press.

Miller, N. W. and Carmona, A. (1967). Modification of a visceral response, salivation in thirsty dogs, by instrumental training. *Journal of Comparative and Physiological Psychology*, **63**, 1–6.

Mowrer, O. H. (1960). *Learning Theory and Behavior*. New York: Wiley.

Ost, J. W. and Lauer, D. W. (1965). Some investigations of classical salivary conditioning in the dog. In: W. F. Prokasy (Ed.), *Classical Conditioning*. New York: Appleton–Century–Crofts, pp. 192–207.

Overmeir, J. B. (1967). Instrumental and cardiac indices of Pavlovian fear conditioning as a function of US duration. *Journal of Comparative and Physiological Psychology*, **62**, 15–20.

Perkins, C. C., Jr. (1968). An analysis of the concept of reinforcement. *Psychological Review*, **75**, 155–172.

Prokasy, W. F. (1965). *Classical Conditioning*. New York: Appleton–Century–Crofts.

Rashotte, M. W. and Amsel, A. (1968). Transfer of slow-response rituals to the extinction of a continuously rewarded response. *Journal of Comparative and Physiological Psychology*, **66**, 432–443.

Rashotte, M. E. and Surridge, C. T. (1969). Partial reinforcement and partial delay of reinforcement effects with 72-hour inter-trial intervals and interpolated continuous reinforcement. *Quarterly Journal of Experimental Psychology*, **21**, 156–161.

Rescorla, R. A. (1967). Pavlovian conditioning and its proper control procedures. *Psychological Review*, **74**, 71–80.

Rescorla, R. A. (1969). Pavlovian conditioned inhibition. *Psychological Bulletin*, **72**, 77–94.

Rescorla, R. A. and Solomon, R. L. (1967). Two-process learning theory: Relationships between Pavlovian conditioning and instrumental learning. *Psychological Review*, **74,** 151–182.

Ross, L. E. (1965). Eyelid conditioning as a tool in psychological research: Some problems and prospects. In: W. F. Prokasy (Ed.), *Classical Conditioning.* New York: Appleton–Century–Crofts, pp. 249–268.

Ross, R. R. (1964). Positive and negative partial-reinforcement extinction effects carried through continuous reinforcement, changed motivation, and changed response. *Journal of Experimental Psychology,* **68,** 492–502.

Schlosberg, H. (1937). The relationship between success and the laws of conditioning. *Psychological Review* **44,** 379–394.

Skinner, B. F. (1938). *The Behavior of Organisms: An Experimental Analysis.* New York: Appleton–Century.

Spence, K. W. (1960). *Behavior Theory and Learning.* Englewood Cliffs, N.J.: Prentice-Hall.

Spence, K. W. (1966). Cognitive and drive factors in the extinction of the conditioned eye blink in human subjects. *Psychological Review,* **73,** 445–458.

Sutherland, N. S., MacKintosh, N. J. and Wolfe, J. B. (1965). Extinction as a function of the order of partial and consistent reinforcement. *Journal of Experimental Psychology,* **69,** 56–59.

Theios, J. (1962). The partial reinforcement effect sustained through blocks of continuous reinforcement. *Journal of Experimental Psychology,* **64,** 1–6.

Thorndike, E. L. (1911). *Animal Intelligence.* New York: Macmillan.

Wagner, A. R., Siegel, L. S. and Fein, G. G. (1967a). Extinction of conditioned response or sign-gestalt? *Psychological Review,* **44,** 195–211.

Traupmann, K. L. and Wong, P. T. P. (1971). Extinction and counterconditioning to specific intensities of anticipatory frustration (in preparation).

Wagner, A. R., Siegel, L. S. and Fein, G. G. (1967a). Extinction of conditioned fear as a function of percentage of reinforcement. *Journal of Comparative and Physiological Psychology,* **63,** 160–164.

Wagner, A. R., Thomas, E. and Norton, T. (1967b). Conditioning with electrical stimulation of motor cortex: Evidence of a possible source of motivation. *Journal of Comparative and Physiological Psychology,* **64,** 191–199.

12

Inhibition in Pavlovian Conditioning: Application of a Theory*

A. R. WAGNER and R. A. RESCORLA

Yale University, New Haven, Connecticut, U.S.A.

I.	Introduction	301
II.	The Model	302
	A. The Basic Proposition	302
	B. The Detailed Model	304
III.	Implications for Inhibition	306
	A. Nonreinforcement and Inhibition	307
	B. Independence-of-Path and Inhibition	308
	C. Measurement of Inhibition	310
IV.	Basic Data	310
	A. Extinction	311
	B. Conditioned Inhibition	312
V.	Additional Inhibitory Procedures Involving Nonreinforcement	314
	A. Negative Correlation Between CS and US	315
	B. Discriminative Conditioning	318
	C. Inhibition of Delay	320
VI.	Inhibitory Procedures Involving Reinforcement	320
	A. Variation in US Magnitude	321
	B. "Overexpectation" of the US	323
VII.	Repeated Nonreinforced Presentation of a Stimulus	325
	A. Latent Inhibition	326
	B. Extinction of an Excitatory Stimulus	330
	C. Extinction of an Inhibitory Stimulus	331
VIII.	Conclusion	333
References		334

I. Introduction

One of the apparent advantages of a model of Pavlovian conditioning that we have recently presented (Rescorla and Wagner, 1972) is that it accounts rather effortlessly for certain inhibitory phenomena. The model was designed to accommodate a central proposition concerning the necessary

*Preparation of this manuscript and the research reported were supported in part by National Science Foundation Grants GB-12897 and GB-14384. This paper and a previous one (Rescorla and Wagner, 1972) to which it is related were both collaborative efforts in which both authors contributed equally. Order of authorship on this paper indicates only our reaction to the chance ordering of authorship on the earlier paper.

conditions for associative-learning to which we had each been led (e.g. Rescorla, 1969b; Wagner, 1969a, b) but required a reasonable number of auxiliary assumptions to render it as unambiguous as possible. At certain steps the choice of assumption was determined by our predilections concerning Pavlovian Inhibition, in other cases the model turned out to have important implications that we did not necessarily anticipate.

Since the model has thus far fared quite well in accounting for a variety of data from Pavlovian conditioning (e.g. Rescorla, 1970; Rescorla and Wagner, 1972; Wagner, 1971) we are encouraged to rehearse its development, pointing separately to the major proposition and certain of the auxiliary assumptions. In this manner we will attempt to make evident the rationale, as well as the substance of our present treatment of inhibition. We shall then marshal those data which show off the real advantages of the model in accounting for decremental learning and inhibition, as well as indicate certain data areas in which the model, without modification, may be less successful.

II. The Model

A. THE BASIC PROPOSITION

The most direct way to approach the model is by way of comparison with those familiar theories (e.g. Hull, 1943; Estes and Burke, 1953; Bush and Mosteller, 1955; Spence, 1956) all of which have commonly assumed that successive CS-US pairings lead to a negatively accelerated growth in some associative tendency. If we adopt a common notational system which ignores certain differences in the nature of the associative variable, each of the theories assumes that when a particular CS, A, is repeatedly paired with a US, that the associative strength of that CS, V_A, will eventually approach some value λ, with the increments in V_A on each trial being $\Delta V_A = \phi (\lambda - V_A)$. That is, the increments in V_A are taken to be a decreasing linear function of the difference between V_A and the fixed-point value towards which it may grow as a consequence of such trials. It is generally assumed that the latter value, λ, is greater the greater the intensity of the US involved (e.g. Hull, 1943) so that one may account both for different asymptotic levels of responding with different US values, and for changes in conditioned responding when US values are increased or decreased.

Now, an interesting option is presented to such a theory when not just a single CS, but several CSs are concurrently present on a trial. That is, suppose that two cues A and B are presented in compound and followed by a US. Should we assume that the associative value of the components will be modified until each individually reaches λ? Or should we assume that the associative values will be modified only until the collective value of the compound reaches λ? There is nothing intrinsic to the theories we have mentioned which necessarily implies either possibility, but all have none the less followed the former option. And what basically sets our model apart is that we have chosen to follow the latter alternative.

If there are no reasons of internal consistency to favour choosing one of these options over the other, one may ask why the one has been uniformly followed and why we would now advocate the alternative. Wagner (1971) has argued that certain presystematic notions have played a major role in this choice. As repeated CS-US pairings produce smaller and smaller increments in associative strength, it is easy to see this in terms of a saturation-like process: As the individual CS acquires more and more associative strength, it becomes less and less possible for that CS to acquire further strength by pairing with a designated US. According to this view, it is reasonable to expect that when multiple CSs, e.g. A and B, are present on a conditioning trial that each should be independently incremented according to the distance from its own saturation level. This "saturation" viewpoint has apparently dominated previous theorizing, and would probably not have been challenged by us, had Kamin (1968, 1969) not called our attention to another intriguing viewpoint. Quite simply, perhaps repeated CS-US pairings produce smaller and smaller increments, not because the associative strength of the CS is becoming less and less capable of being incremented, but because the US is becoming less and less effective, as it is announced by a cue with increasingly greater associative strength. Or, as Kamin has proposed, perhaps a US is reinforcing only to the degree that it is "surprising" on that occasion. According to this view it is more reasonable to assume that when multiple CSs are present on a conditioning trial that the associative strength of each should be commonly incremented according to the surprisingness of the US, which in turn should be a function of the aggregate associative strength of all of the cues which announced that US.

There are also, of course, data that appear to favour one or the other alternative. It is unlikely that previous theorists ignored the fact (e.g. Miller, 1939; Hull, 1940) that when a compound of CSs is paired with a US that conditioned responding is acquired more rapidly than when only one of the components is employed as the CS. This seems to suggest that the associative strength of each cue placed in the position of a CS is independently being incremented towards λ and that in the case of the compound, the several component associative strengths have an additive effect upon responding. Recently, however, a number of authors (e.g. Sutherland and Mackintosh, 1964; Trabasso et al., 1966) have pointed out that this observation can be accounted for in other ways, as for example by assuming that the greater the number of cues which is made available, the more likely it is that the subject will be provided (and perhaps ideosyncratically so) with a single salient cue to which conditioning can rapidly occur. At the same time a variety of recent investigations (see Rescorla and Wagner, 1972) appear to support the view that it is the aggregate associative strength of the stimulus compound which approaches λ. The most influential observation has probably been the so-called "blocking-effect" demonstrated by Kamin (e.g. 1968, 1969). In his now-familiar, basic manipulation, Kamin trained two groups of subjects in a conditioned suppression situation with a compound CS, AX, consistently reinforced, and then tested the effectiveness of the X component alone. The only difference between the two groups was that one had received a series of reinforced trials to A alone prior to the compound phase. The results were dramatic in that whereas the nonpretrained group evidenced considerable conditioning to X, the pretrained group showed little or none. This is clearly what one would expect if during compound training it is the compound associative strength, V_{AX}, which approaches λ. For the pretrained group, V_{AX} should already have been high due to the contribution of V_A to the compound strength, and hence there should have been little opportunity for V_A or V_X to be further incremented. Or as Kamin proposed, in the pretrained group the US was well-predicted by A, and hence was relatively ineffective for producing further associative learning during compound training.

B. The Detailed Model

The general form of the linear model to which the foregoing arguments have led us is one which assumes that when several CSs are presented in compound and paired with a US that the changes in any component, CS_i, may be expressed as $\Delta V_i = \phi (\lambda - \bar{V})$, where $\bar{V}$ represents the aggregate associative strength of all of the cues present on that trial. The most important properties of the model are that the increments, ΔV_i, in each component decrease as $\bar{V}$ approaches λ, and that with extensive training $\bar{V}$, rather than V_i, will thus approximate λ.

Since the several cues in a compound may be expected to vary in their intensity or salience, one would not like to assume that the associative strength of each will be equally effected by a conditioning trial. It also seems possible that different USs will dictate different rates of learning as well as different asymptotes. Hence, we have replaced the rate parameter, ϕ, by the product of two parameters, α, which is assumed to be determined by the properties of the CS, and β, which is assumed, like λ, to be determined by the properties of the US. Thus when several CSs, A, B, C, ..., X, are paired with a US on a trial it is assumed that

$$\Delta V_A = a_A \beta_1 (\lambda_1 - \bar{V})$$
$$\Delta V_B = a_B \beta_1 (\lambda_1 - \bar{V})$$

. . . .

. . . .

. . . .

$$\Delta V_X = a_X \beta_1 (\lambda_1 - \bar{V}).$$

These changes are assumed to be occasioned by reinforced trials. In terms of the presystematic view which guided the theory, it also seemed appropriate to suppose that nonreinforcement would promote learning only when it was "surprising". And, in terms of the linear model, it seemed appropriate to write an equation of the same form as that above, in which the amount of learning accruing to any component of a nonreinforced compound would vary inversely with the degree to which the aggregation of cues present had an *association with nonreinforcement*. But what then is the relationship between that learning which occurs on reinforced trials and that which occurs on nonreinforced trials, and how (if at all) do the two combine to influence the learning which occurs on subsequent trials of either variety?

Since these sound like complex issues we were more than happy to try a simple solution. If we follow the common assumption (e.g. Hull, 1943) that λ decreases with decreasing US intensity, then why not assume that nonreinforcement differs from reinforcement only in having a value of λ that would most reasonably be expected to be associated with zero US intensity, i.e. zero? The learning which would occur on such trials would then also be represented in ΔV_i and contribute to influence the learning on subsequent reinforced or nonreinforced trials in terms of its influence on the appropriate $\bar{V}$. The above equations would thus remain perfectly general to any trial type involving a given US or its absence.* This strategy is again not unlike that in various stochastic models (e.g. Estes and Burke, 1953; Bush and Mosteller, 1955) and Wagner (1969a) has suggested that it might then only be preferable to refer to the V dimension as "signal value" to be reminded that it may represent a summary statement of the net effects of the subjects' history with both reinforcement and nonreinforcement.

In following this course we were influenced by the studies of Kamin (1969) and Wagner (1969a). Kamin, in the blocking situation, showed that, if the pretrained cue (A) was first reinforced and then nonreinforced prior to the instituting of compound (AX) training, the blocking effect was

*Although not critical to our present concern, it should be noted that the β associated with nonreinforcement is assumed to be less than the β associated with reinforcement (Rescorla and Wagner, 1972). This may be viewed as consistent with a more general proposition that β, like λ, decreases with decreasing US intensity, although β cannot be assumed to be zero at zero US intensity.

x

removed, i.e. conditioning to X proceeded as though cue A had not been previously reinforced. Wagner showed that concurrent training with cue A nonreinforced and the compound AX reinforced increased the degree of conditioning to cue X as compared to a condition involving only reinforcement of the AX compound. In each case it appeared as though nonreinforcement of A alone reduced the contribution of A to $\bar{V}$ so that ΔV_X was increased on each reinforced compound trial.

The major assumption which must yet be made explicit is the combination rule for determining $\bar{V}$ granted any compound of CSs with separate Vs. If we take as our guideline the manner in which separately reinforced CSs combine to influence conditioned responding (e.g. Hull, 1940; Konorski, 1948), we would infer that the separate Vs combine in some additive fashion up to a limit. We have followed the simplest algebraic assumption which is that $\bar{V} = V_A + V_B + \ldots V_X$, and attributed any limit observed in conditioned responding to the constraints of the response measure employed rather than to any potential bounds upon $\bar{V}$ with conceivable aggregations of cues. The form of the equation may seem too simplistic in view of more elaborate proposals (e.g. Hull, 1943) and the unboundedness assumption may seem exceedingly implausible. We know of no data, however, that would encourage us to trust the greater adequacy of any more complex combination rule. And, the assumption that $\bar{V}$ is at least relatively unbounded for conceivable aggregations of separately trained cues (in comparison to the effective bounds placed upon $\bar{V}$ of any training compound by λ) leads, as we shall demonstrate, to interesting and easily testable implications.

It will follow also from the model, as we will later emphasize, that under certain conditions of training with a US and its absence, component Vs should become negative. Following the same guidelines concerning the manner in which separately trained CSs combine to influence conditioned responding (e.g. Konorski, 1948; Pavlov, 1927), we have assumed that negative Vs simply reduce $\bar{V}$ according to the same general principle that $\bar{V} = V_A + V_B + \ldots V_X.$*

III. Implications for Inhibition

Included in the above set of assumptions is a particular characterization of decremental learning and inhibition in Pavlovian conditioning. The

---

*This combination rule should be read so as to include in the summation the Vs of *all* effective cues, whatever their source. Thus, for example, in some situations such as in "conditional discrimination" (e.g. Saavedra, 1971) or "negative patterning" (e.g. Woodbury, 1943), "configurational" cues may play an important role. As Wagner (1971) has indicated, such cues should be treated as any other component contributing to the determination of $\bar{V}$. We ignore them here for simplicity of exposition, and because available data (e.g. Saavedra, 1971) suggests that they are probably relatively inconsequential in the kinds of studies we will discuss.

most important proposition is, of course, that what is learned on any Pavlovian trial, reinforced or nonreinforced, will depend upon the aggregate associative strength of all of the cues present on that trial. The effect of nonreinforcing a particular CS, possessing a specified associative strength, should not be constant but should depend upon the associative strength of the other cues with which it is in compound.

The theory appeals to no special inhibitory process. A single associative-strength variable, V, identified with each component CS is assumed to be decreased, just as it may be increased, according to the relationship $(\lambda - \bar{V})$ appropriate for that trial. To speak of "inhibition" in the context of this model is simply to speak of a range of values along the associative-strength continuum where V is negative, as revealed by the decrement in $\bar{V}$ when a cue with such value is added to a compound of cues.

A. NONREINFORCEMENT AND INHIBITION

By assuming that the λ associated with nonreinforcement is zero, we have specifically arranged that the model *does not* predict that simply nonreinforcing a CS *in isolation* will result in an inhibitory (negative V) cue. In order for nonreinforcement to produce a decremental effect, $(\lambda - \bar{V})$ must be negative. Thus, for a neutral cue to be made inhibitory as a result of nonreinforcement, it must be nonreinforced in compound with other cues which make $\bar{V}$ positive. This point is central to many implications of the model which we will later consider.

The model, moreover, assigns no unique status to nonreinforcement in regard to producing decremental learning or inhibition. It is assumed to be a perfectly general proposition that whenever $(\lambda - \bar{V})$ is negative that the component CSs on that trial will be decremented in proportion to the discrepancy involved. Such decrement may be likely to occur on nonreinforced trials since λ is then especially low, but it may also occur when US magnitude is reduced in the presence of a compound that has been trained to some value greater than the λ associated with the low value US. And such decrement may also occur when $\bar{V}$ is made greater than λ, not by changing the US event involved but by changing the cues present on the trial so that $\bar{V}$ is especially large.

To dispel further the notion that there is any special relationship between nonreinforcement and inhibition, it should be noted that the model allows the possibility that nonreinforcement may have an *incremental* effect upon the cues present, if $(\lambda - \bar{V})$ has a positive value. This should occur if $\lambda = 0$, and $\bar{V}$ is *negative*. We will have more to say about each of these implications of the model in connection with various data we will consider.

B. Independence-of-Path and Inhibition

We recognize that this treatment of inhibition is unusual in many respects. It may be disturbing that, among other features, it appears to run counter to a major theme set by Pavlovian theory (e.g. 1927), that we must recognize decremental learning and inhibition as involving a separate process distinct from incremental learning and excitation. We have been willing to ignore this theme simply because the data with which we have been concerned, involving the effects of reinforcement and nonreinforcement in compound conditioning, have not appeared to imply it. Perhaps future data will. Beyond this, whether or not a model of Pavlovian conditioning without a special inhibitory process is generally tenable is a larger issue on which we have not committed ourselves.

The critical question, asked in one form or another, is always whether or not there is independence-of-path. That is, can we maintain that as a result of prior training with a given US and its absence that the associative tendency to any CS may be indicated by a single construct, e.g. V, so that we may, for purposes of predicting future actions of that CS, ignore the path of training which established that V? We have already alluded to this reasoning in discussing the impact of the Kamin (1968) and Wagner (1969a) data upon our theorizing. The V of any component CS influences, within the model, the $\bar{V}$ determining the changes in associative strength which accrue on that trial. It might have been the case, for example, that a component CS first reinforced and then nonreinforced would contribute quite differently to $\bar{V}$ than would a nontrained CS, for determining the $\triangle V$ of an added CS when the two are reinforced in compound. The Kamin data suggested that we could ignore the path by which the CS was rendered neutral, for purposes of predicting $\varDelta V$.

Much more exhaustive tests of this assumption need to be made over a greater range of conditions. For example, can we assume that when a neutral cue is reinforced in a compound arranged to have a designated aggregate $\bar{V}$, that the incremental effects will be indifferent to the way in which the remaining cues have been constituted so as to assure the $\bar{V}$ presumably involved? Suppose, for example, that we were to reinforce a novel cue X in compound with CSs A and B. Would it matter if A and B were both mildly "excitatory", as opposed to the case in which A was highly "excitatory" and B was somewhat "inhibitory", even though the two AB compounds otherwise appear to have equal "strength", e.g. produce the same degree of conditioned responding? If the increments in V_X were different in the two cases, we would need to reconsider our assumption.

The independence-of-path assumption has often been evaluated in ways which are fraught with interpretive problems. For example, it is well known (e.g. Konorski and Szwejkowska, 1952) that a CS which is reinforced, and then nonreinforced until conditioned responding no longer occurs, will show faster subsequent conditioning than will an untrained CS. This fact has frequently been taken to indicate that reinforcement first produces excitatory learning, that nonreinforcement then produces a separate inhibitory learning, and that the two remain in opposition until the more fragile inhibitory tendency is superseded by the new excitatory learning. It is just as reasonable to assume, however, that the previously reinforced cue simply was not rendered neutral by the number of extinction trials administered but still possessed positive V — not sufficient to elicit measurable conditioned responding alone, but perhaps detectable via a summation test with other CSs. Or it is reasonable to assume that part of the compound CS, in the presence of which the subject was originally reinforced, involved traces of the preceding reinforcements. As extinction involves a removal of this component cue from the situation, the associative tendency to it should not be extinguished. And as reacquisition training involves reinstating this cue, reacquisition may proceed faster than original acquisition simply as a result of their being in compound with the CS, a cue which has appreciable associative strength.

This may be simply to say that we have been cautious in rejecting the independence-of-path assumption and in accepting a more complex duo-process theory without relatively unambiguous data to force the issue. In the context of our model such data may be especially hard to come by, since, although a component V presumably retains no memory of how it got to that value, a compound $\bar{V}$ may retain such memory in the distribution of strengths among the several components. Consider, for example, the two treatments involved in the Kamin blocking procedure, one receiving cue A reinforced, then the compound AX reinforced, while the other receives only compound training with AX reinforced. At the end of compound training $\bar{V} = V_A + V_X$ should approach λ in both groups, but as we have well rehearsed, there should be different strengths of the V_A and V_X involved in the two cases. In the nonpretrained group V_A and 8_X should be relatively equal (assuming equal a values of the two cues). In the pretrained group V_A should be relatively high and V_X relatively low. Now suppose we nonreinforce the AX compound in both cases. Then $\bar{V} = V_A + V_X$ should approach zero in both groups. But V_A and V_X should *not* be extinguished to the same level in each case. In the nonpretrained group V_A and V_X should both be extinguished to zero. In the pretrained group V_A and V_X will also be commonly decremented on each trial, but this means that when $\bar{V}$ reaches zero, V_A will still have a positive value and V_X will have a negative value. Now, certain tests such as presenting A alone or presenting a generalization test in which X is modified (thus depreciating

V_X) would be expected to reveal quite different levels of responding, of the sort that in other theoretical contexts one might wish to take as evidence against the independence-of-path assumption, and as evidence in favour of two separate learning processes possessing different properties.

C. MEASUREMENT OF INHIBITION

A final note is in order concerning the measurement of inhibition. A CS with a negative V is presumed to be indistinguishable from a CS with a neutral V in terms of its tendency to elicit conditioned responding in isolation. Each should be associated with zero CRs. The most natural way to detect inhibition is in the contribution of a CS to $\bar{V}$. Thus, for example, we should see evidence of inhibition in a decrement in conditioned responding when a negative CS is combined with a compound of cues, the $\bar{V}$ of which is otherwise sufficiently positive to produce conditioned responding. This is the conventional "summation" test (Rescorla, 1969c).

A second conventional test is the "retardation" evaluation (Rescorla, 1969c). A CS with a negative V should be slower to acquire positive V, and hence conditioned responding, as a result of reinforced trials than should a neutral CS. Rescorla (1969c) has argued that a combination of the summation and retardation tests offers the possibility of the most conclusive evidence of learned inhibition (see also Hearst et al., 1970). Either alone could produce apparent evidence of inhibition that we might wish to attribute to other processes, e.g. generalization decrement in the case of the summation test or decreased attention in the case of the retardation test. But, many such alternatives can be eliminated if a CS produces both a decrement in conditioned responding to other cues and is itself retarded in the development of conditioned responding.

Hearst (Chapter 1) has considered these issues in considerable detail and we are generally in agreement with his conclusion that converging operations are required to demonstrate the involvement of "inhibition" as opposed to various alternative effects. In the context of a relatively precise model a further evaluative strategy takes on more significance, however. That is, do the results from a summation or retardation test, or their combination, show greater evidence of inhibition the more favourable have presumably been the conditions for the acquisition of such inhibition? It is such a question which we will generally be asking as we turn to a consideration of relevant data.

IV. Basic Data

Two experiments will serve to exemplify the major advantages of the model in accounting for decremental learning and inhibition. Both experiments are concerned with the effects of nonreinforcement and with the fundamental expectation that the decrement in associative strength accruing to a component CS should be greater the greater the associative strength of the compound of cues in which that CS is embedded at the time of nonreinforcement. The first study illustrates such a phenomenon in the case of simple extinction. The second study illustrates the same phenomenon in the development of "conditioned inhibition".

A. EXTINCTION

Wagner, Saavedra and Lehmann (Wagner, 1969b) employed eyelid conditioning in the rabbit to provide a simple test of our assumptions. The plan was first to train the subject to respond to some CS, X, then to combine X with a second CS which had been arranged to possess either relatively high or relatively low associative strength and nonreinforce the compound, and finally to test the degree of subsequent responding to X alone to determine the degree of decrement resulting from the nonreinforced compound trials. According to the theory, since $(\lambda-\bar{V})$ should have been more negative in that group in which X was nonreinforced in compound with the relatively strong cue, that group should also have shown the greater extinction of responding to X.

Thirty-six rabbits were first conditioned to three separate, 1100-msec, CSs which will be referred to as A, B, and X. Over the course of two days' training there were 224 A, 28 B, and 224 X trials, irregularly ordered, in which the respective cues were presented alone and each reinforced with a 100-msec, 4·5-ma shock US to the area of the eye.

The A and B cues, by virtue of the different numbers of reinforcements in their presence, were designed to have different associative strengths, i.e. A was designed to be a relatively strong cue, and B a relatively weak cue by the end of acquisition. For half of the subject's A was a flashing light and B was a vibration applied to the subject's chest. For the remaining subjects the nature of the cues was reversed.

The X cue, which for all subjects was a 3160-Hz tone, was the element of special interest. Immediately following acquisition, subjects were assigned to one of two treatment conditions and administered 32 extinction trials, in which X was presented and nonreinforced. For half of the subjects X was presented during extinction in compound with the A cue, while for the remaining 18 subjects it was presented in compound with the B cue. On the 32 trials immediately following the extinction phase, X was again presented alone to all subjects and was reinforced. Comparison of the responding of the two groups during this reacquisition phase allowed a determination of the decremental effects suffered as a result of the preceding extinction with either of the two compounds containing X.

Figure 1 represents the mean percentages conditioned eyeblink responses to the several CSs during the three phases of the experiment. The acquisition functions, which summarize the responding of all 36 subjects prior to differential treatment, indicate that there was appreciable acquisition to X, and importantly, different amounts of acquisition to the A and B cues. Further evidence that A and B attained different associative strengths may be seen in the extinction phase panel of Fig. 1. That group which received X in compound with the A cue responded more frequently during extinction than did that group which received X in compound with the presumably weaker, B cue.

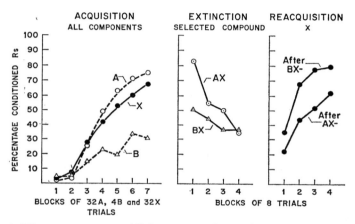

FIG. 1. Mean percentage eye-blink responses during three training phases, involving acquisition to each of three separate component CSs, extinction with one of two compounds formed from the acquisition components, and reacquisition to the component common to the two extinction compounds (from Wagner, 1969b).

The data of major interest, however, are depicted in the reacquisition functions which summarize the subsequent responding to X alone in each of the two treatment groups. As is apparent, there was *less* responding to X following the AX extinction than following the BX extinction condition. That group, in which the 32 nonreinforced exposures to X involved a relatively strong compound containing the A cue, experienced a significantly greater decrement in responding to X than did that group in which the same nonreinforced exposures to X involved a relatively weak compound containing the B cue.

B. CONDITIONED INHIBITION

We have indicated that one way to produce an inhibitory cue, that is a cue with a negative V, is to nonreinforce a neutral cue in compound with another CS which has a positive value of V. This is explicitly what is done in the procedure known to produce a "conditioned inhibitor" (e.g. Pavlov, 1927; Konorski, 1948; Rescorla and LoLordo, 1965). The only difference is that it is usually arranged that the subject receives intermixed trials in which one CS, e.g. A, is reinforced and a compound of that CS and another CS, e.g. X, is nonreinforced. This procedure should be especially effective in making X inhibitory in that each reinforcement of A alone tends to maintain V_{AX} above zero and hence, insure that V_X will be further decremented on each nonreinforced compound trial.

If our reasoning is correct, however, we should be able to demonstrate not only that discrimination training with A reinforced vs. AX nonreinforced will make X an inhibitory cue, but that X will be more inhibitory the greater the associative strength of A in compound with which X is nonreinforced.

To evaluate this proposition Wagner and Saavedra (Wagner 1971) only slightly modified the procedure of the Wagner, Saavedra and Lehmann study referred to above. During an initial acquisition phase cues A and B were again trained as a result of differential numbers of reinforced trials (240 vs. 8) to have different associative strengths, and a third cue, C, necessary for the test phase was also highly trained (548 reinforced trials).

Following such training, a novel cue X was introduced in compound with either A or B for different groups of 20 subjects and the compound was nonreinforced. Sixty-four such nonreinforced trials were irregularly intermixed with a similar number of trials in which the cue paired with X continued to be presented alone and reinforced.

The X cue should have become a "conditioned inhibitor" as a result of either training schedule. The question, again, was whether or not X would become more inhibitory as a result of being nonreinforced in compound with the stronger A cue, as compared to the weaker B cue. This was evaluated by returning the C cue and determining in both groups the reduction in responding to C when in compound with X. This final test phase involved 16 reinforced presentations of C and of the CX compound.

For all subjects C was a flashing light, X a vibratory stimulus, and A and B dissimilar auditory cues, the identification of the two as A and B counterbalanced within experimental groups. Conditioned responding during the initial training phases was appropriate to the experimental intention that A have a greater associative strength than B: prior to the introduction of X all subjects were responding at a higher level to their A cue than to their B cue, and a similar difference in responding to the two cues was continued in the performance of the separate groups subsequently receiving A reinforced vs. AX nonreinforced or B reinforced vs. BX nonreinforced.

Figure 2 presents the data of major interest from the final test phase. The two groups responded at the same high level to the C cue alone. The addition of the X cue, however, decreased this responding considerably (and reliably) more in the case of that group which had experienced the nonreinforcement of X in compound with the relatively strong A cue, than in the case of that group which had experienced the nonreinforcement of X in compound with the relatively weak B cue.

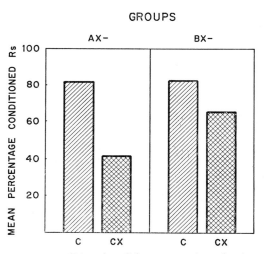

Fig. 2 Mean percentage conditioned eyelid responses, in evaluation of the conditioned inhibitory properties of X in two groups. In one group X had been nonreinforced in compound with a relatively excitatory cue, A, while in the other group X had been nonreinforced in compound with a less excitatory cue, B (from Wagner, 1971).

This experiment in conjunction with the preceding study offers strong support for the basic expectation of the model that the degree of decrement in associative strength and the amount of inhibition that may accrue to a stimulus as a result of its nonreinforced presentation depends systematically upon the associative strength of the compound in which it is embedded.

V. Additional Inhibitory Procedures Involving Nonreinforcement

It should be clear that according to the present theory an especially effective condition for establishing inhibition is the nonreinforcement of a cue in compound with an otherwise reinforced second cue. There are other procedures, however, which are known to establish inhibition but which do not explicitly involve such nonreinforcement of stimulus compounds. In many cases these procedures can still be construed as involving the same basic learning conditions. In this section, we attempt to describe several such situations in terms compatible with the present theory, thereby providing a more general account of conditioned inhibitory phenomena.

A. NEGATIVE CORRELATION BETWEEN CS AND US

Rescorla (1967a) has suggested a view of conditioning which differs from those commonly employed. According to that view, the important relationships in a conditioning situation involve the correlation or contingency between CS and US. It is argued that attention to the correlational aspects of the two events generates three types of procedures: positive correlations, no correlation and negative correlations. The former, in which the probability of a US is greater during the CS than at other times, is thought to generate conditioned excitation; the second, in which the probability of the US is equal in the presence and absence of the CS, is supposed to leave a neutral stimulus; and the third, in which the US probability is greater in the absence of the CS, is thought to generate conditioned inhibition.

There is now a reasonable amount of evidence to support the last claim that a conditioned inhibitor can be created by simply arranging a negative correlation with the US. Typical experiments (e.g. Hammond and Daniel, 1970; Rescorla, 1969a) involve conditioned suppression procedures in which brief shocks are programmed randomly in time. Occasional CSs are presented, during which shock presentation is discontinued. When these CSs are later tested in either a summation or retardation procedure, they show evidence of inhibition compared with stimuli treated according to a number of different control procedures.

Although in these experiments only one explicit CS is presented, it seems pertinent to notice that the animal is continually exposed to other stimuli not under our control. Whenever the animal is in the conditioning chamber, it is subjected to a variety of stimuli in many different modalities, so-called background stimuli. One way of conceptualizing the presentation of an explicit CS is as transforming the stimulation which the subject receives from background stimuli alone into a stimulus compound consisting of the background plus the explicit CS. If we identify the background stimulus as A and the CS as X, presentation of the CS transforms the stimulation from A into AX. The arrangement of a negative correlation between a CS and US then involves sometimes reinforcing the background stimuli, A, but never when they are presented in compound with the CS, AX. Viewed in this way, the case of negative correlation becomes simply an example of the fundamental conditioned inhibition paradigm deduced from the present theory.

Rescorla and Wagner (1972) have discussed this analysis of negative correlations in some quantitative detail, indicating how the notion of contingency can be reduced to the kind of pairing operations discussed by the present theory. It seems relevant to mention here only a few of the implications of that analysis. First, according to the present theory, conditioning should occur to the background stimuli; Dweck and Wagner (1970) have presented evidence that this does occur with such correlational treatments in a conditioned suppression situation. Secondly, the model correctly predicts certain parallels between positive and negative CS–US correlations in the effects of parametric variations. For instance, increasing the degree of negative correlation between the CS and US by presenting more USs in the absence of the CS yields a more inhibitory CS (Rescorla, 1969a). On the present model this results from the greater excitatory conditioning of background cues, A. The X is then nonreinforced in the presence of a larger $\bar{V} = V_A + V_X$. Furthermore, the blocking which Kamin (1968, 1969) obtained for positive correlations should be observable with negative correlations. If one cue, e.g. Y, is first negatively correlated with the US, the associative value of that cue, V_Y, should become sufficiently negative that $V_A + V_Y$ will be close to the zero λ appropriate to nonreinforcement. If a neutral X is then presented in conjunction with Y and the same negative correlation continued, no further decrements should occur so that X should not become inhibitory. Suiter and LoLordo (1971) have confirmed this prediction in a conditioned suppression situation. Finally, Rescorla and Wagner (1972) derived from the model the prediction that under some circumstances the initial effect of subjecting an animal to a negative correlation should be excitatory conditioning. This can occur whenever shock probability during the CS is nonzero, although lower than that in the absence of the CS. In such cases it is only later in conditioning, when the background cues are too excitatory for the reinforcement schedule during the CS to support, that inhibition should develop to the CS. No evidence is available on this interesting prediction.

Two special cases of inhibition resulting from higher US probabilities in the absence of the CS than in its presence are worth mentioning. A control procedure in common use in Pavlovian conditioning experiments involves separate presentation of the CS and US in such a way that they are explicitly unpaired. Although USs are not distributed randomly in time with this procedure, it does result in a negative correlation between CS and US. The US is never presented during the CS, although it occurs at other times. In agreement with the deduction from the present theory, there is evidence that this control procedure yields a conditioned inhibitor, at least in fear conditioning experiments (e.g. Rescorla and LoLordo, 1965). It may be noted that the fact that USs are not randomly delivered in time in the explicitly unpaired procedure may somewhat complicate the theoretical analysis. With regular spacing of the USs, temporal components of the background stimuli may become important; in some analyses, therefore, it may be necessary to distinguish background stimuli from one another according to their temporal location.

A second procedure which may be viewed as arranging a higher US probability during the CS than in its absence is more typically described as presentation of the CS at the end of the US. The CS may either be initiated at the termination of the US (backward conditioning) or it may precede US termination (cessation conditioning). Most authors working with such paradigms have emphasized the relation between the CS and the end of the US and many have argued that such an arrangement endows the CS with an inhibitory character. Indeed, Konorski (1948) cites this as the paradigmatic case for establishing conditioned inhibition. However, examination of the relation between the CS and the *onset* of the US reveals that the probability of a US onset is less during (and just following) a CS than at any other time in the session. Again, the procedure is not derived from presentations of USs randomly in time but, nevertheless, it results in a reduced probability of US onset during the CS. There does seem to be some suggestive evidence that these arrangements may generate conditioned inhibitors (e.g. Segundo *et al.*, 1961; Siegel and Domjan, 1971; Zbrozyna, 1958a, b), but it is not clear whether they do so because the CS occurs in conjunction with US termination or because the CS precedes a period in which the probability of US onset is low.

A recent fear conditioning experiment by Moscovitch and LoLordo (1968) is relevant. Noting the above mentioned confounding, they compared two groups of dogs for both of which a CS occurred in conjunction with US termination. For one group the time between that CS and the next US onset was random, thus removing the lowered probability of a shock after a CS; for the other group, standard inter-trial intervals were used, thus preserving that probability. Both groups then received a summation test for the inhibition controlled by the CS. Despite the association with US termination in both groups, only the group which also had the CS consistently precede a shock-free period showed signs of inhibition. A similar but more extensive experiment by Weisman and Litner (1971) supports this conclusion. Thus, the available evidence appears to indicate that associating a CS with US termination has no special consequences aside from those resulting from the confounded association with a diminished probability of US onset.

In any case, it is clear that the data obtained from negatively correlating a CS and US is quite compatible with the present theory. Whether stimuli associated with US-termination will require additional assumptions must await further evidence.*

---

*It would be possible to find a place for possible US-termination effects within the present model. We have assumed that the λ associated with the occurrence of a US is

B. DISCRIMINATIVE CONDITIONING

A commonly employed conditioning procedure involves following one stimulus (CS+) with reinforcement while separately presenting a second stimulus (CS−) without reinforcement. Under these circumstances the second stimulus may initially develop an excitatory conditioned response, presumably as a result of generalization from the reinforced stimulus. But eventually the response to the nonreinforced stimulus will fall, and in some circumstances even become an inhibitor. Indeed, this is one of the procedures originally described by Pavlov (1927) as establishing an inhibitor. There is now considerable evidence from both summation and retardation techniques that such a procedure does generate conditioned inhibition (e.g. Bull and Overmier, 1968; Hammond, 1968; Konorski and Szwejkowska, 1952; Rescorla and LoLordo, 1965; Szwejkowska and Konorski, 1959).

It is also possible to analyse this procedure in terms of the primary condition for inhibition presented here; i.e. the nonreinforcement of a stimulus compound, one element of which is otherwise reinforced. Rescorla and Wagner (1972) followed Konorski (1948) in suggesting that generalization between the CS+ and CS− may be represented in terms of unique and common elements of those stimuli. Discriminative conditioning can then be viewed as an AX+, BX− procedure. According to the present theory, V_{AX} will become large while V_{BX} will at first rise, as V_X grows, and then fall off to zero. Furthermore, in agreement with Konorski's (1948) deduction, V_B should become negative since it is repeatedly nonreinforced in conjunction with X. However, considering only these features would necessarily lead to the prediction that the total compound comprising CS− will simply return to zero, i.e. will not become inhibitory since conditioning will stop when $(0 - V_{BX})$ becomes zero. In contrast, the available evidence indicates that CS− becomes inhibitory.

---

high, while that associated with the nonoccurrence of a US is zero. One way of viewing a US is as an event involving a transition from one state to another. Each transition (such as from no shock to shock) may have associated with it a particular λ defining not only an appropriate magnitude but implying a particular scale of associative strength. The absence of a transition (nonreinforcement) may be associated with zero on all such scales. Viewed in this way, stimuli preceding transitions which involve the termination of our normal USs would develop associative strengths appropriate to the λs established by those transitions. The consequences of that learning in either a summation or retardation test of inhibition would then depend upon the relation between the scales established by the various λs. In the extreme case, the λ associated with US termination might be directly antagonistic to that associated with US onset; i.e. they would be negatives of one another. This apparently is the assumption which Konorski (1948) made. In that case, associating a stimulus with termination of a US would create a conditioned inhibitor as measured by summation with a stimulus associated with the onset of that US. However, these relations seem too far from being worked out to permit any such firm predictions at this time.

To account for this fact, we must again appeal to background stimuli. It may be helpful to notice that a discriminative conditioning procedure is identical to the explicitly unpaired procedure discussed in the previous section, with the exception that a second stimulus precedes the reinforcer. That is, discriminative conditioning involves a negative correlation between the CS— and the US. Despite the fact that USs are regularly preceded by another stimulus in compound with background cues, we may expect the background cues to acquire some excitatory strength, at least early in the learning process. Presentation of CS— would then involve its nonreinforcement in the presence of excitatory background stimuli, thus generating conditioned inhibition. On this view, discriminative inhibition is only a special case of negative correlation.

This analysis of inhibition resulting from discrimination training makes sense out of the finding that CS+ develops excitation before CS— develops inhibition (e.g. Weisman and Litner, 1970). The CS— can only develop inhibition after the background cues first become excitatory; presumably, the CS+ will condition at least as fast as those background cues, and therefore show excitation before CS— shows inhibition. Furthermore, the analysis makes understandable the finding of "primary inhibitory conditioned stimuli" which puzzled Konorski (1967) and was instrumental in his rejection of a theory very similar to that given here. Konorski and Szwejkowska (1952) found that a CS— could become an inhibitor even though it showed no initial stimulus generalization from CS+. Because excitation from background cues, rather than generalization from CS+, is critical to generating inhibition to CS— according to the present theory, such purely inhibitory stimuli should be observable.

It is important to note, however, two ways in which discriminative conditioning deviates from the simple case of negative correlation. First, because all USs are preceded by another stimulus, we may expect the background cues to receive less total conditioning during discriminative conditioning than in the simple negative correlation case. Consequently, this procedure should not be as powerful in establishing an inhibitor as the previously discussed cases. Although direct comparisons between conditioned inhibition and discrimination procedures are rare, the results of Weisman and Litner (1970) agree with that deduction. Indeed, according to the present theory, any procedures which facilitate "overshadowing" of background cues by CS+ should reduce the inhibition to CS—. Secondly, because the background cues occur not only in compound with CS+ and CS— but are also nonreinforced when presented alone in the intertrial interval, the present theory anticipates that they will eventually return to zero associative strength. The consequences of this for discriminative inhibition are discussed in a later section.

C. Inhibition of Delay

Pavlov described yet another procedure for the establishment of inhibition, reinforcement of a long-delay stimulus. He noted that when a very extended CS preceded the US, initially the conditioned response occurred throughout the CS; however, with the extended training, the response early in the CS was reduced and the CR became confined to the later part of the stimulus. More important in the present context, he claimed that the early part of the CS was not simply neutral but actually became a conditioned inhibitor. Some recent experiments with fear conditioning from Rescorla's laboratory (Rescorla 1967b) support Pavlov's claim, using a summation assessment technique.

Without analysing this situation in detail, it can be pointed out that an extended CS may be conceptualized as having partially discriminable subparts, occurring sequentially in time. An extended CS is then a special case of discrimination training in which the early part of the CS is nonreinforced and the later part is reinforced. The inhibition accruing to the early part of the CS then results from its nonreinforcement in conjunction with background cues in much the same way as that of the CS— in discrimination training. Just as with discrimination, the present theory anticipates that inhibition early in the long-delay CS should require a large number of trials to develop (Rescorla, 1967b).

Thus, the analyses presented in this section indicate that the present theory can generate the occurrence of inhibition in a number of known paradigms. All three of the cases discussed here, negative correlation, discriminative conditioning, and inhibition of delay, involve appeal to the conditioning of background stimuli. These stimuli play the important role of providing a level of excitation in the presence of which the critical stimulus is nonreinforced.

Another feature common to all of these paradigms is that inhibition results from the application of nonreinforcement. In the next section we deal with the possibility of generating inhibition from reinforcement.

VI. Inhibitory Procedures Involving Reinforcement

As noted earlier, according to the present theory, decrements in associative strength occur whenever the quantity $(\lambda - \bar{V})$ is negative. The conditioned inhibition procedure is paradigmatic because it ensures that this condition will be met by arranging $\lambda = 0$ while producing a high value for $\bar{V}$. Nevertheless, it is only the *relation* between these two terms that determines the direction of change resulting from a trial. Consequently, no special place is given within the present theory to the zero λ resulting from nonreinforcement. Decrements and, under the appropriate circumstances, inhibition should be producible whenever the expression $(\lambda - \bar{V})$ is negative, even if that value results from a reinforced trial. The present section points to two cases in which this outcome may be achieved.*

A. Variation in US Magnitude

We have noted earlier that λ is presumed to be related to the magnitude of the US, stronger USs yielding higher asymptotes of conditioning. This assumption seems well-grounded in available evidence (e.g. Annau and Kamin, 1961; Ost and Lauer, 1965; Wagner et al., 1964). Consider, then, a situation in which conditioning is carried out to a single stimulus, A, with one level of US, yielding an asymptotic V_A close to the appropriate λ. According to the present model, if we then shift the magnitude of the US either up or down, the level of conditioning to A should shift to conform to the current level of λ. In the case of an increase in US magnitude, this may be viewed as additional excitatory conditioning. But if the US is reduced in magnitude, we anticipate a decrement in V_A. Although experiments reducing reinforcement magnitude are common in instrumental training situations, there is surprisingly little evidence bearing on this prediction for Pavlovian conditioning. What is available, however, seems confirmatory (e.g. Klestchov, 1936), and it is interesting to note that despite the relative lack of evidence, theorists generally agree that such decrements should occur (e.g. Hull, 1943; Konorski, 1948; Spence, 1956).

The present theory, however, predicts not only decrement, but also inhibition, from appropriate reduction in US magnitude. Suppose that A is associated with a high US magnitude but that AX is followed by a US of lower magnitude. In a manner analogous to that of the conditioned inhibition paradigm, V_A would approach a high asymptote (λ_1) and $V_{AX} = V_A + V_X$ a lower asymptote (λ_2). The only way for this to occur is obviously for V_X to become negative. As soon as V_A exceeds λ_2, $(\lambda_2 - \bar{V})$ on AX trials will become negative, and V_A and V_X will each be decremented. As each A trial again raises V_A and each AX trial decreases V_A and V_X, they should eventually drive V_A towards λ_1, and V_X towards $(\lambda_2 - \lambda_1)$.

An unpublished experiment recently carried out in Rescorla's laboratory employing different durations of a shock US provides some support for this

---

*The occurrence of inhibition with reinforcement discussed in this section should not be confused with the phenomenon of "extinction with reinforcement", described by Pavlov (1927). A number of authors have reported that with extended training, a CS may cease evoking CRs anticipatory to the US even though it continues to be regularly followed by reinforcement. It seems plausible to interpret that result, when it occurs, in terms of the development of a precise discrimination of the specific location within the CS at which reinforcement is delivered. The report by Pavlov that extension of the duration of the CS leads to a return of the CR supports such an interpretation. The predictions described here are concerned with conditioned responding which is too great for the asymptote which the current US will support, not with such fine temporal discriminations.

deduction. Three groups of rats were trained to barpress for food on a VI schedule, in preparation for conditioned suppression training. They were then subjected to fear conditioning in the absence of the opportunity to barpress. In all cases the US was a 0·5-ma shock (of a duration specified), while cue A was an 1800-Hz tone, cue B an interrupted 250-Hz tone, and cue X a 1/sec flashing light, each of 30 sec duration.

In the first conditioning phase Group E received cue A ending in a 5·0-sec US and the compound AX ending in a shorter, 0·5-sec US. Group C_1 and C_2 also received both A and AX trials, but did not have different US durations associated with the two. For Group C_1 both trials ended in the 0·5-sec US; for Group C_2 half of each trial type ended in the short US and half in the long US. All groups received nine trials of each type on each of nine conditioning days. It was anticipated that in Group E, but in neither of the control groups, the light (X) should become an inhibitor of fear.

To assess possible conditioned inhibition controlled by X, a savings test was employed. All rats were given the opportunity to barpress for food. Superimposed on that behaviour were reinforced (0·5-sec shock) presentations of B and nonreinforced presentations of BX. Two B+ and six BX— trials were given per day. Again the measure of fear employed was suppression of barpressing during stimulus presentations. To the degree that X is inhibitory, it should alleviate that suppression. Under this testing treatment, X was expected to acquire inhibition in all groups. The question of interest was whether or not the acquisition of inhibition would be more rapid in Group E, thereby indicating that the previous association with US magnitude reduction had produced some inhibition to X in that group.

Figure 3 shows the data for the BX compound trials throughout the savings test. The data are plotted in suppression ratios of the form $R_2/(R_2 + R_1)$ where R_2 is the response rate during the CS and R_1 is the rate in a comparable period prior to the CS. This ratio has the properties that complete suppression (high excitatory conditioning) yields a value of zero while absence of suppression yields a value of 0·5. All groups showed complete suppression to the B cue when presented alone; consequently, only the compound trials are presented. Through the course of the savings test, all three groups began to respond on the BX trials; however, it is clear that this learning was more rapid in Group E than in either of the control groups. Apparently, the prior association of X with reduced US magnitude gave it some inhibitory control.

Some caution should be exercised, however, in interpreting these data. First, a set of animals which received no experience with X prior to the savings test was run concurrently with the groups shown in Fig. 3. Group E did not acquire the conditioned inhibition faster than that group. However, data reported below on "latent inhibition" suggest that this novel CS

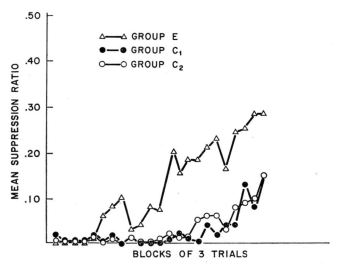

FIG. 3. Acquisition of conditioned inhibition following association with US magnitude reduction. Group E, but not Groups C_1, or C_2, received X paired with a reduced shock duration. Data are from nonreinforced BX trials which were intermingled with B reinforced trials.

group does not provide an easily interpretable comparison condition for animals which have experienced the CS. Secondly, the present learning assessment of conditioned inhibition is open to alternative interpretations. For instance, since during initial training X is uncorrelated with US events in the two control groups, but not in Group E, subjects in the former groups may have learned not to attend to the X cue. Consequently, during the savings test with the X cue the learning of the control groups may have been retarded compared with that of Group E. The present data do not preclude such an attentional account. It is clear that a summation test of conditioned inhibition would provide important data on the choice between these interpretations.

Thus, at present there appears to be only sparse evidence on the theory's predictions concerning the effects of reduced US magnitude. The meagre available data do agree with expectations that reduced US magnitude will produce a decrease in the CR. Furthermore, there is suggestive evidence that if a neutral cue is correlated with that reduction, it will become a conditioned inhibitor.

B. "Overexpectation" of the US

There is a second way to arrange that the quantity $(\lambda - \bar{V})$ is negative despite reinforcement. Consider a procedure in which A and X are both presented separately and each reinforced; V_A and V_X should both approach asymptote at the appropriate λ. If we then present the AX compound and follow it with the same reinforcer, the expression governing the changes in associative strength to A and X will be $\lambda^- (V_A+V_X)$, which should initially be very *negative*. That is, the result of application of the reinforcer to this compound will be to *decrement* the associative strength of each of the elements. Speaking casually, as a result of separate training with the elements, the subject will "overexpect" the US when presented with the compound, and compound reinforcement will act to bring that expectation into line. Both Rescorla (1970) and Wagner (1971) have reported evidence supporting this deduction in a CER situation. The results of Wagner's experiment are shown in Fig. 4.

In this experiment four groups of rats received different fear conditioning treatments with a 2-min flashing light (A) and a 2-min tone (B) preceding a 0·5-sec, 0·5-ma shock US, which could be expected to produce only a modest terminal level of suppression. Groups A+B+ and A+B+/AB+ received 40 reinforced presentations each of the A and B cues. Following that, Group A+B+/AB+ received 40 reinforced presentations of the AB compound, in an attempt to reduce the associative strengths of A and B. Two comparison groups received training only with the compound; Group AB+ received 80 reinforced trials while Group AB+/AB+ received those 80 trials plus 40 additional reinforced trials. All groups then received 16 nonreinforced presentations of the AB compound while barpressing for food, so that the degree of suppression produced by the compound could be assessed.

It is clear from Fig. 4 that Group A+B+ showed considerably more suppression to the compound than did the other groups, which were approximately equal to one another. This confirms two important predictions from the theory. First, the superior suppression of Group A+B+ compared with that of Group AB+ indicates that the same number of reinforcements produced more learning when administered to the stimuli presented separately rather than in compound. Secondly, the attenuated suppression of Group A+B+/AB+ compared with that of Group A+B+ indicates that added reinforcement of the compound in the former group reduced suppression. Furthermore, in accordance with the model, that reduction brought conditioning in Group A+B+/AB+ to a level similar to that of the two AB+ control groups. Because suppression to the AB compound is measured in this experiment, the superiority of A+B+ to groups which received compound training cannot be attributed to differential stimulus generalization decrement from conditioning to test procedures. That suppression to the separate elements is also reduced by such a procedure is confirmed in the similar experiment by Rescorla (1970).

These experiments indicate that under the appropriate conditions of "overexpectation", reinforcement can produce response decrements. Again, however, the theory makes the stronger prediction that inhibition can also be produced under these circumstances. Suppose, for instance, that instead of following A+B+ training with AB+, we had followed it with ABX+, in which X was initially a neutral cue. We would then expect all three cues to be decremented, resulting in the establishment of

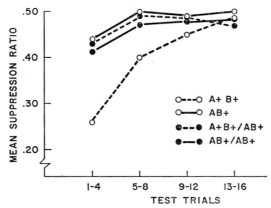

FIG. 4. Conditioned suppression to the nonreinforced AB compound. The groups are distinguished by whether they had been conditioned separately to the elements of the compound (A+B+) or conditioned to the compound (AB+). See text. (After Wagner, 1971.)

conditioned inhibition to X. Unfortunately, there is no evidence available on this prediction.

The analyses presented in this section most clearly indicate the special kinds of deductions which follow from the present theory. By suggesting that a particular discrepancy is important for the establishment of inhibition, the theory denies a unique role to nonreinforcement in producing inhibition. It suggests that inhibition may result from a considerably wider range of procedures than are generally used.* Should future research continue to bear out such deductions, it would provide strong support for the present theory.

VII. Repeated Nonreinforced Presentation of a Stimulus

Some authors have suggested a procedure for the development of conditioned inhibition which is apparently simpler than those we have thus far

*We have not specifically considered a case similar to reduction in reinforcement magnitude which is of some interest, namely reduction in reinforcement *probability*. This case should also occasion decremental learning and inhibition, but can be viewed simply in terms of the changing relative frequency of reinforcement and nonreinforcement occasions, with decremental learning occurring on the latter instances only.

considered. It has been argued by Pavlov (1927), Hull (1943), and others that the simple repeated presentation of a CS without the necessity of reinforcement experience, should endow that stimulus with conditioned inhibitory properties. In this section, we discuss three special cases of this procedure, separated according to the associative value of the stimulus prior to this repeated nonreinforcement.

A. LATENT INHIBITION

The simplest case is one in which an originally novel stimulus is simply presented repeatedly to the subject without reinforcement. This "habituation" procedure has been shown with a number of different response systems to result in retarded learning when that stimulus is subsequently reinforced (e.g. Carlton and Vogel, 1967; Lubow and Moore, 1959; Siegel, 1969). One interpretation of this outcome is that simple repeated presentation sets up a kind of inhibition to a CS which is comparable to that established by the procedures discussed earlier in this paper. It has been noted that such an interpretation would make these data at variance with the present theory. According to the theory, the associative changes induced in a stimulus by repeated nonreinforcement are governed by the expression $(0-\bar{V})$. Asymptotically such a stimulus would not have a negative V or be inhibitory, but would simply have zero associative strength.

However, another interpretation has been given to these data (e.g. Rescorla, 1969c; Siegel, 1969). It seems possible that repeated exposure does not establish negative associative strengths upon particular response scales; rather, it may lead to a general decrease in the ability of that stimulus to serve as a CS. In terms of the present theory, repeated exposure may reduce the learning rate parameter, a, associated with the CS. In more general terms, it may reduce the salience of the stimulus or the attention which the organism gives to that stimulus. In the light of this alternative, it is interesting to note that the available evidence demonstrating "latent inhibition" comes only from the retardation measure of inhibition; with that procedure the two interpretations predict similar outcomes. However, a summation test would separate the alternatives. If repeated presentation of a CS establishes inhibition, the CS should interfere with excitation in a summation test; if it only reduces the degree of attention given to the stimulus, or reduces its salience, little such interference would be expected. Both Reiss and Wagner (1972) and Rescorla (1971) have reported such summation tests of latent inhibition, the former with the eyeblink response and the latter with conditioned suppression.

Reiss and Wagner (1972) used eyeblink conditioning procedures in the rabbit similar to those employed by Wagner and Saavedra as described above. An initial experiment was conducted to determine that the conventional retardation of acquisition findings could be replicated under the special conditions necessary to perform a summation test. In this experiment all subjects initially received 1,380 nonreinforced exposures to stimulus A and 12 nonreinforced exposures to stimulus B over four days of training. They then received 120 reinforced presentations of a third stimulus C, prior to reinforced acquisition training on all three cues, A, B, and C. In accordance with previous findings, conditioned responding was slower to develop to the more frequently pre-exposed A cue than to the less frequently pre-exposed B cue.

To allow a summation evaluation of any differential inhibition that may have accrued to A and B, it was necessary only to change the last phase of this procedure so that subjects could be tested for their responsiveness to C, AC, and BC. If the more frequently pre-exposed A cue had become a greater conditioned inhibitor, there should have been not only less responding to AC than to C alone, but less responding to AC than to BC. This testing procedure was followed in the second experiment which was otherwise identical to that in which the retardation test had shown "latent inhibition". All animals received testing with five presentations each of stimulus C, AC, and BC in each of five blocks of fifteen trials. For all animals, C was reinforced when presented alone during testing; for half of the rabbits AC and BC were also reinforced, the other half received the compounds nonreinforced. For all animals C was a flashing light; the A and B cues were a vibratory and auditory stimulus, counterbalanced across animals.

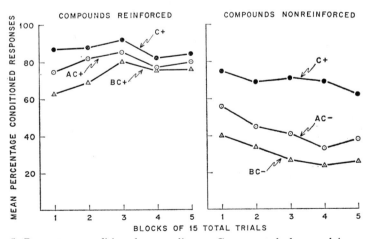

FIG. 5. Percentage conditioned responding to C, presented alone and in compound with A or B. The A and B cues are distinguished by the amount of pre-exposure. For the animals depicted on the left AC and BC were reinforced during testing; for those on the right, they were nonreinforced. (After Reiss and Wagner, 1972.)

Figure 5 shows separately the results of the summation test for animals receiving the compounds reinforced and those receiving the compounds non-reinforced. For both groups the C cue continued to produce substantial conditioned responding during the test. Also in both testing procedures, responding to the compounds was less than that to the C cue alone. However, the magnitude of the interference with responding was greater in the case of the B stimulus, which had received *less* pre-exposures, than it was in the case of the A stimulus. Apparently in this situation the initial effect of a novel stimulus is to disrupt responding. The effect of pre-exposure reduced, rather than increased, the effect of that stimulus in a summation test for inhibition. This outcome is inconsistent with the interpretation that pre-exposure produces conditioned inhibition.

A pair of experiments by Rescorla (1971) using a conditioned suppression situation yielded results in agreement with these. Of particular interest is an experiment involving transfer from a latent inhibition treatment to a conventionally conditioned inhibition training procedure. It was reasoned that if pre-exposure produces inhibition, such a shift should yield positive transfer; on the other hand, if pre-exposure reduces the salience of a stimulus, such a stimulus should also be retarded in the development of inhibition, producing negative transfer. Rats were first trained to barpress for food reward on a VI 2 min schedule. They were then confined to conditioning chambers and half of the animals were exposed to 72 2-min presentations of an 1800-Hz tone, X, over the course of three 2-hr sessions. Next, both groups were returned to the barpressing situation and given conditioned suppression training to a 2-min light CS, A. Over two days they received eight presentations of the A cue ending in a 0·5-ma, 0·5-sec foot shock. Finally, all groups received eight days of conditioned inhibition training superimposed on barpressing. Each day involved one A presentation ending in shock and three nonreinforced AX presentations.

Figure 6 shows separately the results for the animals receiving the pre-exposure (Group T) and those without pre-exposure (Group C) over the terminal conditioned inhibition training. Substantial and about equal suppression occurred to the A cue when presented alone in both groups. Initially the X cue was apparently not inhibitory in either group as there was as much suppression of barpressing in the presence of AX as in the presence of A alone. Most interesting, however, is the observation that although Group C subjects did eventually come to barpress more in the presence of AX than to A alone, such did not occur in Group T subjects. It is clear that the acquisition of inhibition to X was retarded in Group T. This outcome seems inconsistent with an interpretation of the effects of pre-exposure in terms of the development of conditioned inhibition, but suggests that pre-exposure does reduce stimulus salience.* In a parallel experiment, Rescorla (1971) demonstrated that pre-exposure led to substantially retarded acquisition of conditioned excitation in this same situation. Taken together the results suggest that pre-exposure reduces the animal's ability to develop conditioning to a stimulus, regardless of whether that conditioning is of an excitatory or inhibitory type.

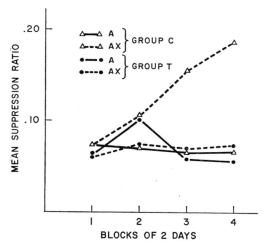

FIG. 6. Acquisition of conditioned inhibition follow either pre-exposure to X (Group T) or no pre-exposure (Group C). Data are plotted separately for reinforced A alone trials and nonreinforced AX trials. (After Rescorla, 1971.)

Within the present model, a stimulus which is slow in the acquisition of both excitation and inhibition would have not a negative V, but a low learning rate parameter, a. However, the current theory, while providing for different stimuli to have different a values, does not provide for modification of the learning rate parameter associated with a particular stimulus. The results of these experiments suggest that repeated CS presentation is one procedure which does change a. It does not seem unreasonable that other effective procedures will yet be discovered. Apparently, the present model will require modification in order to accommodate such data, perhaps along the "attentional" lines suggested by Sutherland and Mackintosh (1971). At the present time, we prefer to simply acknowledge this need for modification and await more detailed experimental results describing the

*It should be noted that in the Reiss and Wagner (1972) experiment the testing procedure in which the C cue was reinforced while the AC and BC compounds were nonreinforced also constituted a conditioned inhibition procedure. Apparently, however, the test procedure was too brief to permit observation of differential rates of development of inhibition to B and C.

conditions which modify the rate at which a stimulus can become conditioned. Admitting the possibility of a changes, as a result of nonreinforced exposures, obviously complicates the arguments we have raised concerning independence-of-path. Thus, while we have been reluctant to accept the necessity of adopting a special "inhibition" learning construct, we are apparently being led towards adopting a special "attentional" learning construct. However this may turn out, it should be noted that the available evidence that pre-exposure leads to retarded acquisition but to little effect in a summation test is entirely consistent with the conditions for developing inhibition described by the present theory.

B. Extinction of an Excitatory Stimulus

Nonreinforced exposure to a stimulus may also be given following prior reinforcement of that stimulus. There can be little question that this procedure produces decrements in responding in virtually all response systems so far studied. Furthermore, there is evidence that the magnitude of the decrement produced by nonreinforcement depends upon the current associative strength of all stimuli present during nonreinforcement. One such example is to be seen in the findings of Wagner, Saavedra and Lehmann described above, in which the decrement to X as a result of its nonreinforcement depended upon the level of excitation evoked by concurrently present stimuli. A parallel example is the case of "protection from extinction" in which the decrement to X is attenuated if it is nonreinforced in the presence of an inhibitory stimulus (Chorazyna, 1962). In the latter case, changes in associative strength to X are governed by $(0-\bar{V})$, but $\bar{V} = V_A + V_X$ is reduced because of the presence of the inhibitory A. Consequently, less extinction to X would be expected.

However, a separate question of interest in the present context is whether repeatedly nonreinforcing a previously reinforced stimulus in isolation can result in a net inhibitory value for that stimulus. According to the present theory it should not, but some earlier authors (e.g. Pavlov, 1927) have asserted that an extinguished stimulus does become a conditioned inhibitor.

One kind of evidence that has been taken as indicating that extinction results in a net inhibitory value for the CS is "extinction below zero". Pavlov (1927) reported that once a stimulus had been extinguished to the point of no response, continued nonreinforced presentation resulted in greater extinction. This greater extinction was manifested when an attempt was made to retrain the stimulus; stimuli with extinction below zero were harder to retrain than stimuli simply extinguished to zero. The use of the term "zero" presumably reflects the assumption that when responding stopped, excitation and inhibition were balanced; further extinction then yielded a net inhibitory stimulus.

On the basis of such evidence, however, there is no need to assume that net inhibition is involved in extinction below zero. It may only represent a further reduction in undetected excitation. This interpretation is supported by the absence of any data indicating that an extinguished stimulus is more inhibitory than appropriate controls. For instance, using a summation procedure, LoLordo and Rescorla (1966) found only a return to no effect when a previous fear elicitor was extinguished. With a retardation procedure, the available evidence is that an extinguished stimulus can be reconditioned *faster* than a previously untrained stimulus (e.g. Konorski and Szwej-kowska, 1950, 1952). We have earlier noted the difficulties in interpreting such results. But in any case there is no evidence that we know of in Pavlovian conditioning that simple extinction generates a conditioned inhibitor.

It is important to differentiate a simple extinction procedure, in which no reinforcement is delivered, from a discrimination procedure, in which some other stimulus continues to receive reinforcement. This is particularly critical in interpreting some early Eastern European studies; often what is described as an extinction procedure actually involves discrimination training because other stimuli continue to be reinforced within the same experimental situation. Although the present theory predicts only a return to zero when a stimulus is extinguished, it does predict the development of conditioned inhibition when other stimuli are concomitantly reinforced.

C. Extinction of an Inhibitory Stimulus

According to the present theory, any simple nonreinforcement of a cue will result in the movement of the associative strength of that cue towards zero. This is no less true for a stimulus which has previously been made an inhibitor than it is for an excitor or neutral stimulus. Thus, far from generating conditioned inhibition, according to the present theory, repeated nonreinforcement should "extinguish" inhibition. This prediction is of considerable interest because very little has been said about the conditions under which inhibition may be expected to be destroyed; nevertheless, any reasonably complete theory of inhibition must specify the conditions under which it can be removed as well as those under which it can be generated. It should be apparent from what has been said here and elsewhere (Rescorla and Wagner, 1972) that either repeatedly reinforcing a stimulus or de-correlating the stimulus with the US should remove any inhibition which it controls. But the most straightforward way in which loss of inhibition should be accomplished is simply nonreinforced presentation of the stimulus.

There are very few data available on the possibility that repeated non-reinforcement removes inhibition. Rescorla and LoLordo (1965) carried out extensive testing of inhibitors established by a variety of procedures. This testing involved repeated nonreinforced presentation of the inhibitors superimposed on an avoidance response; inhibition was measured by re- duction in response rate. Despite this nonreinforced testing, they observed no tendency of the inhibitor to lose its effects. On the other hand, Weisman and Litner (1970) carried out a highly similar experiment and did observe loss of the suppressive effects of the inhibitor during considerable yet more extensive testing. It is relevant to note, however, that the Weisman and Litner study involved superimposition of the CS on an active avoidance schedule. That is, shocks could occur during the inhibitor, if avoidance responding were depressed. This operant contingency was not operative during the Rescorla and LoLordo study. The recovery of response rate during the inhibitor in the Weisman and Litner study may thus have re- presented the assertion of control by the operant contingencies.

We have collected, in our separate laboratories, more direct data rele- vant to this issue. However, the results of those experiments are contra- dictory. In some experiments, such extinction seems to occur, while in others no extinction can be detected. At present we do not know what condi- tions are responsible for the disagreement; consequently, we can do little more than raise the issue here. It should be pointed out, however, that interpretation of the results of such experiments is extremely difficult. At the heart of the problem are two issues which have been recurrent in the preceding discussion. On the one hand, if extinction of inhibition apparently occurs, an alternative interpretation in terms of attention changes is pos- sible; perhaps the repeated nonreinforced presentation has only reduced the degree to which the subject attends to the inhibitor, while leaving intact its inhibitory power. Reduction in the effectiveness of the stimulus in a sum- mation test procedure could be attributed to either process. On the other hand, suppose that no extinction is observed. Then it seems conceivable that, although the stimulus was repeatedly nonreinforced, its presentation occurred in conjunction with slightly excitatory background cues. Such cues may be sufficient to prevent extinction, since the associative strength of the stimulus V_X may remain negative while $V_A + V_X$ approaches zero as long as the strength of background cue, V_A, remains positive. Eventually, the background cues should lose their power, but it is difficult to assess their status for any given amount of extinction. We are currently involved in a number of experiments to clarify the issue, experiments which are less subject to these alternative interpretations. But it is too early to describe the outcomes.

It is worth pointing out that the issue of whether or not there is a loss of inhibition with simple repeated nonreinforcement has broad implications for the characterization of inhibition. For instance, if inhibition does extinguish, then some experimental procedures which initially establish it may be un- able to maintain it. In discriminative conditioning, for example, CS$-$ is thought, according to the present theory, to become inhibitory because of excitatory background cues. Eventually, the latter cues should lose their excitation because of their repeated nonreinforcement. When that happens, the discrimination procedure should become an extinction of inhibition procedure and the theory predicts loss of the inhibition. A similar deduction follows for inhibition of delay. Again, there is little data available, but the ability to maintain both discriminative inhibition and inhibition of delay over long training procedures (Szwejkowska and Konorski, 1959; Rescorla, 1967b) may point to an instance in which modification of the theory will become necessary.

Despite the uncertainty with regard to the conditions destroying inhibition, the results discussed in this section are in general agreement with the model that simple nonreinforcement does not invariably establish inhibition. Simply nonreinforcing a stimulus in isolation, whether it be following prior excitatory training, prior inhibitory training, or without prior training, will not make that stimulus a *stronger* conditioned inhibitor. Just as the theory makes understandable the success of certain procedures described in previous sections in establishing inhibition, so here it makes understandable the failure of certain similar procedures to generate inhibition. It is this ability to accurately partition these procedures that makes the present theory powerful in accounting for inhibitory phenomena in Pavlovian conditioning.

VIII. Conclusion

We have described the application of a relatively well-specified theory of Pavlovian conditioning to the special problems of decremental learning and conditioned inhibition. The basic proposition of this theory is that changes in associative strength of a stimulus, resulting from a conditioning trial, depend upon the total associative strength of all stimuli present on that trial. We have described in some detail how such a theory provides an account of the development of conditioned inhibition when certain traditional paradigms are employed. Furthermore, we have emphasized that this theory denies any special relationship between inhibition and nonreinforcement. We have pointed to paradigms predicted to yield inhibition despite reinforcement, as well as to paradigms which fail to yield inhibition despite repeated nonreinforcement.

Throughout the discussion we have discovered a number of points at which the theory seems to need elaboration. But even in its present form, it is clear that the theory provides a comprehensive account of the major phenomena of conditioned inhibition. This is especially encouraging because the propositions discussed here fit easily into a general theory of the operation of reinforcement and nonreinforcement in Pavlovian conditioning.

References

Anderson, N. H. (1970). Functional measurement and psychophysical judgment. *Psychological Review*, **77**, 153–170.

Annau, Z. and Kamin, L. J. (1961). The conditioned emotional response as a function of intensity of the US. *Journal of Comparative and Physiological Psychology*, **54**, 428–432.

Bull, J. A., III and Overmier, J. B. (1968). Additive and subtractive properties of excitation and inhibition. *Journal of Comparative and Physiological Psychology*, **66**, 511–514.

Bush, R. R. and Mosteller, F. (1955). *Stochastic Models for Learning*. New York: Wiley.

Carlton, P. L. and Vogel, J. R. (1967). Habituation and conditioning. *Journal of Comparative and Physiological Psychology*, **63**, 348–351.

Chorazyna, H. (1962). Some properties of conditioned inhibition. *Acta Biologiae Experimentalis*, **22**, 5.

Dweck, C. S. and Wagner, A. R. (1970). Situational cues and correlation between conditioned stimulus and unconditioned stimulus as determinants of the conditioned emotional response. *Psychonomic Science*, **18**, 145–147.

Estes, W. K. and Burke, C. J. (1953). A theory of stimulus variability in learning. *Psychological Review*, **60**, 276–286.

Hammond, L. J. (1968). Retardation of fear acquisition by a previously inhibitory CS. *Journal of Comparative and Physiological Psychology*, **66**, 756–759.

Hammond, L. J. and Daniel, R. (1970). Negative contingency discrimination: Differentiation by rats between safe and random stimuli. *Journal of Comparative and Physiological Psychology*, **72**, 486–491.

Hearst, E., Besley, S. and Farthing, G. W. (1970). Inhibition and the stimulus control of operant behavior. *Journal of the Experimental Analysis of Behavior*, **14**, 373–409.

Hull, C. L. (1940). Explorations in the patterning of stimuli conditioned to the G. S. R. *Journal of Experimental Psychology*, **27**, 95–110.

Hull, C. L. (1943). *Principles of Behavior*. New York: Appleton–Century–Crofts.

Kamin, L. J. (1968). "Attention-like" processes in classical conditioning. In: M. R. Jones (Ed.), *Miami Symposium on the Prediction of Behavior: Aversive Stimulation*. Miami: University of Miami Press.

Kamin, L. J. (1969). Predictability, surprise, attention, and conditioning. In: B. A. Campbell and R. M. Church (Eds.), *Punishment*. New York: Appleton–Century–Crofts.

Klestchov, S. V. (1936). The dependence of the magnitude of conditioned food reflexes upon the amount of unconditioned reinforcement. *Trudy Fizio Lab Pavlova*, **6**, 27–53.

Konorski, J. (1948). *Conditioned Reflexes and Neuron Organization*. Cambridge: Cambridge University Press.

Konorski, J. (1967). *Integrative Activity of the Brain*. Chicago: University of Chicago Press.

Konorski, J. and Szwejkowska, G. (1950). Chronic extinction and restoration of conditioned reflexes, I: Extinction against the excitatory background. *Acta Biologiae Experimentalis*, **15**, 155–170.

Konorski, J. and Szwejkowska, G. (1952). Chronic extinction and restoration of conditioned reflexes, IV. The dependence of the course of extinction and restoration of conditioned reflexes on the "history" of the conditioned stimulus (The principle of the primacy of first training) . . . *Acta Biologiae Experimentalis*, **16**, 95–113.

LoLordo, V. M. and Rescorla, R. A. (1966). Protection of the fear-eliciting capacity of a stimulus from extinction. *Acta Biologiae Experimentalis*, **26**, 251–258.

Lubow, R. E. and Moore, A. U. (1959). Latent inhibition: The effect of non-reinforced pre-exposure to the conditioned stimulus. *Journal of Comparative and Physiological Psychology*, **52**, 415–419.

Miller, J. (1939). The rate of conditioning of human subjects to single and multiple conditioned stimuli. *Journal of Genetic Psychology*, **20**, 399–408.

Moscovitch, A. and LoLordo, V. M. (1968). Role of safety in the Pavlovian backward fear conditioning procedure. *Journal of Comparative and Physiological Psychology*, **66**, 673–678.

Ost, J. W. P. and Lauer, D. W. (1965). Some investigations of classical salivary conditioning in the dog. In: W. F. Prokasy (Ed.), *Classical Conditioning: A Symposium*. New York: Appleton–Century–Crofts.

Pavlov, I. P. (1927). *Conditioned Reflexes*. London: Oxford University Press.

Reiss, S. and Wagner, A. R. (1972). CS habituation produces a "latent inhibition effect" but no active conditioned inhibition. *Learning and Motivation* (in press).

Rescorla, R. A. (1967a). Pavlovian conditioning and its proper control procedures. *Psychological Review*, **74**, 71–80.

Rescorla, R. A. (1967b). Inhibition of delay in Pavlovian fear conditioning. *Journal of Comparative and Physiological Psychology*, **64**, 114–120.

Rescorla, R. A. (1969a). Conditioned inhibition of fear resulting from negative CS–US contingencies. *Journal of Comparative and Physiological Psychology*, **67**, 504–509.

Rescorla, R. A. (1969b). Conditioned inhibition of fear. In: W. K. Honig and N. J. Mackintosh (Eds.), *Fundamental Issues in Associative Learning*. Halifax: Dalhousie University Press.

Rescorla, R. A. (1969c). Pavlovian conditioned inhibition. *Psychological Bulletin*, **72**, 77–94.

Rescorla, R. A. (1970). Reduction in the effectiveness of reinforcement after prior excitatory conditioning. *Learning and Motivation*, **1**, 372–381.

Rescorla, R. A. (1971). Summation and retardation tests of latent inhibition. *Journal of Comparative and Physiological Psychology*, **75**, 77–81.

Rescorla, R. A. and LoLordo, V. M. (1965). Inhibition of avoidance behavior. *Journal of Comparative and Physiological Psychology*, **59**, 406–412.

Rescorla, R. A. and Wagner, A. R. (1972). A theory of Pavlovian conditioning: Variations in the effectiveness of reinforcement and nonreinforcement. In: A. Black and W. F. Prokasy (Eds.), *Classical Conditioning II*. New York: Appleton–Century–Crofts.

Saavedra, M. (1971). Pavlovian compound conditioning. Unpublished Ph.D dissertation, Yale University.

Segundo, J. P., Galeano, C., Sommer-Smith, J. A. and Roig, J. A. (1961). Behavioral and EEG effects of tones reinforced by cessation of painful stimuli. In: J. F. Delafrensaye (Ed.), *Brain Mechanisms and Learning*. Oxford: Blackwell.

Siegel, S. (1969). Effect of CS habituation on eyelid conditioning. *Journal of Comparative and Physiological Psychology*, **68**, 245–248.

Siegel, S. and Domjan, M. (1971). Backward conditioning as an inhibitory procedure. *Learning and Motivation*, **2**, 1–11.

Spence, K. W. (1956). *Behavior Theory and Conditioning.* New Haven: Yale University Press.

Sutherland, N. S. and Mackintosh, J. (1964). Discrimination learning: Non-additivity of cues. *Nature,* **201,** 528–530.

Sutherland, N. S. and Mackintosh, N. J. (1971). *Mechanisms of Animal Discrimination Learning.* New York: Academic Press.

Suiter, R. D. and LoLordo, V. M. (1971). Blocking of inhibitory Pavlovian conditioning in the conditioned emotional response procedure. *Journal of Comparative and Physiological Psychology,* **76,** 137–144.

Szwejkowska, G. and Konorski, J. (1959). The influence of the primary inhibitory stimulus upon the salivary effect of excitatory conditioned stimulus. *Acta Biologiae Experimentalis,* **19,** 162–174.

Trabasso, T., Bower, G., Gelman, R. and Schaeffer, B. (1966). Selectivity and additivity of cues in concept identification. Proceedings 74th Annual Convention, American Psychological Association, 35–36.

Wagner, A. R. (1969a). Stimulus validity and stimulus selection. In: W. K. Honig and N. J. Mackintosh (Eds.), *Fundamental Issues in Associative Learning.* Halifax: Dalhousie University Press.

Wagner, A. R. (1969b). Stimulus selection and a "modified continuity theory". In: G. H. Bower and J. T. Spence (Eds.), *The Psychology of Learning and Motivation,* Volume 3. New York: Academic Press.

Wagner, A. R. (1971). Elementary associations. In: H. H. Kendler and J. T. Spence (Eds.), *Essays in Neobehaviorism: A Memorial Volume to Kenneth W. Spence.* New York: Appleton–Century–Crofts.

Wagner, A. R., Siegel, S., Thomas, E. and Ellison, G. D. (1964). Reinforcement history and the extinction of a conditioned salivary response. *Journal of Comparative and Physiological Psychology,* **58,** 354–358.

Weisman, R. G. and Litner, J. S. (1969). The course of Pavlovian excitation and inhibition of fear in rats. *Journal of Comparative and Physiological Psychology,* **69,** 667–672.

Weisman, R. G. and Litner, J. S. (1972). Role of the intertrial interval in Pavlovian differential conditioning of fear in rats. *Journal of Comparative and Physiological Psychology,* **74,** 211–218.

Woodbury, C. B. (1943). The learning of stimulus patterns by dogs. *Journal of Comparative Psychology,* **35,** 29–40.

Zbrozyna, A. W. (1958a). On the conditioned reflex of the cessation of the act of eating, I: Establishment of the conditioned cessation reflex. *Acta Biologiae Experimentalis,* **18,** 137–162.

Zbrozyna, A. W. (1958b). On the conditioned reflex of the cessation of the act of eating, II: Differentiation of the conditioned cessation reflex. *Acta Biologiae Experimentalis,* **18,** 163–164.

A Simple and Accurate Stimulator of the Wayner and Rescorla Equations

Appendix

A. M. UTTLEY

University of Sussex, Brighton, Sussex, England

$$\triangle V_A = a_A\beta\,(\lambda - \overline{V_A + V_x}) \tag{1a}$$
$$\triangle V_x = a_x\beta\,(\lambda - \overline{V_A + V_x}) \tag{1b}$$

where

V_A = associative strength of conditioned stimulus (CS) A
V_x = associative strength of CS X
a_A = salience or learning rate parameter of CS A
a_x = salience or learning rate parameter of CS X
β = scaling factor or learning rate parameter of unconditioned stimulus (US)
λ = asymptotic level of associative strength which US will support

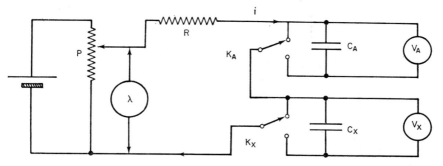

In the above circuit
the voltage across the potentiometer P represents λ
the resistor R represents $1/\beta$
the non-polarized electrolytic capacitors C_A and C_x
   represent $1/a_A$ and $1/a_x$
the voltages across the capacitors represent V_A and V_x
   Depressing keys K_A and K_x represents trials with CS A and X respectively (at about one trial per second with the component values used).

z

I. Circuit Principles

The rate of change of voltage across a capacitor is proportional to the current flowing into it, and inversely proportional to its capacity;

hence
$$\frac{dV_A}{dt} = \frac{i}{C_A} \text{ and } \frac{dV_x}{dt} = \frac{i}{C_x}$$

The current flowing is proportional to the voltage across R;

i.e.
$$i = \left\{ \frac{\lambda - \overline{V_A + V_x}}{R} \right\}$$

therefore
$$\frac{dV_A}{dt} = \frac{1}{C_A} \cdot \frac{1}{R} \left\{ \lambda - \overline{V_A + V_x} \right\} \tag{2a}$$

$$\frac{dV_x}{dt} = \frac{1}{C_x} \cdot \frac{1}{R} \left\{ \lambda - \overline{V_A + V_x} \right\} \tag{2b}$$

The difference equations (1a) and (2b) define the changes in associative strength of stimuli A and X, after one trial.

The continuous differential equations (2a) and (2b) define the rates of change of strength for trials at a constant rate.

The circuit can be extended to include any number of CS.

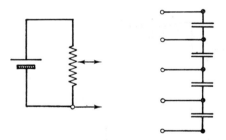

II. Technical Details

The resistance of the voltmeters V_A and V_x must be large compared with R, which in turn, must be large compared with the resistance of the potentiometer.

$$\lambda \max = 6 \text{ volts}$$
$$P = 10000 \ \Omega$$
$$R = 28700 \ \Omega$$
$$C_A = C_x = 400 \ \mu F \text{ non-polarized electrolytic (40v).}$$

III. A Typical Simulation

1. Set λ to maximum value to simulate reinforcement.
2. Depress key K_A to simulate trials with CS A only.
3. After V_A has approached its maximum value raise key K_A to stop trials.
4. Set λ to zero to simulate nonreinforcement.
5. Depress keys K_A and K_x to simulate trials with the combined stimuli A and X.

Note that V_A drops to half value and that V_x goes negative.

Press the reversing button on the avometer to read negative values of V.

Some Ideas Concerning Physiological Mechanisms of so-called Internal Inhibition

13

J. KONORSKI

Department of Neurophysiology, Nencki Institute of Experimental Biology, Warsaw, Poland

I. Introduction 341
II. Experimental Data on the Transformations of Excitatory into Inhibitory
CRs, and Vice Versa 343
III. A New Theory of Internal Inhibition 347
IV. The Problem of Motor-act Inhibition 351
V. Conclusion 353
VI. Postscript 354
References 356

I. Introduction

When discussing the physiological mechanisms of inhibitory processes involved in learning we should begin with a short survey of the occurrence of these processes in more fundamental functions of the nervous system observed mostly in acute experiments performed in anaesthetized or immobilized animals. For these experiments give us indubitable evidence that inhibitory processes are no less, and may be even more, ubiquitous than excitatory processes, and that the normal activity of the nervous system is thoroughly impregnated by their presence.

If we try to categorize the conditions in which inhibitory processes occur, we may specify at least the four following cases.

1. Reciprocal inhibition. There is a great body of evidence to show that most nervous "centres" (i.e. sets of neurons endowed with the same functions) are arranged in antagonistic pairs, such that excitation of one centre inhibits the other one and vice versa. The first example of this general rule was provided by Sherrington (1947) in spinal reflexes with the help of crude stimulus-response techniques; methods of detecting this type of inhibition have since become more and more refined and include the method of recording hyperpolarization in nerve cells by intracellular microelectrodes (Eccles, 1964). Typical examples of this reciprocal inhibition at various levels of the nervous axis are: flexion versus extension of the limbs,

inspiration versus expiration, hunger versus satiation, reciprocal relations of centres controlling bodily temperature, and last but not least, arousal versus somnolence. This type of inhibition is characterized by the reciprocity of the mutual relations between a pair of centres, which Sherrington used to call "subcentres".

2. Antagonisms between centres (or rather functional systems) which are not specifically paired. Again the simplest Sherringtonian model of this relation is inhibition of the scratch reflex, produced by a nociceptive stimulus. To turn to a higher level of nervous integration, we can indicate the inhibitory influence of fear reflexes upon *any* other drive reflexes (hunger, anger, somnolence, sexual drive).

3. Unidirectional inhibition. There are structures in the nervous system which exert overall inhibitory effects upon other structures. In the majority of cases we deal here with the inhibitory influence of higher structures, including the cerebral cortex, upon lower structures. Disinhibition of the function of these lower centres by the removal of the higher centres is called the "release phenomenon". Decerebrate rigidity and sham rage are typical examples of this release.

4. Lateral inhibition. This is probably the most ubiquitous type of inhibitory process within the nervous system. It is produced by a special type of inhibitory neurons with short and widely ramifying axons, exerting inhibitory influence upon neighbouring long-axon neurons. Lateral inhibition accounts for delicate motor adjustments both in the spinal cord and the motor cortex, as well as for the sharpening of contrast in afferent functions. Konorski (1967) emphasized the important role of lateral inhibition in perceptual processes at the highest levels of the nervous hierarchy.

Keeping in mind these four (at the minimum) categories of inhibitory process, we turn now to the discussion of inhibitory processes as they are manifested in complex forms of behaviour in higher animals.

There is no doubt that Pavlov was virtually the first scientist who utilized the concept of inhibition in behavioural experimentation by introducing his notions of external and internal inhibition. By internal inhibition he meant those inhibitory processes which are not ready-made as a result of ontogenetic development (as is the case with external inhibition), but which are learnt whenever the external conditions require the animal to suppress some of its inborn or acquired behavioural acts. According to various inhibitory training procedures he distinguished extinction, differentiation (including so-called conditioned inhibition), and inhibition of delay.

I shall not dwell upon the original Pavlovian theory of internal inhibition, an evaluation of which was presented in my monograph published in the forties (Konorski, 1948). In that monograph I put forward a concept of the mechanism of internal inhibition which assumed that it consists in the formation of inhibitory synaptic connections between the "centre" of the conditioned stimulus (CS) and the centre of the unconditioned stimulus (US). An important assumption, based on relevant experimental evidence, was that the formation of an inhibitory conditioned reflex (CR) does not consist in the *transformation* of excitatory synaptic paths between the two centres into inhibitory ones, but rather in the *addition* of inhibitory connections to the previously developed excitatory connections. To put it in a different way, we may say that the "inhibitory CR" established by the procedure of extinction, differentiation or inhibition of delay is, as a matter of fact, a mixed excitatory-inhibitory CR, its reflex-arc consisting of both types of synaptic connection between the CS centre and the US centre.

This assumption accounts for the gradual elaboration of the inhibitory CR and its "disinhibition" (temporary or permanent) whenever the newly established inhibitory connections are for some reason outweighed by previously established excitatory connections. My previous monograph (Konorski, 1948) was mainly concerned with demonstrating that the great bulk of data on internal inhibition gathered in Pavlov's laboratories could be satisfactorily accounted for by this concept. Thus it was postulated that both excitatory and inhibitory synaptic connections are established either in the course of phylogenetic development, or in the individual life of the organism as a result of his experiences.

My previous concept was developed about 25 years ago, before the postwar work of our laboratory started in the Nencki Institute. It now appears to be inadequate and has been replaced by a quite different concept, which seems to me both more adequate for the explanation of numerous experimental facts gathered in the meantime, and more reasonable from the physiological point of view. This new concept has been described in detail (Konorski, 1967), and since I have not so far changed my views upon this subject, the present considerations will be based on the same ideas and experimental evidence which were discussed in that book.

II. Experimental Data on the Transformations of Excitatory into Inhibitory CRs, and Vice Versa

When testing my previous hypothesis concerning the mechanism of internal inhibition, Konorski and Szwejkowska (1950) came across the following facts:

In experiments on dogs in a standard CR chamber a number of classical food CRs were established and measured by the magnitude of salivary response. When the CRs became stable, one of the CSs was presented once or twice per session, without reinforcement, while other CSs continued to be reinforced. This chronic extinction lasted for about one month until a definite extinction level was reached. Thereupon the excitatory CR to that CS was restored by reinforcing it again in similar conditions. It was found that while resistance to extinction of the excitatory CR was considerable, resistance to its restoration was minimal, since after one or two reinforced trials the previous level of the salivary response was attained (Fig. 1).

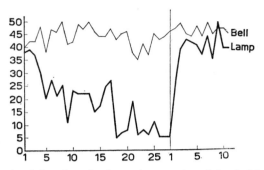

FIG. 1. An example of chronic extinction and restoration of classical food CR. Abscissa: experimental sessions with one extinction trial per session. Ordinate: conditioned salivation in arbitrary units. The vertical line denotes the beginning of restoration of the CR to lamp. Lamp is the extinguished CS; Bell is the control CS, which always just precedes an extinction trial. Note that the process of extinction is slow and irregular, while restoration of the extinguished CR is immediate (from Konorski, 1967).

The same asymmetry of the rate of extinction and restoration was obtained in experiments by Konorski and Szwejkowska (1952a) with defensive classical CRs, the unavoidable US being a shock delivered to the paw (Fig. 2).

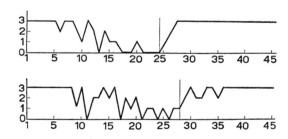

FIG. 2. Chronic extinction and restoration of classical defensive CR. Abscissa: experimental sessions. Ordinate: the number of positive responses to the extinguished and restored CS. In each session this CS was presented three times among positive CSs. The vertical line denotes the beginning of restoration of the CR. Each graph denotes the experimental results from one dog. Note the slow and irregular course of extinction and much more rapid course of restoration of the CR (from Konorski and Szwejkowska, 1952a).

In another series of experiments a bell (S_1) was a positive (excitatory) CS signalling food. When the CR to this CS was firmly established, a bell

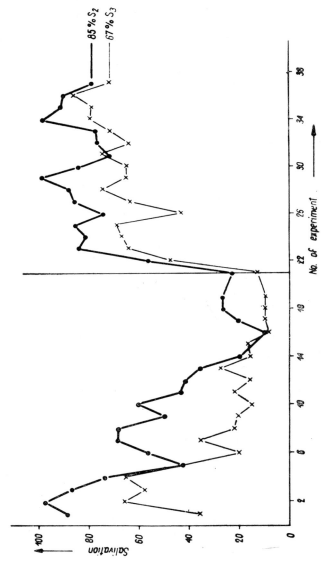

Fig. 3. Extinction of two stimuli similar to a positive CS and their transformation into positive CSs. Abscissa: experimental sessions. Ordinate: salivation as a percentage of the effect of the positive CS (S_1). The vertical line denotes the beginning of positive conditioning. Note the stronger resistance to extinction of a CR to a stimulus more similar to the positive CS, S_2, than to a stimulus less similar, S_3, and the weaker resistance to conditioning of S_2 than to conditioning of S_3 (from Szwejkowska, 1959).

of different sound (S_2) and a buzzer (S_3) were presented without reinforcement among other positive CSs. As seen in Fig. 3, S_3 was less similar to S_1 than S_2, as judged by weaker generalization and weaker resistance to extinction. When both S_2 and S_3 were converted into positive CSs by reinforcing them, it appeared that resistance to conditioning was much weaker for S_2 than for S_3, that is the closer the differentiated CS to the original CS, the easier its transformation into the positive CS (Szwejkowska 1959).

Finally, in the third series of experiments, after the formation of an excitatory food CR to a given stimulus, a stimulus quite different from the original CS (as judged by the lack of generalization) was introduced and repeatedly presented without reinforcement. When, after this nonreinforced training, the stimulus was converted into an excitatory CS by food reinforcement its resistance to conditioning was extremely strong, and this stimulus practically never produced a strong and regular conditioned response (Fig. 4). It should be noted that in the presence of that stimulus the animals refused to take food, waiting till the stimulus was discontinued.

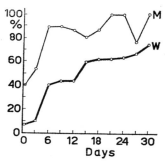

FIG. 4. The formation of classical food CR to a new stimulus (Metronome) and to a stimulus repeatedly presented without food reinforcement (Whistle). Abscissa: experimental sessions. Ordinate: conditioned salivation as a percentage of that of a well-established CR. Note that a new stimulus (M) elicits from the very beginning considerable salivation (pseudo-conditioning), rapidly attaining the level of the control CR, whereas the nonreinforced stimulus (W) originally elicits a negligible salivary response which very slowly increases when the stimulus is reinforced. The irregularity of the responses is not seen, because each point denotes the average of three sessions (from Konorski, 1967).

Experimental neuroses developed occasionally under these conditions (Konorski and Szwejkowska, 1952b).

An important conclusion drawn from these experiments is that a stimulus presented without reinforcement among other stimuli which are duly reinforced, and being outside the field of their generalization, is not a "neutral" stimulus (as was thought before), but acquires strong inhibitory properties, as judged from its resistance to conditioning. Thus, while a stimulus which had previously signalled the US, and then stopped doing so because of nonreinforcement, easily regains its signalling capacity, a stimulus which was presented among positive CSs but always signalled the lack of the US, could not thereafter be converted into a regular and reliable signal heralding the occurrence of the US.

According to these data the original version of the concept of inhibitory conditioning should be modified by distinguishing secondary inhibitory CRs which arise when excitatory CSs cease to be reinforced by the US, and primary inhibitory CRs, which arise when the corresponding CSs are never reinforced. Although the primary and the secondary CSs may be phenomenologically indistinguishable, because both of them produce no salivary response, they *can* be distinguished when we convert them into excitatory CSs. While the secondary inhibitory CS is very quickly transformed into the excitatory CS, the primary inhibitory CS is resistant to such a transformation.

III. A New Theory of Internal Inhibition

We might be satisfied with this improved concept of internal inhibition when dealing with transformations of *homogeneous* CRs, either alimentary, or defensive. The situation is, however, changed, when we deal with transformations of *heterogeneous* CRs, for instance if we transform alimentary CRs into defensive CRs and vice versa (Konorski and Szwejkowska, 1956; Konorski, 1967). It has been found that the same rules stated above for excitatory and inhibitory CRs hold true with regard to food-excitatory and shock-excitatory CRs. In fact, whereas the *formation* of either alimentary or defensive CRs to new stimuli is generally rapid, the *transformation* of CSs from one of these categories into the other one encounters great resistance and the new CR is never fully attained. Moreover, it has been found that a transformed CS has a mixed nature, being both alimentary and defensive, and this or that aspect of this CS may become manifest, depending on whether it is presented against an alimentary background or against a defensive background.

This being so, one is tempted to propose a theory which would account in the same manner for both kinds of transformation, namely excitatory-inhibitory transformations in homogeneous CRs and alimentary-defensive transformations in heterogeneous CRs. Such a theory can indeed be established if we admit that non-reinforcement of a given stimulus, in a situation in which other stimuli *are* reinforced by a definite US, means that this stimulus is reinforced by the *lack of the US* (denoted as no-US). In physiological terms it may be assumed that there are two reciprocally related centres (for instance, food and no-food centres), the first one being activated by the taste of food and the other by no-food in the mouth. The "excitatory" CS is a CS the centre for which is connected with the US centre, whereas the "inhibitory" CS is a CS the centre for which is connected with the no-US centre. This theory has been recently developed (Konorski, 1967), and it has been found that it accounts much better for the available experimental data than does the previous theory, which postulated the formation of both excitatory and inhibitory connections between the CS centre and a unique US centre.

In order to show the advantages of the new concept over the previous one, let us consider in more detail the processes of the formation of excitatory and inhibitory CRs and their mutual transformations on the basis of the experimental data described above. As explained above, the formation of a primary excitatory CR carried out by pairing the CS with the US is generally a rapid process requiring a small number of trials. Extinction of the CR, on the contrary, is a rather lengthy process requiring several dozen non-reinforced trials (cf. Figs. 1 and 2). If extinction is supposed to be due to the formation of connections between the CS centre and the no-US centre, this slowness is understandable, as a result of the antagonistic relationship between the US and the no-US centres. In fact, in the first stage of extinction the CS strongly activates the US centre, which in turn strongly inhibits the no-US centre. Accordingly, although the pairing of the CS and the no-US does occur, the connections between the two centres cannot be formed because of the nonreactive state of the no-US centre. This situation, however, cannot last indefinitely. After all, the US does *not* follow the CS and accordingly the activation of the no-US centre begins to take place, first after the cessation of the CS and then in the presence of the CS itself. This activation, in turn, inhibits the US centre and thus more and more gives an upper hand to the no-US centre and allows connections between the CS centre and the no-US centre to be formed. Finally, these connections become so abundant that the US centre becomes completely inhibited during the action of the CS.

What are the experimental consequences of the proposed mechanism in comparison with the hypothesis assuming the formation of inhibitory connections between the CS centre and the US centre, as postulated by the previous theory?

First, the theory assuming the formation of inhibitory connections between the CS and US centres would predict a regular and rather linear decrease of the magnitude of the conditioned response, since each non-reinforced trial adds a "quantum" of inhibition to the CS–US connections. On the contrary, the theory of two reciprocal centres being involved in extinction predicts a quite different course of events: the process of extinction should be very slow in the first extinction trials and then should gain momentum in later trials, thus being completely non-linear.

Secondly, in the middle of the process of extinction, when there is a balance between the CS–US connections and the CS-no-US connections, the process *must* be utterly irregular because even a small dominance in the activation of one of the two centres would immediately give it the upper hand, because of the reciprocal inhibition of the other centre. Thus oscillations in the magnitude of conditioned responses should in the transition stage, be much above the reasonable chance level, because each oscillation is amplified by positive feedback due to the instability of the whole system.

Thirdly, if the duration of the CS on each trial lasts a dozen seconds or more, as is the case in most experiments with salivary CRs, then the irregularity of conditioned responses should be observed not only between successive trials but also within trials. For instance, at the beginning of its action the CS might produce a full-sized salivary response, which may stop abruptly after a few seconds when the inhibitory process starts to dominate the excitatory process, or, more rarely, the sequence of the processes may be the reverse.

My own experience in CR experimentation, acquired before the present concept had been developed, is in full agreement with these predictions and in full conflict with the previous theory. Like all learning theorists who tried arduously to construct "learning curves" by smoothing down all the irregularities of learning processes, I had also believed in the real existence of these curves and that they reflected the "true" course of learning. Now I think, on the contrary, that these curves falsify reality by concealing the irregularity of the learning process, an irregularity which is inherent in its very nature.

Now, what is the situation when the extinguished CR is restored by reinforcement of the CS? According to our previous view this restoration should work in the opposite direction to extinction, adding an excitatory quantum in each successive trial. In consequence the process should again be linear and perhaps symmetrical to the process of extinction, if excitatory quanta and inhibitory quanta are of equal value. On the other hand, according to our present view, the situation is as follows: the CS centre is now connected with the US centre and the no-US centre, and therefore the dominance of one of those connections over the other one depends on a relatively small difference. The system, therefore, becomes bistable with a relatively strong preponderance of one of the two states depending on minor factors.

We are confronted with a quite different situation when dealing with a primary inhibitory CS, namely a stimulus which is presented among excitatory CSs reinforced by a given US, but is never followed by this US.

In that case the non-reinforced CS becomes a consistent signal for the no-US, which means that its centre forms connections with the no-US centre only. Again, this CS does not differ very much from an extinguished CS, unless it is converted into the excitatory CS. Then we may notice that its resistance to conditioning is exceedingly strong and it hardly ever acquires the stability and reliability of a primary excitatory CS. The reason for this resistance to conditioning lies in the fact that the activation of the no-US centre produced by this CS strongly inhibits the US centre and thus prevents the formation of connections between the CS centre and the US centre. When the excitatory CR to the former inhibitory CS is eventually established it is, as a rule, irregular because whenever for some reason the US centre is not activated this immediately leads to the activation of the no-US centre which further inhibits the US centre.

The assumption that, apart from the units activated by actual stimuli of various modalities, there are units which are thrown into action when these stimuli are discontinued, or even not operating at all for a length of time, may seem paradoxical, but only at first glance. As a matter of fact, there exist numerous units in the perceptual areas of the brain which discharge "spontaneously", in spite of the absence of any observable actual stimuli, but are immediately silenced, when a given stimulus is presented. When this stimulus is discontinued, the unit resumes its activity with an increased rate (the so-called "off-effect"), returning thereafter to its "spontaneous" moderate rate of firing. In other words, such an "off-unit" behaves exactly in the same way as an "on-unit", except that it does not react to an actual stimulus but to its absence. These off-units obviously play a most important role in perceptual processes, because they actively announce that "nothing happens" in the given perceptual field, information which may be as valuable as that something does happen. Accordingly, when we claim that along with "centres" (that is groups of units) representing tastes of particular kinds of food, there are "centres" which represent the absence of food in the mouth, we stick to a general principle of the activity of the nervous system. We should add only that the absence of food in the mouth activates the off-taste units only when the subject turns its attention to its gustatory perceptual field, which normally occurs when it is hungry. This is why one is aware of the emptiness of one's mouth when one is looking for food.

The hypothesis proposed above is in good agreement with the fact that, as found in many experiments on various species of animals (cf. Brutkowski, 1965), ablation of a specific area within the prefrontal cortex leads to a dramatic impairment of inhibitory alimentary CRs. Our explanation of this phenomenon is as follows (Konorski, 1967, 1971): it is assumed that the orbital part of the prefrontal area in monkeys and the medial part of this area in dogs is an extension of the limbic system. Its role is the higher control of alimentary behaviour and, in particular, inhibition of conditioned alimentary responses, in spite of humoural hunger, in those situations in which food is completely unavailable. In other words this area becomes connected with centres of all those external stimuli which signal the unavailability of food, and its activation exerts an inhibitory influence upon humoural hunger centres. Accordingly, if this area is removed, the animal is

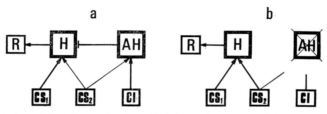

FIG. 5. Block model of the mechanism of inhibitory instrumental CR (a) and its impairment after prefrontal lesion (b). CS_1, excitatory CS centre; CS_2, inhibitory CS centre; CI, conditioned inhibition centre; H, hunger system; AH, antihunger centre situated in the prefrontal extension of the limbic system; R, instrumental response centre. Arrows, excitatory connections; stopped lines, inhibitory connections. Thin lines denote weak connections.

unable to suppress hunger by no-food CSs, and this deficit is manifested under experimental conditions by disinhibition of inhibitory CRs. The model of this action is shown in Fig. 5.

IV. The Problem of Motor-act Inhibition

The important conclusion which follows from our considerations is that plasticity of the brain consists in the formation of only excitatory synapses, while inhibitory CRs *utilize* inborn inhibitory connections which link either reciprocally related centres or higher inhibitory centres with subordinate ones. Of course, we cannot generalize this thesis until we can prove that there are no instances of learning based on the formation of new inhibitory synaptic contacts.

So far we have been concerned only with inhibitory effects exerted upon US centres and drive centres. However, animal and human behaviour consists mainly of purposeful (voluntary) movements, represented in a simplified model by instrumental conditioned responses. Shaping this behaviour includes not only learning *to perform* particular motor acts in response to particular situations, but also *not* to perform these acts in the presence of "prohibitions" commanding: don't do this or that, because if you don't you may get a reward, but if you do you will be punished (either on earth or in hell). Thus we have learnt during life to restrain many motor activities, and the problem arises whether all these restraints are established by the formation of direct inhibitory synapses on the neuronal groups controlling these activities, or whether excitatory synapses are formed on the neuronal groups controlling antagonistic activities.

To avoid misunderstanding, the present discussion is not concerned with the inhibition of instrumental responses when the animal stops performing a movement which is not rewarded. Here the performance of the movement is discontinued because the *drive* CR is extinguished, that is, there is no motivation which is the *spiritus movens* of the performance of any instrumental act. On the contrary, we shall now deal with the situation where the non-performance of the movement *is* motivated, that is it is followed by reward or absence of punishment, and we ask what is the mechanism of *that* sort of inhibition of motor acts. Let us discuss two experimental procedures illustrating this situation.

1. The animal is subjected to discrimination training in which he is required, in order to receive food, to perform a given movement (say, leg flexion) in response to one stimulus, while in the presence of the other stimulus he is obliged not to perform that movement in order to receive food. This training leads to the animal actively refraining from the performance of that movement by executing the antagonistic movement (extension). We have good evidence to show that in this type of procedure a different mechanism is in operation from that involved in the Pavlovian type of differentiation (when the negative CS is simply not reinforced), because the symmetrically reinforced differentiation task is impaired after quite different prefrontal lesions (Dabrowska, 1971).

2. The dog is trained in classical alimentary conditioning to a certain CS. Now, from time to time, in the presence of that CS we passively lift the dog's left foreleg with the aid of some apparatus, and if the leg is lifted food is not offered. Very soon we notice that the animal keeps his left foreleg immobile throughout the experimental session; at the onset of the CS the leg is extended and the extension grows stronger when the leg is pulled upwards. It is clear that the animal resists the bending of his foreleg with his whole strength (Konorski and Miller, 1936).

The situation is roughly the same when the animal refrains from performing a certain movement because this movement is followed by a noxious stimulus. Here too we observe the performance of the antagonistic movement which increases in strength whenever the animal is pulled or pushed to perform the danger-provoking motor act.

As we see, in all these situations we have clear evidence that the muscles antagonistic to those participating in the performed motor act are brought into action and that this is the way by which this motor act is inhibited. Therefore, again we have no evidence to show that new inhibitory synaptic connections are formed between the CS centre and the centre of the inhibited motor act. This finding suggests that perhaps in *all* cases of motor-act inhibition the mechanism is the same and this inhibition occurs by the mediation of excitation of groups of neurons antagonistic to those eliciting that motor act.

V. Conclusion

If we try to explain in physiological terms the class of phenomena referred to as inhibitory CRs on the basis of a connectionist theory of the functioning of the nervous system, we are confronted with the following problem.

We have good reason to believe that conditioning and learning are based on the increase of transmissibility of synaptic contacts between particular groups of neurons, regardless of the detailed nature of this process. Thus, all excitatory CRs and, more generally, all associations can be understood by reference to this concept, again regardless of what groups of neurons take part in particular learning processes.

On the other hand, in experiments on CRs (including habit formation) we encounter a sort of "negative learning" when a subject is trained to suppress his response, if it is for some reason maladaptive. To account for this phenomenon we have to choose between two possible mechanisms. One mechanism, in which I believed for many years, is that learning consists in the formation of either excitatory or inhibitory synaptic contacts between the CS centre and the US centre, the former being responsible for excitatory CRs, the latter for inhibitory CRs. My previous monograph (Konorski, 1948) advocated this approach, which I tried to support by the known experimental data. The second possible mechanism is based on the assumption that inhibitory CRs are established by the formation of excitatory connections between the CS centre and the no-US centre, the latter centre being reciprocally related to the former one. In our preceding discussion we have seen that the latter theory accounts much better for experimental data concerning inhibitory CRs than does the previous theory based on the formation of inhibitory synapses between the CS and the US units.

Now, analysing in more detail inhibitory CRs we may find that they can be divided into three somewhat differing groups:

First, we may deal with inhibition in classical consummatory CRs, as represented by food CRs, measured by salivation, or shock CRs measured by flexion of the leg to which shock is delivered. Here, as we said before, the inhibitory CR is established by formation of connections between the central representation of a given CS and that of no-food or no-shock, respectively.

Secondly, we may deal with inhibition within drive CRs, as represented by hunger CRs or fear CRs. As we know, instrumental responses in approach or avoidance training, respectively, are the best overt indicators

AA

of these CRs. If in a given drive situation a given CS is never reinforced by food or by a noxious agent, respectively, then this CS becomes a signal of hunger anti-drive or fear anti-drive, manifested by the absence of instrumental approach responses or avoidance responses. Of particular interest are the anti-drive hunger CRs when a subject is confronted with a situation in which food is completely unavailable, and therefore his hunger drive is inhibitied by the action of a higher order inhibitory centre localized in the prefrontal cortex.

Finally, we may deal with inhibition within instrumental responses themselves, when the performance of a given motor act is maladaptive and therefore should be inhibited. According to the experiments involving such a situation in animals, we have many reasons to believe that inhibition of the maladaptive motor acts occurs owing to excitation of neurons eliciting antagonistic motor acts. We cannot, however, be certain whether this is the only way of opposing the maladaptive behaviour, or whether there exists a direct inhibitory mechanism controlling this behaviour.

VI. Postscript

The above concept concerning the physiological mechanism of internal inhibition seems to be suitable for the explanation of a number of facts presented by other contributors. I shall discuss a few of these facts and try to show how I would explain them within the framework of my concept.

I shall begin with a discussion of Bitterman's data (Chapter 6) concerning the repeated reversal training of the Go; No go differentiation, in which, of the two CSs (for instance, red and green), either one or the other was reinforced by food. It has been found that the first reversal takes longer to train than the following ones. The explanation of this is as follows. In the original training the positive CS centre became connected with the US centre, and the negative CS centre, with the no-US centre. On the other hand, in the first reversal, the so far positive CS centre must have become connected with the no-US centre, while the so far negative CS centre must have become connected with the US centre. As shown in my chapter, this training encounters inherent resistance. However, after the first reversal, and even more after a few successive reversals, the situation changes: now *each* of the two CSs is connected both with the US centre and the no-US centre, and therefore the slight dominance of one of the respective connections, produced by one or a few appropriate trials is sufficient for the animal's correct response.

The fact that a pigeon develops a "positive presumption" in response to both CSs, tending at the beginning of each reversal to react to both of them, and then eliminating the conditioned response to the now negative CS, is understandable. For, other things being equal, the connections of both CS centres with the US centre are slightly stronger than those with the no-US centre.

I should now like to turn to the results reported by Wagner and Rescorla (Chapter 12), and discuss their beautiful experiments on conditioned inhibition. In one experiment A is a strong fear CS and B is a weak one; the stimulus X precedes trials in which the shock to A or B is not given. According to our concept X forms "pure" connections with the no-fear (or safety) centre. Wagner and Rescorla show that X becomes a stronger inhibitory CS when it is paired with A than when paired with B. This fact may be explained by reference to our thesis that all types of connections (whether with US or no-US) are better developed against the background of a strong drive, than against the background of a weak drive. Since X is a primary inhibitory CS (and not a secondary inhibitory CS *transformed* from the primary excitatory CS) it is clear that this CS does not form connections with the US centre which would dwarf the connections established with the no-US centre.

Finally, I wish to comment on the results described by Halliday and Boakes (Chapter 3), and by Terrace (Chapter 4), concerning the presence or absence of the "behavioural contrast phenomenon" in discrimination learning depending on different experimental procedures.

In my recent monograph I have explained the contrast phenomenon as due to the fact that occasional lack of reinforcement of a CS increases the hunger drive for a whole experimental session (Konorski, 1967). Therefore, when we train an animal in Pavlovian differentiation of two similar stimuli CS + and CS —, the centre of CS —, is connected with the US centre, owing to generalization, and with the no-US centre, owing to nonreinforcement of that stimulus by food. Since CS— was originally an excitatory CS as a result of generalization it still elicits a conditioned drive reflex, which is not inhibited by the consummatory food response, and therefore increases the drive level of the subject. This is why, according to Terrace, "subjects who learn with errors exhibit emotional responses in the presence of S⁻".

On the other hand, when the animal learns the discrimination "without errors", CS— is outside the field of generalization of CS+, being what I have called a "primary inhibitory CS" (cf. Konorski, 1967). Since such a stimulus was never connected with either food, or hunger drive, its properties are quite different from those of the extinguished CS, because it not only fails to increase the hunger drive, but may even decrease it. This is why the subject "tends to squat down . . . and quietly await the next presentation of S+" (Terrace).

The situation encountered in the Halliday and Boakes experiments is somewhat different. These authors first trained the pigeons to peck the key to S₁, and S₂, and thereafter in the presence of S₂, either withheld reinforcement (extinction subjects), or offered "free reinforcement" (Free VI subjects). It appears that contrast in S_1 trials was observed only when food was withheld, but not when given gratis in the presence of S_2.

How are these facts to be explained? As far as the extinction subjects are concerned, extinction of the instrumental response to S_2 leads, in our view, to an increase of the hunger drive manifested by the increased rate of keypecking in response to S_1. With regard to Free VI subjects, the situation is different. Since food is offered gratis in the presence of S_2, a classical CR is established to this stimulus, owing to which the instrumental CR is suppressed but not extinguished (cf. Konorski, 1967). Accordingly, S_2 in no way produces an increase in the hunger drive, since it is accompanied by the consummatory food response.

To sum up, in the above experiments we were confronted with three types of "negative" stimuli (with regard to the instrumental response):

(i) a stimulus which stopped eliciting a response because of the withholding of reinforcement;

(ii) a stimulus which stopped eliciting a response because food was offered gratis;

(iii) a stimulus which never elicited a response because, owing to a special procedure, it was outside the field of generalization of a positive CS.

According to my view, only the first type of stimulus produces an increase in hunger drive when it is presented along with positive CSs. The second and third type do not produce this effect, because, respectively, either drive is satisfied by presentation of food gratis, or the subject does not hope to receive food, since it was never presented in the presence of that stimulus.

References

Brutkowski, S. (1965). Functions of prefrontal cortex in animals. *Physiological Review*, **45**, 721–746.

Dabrowska, J. (1971). Dissociation of impairment after lateral and medial prefrontal lesions in dogs. *Science*, **171**, 1037–1038.

Eccles, J. C. (1964). *The Physiology of Synapses*. Berlin, Gottingen Heidelberg: Springer Verlag.

Konorski, J. (1948). *Conditioned Reflexes and Neuron Organizations*. London: Cambridge University Press; second printing New York and London: Hafner Publishing Company, 1968.

Konorski, J. (1967). *Integrative Activity of the Brain*. Chicago and London: The University of Chicago Press; second printing, 1970.

Konorski, J. (1971). The role of prefrontal control in programming of motor behaviour. In: J. D. Maser (Ed.), *Efferent Organization and Integrative Behaviour*.

Konorski, J. and Miller, S. (1936). Conditioned reflexes of motor analyser. (In

Russian with English summary.) *Trudy fiziologitcheskikh laboratoryi akademika J. P. Pavlova*, **6/1**, 119–278.

Konorski, J. and Szwejkowska, G. (1950). Chronic extinction and restoration of conditioned reflexes. I. Extinction against the excitatory background. *Acta Biologiae Experimentalis*, **15**, 155–170.

Konorski, J. and Szwejkowska, G. (1952a). Chronic extinction and restoration of conditioned reflexes. III. Defensive motor reflexes. *Acta Biologiae Experimentalis*, **16**, 91–94.

Konorski, J. and Szwejkowska, G. (1952b). Chronic extinction and restoration of conditioned reflexes. IV. The dependence of the course of extinction and restoration of conditioned reflexes on the "history" of the conditioned stimulus. *Acta Biologiae Experimentalis*, **16**, 95–113.

Konorski, J. and Szwejkowska, G. (1956). Reciprocal transformations of heterogenous conditioned reflexes. *Acta Biologiae Experimentalis*, **17**, 141–165.

Sherrington, C. S. (1947). *The Integrative Action of the Nervous System*. 7th Ed. London: Cambridge University Press.

Szwejkowska, G. (1959). The transformation of differentiated inhibitory stimuli into positive conditioned stimuli. *Acta Biologiae Experimentalis*, **19**, 151–159.

Excitatory and Inhibitory Processes in Hypothalamic Conditioning

14

E. THOMAS

Bryn Mawr College, Bryn Mawr, Pennsylvania, U.S.A.

I. Introduction 359
   A. Behavioural Inhibition 359
   B. Neurophysiological Inhibition 361
   C. The Neurological Basis of Behavioural Inhibition . . . 362
II. Experiment I 363
III. Experiment II 371
IV. General Discussion 376
Acknowledgements 379
References 379

I. Introduction

The task of identifying the neural substrates of inhibition is made difficult by the multitude of uses of the term inhibition both in the field of learning and in neurophysiology. The purpose of this chapter is to attempt to establish a frame of reference for the use of the concept which emphasizes features which are common to both fields, and within such a framework to present evidence concerning the dynamics of inhibition in Pavlovian conditioning. In order to specify what behavioural inhibition and neurophysiological inhibition have in common, it will be useful to outline some applications of the term inhibition as they have developed in these fields.

A. BEHAVIOURAL INHIBITION

Several factors appear to predispose theorists to the use of the term inhibition in a behavioural context. One of these is the absence of observed responding in a learning situation where responding is expected or where the potential for making a response is presumed to be present. Pavlov's (1927) concepts of external and internal inhibition represent such a use of the term. Thus, the importance of many of the characteristics of internal inhibition (spontaneous recovery, susceptibility to disinhibition, and speedy reacquisition after extinction) was that they demonstrated that even though conditioned responding was not observed to a given CS the potential for making that response remained. While not explicitly stated, Hull's (1943) use of the term inhibition appears to rest on the same grounds as that of Pavlov. In fact, Hull considered it important that his concepts of I_R and $_sI_R$ could explain Pavlov's results of spontaneous recovery and disinhibition. These criteria for inhibition, however, provide little basis for common ground with neurophysiology. For one thing, models of learning which do not posit active inhibition as a mechanism for extinction (e.g. Estes, 1959) have little difficulty incorporating most of the phenomena listed above.

In the context of operant conditioning, the use of the term inhibition by Terrace (Chapter 4) when comparing properties of negative stimuli in errorless discrimination learning with discrimination learning with errors appears to be partially based on the observation of reduced responding where the potential for greater responding is presumed to be present. An example of this is the demonstration of a peak shift in learning with errors. Thus, if a discrimination is learned with errors between S^+ and S^- on the same continuum, and subsequently a generalization gradient is determined around S^+, the greatest responding will not be to S^+, but to a stimulus on the continuum on the side of S^+ distal from S^-. The fact that the greatest responding is not to S^+ but to a different stimulus suggests that there is a greater potential for responding to S^+ than is exhibited. The presumption is that the reduced rate of responding to S^+ is due to the generalization of inhibitory effects from S^-. By way of contrast the absence of a peak shift in errorless discrimination learning was an important part of the evidence suggesting to Terrace that S^- in errorless discrimination learning does not have inhibitory properties. Similarly, Jenkins' (1965) concept of an inhibitory stimulus as one that controls nonresponding is based upon the demonstration of a potential for responding in the absence of actual responding. In this case the potential for responding is indicated by an inhibitory generalization gradient around S^-. While exceedingly important for behavioural considerations, the concept of inhibition in the context provided by Terrace and Jenkins appears to yield little basis for common usage with neurophysiology.

A second broad category of data disposing theorists to the term inhibition is the demonstration of active suppression of behaviour by stimuli which have had a history of nonreinforcement. Here again the original observations come from Pavlov (1927) who observed that a conditioned inhibitor established in one context could suppress responding to other CSs and even suppress the unconditioned salivary response to food. A remarkably thorough review of the concept of inhibition as active suppression of behaviour has been provided by Rescorla (1969). As a behavioural concept this use of the term inhibition appears to come closest to inhibition as used by neurophysiologists and probably provides the best basis for the correlation of physiological events with behavioural events. Statements concerning the active suppression of behaviour by CSs with inhibitory significance are, as we shall see, easily translated into statements concerning the suppressing effect of these stimuli on brain structures concerned with the production of that behaviour.

B. NEUROPHYSIOLOGICAL INHIBITION

Ever since Brunton (1883) provided his classic definition of inhibition, that term, from a neurophysiological point of view, has meant the arrest of function of one neural structure by the activity of another neural structure. The concept thus defined is equally applicable to neural functioning at all levels within the nervous system from single unit activity to the level of the nucleus and presumably to even larger functional systems. While many measures of this "arrest" function are available, the most profitable measure has come from the standard neurophysiological conditioning-test technique. The technique consists, simply, of presenting a volley of stimulation to one structure (conditioning volley) followed at specified intervals thereafter by a volley to a second structure (test volley). Inhibition is reflected in the diminution of electrophysiological responses to the test volley as a result of the previous conditioning volley.

Good examples of the use of this technique at the levels of the single neuron are the experiments by Frank and Fuortes (1957) and Eccles *et al.* (1961) which demonstrated the depression of monosynaptic EPSPs by conditioning volleys to a nerve from an antagonistic muscle. Using the same techniques, Lloyd (1941, 1946) and Renshaw (1941) were able to demonstrate many of the characteristics of inhibition in the spinal reflex arc. At a higher neural level, recent experiments by Nakamura *et al.* (1967) provide a good example of the effect of a conditioning volley to the cortex upon a brainstem reflex elicited by a test volley made to the trigeminal mesencephalic nucleus. The examples cited above represent only a very small portion of the kinds of experiment which demonstrate active neurological inhibition by the conditioning-test technique, and which show the wide range of applicability of the technique to all levels of neural functioning.

An exceedingly important concept with regard to the neurophysiological basis of behavioural inhibition was first elaborated by Sechenov (Beritov, 1968; Sechenov, 1956). Using what was essentially an early version of the conditioning-test technique, Sechenov observed that stimulation of the brainstem of the frog caused widespread inhibition of reflex activity. This phenomenon was termed "general inhibition". In modern terms we may invoke the concept of general inhibition when a conditioning volley to a particular structure will cause diminution in responding to test stimuli in a large variety of other structures. Experiments in many laboratories, including our own, would suggest the septal area as one of these general inhibitory areas. There is increasing evidence that general inhibitory areas such as the septal area may be importantly involved in learned inhibition.

C. The Neurological Basis of Behavioural Inhibition

An important concept of the relation of neural inhibition to behaviour comes from the tradition of clinical neurology and especially the writings of Hughlings Jackson (1958). The basic tenet is that a structure has inhibitory influence over a given behaviour if the behaviour is released when the particular structure is injured. This has been the guiding principle behind a large number of experiments in which inhibitory function is inferred on the basis of lesioning experiments. Good examples of this approach are the many experiments on the effect of frontal cortical ablations on behavioural inhibition in a variety of learning situations (for example, see Warren and Akert, 1964). While such experiments have provided much valuable information concerning the neurology of inhibition, the major problem posed by these experiments is, exactly what is inhibited? To say merely that some aspect of behaviour is inhibited by a given structure is in some ways misleading, since what is implied is that some structure concerned with the production of the behaviour in question is what is inhibited. The problem is that, in the final analysis, we know very little about how various brain structures are involved in the production of learned behaviour. The various theories concerning what is disinhibited by frontal ablation (act inhibition, drive inhibition, stimulus inhibition, etc.) reflect, I think, this lack of knowledge. It should be added that experiments employing gross electrophysiological correlates of behavioural inhibition, especially as indicated by hypersynchrony of the EEG (Gluck and Rowland, 1959; Kogan, 1960), run into a similar problem of determining precisely what is inhibited.

What is needed, then, is an experimental paradigm that will permit answers to the questions posed by lesioning and other neurological techniques. This chapter is concerned with such answers, at least at the level of Pavlovian conditioning. The present experiment suggests a threshold probe technique, the elaboration of which may provide answers to such questions. The technique is rather simple in concept and consists of measuring changes in the threshold for brain stimulation in the presence of CSs with various reinforcement histories. In certain respects it may be considered to be a hybrid version of the standard neurophysiological conditioning-test technique. It is hybrid in the sense that the conditioning stimulus (in the neurophysiological sense) is a stimulus of behavioural significance, whereas the test stimulus is of neurophysiological significance.

Specifically, we may regard the CSs in a Pavlovian conditioning paradigm as being equivalent to neurophysiological conditioning stimuli, and electrical stimulation of the hypothalamus and other structures in the presence of the CSs as test stimuli. By measuring responsivity of the various brain structures in the presence of the CSs we may obtain an index of the excitatory and inhibitory influences of the CSs upon these structures. A decrease in the threshold for brain stimulation may be regarded as reflecting an excitatory effect of the stimulus, whereas an increase in the threshold may be regarded as reflecting an inhibitory effect of the CS.

In a Pavlovian conditioning situation we often say that CS+ acquires excitatory tendencies and CS− acquires inhibitory tendencies. The important question, however, is excitatory to what, inhibitory to what? I would suggest that if the CSs may be considered as conditioning stimuli in the neurophysiological sense, then the "to what" may be determined by suitable application of electrical stimulation to various areas of the brain and testing for responsivity of these areas. That, basically is the plan of the experiments to be described below.

In two previous experiments by Wagner *et al.* (1967) and Thomas (1971), such a technique was employed in a Pavlovian discrimination experiment, where the US was electrical stimulation of the motor cortex. In these experiments CS+ tended to potentiate responding to a threshold value of the US whereas CS− tended to inhibit such responding. The experiments to be reported here represent an extension of the threshold probe technique to experiments where the US is electrical stimulation of the hypothalamus. The purpose of these experiments was to determine under what conditions nonreinforced stimuli come to acquire inhibitory properties and to provide some additional information on the nature of these inhibitory properties.

II. Experiment I

In the Pavlovian discrimination experiment by Thomas (1971), CS+ and CS− were easily discriminable (tone vs. clicks). As a result, CS− elicited virtually no generalized responding and presumably, therefore, had no history of a strong excitatory tendency. Stimuli with such histories have been termed by Konorski (Chapter 13) "primary inhibitory stimuli". Konorski suggests that such stimuli may have quite different inhibitory properties than stimuli with previous histories of excitation. Therefore, the first experiment was designed to permit comparison of the inhibitory properties of negative stimuli which have had a previous history of excitation with stimuli that have had no such previous history.

The subjects for the first experiment were eight adult cats of mixed breed, four male and four female. Chronic stimulating electrodes were implanted under aseptic procedures in the lateral hypothalamic area and posterior hypothalamic area. The electrodes were made from stainless steel wire ·25 mm in diameter and insulated with enamel to the tip. The electrodes were connected to a 14-prong female Amphenol connector anchored to the skull with several stainless steel screws and dental cement. A length of wire connected to one of the anchoring screws served as the indifferent electrode for monopolar stimulation.

The subjects were stimulated with a 100 Hz, 1 msec, monophasic, monopolar square wave provided by a Grass model SD 5 stimulator. Stimulating currents ranged from 0·22 to 1·7 ma.

Not less than one week following surgery, the electrode sites were tested for responses to stimulation. Sites which upon stimulation gave responses that could be clearly categorized as either "fear" or "rage" were chosen for use in the conditioning experiments. Fear was indicated by crouching and attempts to escape from the chamber. Rage was indicated by hissing, spitting, and a sham attack, usually at the door of the experimental chamber. In four of the subjects stimulation of the fear sites served as the unconditioned stimulus and in four of the subjects stimulation of the rage sites served as the unconditioned stimulus.

At the end of the experiments the subjects were sacrificed and the brains perfused with normal saline and formalin. Serial frozen sections were taken at 40 microns and stained according to the method of Weil to permit location of the electrode tips. The tips of all electrodes used in this experiment were found to be in the lateral hypothalamic area or the posterior hypothalamic area. The rage sites were in the lateral hypothalamus, lateral and dorsal to the fornix. The fear sites were in the posterior hypothalamus about 2–3 mm dorsal to the mammillary bodies and 1·5 mm from the midline.

The CSs were two tones of 2000 Hz and 500 Hz, and a 60-watt incandescent lamp located at the front of the experimental chamber. The duration of the CS was 5 sec. When reinforced, the onset of the CS was followed 3 sec later by a 2-sec hypothalamic US, the CS and US terminating together.

Responses were recorded by means of a strain gauge transducer epoxied to a rubber strap which was placed around the subject's chest. The strain gauge was connected through a Wheatstone bridge to the DC preamplifier of a Grass Model 5 polygraph. The chest band assembly was highly sensitive to gross movements of the animal and provided a reliable index of conditioned responding. Any movement that produced a deflection of 1 cm or greater on the polygraph was classified as a response. Such a criterion allowed for the distinction between the large deflections due to movements evoked by hypothalamic stimulation and the small deflections produced by breathing and normal head movements on the part of the animal.

There were two kinds of sessions during the experiment: conditioning sessions and threshold probe test sessions. Figure 1 presents a diagram of the sequence of events characterizing conditioning trials and threshold probe test trials.

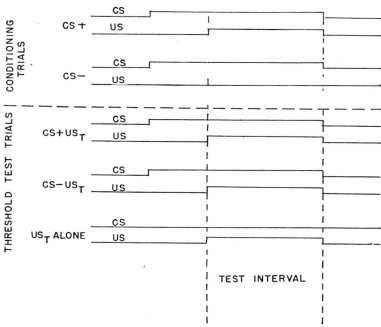

FIG. 1. Temporal sequence of events on conditioning trials and on threshold probe test trials.

Each of the daily conditioning sessions contained 30 trials. On half of the trials one CS (CS+) was reinforced by a presentation of the US, and on half the trials a second CS (CS−) was presented unreinforced by the US. For one half of the subjects both CS+ and CS− were in the same modality (i.e. 2000 Hz tone vs. 500 Hz tone) while for the other subjects CS+ and CS− were from different modalities (i.e. 2000 Hz tone vs. light). Each experimental condition contained an equal number of male and female subjects and an equal number of rage and fear electrode sites. In each group one CS was positive for one half of the subjects and the other

CS positive for the other half of the subjects. The inter-trial interval ranged from 2 to 4 min with a mean inter-trial interval of 3 min.

It was in the threshold probe test session that the hybrid version of the conditioning-test technique was used. At the beginning of each test session the threshold value of the US (US_T) was determined by adjusting the US_T intensities until it would elicit the criterion response of 1 cm approximately 50% of the time. Subsequent to threshold determination, 30 threshold probe test trials were administered to the subjects. These trials were of three kinds, (1) CS+ paired with US_T in the same temporal sequence as with the usual suprathreshold US in the conditioning session ($CS+US_T$), (2) CS— similarly paired with US_T ($CS-US_T$), (3) US_T presented alone. On these test trials the responses of interest were those recorded during the period of action of US_T either when presented alone or in combination with the CSs. This period is termed the test interval and is depicted in Fig. 1.

In the test sessions each inter-trial interval was exactly 3 min to keep constant any temporal effect of the presentation of one US_T upon subsequent response thresholds. Each group of three test trials contained all three test conditions. The order of the conditions within the groups of three trials was varied randomly.

Threshold test sessions were interspersed among conditioning sessions according to the following schedule: threshold session 1 was given prior to the first conditioning session, in order to assess the initial effects of the CSs upon threshold responding; test session 2 was given after conditioning session 5 to test for the effects of the CSs early in conditioning; test sessions 3, 4, and 5 were given after conditioning sessions 20, 25, and 30, to test for the effects of the CSs late in conditioning.

1. *Results*

Daily conditioning scores were derived for each of CS+ and CS— by subtracting from total number of responses recorded for that CS during the CS-US interval the total number of responses recorded during equivalent pre-CS periods. According to this method of scoring, responding during the pre-CS period could serve as a baseline against which inhibitory properties of CS— might be reflected as a lower probability of responding in the CS-US interval as compared to pre-CS responding. Such a case would yield a negative conditioning score.

Figure 2 presents the mean percentage of responses during the CS-US interval minus the mean percentage of responses in the pre-CS period over six blocks of five sessions each. It can be seen that while the learning curves for CS+ are similar for the two groups there is a marked difference in the curves for CS—. In the intramodal group there is evidence of appreciable generalized responding to CS— early in conditioning and especially in the second block of trials. By contrast, in the intermodal group there is virtually no generalized responding and the percentage of responding over all six blocks of trials approximates zero. The difference in generalized responding to CS— is reflected in a statistically significant trials by groups interaction for CS— (F = 3·33, df = 5·30, p < ·05). There is no evidence in either group that CS— reduces the probability of making a response in that there are no appreciable negative conditioning scores.

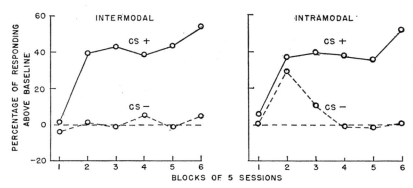

FIG. 2. Percentage of responses during CS-US interval minus percentage of responses in pre-CS period for CS+ and CS—.

The topography of the observed CR could not be distinguished visually according to the kind of UR upon which conditioning was based. A typical CR for both fear and rage sites was a general body movement and alerting. No gross components of the UR such as hissing, spitting, unsheathing of the claws, cringing, or attempts to escape could be detected.

Figure 3 presents the mean percentage of responses made to each of US_T. $CS+US_T$, and $CS-US_T$ during the test intervals on threshold test days 3, 4, and 5 averaged together. In both groups there were significantly more responses to $CS+US_T$ than to US_T alone ($t = 6·62, df = 3$, p < ·01 for the intramodal group and $t = 4·75, df = 3$, p < ·02 for the intermodal group). When responding to $CS-US_T$ is compared to responding to US_T alone, there is a striking difference in the direction of responding between the two groups. In the intramodal group there is significantly more responding to $CS-US_T$ than to US_T alone ($t = 6·47, df = 3$, p < ·01). In the intermodal group, however, there is significantly less responding to $CS-$ US_T than to US_T alone ($t = 5·54, df = 3$, p < ·02).

Mean test trial performance for each of the five test days is depicted in Fig. 4. In this case, the daily test trial score for each subject was computed

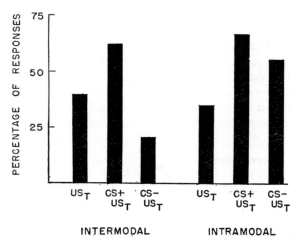

FIG. 3. Percentage of responses during the test interval for each of $CS+US_T$, $CS-US_T$ and US_T alone for the intermodal and intramodal groups.

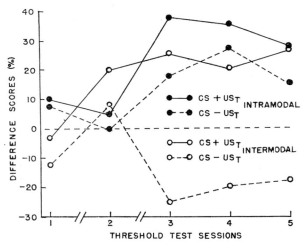

FIG. 4. Difference scores (in percentage) between $CS+US_T$ and US_T alone, and between $CS-US_T$ and US_T alone, for each test session.

as a difference in percentage of responses between either $CS+US_T$ or $CS-US_T$ and US_T alone. Points above the baseline represent a potentiating effect of the CS, whereas points below the baseline represent inhibitory effects of the CS. It should be noted that the abscissa on this graph is not linear since there were not an equal number of days between all of the test sessions. The important facets of the test trial data, however, are made clear by this graph. First of all, the points for the first test session which was carried out before any conditioning suggests that there are negligible initial effects of the CSs on the US threshold. Secondly, the curve for CS— demonstrates that the group difference in the effect of CS— on the threshold for the US is maintained until the end of the experiment, at least 450 trials beyond the point where the percentage of anticipatory CRs to CS— is essentially zero in both groups.

2. *Discussion*

While the present experiment was not directed towards the question of the conditionability of responses based upon stimulation of the hypothalamus, it does bear upon that question and is worth considering briefly in that light. The results clearly show that both "fear" and "sham rage" elicited by hypothalamic stimulation are conditionable. A number of previous experiments have shown the fear response to be conditionable (e.g. Delgado *et al.*, 1954; Nakao, 1958), however the literature with regard to rage appears to be equivocal. In an early experiment, Masserman (1941) claimed to be unable to condition such responses. Delgado (1964), on the other hand, distinguished on the basis of a number of criteria between "true rage" and "false rage" and has suggested that only true rage is conditionable. The main criterion was whether or not the rage response was appropriately directed at an object in the environment. Only directed responses represent "true rage". According to that criterion, the rage responses obtained upon stimulation of the hypothalamus in this experiment corresponded to Delgado's false rage. The data presented here suggest that if the measure is sensitive enough, conditioning even of false rage may also be obtained. In fact, out of an exceedingly large number of cats conditioned with a hypothalamic US, we have never had a failure to condition. However, the CR is not a response that closely resembles the UR, but is rather a general agitation and alerting of the kind that is only likely to be measurable by a sensitive movement transducer. It appears likely that, provided the measure is sensitive enough, conditioning may be obtained from any electrical stimulation of the brain which elicits a response.

The major conclusions of this experiment are that, consistent with previous findings, CSs in a conditioning experiment have a profound effect upon responsivity to electrical stimulation of the brain and that the nature of threshold changes, especially to CS—, are likely dependent upon the conditioning history of the CS.

If, early in conditioning, a CS— has a history of eliciting appreciable generalized responding, there is a persistent tendency for that CS to potentiate responding to a threshold US. On the other hand, if the history of the

CS is characterized by an absence of generalized responding, then the CS has an inhibitory effect upon responding to the threshold US. These results conform rather closely to what might be expected from Konorski's theory of "primary inhibition" (Konorski, 1967; Szwejkowska, 1959). Konorski (1967) summarizes that theory in the following manner: "A stimulus consistently presented without reinforcement in a situation in which a given unconditioned activity (alimentary, defensive, and so on) is displayed has been called a 'primary inhibitory stimulus' [as would be the case for CS— in the intermodal group] whereas a stimulus which was previously a positive CS but has lost its conditioned response by extinction training has been called a 'secondary inhibitory stimulus' [as would be the case by virtue of stimulus generalization for CS— in the intramodal group]. We have seen that the properties of the primary and secondary inhibitory stimuli are quite different . . . this fact really indicates that the 'history of a stimulus' plays an important role in determining its actual properties."

It seems reasonable to presume that the absence of responding to CS— in both groups represents inhibitory processes. In the intramodal group, however, inhibition must compete with generalized excitation and the net effect is in essence mixed. On the basis of the threshold probe data, it appears that the residual excitatory effect still predominates. The inhibitory effect of CS— in the intermodal case is presumably relatively "pure", that is, not competing with an excitatory effect, and therefore the net effect is inhibitory.

It is of interest to note at least a superficial similarity between the results obtained here and the phenomenon of "errorless discrimination" in operant conditioning (Terrace, Chapter 4, this volume). In one sense the results may seem paradoxical in that Terrace found evidence of inhibition not in errorless discrimination but in discrimination with errors, a result apparently opposite to that obtained here. For several reasons, however, it would be unwise to consider the two cases of errorless discrimination learning as identical. For one thing, the definition of inhibition in the two kinds of experiment differed widely and therefore may or may not represent the same processes. Even if we presume that they do represent similar processes, the procedures involved are widely disparate. It seems clear that the absence of errors in the Terrace procedure is due to the fact that "fading in" renders the negative stimulus essentially a nonsignal or neutral. In the case of the present experiment the absence of errors is due to the lack of stimulus generalization. Nevertheless, it seems likely, as Rescorla (1969) has suggested, that the CS— has important signal value concerning the postponement of the US, and as a result acquires its inhibitory properties. Interestingly enough, based upon the peak shift phenomenon, Hoffman (1969) found evidence of inhibitory properties of CS— in errorless discrimination based upon aversive Pavlovian conditioning.

The present experiment has important implications for the use of the threshold probe technique in studying inhibitory processes in the brain. To be of optimal use, the negative CS should have unmixed effects, that is, its inhibitory effects should not be contaminated by residual excitory effects. It is important, therefore, to ensure that there is little or no generalization to CS— as a result of the conditioning regime. Selecting CSs from different modalities appears to ensure this, and therefore subsequent experiments employed only intermodal discrimination.

III. Experiment II

In subsequent experiments using the threshold probe technique, the recording of gross somatic responses was discarded in favour of recording autonomic responses. In the present experiment the autonomic response recorded was blood volume measured by the photoplethysmograph. Recording autonomic responses has several inherent advantages over recording gross movement. First, autonomic responses may be bidirectional, allowing for the possibility of recording inhibition as qualitatively different than excitation. Secondly, the use of a probability measure for movements (within practical limits the only feasible measure) precludes important information that may be obtained from amplitude measures. The probability measure also precludes data on the time course of inhibitory effects during a given trial. From a practical point of view the use of an autonomic response permitted a modification of the definition of "threshold" from a 50% probability of responding to a consistent response of small amplitude produced by stimulation. Thus, the time expended determining the threshold was considerably reduced. The purpose of this second experiment, then, was to determine the usefulness of autonomic measures in the threshold probe technique and to examine in further detail some of the properties of inhibition.

The subjects were eight female adult cats of mixed breed. The surgical procedures in this experiment were precisely the same as those in the previous experiment with electrodes implanted in the lateral and posterior hypothalamus. Blood volume responses were recorded by means of a photoplethysmographic transducer clipped to the subject's ear. The transducer was connected through a Wheatstone bridge to the Grass polygraph. All electrodes when stimulated elicited large reliable vasoconstrictions at response levels well below that which would produce overt movements. During conditioning, the subjects were restrained in a hammock arrangement with their legs suspended through holes in the hammock. The restraining procedure was similar to that employed by

Wickens *et al.* (1963). It took approximately one week to adapt subjects to accept this restraint without struggling.

As in Expt I, the sessions were of two kinds: conditioning sessions and threshold test sessions. The conditioning sessions were standard Pavlovian discrimination conditioning with a light and tone as CSs, counterbalanced as in the previous experiment. There were 30 trials per session, 15 positive and 15 negative. The mean inter-trial interval was 1½ min, varying from 1 min to 2 min. The CS-US interval was 5 sec. The duration of the US was 10 sec with the CS overlapping for the entire duration of the US, both CS and US terminating together. Threshold test sessions occurred before conditioning Day 1 and after conditioning Days 5, 15, 20, and 25. Prior to testing, the "threshold" was determined as that level of hypothalamic stimulation which produced a vasoconstriction amounting to a deflection of approximately 3 mm of the polygraph pen. The choice of the 3 mm deflection criterion was based upon work with pilot animals and was designed to assure that the response would be large enough to occur on every trial yet near enough to the threshold to be maximally sensitive to the excitatory and inhibitory effects of the CSs.

1. *Results*

The relative magnitude of blood volume changes were represented as integrated areas under the polygraph tracing as measured by a polar planimeter. For anticipatory conditioning the measure was the area under the tracing during the CS-US interval. On the threshold test trials, the measure was the area under the tracing during the test interval, as defined

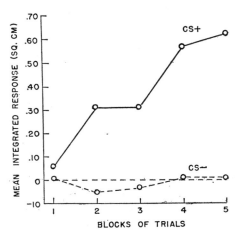

Fig. 5. Anticipatory conditioning of blood volume responses to CS+ and CS−.

in Expt I and depicted in Fig. 1. If the pen deflection was in the direction of vasoconstriction then the area of the curve was arbitrarily assigned a positive score; if the deflection was in the direction of vasodilatation the area was assigned a negative score.

Figure 5 presents the mean integrated anticipatory conditioning scores to CS+ and CS— over blocks of five sessions. Here again, two aspects are of interest. First, it can be seen that there is virtually no generalized responding to CS— at any point in conditioning. Secondly, there appears to be no direct evidence of inhibition in anticipatory conditioning as might be reflected in conditioning scores below the baseline (an index of net vasodilatation).

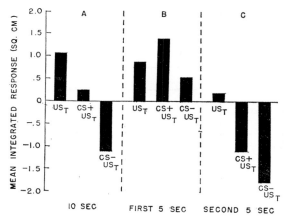

FIG. 6. Integrated threshold test responding. A. Responding during entire 10 sec of test interval; B. Responding during first 5 sec of test interval; C. Responding during second 5 sec of test interval.

In Fig. 6A, mean integrated responses during the test interval to CS+US_T, CS—US_T, and US_T alone are presented, averaged over the last three test sessions. There are a number of puzzling and interesting aspects to these data. First, the response to CS—US_T is clearly in a direction opposite to that of US_T alone, and is significantly different ($t = 6.89$, $df = 7$, p < ·01). That is, US_T, when presented alone, causes a net vasoconstriction, but when presented in combination with CS— it produces a net dilatation even though, as can be seen from Fig. 5, CS— shows no particular tendency to cause a dilatation by itself. It appears as though the very nature of response to brain stimulation can be altered by inhibitory stimuli. A second puzzling fact is that the net response to CS+US_T is smaller than that to US_T alone, though not significantly

($t = 2\cdot22$, $df = 7$, $p < \cdot10$). If the 10-sec duration of the test interval is divided into two halves it may be seen that the apparent suppression observed in the case of $CS+US_T$ is due to an interesting temporal effect. Figure 6B shows the area under the polygraph tracing for the first 5 sec of the test interval. It can be seen that in the first 5 sec the relations between $CS+US_T$, $CS-US_T$, and US_T alone are in the expected directions. The response to $CS+US_T$ is significantly greater than to US_T alone ($t = 2\cdot83$, $df = 7$, $p < \cdot05$) and the response to $CS-US_T$ is significantly less than to US_T alone ($t = 3\cdot35$, $df = 7$, $p < \cdot05$). It may be noted that during the first 5 sec of US_T both the responses to $CS+US_T$ and $CS-US_T$ are in the same direction as US_T alone, that is, in the direction of vasoconstriction.

As may be seen in Fig. 6C, there are clearly some important inhibitory events taking place during the second 5 sec of the test interval, both to $CS+US_T$ and to $CS-US_T$. It appears as though a "stop" mechanism

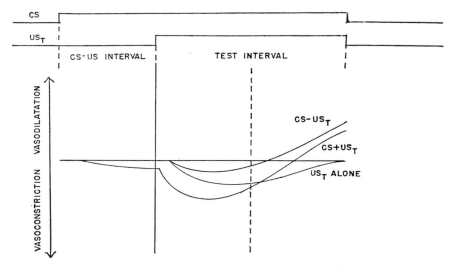

Fig. 7. Idealized diagram of typical blood volume responses during the test interval on threshold probe test trials.

comes into action actively suppressing responding to US_T and even reversing its direction. This process is much more profound for $CS-US_T$ than for $CS+US_T$, but is appreciable even for $CS+US_T$. In fact, as may be seen in Fig. 6C, there is a net dilatation to $CS+US_T$ as well as to $CS-US_T$ during the second 5 sec of the test interval. Both $CS+US_T$ and $CS-US_T$ are significantly different than responses to US_T alone in the second 5 sec of the test interval ($t = 3\cdot49$, $df = 7$, p $< \cdot01$ for $CS+US_T$, $t = 3\cdot45$, $df = 7$, p $< \cdot01$ for $CS-US_T$). It is of importance to note that a rebound effect above the baseline is virtually never seen to US_T alone. Figure 7 presents in idealized form a representation of a typical response in test trials to $CS+US_T$, $CS-US_T$, and US_T alone.

Discussion

It is interesting at this point to speculate upon what might be occurring in the nervous system corresponding to the observed effects on the threshold test trials. It is known that stimulation of the very same hypothalamic area can lead to both sympathetic and parasympathetic discharges depending upon conditions (e.g. Gellhorn et al., 1941). These effects are presumably mediated by different subsets of neurons under the electrode site. Under normal conditions the sympathetic discharge predominates. Thus, in the experiment by Gellhorn et al. (1941), evidence for parasympathetic activity was observed only after adrenalectomy. Since the response conditioned in the present experiment was sympathetic, it may very well be that the inhibition built up to $CS-$ is specific to the sympathetic discharges. With the sympathetic discharges from the hypothalamus inhibited in the presence of $CS-$, low level stimulation may selectively activate the parasympathetic neurons leading to a predominantly parasympathetic discharge. The parasympathetic discharge would lead to a loss of normal sympathetic vasoconstrictor tone and therefore to the vasodilatation observed especially during the second portion of the test interval.

The interesting response to $CS+US_T$ allows us to speculate upon a possible mechanism for the acquisition of inhibitory effects (i.e. extinction). During the course of normal conditioning $CS+$ is followed by a large suprathreshold US. On test days, however, the large suprathreshold US is substituted for by a value of the US that is barely at threshold for producing a response. Such stimulation is very unlikely to be an efficacious reinforcer. If this is the case, then what is being observed during the test interval on a $CS+US_T$ trial is a response characteristic of extinction. What appears to be happening during nonreinforcement is an initial excitatory event characterized by potentiation in the first 5 sec of the test interval followed by an inhibitory effect characterized by suppressed responding in the second 5 sec of the test interval. This inhibitory event or "stop" mechanism as a result of repetitions may become anticipatory and eventually compete with the original anticipatory excitation. Thus, extinction may be anticipatory conditioning of the inhibitory "stop" response observed late in the test interval.

IV. General Discussion

We have seen that CSs, both excitatory and inhibitory, have profound effects upon responsivity to hypothalamic stimulation. However, many questions remain as yet unanswered. For instance, what is the specificity of the excitability change? Several alternatives are open. The effector response measured in the present experiments represents the end-point of a final common path from a large number of structures. Therefore, the change in responsivity to hypothalamic stimulation may be the result of excitability changes in very remote parts of the nervous system. One extreme possibility is that no matter what the site of the US, CS+ would potentiate the response of any structure concerned with the production of the response in question and, conversely, CS— would inhibit such responding. On the other hand, there is the possibility that only the very specific site of stimulation is altered and that the facilitatory and inhibitory effects are only obtainable with the electrode used as the site of the US. We are now near the completion of a series of experiments designed to test this possibility, and while the collection of data is not entirely complete, there are a number of trends in the data that are clear.

It appears that if the electrodes are in structures that upon gross observation elicit similar reactions, for instance, defensive reactions, then there is, indeed, transfer of effects from one electrode to another. So, for instance, if conditioning is carried out with stimulation of the lateral hypothalamus as the US, and threshold probe tests are carried out with stimulation in the posterior hypothalamus, then there is transfer of both the excitatory and inhibitory effects to the posterior hypothalamus. Transfer in the opposite direction also appears to be the case.

We also have data where during conditioning the US is hypothalamic stimulation and the test stimulation is in the septal area, both eliciting the same autonomic response (in this case, the GSR). Here the data seem quite clear that there is no transfer of potentiating or inhibiting effects of CSs based upon hypothalamic USs to electrode sites in the septal area.

In sum, preliminary evidence points to a position somewhere between the two extremes outlined, that is, not all electrode sites that elicit the GSR are affected by CSs conditioned to one of the sites, but neither is the effect limited to the site of the electrode used as the US.

As a first approximation one may assume that what is affected by the CS is a functional system of synergists involved in the mediation of a particular type of response, such as a defensive reaction. One might presume that when one portion of the functional system is used as a US, excitability changes may be detected throughout that system, but not in other, independent systems.

While the transfer tests outlined above provide important information concerning possible functional systems involved in the production of CRs, we still do not have a direct test of the alteration of the excitability of specific structures. The transfer experiments, for instance, cast no light on precisely which of the synergistic systems of structures are altered in excitability. We think, however, we have a technique which may provide answers to this important question.

If two pairs of electrodes are inserted into a structure close together (approximately 1 mm apart), by stimulating one pair and recording from the other, we can record local evoked responses which provide a direct index of the excitability of the neuropil in the proximity of the electrode site. That such local evoked potentials are alterable by exteroceptive stimuli has been demonstrated by Hernández-Peón and Guerrero-Figueroa (1965). Alteration in the size of these local evoked potentials by CSs in a conditioning experiment may provide us with the direct evidence of excitability changes in particular structures that is needed.

Another important question remaining as yet unanswered concerns the structures involved in the observed suppression of responding to hypothalamic stimulation by CS—. From the principal of neurophysiological inhibition espoused since the time of Brunton, it must be assumed that the observed inhibition is a result of increased activity in a structure which has inhibitory connections to the functional system involved in producing the conditioned behaviour. In initial speculations about what structures might be involved, it seemed likely that there would be rather specific inhibitory centres for particular portions of the hypothalamus, akin to the various specific "no-US" centres postulated by Konorski (Chapter 13).

However, some incidental observations of the general behaviour of cats during presentation of CS— suggested an alternative mechanism. It was noticed, especially in the autonomic conditioning experiment, that during the presentation of CS— the cats exhibited a behaviour that could be best described as a general "arrest". That is, gross somatic movements in which the animal was engaged were arrested during the presentation of CS— even though such somatic responses were neither elicited by the US nor part of the conditioned behaviour. The arrest properties of CS— were so profound as to inhibit ongoing behaviour that was often extremely vigorous. As an example, every so often, a cat would make vigorous attempts to escape from the restraints of the hammock. Invariably, if CS— were presented during the escape attempts, these escape behaviours were completely arrested, and the animal became motionless. This complete arrest impressed us as being very similar to the general arrest we have obtained upon electrical stimulation of the septal area.

On the basis of stimulation experiments, the septal area would have to be classified as a general inhibitory area. That is, stimulation of the septal area inhibits responses to stimulation of a wide variety of other brain structures. Thus, for instance, stimulation of the septal area may inhibit cortically evoked reflexes and knee-jerk reflexes (Hodes et al., 1951; Kaada, 1951) as well as more molar behaviour such as hypothalamically elicited attack (Siegel and Skog, 1970). In addition, septal stimulation may have a depressor effect upon blood pressure (Covian et al., 1964) and may induce bradycardia (Malmo, 1964). Furthermore, it appears from experiments carried out in our laboratory that septal stimulation inhibits all responses elicited by stimulation of a variety of different areas in the hypothalamus and that both autonomic and somatic responses are inhibited. Interestingly enough, based upon GSR recordings, it appears as though prior septal stimulation can even reverse the direction of the response originally elicited by hypothalamic stimulation, much as did CS— in the conditioning experiments described above.

There are two lines of evidence that may cast light upon the role of the septal area as a general inhibitor in Pavlovian conditioning, one indirect and one direct. An indirect test is to compare certain temporal properties of septal effects upon responding to hypothalamic stimulation with effects of CS—. Thus, for instance, if septal stimulation is applied simultaneously with hypothalamic stimulation, facilitation of a hypothalamically elicited GSR is obtained, even when we use septal stimulation which in itself does not elicit the GSR. Septal stimulation must in fact precede hypothalamic stimulation by a few seconds (approximately 1–3) in order for septal inhibition of hypothalamic responses to be obtained. We would predict that a similar time course might obtain for CS—, that is, that CS— presented simultaneously with hypothalamic US_T would potentiate responding and that maximum inhibition would occur only about 1–3 sec after the onset of CS—. A more direct test of septal mediation of inhibitory effects of Pavlovian conditioning is to use the technique of local evoked potentials described above. An interesting prediction is that CS—, while inhibiting local evoked potentials in the hypothalamus, will potentiate such responses in the septal area.

One of the most elementary questions that has been with us since Pavlov's original experiments and which has yet to be satisfactorily answered is how CSs gain access to the structures which are responsible for producing and integrating conditioned responses. The present series of experiments represents a somewhat new approach to the problem and may provide some important answers concerning conditioning. The endpoint of such research may very well result in a functional architecture of the conditioned response about which much has been speculated but little demonstrated.

Acknowledgements

Support for the preparation of this paper was provided by Grant MH-15946 from the National Institute of Mental Health. Thanks are due to William J. Carmint for his excellent services in performing the histologies reported here.

References

Beritov, I. S. (1968). Central inhibition according to I. M. Sechenov's experiments and concepts, and its modern interpretation. In: E. A. Asratyan (Ed.), *Brain Reflexes*. London: Elsevier Publishing Co., pp. 21–31.

Brunton, T. L. (1883). On the nature of inhibition, and the action of drugs upon it. *Nature*, **27**, 419–422.

Covian, M. R., Antunes-Rodrigues, J. and O'Flaherty, J. J. (1964). Effects of stimulation of the septal area upon blood pressure and respiration in the cat. *Journal of Neurophysiology*, **27**, 394–407.

Delgado, J. M. R. (1964). Free behavior and brain stimulation. In: C. C. Pfeiffer and J. R. Smythies (Eds.), *International Review of Neurobiology*. New York: Academic Press, pp. 349–449.

Delgado, J. M. R., Roberts, W. W. and Miller, N. E. (1954). Learning motivated by electrical stimulation of the brain. *American Journal of Physiology*, **179**, 587–593.

Eccles, J. C., Eccles, R. M. and Magni, F. (1961). Central inhibitory action attributable to presynaptic depolarization produced by muscle afferent volleys. *Journal of Physiology (London)*, **159**, 147–166.

Estes, W. K. (1959). The statistical approach to learning theory. In: S. Koch (Ed.) *Psychology: A Study of a Science*, Vol. 2. New York: McGraw-Hill, pp. 380–491.

Frank, K. and Fuortes, M. G. F. (1957). Presynaptic and postsynaptic inhibition of monosynaptic reflexes. *Federation Proceedings*, **16**, 39–40.

Gellhorn, E., Cortell, R. and Feldman, J. (1941). The effect of emotion, sham rage, and hypothalamic stimulation on the vago-insulin system. *American Journal of Physiology*, **132**, 532–541.

Gluck, H. and Rowland, V. (1959). Defensive conditioning of electrographic arousal with delayed and differentiated auditory stimuli. *Electroencephalography and Clinical Neurophysiology*, **11**, 485–496.

Hodes, R., Peacock, S. M. and Heath, R. G. (1951). Influence of the forebrain on somato-motor activity. I. Inhibition. *Journal of Comparative Neurology*, **94**, 381–408.

Hoffman, H. S. (1969). Stimulus factors in conditioned suppression. In: B. A. Campbell and R. M. Church (Eds.), *Punishment and Aversive Behavior*. New York: Appleton–Century–Crofts, pp. 185–234.

Hernández-Peón, R. and Guerrero-Figueroa, R. (1965). Modifications of local amygdaloid evoked responses during wakefulness and sleep. *Acta Neurologica Latinoamerica*, **11**, 222–233.

Hull, C. L. (1943). *Principles of Behavior*. New York: Appleton–Century–Crofts.

Jackson, J. H. (1958). *Selected Writings*. Basic Books, New York.

Jenkins, H. M. (1965). Generalization gradients and the concept of inhibition. In: D. I. Mostofsky (Ed.) *Stimulus Generalization*. Stanford: Stanford University Press.

Kaada, B. R. (1951). Somato-motor, autonomic, and electrocorticographic responses to electrical stimulation of "rhinencephalic" and other structures in primates, cat, and dog. *Acta Physiologica Scandinavica*, **24,** *Suppl.* 83, 1–258.

Kogan, A. B. (1960). The manifestations of processes of higher nervous activity in the electrical potential of the cortex during free behavior of animals. In H. H. Jasper and G. E. Smirnov (Eds.). Moscow colloquium on electroencephalography of higher nervous activity. *Electroencephalography and Clinical Neurophysiology*, Supplement 13, 51–64.

Konorski, J. (1967). *Integrative Activity of the Brain*. Chicago: University of Chicago Press.

Lloyd, D. P. C. (1941). A direct central inhibitory action of dromically conducted impulses. *Journal of Neurophysiology*, **4,** 184–190.

Lloyd, D. P. C. (1946). Facilitation and inhibition of spinal motoneurons. *Journal of Neurophysiology*, **9,** 421–438.

Malmo, R. B. (1964). Heart rate reactions and locus of stimulation within the septal area of the rat. *Science*, **144,** 1029–1030.

Masserman, J. H. (1941). Is the hypothalamus a center of emotion? *Psychosomatic Medicine*, **3,** 3–25.

Nakamura, Y., Goldberg, L. J. and Clemente, C. D. (1967). Nature of suppression of the masseteric monosynaptic reflex induced by stimulation of the orbital gyrus of the cat. *Brain Research*, **6,** 184–198.

Nakao, H. (1958). Emotional behavior produced by hypothalamic stimulation. *American Journal of Physiology*, **194,** 411–418.

Pavlov, I. P. (1927). *Conditioned Reflexes*. Trans. by G. V. Anrep. Oxford: Clarendon Press.

Renshaw, B. (1941). Influence of discharge of motoneurons upon excitation of neighbouring motoneurons. *Journal of Neurophysiology*, **4,** 167–183.

Rescorla, R. A. (1969). Pavlovian conditioned inhibition. *Psychological Bulletin*, **72,** 77–94.

Sechenov, I. M. (1956). *Selected Physiological and Psychological Works*. Moscow: Foreign Languages Publishing House.

Siegel, A. and Skog, D. (1970). Effects of electrical stimulation of the septum upon attack behavior elicited from the hypothalamus in the cat. *Brain research*, **23,** 371–380.

Szwejkowska, G. (1959). The transformation of differentiated inhibitory stimuli into positive conditioned stimuli. *Acta Biologiae Experimentalis*, **19,** 162–174.

Thomas, E. (1971). The role of postural adjustments in conditioning with electrical stimulation of the motor cortex as the unconditioned stimulus. *Journal of Comparative and Physiological Psychology* (in press).

Wagner, A. R., Thomas, E. and Norton, T. (1967). Conditioning with electrical stimulation of the motor cortex: Evidence of a possible source of motivation. *Journal of Comparative and Physiological Psychology*, **64,** 191–199.

Warren, J. M. and Akert, K. (Eds.) (1964). *The frontal granular cortex and behavior*. New York: McGraw-Hill.

Wickens, D. D., Born, D. G. and Wickens, C. D. (1963). Response strength to a compound conditioned stimulus as a function of the element interstimulus interval. *Journal of Comparative and Physiological Psychology*, **56,** 727–731.

Genesis and Localization of Conditioned Inhibition

15

E. A. ASRATIAN

Institute of Higher Nervous Activity and Neurophysiology, U.S.S.R. Academy of Sciences, Moscow, U.S.S.R.

I.	Introduction	381
II.	Localization of Internal Inhibition	382
III.	Mechanism of Internal Inhibition	387
IV.	Conclusion	394
	References	395

I. Introduction

Pavlov's contribution to the experimental and theoretical study of cortical inhibition is exceptionally great. We are indebted to him for discovering new kinds and varieties of such inhibition, defining their specific characteristics and their classification, formulating the principles and conditions of their genesis and development, establishing their role in higher nervous activity, and revealing its protective-restorative role—a fundamentally new neurophysiological part played by inhibition. By all these outstanding achievements Pavlov ushered in a new era in the history of studying the problem of inhibition, that major and ever pertinent problem of neurophysiology as a whole. Nevertheless, as is well known, Pavlov was very critical in appraising his own achievements in attacking this problem. He was constantly dissatisfied with his knowledge of the problem and formulated his views on various points of cortical inhibition with invariable caution, reservations and doubts, frequently going so far as to revise them. He gave as a reason for this the paucity of the available factual material, the insufficiency of precise knowledge, and the extreme complexity of the problem. Pavlov justly called the problem "accursed".

After his death interest in the problem of inhibition in higher nervous activity has been steadily growing not only among his followers, whose number is now great the world over, but also among representatives of other traditions in physiology and psychology. The investigations they have carried out in the last few decades have led to the establishment of a multitude of new and valuable facts on the role of inhibition in brain activity and neurophysiology as a whole, and also to the development of new and interesting concepts on the subject. Many of these facts and concepts may by right be regarded as further elaborations of Pavlov's evidence and ideas. For example, the findings and ideas presented by present-day authors (Thorpe, 1965; Kandel and Spencer, 1968; Sokolov, 1969) regarding the mechanism of habituation (or negative learning) corroborate and advance Pavlov's own findings and ideas to the effect that the phenomenon of extinction of the orienting reflex as a result of its frequent occurrence is based on the development of internal inhibition. There are also some concepts and evidence which are essentially new, but may be considered as an appreciable addition to and development of those expounded by Pavlov. An example is provided by the findings and views of Simonov (1962) on preventive, or adaptive, inhibition emerging initially in the cortex under the action of very weak stimuli and restraining the substrate from useless activity. Similar also are the findings of Rabinovich (1970) that an analogue of internal inhibition can be elaborated in cortical neurones, not only by eliminating reinforcement of the conditioned stimulus, but also by combining an indifferent stimulus with the initially inhibiting effect of an unconditioned stimulus on the neurone.

The evidence and concepts of present-day authors on cortical inhibition also comprise certain of Pavlov's initial views on the subject, although some are not quite in harmony with, or even contradict them. Furthermore, there are also cases when new facts and ideas run counter to Pavlov's ideas regarding secondary aspects of cortical inhibition, but confirm and further develop his essential facts and postulates on the more important aspects of the problem. And this communication is devoted precisely to such a case.

This communication is mainly concerned with findings and concepts regarding the mechanism of the genesis and localization of internal inhibition which, according to Pavlov, occupies a place of the utmost importance among the varieties of cortical inhibition. For the sake of simplicity and convenience in outlining the data, we shall present the material on localization of inhibition before that on the mechanisms of its origin. The history and present-day state of our knowledge of each of these points will be presented in a very general way. Those who take a special interest in this aspect of the matter as outlined by the author may be referred to his publications both in Russian and English (Asratian, 1961, 1969, 1970).

II. Localization of Internal Inhibition

Pavlov held the view that "inhibition takes place precisely in the nerve cell, and not at the connecting point or on the path between the cell of the conditioned stimulus and that of the special unconditioned stimulus'.

(Pavlov, 1947). One of the most notable features of the modern state of knowledge about internal inhibition is the view, very popular among specialists on higher nervous activity, that conditioned inhibition appears and is initially localized not at the cortical point of the conditioned stimulus, as upheld by Pavlov and many of his disciples, but at one of the subsequent elements of the conditioned reflex arc. This view has been substantiated by old and new evidence showing that:

(a) inhibitory conditioned stimuli induce an active motor reaction of a kind antagonistic to the reaction to positive conditioned stimuli (Mishtovt, 1907; Terrace, Chapter 4, this volume);

(b) that during conditioned inhibition the components of a multi-effector conditioned reflex are inhibited at different times and to different degrees (Voskresensky and Pavlov, 1917; Fursikov, 1924; Anokhin, 1932);

(c) that in conditioned switching over,* stimuli with a double signal significance elicit either one of the conditioned reflexes and inhibit the other one depending on the situation (Asratian, 1941);

(d) that in binary conditioned reflexes to one and the same conditioned stimulus it is possible, by eliminating reinforcement of one of the reflexes, to inhibit it selectively while preserving that other reflex to the same stimulus (Asratian, 1961);

(e) that after elaborating two different electro-defensive motor conditioned reflexes to one and the same stimulus, it is possible to inhibit one of the reflexes while retaining the other (Khodorov, 1955).

This view has also been corroborated by electrophysiological data, Thus, it has been established that the action of inhibitory conditioned stimuli is attended by an activation reaction and the appearance of evoked responses in the electrocorticogram similar to the action of positive conditioned stimuli (Laptev, 1949; Kogan, 1962; Roitbak, 1962), and that conditioned inhibition even considerably enhances the excitability of the cortical structures of the inhibitory stimulus (Chistovich, 1955; Kratin, 1967; Gasanov, 1968). Also of significance are some data on this subject obtained by various authors on children and adults, which show that inhibitory conditioned stimuli are subjectively perceived as well as positive ones.

Authors sharing a similar view on the subject differ in their standpoint regarding the following question: in which of the subsequent links of the conditioned reflex arc does conditioned inhibition appear and is localized? Some present-day authors follow the suggestion of Perelzweig (1907) and Kasherininova (1909) and localize this inhibition in the cortical and even

---

*Asratian and co-workers (Asratian 1941, 1970) used an experimental design with conditioned stimuli possessing a double signalling role which switched according to the changes of experimental situation; these stimuli in one situation elicited one conditioned reflex and inhibited the other, while in the second situation they inhibited the first conditioned reflex and elicited the other.

subcortical nervous structures of the unconditioned reflex; others localize it in the brain structures of both the signal and reinforcing stimuli (Kupalov and Ushakova, 1931); still others share the view expounded by the author that conditioned inhibition appears and is initially localized in the elements of the conditioned connection itself (Asratian, 1941, 1961, 1969).

What then are the facts and reasons that justify our questioning the correctness of the view that the initial appearance and localization of internal inhibition is in the cerebral structures of the unconditioned reflex? Are they a convincing scientific substantiation of the viewpoint we have advanced on localization of inhibition in the nerve elements of the conditioned connection itself?

In reply to these questions, some findings from our laboratory are given below, some of which will also be used subsequently in outlining and substantiating our concept of the mechanism of the appearance of internal inhibition.

Our collaborator Struchkov (1955) succeeded in setting up a conditional discrimination of the following sort: in one situation a buzzer elicited in dogs an alimentary conditioned reflex, and a form of mechanical stimulation elicited an electro-defensive one; in another chamber, on the other hand, the first stimulus elicited an electro-defensive reflex, and the other, an alimentary reflex. In either situation the cortical points of both conditioned stimuli must have been free from inhibition, and also those of both the alimentary and electro-defensive unconditioned reflexes must have been similarly free, since conditioned reflexes of both kinds were obtained in both the first and the second situations. There is reason, therefore, to believe that inhibition is localized in the intermediate link of the conditioned reflex arc. Furthermore, in order to study conditioned reflexes with a two-way conditioned connection, we have combined pairs of different kinds of unconditioned stimuli, namely: food, electrostimulation of a leg, air-puff into the eye, local thermostimulation of the skin, etc., each eliciting the appropriate unconditioned reflex, namely, alimentary, electro-defensive, eyelid, local, vasomotor, etc. (Asratian, 1961, 1968). With this procedure a two-way conditioned reflex is established; each of the combined pair of stimuli mutually becomes a conditioned signal for the partner's reflex, conditionally eliciting its effect. Figures 1 and 2 show fragments of a kymogram of such an experiment by our collaborators Struchkov and Rudenko, and Fig. 3 presents a diagram of the arc of such conditioned reflexes. The following data from among those obtained in these studies are of special interest for the question under discussion. After complete extinction of one of the oppositely directed conditioned reflexes, the second reflex, far from being reduced, is often even enhanced; Fig. 4 shows fragments of kymograms of two such experiments. This would apparently have been

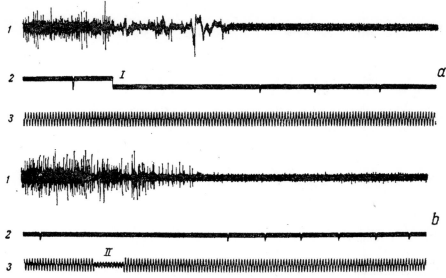

FIG. 1. Conditioned reflex with a two-way connection obtained by systematic pairing of the passive lifting of the leg with food. a, passive lifting of the paw (I) together with the unconditioned disappearance of potentials in the EMG elicits a conditioned salivary response (a forward conditioned connection). b, food (II) elicits unconditioned salivation and in addition causes a conditioned disappearance of the EMG potentials (a backward conditioned connection). 1, EMG. 2, salivation in drops. 3, time (larger deflections) and eating (smaller deflections). From Struchkov (1955).

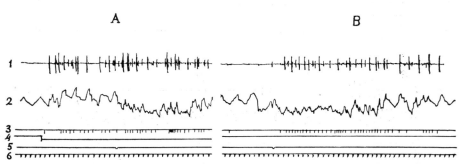

FIG. 2. Forward and backward connections obtained by pairing of two unconditioned stimuli: an air-puff to the eye and food. A, air-puff to the eye evokes the adequate UR, the eye-blinking and elicits a CR, salivation (a forward conditioned connection). B, eating produces salivation and elicits conditioned eye-blinking (a backward conditioned connection). 1, eye-blinking; 2, chest breathing; 3, salivation; 4, conditioned stimulus; 5, delivery of food; 6, time in seconds. From Rudenko (1970).

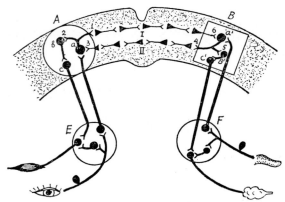

FIG. 3. Schematic representation of the conditioned reflex arc with a two-way connection. A, cortical point of the eye-blink reflex. a, afferent neuron; b, interneuron; c, efferent neuron; 1 and 2, synaptic contacts of collaterals of the afferent neuron with interneurons; 3, synaptic junction between the interneuron of the backward conditioned connection and the afferent neuron of the signalling stimulus. B, cortical point of the food reflex. a′, afferent neuron; b′, interneuron; c′, efferent neuron; 4 and 5, synaptic contacts of collaterals of the afferent neuron with interneurons; 6, synaptic contacts between the interneuron of the forward conditioned connection and the afferent neuron of the reinforcing stimulus. I, forward conditioned connection; II, backward conditioned connection; E, subcortical centre of the eye-blink reflex; F, sub-cortical centre of the food reflex.

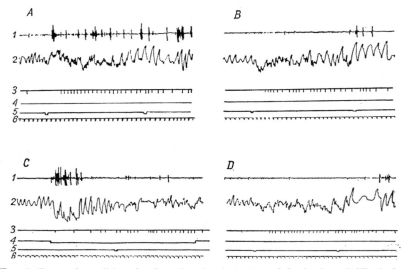

FIG. 4. Forward conditioned reflex after the extinction of the backward CR. A, backward CR (eye-blinking) before extinction. B, extinguished backward CR. C, testing the forward CR (salivation) after the extinction of the backward CR; the forward CR remains intact. D, backward CR on the next trial is still inhibited. Other explanations as in Fig. 2. From Rudenko (1970).

impossible if the inhibition had been localized, not in the conditioned connection, but at the cortical point of one or the other stimulus.

However, according to the data obtained by Davidova (1971) very considerable deepening of extinction of such a reflex leads to the inhibition of the backward connection as well. Proceeding from these and some other data we believe that, although internal inhibition appears and is localized initially in the conditioned connection itself, nevertheless, when considerably deepened, it may subsequently also spread to the cortical points of both conditioned and unconditioned stimuli. This is also attested by the fact that deep extinction of a defensive motor reflex leads to a considerable decrease in the excitability of the cortical point of the conditioned response as detected by its direct electrical stimulation (Asratian, 1961). The same is true of the excitability of the cortical point of the conditioned stimulus of the eyelid reflex following deep extinction (Gasanov, 1968).

Studies of the electrophysiological manifestations of conditioned reflexes and of their inhibition have been conducted in our laboratory as well as in many others. Without going into details, we should like to note some of the facts we have established that are relevant to the questions under discussion and that support the assumptions we have made above. In our experiments we use as indicators electrophysiological phenomena of different origin and types (common evoked potentials, so-called recruiting potentials, augmenting potentials, etc.), recording them at the exact cortical points of those stimuli which are combined in the process of conditioning. The basic fact we have established is that elaboration of an appropriate conditioned reflex leads, in addition to the primary response, to a gradual development of a relatively stable surface-negative potential at the cortical point of the conditioned stimulus, or to a gradual strengthening of the late responses up to a considerable magnitude (Figs. 5 and 6, upper rows). There are reasons for considering the primary response to be an electrophysiological manifestation of the inherent unconditioned reflex evoked by the stimulus applied, and the newly-formed or sharply strengthened surface-negative wave as an electrophysiological manifestation of the conditioned reflex it elicits. It has been established by our collaborators that during extinction of the conditioned reflex the additional wave of indicator evoked potentials first weakens and disappears, while considerable deepening of extinction results in sharp weakening of primary responses as well (Figs. 5 and 6, lower rows).

III. Mechanism of Internal Inhibition

As a brief introduction to the second subject of this communication, namely, the mechanism of the origin of internal inhibition, we should like to begin with a reminder of Pavlov's views, since they gave origin to the

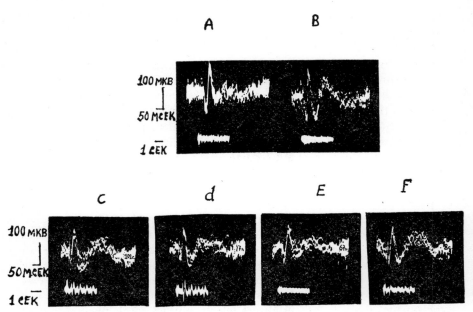

FIG. 5. Evoked responses to click in the auditory cortex of a cat before A and after B, elaboration of eyelid conditioned reflex. The same potentials during extinction C, D, E, and recovery F, of the conditioned reflex.

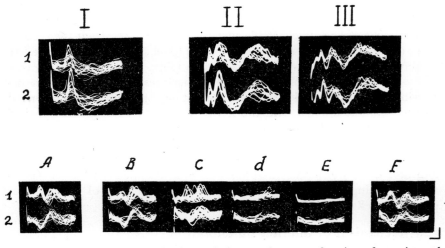

FIG. 6. Recruiting responses in the cortical motor 1, sensory 2, points of experimental paw of a dog before I, and after II, III, elaboration of alimentary conditioned motor reflex. The same potentials during extinction A, B, C, D, E, and recovery F, of conditioned reflex.

author's own views, and also since they have been buried in oblivion even by some of his pupils and followers. Underlying Pavlov's ideas of the mechanism of conditioned inhibition in the cells of the conditioned stimulus is his profound and original concept of the protective and restorative role of *transmarginal inhibition*. According to Pavlov's view when cortical cells are over-excited by an exceptionally strong appropriate stimulus they become fatigued and exhausted and as a result there arises in them an inhibition with a protective role, which he termed *transmarginal inhibition*. "One might think," he wrote, "that peculiar internal inhibition is also transmarginal inhibition, the intensity of stimulation being replaced, as it were, by its duration" (Pavlov, 1949). He believed that in ordinary conditions the normal state and efficiency of the highly reactive and fragile cortical nerve cells is ensured by two mechanisms. First, by the fact that during reinforcement a strong induction or external inhibition of the excited cortical cells of the conditioned stimulus develops during the presentation of the unconditioned stimulus; their work discontinues, this wards off their possible exhaustion and functional destruction and provides them with well-deserved rest and long-lasting efficiency. Thus he saw the reinforcing unconditioned reflex as having a beneficial effect on the stability and preservation of conditioned reflexes. With the abolition of reinforcement, these fragile cells remain for a long time in a state of trace excitation following each action of the conditioned reflex and as a result of this they gradually become fatigued. With further repetition of the conditioned stimulus without reinforcement there is a danger of their extreme exhaustion and functional destruction. It is here that he saw the second protective mechanism, warding off such a danger, as coming into action; this is protective inhibition which is transformed into internal inhibition. Without elaborating on this point, we should like to note that even in Pavlov's lifetime his collaborators obtained findings which disagreed with these views. As a consequence, he made some minor departures from his basic propositions, realizing, however, that these were only half measures and that a clearer and more satisfactory solution of the "accursed" problem was a task for the future.

Perelzweig (1907) and, following him, Anokhin (1968), Kupalov (1955) and Hilgard and Marquis (1940) in general share the view that internal inhibition originates as a result of a struggle, a competition and a collision between two different reflexes. This general view proposes for internal inhibition the same mechanism by which, in Pavlov's opinion, external inhibition occurs. However, each of the above authors has his own ideas regarding this struggle. According to Perelzweig, the struggle is waged between the centre of the conditioned reflex and that of the unconditioned reflex. In the opinion of the other authors, it takes place between the excited nervous structures of the alimentary conditioned reflex and the orienting reflex evoked by the abolition of reinforcement. One view which is rather popular among present-day authors is that the development of internal inhibition is due to the existence of special inhibitory structures; for example, inhibitory synapses, inhibitory interneurones or inhibitory half-centres, which are activated after elimination of reinforcement and which form inhibitory conditioned connections (Konorski, 1948, 1967; Aleksanian, 1958; Sokolov, 1965).

We regard our concepts of the mechanism of the origin of internal inhibition as a development of Pavlov's ideas on this subject. We also think, following Pavlov, that protective inhibition underlies the development of this kind of inhibition. During extinction this protective inhibition is brought about by a certain degree of fatigue and exhaustion of nervous structures deprived, owing to the abolition of reinforcement, of the beneficial influence of inductive inhibition produced by the reinforcing unconditioned reflex. But our viewpoint differs from Pavlov's as to precisely which elements of the conditioned reflex arc are subjected to fatigue and exhaustion and, consequently, are the site of the origin and localization of inhibition. Unlike Pavlov, we believe that it is not the cortical cells of the conditioned stimulus which are the first nervous structures to be exhausted and in which inhibition appears and is localized, *but it is the nervous structures of the middle link of the conditioned reflex arc that are exhausted, i.e. the nerve elements of the conditioned connection itself* in which, as stated above, inhibition originates and is localized.

We have at our disposal the following facts and reasons to support such an assumption. By combining the stimuli which elicit heterogeneous unconditioned reflexes in order to elaborate two-way conditioned reflexes, we are in a position to trace, graphically record and analyse, not only the process of elaboration and accomplishment of such conditioned reflexes, but also the dynamics of changes occurring in the respective innate unconditioned reflexes of the paired stimuli. The material we obtained in these experiments also contains data relevant to the question under discussion on the mechanism of the origin of internal inhibition. Some of the data will be discussed now in a brief outline of our views on this subject. In the following discussion we shall refer to the diagram of the conditioned reflex arc with two-way conditioned connections (Fig. 3 above).

We have studied quite comprehensively the long known phenomenon of the weakening of the orienting reflex to a new stimulus as it becomes conditioned, which found its most vivid expression in Erofeyeva's famous early experiments (1913) on alimentary conditioning in dogs to electrocutaneous stimulation of a paw. In the experiments carried out by our collaborators, the inherent (i.e. unconditioned) reflex to the stimulus which occurs first in time (A in Fig. 3) regularly diminishes as, in the course of pairing with the succeeding stimulus (B in Fig. 3), it acquires a signal significance and begins to elicit the reflex of the latter in a conditioned way. It is worth noting that this is an increase in latency and threshold of excitability of the unconditioned reflex to the first stimulus. Figure 7 presents data showing this from experiments conducted by Rudenko

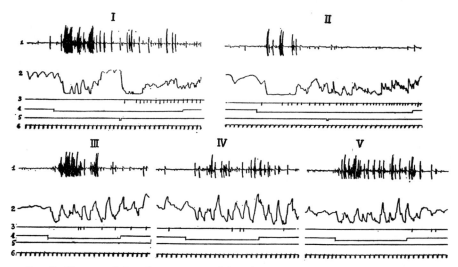

FIG. 7. Changes of the adequate unconditioned reflex of the signalling stimulus during acquisition and extinction of the conditioned food reflex to the air-puff into the eye. I, intensive blinking before the acquisition of the food CR. II, after establishing the food CR blinking is partially inhibited. III, IV, V recovery of the blinking response during the extinction of the conditioned food reflex. Other explanations as in Fig. 2. From Rudenko (1970).

(1970). In our view this phenomenon is also demonstrated by results from our laboratory which show that, as the conditioned reflex is elaborated and stabilized, the primary responses of the electrophysiological indicators that we use diminish in amplitude, while additional, or late potentials grow in amplitude.

We account for these facts and for similar findings of other authors in terms of the repeated occurrence of inductive inhibition of the intermediate link of the unconditioned reflex to the first stimulus arising from the presentation of the second (reinforcing) stimulus. In Fig. 3 it will be synapse 2 between the afferent neurone and the interneurone of the arc of this reflex which is affected by this inhibition. It is impossible to account for the facts in terms of inductive inhibition of the afferent link of the innate reflex arc of the first stimulus (i.e. neurone *a* in Fig. 3), since this would prevent elaboration and accomplishment of the conditioned reflex. Such a view would also fail to account for the dependence of the strength of the conditioned reflex on the duration of the combined action of the conditioned and unconditioned stimuli (Maiorov, 1928). Moreover, data are available (Gershuni, 1947; Giurdzhian, 1954; Gasanov, 1968; Kratin, 1967) attesting that the excitability of the cells perceiving the stimulus is enhanced when it becomes a signal stimulus. As to the appearance of this type of inhibition in the efferent or effector arc links of the first stimulus' own reflex, this is out of the question.

As we see it, this is precisely the link between the mechanism of external inhibition and that of the formation of the conditioned reflex referred to by Pavlov; but inhibition develops not in the neurones of the signal stimulus, as he believed, but in the intermediate structures of the signal stimulus' own reflex. For this reason it does not hinder but, quite the contrary, even favours the formation and accomplishment of the conditioned reflex.

The following fact which we observed in our laboratory is of considerable interest (Verga and Pressman, 1963; Rudenko, 1970): during the extinction of the conditioned reflex, as the first stimulus evokes the reflex of the partner stimulus to an ever lesser degree, its own reflex once more gradually becomes stronger (III, IV, V in Fig. 7).

Proceeding from these and other findings, we arrive at the conclusion that, after conditioning, the conditioned stimulus tends to elicit two reflexes, its own innate reflex and the reflex to the unconditioned stimulus, both these reflexes tending to be aroused by a common afferent path. However reciprocal-inhibitory interrelations are established between the intermediate links of the arcs of these two reflexes with a common afferent link; namely between the intermediate link connecting the cortical point of the conditioned stimulus with that of the reinforcing unconditioned reflex, and the intermediate link of the arc of the inherent unconditioned reflex of the conditioned stimulus (synapses 1 and 2 in Fig. 3). Apparently this is a specific example of the general neurophysiological law so thoroughly investigated by Sherrington (1906) in spinal reflexes. Furthermore, according to Konorski (1948) and Skipin (1956), to our laboratory and to some other authors, it is a well known fact that, if alimentary local motor instrumental conditioned reflexes in dogs, evoked by surrounding or other secondary conditioned stimuli, are inhibited by alimentary reinforcement, in the course of actually eating, they are at once renewed with still greater strength upon the end of feeding. This fact reveals quite clearly not only the inhibitory action of the reinforcing unconditioned reflex on the middle link of the signal stimulus' own reflex—in this case, local movement—even if this link is excited in a conditioned reflex way; it also manifests another well-known neurophysiological phenomenon, *rebound*, or the increased excitation of inhibited structures as soon as the action of the factor generating this inhibition ceases. It is worth noting that the phenomenon of post-inhibitory rebound is also observed in experiments involving the elaboration of an analogue of conditioned reflexes in cortical neurones (Rabinovich, 1970).

These two findings, together with some others, underlie our concept of the mechanism of the beneficial stabilizing effect of reinforcement on the conditioned reflex and of the origin of internal inhibition when reinforcement is abolished. Our idea is as follows:

(a) During reinforcement of the conditioned reflex, under the influence of the strongly excited centre of the unconditioned reflex, there develops an inductive inhibition of the middle link of the arc of the inherent (i.e. unconditioned) reflex to the conditioned stimulus (synapse 2 in Fig. 3), while the cells perceiving the stimulus and the elements of the conditioned connection in this case remain free of inhibition and efficient.

(b) After cessation of the reinforcing unconditioned stimulation and during considerable weakening of excitation in its central structures, its inhibitory action on the middle link of the arc of the unconditioned reflex inherent to the conditioned stimulus disappears.

(c) In virtue of this, there appears in the latter a state of post-inhibitory increase in excitation, a "rebound", which in its turn inhibits inductively the conditioned connection, mainly, it appears, in its initial elements (synapse 1 in Fig. 3). Thus, as we understand it, inductive inhibition of the conditioned connection does not occur while the unconditioned stimulus is present and does not arise directly from excitation in its structures. It only appears when the unconditioned stimulus ceases to act. Furthermore, it appears indirectly as a result of the consequent increased excitation of the middle link of the arc of the conditioned stimulus' own reflex, which prior to this was inhibited by the action of the reinforcing unconditioned stimulus. This indirect inductive inhibition puts an end to trace excitation of the conditioned connection, prevents the danger of possible fatigue and exhaustion of its elements and thereby eliminates the necessity for the appearance of internal inhibition.

(d) When reinforcement of the conditioned reflex is omitted, this whole chain of events is disrupted. As there is no strong excitation of the structures of the reinforcing unconditioned reflex, the middle link of the arc of the conditioned stimulus' own reflex is not inhibited. As a result no state of post-inhibitory increase in excitation appears and hence there is no inductive inhibition of the elements of the conditioned connection, the latter remaining in a state of prolonged trace excitation. With repeated omission of reinforcement (which is necessary for elaboration of internal inhibition), the long duration of the state of excitation of the nerve elements of the conditioned connection results in their ever-increasing and deepening fatigue and exhaustion. This results in the appearance in them of internal inhibition as a protective-restorative process which subsequently acquires a co-ordinating significance and an "economical" character.

IV. Conclusion

Of course, we are far from believing that the approach that we have outlined thoroughly elucidates all aspects of the "accursed" problem and satisfactorily explains all the facts about the origin and localization of internal inhibition. It appears to us, however, that while preserving Pavlov's basic ideas on this subject, but shifting the centre of gravity of the events occurring during the development of internal inhibition from the cortical cells of the conditioned stimulus to the elements of the conditioned connection itself (i.e. to the intermediate link of the conditioned reflex arc), we bring this process into stricter conformity with the majority of well established facts about the subject. In addition we bring the theory of this subject closer to the facts and ideas of modern neurophysiology about the important role of interneurones in the kaleidoscope of excitatory and inhibitory processes in the activity of the central nervous system and about the role of afferent neurones in controlling them.

It may be seen that so far our approach to the subject is at the same "level" as that of Pavlov, Sherrington and other classical neurophysiologists. As in classical neurophysiology the scheme of the conditioned reflex arc with a two-way connection comprising different neurones and synapses was developed, and the suggestions on changes in their functional state were derived, mainly on the basis of facts about the input to the "black box" and the output from it.

As to the lower, and to some extent to the higher, parts of the central nervous system, modern neurophysiology has already attained considerable successes in studying, by means of the finest micro-electrophysiological, cytochemical and electron-microscopic methods, the problem of inhibition at the "level" of the physiology of neurones and synapses. Presynaptic and post-synaptic forms of inhibition have been revealed, as has their physiological significance and, to some extent, their structural, physiochemical and biochemical basis, and the concept of inhibitory pathways has been developed. But it seems to us that an attempt to utilize these highly valuable data with the aim of elucidating more completely and amply the mechanisms of internal inhibition as a specifically cortical phenomenon would as yet be mainly of a speculative nature. Moreover, although many present-day authors have succeeded in elaborating a conditioned reflex (or its analogue) at the neuronal level and proved the possibility of its extinction, restoration and differentiation, nevertheless, according to many authors (Jasper, *et al.*, 1958; Hori, *et al.*, 1968; Rabinovich, 1970), no considerable change in the ratio between excited and inhibited cortical neurones has been recorded during behavioural manifestations of internal inhibition, compared with what occurs during behavioural manifestations of a positive conditioned reflex. Hence, no appreciable benefit can be drawn from these data for the understanding of the detailed mechanism of internal inhibition in integrated conditioned activity. However, it can be stated at present that these outstanding achievements of modern neurophysiology testify to the onset of an era of bold destruction of demarcation lines between different "levels" for studying the functions of the cerebrum, including the problem of inhibition in higher nervous activity, as prophetically foreseen by Pavlov's genius as long as half a century ago.

References

Aleksanian, A. M. (1958). On the mechanism of internal inhibition. *Zhurnal Vysshei Nervoni Deyatelnosti*, **8**, 64–72.

Anokhin, P. K. (1932). Study of the dynamics of higher nervous activity. *Nizhnegorodskii Medzhurnal*, **7-8**, 42–49.

Anokhin, P. K. (1968). *Biologiia i Neurofiziologiia Uslovnogo Refleksa*. (The Biology and Neurophysiology of the Conditioned Reflex.) Moscow: Meditsina.

Asratian, E. A. (1941). On the principle of "switching over" of conditional reflex activity. *Fiziologicheskii Zhurnal SSSR*, **30**, 13–18.

Asratian, E. A. (1953). *I. P. Pavlov, His Life and Work*. Moscow: Foreign Languages Publishing House.

Asratian, E. A. (1961). The initiating and localisation of cortical inhibition in the conditioned reflex arc. *Annals of the New York Academy of Sciences*, **92**, 1141–1159.

Asratian, E. A. (1968). Some peculiarities of formation, function and inhibition of conditioned reflexes with two-way connections. In: E. A. Asratian (Ed.) *Brain Reflexes*. Amsterdam: Elsevier, pp. 8–20.

Asratian, E. A. (1969). Mechanism and localization of conditioned inhibition. *Acta Biologica Experimentals*, **29**, 271–291.

Asratian, E. A. (1970). *Ocherki po Fiziologii Uslovnikh Fefleksov*. (Essays on the Physiology of Conditioned Reflexes.) Moscow Izdatelstvo Nauka.

Chistovich, L. A. (1955). On changes in the discriminative threshold of the acoustic stimulus during changes in its signal meaning. *Fiziologicheskii Zhurnal SSSR*, **41**, 485–492.

Davidova, E. K. (1971) (in press).

Erofeyeva, M. N. (1913). Contribution to the physiology of conditional reflexes to injurious stimuli. *Trudy Obschestva Russkikh Vrachei v Petrograde*, **80**, 278–287.

Fursikov, D. S. (1924). On the relation between processes of excitation and inhibition. *Trudy Laboratorii I. P. Pavlova*, **1**, 3–45.

Gasanov, U. G. (1968). The Neurophysiological Mechanism of Internal Inhibition Thesis. Moscow.

Gershuni, G. V. (1947). A study of subsensory reactions during the activity of the sense organs. *Fiziologicheskii Zhurnal SSSR*, **33**, 393–412.

Giurdzhian, A. A. (1954). Sense-organ sensibility changes due to transformations of conditional stimuli. *Doklady Akademii Nauk SSSR*, **96**, 1273–1275.

Hilgard, E. R. and Marquis, D. C. (1940). *Conditioning and Learning*. New York: Appleton–Century–Crofts.

Hori, Y., Toyohara, I. and Yoshii, N. (1967). Conditioning of unitary activity by intra-cerebral stimulation in cats. *Physiology and Behaviour*, **2**, 255–259.

Jasper, H. H., Ricci, G. F. and Doane, B. (1958). Patterns of Cortical neuronal discharge during conditioned responses in monkeys. In: G. E. W. Wolstenholme and C. M. O'Connor (Eds.), *The Neurological Basis of Behaviour*. London: Churchill, pp. 277–294.

Kandel, E. R. and Spencer, W. A. (1968). Cellular neurophysiological approaches to the study of learning. *Physiological Reviews*, **48**, 65–134.

Kasherininova, N. A. (1909). Contributions to the study of salivary conditioned reflexes in response to tactile stimuli in the dog. Thesis. St Petersburg.

Khodorov, B. I. (1955). On the analysis of the spatial localisation of internal cortical inhibition. *Doklady Akademii Nauk SSSR*, **103**, 1119–1122.

Kogan, A. B. (1962). The manifestation of processes of higher nervous activity in the electrical potentials of the cortex during free behaviour of animals. In: G. D. Smirnov (Ed.) *Elektroensefalograficheskoe Izuchenie Nervnoi Deiatelnosti*. (The Electroencephalographic Study of Higher Nervous Activity) Moscow: Izdatelstvo Academii Nauk SSSR, pp 42–55.

Konorski, J. (1948). *Conditioned Reflexes and Neuron Organisation*. London: Cambridge University Press.

Konorski, J. (1967). *Integrative Activity of the Brain*. Chicago: University of Chicago Press.

Krasnogorski, N. I. (1958). *Vysshaia Nervnaia Deiatelnost Rebenka* (Higher Nervous Activity in Children). Moscow: Medgiz.

Kratin, Y. G. (1967). *Elektricheskie Reaktsii Mozga na Tarmoznye Sygnaly* (Electrical Reaction of the Brain to Inhibitory Signals.) Moscow: Izdatelstvo Nauka.

Kupalov, P. S. (1955). General results of the study of cerebal inhibition. *Zhurnal Vysshei Nervnoi Deiatelnosti*, **5**, 157–172.

Kupalov, P. S. and Ushakova, A. M. (1931). Concerning the localization of differential inhibition. *Archiv Biologicheskikh Nauk*, **31**, 429–431.

Laptev, I. I. (1949). An experience of the study of conditioning in dogs by electro-encephalographic methods. In: P. K. Anokhin (Ed.) *Voprosy Vysshei Nervnoi Deiatelnosti* (Problems of Higher Nervous Activity). Moscow: Izdatelstvo Akedemii Nauk SSSR.

Maiorov, F. P. (1928). On the influence of the duration of conditional and unconditional reflex value. *Trudy Laboratorii I. P. Pavlov*, **3**, 125–128.

Mishtovt, G. W. (1907). Development of inhibition of an artificial conditioned reflex (auditory) by means of different stimuli. Thesis, Petrograd.

Pavlov, I. P. (1947). *Polnoe Sobranie Trudov* (Complete Works), Vol. IV. Moscow.

Pavlov, I. P. (1949). *Polnoe Sobranie Trudov* (Complete Works), Vols. III and V. Moscow.

Perelzweig, I. J. (1907). Contributions to the study of conditioned reflexes. Thesis, Petrograd.

Rabinovich, M. J. (1970). Microelectrode studies of the neuronal mechanisms of the conditioned reflex. *Zhurnal Vysshei Nervnoi Deyatelnosti*, **20**, 303–316.

Roitbak, A. I. (1962). Electrical phenomena in the cerebral cortex during the extinction of orienting and conditioned reflexes. In: G. D. Smirnov (Ed.) *Elektroensefalograficheskoe Izuchenie Vysshei Nervnoi Deiatelnosti* (The Electroencephalographic Study of Higher Nervous Activity). Moscow: Izdatelstvo Academii Nauk SSSR.

Rudenko, L. P. (1970). Changes in the unconditional response to the signalling stimulus in the process of simple and complex conditioning. *Zhurnal Vysshei Nervnoi Deiatelnosti*, **20**, 923–931.

Sherrington, C. S. (1906). *The Integrative Activity of the Nervous System*. London: Cambridge University Press.

Simonov, P. V. (1962). On the mechanism of extinction of the conditioned reflex. *Zhurnal Vysshei Nervnoi Deiatelnosti*, **12**, 248–256.

Skipin, G. V. (1956). On the localization of inhibition in the dog. *Zhurnal Vysshei Nervnoi Deiatelnosti*, **6**, 22–31.

Sokolov, E. N. (1965). Perception and the conditioned reflex. *Zhurnal Vysshei Nervnoi Deiatelnosti*, **15**, 249–256.

Sokolov, E. N. (1969). *Mekhanismy Pamiati* (Mechanisms of Memory). Moscow: Moscow University Press.

Struchkov, M. I. (1955). Switching over of heterogenous conditioned reflexes. *Zhurnal Vysshei Nervnoi Deyatelnosti*, **5**, 547–554.

Thorpe, W. H. (1965). The ontogeny of behaviour. In: J. A. Moore (Ed.) *Ideas in Modern Biology. Proceedings of the XVI International Congress of Zoology*. New York: Natural History Press, pp. 483–518.

Verga, M. E. and Pressman, Y. M. (1963). Some functional peculiarities of direct and reversed conditional connections. In: E. A. Asratian (Ed.) *Nervnye Mekhanismy Uslovnykh Refleksov* (Nervous Mechanisms of the Conditioned Reflex). Moscow: Izdatelstvo Academii Nauk SSSR, pp. 3–28.

Voskresensky, L. N. and Pavlov, I. P. (1917). Contributions to the physiology of sleep. *Izvestiia Petrogradskoi Bioloicheskoi Laboratorii*, **16**, 3–12.

D | Physiological Mechanisms of Behavioural Inhibition

D

The chapters in this section are concerned with the physiological processes underlying the behavioural effects associated with inhibition. In each chapter behavioural evidence is discussed and explanations of the evidence are proposed in terms of physiological mechanisms and processes.

Molnar and Grastyan, in Chapter 16, present evidence about the complex but systematic behavioural effects produced by stimulation of the upper brain stem in cats, and show how these behaviours can be related to rather general theoretical ideas about approach and withdrawal during appetitive behaviour. They suggest, like Konorski, that many of the behavioural manifestations of internal inhibition may best be understood by considering innate inhibitory connections within motivational systems.

In Chapter 17 Warburton investigates the role played by cholinergic transmitters in internal inhibition. Analysis of the experimental results in this area leads him to propose that, in so far as the cholinergic system does improve inhibitory stimulus control, this is probably due to the control of the appropriate sensory inputs via the ascending cholinergic pathways.

The last three chapters of this section are concerned with the effects of brain lesions on inhibition, and in particular lesions of the septal area and hippocampus. In Chapter 18 Dickinson reports a number of experiments designed to identify the mechanisms responsible for the persistence of responding in extinction commonly found in rats with septal lesions. He concludes that this persistence cannot be explained as a failure of some general inhibitory process, and attempts to develop an alternative account making use of Amsel's frustration theory.

Isaacson, in Chapter 19, starts by presenting evidence from rats showing deficits following certain treatments applied to the hippocampus; these effects appear very similar to the hippocampal memory deficit found in humans. He then uses this evidence to develop a theory of the functioning of the limbic system, based on a basic division between ergotropic and trophotropic functions; within this system the hippocampus is seen as playing a central role in inhibiting ergotropic activity.

Douglas also presents a rather general model of brain function in Chapter 20. He draws on behavioural, pharmacological and developmental data to support a theory which, though it differs very considerably from that presented by Isaacson, also suggests that the central structure involved in the inhibition of behaviour is the hippocampus.

The Significance of Inhibition in Motivation and Reinforcement

16

P. MOLNÁR and E. GRASTYÁN

Institute of Physiology, University Medical School, Pécs, Hungary

I. Introduction 403
II. Experiment I: Characteristics of the Locomotor Responses Elicited
   by Electrical Stimulation of the Upper Brain Stem . . . 408
   A. Experimental Design and Technique 408
   B. Behavioural Observations 409
III. Experiment II: A Dual Motivating and Sleep-inducing Effect of
   Ipsiversive Stimulation 419
IV. Experiment III: Behavioural and Electrical Accompaniments of the
   Restraint and Release of an Instrumental Approach Reaction . 422
V. Conclusions 425
   A. Experiment I 425
   B. Experiment II 426
   C. Experiment III 427
Acknowledgements 428
References 428

I. Introduction

The notions of excitation and inhibition were introduced into the explanation of learning processes by Pavlov (1927) partly on the basis of analogies
between spinal reflexes and conditioning.

The justification for this has often been questioned in the past, the most
serious objection being that the inhibitory process conceived by Pavlov
was inferred from gross behavioural observations and not based on direct
indices of neural function. This objection was less reasonable in the pioneer
days of reflexology than now when indicators of inhibition have become
accessible at the level of the single neuron. In fact, Sherrington's conception of excitatory and inhibitory states even if on a more elementary level,
was also based on behavioural signs and not on direct neural indicators.
There is, however, a particular aspect of Sherrington's inhibitory concept,
not necessarily present in the Pavlovian concept, which needs further

consideration if the extension of the spinal analogy to higher behavioural processes is to be justified.

Spinal inhibition is derived from a complex mechanism (reciprocal inhibition), by which antagonistic muscular contractions, like extension and flexion, become organized into adaptative patterns. In other words inhibition is not an independent process but is always part of a behaviourally meaningful motor pattern brought about by fixed neuronal circuitry. Now if we extend the spinal inhibitory concept to complex behavioural processes we should face the question whether inhibition at this higher level is also a part of fixed behavioural patterns and arises as a consequence of wired-in neuronal connections. The variability and flexibility of learned behaviour could hardly be reconciled with such an expectation. If Pavlov did not become aware of this difficulty, this may have been a consequence of his preoccupation with the importance of unconditioned reflexes in conditioning. Some of the difficulties seem to be resolved, indeed, by assuming that inhibitory processes are elements of unconditioned mechanisms. The relatively rigid, stereotyped character of unconditioned reflexes leaves no doubt that their organization is established with fixed neuronal connections. Even if this consideration were valid in the case of classical conditioning it evidently fails to apply to instrumental learning.

These are issues which in Pavlov's days could not have emerged, partly because the mechanism of inhibition postulated by Pavlov was different in principle from our current notions. The fundamental mechanism of the Pavlovian concept of inhibition was necessarily based on indirect inhibition, as revealed by Wedensky, and not on direct inhibition, the intricacies of which were uncovered only in the early forties, following the basic discoveries of Renshaw (1941) and Lloyd (1943).

The early neurophysiological concept of inhibition was inseparably connected with excitation. The only available model of the mechanism of inhibition—clearly demonstrable in peripheral nerves—was based on the periodic changes of excitability accompanying excitatory processes. That is why we now call this indirect inhibition. The demonstration of direct inhibition, that is an inhibitory process independent of any preceding excitatory action, had to await the advent of sophisticated electrophysiological measurements capable of indicating events within the CNS.

It is logical that the early concept of inhibition necessarily limited all the contemporary views about its functional significance, but it seems that our present-day learning theories have been slow to recognize all the consequences stemming from the recent dramatic change in inhibitory concepts.

If inhibition is an indirect process then in principle every nerve cell can exert an inhibitory action and can also be a target for inhibition. Consequently the question of fixed patterns of inhibition and excitation becomes senseless. It is not surprising that observations often made in conditioning, such as a stable negative stimulus, disused for several months, eliciting an immediate inhibitory action on its very first reapplication, remained an insurmountable enigma for Pavlov (1927).

Though the active nature of inhibition was often emphasized by Pavlov it would be a mistake to believe that he attributed inhibition to independent neural elements or wanted to hint at such a mechanism. It seems that for many behavioural physiologists this emphasis laid upon the active nature of inhibition obscured the differences between the two types (indirect and direct, respectively) and thus has delayed examination of possible theoretical consequences which follow from such a distinction. We should not forget, however, that hardly more than a decade has passed since the first explicit statement about the existence of separate inhibitory nerve cells became possible (Eccles, 1957).

If the mechanism of direct inhibition had been known at Pavlov's time then such questions as whether the function of a common neural substrate might be implicated behind all the different forms of internal inhibition would most probably have been raised. The assumption that excitation and inhibition are attributed to different types of neurons certainly does not exclude the implication of indirect inhibition in physiological processes. We still do not know when, and behind what kind of behavioural inhibition, we should look for one or the other kind of inhibitory mechanism. The problem has become even more complicated with the discovery of pre-synaptic inhibition (Eccles, 1964).

If excitation and inhibition are tied to the function of special types of neurons, then, in principle, the notion of excitatory and inhibitory systems also becomes justified. Since the fifties these notions have emerged more and more often in the neurophysiological literature (Magoun and Rhines, 1946; Rhines and Magoun, 1946; Moruzzi, 1963; Parmeggiani, 1962; Sterman and Clemente, 1962; Jouvet, 1962, 1967). If, however, we accept that there are really excitatory and inhibitory systems in the brain stem, then we should ask what coherent and behaviourally characteristic functions they might correspond to. We do not know of any such pure inhibitory or excitatory behavioural process. The question is whether unified patterns of behaviour reflect the interaction between systems each of which, while presumably composed of both inhibitory and excitatory elements, is either predominantly excitatory or predominantly inhibitory in its mode of action.

On the one hand the fact that, with the repeated elicitation of any form of internal inhibition, sleep can be induced, and on the other that in the regulation of sleep certain definite brain structures play a critical role

(Jouvet, 1967), would suggest that the same neural elements may participate in all the different forms of internal inhibition. If the excitatory and inhibitory elements of the sleep-wakefulness regulating mechanism also participate in other acts of behavioural adaptation then the question arises again: what basic behavioural patterns might correspond to the excitatory and inhibitory mechanisms represented by fixed neural connections?

The spinal analogy would suggest that the basic patterns of excitation and inhibition at the higher levels of the brain should be looked for in the seemingly basic patterns of locomotion, in approach and withdrawal. We might wonder, however, whether these two categories really correspond to independent functional entities.

We know that the integration of locomotion occurs at a definite level of the neuraxis. We still do not know, however, whether locomotion can be reduced to basic components or corresponds to an undifferentiated single tendency to move, subject to the modifying influences of the environment. The assumption that all highly organized behavioural acts can be reduced to simple approach-withdrawal (adient-abient) events is not a recent idea in psychology. It was Schneirla (1959), however, who first proposed, on the basis of evidence obtained in comparative behavioural studies, that the unique process of motivation corresponds to biphasic approach-withdrawal mechanisms at all phylogenetic levels. According to him the appearance of approach or withdrawal is basically determined by the intensity of stimuli acting on the organism. It follows logically from this that the two phases of motivation are the consequences of regulation of motor function in a homeostatic sense. This position gains support from the consideration that centrally induced complex and co-ordinated approach-withdrawal effects overlap homeostatic functions in their anatomical representation. Against this, however, is the fact that most of the homeostatically regulated basic drives (eating, drinking, elimination, etc.) are obviously expressed in highly specific and characteristic somato-motor patterns and not simply in approach-withdrawal sequences.

Our knowledge about the relationship between consummatory actions and approach-withdrawal responses is very scanty. Complex species-specific consummative responses (eating automatisms, defecation, urination, copulation, grooming activities, etc.) can be elicited from many subcortical loci as immediate effects of stimulation, that is in the absence of special environmental cues. Other loci within the same structure may produce diffuse orienting, exploratory behaviour which in certain cases, if stimuli of the external environment afford the possibility, are readily transformed into consummatory processes. This latter fact is, however, still not direct evidence that the two functions belong together. According to our own former findings (Grastyán *et al.*, 1965), loci able to produce diffuse orienting-exploratory behaviour, are, if the environment allows, capable of motivating conditioned responses terminated in markedly different consummatory goals. Similar inferences might be drawn from the recent experiments of Valenstein *et al.* (1968, 1969; see also Cox *et al.*, 1969), according to which the majority of centrally induced consummatory actions appear as the consequence of experience obtained in the course of stimulation in the experimental environment rather than locus-specific responses.

These facts strongly suggest that the centrally induced general arousing, motivating, exploratory effects are not necessarily the accessories of the specific drives which they seemingly serve, or in other words they are not the products of the neural substrate of the specific drives but represent a separate function. By this statement, of course, we do not want to deny the close interdependence of the two functions.

Our argument is also supported by the now traditional classification of complex behavioural processes into appetitive and consummatory phases, an idea originally proposed by Sherrington (1906) on the basis of neuro-physiological considerations. There can be no doubt that the biphasic motivational process proposed by Schneirla (1959) conforms better to the appetitive, or preparatory, than to the consummatory phase of behaviour, and, moreover, that most of the learned adaptative processes are also related to the former. Consequently the conclusion seems sound that the excitatory-inhibitory states occurring during conditioning are related to the mechanisms of this general motivational function rather than to those of specific drives or consummatory actions.

The question then arises whether there are reliable indicators of this aspecific motivating process which might help to reveal its underlying mechanism. One of the greatest obstacles to the analysis of appetitive functions consists in their apparent irregularities. This concerns both natural and centrally induced appetitive responses. Reactions elicited from the hypothalamus and mesencephalic reticular formation under the usual experimental conditions most often impress by their confusing character. As the experiments to be described below are intended to show, however, surprising regularities of centrally induced exploratory-locomotor reactions can consistently be demonstrated with methods adapted to the nature of these reactions, by keeping environmental influences at a minimum, and by using adequate behavioural recording techniques. These results suggest that there really are fixed patterns and neural circuits behind the aspecific motivational effects.

The three groups of experiments to be described below contain findings which show:

(a) that approach and withdrawal are an interdependent pair of functions, the latter inhibiting the former, and that the positive and negative character of motivation and the process of reinforcement are products of the interaction of their mechanisms;

(b) that the withdrawal (inhibitory) function may play a critical role in the triggering mechanism of sleep;

(c) that critical events for learning, which are demonstrable with electrical stimulation, can also be revealed under natural conditions.

II. Experiment I: Characteristics of the Locomotor Responses Elicited by Electrical Stimulation of the Upper Brain Stem

A. Experimental Design and Technique

Centrally elicited locomotor responses are subjected to manifold modification by environmental stimuli. This fact very often makes it rather difficult, or even impossible, to decide what components of the overt responses are due purely to the excitation of the neuronal elements of the stimulated loci. The animal may prefer certain stimuli in the environment, the environment can mechanically interfere with the elicited responses, and finally learned consequences of stimulation can unpredictably modify the character of further responses.

To minimize these modifying effects the following experimental situation was used:

Starting from the common experience, that unilateral subcortical stimulations usually result, not in rectilinear, but circular movements, stimulation was carried out in a circular screened cage of 150 cm diameter and 120 cm height with a smooth continuous wall. Recording of the elicited movements was made with the help of an electronic device (Grastyán et al., 1968). A light-weight (5 g) flexible cable, allowing free locomotion, connected the animal with the stimulator and the recording instruments.

In the second stage of the experiment, an easily discernible 5-mm thick switching device (pedal) with a 15 × 20 cm surface, working on capacitive principles, was placed on the floor of the circular cage. Stimulation was always started by the experimenter and the pedal served to switch off stimulation when the animal touched it or jumped over it in the course of the induced movements (pedal switch-off technique). In the final stage of the experiment the self-stimulation characteristics of the stimulated areas were analysed in a second, smaller, cage. A gentle press on a 3 × 15 cm pedal, fixed to one of the narrower side walls of the cage, triggered off a train of impulses preset by the experimenter.

Two to three weeks before stimulation, the animals (a total of 43 grown-up cats of both sexes) were implanted stereotaxically with 2–4 pairs of hypothalamic and/or mesencephalic stimulating, and 2–4 pairs of hippo-campal recording electrodes. The animals survived the implantation by 1–18 months during which period of time they were repeatedly tested in each of the three phases of the Expt I.

B. Behavioural Observations

In accordance with our expectations, the locomotor responses induced in the above mentioned uniform situation showed little variability during their repeated elicitation, and thus were available for systematic measure-ment.

Before going into a detailed description of the findings a short clarifica-tion of the terminology we adopted to characterize the effects and after-effects of stimulation and their relationship seems necessary. The terms "ipsiversive" and "contraversive" always refer to the stimulated hemis-phere. For example, if stimulation of the left hemisphere induces a circular motion to the left, it is an ipsiversive effect, if to the right it is a contra-versive effect. The terms "hetero-rebound" and "auto-rebound" are used to describe the immediate motor after-effects of stimulation and always refer to the preceding movement, that is to the direction of movement occurring during stimulation. For example, if a contraversive locomotor effect is followed by an ipsiversive after-effect, then it is a hetero-rebound. If a contraversive locomotor effect is followed by a contraversive after-effect, then it is an auto-rebound.

We believe that we can show experimental evidence, suggesting that stimulation which produces ipsiversive movements corresponds to with-drawal and a negative motivational condition, while the presence of contraversive movements, especially of rebound character, indicates approach and a positive motivational state.

The motor reactions elicited from hypothalamic and mesencephalic tegmental loci could be classified, on the basis of their constant character-istics, into three groups.

Loci, comprising the first group were mainly in the lateral hypothalamus and were characterized by an initial contraversive movement elicited with widely different stimulus parameters. During prolonged (5–120-sec) stimulation, however, the spatial direction and speed of movement showed regular changes, notably an abrupt change of the locomotion into the opposite direction would take place during the course of stimulation. The occurrence of these "reaction reversals" and their latency was a function of the intensity of stimulation: low voltage produced quick reversals, inter-mediate ones slower reversals and high voltage quick reversals once again.

Plotting the latencies of these reaction-reversals, characteristic curves were drawn (Fig. 1. A). The reaction reversals were regularly preceded

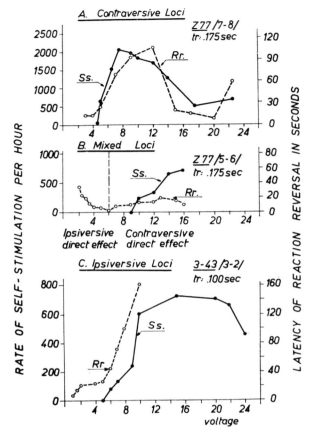

FIG. 1. Three hypothalamic loci showing characteristic differences in the reversal of the direction of locomotion on prolonged stimulation and in the rate of self-stimulation. The dashed lines (Rr) represent curves obtained by plotting the latency of the reversal in direction of movement (ordinate on the right) against stimulation voltage. The continuous lines (Ss) represent rates of self-stimulation (ordinate to the left) obtained in a different situation. The uppermost curves (A) represent a pure contraversive locus where the immediate effect of stimulation was always contraversive circling. The threshold of self-stimulation (of a stable type) corresponds to a value 4·5 V at which the contraversive rebound effect first appeared (cf. Fig. 5; further explanation in the text). The rate of self-stimulation declines where (14 V) the latency of the reaction reversal becomes shorter and the ipsiversive rebound reactions reappear. The middle curves (B) represent a mixed ipsi-contraversive locus. The threshold of self-stimulation corresponds to a value (9 V) at which the contraversive rebound reaction appeared as an auto-rebound effect. The lowermost curves (C) represent a pure ipsiversive locus where the immediate effect of stimulation was always ipsiversive circling. The threshold (5 V) of self-stimulation (of a labile type) corresponds to that of a strong contraversive rebound effect. Ss: self-stimulation; Rr: reaction reversal; tr: train of impulses. (Redrawn from Grastyán et al., 1968.)

by a decrease of the speed of the movement. In the course of longer-lasting (up to 4 min) stimulation the development of a state closely resembling adynamia (Hess, 1957) was often observed. At the termination of the stimulation an immediate and rapid recovery appeared clearly showing that the adynamia was not an effect of fatigue. The *loci* showing such characteristics were labelled as dominantly contraversive loci (Fig. 1, top graph).

Loci allocated to the second group, produced, at or slightly above threshold intensities, initial ipsiversive effects and at higher intensities initial contraversive effects. During prolonged stimulation, changes in the speed of movement and reaction reversals were observed, as in the first group. Loci producing this type of response were labelled as the mixed group (Fig. 1, middle graph).

Loci of the third (pure ipsiversive) group produced, with all parameters, a primary ipsiversive motion. During prolonged stimulation, however, they also showed regular reaction reversals (Fig. 1, bottom graph).

In our earlier stimulation experiments, we often observed that the movements produced by stimulation were abruptly followed at offset by very fast movements occurring in an opposite direction. Since these after-effects were consistently produced from certain loci and showed regular modification with the changes of the stimulus parameters no doubts remained that they represented real rebound effects.

In the present experiment the sensitive electronic technique for recording movements made it possible to recognize an additional type of rebound after-effect. This phenomenon, which we shall call "auto-rebound", in contrast to the "hetero-rebound" just described, was overlooked both by us and others, because its direction coincided with the direction of the movement elicited by the stimulation, and so it gave the impression of a progressively dampening continuation of the direct effect. The electronic recording of the movement, however, definitely excluded this possibility, showing that the speed of this later contraversive (or ipsiversive) rebound movement was several times greater than, that of the contraversive (or ipsiversive) direct effect (Figs. 2b and c).

By systematic analysis of the rebound effects we established that the cessation of stimulation at different moments, could be followed by rebound effects of opposite directions. A closer analysis of locomotion in these cases revealed a correlation between the changes in the velocity of motion and the direction of the rebound. If the stimulation was interrupted during the accelerating or steady phase of motion there was an auto-rebound, while if interrupted during a decelerating phase a hetero-rebound appeared (Fig. 3).

The assumption that the fluctuation of opposing response tendencies

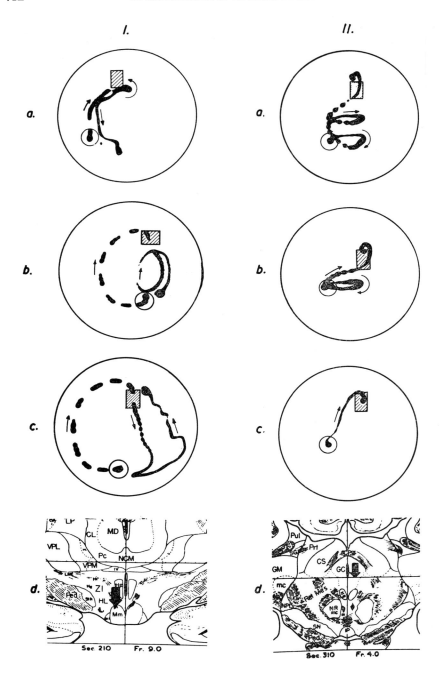

against a background of steady stimulation is due to the physiological interaction between two systems rather than to the artificial effect of stimulation is supported also by the finding that a strong rebound effect often influences the direct effect of the subsequent stimulus, even in the absence of any overt trace of the after-effect. Thus a stable initial ipsiversive effect may become contraversive if stimulation is applied close enough to a strong contraversive rebound or vice versa. This residual influence of the rebound progressively decreases with time, in the present experiment its maximum duration was 55 secs.

We began to pay particular attention to the rebound responses in the second stage of our experiments when, by applying the pedal switch-off technique, it turned out that a strict correlation exists between the type of rebound response and the learned approach and avoidance consequences of stimulation. In these experiments stimulation was switched on by the experimenter, and was switched-off by the animal, when it touched or passed over the pedal. By varying the distance between the start and the position of the rebound reactions of any desired character could be induced repeatedly. This procedure allowed us to establish that, irrespective of the immediate effects of stimulation, after the repeated appearance of contraversive rebound effects a permanent pedal approach occurred and after ipsiversive rebound effects a pedal avoidance reaction developed (Fig. 4). More concretely, during subsequent stimulations the animal began to approach or avoid the pedal with progressively decreasing latencies or offered resistance to attempts at being removed from, or forcefully put on it.

The direction of movement and the presence of rebound reactions, were found to be of special importance in self-stimulation as well. We established that all of the loci showing optimal self-stimulating characteristics belonged to the dominantly contraversive loci; further, stimulation

---

FIG. 2. The behavioural direct effect and after-effects of the stimulation of pure contraversive (I) and ipsiversive (II) loci recorded with the electronic device. A dash in the track of motion corresponds to 50 m sec, the smaller points seen in the after-effect to 10 m sec. The larger circles represent the experimental cage viewed from above, the small circle in it the place where stimulation was started, and the rectangle the pedal which interrupted stimulation. I (a). Interruption of a mild stimulation producing contraversive locomotion results in an ipsiversive (hetero-rebound effect). I (b). Interruption of a stronger stimulation produces a contraversive (auto-) rebound effect. I (c). A very strong stimulation is followed by the alternation of auto-and hetero-rebound effects. II. Interruption of an ipsiversive direct effect is followed by a contraversive (hetero) rebound effect both after a longer (a) and a shorter (b) stimulation. After four subsequent stimulations a spontaneous pedal approach (c) reaction developed. Placement of the stimulating electrodes projected on the corresponding figures of the Jasper-Ajmone-Marsan atlas is shown below. One electrode located just above the mammillary bodies (*left*) produces stable, the other located in the region of the substantia grises centralis (*right*), unstable self-stimulation. Grastyán *et al.*, 1968.

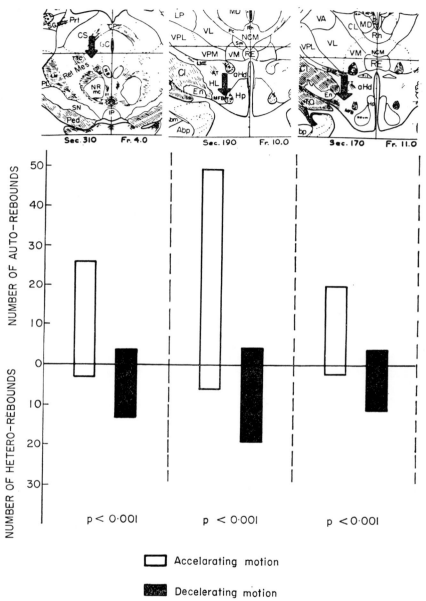

FIG. 3. The statistical relationship between speed of motion at the time of interruption of stimulation of one mesencephalic and two hypothalamic loci, and the direction of the rebound effect. Auto-rebound reactions are significantly related to the accelerating, hetero-rebounds to the decelerating phases of motion. Each of the three columns are based on recordings from a single cat. (Grastyán *et al.*, 1968.)

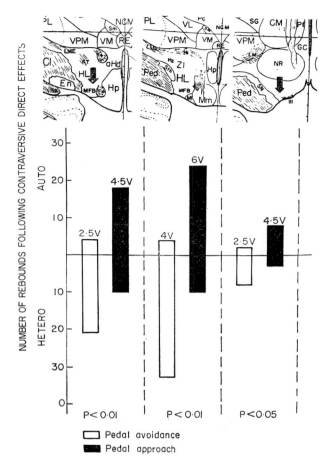

FIG. 4. The statistical relationship between ipsi- and contraversive rebound effects and the lasting behavioural consequences of the stimulation of one mesencephalic and two hypothalamic loci of three different cats. Pedal switch-off experimental situation. Avoidance reactions correlate with ipsiversive, approach reactions with contraversive rebound effects. Note also that hetero- and auto-rebounds are mainly related, respectively, to mild or stronger stimulation of the same locus. (Grastyán et al., 1968.)

parameters producing self-stimulation were invariably accompanied by marked contraversive rebound effects. The threshold of self-stimulation and the appearance of the contraversive rebound effects strictly coincided and both were well above the threshold of locomotor responses (Fig. 5).

The following experiment, devised on the basis of a fortuitous observation, offered seemingly direct evidence that the rebound might correspond

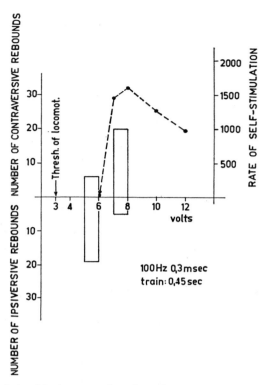

FIG. 5. The relationship between the rebound reactions and self-stimulation. The threshold of self-stimulation coincides with the threshold voltage of the contraversive (auto-) rebound effects, and the maximum rate of self-stimulation with the voltage at which the contraversive rebound becomes dominant with any stimulus parameters. Note also that the threshold of self-stimulation (6 V) is well above the threshold voltage of locomotion (3 V). Stimulation was produced with the parameters which are indicated in the Figure which were found to be most favourable to the rate of pedal pressing. (Grastyán *et al.*, 1968.)

FIG. 6. Transfer of pedal-pressing behaviour to indifferent objects in the self-stimulation environment under the influence of the contraversive auto-rebound. A. The characteristic leg movements developing during the rebound phase of a longer stimulus train (2 sec), and the accompanying afterdischarge in the dorsal hippocampus. Site of stimulation: lateral hypothalamus, in the region of the mammillary bodies. I. Pedal-pressing behaviour on the real self-stimulating pedal (B) and on indifferent objects (C, D) seen during the rebound effect to stimulations of different duration. II. Two equal triangular screens placed crosswise in the middle of the circular cage floor, creating four equal partitions. The space between the cage wall and the edges of the screens allows the cat to move freely around the partitions. Each of the four partitions has an object in it, one of which is a self-stimulating pedal. This arrangement prevents the cat from seeing more than one object during the rebound reaction. The cat never pedals on an object which it has seen only during locomotion (right upper partition cell) but only on such as it has seen during the rebound effects (the rest of the partitions cells). (Grastyán *et al.*, 1968.)

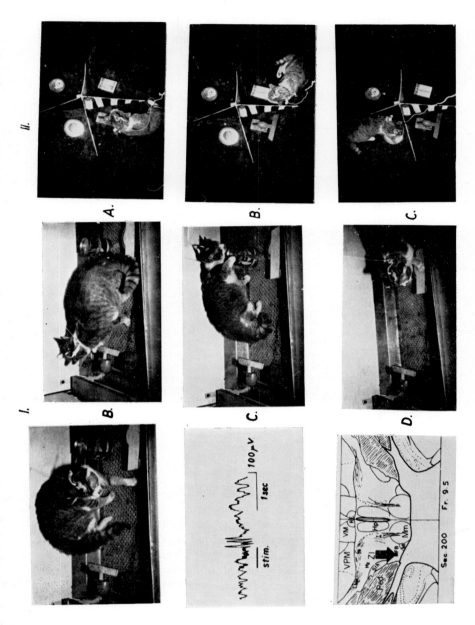

EE

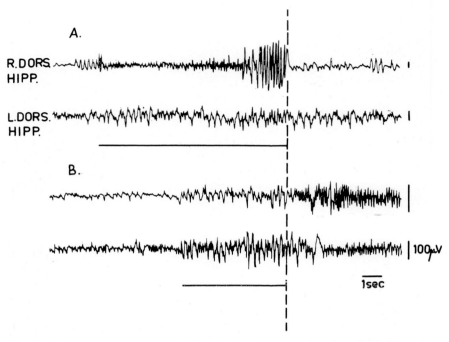

FIG. 7. Hippocampal paroxysmal discharges during centraversive phases of motion.
A: The change of the primary ipsiversive effect of stimulation to contraversive motion is
accompanied by a sustained paroxysmal burst in the right dorsal hippocampus, corresponding to the side of the stimulated hypothalamus. In response to the interruption of
stimulation, simultaneously with the appearance of an ipsiversive rebound, this burst
comes to a sudden halt. B: A sustained epileptic discharge develops when the pure ipsiversive effect of stimulation is followed by a strong contraversive rebound. (Grastyán
et al., 1968.)

to the critical reinforcing event in self-stimulation. If in the course of
a stable self-stimulation process the duration of the stimulus train is
abruptly increased from the usual value (a few tenths of a second) to one
or two seconds then the locomotion induced by the continuous stimulus
removes the animal from the vicinity of the pedal and the rebound motion
appears in the neighbourhood of an indifferent object in the experimental
situation. By applying this procedure the curious finding was made that
manipulation of the pedal becomes transferred to the formerly indifferent
object glimpsed by the animal during the rebound process. With appropriate selection of the duration of the stimulus train a transfer of pedal

manipulation was obtained at will to any object within the experimental environment in four stable cases of self-stimulation (Fig. 6).

The above account should be supplemented by an interesting finding concerning hippocampal electrical activity, since it sheds some light on the differences in functional organization of the systems involved in the contra-, and ipsiversive-patterns of movement. Certain hypothalamic *loci* consistently induced paroxysmal discharges in the hippocampus and their appearance strictly correlated with contraversive phases of locomotion both during and after stimulation (Fig. 7). The fact that only contraversive effects were consistently accompanied by after-discharges indicated positive feedback like connections underlying the contraversive locomotor mechanisms and the lack of such connections in the ipsiversive case.

III. Experiment II: A Dual Motivating and Sleep-inducing Effect of Ipsiversive Stimulation

In connection with a study of the motivational effects of medial thalamic stimulation Kopa *et al.* (1962), described a peculiar dual effect elicited with high frequency (100 Hz) stimulation in the background of a previously elaborated avoidance conditioned reflex from the region of the centrum medianum.

By stimulating the animal while in the danger zone of a one-way active avoidance apparatus (i.e. when the cat was on the electrified grid) it carried out the instrumental avoidance reflex in the absence of the warning signal. The performance of the reflex was preceded and accompanied by overt signs of fear. If, however, applied in the safety zone of the cage, the same parameters of stimulation within several seconds elicited relaxation and the species specific posture of sleep. At the termination of the stimulation, arousal reactions of a rebound character appeared consistently.

Recently we have reinvestigated this dual effect with improved technical means, in order to localize it more precisely as well as to obtain further knowledge about the electrographical and mainly the motor accompaniments of this phenomenon.

Twenty-five chronic cats, supplied with altogether 63 pairs of subcortical stimulating electrodes were used; 15 of the points showed pure ipsiversive effects, 25 contraversive effects if stimulated, while in 23 mesodiencephalic loci mixed stimulational effects were found (Fig. 8).

As a result of this study we established that the dual effect is a peculiar characteristic of the ipsiversive loci: having wide anatomical distribution, but focusing in the pretectal region in the vicinity of the posterior commissure.

Stimulation in the indifferent situation (i.e. in the round cage, described in the previous section) in all of the 15 pairs of electrodes showing the dual effect, elicited ipsiversive circling, or flexion of the head and forelimb and/or withdrawal and backing movements. On changing the parameters of the stimulation, the effects showed regular alterations of a quantitative but not a qualitative character. The following new observation was made in the one-way active avoidance apparatus. By feeding the animal several

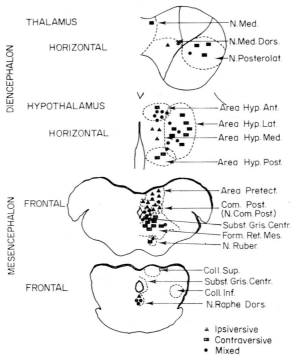

FIG. 8. Anatomical distribution of the ipsiversive (triangles), contraversive (squares) and mixed (circles) loci in the mesodiencephalic structures. (Molnár *et al.*, 1971.)

times in the safety zone of the cage instead of sleep the stimulation elicited diffuse exploration and food seeking behaviour (Fig. 9). Electrical activities of diametrically opposite character were recorded from the neocortex and hippocampus in the two compartments of the cage. Namely a net desynchronization or depression of hippocampal theta rhythm in the danger zone and a desynchronizing effect in the safety zone of the avoidance situation (Fig. 10).

V. Conclusions

A. Experiment I

It is difficult to understand that in the majority of studies locomotor effects are often neglected, or regarded as insignificant, or even undesirable, side-effects of centrally induced species typical reactions (Roberts, 1970). This is all the more surprising since the notion of motivation in its original sense refers to an urge for locomotion; moreover, the integrative level of locomotion anatomically coincides with that of motivation. The findings of Expt I definitely indicate that centrally induced locomotor effects are not fortuitous in their appearance. If the distortions caused by uncontrollable environmental influences are minimized, stable regularities come to light. As a consequence of this, stable correlations could be found between definite patterns of locomotion and qualities of motivation.

These regularities of locomotion are regarded as important since:

(1) they may present advantageous indicators for approaching the morpho-physiological characteristics of the motivational system (for example, it is conceivable that contra- and ipsiversive effects are related to the neural representations of dominantly crossed and uncrossed efferent pathways, respectively);

(2) spatial direction and speed of locomotion may prove to be more reliable indicators of motivational qualities than those traditionally used in experimental psychology.

The findings that contra- and ipsiversive patterns of motion correlated with approach and withdrawal behaviour, respectively, and resulted in corresponding learned responses becomes more acceptable with the following reasoning. The fact that most of the centrally induced locomotor effects involve circling is a consequence of unilateral, that is asymmetrical, brain stimulation. Bilateral stimulation would require symmetrical implantation of electrodes, which is difficult even with careful application of stereotaxic techniques. It seems, however, highly probable that the simultaneous stimulation of two symmetrically contraversive loci would produce rectilinear, progressive motion, that of two symmetrically ipsiversive loci rectilinear, withdrawal movements. The experimental verification of this assumption remains to be made, but it is supported by the fact that rectilinear movements were most commonly elicited by electrodes close to the midline or in the vicinity of commissural pathways.

If the above explanation proves to be valid then the correlation between the direction of movement and the quality of motivation is also supported by Valenstein's (1964) finding that all self-stimulating loci produce advancing locomotion.

It is important to point out that the recognition of the significance of the spatial direction of movement was rendered possible only with the help of the rebound phenomena. This becomes understandable if we consider that the rebound is a release phenomenon, in which the contra- and ipsiversive motor patterns appear in a much more pronounced and pure form than during the immediate effects of stimulation. The rebound effect in itself seems to prove that there is an inhibitory relationship between the two systems representing the two patterns of locomotion.

It remains, however, to be disclosed whether it is a mutual or one-way inhibitory process. Because of the artificial character of electrical stimulation we might also surmise that the rebound is the outcome of mechanical interference by simultaneously elicited antagonistic motor patterns. The available physiological evidence, however, does not support this simple explanation.

On the level of the nerve cell membrane the rebound is related to post-anodal exaltation (Andersen and Eccles, 1962) and thus it is a consequence of a physiological inhibitory mechanism. The consistent and regular changes of speed of locomotion occurring during stimulation also point to a common regulating mechanism lying behind the two basic patterns of locomotion.

In these stimulation studies the rebound was also revealed as a critical event of reinforcement. If this finding proves to be valid, important consequences relevant to one of the most important theories of reinforcement, the drive reduction hypothesis (Hull, 1943), may be derived from it. According to the mechanism of the rebound process the mechanism of reinforcement would correspond to a short lasting but strong excitatory state of one of the two phases of motivation induced by a preceding inhibitory process.

It is evident that in this mechanism the inhibitory process indirectly becomes an indispensable factor in reinforcement. Accordingly the drive reduction hypothesis of reinforcement would, in neurophysiological terms, correspond to a disinhibition, drive induction or inhibition reduction hypothesis.

B. EXPERIMENT II

On the basis of the correlation found between ipsiversive locomotion and avoidance behaviour, the fact that stimulation of ipsiversive loci also induced sleep seems to be paradoxical. This paradox can be resolved by assuming that the ipsiversive locomotion *in itself* does not correspond to an aversive motivational mechanism. The ipsiversive mechanism only contributes to an aversive motivational state if it meets a simultaneous approach tendency. We assume that it is this interaction between the two mechanisms which is the basic condition for the development of an aversive state. With that assumption the first phenomenon of the dual effect is readily explained. In the danger zone of the avoidance situation the animal has a strong urge to approach the safety zone. Stimulation applied in the danger zone inhibits this approach tendency and, as the overt manifestations clearly show, creates a state of high tension from which finally an escape reaction develops even in the absence of the conditional warning stimulus.

In the safety zone of the avoidance situation there is no approach tendency to be opposed, consequently ipsiversive inhibition becomes dominating and the animal falls asleep. If, however, an approach tendency is established by feeding the hungry animal several times in the safety zone, then the ipsiversive effect by inhibiting this approach tendency, again creates an aversive motivational state, in this case hunger. Thus stimulation, instead of inducing sleep, results in food seeking behaviour.

According to this explanation of the findings the aversive motivational state can be interpreted as the inhibition of an approach tendency, that is as a result of an interaction of the contra-, and ipsiversive systems.

C. Experiment III

This experiment actually corresponds to a reconstruction of the above suggested mechanism under natural circumstances. In the first stage of the experiment a stable approach reaction is brought about and later mechanically obstructed by placing the animal in a restraining cage. It is reasonable to suppose that the neural elements representing the approach tendency become inhibited in a physiological sense under the effect of stimuli connected with the obstacles. In other words, mechanical obstruction becomes translated into inhibition in the brain. This assumption is supported by the common observation that following frustrating attempts to get food in a given situation even hungry animals finally become quiet and fall asleep (Campbell and Sheffield, 1953). We suppose that an inhibitory state of a similar character is built up in the restraining cage and disappears suddenly when the door opens as a consequence of a definite action by the animal. The perseveration of the response instrumental in the release of the animal so closely resembles the auto-rebound process of the stimulation experiments that it would be hard to resist asserting a relationship. We hope this may be verified with the help of the accompanying electrical manifestations of the two phenomena. At the moment our evidence is scanty.

A second important conclusion derived from this experiment is based on the behaviour which follows the release of the animal from the restraining cage. The fact that the attention of the animal gets strongly concentrated on objects related to its release instead of those related to food (that is to the primary aim of the preceding behaviour) indicates that when a specific approach tendency becomes released from inhibition, a peculiar, aspecific motivational state develops, which is independent of the original specific drive and corresponds in its overt manifestations to exploratory behaviour. This conclusion coincides with the suggestion made in the introduction that the learning process is related to an aspecific motivational state, the neural substrate of which is not identical with those of primary drives and consummatory responses.

The findings of the first and second experimental groups suggest that the highly complex and varied behavioural manifestations of this aspecific motivational state, or appetitive phase of behaviour, can still be reduced to the basic and fixed behavioural patterns of approach and withdrawal. Approach and withdrawal represent opposite behavioural manifestations of a complex regulatory system, the corresponding sub-systems of which are endowed with one way excitatory-inhibitory connections. It is tempting to conclude that all those complex behavioural manifestations usually subsumed under the term of internal inhibition are related to the intersystemic inhibition of the complex motivational regulating system. This assumption would justify the usage of behavioural inhibition in a neurophysiological sense.

Acknowledgements

The present paper was based on the results of three independent series of experiments. The first, recently fully published study was made in collaboration with Dr I. Szabó and Mr P. Kolta; the second one with Dr L. Lénárd; and the third, hitherto unpublished one, with Drs L. Lénárd and Csilla Trinn. Their contribution and useful suggestions are acknowledged here.

We are indebted to Drs R. A. Boakes and M. S. Halliday for their valuable editorial assistance in the preparation of the final draft for publication.

References

Andersen, P. and Eccles, J. C. (1962). Inhibitory phasing of neural discharge. *Nature*, **196**, 645–647.
Campbell, B. A. and Sheffield, P. D. (1953). Relation of random activity to food deprivation. *Journal of Comparative and Physiological Psychology*, **46**, 320–322.
Cox, C. V., Kakolewski, J. W. and Valenstein, E. S. (1969). Inhibition of eating and drinking following hypothalamic stimulation in the rat. *Journal of Comparative and Physiological Psychology*, **68**, 530–535.
Eccles, J. C. (1957). *The Physiology of Nerve Cells*. Baltimore: Johns Hopkins Press.
Eccles, J. C. (1964). *The Physiology of Synapses*. New York: Academic Press.
Hess, W. R. (1957). *The Functional Organization of the Diencephalon*. New York: Grune and Stratton.

Hull, C. L. (1943). *Principles of Behavior.* New York: Appleton Century.

Grastyán, E., Czopf, J., Ángyán, L. and Szabo, I. (1965). The significance of sub-cortical motivational mechanisms in the organization of conditioned connections. *Acta physiologica Academiae Scientiarum hungaricae,* **26,** 9–46.

Grastyán, E., Szabo, I., Molnár, P. and Kolta, P. (1968). Rebound, reinforcement and self-stimulation. *Communications in Behavioral Biology, Part A,* **2,** 235–266.

Jouvet, M. (1962). Recherches sur les structures nerveuses et les mechanismes responsables des differentes phases du sommeil physiologique. *Archives italiennes de Biologie,* **100,** 125–206.

Jouvet, M. (1967). Neurophysiology of the states of sleep. *Physiological Reviews,* **47,** 117–177.

Kopa, J., Szabo, I. and Grastyán, E. (1962). A dual behavioral effect from stimulating the same thalamic point with identical parameters in different conditional reflex situations. *Acta physiologica Academiae Scientiarum hungaricae,* **21,** 207–214.

Lloyd, D. P. C. (1943). Reflex action in relation to pattern and peripheral source of afferent stimulation. *Journal of Neurophysiology,* **6,** 111–120.

Magoun, H. W. and Rhines, R. (1946). An inhibitory mechanism in the bulbar reticular formation. *Journal of Neurophysiology,* **9,** 165–171.

Molnár, P., Lénárd, L. and Grastyán, E. (1971). Motivating and sleep inducing effects elicited by high frequency stimulation of the same midbrain tegmental region. Lecture held at the *XXV International Congress of Physiological Sciences,* Munich.

Moruzzi, G. (1963). Discussion of the sleep mechanisms. In: G. Moruzzi, A. Fessard, and H. H. Jasper (Eds.) *Brain Mechanisms.* Amsterdam: Elsevier, pp. 438–439.

Parmeggiani, P. L. (1962). Sleep behavior elicited by electrical stimulation of cortical and subcortical structures in the cat. *Helvetica physiologica et pharmacologica Acta,* **20,** 347–367.

Pavlov, I. P. (1927). *Conditioned Reflexes: An Investigation of the Physiological Activity of the Cerebral Cortex.* London: Oxford University Press.

Renshaw, B. (1941). Influence of discharge of motoneurone upon excitation neighbouring motoneurons. *Journal of Neurophysiology,* **4,** 167–183.

Rhines, R. and Magoun, H. W. (1946). Brain stem facilitation of cortical motor responses. *Journal of Neurophysiology,* **9,** 219–229.

Roberts, W. W. (1970). Hypothalamic mechanisms for motivational and species—typical behavior. In: *The Neural Control for Behavior.* R. E. Whalen, R. F. Thompson, M. Verzeano, and N. M. Weinberger (Eds.) New York: Academic Press, pp. 175–208.

Schneirla, T. C. (1959). An evolutionary and developmental theory of biphasic processes underlying approach and withdrawal. In: M. R. Jones (Ed.) *Nebraska Symposion on Motivation.* Lincoln: University of Nebraska Press, pp. 1–42.

Sherrington, Ch.S. (1906). *The Integrative Action of the Nervous System.* New York: Charles Scribner.

Sterman, M. B. and Clemente, C. D. (1962). Forebrain inhibitory mechanisms: sleep patterns induced by basal forebrain stimulation in the behaving cat. *Experimental Neurology,* **6,** 103–117.

Valenstein, E. S. (1964). Problem of measurement and interpretation with reinforcing brain stimulation. *Psychological Reviews,* **71,** 416–437.

Valenstein, E. S., Cox, V. S. and Kakolewski, J. W. (1968). Modification of motivated behavior elicited by electrical stimulation of the hypothalamus. *Science*, **159**, 1119–1121.

Valenstein, E. S., Cox, V. S. and Kakolewski, J. W. (1969). The hypothalamus and the motivated behavior. In: J. Tapp (Ed.) *Reinforcement and Behavior*. New York: Academic Press.

17 | The Cholinergic Control of Internal Inhibition

D. M. WARBURTON

University of Reading, Reading, England

I. Introduction		431
II. Acquisition of Single Alternation		433
A. The Acquisition Model		435
B. Evaluation of Cholinergic Drug Effects on Acquisition		438
III. Cholinergic Effects on Stable Baselines		442
A. Single Alternation		442
B. Stimulus Detection		443
IV. Ascending Reticular Pathways		449
A. Cholinergic Changes in the Reticular Formation		450
B. Cholinergic Changes in the Hippocampus		452
C. Cholinergic Changes in the Septal Nuclei		453
V. Ascending Reticular Activation and Discrimination		454
VI. Concluding Remarks		457
Acknowledgements		457
References		458

I. Introduction

The papers throughout this symposium have discussed the various manifestations of behavioural inhibition where inhibition has been used to describe the process underlying a reduction in the frequency and, or, intensity of a response. Many of the experiments discussed could be considered as examples of Pavlov's internal inhibition (Pavlov, 1927). This behavioural inhibition was believed by Pavlov to be the result of an inhibitory process at the cortex. It was inferred that this process was centred on the sensory analysers of the inhibitory stimulus at the cortex from which it irradiated to other parts of the cortex (Pavlov, 1927). However at this time the precise mechanism or location of the processes mediating internal inhibition were unknown and it was certainly not clear that the behavioural phenomenon was due to a physiological process of inhibition. At the beginning of the 1960s the first suggestion was made about the neurochemical systems controlling behavioural inhibition (Michelson, 1961). He summarized the recent work from his own laboratory and others in the Soviet Union which pointed to the idea that there was a cholinergic system in the brain involved with the processes of internal inhibition. He cited studies which showed that intensified cholinergic activity strengthened the processes of differential and extinctive inhibition while muscarinic cholinolytics weakened both forms of internal inhibition. As a result he concluded that these effects were the result of the action of drugs on cholinergic systems, at the cerebral cortex and in the reticular formation.

The series of experiments discussed in this chapter were designed to investigate these hypotheses and to determine the nature of the mechanism underlying internal inhibition. This mechanism could be acting either at the response output or the stimulus input. Thus an impairment of internal inhibition would result from a loss of suppression of the motor systems, and this impairment would be manifested in locomotor hyperactivity. Alternatively the inhibition could result from a selection from the stimulus input, and impairment would be demonstrated by inappropriate responding to the impinging stimuli. The later experiments with cholinergic drugs will be discussed with reference to these competing hypotheses.

Historically the first working hypothesis about these studies was that the cholinergic system was involved in the inhibition of responses (Bignami, 1967; Russell, 1966; Warburton, 1967). In one version of this hypothesis, Russell (1966) put forward the idea that the cholinergic system was essential for the inhibitory control of all competing responses. He argued that during training an increase in probability of one response depends on the suppression of the array of irrelevant responses also available in the situation. In contrast behavioural extinction results from the interference of competing responses with the previously reinforced response resulting in the decreased probability of this response. If cholinesterase activity was reduced then the increased cholinergic function would enhance the suppression of competing responses and so the latter would not intrude to reduce the probability of responses in an extinction situation. On the basis of this interpretation, cholinolytics might be expected to have opposite effects but in fact cholinolytics retard extinction as well. Soon afterwards, Warburton (1967) proposed a revision of this idea by suggesting that the cholinergic system was involved with the inhibitory control of both competing and dominant responses. Thus a blockade of cholinergic function by cholinolytics and high doses of anticholinesterases would result in an increase in all responses but with a proportionally greater increase in the lower probability responses. However small doses of anticholinesterases would produce improved response withholding and so facilitate extinction as Russell et al. (1961) found. This would explain why Stone (1964) had found that cholinolytics could produce either consistent increases in avoidance responding, consistent decreases in responding, or inverted U-shaped dose response curves depending on the initial baseline response rate of the subject.

In our first investigation of this hypothesis a number of cholinergic drugs were tested using a Go; No go single alternation situation (Heise, et al., 1969). This schedule was selected because it depended on two sorts of inhibited responding. The first type, inter-trial interval responding was extinguished prior to single alternation training and was controlled by an exteroceptive cue. The second type was the nonreinforced responses during the No go trials. The first study examined in detail the acquisition of the alternation behaviour and the various stimuli controlling performance. This acquisition baseline was then used to examine the facilitatory effects of small doses of the anticholinesterase, physostigmine.

II. Acquisition of Single Alternation

In all experiments, naïve male Sprague-Dawley (Simonsen) rats approximately 90 days old at the beginning of the experiments, were used. All animals were deprived of water between sessions and received a 5-min supplement after each daily session. The apparatus consisted of three response chambers with the following dimensions: floor $6\frac{3}{4} \times 5\frac{5}{8} \times 8$ in with a Gerbrands lever on the right side of the chamber. These were contained in cabinets so that external stimuli were partially masked by the noise of the exhaust fan. The beginning of each trial was indicated by the onset of a light which provided the only illumination in the chamber. Leverpressing was reinforced with a drop of 9% sucrose solution delivered by means of a Skinner valve. The schedule was programmed by means of solid state circuitry (Digibits 100 series) and the data recorded with Esterline Angus event recorders. The various schedules programmed are outlined below.

All animals were pretrained to press the lever ten times for reinforcement (FR 10) during the 10-sec trial period. Responding during the 10-sec ITI postponed the onset of the reset trial for 10 sec, so that ITI responding was reduced to a low level. When the animals responded on 90% or more of the 480 daily trials for each of five consecutive days, acquisition trials were begun. The alternation schedule consisted of alternate trials when ten leverpresses still resulted in reinforcement and trial termination, whereas during the remaining trials ten responses did not result in reinforcement and did not terminate the trial. The same discriminative stimulus signalled the beginning of both reinforced and nonreinforced trials. Following the initial acquisition session, the animals were given six more daily sessions of 480 trials.

All 32 animals learned on the FR 10 schedule to respond on 90% of the trials within two weeks of shaping. All measures were taken from the time

FF

when the animals began responding on more than 50% of a block of 40 trials. From this point, it was possible to calculate the preacquisition level of performance, in terms of the probability of an error, i.e. the conditional probability of a response (ten presses) on a nonreinforced trial given that a response was made on the previous reinforced trial. Having been pre-trained to respond on 90% of the trials, all animals responded initially with an error probability of approximately 0·9. This conditional error probability was computed for blocks of 40 trials shifted four at a time and plotted in Fig. 1 as a centred moving average. Thus, the first point on the graph represents the probability of an alternation error computed for Trials 1–40, the second point represents the error probability for Trials 5–44, the third point represents Trials 9–48, and so on. One representative animal has been selected from the control animals in order to show the precise form of the acquisition performance which was similar for all subjects. All

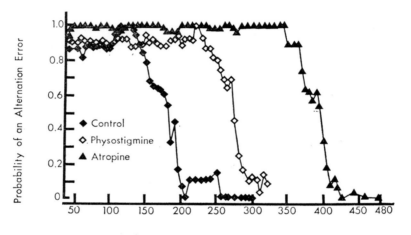

Trials (Blocks 40 shifted 5 at a time)

FIG. 1. Acquisition of single alternation by three subjects injected intraventricularly with either normal saline, physostigmine sulphate, or atropine sulphate.

animals began the acquisition session with a high probability of an alternation error, but after a number of trials, the error probability suddenly decreased at a rapid rate to reach a low probability by the end of the 480 trial session. These similarities were explored further by means of a descriptive mathematical model derived from Warburton and Greeno (1970). In the paragraphs which follow, learning is described in terms of decreasing errors in order to show the relation between the model and the learning curve shown in Fig. 1.

A. The Acquisition Model

According to the model the subject is in either one of two states, an un-learned state or a learning state, where the transition occurs on trial k. In the unlearned state, the probability of an error on trial n, $p(n)$, is constant and equal to $p(1)$, but during learning, $p(n)$ decreases as a function of $(n-k)$ to an asymptotic response level $p(\infty)$. In the single alternation situation, there are a relatively large number of trials prior to the trial k on which behaviour first changes and so the initial response level $p(1)$ is estimated from $(k-1)$ trials. Thus we have a two phase model, where:

$$p(n) = \begin{cases} p(1) & \text{for } n \leqslant k \\ p(\infty) - [p(\infty) - p(1)]\, f(n), & \text{for } n > k \end{cases} \qquad (1)$$

In simple situations, $f(n)$ can be set equal to some relation between a learning rate parameter θ, and the trial n. In our studies we used $f(n) = \theta^{(n-k)}$ from the single linear operator model of Bush and Sternberg (1959).

The special assumption of a linear operator to describe the learning process gives the following expression.

$$p(n) = \begin{cases} p(1) & \text{for } n \leqslant k \\ p(\infty) - [p(\infty) - p(1)]\, \theta^{(n-k)} & \text{for } n > k \end{cases} \qquad (2)$$

This model specifies the behaviour of an organism in terms of four para-meters—$p(1)$, $p(\infty)$, k, and θ. The data of an experiment were then fitted by the model to determine its usefulness as a description of single alternation acquisition. Estimation of parameters was accomplished using a computer program, STEPIT, that minimizes functions of continuous parameters like $p(1)$, $p(\infty)$, and θ. The trial of first learning, k, is not continuous, but satisfactory results were obtained by trying several values of k and finding optimal values of the other parameters in each case. This technique pro-vided maximum likelihood estimates of the parameters, failing only if the best value of k is missed in the set of values tried.

1. Comparison of Data and Predicted Observations

In order to determine the degree of fit of the model some comparisons have been made between some actual and predicted statistics and these are shown in Table I. The predictions made were based on computational convenience and the data available and thus some interesting sequential statistics, such as expected run lengths, have not been calculated. (a). *Presolution phase.* The initial response level, $p(1)$ was calculated from the trials 1 to k and it is assumed that there is no change in $p(n)$ over this period i.e. there is stationarity in the data. There are a number of tests for stationarity of presolution responses. One simple method compares the number of errors in the first and second half of the presolution phase and is sensitive to trends in the response sequences. A paired observation t-test showed that there were no significant differences between these error probabilities for the eight subjects. We thus have no evidence from the performance to suggest that the data from this period are heterogeneous or that learning is occurring during this phase.

TABLE I

Parameter estimates and comparisons of observed and predicted means for various statistics

	Observed Means	Predicted Means
Summary Statistics (n = 8)		
Initial Response Level, p(1)	0·96	—
Transition Trial, k	75	—
Learning Parameter, θ	0·87	—
Asymptotic Response Level, p(∞)	0·11	—
Erorr Trials		
First Quarter of Presolution Phase	17·5	18
Second Quarter of Presolution Phase	17·8	18
Third Quarter of Presolution Phase	18·4	18
Fourth Quarter of Presolution Phase	18·3	18
Total Number per Session	92	88·25
Trial of First Success	5·33	3·47
Learning Curve After k		
Probability of Error for Block k+4	0·82	0·72
k+8	0·62	0·50
k+12	0·34	0·32
k+16	0·24	0·21
k+20	0·16	0·14
k+24	0·12	0·12
k+28	0·08	0·11
k+32	0·11	0·11
k+36	0·13	0·11
k+40	0·14	0·11

b. *Total number of errors.* The total number of errors was computed from the presolution phase and the "learning" phase with a correction for the fact that the asymptotic response probability was not zero. It can be seen from Table I that this simple model gives a good prediction of the total number of errors. A two-tailed paired comparison t-test of the observed and predicted values was not significant showing that the model neither consistently under-estimated nor over-estimated the total number of errors for the subject. (c). *The learning curve.* The mean scores for trial-by-trial performance by the eight control subjects and the predicted data are shown in Table I. The model reproduced the form of the curve very well which is not surprising since the STEPIT program was designed to select parameters to fit the mean performance curve. It will be noticed however that there is some deviation from the model on the first few trials after k. Over the last 80 trials, the actual performance deteriorated for unknown reasons, perhaps due to fatigue effects. The calculations of the statistics, shown in Table I, were based on the first 400 trials or more precisely the first 200 reinforced-unreinforced pairs of trials from which the conditional probability was computed. (d). *Trial of first success.* This statistic is useful because it is sensitive to the early portion of the learning curve. This can be computed fairly easily if $p(1)$ is close to 1 and an approximate formula is used (see Galanter and Bush, 1959). Using the observed and predicted values for the eight animals a t-test comparison gave $t = 2 \cdot 13$ ($0 \cdot 05 < p < 0 \cdot 1$), suggesting that the model is not giving a precise fit at this point. It must also be stressed that the approximate computational formula tends to give an over-estimate of the statistic and therefore the actual differences are probably even greater.

2. *Behavioural Identity of the Parameters*

Although the model provides a good description of the alternation acquisition situation, this is not surprising in view of the number of parameters used. Thus this descriptive success would be valueless unless the model's parameters could be interpreted in terms of the variables controlling the learning situation. In single alternation, pretraining ensured that the animals responded very little when the light was off and that they responded to over 90% of the trials when the acquisition contingencies were initiated. Heise *et al.* (1969) have analysed the controlling stimuli in single alternation and related situations and have shown that performance depends on the outcome stimuli persisting from the preceding trial. Thus the occurrence of reinforcing stimuli on the previous trial is consistently associated with a nonreinforced trial and the absence of reinforcement always precedes a reinforced trial, provided the rat is responding.

In terms of our model we can ask what happens to performance if we change the "intensity" of the persisting stimuli by either increasing or decreasing the inter-trial interval (ITI). The results are derived from an analysis of acquisition data for different intervals where the 5- and 10-sec data are my own while those for 20 and 40 sec are re-analysed from Heise *et al.* (1969). It was found that only the k parameter changed with the mean values decreasing with the 5-sec ITI and increasing monotonically for the 20- and 40-sec groups in comparison with the 10-sec ITI group. The θ parameter remained constant for all values of ITI examined. In another study (in collaboration with Richard Kolodner) it was found that when a specific exteroceptive cue indicated the reinforced trials the k parameter decreased significantly but had no effect on the θ parameter. As yet no situational variable capable of modifying the θ parameter alone has been found although ablation of the ventral hippocampal formation does increase both k and θ (Warburton, 1969b). In the description of a similar model (Warburton and Greeno, 1970), the rats were assumed to be in an unlearned state prior to trial k and responding to partly relevant or irrelevant attributes of the situation as a result of pretraining. From the above experiments changes in the discriminability of the relevant cue modified the values of the k parameter so it does not seem unreasonable to suggest that the initial state consisted of selection of the relevant stimuli and the response occurred during the learning state, and as a consequence irrelevant responses were inhibited. This sort of hypothesis is similar to the two stage theories of discrimination learning.

B. Evaluation of Cholinergic Drug Effects on Acquisition

Treatment effects on learning can only be evaluated from k, θ and possibly from the asymptotic response level, $p(\infty)$. A procedure facilitating or impairing learning could conceivably change one of these, but not the other two. For example, there could be a change in the trial of transition from the unlearned to the learning state (k) without any effect on the learning rate (θ). Another procedure could change the rate of learning in the learning state (θ), once the transition (k) occurred, but not change the terminal level of performance achieved $p(\infty)$. A third treatment might only improve the final level of performance, $p(\infty)$, reached. In our studies we were interested in both facilitation and impairment of performance and so the experimental conditions were set to enable detection of both these effects. The transition trial k was sensitive to changes in either direction as the studies in the last section showed. The learning rate parameter, due to its dependence on the number of trials, was more sentitive to facilitation than impairment. This is because it represents the slope of the learning curve and is derived from the decrease in probability of an error divided by the number of trials, n. The asymptotic response level was more sensitive to impairment than improvement because it was so close to zero and could be improved very little.

In these studies the amount of functional acetylcholine has been modified by two types of drugs, cholinolytics and anticholinesterases. Cholinolytics block transmission in cholinergic neurons by combining with the receptor sites to give a cholinolytic-receptor complex temporarily preventing depolarization. On the other hand, anticholinesterases inhibit the inactivating enzyme for acetylcholine, cholinesterase, leading to an increase in the available acetylcholine. Small increases up to a critical level (Russell and Warburton, 1971) facilitate synaptic transmission but large increases impair transmission by blocking the receptors (McLennan, 1970). In our studies the specific agents used were the tertiary cholinolytics, atropine sulphate and scopolamine hydrochloride, the tertiary anticholinesterase, physostigmine sulphate and the quaternary cholinolytic, atropine methyl bromide, and the quaternary anticholinesterase, neostigmine bromide. Only the tertiary compounds pass the blood-brain barrier and reach the central nervous system.

1. *Facilitation*

The major study of this paper was the attempt to facilitate the acquisition of single alternation behaviour. Prior to this experiment, encouraging evidence for improvement with anticholinesterase had been reported by Michelson (1961), Russell et al. (1961), Whitehouse (1966) and Banks and Russell (1967). In the two studies in Russell's laboratory, using the anticholinesterase, 00-diethyl-S-ethylmercaptoethanol thiophosphate (Systox), there was a consistent, but non-significant, tendency for improved performance in extinction and sequential problem solving tasks when the levels of ChE were between normal and the critical level of 40% inhibition. Whitehouse (1966) followed up these studies by examining the effects of small doses of physostigmine (0·05 and 0·1 mg/kg) on the acquisition of a black-white discrimination in a T maze. Once again there was a trend in the direction of a facilitation of acquisition by the smallest dose: the number of errors for the first seventy trials was significantly smaller while the number of trials to a criterion, eighteen errorless trials out of twenty, was just short of the $p = 0·05$ significance level. In view of these exciting results, the effects of 0·05 and 0·1 mg/kg of physostigmine were tested on single alternation acquisition and the data analysed by means of the shape function model. Inspection of the k, θ and $p(\infty)$ values gave no clear evidence for facilitation although the mean value (57·75) of k for the 0·05 mg/kg group was clearly below the mean (71·88) of the control subjects. However, a one-tailed t-test of the k parameter values from this group and the control group was not significant at the 0·05 level.

Fortunately in some other recent experiments, to be discussed later, physostigmine produced facilitation of performance in a discrimination situation and so the data were re-examined. A study of the t-test calculations revealed the interesting phenomenon that the variance of the 0·05 mg/kg group was substantially larger than that of the control group. An F max test for homoscedasticity showed that the two groups were not of equal variance (F = 3·81 with p < 0·05) and so it was invalid to use a parametric test. The Mann-Whitney U test performed on the k values disclosed a significant difference (U = 12; p = 0·019) on the one-tailed test for facilitation. Little evidence of improvement was found with the 0·01

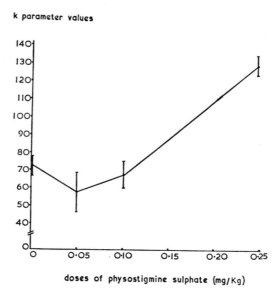

FIG. 2. The changes in the trial (k) when errors began to decrease during single alternation acquisition after doses of physostigmine sulphate.

mg/kg group (U = 17; p = 0·065) and there was no significant difference in the learning rate, θ, for either group, although this parameter was especially sensitive to improvement. From Fig. 2 it can be seen that there was a selective effect on the k parameter, decreasing its mean value but also increasing its variance. An increase in variance would be expected from a system in which there was only a narrow range where facilitation was possible and above a critical level impairment was produced so that the same dose of the drug would increase the ACh sufficiently to facilitate performance in some animals and to produce a receptor blockade in others. Two hypotheses can be put forward to explain the results. First, the drug increased the stimulus intensity in some way, either by enhancing the input, or by improving the short-term storage. Second, the drug could have enhanced the process of response inhibition so that the No go responses decreased earlier. The next experiments examined these two hypotheses by using cholinergic blocking agents.

2. Impairment

In these studies (Warburton, 1969a) the effects of physostigmine and atropine, injected directly into the lateral ventricles of the brain, were compared with those of a quaternary anticholinesterase, neostigmine bromide, and a quaternary cholinolytic, atropine methyl bromide injected intraperitoneally. The quaternary compounds, which did not pass through the blood-brain barrier and so did not reach the brain tissue, had little effect on either of the parameters, k or θ. However, both physostigmine and atropine injected into the brain selectively increased the number of presolution trials, k, but had no effect on the learning rate parameter, θ, as Fig. 1 shows. Thus both drugs at the doses used had qualitatively identical effects on acquisition suggesting that the dose of physostigmine was producing a cholinergic receptor blockade. The dose used here produced a 70% inhibition of cholinesterase (Warburton, 1969a) which exceeded the critical activity level needed to produce a receptor blockade (see Russell and Warburton, 1971). Changes in the k parameter did not occur until the cholinesterase activity fell to 30% of normal. Early interpretations of this data by Russell (1966) stressed the loss of response inhibition and suggested that the cholinergic blockade released previously suppressed responses. However, the latter hypothesis would predict that if the correct stimuli had been learned but could not be inhibited then the rate of decrease in errors, θ, would be faster when the cholinergic system recovered from the effects of the drug This was clearly not the case and, as we pointed out earlier, the learning rate parameter is particularly sensitive to improvement.

In summary, these acquisition studies showed that a small dose of physostigmine facilitated acquisition by reducing the k parameter, representing the number of trials prior to a decrease in the errors, while the rate of decrease in errors remained constant. The studies of impairment by cholinergic blockade enable us to rule out the possibility that the facilitation was due to increased response inhibition. The experiments on behavioural identification of the parameters demonstrated that the k parameter was sensitive to the intensity of the stimulus and so it was concluded that facilitation represented an intensification of the "remembered" stimulus in some sense, but so far we have presented no evidence which will enable us to decide whether cholinergic drugs were modifying the processing of the relevant stimulus input or the short term storage of that stimulus during the inter-trial interval. The next studies of well trained baselines throw some light on this issue.

III. Cholinergic Effects on Stable Baselines

A mass of literature exists on the effects of cholinergic drugs on well-trained performance and it is impractical to mention more than a fraction of it here. Instead the line of research followed in our laboratory will be outlined to show the progressive refinement of hypotheses.

A. SINGLE ALTERNATION

The first studies (Warburton, 1969a) used the single alternation baseline and examined the effects of atropine, and physostigmine injected into the ventricles and intraperitoneal injections of the quaternary compounds, atropine methyl bromide and neostigmine bromide on well-trained single-alternation performance. Three sorts of response were measured for possible drug effects: (1) the Go response controlled by the interoceptive cue from the previous trial; (2) the alternation No go response controlled by a similar interoceptive cue; and (3) the inter-trial interval No go responding under the control of the "blackout", an exteroceptive stimulus. Atropine produced marked increases in the alternation No go responses, very little effect on the Go responses and significant increases in the ITI No go responding. As in acquisition, physostigmine had less marked effects than atropine, but again there was a marked increase in No go responding and little change in Go responding and some increases in ITI responding. No effects were observed with injections of the quaternary compounds or the low doses of physostigmine. The results show that cholinergic blockade in the brain disrupts both the exteroceptive and interoceptive control of No go responding, demonstrating that the phenomenon is not specific to "remembered" cues. Earlier, Laties and Weiss (1966) had observed that behaviour largely controlled by externally based discriminative stimuli was more resistant to cholinergic blockade than responses controlled by internal stimuli. However, they used a fixed interval schedule with and without a "clock" stimulus. It can be seen that this is not a true comparison of interoceptive control and exteroceptive control, but in fact compares control by internal cues with control by an internal plus an external stimulus. In a more recent study Heise, et al. (1970) compared scopolamine's effect on performance when nonresponding was externally controlled by stimuli present at the time of the response and nonresponding which was internally controlled. Both types of responding were impaired and it was concluded that the drug impaired the inhibitory stimulus control of responding. These experiments show that the cholinergic system is involved in both the interoceptive and exteroceptive control of responding and so would be able to produce both inhibition of delay as well as extinctive and differential inhibition. However, these data would be compatible with either of the control mechanisms proposed for mediating internal inhibition and the next studies were designed to examine in more detail the possibility, suggested by the acquisition studies, that control might be on the stimulus input rather than on the response output. In these experiments we used the other two types of situation in which internal inhibition has been observed—responding with reinforcement delay and differential responding.

B. Stimulus Detection

The experiment was part of a series of studies (done in collaboration with K. Brown) examining the control of various kinds of discrimination including temporal (interoceptive) and brightness (exteroceptive) cues. Two of these studies have already been reported elsewhere (Brown and Warburton, 1971; Warburton and Brown, 1971) and they will only be referred to briefly here. The third study was a discrete trial situation with a variable ITI (mean = 15 sec) and reset of the ITI for responses in the last 9 sec of the ITI. The trial was signalled by a light cue which was three times the background illumination giving a signal to noise ratio of three. The animals were trained for 50 days until their performance was very stable and the effects of drugs could be tested.

The discrimination performance was analysed in two main ways. The first was based on the inter-response time (IRT) analysis of Anger (1965) and divided up the time before and after the light onset into 3-sec bands. In our schedule, making a response in one band precludes a response being made in a later band and so a correction had to be made by calculating the IRTs in a band per opportunity of responding in that band. This IRT/Op statistic gives the conditional probability of a response in a band given that the animal reaches the boundary of that interval (Anger, 1956). A portion of this data was used in the second form of analysis which was derived from the theory of signal detectability (TSD).

The form of this analysis was similar to the "method of free response" used previously by Egan et al. (1961) for analysing the detection of tones occurring at random intervals. In order to partition the number of "yes" responses meaningfully between "hits" and "false alarms", they took an interval just after the occurrence of the signal in order to estimate the "hits" and a second equal interval some time after the occurrence of the signal but before the next one for looking at the "false alarms". In the present study we used the 3-sec band after the onset of the light to measure the probability of correct detections and the 3-sec interval just prior to the onset of the light as the period for estimating the probability of a response in the absence of the signal. The selection of the latter interval was somewhat arbitrary but since the probabilities of a response in the other prestimulus intervals were almost identical this choice seems justified. The conditional probabilities for the hit and false alarm intervals under the various drug conditions were plotted on the conventional ROC matrix in order to determine the change in discrimination.

In terms of the IRT/OP analysis it would be predicted that a loss of response inhibition would result in an increase of the conditional probability in any interval while increased response inhibition would reduce these conditional probabilities. In contrast a loss of stimulus sensitivity would tend to produce equal conditional probabilities in all intervals whereas improved signal sensitivity would be reflected in a decreased conditional probability of a response before the light onset and an increased probability after the signal. These predictions are shown in Fig. 3 with the IRT distributions from which they were derived. These hypothetical distributions were based on the assumption that the animal made the same number of responses in each case. Doses of 0, 0·05, 0·1 and 0·25 mg/kg of physostigmine and 0, 0·0625, 0·125 and 0·25 mg/kg of scopolamine were injected into the trained animals. It was found that the pattern of disruption by scopolamine was similar to that found previously (Brown and Warburton, 1971; Warburton and Brown, 1971) when a decrease in stimulus sensitivity was obtained. The values for a representative rat (WBC-7) are shown in Fig. 4. In contrast the changes after 0·1 mg/kg of physostigmine shown in the same figure indicate an improved discrimination with a decrease in both the anticipatory and an increase in the short latency responses. This pattern of change was the same for all the physostigmine injected animals but it was not so clear cut with all animals and all doses. It seemed that seven animals showed a "sharper" discrimination, three were unchanged and two were impaired after the two lower doses of physostigmine while all were impaired after the highest dose (0·25 mg/kg).

The results were then examined using the TSD analysis which enables us to separate the drug effects on response inhibition (criterion changes) from changes in stimulus control (sensitivity changes). The percentage response bias was calculated by the nonparametric method described by Hodos (1970) because no assumptions could be made about the statistical properties of the sensory events underlying the responses. The formula used was

$$\beta = \frac{1-\text{p(hit)}-\text{p(false alarm)}}{1-\text{p(hit)}} \times 100$$

and it would be predicted that this criterion index would get smaller with decreased response inhibition and larger with increased response inhibition. On Fig. 4 the values for the response bias in WBL 7 are shown for the control and the dose of scopolamine and physostigmine. It can be seen that these values are unchanged and this was reflected in the rest of the individual values for the two drugs except that at the highest doses of both drugs

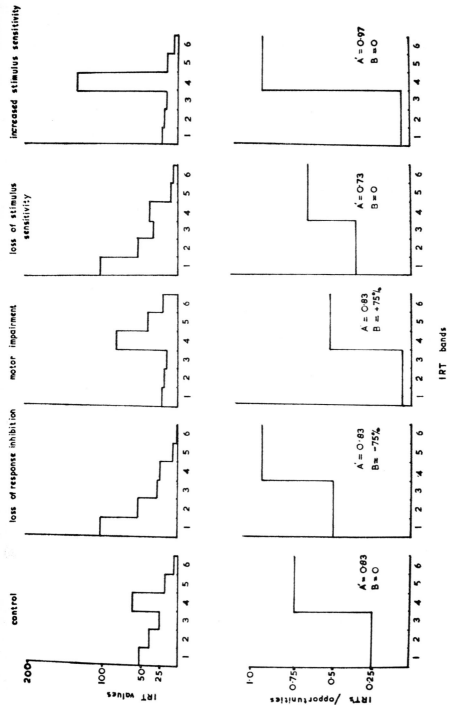

Fig. 3. The predicted changes in the IRT distribution for drug effects on stimulus control and response inhibition mechanisms of internal inhibition. The discriminative stimulus occurred between IRT bands 3 and 4.

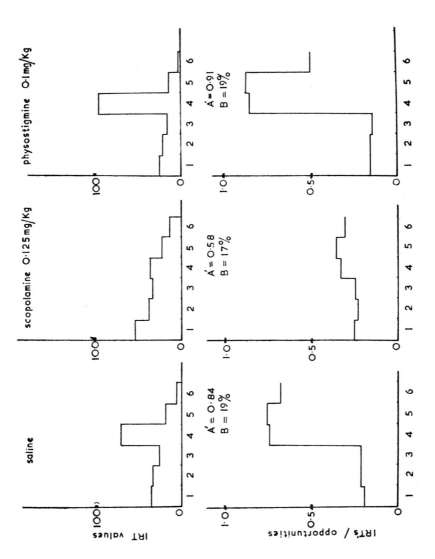

Fig. 4. The observed changes in the IRT distribution of Rat WBC-7 after scopolamine and physostigmine doses.

there was an increase in the criterion, probably due to motor impairment produced by blocking neuromuscular function.

This clear absence of an effect on response bias suggests that the drugs must be modifying the stimulus sensitivity. The false alarms and hit rates for each animal at each dose level were plotted on double probability graph paper and an index of sensitivity, d'_e, was estimated for each one by the procedure suggested by Egon and described by Green and Swets (1966). This method assumes that the underlying noise and signal plus noise distribution are equal and Gaussian, but even if they were not this would only change the values of d'_e but not the relation between the values for each dose. The mean d'_e values for physostigmine are shown in Fig. 5. The upper

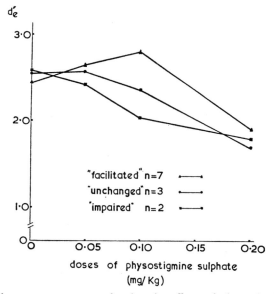

FIG. 5. The dose-response curves showing the effects of physostigmine on stimulus sensitivity. The upper curve represents the seven animals who showed clear facilitation, the middle curve represents the three subjects whose behaviour was changed by the two lowest doses and the lower curve shows the performance of two animals who were impaired by the two lowest doses.

curve represents seven animals who showed clear facilitation, the middle shows the three subjects whose d'_e values remained within their normal range for the 0·05 and 0·1 mg/kg doses while the lower curve shows the mean for the two subjects whose d'_e scores dropped below their normal range for these two doses. This separation was necessitated by the increased variance which was also obtained in the acquisition study with these doses.

It is interesting to note that the unchanged and impaired subjects had higher d'_e values initially compared with the facilitated animals. The significance test for comparing d'_e values (Gourevitch and Galanter, 1967) was used to examine the drug induced shift in the values of d'_e and disclosed a significant improvement in stimulus sensitivity for the 0·05 mg/kg and 0·1 mg/kg doses, the doses used to facilitate single alternation acquisition. Because of the theoretical importance of this study for the mechanisms underlying internal inhibition, the data were also examined using A', the non-parametric index of sensitivity of Pollack and Norman (1964). It was found that eight animals injected with 0·05 mg/kg and seven injected with 0·10 mg/kg showed superior performance to their control values whereas all 12 had poorer stimulus sensitivity at 0·25 mg/kg. These results confirmed the direction of the changes obtained by the conventional TSD performance.

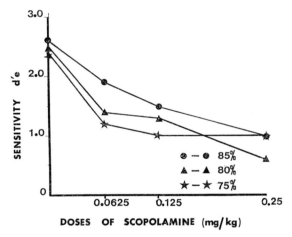

FIG. 6. Changes in the stimulus sensitivity estimates, d'_e, for three motivational levels after injections of scopolamine.

In other experiments scopolamine was tested on the interoceptive control (Brown and Warburton, 1971) and exteroceptive control (Warburton and Brown, 1971) of responding. It is clear from Fig. 6 that there was a decrease in sensitivity for all motivational levels as the dose level increased. Doses as low as 0·0625 mg/kg of scopolamine produced a significant disruption indicating the sensitivity of the technique. These changes in sensitivity were not accompanied by any lowering of the animal's response criterion, on the contrary there was even a tendency for an increase in the criterion with the 0·75 mg/kg dose in the Warburton and Brown (1971) study, giving fewer "hits" but also fewer "false alarms", probably due to motor impairment at this dose. These results demonstrated unequivocally that cholinergic blockade modified behaviour by reducing the signal-to-noise ratio and not by lowering the animal's response criterion. The absence of any decrease in the response criterion contradicted the loss of response inhibition hypothesis which would have predicted an increase in both "false alarms" and "hits". In contrast the results are consistent with the notion that the cholinergic drugs are acting on neural pathways involved with stimulus processing. In perceptual theory, attention has been interpreted as a process of selection produced by increases in the signal-to-noise ratio in sensory systems (Treisman, 1964) and shifts in attention have been found to produce changes in sensitivity with no consistent shift in the response criterion (Broadbent and Gregory, 1963) which was exactly what was found in this study.

These findings suggest very strongly that the phenomenon of internal inhibition as shown in extinction, discrimination and inhibition-of-delay situations is mediated by cholinergic control of the stimulus input. In parallel with the behavioural studies we have been examining the function of specific cholinergic pathways in the brain and attempting to elucidate the involvement of the ascending reticular systems with internal inhibition.

IV. Ascending Reticular Pathways

These pathways consist of the dorsal tegmental system, the ventral tegmental system and a hippocampal circuit. The dorsal tegmental system projects from the dorsal tegmental nuclei to the thalamic nuclei and corresponds to the thalamic reticular activating system of Starzl et al. (1951), although the thalamocortical pathway appears to be noncholinergic (Shute and Lewis, 1967). The ventral tegmental system projects to the neocortex, caudate, and receives inputs and sends outputs to hypothalamic nuclei. The ventral tegmental area is also the origin of the hippocampal circuit which passes from there to the hippocampal formation via the medial septal nuclei. From the hippocampus there are noncholinergic efferent fibres returning to the tegmental area and hypothalamus via the fornix giving the limbic-midbrain circuit of Nauta (1963). The latter author has suggested that reticular function could be characterized as postural in the sense of maintaining stability in the major control systems for behaviour. Thus projections to the cortex influence cortical stability in the sense of electrocortical arousal while hypothalamic projections would help to maintain visceroendocrine stability, i.e. homeostasis. Similar postural functions have also been attributed to the limbric midbrain as they seem to provide stability by diminishing the response to recurrent events in the external and internal milieu (Pribram, 1969). On the basis of these ideas the following hypotheses about the function of the hippocampal and ventral tegmental systems were devised and tested. (1) The ventral tegmental system modulates the organisms sensitivity to the external environment by controlling tonic electrocortical arousal, and to the internal environment via its hypothalamic projections. (2) The hippocampal circuit can be characterized as a feedback loop providing recurrent inhibitory regulation of the internal and external inputs to the ascending cholinergic arousal systems, so that, for example, redundant stimuli from the external and internal milieu are prevented from arousing the cortex. This implies that the system is more than a simple negative feedback loop because there is some sort of storage of information about stimulus regularities (see Douglas, Chapter 20, this volume). These hypotheses have been tested by direct injection of cholinergic drugs into three regions of these systems so far.

A. Cholinergic Changes in The Reticular Formation

In the first study a solution of carbamylcholine chloride (carbachol), a cholinomimetic, and atropine methylbromide, a cholinolytic, were injected bilaterally into, or close to, the ventral tegmental nuclei of the midbrain reticular formation. The effects of these drugs were tested on the stable Go; No go alternation performance used in the previous experiments. It will be remembered that responses on "odd" numbered trials were reinforced while responses on an "even" trial had no programmed consequences. Correct responding in the trials depended on the animal "remembering" the outcome of the preceding trial since no exteroceptive cue was given. Inter-trial responding was controlled by an exteroceptive cue, a blackout, and responses during this period were punished by resetting the interval. Unfortunately the cannula itself produced lesion effects resulting in an impairment of responding so that all of the data in Figs 7 and 8 are considered as per cent of the saline injected baseline. The effects of atropine methylbromide were unequivocal and in Fig. 7 it can be seen there is an increase in both the internally cued No go responding and the externally cued ITI responding at the 4, 8 and 12 microgram doses. However, Fig. 8 shows that the effects of carbachol were less clear cut; at the lowest dose 0·10 micrograms, some animals showed a decrease in errors (i.e. No go responding and ITI responding), but, at the two higher doses 0·20 and 0·40 micrograms, there were decreases in the reinforced, exteroceptively cued, Go responding as well.

The interpretation of the atropine effects can be made simply in terms of an impairment of stimulus control by the interoceptive and the exteroceptive cues and supports the idea that the ventral tegmental system is involved in the control of stimulus input. The improved performance with the lowest dose of carbachol is consistent with this finding but the overall decrease in responding with higher doses could be due to either a blockade of neural

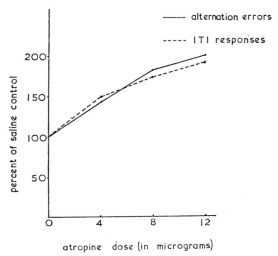

FIG. 7. The effects of injecting atropine bilaterally close to the ventral tegmental nuclei on single alternation performance, both ITI and alternation responses.

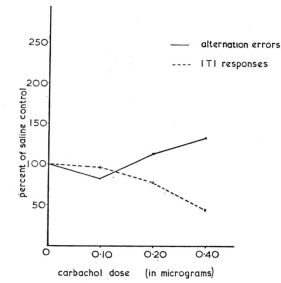

FIG. 8. The effects of carbachol injected bilaterally close to the ventral tegmental nuclei on both alternation and ITI responses in the single alternation situation.

function by the carbachol, activation of competing behaviours or some effect of high cholinergic activation. The first explanation is unlikely in view of the effectiveness of these doses in eliciting drinking (e.g. Russell, 1966) and in stimulation of the hippocampus, as we shall see in the next experiment. The hypothesis of activation of other systems seems more probable in view of the projections to the hypothalamic motivational networks and the basal ganglia. There is also a third explanation discussed in the final section.

B. Cholinergic Changes in the Hippocampus

The multiple effects observed after injection into the ventral tegmental nuclei were not found after injection into the hippocampal circuit. In a preliminary report, Warburton and Russell (1969) demonstrated differential effects of 4·0 micrograms of atropine and 0·43 micrograms of carbachol on single alternation when these drugs were introduced into the ventral portion of the hippocampal formation. It can be seen from Figure 9 that

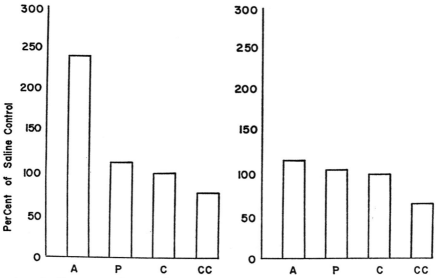

FIG. 9. Changes in alternation errors (*left*) and inter-trial interval (ITI) responding (*right*) following intrahippocampal injection of atropine (A), physostigmine (P), normal saline control (C) and carbachol (CC).

atropine increased both No go and inter-trial interval responding while carbachol reduced both. The effects of this dose of 0·40 micrograms of physostigmine were equivocal in the sense of improving performance in two animals, impairing performance in two others, while one animal showed no change in responding. Again we have found the same dose of physostigmine producing variable responses in different animals.

In a specific study of the effects of a cholinesterase inhibitor, di-iso-propylfluorophosphate, on discrimination learning after minimal training and overtraining (Leibowitz, 1968), it was found that the number of discrimination errors was reduced when the injection was given after minimal training, but that errors were increased by the injection in the overtrained subjects. Thus we have both facilitation and impairment with a dose of the drug depending on the amount of training given to the subjects. Clearly the effects of increasing the amount of acetylcholine is not a simple matter of facilitation or impairment depending only on whether transmission was improved or blocked. In addition to the data on stable performance some pilot studies were performed on single alternation acquisition. Two out of three of the carbachol-injected animals had k values below the range of the control animals while all three of the atropine subjects had greater k values. This is not strong evidence for facilitation but taken in conjunction with the other data it suggests that stimulation of the hippocampal circuit may improve acquisition as well as already established ITI and No go responses.

C. CHOLINERGIC CHANGES IN THE SEPTAL NUCLEI

The hippocampal circuit has its origins in the medial septal nuclei (Shute and Lewis, 1967) and cholinergic stimulation of these nuclei produced increased theta activity in the hippocampal formation analogous to that produced by sensory stimulation (Stumpf, 1965). Stimulation of the septal nuclei with carbachol (0·5–5·0 micrograms) produced a decrease in lever-pressing while similar doses of atropine sulphate increased the response rate (Grossman, 1964) in the same way as intraperitoneally injected atropine. The results of the hippocampal and septal studies confirm that the hippocampal circuit is not a simple inhibitory feedback loop controlling stimulus selection. If it was, it would have been expected that blockade of the pathway with atropine would have produced effects opposite to those resulting from cholinergic blocking of the ventral tegmental nuclei. This evidence is supported by the similarities in the behavioural effects of lesions in the hippocampus (Isaacson et al., 1961) and the ventral tegmental area (Le Moal et al., 1969) and of epileptogenic foci in these same regions (Isaacson, Chapter 19 this volume). As Douglas (Chapter 20) mentions the effects do not appear to be mediated by blocking sensory input in the classical pathways and hippocampal stimulation only seems to modify the late components of the sensory potentials. We would argue that these effects are due to the reticular projection of the hippocampus.

A number of interesting results have emerged from the intracerebral injection studies including the reproduction of the major effects observed after intraperitoneal injections. (1) Improvement of discrimination performance was obtained by drugs which increase the activity in cholinergic neurons. However, with central injection there was not a simple increase in facilitation with increasing doses of carbachol in the ventral tegmental nuclei. This was probably not due to a blockade of function since the same doses in the hippocampus produced effects opposite to those of cholinergic blockade. (2) Cholinergic blocking agents produced impairment similar to that resulting from peripheral injections. (3) An unexpected finding was the similarity in the effects of injections into the ventral tegmental area, the ventral hippocampal formation and the septal region. It is possible that this was due to the drug diffusing to some common site but it seems more likely that the drug was acting on the cholinergic sites closest to the cannula. If this finding is substantiated then it indicates that the cholinergic portion of the hippocampal circuit is not a simple negative feedback pathway.

V. Ascending Reticular Activation and Discrimination

We have presented strong evidence of facilitation of learned performance by cholinergic stimulation of the ascending reticular pathways. Unfortunately it is difficult to relate these studies to the other reports of improved performance after midbrain reticular stimulation, because it is hazardous to draw conclusions from stimulation of areas other than the locus of our cannula. For example, Grossman injected carbachol into a region about 1·5 mm above our placements and obtained facilitation of the acquisition of discriminated avoidance when low shock intensities were used (Grossman and Grossman, 1966) and of a T maze discrimination (Grossman, 1964). However, carbachol impaired the performance of already established behaviour in both these situations. It will be remembered that although we found both facilitation of acquisition and well-trained performance with the same doses there was also impairment with the high doses of carbachol injected into the ventral tegmental nuclei. Nevertheless Grossman's injections were not in the same site as ours and we cannot draw firm parallels.

In studies of electrical stimulation of the midbrain reticular formation both facilitation of acquisition and well-trained performance have been obtained. In experiments on the corneal conditioned reflex of dogs, Zuckerman (1959) applied weak (0·1–0·3 V) stimulation to the subject after 18–30 associations, before the response had appeared, and then presented the previously neutral stimulus which elicited the reflex. Retesting without reticular stimulation immediately after this showed that the response had not been established yet and that the effects of stimulation were transitory. Tests of discrimination showed that the effects were not a response phenomenon because there was both an increase in the reflexive response to the positive stimulus as well as a decrease in the response to the negative stimulus. This fits with our finding of facilitated discrimination with low doses of physostigmine which was manifested in a reduction of errors and an increase in the correct detections of the stimulus. At higher levels of stimulation over 0·8 V, Grastyán observed disruption of the conditioned response to a sound stimulus. This is not a general inhibition of all responding because the animal responds readily to irrelevant stimuli which are presented to it (Grastyán et al., 1956).

Other studies of facilitation of discriminations by midbrain reticular stimulation were performed by Lindsley and his group in Los Angeles. Fuster (1958) trained monkeys on an object discrimination task where the cues were presented only briefly. In the unstimulated condition, performance fell to chance levels when the exposure time was as brief as 10 msec, but reached about 85% at 40 msec. Reticular stimulation produced a constant increment of about 5–7% in the correct responses at each exposure time. Not only that, stimulation also decreased the reaction time so that it looked as if it is central integration processes that are being improved rather than a direct enhancement of either sensory input or motor output.

Another type of discrimination, investigated by Lindsley (1958) was the cortical resolution of two flashes which were presented 50 msec apart. Normally the cat's cortical response was a single evoked potential but after reticular stimulation there were two evoked responses showing better cortical resolution. At about the same time, Bremer and Stoupel (1959) found a marked enhancement of visual evoked potentials by midbrain reticular activation and this facilitation was paralleled by electrocortical arousal in the EEG. It is significant that Bremer and Stoupel observed that the maximum length of facilitation was prolonged by an injection of physostigmine.

As we commented earlier it is difficult to draw conclusions from stimulation of unspecified nuclei in the midbrain reticular formation. This region of the brain is the origin of many ascending pathways, only some of which are cholinergic and it is quite likely that several of these pathways will be activated by the same stimulating electrode. However, the results just discussed indicate that facilitation of sensory processes is possible, that this enhancement was paralleled by electrocortical arousal and that cholinergic drugs prolonged the effects. It has been thought for some time that desynchronization of the cortex was mediated by a cholinergic system (Funderbunk and Case, 1951). In support of this hypothesis electrocortical arousal produced by stimulation of the tegmental nuclei in the midbrain reticular formation was correlated with a large increase in the rate of release of ACh from the cortex (Kanai and Szerb, 1965). About 15 to 25% of the cortical cells, mainly in the sensory cortex, are excited by direct application of ACh and this excitation is blocked by atropine and potentiated by physostigmine (Krnjevic and Phillis, 1963 a, b). The latter authors concluded that desynchronization was due to an increase in the random spontaneous activity and that ACh was involved in the control of this activity rather than acting as a mediator from the specific sensory terminals.

Recently Krnjevic and his co-workers have confirmed the excitatory action of ACh on cortical neurons with intracellular recording (Krnjevic, *et al.*, 1971). It appears that ACh lowers the resting membrane conductance of the cortical cells for potassium as well as the delayed potassium currents associated with the cortical action potential. The net result of these changes is a "marked enhancement of the excitatory action of other inputs, with a particularly striking prolongation of evoked discharges" (Krnjevic *et al.*, 1971). In studies of the nature of stimuli required for human subjects to recognize a stimulus it has been found that the cortical activation must last from 0·5–1·0 sec depending on the stimulus intensity for any effect to be perceived (Libet, 1965). Obviously any mechanism which prolongs the after discharge of liminal evoked potentials will increase the probability of them being detected. It appears that the ascending cholinergic reticular pathways by releasing ACh at the cortex provide such a mechanism. Spehlmann (1969) observed that acetylcholine applied to the visual cortex prolonged both the discharge after mesencephalic reticular stimulation and the after-discharge of stimulating the visual afferent pathways. Atropine had the opposite effects on the evoked potential discharge. In addition muscarinic cholinolytics increase the threshold of facilitation of neuronal discharges by electrical stimulation of the midbrain reticular formation (Il'yutchenok and Gilinskii, 1969). These electrophysiological data parallel remarkably the behavioural results reported earlier. In both sets of experiments increases in cholinergic activity, which intensify electrocortical arousal, produce enhanced responsiveness to stimuli while diminished cholinergic activity reduces the sensitivity to stimuli. There is one complication to this simple picture and that is the impairment of discrimination by strong electrical and chemical stimulation of the ascending reticular pathways. Corresponding to these behavioural findings Bremer (1961) reported that high level reticular activation did not increase subliminal excitability of the cortex but resulted in occlusive interaction with the sensory inputs. Perhaps it is this occlusive mechanism which effectively masks the irrelevant stimuli and prevents them influencing responding when there is strong reticular stimulation.

In normal conditions the activity in the pathway will be determined by inputs from the organism's external and internal environments into the ascending reticular pathways. With drugs, facilitation of this system will produce better performance, both in acquisition and stable performance, by enhancing the cortical consequences of sensory stimulation. However, high levels of activation in this system could result in disrupted performance where the relevant stimuli are masked as well, which would explain the experiments on the ventral tegmental nuclei discussed earlier. In contrast, cholinergic blockade will produce a different sort of impairment where less intense, irrelevant, stimuli will not be inhibited and so become part of the subject controlling behaviour.

In the experimental situations of extinction, discrimination and reinforcement delay that Pavlov (1927) characterized as cases involving internal inhibition, the cholinergic system will modulate behavioural inhibition by controlling the cortical effects of the inhibitory stimulus and its competing responses. Since this mechanism is acting at the cortex and not on the primary sensory pathways it will be equally effective in modulating inhibitory control by the internal stimulation, in delay situations as well as by the external stimuli involved in discrimination and extinction.

VI. Concluding Remarks

These studies have shown how a combination of behavioural and neurochemical analysis has enabled a teasing out of the processes underlying internal inhibition. It was shown that small doses of anticholinesterases likely to improve cholinergic transmission facilitated inhibitory stimulus control whereas cholinergic blockade impaired stimulus control of behavioural inhibition. This change in stimulus control was interpreted as a modification in the processes of stimulus selection or "attention" and not as a change in response inhibition. An investigation of the ascending cholinergic pathways by direct injection of cholinergic drugs suggested that this system was involved in the facilitation of stimulus inhibition and thus selection of the relevant stimuli. This pathway is believed to control the spontaneous activity at the sensory cortex and so it could modulate the evoked potentials. Anatomically the pathway is in a unique position for modifying stimuli from both the external and internal environments. As far as the hippocampus is concerned, it would seem to be some sort of feedback circuit modulating arousal but certainly cholinergic stimulation in the ventral hippocampal formation does not inhibit the ventral tegmental pathway.

Acknowledgements

I am indebted to Professors Michel Treisman and George Heise, Paul Kenyon and to Drs Elizabeth and David Gaffan for helpful suggestions in the preparation of this manuscript.

458 D. M. WARBURTON

References

Anger, D. (1956). The dependence of interresponse times upon the relative reinforcement of different interresponse times. *Journal of Experimental Psychology*, **52**, 145–161.

Banks, A. and Russell, R. W. (1967). Effects of chronic reductions in acetylcholinesterase activity on serial problem solving behavior. *Journal of Comparative and Physiological Psychology*, **64**, 262–267.

Bignami, G. (1967). Anticholinergic agents as tools in the investigation of behavioural phenomena. In: *Proceedings of the Vth International Congress of the Colleqium Internationale Neuropharmaclogicum*. Amsterdam: Excerpta Medica, I.C.S., **129**, pp. 819–830.

Bremer, F. (1961). Neurophysiological mechanisms in cerebral arousal. In: G. E. W. Wolstenholme and M. O'Connor (Eds.) *The Nature of Sleep*. Boston: Little, Brown and Co, pp. 30–56.

Bremer, F. and Stoupel, N. (1959). Etude pharmacologique de la facilitation des résponses corticales dans l'éveil reticulaire. *Archives Internationales de Pharmacodynamie*, **122**, 234–248.

Broadbent, D. E. and Gregory, M. (1963). Division of attention and the decision theory of signal detection. *Proceedings of the Royal Society*, B, **158**, 222–231.

Brown, K. and Warburton, D. M. (1971). Attenuation of stimulus sensitivity by scopolamine. *Psychonomic Science*, **22**, 297–298.

Bush, R. R. and Sternberg, S. H. (1959). A single operator model. In: R. R. Bush, and W. K. Estes (Eds.) *Studies in Mathematical Learning Theory*. Stanford: Stanford University Press, pp 204–214.

Egan, J. P., Greenberg, G. Z. and Schulman, A. I. (1961). Operating characteristics, signal detectability and the method of free response. *Journal of the Acoustical Society of America*, **33**, 993–1007.

Funderbunk, W. H. and Case, T. J. (1951). The effect of atropine on cortical potentials. *Electroencephalography and Clinical Neurophysiology*, **3**, 213–223.

Fuster, J. M. (1958). Effects of stimulation of the brain stem on tachistocopic perception. *Science*, **127**, 150.

Galanter, E. and Bush, R. R. (1959). Some T maze experiments. In: R. R. Bush and W. K. Estes. *Studies in Mathematical Learning Theory*. Stanford University Press, pp 265–289.

Gourevitch, V. and Galanter, E. (1967). A significance test for one parameter isosensitivity functions. *Psychometrika*, **32**, 25–33.

Grastyán, E., Lissák, K. and Kékesi, F. (1956). Facilitation and inhibition of conditioned alimentary and defensive reflexes by stimulation of the hypothalamus and reticular formation. *Acta Physiologica Hungaricaes*, Acadamiae Scientiarum, **9**, 133–151.

Green, D. M. and Swets, J. A. (1966). *Signal Detection Theory and Psychophysics*. New York: Wiley.

Grossman, S. P. (1964). Effect of chemical stimulation of the septal area on motivation. *Journal of Comparative and Physiological Psychology*, **58**, 194–200.

Grossman, S. P. (1966). Acquisition and performance of avoidance responses during chemical stimulation of the midbrain reticular formation. *Journal of Comparative and Physiological Psychology*, **61**, 42–49.

Grossman, S. P. and Grossman, L. (1966). Effects of chemical stimulation of the midbrain reticular formation on appetitive behavior. *Journal of Comparative and Physiological Psychology*, **61**, 333–338.

Heise, G. A., Keller, Connie, Khavari, K. A. and Laughlin, N. (1969). Learning of discrete trial, go-no go alternation patterns by the rat. *Journal for the Experimental Analysis of Behavior*, **12**, 609–622.

Heise, G. A., Laughlin, N. and Keller, C. (1970). A behavioral and pharmacological analysis of reinforcement withdrawal. *Psychopharmacologia* **16**, 345–368.

Hodos, W. (1970). A non parametric index of response bias for use in detection and recognition experiments. *Psychological Bulletin*, **74**, 351–354.

Hodos, W. and Valenstein, E. (1962). An evaluation of response rate as a measure of rewarding intracranial stimulation. *Journal of Comparative and Physiological Psychology*, **55**, 80–84.

Il'yuchenok, R. Yu. and Gilinskiĭ, M. A. (1969). Deĭstvie kholinoliticheskikh veschestv na spontannuyu i vyzannuyu aktivnost, karkovykh neĭronov. *Farmakologiya i Toksikologiya*, **32**, 515–519.

Isaacson, R. L., Douglas, R. J. and Moore, R. Y. (1961). The effect of radical hippocampal ablation on acquisition of avoidance response. *Journal of Comparative and Physiological Psychology*, **54**, 625–628.

Kanai, T. and Szerb, J. C. (1965). Mesencephalic reticular activating system and cortical acetylcholine output. *Nature*, **205**, 81–88.

Krnjević, K. and Phillis, J. W. (1963a). Acetylcholine sensitive cells in the cerebral cortex. *Journal of Physiology*, **166**, 296–327.

Krnjević, K. and Phillis, J. W. (1963b). Pharmacological properties of acetylcholine-sensitive cells in the cerebral cortex. *Journal of Physiology*, **166**, 328–350.

Krnjević, K., Pumain, R. and Renaud, L. (1971). The mechanism of excitation by acetylcholine in the cerebral cortex. *Journal of Physiology*, **215**, 247–268.

Laties, V. and Weiss, B. (1966). Influence of drugs on behavior controlled by internal and external stimuli. *Journal of Pharmacology and Experimental Therapeutics*, **152**, 388–396.

Leibowitz, S. F. (1968). Memory and emotionality after anticholinesterase inhibition in the hippocampus: inverse function of prior learning level. New York University: Unpublished Doctoral Thesis.

Le Moal, M., Cardo, B. and Stinus, J. (1969). Influence of ventral mesencephalic lesions on various spontaneous and conditioned behaviors in the rat. *Physiology and Behavior*, **4**, 567–573.

Libet, B. (1965). Cortical activation in conscious and unconscious experience. *Perspectives in Biology and Medicine*, **9**, 77–86.

Lindsley, D. B. (1958). The reticular system and perceptual discrimination. In: H. H. Jasper and others (Eds.) *Reticular Formation of the Brain*. Boston: Little, Brown, pp. 513–534.

McLennan, H. (1970). *Synaptic transmission*, Philadelphia: Saunders.

Michelson, M. J. (1961). Pharmacological evidences of the role of acetylcholine in the higher nervous activity of man and animals. *Activitas Nervosa Superior* (Prague), **3**, 140–147.

Nauta, W. J. H. (1963). Central nervous organization and the endocrine motor system. In: A. V. Nalbandov (Ed.) *Advances in Neuroendocrinology*. Urbana, Illinois: University of Illinois Press, pp. 5–21.

Pavlov, I. P. (1927). *Conditioned Reflexes*. London: Oxford University Press.

Pollack, I. and Norman, D. A. (1964). A non-parametric analysis of recognition experiments. *Psychonomic Science*, **1**, 125–126.

Pribram, K. H. (1969). The neurobehavioral analysis of limbic forebrain mechanisms: revision and progress report. In: D. Lehrman (Ed.) *Advances in the Study of Behavior*, Vol. 2, New York: Academic Press.

Russell, R. W. (1966). Biochemical substrates of behavior. In: R. W. Russell (Ed.) *Frontiers in Physiological Psychology*. New York: Academic Press, pp. 185–246.

Russell, R. W. and Warburton, D. M. (1971). Biochemical bases of behavior. In: B. Wolman (Ed.). *Handbook of Psychology*. New York: Prentice-Hall.

Russell, R. W., Watson, R. H. J. and Frankenhauser, M. (1961). Effects of chronic reduction in brain cholinesterase activity on acquisition and extinction of a conditioned avoidance response. *Scandinavian Journal of Psychology*, **2**, 21–29.

Shute, C. C. D. and Lewis, P. R. (1967). The ascending cholinergic reticular system: neocortical, olfactory and subcortical projections. *Brain*, **90**, 497–520.

Spehlmann, R. (1969). Effect of acetylcholine and atropine upon excitation of cortical neurons by reticular stimulation. *Federation Proceedings*, **28**, 795.

Starzl, T. E., Taylor, C. W. and Magoun, H. W. (1951). Ascending conduction in the reticular activating system, with special reference to the diencephalon. *Journal of Neurophysiology*, **14**, 461–467.

Stone, G. (1964). Effects of drugs on non-discriminated avoidance behaviour, I. Individual differences in dose-response relationships. *Psychopharmacologia* **6**, 245–255.

Stümpf, C. (1965). Drug action on the electrical activity of the hippocampus. *International Journal Neurobiology*, **8**, 77–138.

Treisman, A. (1964). Selective attention in man. *British Medical Bulletin*, **20**, 12–16.

Warburton, D. M. (1967). Some behavioral effects of central cholinergic stimulation with special reference to the hippocampus. Indiana University: Unpublished Doctoral Thesis.

Warburton, D. M. (1969a). Behavioral effects of central and peripheral changes in acetylcholine systems. *Journal of Comparative and Physiological Psychology*, **68**, 56–64.

Warburton, D. M. (1969b). Effects of atropine sulfate on single alternation in hippocampectomised rats. *Physiology and Behavior*, **4**, 641–644.

Warburton, D. M. and Brown, K. (1971). Scopolamine-induced attenuation of stimulus sensitivity. *Nature*, **230**, 126–127.

Warburton, D. M. and Greeno, J. G. (1970). A general shape function model of learning with applications in psychobiology. *Psychological Review*, **77**, 348–352.

Warburton, D. M. and Russell, R. W. (1969). Some behavioural effects of cholinergic stimulation of the hippocampus. *Life Sciences*, **8**, 617–627.

Whitehouse, J. M. (1966). The effects of physostigmine on discrimination learning. *Psychopharmacologia*, **9**, 183–188.

Zuckerman, E. (1959). Effect of cortical and reticular stimulation on conditioned reflex activity. *Journal of Neurophysiology*, **22**, 633–643.

18

Septal Damage and Response Output Under Frustrative Nonreward

A. DICKINSON

University of Sussex, Brighton, Sussex, England

I. Introduction 461
II. General Experimental Procedures and Results 463
III. Septal Damage and Control of Response Output 463
IV. Theoretical Interpretations of Nonreward Persistence . . . 469
    A. Deficit Dissociations 470
    B. Nonreward Persistence and Frustration 472
V. Frustration Attenuation 473
    A. Method 475
    B. Results and Discussion 478
VI. Frustration Potentiation 481
    A. Method 484
    B. Results and Discussion 485
VII. Concluding Comments 489
Acknowledgements 493
References 493

I. Introduction

One of the fundamental features of adaptive behaviour is that animals cease performing an appetitively-motivated instrumental response when the emission of the response no longer produces the appropriate reward. Although the explanation of such response decrements constitutes a crucial area for any general theory of behavioural adjustment, there is, as yet, little general agreement about the nature of the main mechanisms involved. Faced with the problem of instrumental extinction and related phenomena, learning theorists have proposed basically two types of explanation. The first assumes that the withdrawal of reward does not bring into operation any new behavioural mechanism and that the response decrement can simply be understood in terms of the removal of response-maintaining processes and stimuli associated with reward. Thus, for example, Hull (1943) identified the "reactive inhibition" resulting solely from the repeated performance of a response as the causal mechanism of response decrement, whilst others have emphasized the generalization decrement due to the change in the conditioned-stimulus complex produced by the omission of reward. The second class of theories has typically proposed that the withdrawal of reward brings into play a new mechanism, some features of which are specifically related to conditions of nonreward. For instance, Spence suggested that the "weakening is due to an active, negative process, inhibition, which adding itself in an algebraic fashion to the positive excitatory tendencies, results in lowered strength values" (Spence, 1936). A concern with the existence and nature of such response-controlling processes obviously represents a focal interest of this volume.

In recent years, a number of ablation studies have shown that damage to certain subcortical structures produces behavioural dysfunctions in situations where intact animals exhibit a response decrement following the removal of reward. For example, abnormal response persistence has been found in such situations following ablations of the hippocampus and septum. Douglas (Chapter 20, this volume) describes the behavioural pattern of hippocampal animals, and I shall concentrate exclusively on attempting to elucidate the nature of the persistence shown by septal rats under nonreward. This deficit pattern is typically represented by the prolonged responding of septal rats in simple extinction (e.g. Schwartzbaum, et al., 1964; Raphelson, et al., 1966), their inefficient pattern of responding on schedules of positive reinforcement which require a low rate of responding (e.g. Ellen, et al., 1964), and their relative difficulty in learning the reversal of a simultaneous discrimination (e.g. Schwartzbaum and Donovick, 1968). On a very general level of analysis, the appropriate behavioural adjustment in all these tasks requires that the tendency to emit a pre-potent response, established under positive reinforcement, is decreased when nonreward is introduced, and I shall refer to this deficit pattern as "nonreward persistence".

The significant feature of these deficits is that the persistence appears to be unaccompanied by any general distortions of the acquisition or maintenance of response patterns in situations that do not obviously require a reduction of response output under nonreward and in which the animal has an opportunity to make an active, reinforced response on each trial or occasion. Septal animals show normal acquisition functions in a variety of simultaneous discriminations (e.g. Schwartzbaum and Donovick, 1968) and response-sequencing tasks (Carlson and Cole, 1970). Perhaps the strongest evidence that septal damage does not result in any general learning deficit comes from the similarity of the acquisition functions of septal and intact rats in a complex maze (Ain, et al., 1969). On the most general level, the selectivity of these ablation effects supports the contention that at least some of the mechanisms which take part in the control of normal response decrements under nonreward are minimally involved in acquisition processes. Furthermore, if the effective lesions can be assumed to disturb the proper functioning of such mechanisms, a behavioural analysis of the dysfunctions produced by these lesions in nonreward situations may help to elucidate the nature of these mechanisms as well as the function of the systems represented within the septum. The studies reported within this chapter are directed towards this end.

II. General Experimental Procedures and Results

Before describing any of the experiments, the procedures and results which are common to the series of studies reported in this chapter will be outlined.

The subjects were naïve, male, hooded Lister rats. Before the start of an experiment they were reduced to 85 % of their free-feeding weight by food deprivation and were then maintained at this level throughout the experiment except during the post-operative recovery period. Primary reinforcement consisted of the delivery of a single 45-mg food pellet.

The rats in the septal group were given bilateral, electrolytic lesions of the septal nuclei by passing a 2-ma dc anodal current for 20 sec through the 0·5 mm uninsulated tip of a stainless steel electrode which was positioned in the brain stereotaxically. All subjects were given 10–12 days post-operative recovery before being returned to the experimental conditions. During the first 6–8 days of the recovery period they had free access to food and water before being returned to 85% of their pre-operative free-feeding weight. The lesioned animals typically showed the septal hyperemotionality syndrome (Brady and Nauta, 1953) following surgery. However, the syndrome had considerably abated by the end of the post-operative recovery period. In fact, by the time that the main experimental manipulations were instituted the septal animals were often more placid than controls when handled.

All the lesions destroyed most of the pre-commissural septum from the genu of the corpus callosum to the crossing of the anterior commissure, and were fairly typical of the large septal lesions reported in previous studies. Also, the nucleus and tract of the diagonal band of Broca and the dorso-medial tip of the nucleus accumbens usually sustained some damage. In certain cases the lesion extended beyond the pre-commissural septum involving damage to the hippocampus pars anterior and the medial parolfactory area in the anterior direction and to the supracommissural septum and the descending columns of the fornix in the posterior direction.

III. Septal Damage and Control of Response Output

The behavioural adjustment of intact animals to nonreward must involve a large number of complex and interacting mechanisms, each having different functional properties, and one of the first problems in an analysis of septal nonreward persistence is to determine the general type of functional mechanism disturbed by the damage. The basic phenomena of persistence could be ascribed to the disruption of a variety of different classes of mechanisms. Although the evidence so far considered indicates that septal damage does not interfere with learning under positive reinforcement, it remains possible that the ablation disturbs some processes generally involved in the adjustment to nonreward but not specifically mediating the reduction in the output of nonreinforced responses. Septal animals may be, in some sense, unable to register the change in conditions associated with the withdrawal of reward or to store information about such changes across inter-sessional or inter-trial intervals. On the other hand, the persistence may arise from the disruption of a system directly involved in controlling response reductions under nonreward.

The fact that nonreward persistence *per se* is compatible with a number of such explanations is illustrated by the performance of septal and intact rats during the acquisition of a free-operant, successive discrimination. Six septal and six control rats were reinforced for leverpresses on a *mult* VI 45 sec VI 45 sec schedule. A daily session consisted of 12 successive presentations of each component in a semi-random order. During one of the components a stimulus light was illuminated and during the other component this light was out. The duration of each component was 120 sec and successive components were separated by a 10-sec blackout period during which the stimulus and houselights were out and responding had no programmed consequences. After the response rates had stabilized for all subjects, the schedule was changed to *mult* VI 45 sec EXT and training continued for a further 30 sessions by which time performance had again stabilized. The components in which responding was extinguished will be referred to as S^- components, and those in which responding was reinforced as S^+ components. For half the subjects in each group the S^- components were signalled by the presence of the stimulus light, and for the remaining subjects by its absence.

When the discrimination was introduced the septal rats showed sustained nonreward persistence in that they maintained a much higher response rate in S^- components than control animals even when the performance had reached asymptote. There was no overlap between the response rates of the septal and control subjects in S^- components on any of the last 10 discrimination sessions. The nature of this persistence is illustrated in Fig. 1 which shows the cumulative records of representative subjects during the whole of one discrimination session when performance had stabilized. The presence of an S^- component is indicated by the downward excursion of the event pen below each record, and transitions between S^+

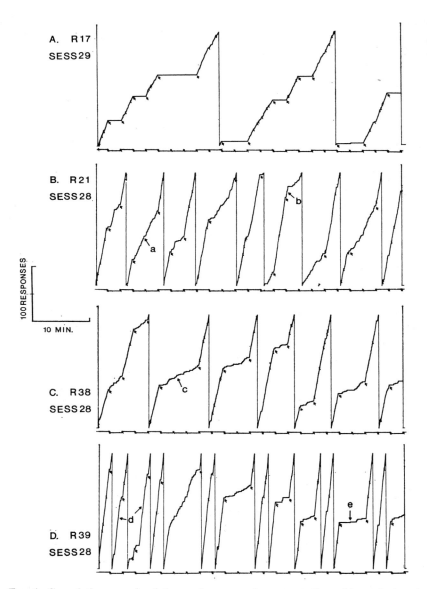

FIG. 1. Cumulative records of the performance of representative subjects during the whole of one discrimination session when performance had stabilized. For further details see text.

and S$^-$ components are marked by small arrows on the records themselves. Fig. 1A shows the record of a control subject and illustrates the almost total absence of S$^-$ responding typically shown by normal subjects when discriminative performance had stabilized. Figures 1B, C, and D show the records of three septal rats and illustrate the elevated level of septal responding in S$^-$ components. Another factor distinguishing septal and intact animals was that the lesioned subjects also emitted a higher response rate in S$^+$ components. This elevation primarily arose from the fact that septal animals developed a significantly higher rate during baseline training which was then sustained in S$^+$ components during discrimination training rather than from any lesion-induced change in the magnitude of behavioural contrast (Reynolds, 1961). However, the elevated S$^+$ response rate *per se* was not a causal factor in the nonreward persistence. When the baseline response rates of the septal and control subjects were equated by selecting intact animals with a high baseline rate, the effect of the lesion on S$^-$ responding was still present even though the septal and control rats emitted similar response rates in S$^+$ components (Dickinson, 1971).

The main question of interest is whether the pattern of septal persistence shown in Fig. 1 gives any indication of the type of processes disrupted by the lesion. Two basic within-session patterns of S$^-$ responding were shown by the septal animals. The first, illustrated in Figs 1B and C, was represented by a steady low rate of responding throughout S$^-$ components (points a and c) which remained relatively constant across successive components of the session. The S$^+$ and S$^-$ response rates were differentiated during the initial components of the session suggesting that the persistence was not due to a failure of inter-sessional retention. Also the abrupt change in response rate which occurred at transitions between the two types of components, except where there were occasional "run-through" effects (point b), indicates that the persistence did not arise from a gross failure of responding to come under the control of the programmed exteroceptive stimuli. This pattern of persistence is in general agreement with the hypothesis that septal damage actually affects some processes involved in reducing response output.

However, the implications of the second septal pattern, shown in Fig. 1D, for the interpretation of the persistence are more ambiguous. During the initial components of a session, there was little differentiation between the response rates in S$^+$ and S$^-$ components (point d). The S$^-$ response rate then progressively declined across successive components until, in the terminal components of the session, the septal animal exhibited a level of suppression comparable to that of an intact subject (point e). This is just the pattern of responding which would be expected if the lesion produced a deficit in the retention of the information about the contingencies associated with S⁻ components across the inter-sessional intervals. Thus, in spite of the magnitude and sustained nature of the deficit, it remains unclear whether the persistence results from the disturbance of a system directly involved in modulating the output of nonreinforced responses.

Having demonstrated septal persistence in a Go, No go discrimination, one way of investigating the type of underlying functional disturbance would be to compare the discriminative performance of septal and intact rats in a similar situation which does not require the animal to reduce response output under nonreward. This was done by running septal and normal rats in a discriminative procedure identical to that employed in the previous experiment except for the presence of an alternative response, a *switch* response. Performance of this response during an S⁻ component terminated the conditions associated with that component and produced the conditions associated with the S⁺ component for a fixed period of time. Thus an animal could show discriminative performance by increasing *switch* responding in S⁻ components without changing the rate of emission of the previously reinforced response. This situation bears considerable resemblance to the "advance" procedure reported by Honig and his colleagues (Chapter 2, this volume). If septal rats were found to emit a level of *switch* responding in S⁻ components comparable to that of controls, it would be difficult to argue that the lesion had disturbed any general mechanism concerned with the processing and storage of information about the withdrawal of reward.

Three septal and four control subjects were trained on a *mult* VI 45 sec VI 45 sec schedule until performance stabilized and were then switched to a *mult* VI 45 sec EXT schedule as in the previous experiment. Except for the presence of an extra lever in the chamber, the apparatus and the component stimuli, duration, and sequencing were identical to those employed in the previous experiment. A single response on this additional lever (a *switch* response) in an S⁻ component instituted a 20-sec *switch* period during both the baseline and discrimination sessions. During a *switch* period the stimuli associated with S⁺ components were presented and responses on the original lever reinforced according to the schedule of primary reinforcement associated with S⁺ components. After a *switch* period had elapsed, the stimuli and reinforcement conditions associated with S⁻ components were again presented. The timer determining the duration of the components continued to run during *switch* periods. If a *switch* period was instituted when there was less than 20 sec of the current S⁻ component duration to run, the *switch* period was terminated by the inter-component blackout when the programmed duration of the S⁻ component had elapsed. The emission of *switch* responses during S⁺

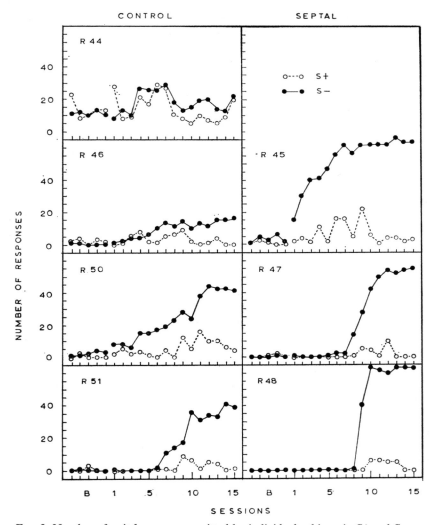

FIG. 2. Number of *switch* responses emitted by individual subjects in S+ and S− components during the last five baseline sessions (plotted against the points marked B on the abscissa) and all the discrimination sessions.

components and *switch* periods produced no change in the stimulus conditions or reinforcement schedules.

The discriminative performance of the subjects in terms of *switch* responding is illustrated in Fig. 2. This figure shows the number of *switch* responses emitted by individual subjects in S+ and S− components during the last five baseline sessions (plotted against the points marked B on the abscissa) and during the 15 discrimination sessions. The maximum possible number of *switch* responses per session in S⁻ components was 72. During the baseline sessions both groups maintained a low level of *switch* responding. However, when primary reinforcement was withheld in S⁻ components during the discrimination sessions, the emission of *switch* responses in these components increased above the level maintained in S⁺ components for all subjects except one control rat (R 44). The main feature of *switch* responding, though, was that all three septal animals emitted more *switch* response in S⁻ components during the terminal discrimination sessions than any of the controls. The mean number of *switch* responses emitted in S⁻ components over the last five discrimination sessions by the septal animals was significantly higher than that emitted by the three control subjects (R 46, R 50, and R 51) who showed discriminative performance in terms of *switch* responding (p < 0·05, two-tailed t-test). As there was little difference between the number of *switch* responses emitted by the septal and control subjects in S⁺ components, the difference in S⁻ components suggests that if the animal is not required to demonstrate discriminative performance by a response decrement, septal rats, if anything, show better discrimination on this successive procedure than intact rats. The septal deficit in adjustment to reward withdrawal appears to be limited to situations in which intact animals reduce their response output. Consequently, it would seem reasonable to assume that the septal deficit arises from the disturbance of a system directly involved in the control of such adjustments.

Before leaving this experiment one feature of *switch* responding, which will be of significance in discussing a later experiment, should be noted. Fig. 2 shows that there was considerable between-subject variance in the point at which animals who exhibited discriminative performance started to emit *switch* responses in S⁻ components. Two control animals (R 46 and R 50) and one septal (R 45) showed an increase in S⁻ *switch* responding during the initial discrimination sessions, whilst the remaining subjects (R 51, R 47, and R 48) showed a delayed development. As these latter subjects also emitted the lowest total number of *switch* responses during the baseline sessions, it appears that the point at which an animal will start to perform an alternative response depends upon the extent to which it has experienced the contingencies associated with this response previously.

IV. Theoretical Interpretations of Nonreward Persistence

Given that there are good reasons for believing that septal nonreward persistence is due to the disruption of a system directly related to the control of response output, a further question of importance concerns the extent to which the operation of such a system is limited to nonreward situations. Most previous accounts of septal dysfunctions (e.g. Gerbrandt, 1965; McCleary, 1966) treat nonreward persistence as an example of a more general disruption of the ability to reduce or withhold pre-potent responses under a number of different contingencies. These formulations typically explain the persistence by appealing to the destruction of some "inhibitory" mechanism which is involved in the control of general response output. The empirical basis for these general "inhibitory" theories is that large septal lesions as well as producing nonreward persistence result in a number of other changes in response output. Two of the most notable are the retarded acquisition of passive-avoidance behaviour (e.g. Kaada, *et al.*, 1962) and the enhanced acquisition of two-way active avoidance behaviour in a shuttle box (e.g. King 1958). However the pattern of deficit dissociation found in a number of recent studies, using anatomically discrete lesions within the septal nuclei and related structures, suggests that nonreward persistence may be mediated by the disruption of functional systems which are independent of those underlying the changes in active and passive avoidance.

A. Deficit Dissociations

The evidence for the dissociations between the various septal dysfunctions is fairly extensive. Donovick (1968) compared the effects of various discrete lesions within the septum on the acquisition of two-way discriminated avoidance and the reversal of a simultaneous-position discrimination. Whilst the enhanced avoidance was found following a wide range of restricted septal damage, only lesions involving destruction of the anterior part of the medial septal nucleus and the diagonal band of Broca resulted in the reversal deficit. Similar dissociations between position-habit reversals and active-avoidance acquisition have also arisen from the comparison of the behavioural effects of bilateral and unilateral lesions (Green and Schwartzbaum 1968; Hamilton, 1970; Hamilton, *et al.*, 1970). These studies all used position-habit reversal performance as an index of nonreward persistence. However, comparable dissociations occur when DRL schedule performance is employed. In two studies, MacDougall, Van Hoesen and Mitchell (MacDougall *et al.* 1969a; Van Hoesen *et al.*, 1969) compared the effects of lesions of the stria medullaris and habenular nuclei, representing the diencephalic projections of the posterior septum, with those of fornical damage. This latter tract carries, among other fibres, hippocampal afferents originating in the medial septal nucleus and associated structures. Whilst the destruction of both tracts enhanced active-avoidance acquisition to a similar degree as full septal damage, the stria medullaris-habenular damage resulted in less disturbance of DRL schedule performance than full fornical or septal destruction.

Thus, it appears that nonreward persistence depends upon insult to discrete anatomical systems within the septum and related structures. The enhanced avoidance performance, on the other hand, follows a much wider range of damage. The passive-avoidance deficit, like nonreward persistence, seems to be mediated by the destruction of localized septal structures. However, the sites of maximum effect for these two tasks differ. Lesions of the stria medullaris and habenular have the major effect on passive-avoidance acquisition whilst damage to the fornix produces little deficit (Van Hoesen, et al., 1969). This is the opposite pattern to that found in the case of DRL schedule performance (MacDougall, et al., 1969a). Similar dissociations between passive-avoidance acquisition and position-habit reversals have also been shown following restricted lesions within the septum itself (Hamilton, 1970; Hamilton, et al., 1970).

Two tentative conclusions can be drawn from the results of these dissociation studies. (1) There is some justification for the classification of the lesion-induced deficits in situations with as widely divergent task requirements as DRL schedules and reversal acquisition under the single category of "nonreward persistence". Both deficits appear to be mediated by the destruction of a common anatomical system which is, at least partially, represented within the medial septum and the diagonal band of Broca and involves septal projections to the hippocampus via the fimbria and fornix. The finding that prolonged extinction also occurs after discrete medial lesions (Clody and Carlton, 1969) provides a rationale for including this septal deficit in the same category. (2) Nonreward persistence appears to arise from the destruction of a functional system which is independent of those mediating other septal changes in response output. Consequently, an adequate account of septal nonreward persistence is not required to explain the other behavioural changes which lie outside that category. In fact, any theoretical account is inadequate to the extent that it fails to take cognizance of the independence of the different behavioural dysfunctions.

The pattern of dissociations revealed by the above studies is also of significance in determining the critical features of the situations which give rise to nonreward persistence. The system underlying the dysfunction must be involved in the regulation of behaviour in such diverse tasks as DRL schedule performance, simple extinction, and habit reversal, but only minimally involved in the control of responding in active and passive avoidance. The similarity of the response changes found in simple extinction and passive-avoidance learning suggests that the differentiation is not related to the actual nature of the motor or response modification required by the task. Both demand that the animal stops performing a pre-established response. This point is made even more strongly with respect to septal lesions in general by a comparison of the performance of septal animals on DRL and free-operant avoidance schedules. Both situations require the animal to space its responses in time to achieve optimal performance, and yet septal damage decreases efficiency in the appetitively-motivated task whilst increasing it in the aversively-motivated one (Morgan and Mitchell, 1969; Sodetz, 1970). It might be argued that the critical feature of procedures producing nonreward persistence is that they simply involve the removal of the contingencies under which responding was acquired and maintained. However, another dissociation result suggests that this is not so. Van Hoesen, *et al.* (1969) showed that simple, massed extinction of a two-way active avoidance response was prolonged by stria medullaris-habenular damage as much as by full septal lesions. The fact that the former lesion has a minimal effect on the maintenance of DRL schedule performance (MacDougall, *et al.*, 1969a) suggests that this extinction effect is part of the deficit pattern represented by the enhanced active-avoidance acquisition rather than nonreward persistence.

If neither the nature of the required response change nor the withdrawal of *general* response-maintaining contingencies is the critical feature of situations producing nonreward persistence, the next most obvious factor distinguishing these situations is the type of event employed to establish the response, positive reinforcement. Thus, it is possible that nonreward persistence results from the disturbance of a system which selectively mediates response changes when positive reinforcement or reward is withheld.

B. NONREWARD PERSISTENCE AND FRUSTRATION

A theory of instrumental response changes under nonreward has been proposed by Amsel (1958). This theory is formulated within the terms of a general two-process theory of instrumental conditioning. It assumes that instrumental behaviour is mediated by a learned expectancy of reward, as described by Spence (1956), and that this expectancy is the mechanism by which incentive variables come to affect instrumental performance. The critical feature of the theory is the proposal that, if nonreward occurs in the presence of this expectancy (frustrative nonreward), a transitory, unconditional emotional response, frustration, occurs. Further, it is assumed that the occurrence of this response plays a causal role in controlling response output under nonreward. As frustration theory makes special reference to just those situations in which septal nonreward persistence has been found, it is possible that septal damage affects instrumental response output in these situations by altering the magnitude of this primary emotional response to nonreward. This general hypothesis bears some similarities to traditional accounts of limbic function (Papez, 1937) which have assumed that the septum represents part of the neural substrate of emotional behaviour, but differs in suggesting that there are functional systems within the septum which mediate emotional responsiveness to the restricted range of events defined as frustrative nonreward.

Two main properties are usually ascribed to primary frustration; firstly, it is an aversive state, and secondly, it is assumed to represent a condition of heightened general drive. Amsel (Chapter 11, this volume) has maintained an interference or avoidance theory of response reduction under nonreward by assuming that conditioned, anticipatory frustration elicits response tendencies which compete with the instrumental behaviour. Although some elegant experiments described by Amsel (Chapter 11) have demonstrated that the association of compatible and incompatible response tendencies with frustrative nonreward can appropriately enhance or attenuate response persistence, it remains unclear whether the development of alternative-response tendencies plays a significant causal role in mediating simple response decrements or modifications under nonreward. If a hypothesis of septal action can be stated within the terms of frustration theory without making specific assumptions about the actual nature of the mechanisms mediating response decrements, it would seem reasonable to leave this question open for the present. There is good evidence that frustrative nonreward is an aversive event on criteria which are independent of any suppressive effects; animals will learn a response in order to escape from frustrative-nonreward conditions and from stimuli which have been paired with such conditions (e.g. Daly, 1969a, b). Consequently, the response decrement which occurs following the withdrawal of reward can be subsumed under a general, empirical, negative law of effect stating that the presentation of an aversive event contingent upon a response decreases the probability of the subsequent emission of that response. If septal damage attenuates the magnitude of the primary emotional reaction elicited by frustrative nonreward for a given level of reward expectancy, the aversive consequences of emitting nonrewarded responses should be reduced for septal animals. The persistence could then be understood in terms of a general relationship between the magnitude of response suppression and the degree of aversiveness of a response-contingent event.

V. Frustration Attenuation

The idea that septal damage alters the magnitude of the emotional reaction to nonreward is not novel. Gray (1970) has suggested that the behavioural effects of nonreward are mediated by the septo-hippocampal system involved in the elaboration of the hippocampal theta rhythm and identified by the dissociation studies as being crucial for septal nonreward persistence.

It follows from this hypothesis that lesions of the medial septal area should attenuate the behavioural effects of frustrative nonreward. Although in a series of ingenious experiments Gray has shown that septal stimulation at certain critical frequencies can simulate and block the effects of frustrative nonreward, the only direct evidence of the attenuating effect of septal damage comes from a study in which he compared the magnitude of the partial reinforcement extinction effect (PRE) exhibited by intact rats with that of animals lesioned in the medial septal area. Whilst showing increased persistence in extinction following CRF training, the septal animals exhibited a reduced PRE. This finding is in general agreement with the results predicted by Amsel's (1958) theory of the PRE on the assumption that the lesion attenuates the magnitude of primary frustration.

In spite of the significance of this finding, more compelling evidence that the persistence is causally associated with an attenuation of frustration would come from the demonstration that septal damage decreases the aversiveness of frustrative nonreward. As the performance of the *switch* response in the previous experiment permitted the rats to escape from the conditions associated with S⁻ components, it might be thought that the higher septal *switch* responding demonstrated that septal animals in fact found the frustrative-nonreward conditions associated with those components more aversive. However, the *switch* response also served to institute conditions associated with S⁺ components, and the septal effect could equally well have arisen through a change in the positive reinforcement associated with S⁺ stimuli and the increased overall frequency of primary reinforcement as through a change in the negative reinforcement associated with escape from the S⁻ components. Rilling, *et al.* (1969) and Terrace (Chapter 4, this volume) have demonstrated that pigeons, trained on a successive discrimination, will acquire an escape response which terminates the S⁻ component conditions and substitutes a time-out period (TO) without altering the overall frequency of primary reinforcement. As the TO has never been associated with primary reinforcement and as the animal does not perform the instrumental response in its presence, it can be argued that the TO is in some sense "neutral" and that the reinforcement for the escape response is provided solely by the termination of the conditions in which the response is performed (Leitenberg, 1965). Since the first experiment of this paper demonstrated that septal rats show sustained persistence in S⁻ components, it was decided to measure any lesion-induced changes in the aversiveness of frustrative nonreward using a similar successive-discrimination procedure.

The pattern of development of S⁻ *switch* responding in the previous experiment indicated that the point at which rats started to emit an alternative response during the acquisition of a discrimination depended upon their prior experience of the contingencies associated with such a response during baseline sessions. In order to ensure that all subjects received such experience in this experiment, a two-lever chamber was used and the side of the response which was rewarded by primary reinforcement was randomly varied across successive components. For any given component the side of the reinforced lever was signalled by a discriminative stimulus, and thus, during the baseline sessions, the subjects were required to learn what was essentially a successive Go; Go discrimination. As responding on the nonreinforced lever in any given component instituted a TO, it was assumed that errors made during the acquisition of this discrimination would ensure that the subjects had been exposed to the contingency associated with the nonreinforced lever before reward for responding on the reinforced lever was withdrawn in S^- components. Also, the response requirement for TO institution was increased on a fixed-ratio schedule to test whether the emission of responses on the nonreinforced lever was under the control of this contingency.

A. Method

The subjects were trained in an operant chamber equipped with two retractable levers and a 3W houselight mounted in the roof. A small circular stimulus panel was mounted in the front wall just above each lever. At any given time one of these two panels could be illuminated by either a constant or a flashing light (2·5 Hz). After magazine training, the subjects were taught to press both levers on a CRF schedule. They were then reinforced for responses on each lever on a VI 15 sec and a VI 30 sec schedule over the next two sessions. During this pretraining only one lever was inserted at a time.

The subjects were then introduced to the general conditions which held throughout the rest of the experiment. Each daily session consisted of the successive presentation of 12 S1 and 12 S2 components in the same semirandom orders as used in the previous experiments. During each component the houselight was on, both levers inserted, and the stimulus panel above one of the levers illuminated. In S1 components this panel was illuminated by the constant light, and in S2 components by the flashing light. For any given component the stimulus panel above the left-and right-hand levers had an equal probability of being illuminated. A response on the lever beneath the illuminated panel in any given component will be referred to as a *sched R* and a response on the other lever as a *TO R*. As in the previous experiments, the duration of each component was 120 sec, and successive components were separated by a 10-sec blackout during which both levers were retracted and the house and stimulus panel lights were out.

*Sched R*s were reinforced by primary reinforcement. *TO R*s in either component instituted a TO of 20 sec during which both levers were retracted and the relevant stimulus-panel light was out. These TOs were differentiated from the inter-component blackouts by the fact that the houselight remained on. After a TO had elapsed, the conditions were returned to those of the component in which the *TO R* had occurred; both levers were reinserted and the component stimulus panel again illuminated. The timer determining the duration of the component continued to run during a TO. If a TO was instituted when there was less than 20 sec of the programmed duration of the current component to run, the TO was terminated by the inter-component blackout when the programmed component duration had elapsed. Reinforcements set up but not delivered before the institution of a TO or before the end of the component were cancelled.

The experiment was divided into eight stages. The schedules of primary reinforcement for *sched R*s and the schedules of TO institution for *TO R*s during the successive stages of the experiment are presented in Table I. Table I also shows the number of sessions for which each stage was in force. Initially the subjects were given pre-operative baseline training

TABLE I

Schedules of response contingencies

Stage	*sched R*s primary reinforcement		*TO R*s TO institution	Sessions
	S⁺	S⁻		
1	VI 45	VI 45	FR 1	20
2	surgery and post-operative recovery			
3	VI 45	VI 45	FR 1	18
4	VI 45	EXT	FR 1	28
5	VI 45	EXT	FR 2	1
6	VI 45	EXT	FR 3	1
7	VI 45	EXT	FR 5	5
8	VI 45	EXT	FR 10	4

(Stage 1) during which *sched R*s were reinforced in both components on independent VI 45 sec schedules. A single *TO R* in either component instituted a TO. The subjects were then assigned to a septal ($N = 4$) and a control group ($N = 4$) for surgery (Stage 2). Following post-operative recovery, further baseline training (Stage 3) was administered under the same conditions as held in Stage 1. During Stages 1 and 3 the subjects had to learn to respond on the lever beneath the illuminated stimulus panel irrespective of its side of presentation. During discrimination acquisition (Stage 4) and all subsequent stages, *sched R*s were no longer reinforced in S1 components for half the subjects in each group, whilst the schedule of reinforcement for *sched R*s in S2 components remained VI 45 sec. For the remaining subjects the opposite relationship was established. Components in which *sched R*s were extinguished will be referred to as S⁻ components and those in which *sched R*s were reinforced as S⁺ components. After the discrimination had been established, the response requirement for instituting TOs was progressively increased from FR 1 to FR 10 during Stages 5 to 8. Since in these stages a *TO R* could be immediately followed by a reinforced *sched R*, there was a possibility that *TO R*s might be "superstitiously" reinforced. To minimize this possibility a changeover delay of 4 sec between *TO R*s and reinforcement of *sched R*s was programmed during Stages 5 to 8.

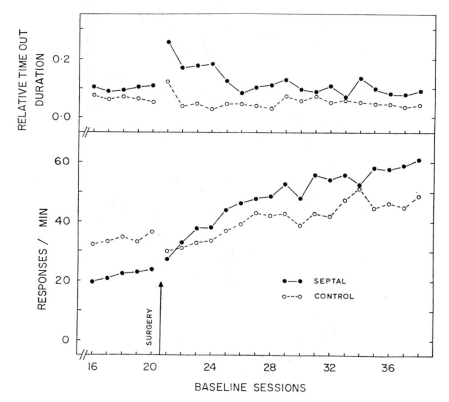

FIG. 3. Mean relative TO duration (upper panel) and mean *sched R* rate (lower panel) during the last five pre-operative (Stage 1; Sessions 16–20) and all the post-operative baseline sessions (Stage 3; Sessions 21–38).

B. RESULTS AND DISCUSSION

Figure 3 illustrates the terminal pre-operative (Stage 1) and the post-operative baseline performance (Stage 3) of both groups. As there was no difference between the performance of either group in the two components during these nondifferential stages, the results have been averaged across the two components. The upper panel of Fig. 3 shows the proportion of the programmed component duration spent in TO (relative TO duration), and the lower panel the *sched R* rate. In calculating all response rates the time during which TOs were instituted was discounted. Although the general pattern of post-operative *sched R* rate change was similar to that

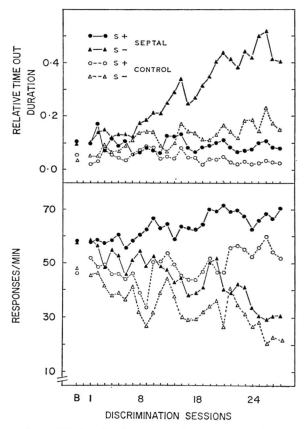

FIG. 4. Mean relative TO duration (upper panel) and mean *sched R* rate (lower panel) in S+ and S− components during the discrimination sessions (Stage 4). The values plotted against point B on the abscissa represent the terminal baseline performance averaged over the last five post-operative baseline sessions (Stage 3).

found in the previous experiments, the difference between the two groups was not significant in this case. There were also no significant differences between the relative TO durations of the two groups during the baseline sessions. Although Fig. 3 shows that the surgical procedure and post-operative recovery period produced a small transient increase in the relative TO duration, the lesion did not significantly affect the magnitude of this increase.

The performance of the two groups during the acquisition of the successive discrimination (Stage 4) is shown in Fig. 4. The values plotted against point B on the abscissa represent the terminal baseline performance averaged over the last five post-operative sessions (Stage 3). The withdrawal of reinforcement for responding in S$^-$ components resulted in a separation of *sched R* response rates in S$^+$ and S$^-$ components. The development of this discrimination was accompanied by a progressive and systematic increase in the relative TO duration in S$^-$ components (F = 7·39, df = 27/162, p < 0·005) to a level above that maintained in the baseline sessions and in the S$^+$ components during the discrimination sessions. On the other hand, there was no evidence for a systematic change in the relative TO duration in S$^+$ components (F < 1) from the baseline level for either group as the discrimination developed. It is unlikely that the increase in S$^-$ relative TO duration could have been a fortuitous consequence of an increase in general activation due to the withdrawal of reinforcement on *TO* responding. Such an interpretation would imply that the *TO R* was not controlled by its outcome, and consequently that changes in the response requirement should not affect its output. Figure 5 shows the mean *TO R* rate as a function of the value of the fixed-ratio response requirement. The response rate for the FR 1 value represents the mean *TO R* rate over the last five sessions of discrimination acquisition (Stage 4). The rates plotted against the other fixed-ratio values represent the mean *TO R* rates over the sessions for which that particular response requirement was in force (Stages 5–8). As Fig. 5 suggests, the *TO R* rate in S$^-$ components increased as the response requirement was raised (F = 8·78, df = 4/24, p < 0·005) demonstrating that the emission of the response was affected by changes in the associated contingency.

The main question of interest in this experiment concerns the manner in which septal damage affected performance during the acquisition of the discrimination. Although Fig. 4 suggests that the lesion increased the *sched R* rate in both S$^+$ and S$^-$ components, neither of these differences was significant. At first sight, the absence of a septal enhancement of S$^-$ *sched R* output appears to be at variance with the persistence shown in the first experiment, and to suggest that the lesions were not effective in producing the deficit of interest. However, the presence of the TO con-

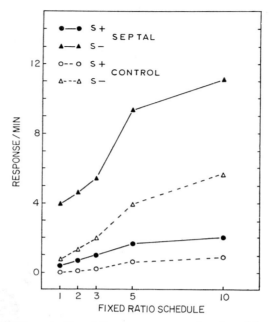

FIG. 5. Mean *TO R* rate in S$^+$ and S$^-$ components as a function of the response require-ment for TO institution.

tingency makes it impossible to draw this conclusion from a comparison of the two experiments. The elevated S$^-$ response rate of the septal animals in the first experiment might have been primarily due to an increase in response output during those periods of S$^-$ components in which *TO R*s would have occurred if such an effective response had been available to the animal. Thus, in the present experiment, the programming of a TO con-tingency may have obscured the septal nonreward persistence.

The most important and surprising finding was that septal animals developed a higher relative TO duration than the controls in S$^-$ com-ponents (F $= 6.32$, df $= 1/6$, p < 0.05) but not in S$^+$ components (F < 1) during the acquisition of the discrimination (Stage 4). This effect is demon-strated clearly in the upper panel of Fig. 4. The absence of a significant difference between the *sched R* rate of the two groups in either component suggests that the septal enhancement of S$^-$ *TO* responding was not secon-dary to a change in *sched* responding. As a *TO R* can be assumed to rep-resent an escape response, reinforced by the cessation of the S$^-$ conditions, the most obvious implication of this result is that septal damage, contrary to the frustration-attenuation hypothesis, actually increases the aversive-ness of frustrative nonreward. Consequently, the nonreward persistence of septal animals cannot be explained by appealing to a decrement in the aversive consequences of emitting a nonreinforced response. In fact, we are apparently left with the surprising conclusion that septal animals persist in performing responses that produce an outcome whose aversiveness appears to be augmented by the lesion.

VI. Frustration Potentiation

By ascribing drive-enhancing as well as aversive properties to frustrative nonreward (Amsel, 1958), frustration theory provides a way of resolving this paradox. In complete contrast to the attenuation hypothesis, Thomas, et al. (1968) and Caplan (1970) have proposed that septal damage actually enhances the reaction to frustrative nonreward. In both cases, the basis of this suggestion comes from an analysis of the performance of septal animals on DRL schedules. On this potentiation hypothesis, the higher response rate and decreased efficiency of septal animals on these schedules result from a lesion-induced enhancement of the transitory, general-drive increment which, according to frustration theory, should occur following the emission of a nonreinforced response and should act to energize the dominant instrumental response, leverpressing. In agreement with this interpretation, experiments of Simmons (reported by Thomas, et al., 1968, and MacDougall, et al. (1969b) have shown that the main factor differentiating the steady-state performance of septal and normal rats on DRL schedules is the higher response rate of the lesioned subjects following the emission of a nonreinforced response. Similarly, Caplan (1970) found that septal rats displayed a greater increment in response rate on a low-valued DRL schedule with the introduction of partial reinforcement of inter-response times (IRTs) which met the schedule criterion. Further, the lesioned rats, unlike the controls, emitted a higher response rate after nonreinforced criterion IRTs than after reinforced criterion IRTs when the overall probability of reinforcement was low. Such a result would be expected if septal damage augmented the energizing effects of frustrative nonreward on subsequent behaviour.

The DRL schedule, by allowing the continued partial reinforcement of the instrumental response and the free emission of responses immediately following nonreinforcement, provides a situation in which the energizing effects of the enhanced-drive level could be expected to predominate over the suppressive effects of increased aversiveness. However, the predicted effects of enhanced frustration on persistence in other nonreward situations, such as simple extinction, are very much dependent upon the specific parameters of the task. As frustration is a transitory response, the drive effects should only be evident in extinction when the opportunities to perform the instrumental response are massed. There is evidence for response-

II

sustaining effects of frustration in free-operant (e.g. Thompson *et al.,* 1963) and massed, discrete-trial extinction (e.g. Sheffield 1950) and it is significant that septal nonreward persistence in simple extinction has typically been demonstrated either in a free-operant situation (Schwarzbaum, *et al.,* 1964) or in a runway with massed trials (Raphelson, *et al.,* 1964; Winocur and Mills, 1969). The only discrete-trial study failing to demonstrate a septal effect used relatively spaced trials in extinction (Wolfe, *et al.,* 1967). If the carry-over of the drive-enhancing effects of frustrative nonreward between successive extinction trials is prevented, then according to the potentiation hypothesis septal animals should in fact show more rapid adjustment to nonreward. This is because the effect of the augmented aversiveness of frustrative nonreward for the septal animals will no longer be counteracted by the change in general-drive level. One way of preventing the carry-over effects would be to employ a single, Go; No go alternation task in which nonreinforced trials are separated by reinforced ones for in this situation any modulation of the drive-enhancing effects of frustrative nonreward will only affect performance on the succeeding reinforced trial. In agreement with this argument Carlson and Norman (1971) have, in fact, shown that septal mice acquire a single Go; No go alternation in an operant situation more rapidly than controls. The lesion advantage was due to both a decreased latency on reinforced trials and an increased latency on nonreinforced trials.

A potentiation account of the simultaneous-discrimination reversal deficit is similar to that employed for the prolonged extinction. It has to assume that, during the initial stages of the reversal, the nonreinforcement accompanying an incorrect response differentially enhances, on the next trial, the tendency to perform the response acquired during acquisition thus increasing the probability of further errors. Although this proposal may seem somewhat implausible, the elicitation of primary frustration does appear to increase competing-response tendencies selectively during the reversal stage. Bruning, *et al.* (1971) have demonstrated that if rats are frustrated just before the choice point in a T-maze on reversal trials, they show more errors than reversed but not frustrated subjects. Significantly, these reversed-frustrated subjects also emit more errors than subjects similarly frustrated during simple discrimination training. Such inter-trial disruptive effects of primary frustration could have been operative in most of the experiments showing a septal reversal deficit. In cases where the inter-trial interval has been reported, the values have been uniformly short. For instance, Schwartzbaum and Donovick (1968) used a discrete-trial, operant procedure with no programmed inter-trial interval, whilst Hamilton, *et al.* (1970) only employed a 20-sec interval in a T-maze study.

In view of this evidence it was decided that a direct measure of the effect of septal damage on the drive-enhancing effects of frustrative nonreward should be made. The increased vigour of responding following nonreward has been termed the frustration effect (FE) (Amsel, 1958). Typically the FE is measured in a double runway in which the omission of reward in the first goal box results in faster running in the second alley (e.g. Amsel and Roussel, 1952). However, as Wagner (1969) has pointed out, the double runway technique of measuring the FE does not permit the dissociation of any nonspecific motivating properties of frustrative nonreward from its aversive properties since the measured response involves locomotion away from the nonreward situation. As the explanation of septal persistence offered by the frustration-potentiation hypothesis rests crucially upon the *general drive-enhancing* effects of nonreward, a situation was required which minimized the possibility of interpreting any lesion effects in terms of other properties of frustrative nonreward. A free-operant analogue of the double runway (e.g. Davenport and Thompson, 1965) seemed to meet this requirement in that it is not clear how an increase in response rate following nonreward can represent escape from a frustrating situation.

In the above discussion, the experiments of Simmons and of Caplan (1970), showing an enhanced septal sensitivity to nonreward on DRL schedules, were interpreted in terms of augmented frustration. However, the results are open to an alternative explanation which makes no reference to the emotional consequences of nonreward. Reinforced responses are more likely to follow a reinforcement than a nonreinforced response on DRL schedules (see Kramer and Rilling, 1970, for review of evidence). This finding can be interpreted in terms of the discriminative control acquired by reinforcement over spaced responding on these types of schedules and the resultant generalization decrement in this control which follows a nonreinforced response. If septal damage increases the degree of discriminative control acquired by reinforcement over the appropriate response pattern relative to other stimuli, the higher septal response rate following nonreinforcement could be due to the greater generalization decrement suffered by these animals. Staddon (1970) has pointed out the possible role of discriminative control acquired by reinforcement in frustration-like effects within the wider context of general FE studies. In the present experiment a special procedure was used to minimize the role of such generalization decrements. Rats were trained on a successive discrimination in which they responded on one lever at a relatively high rate, maintained by a fixed-ratio schedule, in the presence of one stimulus (FR component), and on a second lever at a relatively low rate, maintained by a fixed-interval schedule, in the presence of another stimulus (FI component). In order to minimize the control acquired by reinforcement over response rate, the delivery of reinforcement was equally often followed by the component which sustained a high rate (FR) and by the component which sustained a low rate (FI). As a result, the delivery of reinforcement was not predictive of the subsequent response rate. Furthermore, an attempt was made to determine whether reinforcement came to control post-reinforcement behaviour in general by measuring the extent to which reinforcement omission would disrupt the discrimination between the two bars in the succeeding component.

A. METHOD

The experimental procedure will only be briefly outlined in this presentation. A more detailed description of the pretraining procedure is available elsewhere (Dickinson, 1971).

The subjects were trained in a two-lever operant chamber with a 3 W houselight mounted in the roof and a recessed magazine positioned centrally between the two levers. A small circular stimulus panel was positioned in the front wall just above each lever. These panels could be illuminated concurrently by either a constant or a flashing (2·5 Hz) 3 W light.

Septal (N = 4) and control subjects (N = 4) were trained on a two-component, successive, Go-left; Go-right discrimination in which reinforcement was programmed for responding on opposite levers in the two components. In each component, responses on the reinforced lever will be referred to as *sched R*s, and responses on the nonreinforced lever as *ext R*s. In one component of the discrimination both stimulus panels were illuminated by the constant light, and in the other component by the flashing light. Thus, for example, a given rat had to learn to respond on the left-hand lever for reinforcement when both panels were illuminated by the constant light, and on the right-hand lever when the stimulus on both panels was a flashing light. The side of the lever on which responses were reinforced and the type of stimulus were counterbalanced across the subjects in each group for a given component.

In one component *sched R*s were reinforced on an FR 10 schedule (FR component), and in the other component on an FI 60 sec schedule (FI component). One reinforcement was given per component presentation and each component presentation was terminated by the delivery of this reinforcement. The emission of *ext R*s had no programmed consequences. Successive components were separated by a 6-sec inter-component interval during which the stimulus and houselights were out, the magazine illuminated and response on either bar had no programmed consequences. Each daily session started with two alternations of the FR and FI components followed by 36 presentations of each component in a semi-random order.

The experiment was divided into two stages. First of all the subjects were given 15 baseline sessions during which every component was terminated by reinforcement and performance stabilized. In the second stage eight reinforcement-omission sessions were administered. During these sessions the delivery of reinforcement was omitted on a semi-random basis following half of the FR components which were immediately followed by an FI component. Thus, the effect of omitting reinforcement for responding in an FR component on the subsequent emission of *sched* and *ext* Rs in an FI component could be measured. The inter-component intervals in which reinforcement was omitted were otherwise identical to those accompanied by reinforcement. FI components programmed to be preceded by nonreinforced FR components during the reinforcement-omission sessions will be referred to as N components, and those programmed to be preceded by reinforced FR components will be referred to as R components.

B. Results and Discussion

The subjects in both groups maintained a much higher *sched R* rate in FR components than in FI components during both the baseline and reinforcement-omission sessions. Thus the requirement of the experimental design that reinforcement should be equally often followed by a high and low rate of responding was met. There was no significant difference between the *sched R* rate of the two groups in FR components during either stage of the experiment, and subsequent presentation will only concern performance in R and N components.

Figure 6 illustrates the *sched R* rate of both groups in N and R components during the baseline and reinforcement-omission sessions. Although the septal animals exhibited a significantly higher response rate during the initial baseline sessions, the difference declined with further training. The mean *sched R* rate of the two groups over the last five baseline sessions did not differ significantly ($p > 0.10$, two-tailed t-test) and both groups had equivalent baseline performance levels from which to measure the effects of reinforcement omission. The *ext R* rate is shown in Fig. 7. A comparison of Figs. 6 and 7 shows that the subjects maintained a good discrimination between the two levers in N and R components by the end of baseline training (note the difference in response rate scales in Figs. 6 and 7).

Although there was no difference between the *sched R* rate in N and R components when both were preceded by reinforcement, the omission of reinforcement preceding N components in the test sessions produced a significant increase in response rate in N components above the level maintained in R components ($F = 39.42$, $df = 1/6$, $p < 0.001$). Figure 6 shows that the magnitude of the effect is considerable and that the rate increase occurs on the first sessions and is sustained thereafter. The overall *sched R* rate was analysed into the latency of the first response and the response

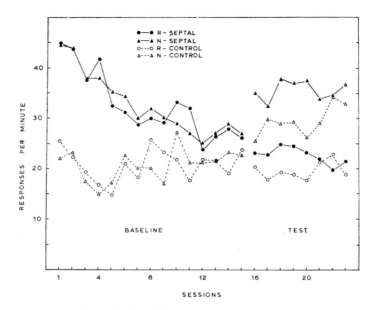

FIG. 6. Mean *sched R* rate in R and N components during the baseline (Sessions 1–15) and reinforcement-omission stages (Sessions 16–23).

rate over the period from the first response to the end of the component (running rate). The effect of reinforcement omission on the overall *sched R* rate was due to a joint change in both these measures. Unlike *sched* responding, the *ext R* rate was unaffected by reinforcement omission (see Fig. 7). In view of this finding it is unlikely that reinforcement-omission effect was due to a generalization decrement in the stimulus control of *sched* responding. The discriminative performance on the two levers bore the same relationship to the presentation of prior reinforcement as did the emission of the *sched R* rate appropriate to the given component. Consequently, if the *sched R* rate had come under control of reinforcement-associated stimuli, so should the differential performance on the two levers. Under these circumstances the effects of reinforcement omission should not have been manifested solely by a change in *sched R* performance, and an elevation of *ext R* rate in N components would also have been expected. Consequently, it would seem appropriate to attribute the increase in *sched R* output in N components to a frustration-produced increase in general drive level.

In spite of the general sensitivity of *sched R* rate to reinforcement omission, the lesion did not significantly alter the magnitude of the effect ($F < 1$). There were also no significant lesion effects in performance in N

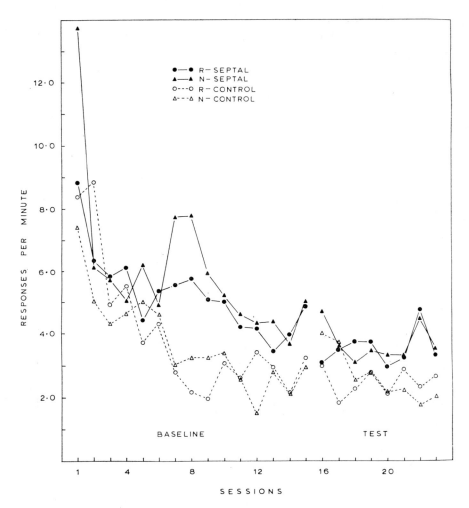

Fɪɢ. 7. Mean *ext R* rate in R and N components during the baseline (Sessions 1–15) and reinforcement-omission stages (Sessions 16–23).

and R components in terms of the latency of the first response or the running rate. The similarity of the reaction of septal and control subjects to reinforcement omission is more convincingly demonstrated when the relative rates are considered. Fig. 8 shows the mean number of *sched R*s emitted in successive 10-sec segments of the fixed interval following reinforcement (R components) and reinforcement omission (N components) expressed as a percentage of the total number of *sched R*s emitted

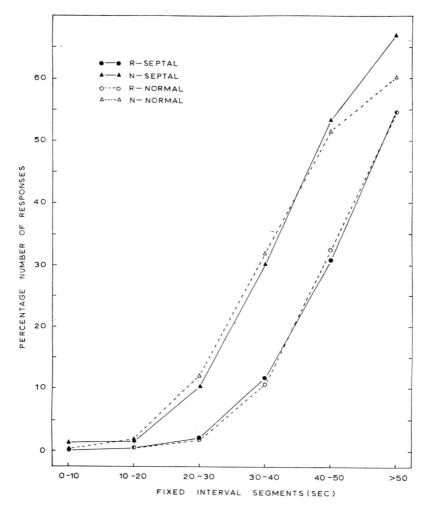

Fig. 8. Mean percentage number of *sched R*s emitted in successive segments of R and N components averaged over the reinforcement-omission sessions.

following reinforcement (R components) per session and averaged over the eight reinforcement-omission sessions. Not only is the overall relative magnitude of the effect similar for the two groups but so is the distribution of the enhanced response output within the fixed interval.

The absence of a significant effect of the lesion on the magnitude of the omission effect provides no support for the hypothesis that nonreward persistence results from a septal enhancement of the drive-incrementing effects of frustrative nonreward. In fact the similarity of the overall relative magnitude and pattern of rate increase produced by reinforcement omission suggests that the energizing properties of frustrative nonreward are equivalent for septal and intact rats. However, this conclusion should be qualified by noting a feature of the experimental design which might have masked an important lesion effect. It is possible that septal damage does in fact enhance the immediate, primary reaction to frustrative nonreward sufficiently to produce perseveration, and that, with the decay of this reaction across time, the levels of frustration sustained by the septal and intact subjects converge. The nature of the schedule used in the N and R components makes it unlikely that a *sched R* measure would have been sensitive to any such immediate and transitory post-omission differences. Assuming that the post-reinforcement pause on a fixed-interval schedule is due to the presence of a low habit strength in the initial segments, then a transitory increase in drive level during these segments would not have been detected by measures of instrumental performance. By the time that the habit strength had gained sufficient magnitude to support responding, the difference between the frustrative-drive level of the two groups could have disappeared. This argument suggests that the effect of septal damage on the FE should be measured using a schedule which maintains responding in the immediate post-omission period; however, since the lesion alters the steady-state performance on variable-interval schedules (as shown in the first experiment), the nature of the appropriate schedule is not immediately apparent.

VII. Concluding Comments

As septal damage did not enhance the FE, the nonreward persistence of septal rats still remains unexplained and paradoxical in view of the evidence that the lesion increases the aversiveness of frustrative nonreward. Although the use of alternative procedures for measuring the FE may provide evidence for the potentiation hypothesis, in the absence of such data it is probably worth speculating about other accounts which might reconcile the results of the experiments reported in this chapter with the basic phenomenon of nonreward persistence.

As was mentioned earlier, frustration theory (see Amsel, Chapter 11, this volume) has usually assumed an interference or avoidance theory of response reduction under nonreward. In this type of theory an important component of the "inhibitory" mechanism is the process by which animals come to anticipate the occurrence of an aversive goal event, such as nonreward, during the performance of the instrumental responses which compose the behavioural sequence leading to that event. It is this anticipatory mechanism which accounts for the emission of competing responses at the appropriate temporal and spatial location in the behavioural sequence so that interference with the instrumental responses can occur. It has usually been assumed that this anticipatory process involves two mechanisms (Amsel, 1958). The first is the classical conditioning of a fractional, anticipatory component of the unconditional response elicited by the goal event to accompanying stimuli, and the second, the primary stimulus generalization of this anticipatory response to stimuli present during the performance of the instrumental behaviour itself. From this model persistence would be predicted if the lesion selectively disrupted either of the processes mediating the anticipation of an aversive event.

There is some evidence that septal damage may affect both these mechanisms in cases where the aversive goal event is electric shock. Duncan (1971) gave rats with septal cannulae pairings of a stimulus and foot-shock following injections of either procaine or saline. When the effects of the procaine had worn off, the amount of conditioned suppression of an operant response produced by the stimulus was measured. He found that the subjects who had received the stimulus-shock pairing whilst under septal procain showed considerably less suppression than controls and interpreted this finding as evidence for a septal disturbance of the mechanism mediating anticipatory aversive conditioning. Another study suggests that septal damage might also alter the generalization of the anticipatory response. Thomas, et al. (1968) reported an experiment by Thomas, Simmons, and Slotnick in which they studied in relative detail the septal pattern of response reduction in a passive-avoidance task. Having been trained to respond in a runway for food reward, the rats were given one trial in which an electric shock was administered as soon as they made contact with the food. Analysis of the response latencies on the first post-shock trial showed that the lesion decreased the latency to reach the goal box without affecting the latency to start eating. On the basis of this result, Thomas, et al., (1968) suggested that septal damage results in a steepening of the avoidance gradient.

Given that the lesion has a similar effect in cases where the aversive goal event is frustrative nonreward, then nonreward persistence would be expected even if the ablation increases the magnitude of the primary reaction to nonreward. Although the dissociation studies considered previously indicated that the effects of septal damage on response reduction under shock (passive avoidance) and frustrative nonreward (nonreward persistence) are mediated by anatomically differentiated systems, there is no reason why these systems should not perform similar functions in the control of behaviour by different primary aversive events. Unfortunately, it is not clear at present how far the parallel between the effects of septal damage on behaviour under the control of shock and frustrative nonreward extends beyond the case of response suppression to that of the escape and avoidance paradigms. The escape experiment indicated that the lesion increases escape from frustrative nonreward, whilst Gotsick, et al., (1971) have reported a septal deficit in the performance of an operant response mediating escape from foot-shock. But the authors themselves noted that the septal deficit may have been due to a greater incompatibility between the septal unconditional motor response to foot-shock and the required instrumental response rather than to a change in learning ability or motivation. Septal damage generally enhances shock-motivated avoidance and, at present, it is not known what effect the lesion has on the avoidance of frustrative nonreward.

A full two-process conditioning account of the extinction of appetitively-motivated responses would seem to require that the expectancy of reward decreases concurrently with the reduction of instrumental responding by the frustration mechanism when reward is withdrawn. Such a change is required if this type of theory is to explain the apparent changes in the effects of nonreward with extended exposure (e.g. Amsel and Ward, 1965). In Chapter 11, Amsel suggests that an actual "inhibitory" process only operates during the reduction of the strength of expectancies established by "pure" classical conditioning, and it is possible that septal damage disturbs the proper functioning of such an inhibitory process in the case of reward expectancy. Within this context it is significant that Thomas (Chapter 14) proposes that septal structures might be involved in mediating the effects of the conditioned inhibitors demonstrated in his hypothalamic conditioning experiments. If it is assumed that septal damage retards the reduction of reward expectancies following the withdrawal of reinforcement, then the increased escape behaviour shown by septal animals can be reconciled with the unchanged magnitude of the FE.

The strength of primary frustration is usually assumed to be a positive function of reward expectancy, and as a result the FE provides a possible indirect measure of the magnitude of this expectancy. Evidence from studies using this measure indicates that relatively high-density partial reinforcement such as 50%, maintains levels of reward expectancy comparable to that of continuous reinforcement (Hug, 1970). On the basis of this finding it can be argued that, in the FE experiment, the shift from 100% reinforcement of responding in the FR components during the baseline sessions to 75% reinforcement during the reinforcement-omission sessions should not have caused intact animals to decrease their expectancy of reward in those components. So if the only effect of the lesion is to retard downward changes in reward expectancy, there is no reason why the magnitude of the FE should have been changed by the lesion.

On this hypothesis, the difference between the reward expectancy sustained by normal and septal subjects might be expected to be maximal when reward is totally withheld in a given situation, such as in the S⁻ component of the escape experiment. Daly has presented evidence indicating that the aversiveness of frustrative nonreward for normal subjects increases with the magnitude of reward expectancy. She found that rats who had received large rewards on reinforced trials escaped more rapidly from situations associated with both simple extinction (Daly, 1969a) and partial reinforcement (Daly, 1969b) than animals who received small rewards. As the septal subjects in the escape experiment should have sustained a larger reward expectancy than controls in the S⁻ components when reinforcement was totally withdrawn, it can be argued that they should have also experienced a higher level of frustration. Thus, like the potentiation hypothesis, this account can explain both the increased septal escape and the nonreward persistency by appealing to the enhanced frustration sustained by septal animals. However, it differs from the potentiation hypothesis by proposing that this increment is mediated through the effect of the ablation on the antecedent conditions for frustration rather than by a direct change in the magnitude of the primary emotional reaction to nonreward for a given level of reward expectancy.

A final possibility is that septal persistence results from the disruption of some system involved in the mediation of response decrements under nonreward in normal animals but not adequately characterized by current behavioural theories. Recently, certain authors (Rachlin and Herrnstein, 1969; Dunham, 1971) have questioned the adequacy of interference or avoidance theories of response suppression by contingent aversive events. One of the main problems with marshalling evidence against this type of theory is that, by postulating unobserved competing responses, the theory becomes almost invulnerable to purely behavioural evidence (Rachlin and Herrnstein, 1969). However, if the implications of the escape experiment are substantiated and septal animals are found to escape from and to avoid frustrative nonreward in a variety of situations at the same or higher level than intact subjects, then septal nonreward persistence would seem to be at variance with an interference theory of extinction. At present the viable theoretical alternatives to an interference theory are relatively few, and it is likely that there are a variety of mechanisms controlling response reduction in different nonreward situations (see Terrace, Chapter 4). One of the most developed alternatives is represented by Konorski's theory of reciprocally interrelated drive and anti-drive centres (Chapter 13). If the escape and avoidance tendencies are not reduced by septal damage, the persistence might well result from the disruption of systems which control actual response-strength weakening or suppression under nonreward, and a comparison of the behaviour of intact and brain-damaged animals in nonreward situations may well provide a valuable source of evidence in specifying the constituent mechanisms of such systems.

At present, the strongest conclusion which can be drawn from the studies presented in this chapter is that septal persistence under non-reward does not appear to be due to a simple, gross change in the primary reactions to frustrative nonreward. The nature of the persistence and the pattern of associated changes, though, do suggest that the continuing study of the effects of septal damage on behaviour in nonreward situations will help to elucidate the type of mechanisms underlying the ability of animals to reduce their response output in these situations as well as the function of the systems represented within the septum.

Acknowledgements

The work reported in this chapter was aided by a grant from the U.K. Medical Research Council.

References

Ain, B. R., Lubar, J. F., Moon, R. D., and Kulig, B. M. (1969). Effect of septal and neocortical damage on complex maze learning. *Physiology and Behavior*, **4**, 235–238.

Amsel, A. (1958). The role of frustrative nonreward in noncontinuous reward situations. *Psychological Bulletin*, **55**, 102–119.

Amsel, A., and Roussel, J. (1952). Motivational properties of frustration: I. Effect on a running response of the addition of frustration to the motivational complex. *Journal of Experimental Psychology*, **43**, 363–368.

Amsel, A., and Ward, J. S. (1965). Frustration and persistence: Resistance to discrimination following prior experience with the discriminanda. *Psychological Monographs*, **79**. No. 4 (Whole No. 597).

Brady, J. V., and Nauta, W. J. H. (1953). Subcortical mechanisms in emotional behavior: Affective changes following septal forebrain lesions in albino rats. *Journal of Comparative and Physiological Psychology*, **46**, 339–346.

Bruning, J. L., Schmeck, R. R., and Silver, A. I. (1971). Frustration, competing responses, and error making. *Psychonomic Science*, **22**, 47–48.

Caplan, M. (1970). Effects of withheld reinforcement on timing behavior of rats with limbic lesions. *Journal of Comparative and Physiological Psychology*, **71**, 119–135.

Carlson, N. R., and Cole, J. R. (1970). Enhanced alternation performance following septal lesions in mice. *Journal of Comparative and Physiological Psychology*, **73**, 157–161.

Carlson, N. R., and Norman, R. J. (1971). Enhanced go, no-go single-lever alternation of mice with septal lesions. *Journal of Comparative and Physiological Psychology*, **75**, 508–512.

Clody, D. E., and Carlton, P. L. (1969). Behavioral effects of lesions of the medial septum of rats. *Journal of Comparative and Physiological Psychology*, **67**, 344–351.

Daly, H. B. (1969a). Learning of a hurdle-jump response to escape cues paired with reduced reward or frustrative nonreward. *Journal of Experimental Psychology* **79**, 146–157.

Daly, H. B. (1969b). Aversive properties of partial and varied reinforcement during runway acquisition. *Journal of Experimental Psychology*, **81**, 54–60.

Davenport, J. W., and Thompson, C. I. (1965). The Amsel frustration effect in monkeys. *Psychonomic Science*, **3**, 481–482.

Dickinson, A. (1971). Behavioural reactions of septal rats to frustrative nonreward. Unpublished doctoral thesis, University of Sussex.

Donovick, P. J. (1968). Effects of localised septal lesions on hippocampal EEG activity and behavior in rats. *Journal of Comparative and Physiological Psychology*, **66**, 569–578.

Duncan, P. M. (1971). Effect of temporary septal dysfunction on conditioning and performance of fear responses in rats. *Journal of Comparative and Physiological Psychology*, **74**, 340–348.

Dunham, P. J. (1971). Punishment: Method and theory. *Psychological Review*, **78**, 58–70.

Ellen, P., Wilson, A. S., and Powell, E. W. (1964). Septal inhibition and timing behavior in the rat. *Experimental Neurology*, **10**, 120–132,

Gerbrandt, L. K. (1965). Neural systems of response release and control. *Psychological Bulletin,* **64**, 113–123.

Gotsick, J. E., Osborne, F. H., Allen, C. J., and Hines, K. M. (1971). Factors affecting performance on a shock escape task in rats with septal lesions. *Physiology and Behavior*, **6**, 199–202.

Gray, J. A. (1970). Sodium amobarbital, the hippocampal theta rhythm, and the partial reinforcement extinction effect. *Psychological Review*, **77**, 465–480.

Green, R. H., and Schwartzbaum, J. S. (1968). Effects of unilateral septal lesions on avoidance behavior, discrimination reversal, and hippocampal EEG. *Journal of Comparative and Physiological Psychology*, **65**, 388–396.

Hamilton, L. W. (1970). Behavioral effects of unilateral and bilateral septal lesions in rats. *Physiology and Behavior*, **5**, 855–859.

Hamilton, L. W., Kelsey, J. E., and Grossman, S. P. (1970). Variations in behavioral inhibition following differential septal lesions. *Journal of Comparative and Physiological Psychology*, **70**, 79–86.

Hug, J. J. (1970). Frustration effects after varied number of partial and continuous reinforcements: Incentive differences as a function of reinforcement percentage. *Psychonomic Science*, **21**, 57–59.

Hull, C. L. (1943). *Principles of Behavior*. New York: Appleton–Century–Crofts.

Kaada, B. R., Rasmussen, E. W., and Kveim, O. (1962). Impaired acquisition of passive avoidance behavior by subcallosal, septal, hypothalamic, and insular lesions in rats. *Journal of Comparative and Physiological Psychology*, **55**, 661–670.

King, F. A. (1958). Effects of septal and amygdaloid lesions on emotional behavior and conditioned avoidance responses in the rat. *Journal of Nervous and Mental Disease*, **126**, 57–63.

Kramer, T. J., and Rilling, M. (1970). Differential reinforcement of low rates: A selective critique. *Psychological Bulletin,* **72**, 225–254.

Leitenberg, H. (1965). Is time-out from reinforcement an aversive event? A review of experimental evidence. *Psychological Bulletin*, **64**, 428–441.

MacDougall, J. M., Van Hoesen, G. W., and Mitchell, J. C. (1969a). Anatomical organisation of septal projections in maintenance of DRL behavior. *Journal of Comparative and Physiological Psychology*, **68**, 568–575.

MacDougall, J. M., Van Hoesen, G. W., and Mitchell, J. C. (1969b). Development of post S^R and post non-S^R DRL performance and its retention following septal lesions in rats. *Psychonomic Science*, **16**, 45–46.

McCleary, R. A. (1966). Response-modulating functions of the limbic system: Initiation and suppression. In: E. Stellar and J. M. Sprague (Eds.), *Progress in Physiological Psychology*. Vol. 1. New York: Academic Press, pp. 209–272.

Morgan, J. M., and Mitchell, J. C. (1969). Septal lesions enhance delay of responding on a free-operant avoidance schedule. *Psychonomic Science*, **16**, 10–11.

Papez, J. W. (1937). A proposed mechanism of emotion. *A.M.A. Archives of Neurology and Psychiatry*, **38**, 725–743.

Rachlin, H., and Herrnstein, R. J. (1969). Hedonism revisited: On the negative law of effect. In: B. A. Campbell and R. M. Church (Eds.), *Punishment and Aversive Behavior*. New York: Appleton–Century–Crofts, pp. 83–109.

Raphelson, A. C., Isaacson, R. L., and Douglas, R. J. (1966). The effect of limbic damage on the retention and performance of a runway response. *Neuropsychologia*, **4**, 253–264.

Reynolds, G. S. (1961). Behavioral Contrast. *Journal of the Experimental Analysis of Behavior*, **4**, 57–71.

Rilling, M. E., Askew, H. R., Ahlskog, J. E., and Kramer, T. J. (1969). Aversive properties of the negative stimulus in a successive discrimination. *Journal of the Experimental Analysis of Behavior*, **12**, 917–932.

Schwartzbaum, J. S., and Donovick, P. J. (1968). Discrimination reversal and spatial alternation associated with septal and caudate dysfunction in rats. *Journal of Comparative and Phsyiological Psychology*, **65**, 83–92.

Schwartzbaum, J. S., Kellicut, M. H., Spieth, T. M., and Thompson, J. B. (1964). Effects of septal lesions in rats on response inhibition associated with food reinforced behavior. *Journal of Comparative and Physiological Psychology*, **58**, 217–224.

Sheffield, V. F. (1950). Resistance to extinction as a function of the distribution of extinction trials. *Journal of Experimental Psychology*, **40**, 305–313.

Sodetz, K. J. (1970). Septal ablation and free-operant avoidance behavior in the rat. *Physiology and Behavior*, **5**, 773–777.

Spence, K. W. (1936). The nature of discrimination learning in animals. *Psychological Review*, **43**, 427–449.

Spence, K. W. (1956). *Behaviour Theory and Conditioning*. New Haven: Yale University Press.

Staddon, J. E. R. (1970). Temporal effects of reinforcement: A negative "frustration" effect. *Learning and Motivation*, **1**, 227–247.

Thomas, G. J., Hostetter, G., and Barker, D. J. (1968). Behavioral functions of the limbic system. In: E. Stellar and J. M. Sprague (Eds.), *Progress in Physiological Psychology*. Vol. 2. New York: Academic Press, pp. 229–311.

Thompson, T., Heistad, G. T., and Palermo, D. S. (1963). Effect of amount of training on rate and duration of responding during extinction. *Journal of the Experimental Analysis of Behavior*, **6**, 155–161.

Van Hoesen, G. W., MacDougall, J. M., and Mitchell, J. C. (1969). Anatomical specificity of septal projections in active and passive avoidance behavior in the rat. *Journal of Comparative and Physiological Psychology*, **68**, 80–89.

Wagner, A. R. (1969). Frustrative nonreward: A variety of punishment? In: B. A.

Campbell and R. M. Church (Eds.), *Punishment and Aversive Behavior.* New York: Appleton–Century–Crofts, pp. 157–181.

Winocur, G., and Mills, J. A. (1969). Hippocampus and septum in response inhibition. *Journal of Comparative and Physiological Psychology*, **67**, 352–357.

Wolfe J. W., Lubar, J. F., and Ison, J. R. (1967). Effects of medial cortical lesions on appetitive instrumental conditioning. *Physiology and Behavior*, **2**, 167–170.

19

Neural Systems of the Limbic Brain and Behavioural Inhibition

R. L. ISAACSON

University of Florida, Gainsville, Florida, U.S.A.

I.	Introduction	497
II.	The Limbic System and Memory	498
	A. The Importance of a Disease Process	500
	B. Behavioural Studies of Animals with Artificially Established Epileptogenic Foci	501
III.	Hippocampal-Hypothalamic Relationships	512
	A. Hess's Model of the Hypothalamus	512
	B. Behavioural Correlates of Ergotropic and Trophotropic Activity	513
	C. Hippocampal Influences on Hypothalamic Mechanisms . .	514
	D. Amygdalar Influences on Hypothalamic Mechanisms . .	515
	E. Single Neuron Activity in the Hypothalamus	515
IV.	Behavioural Evidence for an Ergotropic Balance Following Hippocampal Destruction	516
V.	Evidence for a Trophotropic Balance After Amygdala Lesions .	517
VI.	The Ergotropic-Trophotropic Systems and Memory . . .	520
	A. Post-trial Administration of Stimulants	521
	B. Artificial Epileptogenic Foci	521
	C. Electrical Stimulation of the Limbic System . . .	522
	D. Withholding Responses	523
	E. Electrographic Correlates of Behaviour	523
VII.	Conclusion	525
	Acknowledgements	525
	References	525

I. Introduction

An individual's response to any stimulus is a relative matter: it is relative to the general condition of the organism, the environment, and past experiences. This is a law of nature with wide scope and applicability. For example, electrical stimulation of the motor area of the brain produces a response in the somatic musculature which is dependent upon what the body is doing at the time of stimulation, i.e., if a limb is flexed it will extend, if extended it will flex. Stimulation of the brain which affects the internal organs will produce the same kind of result; if the stomach is

497

contracting, electrical stimulation ends the contractions. If the stomach is quiet, the stimulation may begin contractions.

Observations like these are usually considered to reflect the establishment of sets, dispositions, or the "tuning" of the nervous system. These in turn are explained in terms of changes in the balance between opposing excitatory and inhibitory forces in various neural systems. The conceptual scheme used to describe opposing excitatory or inhibitory influences may be broadly or narrowly defined in terms of the neural systems involved and more or less broadly applied to behaviour. In what follows, I would like to attempt a formulation of how the notion of the opposing excitatory and inhibitory mechanisms of the diencephalon, originally proposed by Hess (1949), can be applied to how the limbic system influences behaviour. It is, perhaps, useful to begin with certain neurological speculations concerning human memory since this provides an historical approach to the problems to be examined.

II. The Limbic System and Memory

Just before the 1950s turned into the 1960s, hopes were being expressed that the study of particular patients who had been subjected to brain surgery for the relief of convulsive disorders (presumed to be of temporal lobe origin) had led to the discovery of anatomical structures involved with "memory," or at least some aspect of memory. The hippocampus and the amygdala, two limbic system structures lying deep within the temporal lobe, were thought to be essential to the formation of new memories. Many types of research programme were aimed at understanding the relationship between the temporal lobe components of the limbic systems and behaviour. In the 1970s most people have concluded that there is little reason to connect the temporal lobe limbic system structures with memory, at least as evaluated from experimental studies with animals of any species other than man. However, the problem remains as to why there are certain patients with behavioural deficits that appear related to a type of memory disorder.

The deficit which has been reported to follow temporal lobe destruction, and especially destruction of the hippocampus, in man is a loss of memory for events intervening between the time of surgery and extending to the span of immediate attention. In general, the amnesic syndrome studied in man which results from medial temporal lobe destruction is not associated with losses in attention, skills, or intelligence. Reasoning and perception seem unaffected, as do memories of the remote past. But, new memory formation is lost or impaired from the time of surgery.

In considering the temporal lobe memory deficit, it should be emphasized that the memory debility found after medial destruction of temporal lobe is not an all-or-none phenomenon. The brain damage is not without other, albeit relatively minor, behavioural effects. Scoville's patient, H.M., the most intensively studied of all such patients, needs to be reminded to shave even though he generally keeps himself neat and tidy. He also needs to be reminded to eat, but when food is placed before him he eats it in a normal manner. Both behaviours are ones with which H.M. was familiar before surgery which occurred, at age 27, and cues are available to remind him of the appropriate occasions for both types of acts.

These observations on H.M. are thought to be representative of a wider class of patients in which recent memories are disturbed, whether in registration or in retrieval from some storage system, by damage to the hippocampal system and the temporal lobes. For the most part, bilateral damage to the hippocampal system is thought to be necessary for the generalized deficit in recent memory, because the occurrence of this debilitating memory loss is a relatively rare occurrence following unilateral temporal lobe destruction. For example, Milner (1959) reported that only two out of 100 patients receiving unilateral temporal lobe removals at the Montreal Neurological Institute demonstrated the memory disorder. What could explain the fact that only these two developed recent memory impairments? "To account for it we have assumed that, in addition to the known epileptogenic lesion of the left hippocampal zone (the one removed surgically), there must have been a second and pre-operatively unsuspected destructive lesion of the opposite (right) hippocampal zone at the time of birth, so that when the surgeon removed the left hippocampal area the patient was functionally deprived of that area on both sides."

The emphasis on the necessity for bilateral destruction also arose from the report of Scoville (1954). In this paper, severe disturbances of recent memory were reported in one psychotic patient and one with an extreme convulsive disorder (H.M.). These two patients had bilateral resections of the medial temporal lobes and were reported to suffer from the recent memory disorder as described above. Milner studied some eight other patients operated upon by Scoville and concluded that disturbances of recent memory were found when the hippocampus had been invaded bilaterally and the amount of disturbance correlated to some degree with the extent to which the hippocampus had been damaged. No memory deficits were found when the removals were restricted to uncus and the amygdaloid areas. It should be remembered that temporal lobe removals are radical procedures and only undertaken when the symptoms are severe and when other procedures have failed to provide relief.

To assume that man is unique among animals in connection with hippocampal function would be unfortunate for many reasons. Most important, it would mean that the information derived from the many kinds of animal

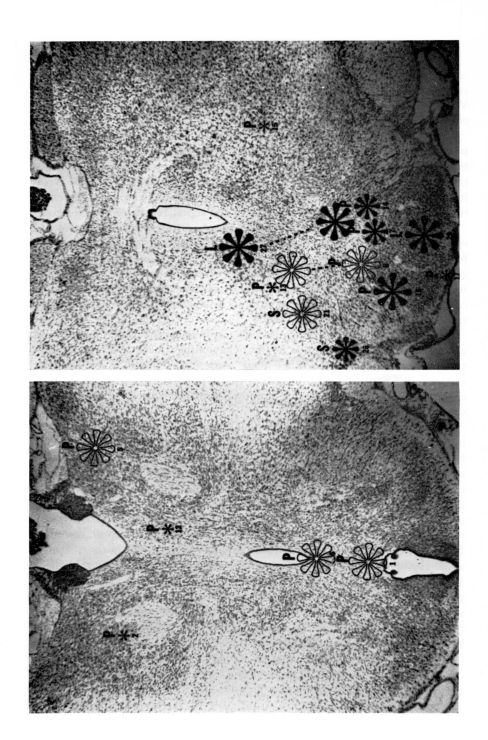

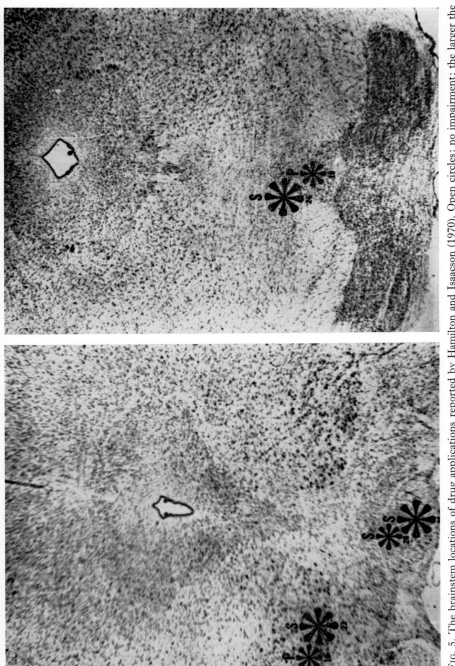

Fig. 5. The brainstem locations of drug applications reported by Hamilton and Isaacson (1970). Open circles: no impairment; the larger the diameter of the black circles, the greater the behavioural impairment. The subject number is given by each circle. P = penicillin; S = sodium sulphadiazene.

III. Hippocampal-Hypothalamic Relationships

Related to my theoretical speculations is the fact that the refinements of the limbic system found in various lines of evolutionary "progress" all converge their influences upon a brain which has reasonably well developed behaviour-control capabilities. The principle of an *hierarchical organization of neural systems is implicit.* "Newer" systems are added "on top of" older systems. The older systems remain intact but are subjected to new regulatory influences. The development of the neocortex adds additional controls upon a limbic-hypothalamic brain. Both the limbic system and the neocortex provide new regulatory mechanisms on to systems already organized at diencephalic and brainstem levels.

What purposes do these new systems fulfil? It seems to me that they add new mechanisms which further refine and adapt the previously existing neural mechanisms to new and more subtle environmental contingencies. New degrees of freedom are added to behaviour. Additional complexities and contingencies can play upon the more fundamental apparati of behaviour. From these considerations, one would expect the capabilities provided the organism by the limbic system and neocortex to be subtle rather than gross, intricate rather than simple.

It is frequently said that the thalamus is the key by which the secrets of the neocortex can be discovered. In a similar fashion, the hypothalamus may hold the key that will unlock the mysteries of the limbic system.

A corollary of the belief that the limbic system can best be understood in its relationship to the hypothamalus is that any model of the limbic system depends upon the model of the hypothalamus selected. For the past several years, I have been impressed by the usefulness of the model stemming from the work of W. R. Hess. In 1949 he proposed two terms that describe some of his conclusions based on numerous studies of the diencephalon. These terms, ergotropic and trophotropic, refer to system-divisions of the hypothalamus.

A. HESS'S MODEL OF THE HYPOTHALMUS

For many years, the association of the anterior hypothalamic regions with parasympathetic activities in the autonomic nervous system and the posterior regions with sympathetic activities has been recognized. Hess's term *trophotropic* includes parasympathetic activities but also includes correlated activities of the somatic musculature that are associated with the conservation of bodily energies and common housekeeping activities of the striate muscles. The term *ergotrophic* includes neural mechanisms regulating both smooth and striate muscle activities which are directed towards the mobilization and expenditure of the body's resources. The hypothalamic regions identified as trophotropic or ergotropic correspond to some extent, to "anterior" and "posterior", but they extend our horizons of the effects controlled by the hypothalamus beyond the autonomic nervous system and even beyond the somatic nervous system. The trophotropic reactions include decreases in electrical arousal of forebrain areas, while ergotropic reactions include increases in the electrical activity of the forebrain. Thus, Hess's terms should be thought of as describing autonomic, somatic, and central nervous system effects.

At this time, it would be a mistake to attempt to make too close an identification of specific hypothalamic locations with the trophotropic and ergotropic reactions. For one reason, I doubt if our knowledge of the anatomy of the diencephalic regions is adequate to the task. Secondly, I think that an overly specific anatomical approach could not be sufficiently general. The distribution of fibres from the fornix shows rather extensive species-specific distribution patterns (e.g. Valenstein and Nauta, 1959). The functional end-targets and results of impulses arriving over the fornix may be similar across many species but the routes whereby the ends are accomplished may show considerable variation. For these reasons, I suspect it will be best to consider the terms ergotropic and trophotropic to refer to systems inhabiting the hypothalamus, but not only the hypothalamus, and not with uniform and consistent anatomical organization in every type of animal.

B. Behavioural Correlates of Ergotropic and Trophotropic Activity

It is possible to make speculations about the role of the ergotropic and trophotropic systems in behaviour. Some have been advanced before by Gellhorn (e.g. 1970), but many have not. Some are based upon intuition concerning both the ergotropic and trophotropic systems and behaviour. Hopefully, the speculations can be subjected to empirical examination using many different techniques.

The ergotropic system seems especially well suited for the activation of behaviours of all varieties. It will be assumed that some critical amount of ergotropic system activity is essential to the *initiation* and the *maintenance* of all behavioural acts. The stronger the ergotropic system activity is the stronger and quicker will be the response. Ergotropic system activity is also essential to the continuation of behavioural episodes.

The trophotropic system, on the other hand, acts in an antagonistic manner to the ergotropic system. Strong activity in the trophotropic system is related to the arrest of overt behaviour and to rest and sleep.

In most circumstances the ergotropic and trophotropic systems co-operate so as to maintain a balance between the two systems appropriate to the environmental circumstances. The greater the activity in one, the less the activity in the other. The two stand in an inhibitory relationship. However, this balance can be upset so that activity can be great in both at the same time as is sometimes found in convulsions.

Again, in most circumstances, behaviour reflects cooperation and amalgamation of activities in trophotropic and ergotropic systems. Male sexual activity depends upon the trophotropic system's physiological preparations for an erection, while the ejaculation of semen requires neural initiation of a sympathetic ergotropic origin. The systems operate within specified sequences.

The terms ergotropic and trophotropic may seem to suggest homogeneous anatomical or functional systems. This need not be the case, however. It may well be that each "system" is really a collection of neural systems of great specificity. These neural systems could be involved with the regulation of specific behavioural components related to well-defined aspects of aggressive, sexual, feeding, drinking, and so forth, behaviours. Each neural system could have inhibitory effects upon antagonistic behaviours or physiological reactions and facilitatory effects on synergistic behaviours or physiological reactions. Perhaps sets of mutually inhibitory highly specific reactions define what has been called the ergotropic and trophotropic systems.

Because of a prolonged interest in one component of the limbic system, the hippocampus, I would like to discuss some of its possible interactions with the ergotropic and trophotropic systems in detail.

C. Hippocampal Influences on Hypothalamic Mechanisms

Stated in the simplest way, the hippocampal influence upon the hypothalamus could be the inhibition of the ergotropic systems in the posterior hypothalamus. When certain conditions arise, the hippocampal "system" becomes activated and this in turn suppresses the on-going activities of the ergotropic system. The occasions in which the hippocampal influences come to be exerted probably correspond to those described by Klüver (1965). He believes that the effective stimulus for hippocampal participation in behaviour is the disruption of expectancies about the environment. This disruption of anticipated events influences the activities of the polysensory and intrinsic nuclei of the thalamus. These changes are then projected to the transitional cortical areas beyond the subicular zones. When things are not as they should be, the hippocampal system acts, and one result of this action is the suppression of activities in the ergotropic hypothalamic regions.

D. Amygdalar Influences on Hypothalamic Mechanisms

Since the hippocampus and amygdala are two of the most significant aspects of the limbic system and since their roles in behaviour are often contrasted and compared, it would be worthwhile to relate the amygdala to the ergotropic and trophotropic systems. Assumptions concerning the role of the amygdala in behaviour are more difficult because this anatomical structure is composed of two (at least) populations of cells with quite different functional properties, as judged on the basis of electrical stimulation of the structure (Ursin and Kaada, 1960). One component probably facilitates the trophotropic system while another component probably exerts a facilitatory effect upon the ergotropic system. Overall, the predominant net effect of amygdala activation is probably one of an ergotropic facilitation, since destruction of the majority of the amygdala usually produces a placid, calm animal which can be presumed to reflect a trophotropic bias.

The occasions in which the amygdala becomes active in regulating the ergotropic and trophotropic system activity are ones concerned with circumstances of vital concern to the animal's preservation of its life and the propagation of the species. Deprivations, rewards, threats, and sexual opportunities, among other things, probably energize specific response systems organized through the amygdala, medial forebrain bundle, and brainstem. These specific neural systems in turn participate in the determination of the balance between the ergotropic and trophotropic systems of the hypothalamus.

Electrical stimulation of both the hippocampus and the amygdala can produce an inhibition in behaviour. After training animals to choose the correct one of two feeding devices on the basis of a visual sign, Endröczi and Lissák (1962), tested the animals during periods in which the dorsal hippocampus or the amygdala was stimulated. Stimulation of both locations produced quite different reactions, however, while interrupting the behaviour. The interruption of behaviour during amygdalar stimulation was associated with fear, rage, and escape-oriented behaviour. The interruption caused by hippocampal stimulation was only associated with a staring expression. These results suggest that the hippocampal stimulation simply turned-off the ergotropic systems while the amygdala systems arrested ongoing behaviour while energizing certain other ergotropic behaviours at the same time.

E. Single Neuron Activity in the Hypothalamus

Reports of single unit activity in the hypothalamus during and following electrical stimulation of the hippocampus are not entirely consistent, perhaps due to species differences. The majority of the evidence, however, points to a suppression of neuronal activities in the hypothalamus following stimulation of the hippocampus (e.g., Stuart *et al.*, 1964). Gergen (1967) found some posterior hypothalamic neurons which showed short latency increased discharges following hippocampal stimulation but the majority evidenced a longer latency inhibitory effect. The short latency neurons which increased in activity could be inhibitory inter-neurons.

The observations of Dafney and Feldmann (1969) seem especially important in this connection. They found inhibitory effects arising from stimulation of both septal and hippocampal sites. However, the two sites produced effects upon different populations of cells. Septal stimulation effects were found in neurons which are also responsive to peripheral stimulation while the hippocampal effects were upon cells unresponsive to peripheral stimulation. Poletti *et al.* (1969, 1970) have recently reported some observations in the monkey which indicate a preponderance of excitatory activity in response to hippocampal stimulation which presently cannot be amalgamated with previous data.

Overall, however, the evidence from single unit experiments does not conflict with an inhibitory hypothesis of the hippocampal effects upon hypothalamic activity. Furthermore, the fact that hippocampal stimulation can inhibit gross electrical responses evoked by peripheral nerve stimulation can be interpreted in the same fashion.

IV. Behavioural Evidence for an Ergotropic Balance Following Hippocampal Destruction

This model of hippocampal function provides us with an explanation of many, if not all, of the behavioural results observed to follow from hippocampal destruction. One of the frequent observations which has been found in several experiments is that animals with hippocampal destruction tend to initiate responses which have been punished in the past in what is called the "passive avoidance paradigm". This observation has been made in rats and cats in several types of training situations.

What is seldom recognized is that the behaviour which is perpetuated by the animals with hippocampal destruction is the *initiation* of the behavioural act. The initiation of behaviour is assumed to be the responsibility of the ergotropic regions of the hypothalamus. The model which I have described would account for this by the release of the ergotropic, response-initiating system from normal inhibitory influences from the hippocampus. Looking at the data of animals in runways where they are trained in passive avoidance tasks for simple extinction paradigms, one finds the greatest perseverative effects are on the *starting latencies*, and a smaller effect upon the running speeds. The animals will often, in fact, slow down on their path to the goal box when long runways are used.

The hippocampally lesioned animals cannot inhibit the beginning of the response sequence. The starting mechanism is not under normal control. Illustrating this in another way, Glickman *et al.* (1970) have reported the effects of radical bilateral hippocampal destruction in the mongolian gerbil *Meriones Unguiculatus.* Several observations were of significance, including the reduction in sleeping time in the evening which could be a sign of a changed balance towards a greater ergotropic balance. Many types of behaviours were sampled and several increased in frequency following the hippocampal lesions. But, as pointed out in the article, the increases were entirely in the frequency with which these behaviours were initiated and not in terms of total time spent performing them. A recent study by Kim *et al.* (1970) supports this general theme in that the behaviours after hippocampal destruction seem to reflect primarily an increase in the frequency of the initiation of the acts.

Some of the most well-established behavioural consequences of hippocampal destruction can be related to an exaggerated ergotropic balance in the hypothalamic mechanisms. The enhanced responding which occurs when an animal with hippocampal destruction is transferred from a continuous reinforcement schedule to an intermittent schedule in which it must wait some number of seconds between barpresses (DRL schedule), originally reported by Clark and Isaacson (1965), could reflect an enhanced ergotropic bias. Later, Schmaltz and Isaacson (1966) discovered that the change from continuous to intermittent schedules of reinforcement probably represented the most important ergotropically stimulating aspect of the training situation, since animals which had never experienced continuous reinforcement showed much less of the "ergotropic" response rate increase.

Of special interest is the observation by Dr Van Hartesveldt (personal communication) that chlorpromazine, a tranquillizing agent thought to affect adrenergic systems primarily, but not exclusively, will lower the response rates of hippocampally lesioned animals on DRL-schedules to approximately those of intact animals.

V. Evidence for a Trophotropic Balance after Amygdala Lesions

By contrast, the animals with destruction of the amygdala have a problem in the initiation of behaviours, whether they be in an avoidance conditioning task or in other types of learning situations. In the two-way active avoidance task, animals with amygdala lesions show a considerable impairment. However, after the first response is made, the animals learn the problem just as fast as intact animals. Here, once again, we see a change in a "starting mechanism" but one in the opposite direction to the result obtained from hippocampal destruction. In a recent experiment by Kemble and Beckman (1970) the greatest deficit observed in animals with amygdala lesions was their refusal to leave the starting compartment of the test chamber. Those that did leave the starting compartment did so with extraordinarily long latencies. These animals were being trained in a T-maze with food reward for correct responses. Deprivation was maintained at 80% of prior body weight and there was no difference in the weights of the animals with amygdala lesions compared with the control groups during the experiment. This suggests that the starting mechanism deficit presumed to be related to an indirect reduction of ergotropic system activity of the animals with the amygdala lesions was not restricted to tasks of an avoidance nature but is also found in tasks performed for food rewards under deprivation.

There are some similarities between the suggestion that amygdala lesions produce a trophotropically tuned organism and the theory advanced by Pribram (1969) concerning the same structure. He suggests ". . . amygdalectomy produces hyperstability by disrupting the temporal organization which has developed by habituation to regularly recurring events such as those derived from visceral activity". Under normal conditions, the amygdala should function to decrease the effects of regularly occurring visceral and external sensory events. Without this suppressive influence Pribram believes a stable framework cannot be achieved for the evaluation of changes in the environment; a stable context for new events will be lacking.

The evidence which led Pribram to this view derives from several sources, including the failure of animals with lesions of the amygdala to show normal amounts of habituation to changes in the environment. Schwartzbaum et al. (1961) found that amygdala destruction produced impaired habituation of locomotor activity. In fact, these authors found the activity of the amygdalectomized monkeys to increase under conditions in which the activity of normal monkeys decreased (habituated). In a related set of experiments (Bagshaw et al., 1965; Bagshaw and Benzies, 1968) interruption of habituation resulted from amygdalectomy as measured by the galvanic skin responses (GSR). Actually, the change found in the amygdalectomized monkeys was a somewhat diminished rate of decrease in the habituation of the GSR response superimposed upon a much greater reduction in overall GSR responsiveness. This reduction in GSR responsiveness would be expected on the basis of an overall bias towards a trophotropic balance.

The *increases* in locomotor activity found when testing for habituation of this response can be explained, if the locomotor activity measured by Schwartzbaum et al. (1961) was one mediated by the trophotropic system.

It seems likely that *exploration and locomotor responses of certain kinds are mediated by the trophotropic system.* In any case, a single failure of an habituation system would be insufficient to explain the *higher* locomotor rates which were found.

Pribram's explanation of the effects of amygdalectomy is based upon the normal role of the amygdala in the habituation or suppression of repetitive events. This suppression is thought to foster a stable neural condition and thus provides a stable neural context for further elaboration of new behaviours. My explanation is also based on the suppression of neural events, particularly those of the trophotropic system, but under conditions of circumstances of great significance to the organism from a biological point of view. Pribram stresses the importance of repetitive events for the habituation events to occur. The Pribram model also indicates that an unstable, labile neural condition should follow amygdala destruction whereas my thought is that a trophotropic balance should prevail after the lesion which should be no more or less stable than before the lesion, except in so far as one suppressive influence on the trophotropic system has been eliminated.

Electrical stimulation of the amygdala has been reported to produce impaired performances indicative of impaired memory consolidation (e.g. Goddard, 1964; Kesner and Doty, 1968). However, in two recent studies data contrary to such an interpretation have been reported. Lidsky and Slotnick (1970) found stimulation of the rat amygdala at subseizure intensities failed to produce any retrograde amnesic effects upon the suppression of a licking response. Stimulation of sufficient intensity to produce a seizure in the amygdala which spread to other brain areas *did* cause impairments in performance but the long-lasting effects of seizure-inducing stimulation of the amygdala made evaluation of specified memory disruptions difficult.

Electrically induced seizures of the inferotemporal cortex in monkeys, but not seizures begun in the amygdalae, interfered with the retention of a conditioned suppression of barpress rate to a visual stimulus. Conditioned suppression of barpress rate to an auditory stimulus was not affected (Levine *et al.*, 1970). The interesting suggestion arising from this series of experiments by Schwartzbaum and his colleagues is that there is a modality specificity memory effect created by seizure activities which arise in the inferotemporal cortex and which spread to the amygdala.

While Lidsky and Slotnick describe their results as a failure to replicate the findings of Goddard in 1964, there were significant procedural differences between the two studies. Both studies evaluated the effects of stimulation of the amygdala upon conditioned suppression of a barpress response. Lidsky and Slotnick studied the suppression of the barpress response which was based upon a sugar–water reward. The earlier Goddard study involved a food pellet reward. The stimulation used by Lidsky and Slotnick was bilateral to the amygdala, that used by Goddard was unilateral. The stimulus associated with electrical shock in the Lidsky and Slotnick experiment was light, while that used by Goddard was a buzzer.

Which of these differences is most significant for producing the discrepant results is unknown. However, the difference in the rewards used in the two studies is the most interesting from the framework of the present theory. There are some reasons to believe that drinking and eating are subserved by different hypothalamic subsystems; drinking by the trophotropic, eating by the ergotropic.

VI. The Ergotropic-Trophotropic Systems and Memory

The model of hippocampal influences on behaviour described above must be extended to provide some working hypotheses concerning the effects of penicillin-induced changes in behaviour, which appear to reflect difficulties in short-term memory. Two alternate hypotheses can be stated as follows.

    1. A "prolonged" period (1 hr or so) of ergotropic activity immediately after a learning experience is essential to the incorporation of that experience into long-term memory storage.

    2. A "prolonged" period of ergotropic activity immediately after an "ergotropic experience" and a "prolonged" period of trophotropic activity immediately after a "trophotropic experience" are essential to the incorporation of the learning experiences into long-term memory storage.

Of course, many of the terms need to be defined in these statements to make them perfectly clear, but the important difference between the two hypotheses is that the first assumes that ergotropic activity must occur after any learning experience for long-term memory to be achieved, whereas the second assumes that there are two types of learning tasks and that the type of hypothalamic activity following each must be of the same quality as was dominant in the training experience. This second hypothesis is based upon the assumption that behavioural tasks can be divided into ones mediated to a greater or lesser extent by the ergotropic or trophotropic systems. But, what basis can be found for such a division? A preliminary suggestion can be made that those tasks which are performed best with increased energy expenditures, tasks in which a high level of arousal and sympathetic-adrenal activation are optimal, should be classified as "ergotropic". Tasks performed optionally with low arousal levels, minimal activation, and perhaps a parasympathetic suppression of autonomic reactivity should be classified as "trophotropic." Under the second hypothesis, ergotropic tasks require an ergotropic state after training for the consolidation of learning. For trophotropic tasks, a trophotropic balance must prevail afterwards to allow consolidation to occur. Under hypothesis one, an ergotropic state should follow training on any type of task in order to facilitate consolidation.

A. POST-TRIAL ADMINISTRATION OF STIMULANTS

From some of the recent results from experiments in which retention of learning can be enhanced by post-training drug administration, it might seem as if hypothesis one is most reasonable. For example, the work of McGaugh and his associates (for a review see McGaugh, 1967) indicates that various types of stimulant drugs when administered after a training experience, can enhance retention. However, the tasks used have been "ergotropic" in nature, for the most part. However, it may be that certain inconsistencies in the literature could be resolved if the ergotropic-trophotropic differences in the task were to be considered.

With these hypotheses in mind it is possible to attempt an interpretation of the results obtained from the application of penicillin to the hippocampus. If destruction of the hippocampus releases the ergotropic zones of the hypothalamus from periodic periods of suppression, what is the effect of the changes produced by the establishment of an artificial epileptic focus? On the other hand, the discharges must disrupt the normal ongoing relationships existing between this portion of the limbic system, the hypothalamus, and the transitional cortex. In animals in which the penicillin has caused and continues to cause periodic spike discharges from the hippocampus, this should produce periodic interruptions of activity in the ergotropic system due to the periodic assaults of massive neural discharges.

B. ARTIFICIAL EPILEPTOGENIC FOCI

This disruption of neural activity at hypothalamic or other levels by artificially established epileptic foci could be interpreted as a disruption in the contextual core of brain activities. The importance of a neural context provided by various brain systems and the autonomic nervous system has been emphasized by Pribram (1971). Massive periodic discharges from any limbic area should alter the ergotropic-trophotropic balance and thus tend to disrupt or destroy the context upon which further elaboration of the neural activities upon which learning and memory are established.

The effects of penicillin application would, perhaps, correspond to the effects produced by low frequency stimulation of the hippocampus. It must be noted that these effects should *not* correspond, however, to those produced by the induction of seizure after-discharges in the hippocampus.

This is because the application of penicillin usually produces single spike discharges which recur in periodic bursts at a rate of about one discharge every two to five seconds. Electrical seizure activities produce large, repetitive discharges at a much higher rate. The electrical activities recorded in these two conditions are quite different, as are the overt behavioural reactions.

C. Electrical Stimulation of the Limbic System

Erickson and Patel (1969) electrically stimulated the dorsal hippocampus at low (30 v AC) and high (200 v AC) intensities (for three seconds) ten seconds after each response in a bar press avoidance task. They used a 30-sec inter-trial interval with a 5-sec buzzer as the CS which preceded the foot shock. They found that the low intensity brain stimulation almost doubled the rate of acquisition of the avoidance task, but that the high intensity brain stimulation was without effect. Furthermore, they found that the systematic administration of a low level (1 mg/kg) of atropine abolished the facilitation produced by the low intensity stimulation of the hippocampus.

According to the present theory, the facilitation of the acquisition of the task used by Erickson and Patel was a result of the elicitation of a bias towards a trophotropic balance which could be offset by the administration of the cholinergic blocking agent, atropine. Rather than assuming the atropine effects to be specific to the hippocampus, I would assume that this drug tended to reduce the activity of the trophotropic system. This counteracted the effects of the low level hippocampal stimulation. The failure to find facilitation in the acquisition of the task as a result of high intensity stimulation could be attributed to the overall disruption of behaviour produced by the intense stimulation and possibly by after-discharges, although the electrical activities of the hippocampus were not recorded in this experiment.

Using a similar approach, Lidsky and Slotnick (1971) have studied the effects of hippocampal stimulation upon the retention of a one-trial *passive* avoidance response. They found that stimulation of this structure produced retention *deficits* similar to those found after ECS (when both are applied at the same time after training). In an extension of this first result, they found (in an unpublished study) that the time course of impairment over various delays between the response and the brain stimulation was almost identical for both the hippocampal and entire brain (ECS) stimulation.

On the other hand, in support of the facilitation in acquisition found by Erickson and Patel, Landfield and McGaugh (personal communication) found that hippocampal stimulation administered after training enhanced memory. They used an *active* shock avoidance problem whereas Lidsky and Slotnick used a passive avoidance problem. Under hypothesis two this difference would be critical.

D. WITHHOLDING RESPONSES

The activation of behavioural sequences could depend upon the activity in the ergotropic systems while the *withholding* of a response could depend upon the dominance of the trophotropic systems. The successful performance of a passive avoidance task would be hindered by destruction (or inactivation) of the hippocampus. If it is assumed that hippocampal theta rhythms represent a period of relative inhibition of hippocampal activities (Grastyán *et al.*, 1959) then conditions which cause theta frequency activities to be prominent in the hippocampus would be ones in which an ergotropic balance was established in the organism. Landfield and McGaugh, personal communication, found that the electrical stimulation which enhanced memory also produced theta wave activity. Since recordings of electrical activities in hippocampus were not made by Erickson and Patel or by Lidsky and Slotnick, it is not possible to determine if their stimulation produced theta activities, after-discharges, or other kinds of electrical changes. In general, the results of studies in which hippocampal seizures or after-discharges have been elicited by electrical stimulation have resulted in impaired responding and an arrest of ongoing behaviours even though there have been negligible effects upon conditioned responses when measured after the seizure had subsided (e.g. Delgado and Sevillano, 1961; MacLean *et al.*, 1956).

The inhibition produced by high frequency stimulation of the hippocampus does not extend only to naturally occurring motor acts. Movements induced by electrical stimulation of the neocortex are also inhibited (Vanegas and Flynn, 1968) as are at least some components of attack behaviours elicited by hypothalamic stimulation (Siegel and Flynn, 1968).

E. ELECTROGRAPHIC CORRELATES OF BEHAVIOUR

Turning to the types of tasks or behaviours which may be assumed to be associated with specific hippocampal rhythms and related hypothalamic tuning, a report by Pond and Schwartzbaum (1970) indicates that rhythmic theta-like activity is obtained by *both* rewarding and aversive stimulation of hypothalamic and midbrain sites. These results cast further doubt upon the generalization of Grastyan and his colleagues (Grastyan *et al.*, 1965, 1966) that hippocampal theta rhythms are associated with approach responses whereas hippocampal desynchronization is associated with withdrawal and escape. Pond and Schwartzbaum found that the hippocampus could reflect either slow wave patterns or desynchronization during electrical stimulation of the brain depending on what area of the brain was stimulated. Rewarding stimulation of the hypothalamus produced theta-like activities in the hippocampus, whereas rewarding stimulation of the septal area produced desynchronization of the hippocampus. The fact that rewarding *and* aversive stimulation can elicit slow wave activity in the hippocampus indicates that the activation of any important motivational sequence of behaviour, whether it be approach or withdrawal oriented, can inhibit activities of the hippocampal system and, as a consequence, elicit rhythmic slow activity in the hippocampus. It should be noted, however, that normal eating behaviours are associated with desynchronized hippocampal activities, whereas eating behaviours elicited by electrical stimulation of the hypothalamus produce synchronized patterns of activity in the hippocampus (Pond *et al.*, 1970). This also reflects a reciprocity of inhibitory influences between the hypothalamus and the hippocampus.

Whether or not the effects of electrical stimulation of the hippocampus will be comparable to the effects of the epileptogenic foci created in the hippocampus by penicillin is uncertain, and quite different results are obtained when the stimulation produces after-discharges as compared with when it does not. At least the present model provides certain working assumptions about the effects of such sites of abnormal activity. In addition the theory offers suggestions for new lines of investigation into the possible interaction between the type of training task used and the effects produced by drugs, brain stimulation, or brain lesions.

At this point, we have completed a circle. The problem that initiated our research concerned the reasons behind recent memory disturbances following "bilateral" temporal lobe surgery in some patients. The original research programme apparently diverged from this central goal, but now, with our studies of the animal with artificially established epileptogenic foci, we find behavioural deficits which seem to be similar to those found in the few patients having a loss in recent memory. In addition, a tentative theory has been generated which has arisen in response to data from many types of experiments and which at least summarizes a large amount of data and which leads to a large number of testable hypotheses concerning the retention of previously acquired habits. It is based upon limbic system activities which converge upon hypothalamic systems presumed to be of fundamental significance to the organism. These convergences are both inhibitory and excitatory, depending upon the systems and tasks under consideration. Within the present framework, no aspect of the limbic system or hypothalamus should be considered to be "inhibitory" or "excitatory" in any absolute sense. Rather, they should be considered to be inhibitory or excitatory relative to the action, task, and disposition of the organism at any moment in time.

The theory presented in this paper is similar in some ways to the one advanced by Molnár and Grastyán (Chapter 16, this volume). The chapter by Douglas (Chapter 20) also reviews many aspects of hippocampal contributions to behaviour related to this theory.

VII. Conclusion

In this paper I have tried to propose mechanisms of limbic system function which may help explain phenomena of memory arising from observations made upon patients with disorders of the temporal lobe. These limbic mechanisms are related to the ergotropic and trophotropic divisions of the hypothalamus whose facilitatory and inhibitory influences on behaviour are well established for certain types of physiological functions but may have relevance to behaviour as well. It was postulated that the hippocampus normally acts to suppress (inhibit) activities in the ergotropic system under conditions of environmental uncertainty. This function would be enhanced under some conditions of hippocampal stimulation but suppressed under others. Lesions of the hippocampus should induce an ergotropic balance under many conditions.

The implications of these speculations were applied to the results of many types of physiological and behavioural experiments.

Acknowledgements

This research was supported in part by Grant NIH-MH-16384-02. I would like to acknowledge the fact that the theoretical speculations have evolved from many discussions of the systems involved with Dr Carol Van Hartesveldt. Her contributions have been most important and she deserves credit for any merit the suggestions may have, although the difficulties and problems in the conceptualizations are undoubtedly ones of my own creation.

References

Bagshaw, M. H. and Benzies, S. (1968). Multiple measures of the orienting reaction to a simple non-reinforced stimulus after amygdalectomy. *Experimental Neurology*, **20**, 175–187.

Bagshaw, M. H., Kimble, D. P. and Pribram, K. H. (1965). The GSR of monkeys during orienting and habituation and after ablation of the amygdala, hippocampus and inferotemporal cortex. *Neuropsychologia*, **3**, 111–119.

Clark, C. V. H. and Isaacson, R. L. (1965). Effect of bilateral hippocampal ablation on DRL performance. *Journal of Comparative and Physiological Psychology*, **59**, 137–140.

Dafney, N. and Feldman, S. (1969). Effects of stimulating reticular formation, hippocampus and septum on single cells in the posterior hypothalamus. *Electroencephalography and Clinical Neurophysiology*, **26**, 578–587.

Delgado, J. M. R. and Sevillano, M. (1961). Evolution of repeated hippocampal seizures in the cat. *Electroencephalography and Clinical Neurophysiology*, **13**, 722–723.

Endörczi, E. and Lissák, K. (1962). Spontaneous goal directed motor activity related to the alimentary conditioned reflex behavior and its regulation by neural and humoral factors. *Acta Physiological Academiae Scientarum Hungariae*, **21**, 265–283.

Erickson, C. K. and Patel, J. B. (1969). Facilitation of avoidance learning by posttrial hippocampal electrical stimulation. *Journal of Comparative and Physiological Psychology*, **68**, 400–406.

Gellhorn, E. (1970). The emotions and the ergotropic and trophotropic systems. *Psychologische Forschung,* **34**, 48–94.

Gergen, J. A. (1967). Functional properties of the hippocampus in the sub-human primate. *Progress in Brain Research*, **27**, 442–461.

Glickman, S. E., Higgins, T. and Isaacson, R. L. (1970). Some effects of hippocampal lesions on the behavior of Mongolian gerbils. *Physiology and Behavior,* **5**, 931–938.

Goddard, G. V. (1964). Amygdaloid stimulation and learning in the rat. *Journal of Comparative and Physiological Psychology*, **58**, 23–30.

Goodfellow, E. F. and Neimer, W. T. (1961). The spread of after-discharge from stimulation of the rhinencephalon in cat. *Electrocephalography and Clinical Neurophysiology*, **13**, 710–721.

Grastyán, E., Lissak, K., Madarasz, I. and Donhoffer, H. (1959). Hippocampal electrical activity during the development of conditioned reflexes. *Electroencephalography and Clinical Neurophysiology*, **21**, 34–53.

Grastyán, E., Karmos, G., Vereczkey, L., Martin, J. and Kellenyi, L. (1965). Hypothalamic motivational processes as reflected by their electrical correlates. *Science*, **149**, 91–93.

Grastyán, E., Karmos, G., Vereczkey, L. and Kellenyi, L. (1966). The hippocampal electrical correlates of the homeostatic regulation of motivation. *Electroencephalography and Clinical Neurophysiology*, **21**, 34–53.

Hamilton, G. L. (1970). Effects of penicillin-induced epileptic foci in the hippocampus. Unpublished doctoral dissertation, University of Florida.

Hamilton, G. L. and Isaacson, R. L. (1970). Changes in avoidance behavior following epileptogenic lesions of the mesencephalon. *Physiology and Behavior*, **5**, 1165–1167.

Hess, W. R. (1949). *Das Zwischenhirn*. Basel: Schwabe.

Isaacson, R. L., Douglas, R. J. and Moore, R. Y. (1961). The effects of radical hippocampal ablation on acquisition of avoidance responses. *Journal of Comparative and Physiological Psychology*, **54**, 625–628.

Kemble, E. D. and Beckman, G. J. (1970). Vicarious trial and error following amygdaloid lesions in rats. *Neuropsychologia*, **8**, 161–169.

Kesner, R. P. and Doty, R. W. (1968). Amnesia produced in cats by local seizure activity initiated from the amygdala. *Experimental Neurology*, **21**, 58–68.

Kim, C., Choi, H., Kim, J. K., Chang, H. K., Park, R. S. and Kang, I. Y. (1970). General behavioral activity and its component patterns in hippocampectomized rats. *Brain Research*. **19**, 379–394.

Klüver, H. (1965). Neurology of normal and abnormal perception. In: P. H. Hoch and J. Zubin (Eds.) *Psychopathology of Perception*. New York: Grune and Stratton.

Levine, M. S., Goldrich, S. G. Pond, F. J., Livesey, P. and Schwartzbaum, J. S.

(1970). Retrograde amnestic effects of inferotemporal and amygdaloid seizures upon conditioned suppression of leverpressing in monkeys. *Neuropsychologia*, **8**, 431–442.

Lidsky, A. and Slotnick, B. M. (1970). Electrical stimulation of the hippocampus and electroconvulsive shock produce similar amnestic effects in mice. *Neuropsychologia*, **8**, 363–369.

Lidsky, A. and Slotnick, B. M. (1971). Effects of post-trial limbic stimulation on retention of a one-trial passive avoidance response. *Journal of Comparative and Physiological Psychology*, (in Press).

MacLean, P. D., Flanigan, S., Flynn, J. P., Kim, C. and Stevens, J. R. (1956). Hippocampal function: Tentative correlations of conditioning, EEG, drug, and radioautographic studies. *Yale Journal of Biology and Medicine*, **28**, 380–395.

Matsumoto, H. and Ajmone-Marsan, C. (1964). Cortical cellular phenomena in experimental epilepsy. *Experimental Neurology*, **9**, 286–304.

McGaugh, J. L. (1967). Drug facilitation of memory and learning. In: D. H. Efron (Ed.) *Proceedings of the sixth annual meeting of the American College of Neuropsychopharmacology*, 891–904.

Milner, B. (1959). The memory defect in bilateral hippocampal lesions. *Psychiatric Research Reports*, **11**, 43–52.

Olton, D. S. (1969). Penicillin and the hippocampus. Unpublished doctoral dissertation, University of Michigan.

Olton, D. S. (1970). Specific deficits in active avoidance behavior following penicillin injection into the hippocampus. *Physiology and Behavior*, **5**, 957–963.

Olton, D. S. and Isaacson, R. L. (1968). Hippocampal lesions and active avoidance. *Physiology and Behavior*, **3**, 719–724.

Poletti, C. E., Kinnard, M. A. and MacLean, P. D. (1969). Effect of hippocampal stimulation on unit activity of hypothalamic, preoptic, and basal forebrain areas. *Electroencephalography and Clinical Neurophysiology*, **27**, 606.

Poletti, C. E., Kinnard, M. A. and MacLean, P. D. (1970). Analysis of hippocampal influence on units of mammillary region in awake, sitting squirrel-monkeys. *Electroencephalography and Clinical Neurophysiology*, **29**, 322.

Pond, F. J. and Schwartzbaum, J. S. (1970). Hippocampal electrical activity evoked by rewarding and aversive brain stimulation in rats. *Communications in Behavioral Biology*, **5**, 89–103.

Pond, F. J., Lidsky, T. I., Levine, M. S. and Schwartzbaum, J. S. (1970). Hippocampal electrical activity during hypothalamic-evoked consummatory behavior in rats. *Psychonomic Science*, **21**, 21–23,

Pribram, K. H. (1969). The neurobehavioral analysis of limbic forebrain mechanisms: Revision and progress report. In: *Advances in the Study of Behavior*, Vol. 2 New York: Academic Press.

Pribram, K. H. (1971). *The Languages of the Brain*. Englewood Cliffs: Prentice Hall.

Schmaltz, L. W. (1968). The hippocampus and recent memory loss. Unpublished doctoral dissertation, University of Michigan.

Schmaltz, L. W. (1971). Deficit in active avoidance learning in rats following penicillin injection into hippocampus. *Physiology and Behavior*, **6**, 667–674

Schmaltz, L. W. and Isaacson, R. L. (1966). The effects of preliminary training conditions upon DRL 20 performance in the hippocampectomized rat. *Physiology and Behavior*, **1**, 175–182.

Schmidt, R. P. and Wilder, B. J. (1968). *Epilepsy*. Philadelphia: F. A. Davis.

Schwartzbaum, J. S., Wilson, W. A. and Marrissett, J. R. (1961). The effects of amygdalectomy on locomotor activity in monkeys. *Journal of Comparative and Physiological Psychology*, **54,** 334–336.

Scoville, W. B. (1954). The limbic love in man. *Journal of Neurosurgery*, **11,** 64–66.

Siegel, A. and Flynn, J. P. (1968). Differential effects of electrical stimulation and lesions of the hippocampus and adjacent regions upon attack behavior in cats. *Brain Research*, **7,** 252.

Stuart, D. G., Porter, R. W., and Adey, W. R. (1964). Hypothalamic unit activity. II. Central and peripheral influences. *Electroencephalography and Clinical Neurophysiology*, **16,** 248–258.

Ursin, H. and Kaada, B. R. (1960). Functional localization within the amygdaloid complex in the cat. *Electroencephalography and Clinical Neurophysiology*, **12,** 1–20.

Valenstein, E. S. and Nauta, W. J. H. (1959). A comparison of the distribution of the fornix system in the rat, guinea pig, cat, and monkey. *Journal of Comparative Neurology*, **113,** 337–363.

Vanegas, H. and Flynn, J. P. (1968). Inhibition of cortically-elicited movement by electrical stimulation of the hippocampus. *Brain Research*, **11,** 489–506.

Walker, A. E., Johnson, H. C., and Kollros, J. J. (1945). Penicillin convulsions. The convulsive effects of penicillin applied to the cortex of monkey and man. *Surgery, Gynecology, and Obstetrics,* **81,** 692–701.

Ward, A. A., Jr. (1969). The epileptic neuron: chronic foci in animals and man. In: Jasper, H. H., Ward, A. A., and Pope, A. (Eds.) *Basic Mechanisms of the Epilepsies*. Boston: Little Brown and Co.

Wilder, B. J. and Morrell, F. (1967). Secondary epileptogenesis in the frog forebrain. *Neurology*, **17,** 1041–1051.

20 | Pavlovian Conditioning and the Brain

R. J. DOUGLAS

University of Washington, Seattle, Washington, U.S.A.

I.	Introduction	529
II.	Internal Inhibition and Excitation	530
III.	Hippocampal Lesions and Behaviour	531
	A. Simple Nonreinforcement	531
	B. Inhibition of Delay	533
	C. Passive Avoidance (plus Active)	534
	D. External Inhibition	535
	E. Differential Inhibition	536
	F. Sleep and Trauma	537
IV.	Behaviour Unaffected by Hippocampal Lesions	538
V.	Excitation and the Mediation of Reinforcement	538
VI.	Association Learning	539
VII.	The Drug Parallel	541
VIII.	Development	543
IX.	The Model: Putting it all Together	544
X.	The Nature of Internal Inhibition	549
	Acknowledgements	550
	References	550

I. Introduction

I originally believed that contributors to this book would write on the same subject, and that the term "inhibition" would at least loosely correspond to Pavlovian internal inhibition. But after reading several chapters my reactions to the frequent need for authors to define inhibition changed from annoyance to sympathy. Several authors have implied, overtly or covertly, that the presence of inhibition can only be inferred from observing the subject strenuously attempt to perform the "opposite" response. Such an idea is, however, neither derivable from Pavlov's definitions nor from "reading between the lines". Instead, it smacks of being a defensive conditioned reflex. While there is nothing intrinsically wrong with calling aversive behaviour "inhibition", it is obviously not internal inhibition. Perhaps we should use "suppression" to cover this behaviour, in accord with clinical usage. I hope to show in this chapter that there is an important difference between inhibition and behaviour based on punishment. I

MM

cannot at this point rigidly define inhibition, however, as one purpose of the entire chapter is to do just that.

My main purpose, however, is to show that all the elements of Pavlov's theory correspond to a true division of labour within the brain. The key point in this argument is the association between internal inhibition and a unique brain structure known as the hippocampus. It has already been pointed out that animals act as if they lack internal inhibition after this structure is massively damaged (Douglas, 1967; Kimble, 1968), but the full extent of this parallel has barely been touched upon. And once it is granted that the hippocampus is, so to speak, the organ of internal inhibition, then everything else in Pavlov's model falls into place. Known relations between the hippocampus and the rest of the brain, and the stipulated relations between Pavlovian variables, conspire to almost force the assignment of other functions to other brain regions. But more, the anatomical and physiological facts about the hippocampus go a long way towards answering the question so frequently asked: "Just what do you *mean* by inhibition?"

II. Internal Inhibition and Excitation

According to Pavlov (1960) internal inhibition is an actively generated brain process based primarily on nonreinforcement. The thing which is inhibited is an opposed process called excitation. Excitation is in some degree a response to any stimulus which can be detected, but the process builds up or becomes more powerful as a consequence of reinforcement. This reinforcement can be either "good" (alimentary) or "bad" (defensive). Internal inhibition is in general much more labile than excitation, and it can be completely (but temporarily) held in check by a distracting stimulus or unexpected event (disinhibition). Excitation and internal inhibition are generated somewhere within a very crude sensory analyser system, and they mutually antagonize and induce each other. The disinhibitory mechanism, in contrast, must be directed by a system capable of very fine-grained sensory analysis.

Our thesis is that the hippocampus is the organ of expression of internal inhibition, and that it is not *directly* involved in the generation of excitation. As a test of this thesis we demand that animals with massive hippocampal damage do poorly on tasks which involve internal inhibition as a positive factor. To the extent that performance is "saturated" with inhibition, animals lacking hippocampi should be deficient. On tasks where internal inhibition is irrelevant or tangential to the problem, hippocampectomized animals should be normal. Finally, these animals should be superior to normal on those problems in which inhibition is a negative factor which detracts from performance in normals. Note that it is not necessary that the lesioned animals be totally incapable of solving tasks even when internal inhibition is undeniably important, because it will later be shown that there is some evidence that there are alternative mechanisms for problem solving. So our first task is to organize the behavioural lesion literature relating to the hippocampus and inhibition.

III. Hippocampal Lesions and Behaviour

A. Simple Nonreinforcement

Since internal inhibition is primarily (but not exclusively) a product of nonreinforcement, we shall first consider the behaviour of hippocampectomized subjects on tasks where this factor is most obviously involved. The following is a list of behaviours which we might conclude from Pavlov, various other theorists, or just common sense, to be importantly based on nonreinforcement:

> habituation
> extinction
> reversal (first stage)
> active error reduction
> inhibitory preconditioning
> spontaneous alternation
> complex maze learning

1. We can dispose of the first three items easily because many experiments have shown deficits in habituation, extinction and reversal learning in a variety of species after hippocampal lesions (see reviews by Douglas, 1967; Kimble, 1968).

2. On many tasks it is difficult to determine one way or another whether a subject has avoided errors by default (due to reinforcement of an alternative) or by an active process, or both. But there are several possible ways to gain an approximation to such a determination, including a study of a generalization curve for the negative stimulus, as has been so profitably exploited by Terrace (Chapter 4, this volume). The closest anyone has come so far to such an investigation with hippocampectomized animals was a study by Douglas and Pribram (1966). In that experiment normal and brain-lesioned monkeys were first trained on a type of two-stimulus discrimination problem. Then, over a series of trials, they were given the opportunity to respond to either the positive stimulus versus a novel stimulus, or the negative versus a novel. Normals preferred the positive stimulus to a novel one, and a novel to the negative. Hippocampectomized monkeys also preferred (responded to) the positive stimulus. But, unlike the normals, they did not prefer a novel to a negative stimulus. Another

way of trying to get at this problem is to examine learning performance as
the number of negative cues is increased. Douglas, *et al.* (1969) trained
monkeys on a series of problems each of which contained just one positive
or rewarded stimulus, but with the number of unrewarded cues varying
from one to four. With only one negative stimulus present the hippocampectomized monkeys were entirely normal, as had been shown many
times previously. But as the number of negative stimuli per problem
mounted the hippocampal group took longer and longer to achieve criterion. Their performance was in fact highly related to the probability of
being correct by chance, as if they profited only from reinforcement. In
contrast, normal and amygdalectomized monkeys learned in about the
same number of trials no matter how many negative cues were used, and
their performance was totally unrelated to chance reinforcement probability. This appears to be strange, but it was confirmed by previously
gathered data from an analogous problem.

3. Inhibitory preconditioning could conceivably be used in conjunction
with conditioned inhibition tests, but the conditioned inhibition procedures employed by Wagner and Rescorla (see Chapter 12, this volume)
involved an entirely different technique. Inhibitory preconditioning has
also been called "latent inhibition", but there is nothing "latent" about it
at all. Inhibitory preconditioning is a very simple procedure in which the
future CS is presented a number of times without reinforcement. It should
therefore generate internal inhibition. After this the stimulus is used as a
positive cue in reinforced excitatory conditioning, with the expected result
being that such conditioning should be retarded in comparison to the case
where inhibitory preconditioning is not employed. In any event, this
procedure is logically based on nonreinforcement and specifically designed
to produce the generation of internal inhibition. Ackil *et al.* (1969) did
find the expected retardation in their control animals, but found that
inhibitory preconditioning apparently had no effect on hippocampectomized rats.

4. Spontaneous alternation is the very epitome of behaviour based on
internal inhibition. According to some theorists (e.g. Glanzer, 1953) spontaneous alternation is merely one form of habituation, and a very pure
one at that. Spontaneous alternation in the general sense refers to the
tendency of most mammals (including man) to systematically vary their
choice behaviour during exploration or manipulation of stimuli. In the rat
this is usually tested by giving the subject two consecutive unrewarded
trials in a T maze. If he chooses to enter the right side alley on trial one,
the chances are about 85 in 100 that he will enter the left alley on the
second trial. A "standard" explanation for this behaviour is that exposure
to, or examination of a stimulus in the absence of reinforcement leads to a

reduction in the excitatory value (or interest) of the stimulus. It has been abundantly proven that spontaneous alternation is not due to inhibition of a "response" but of a choice (Glanzer, 1953; Douglas, 1966). It should also be noted that internal inhibition occurs on the sensory, not the motor, end of behaviour. The importance of spontaneous alternation for present purposes is that there is no behaviour more adversely affected by hippo-campal lesions than this. Extensive damage to the hippocampus totally and permanently abolishes this tendency, while a variety of other brain lesions have no effect whatever (Douglas, et al., 1968). This is true whether the hippocampus is removed in one or two stages, in infancy or adulthood (Douglas and Peterson, 1969a). This behaviour cannot be explained as being "simply" due to loss of memory ability or an inability to tell one alley from the other. The reason is that these animals are entirely normal in learning to go to one alley on the basis of reinforcement. But they entirely lack the normal powerful tendency to choose the unexplored alternative, and there is no contingency between their choices in the absence of reinforcement.

5. Many investigators have reported severe deficits in complex (multi-choice point) mazes after even small lesions of the hippocampus (see Douglas, 1967). The deficit appears to be related to the loss of spontaneous alternation in that the lesioned subjects make repeated re-entries into blind alleys, as if not profiting by previous nonreinforced instances. Many of the old-time maze learning analysts believed error avoidance (inhibition) to be extremely crucial in maze learning. Dennis and Sollenberger (1934) went so far as to claim that complex maze learning consisted almost entirely of the active elimination of erroneous pathways which, it should be noted, far outnumber the one single error-free path.

Thus, hippocampal lesions do indeed result in deficits on this list of tasks or responses believed to involve nonreinforcement in an important way. No brain lesion other than hippocampal produces even this limited constellation of effects, and they would appear to be specifically related to the function of this structure. It should be noted that we are here including the septal region as an integral part of the "hippocampus", as the two are highly related anatomically and physiologically. It is hardly coincidental that septal and hippocampal lesions produce, with very few exceptions, the same general behavioural syndrome characterized as a "loss of inhibi-tion" (e.g. McCleary, 1966). The hippocampal syndrome also appears after injection of anticholinergic drugs, as will be discussed later.

B. INHIBITION OF DELAY

Inhibition of delay, or delay inhibition, is also based on nonreinforcement, but Pavlov saw fit to give it a separate name. Delay inhibition is generated by lengthening a formerly shorter time interval between CS and UCS. A time delay *per se* does not, however, necessarily induce inhibition, because a constant or unchanged delay period can merely be part of a compound CS for excitatory conditioning. Thus, hippocampally lesioned animals should have no problem with long time intervals unless these represent an increase from shorter intervals to which the subject has become accustomed. This is precisely what has been found. Clark and Isaacson (1965) reported that hippocampectomized rats could not learn to wait for 20 secs between barpresses if they had first been trained on a continuous reinforcement schedule. Schmaltz and Isaacson (1966) confirmed the earlier report and showed that rats with this lesion could learn the 20 sec DRL problem normally provided they had not first been trained on a continuous schedule. In both studies hippocampectomized rats were found to be remarkably quick to associate a leverpress with reinforcement, or to shape.

C. PASSIVE AVOIDANCE (PLUS ACTIVE)

In the days when an intuitive belief in "inhibition" was sufficient, passive avoidance was classed as being inhibitory with no second thoughts. But in a Pavlovian framework this is not so. Passive avoidance is presumably based on reinforcement (punishment) and thus is excitatory. Or it would be, were it not for Pavlov's observations in closely analogous situations. Pavlov claimed, and demonstrated, that alimentary and defensive conditioned reflexes followed the same rules. But he convincingly showed that one cannot simply switch from one to the other. That is, if an animal is first reinforced with meat (alimentary conditioned reflex) and then is placed (cold turkey) into a situation in which the very same CS is now reinforced with mild acid (defensive) the result is profound and long-lasting inhibition. The excitatory response (salivation) is reduced to zero and stays there for a long period of many trials. It works the same way when the reverse switch is made, from defensive to alimentary. Thus, we might add another condition (aside from nonreinforcement) in which internal inhibition is powerfully generated: the alteration of the significance of the stimulus. Passive avoidance is little more than a translation of the classical techniques of Pavlov into instrumental behaviour. In the typical passive avoidance task the subject is first taught that a particular spatial location and stimulus complex is associated with food (or water) reinforcement. Then, on a critical trial, that same stimulus complex is defensively reinforced with an electric shock. The result should be internal inhibition. If the approach response is anything like salivation, it should fail to occur (in normal subjects). Under conditions such as those above hippocampectomized rats are very poor passive avoiders compared to controls (Isaacson and Wickelgren, 1962; Snyder and Isaacson, 1965; and Kimble, 1963).

Finally, learning in the shuttle-box has been claimed to involve inhibition in a negative fashion. That is, the same grid region is both safe and dangerous. Animals with intact inhibitory processes (normal on passive avoidance) should have a problem here, while those lacking inhibition should have less trouble (see McCleary, 1966). On the other hand, a one-way version of the shuttle box should not contain this factor. In one-way active avoidance the same stimulus (grid, box) is always either safe or dangerous and never both. Normal animals learn the one-way avoidance problem very much faster than the two-way, while with scopolamine injections or hippocampal lesions we find that the subject takes just about as long to learn either problem (see Suits and Isaacson, 1968). As the present theory would predict, hippocampectomized rats are markedly superior to normals in learning the shuttle box problem (Isaacson *et al.*, 1961). Thus, hippocampectomized animals are indeed superior to normals in at least one case in which inhibition is believed to be a negative factor in learning or performance. There are other examples as well. For instance, Douglas and Pribram (1969) trained normal and lesioned monkeys to perform a sequential response to two stimuli which appeared in sequence. The second (directly reinforced) stimulus did not appear until the first one had been touched. Thus, a response to the first stimulus was not directly reinforced. Theoretically we might then suspect that maybe animals possessing normal internal inhibition might develop a maladaptive tendency to shy away from that first stimulus. In fact, we found that the normals did have a period early in learning in which their response latency went up for the first response. As a result, they took much longer to reach stable levels of speed in the sequential response than did our hippocampectomized monkeys. The latter had marked reductions in latency on all aspects of the sequential response from trial one onwards, and they reached stable asymptotic performance levels much faster than the normals.

D. External Inhibition

External inhibition is mediated by internal inhibition, and so it should be absent in hippocampectomized animals if our thesis is correct. The major difference between internal and external inhibition is that internal inhibition involves only one stimulus (the CS), while external inhibition is the effect of one stimulus (a distractor) upon another (the CS). Although distraction (like the other responses discussed here) is a very complicated subject, we would expect that, by and large, hippocampectomized subjects should be less than normally distracted from an ongoing response by the presence of an "external inhibitor". This is supported by two studies in which attempts were made to distract rats from straight alley running by placing stimuli along the way. In both cases (Wickelgren and Isaacson,

1963; Raphelson *et al.*, 1965) it was found that rats with hippocampal damage were less slowed in their running by the distractor. In the latter study, in fact, they seemed to be speeded up on distraction trials as compared to previous runs. On the other hand, Hendrickson and Kimble (1966) found that rats with hippocampal lesions actually reacted more strongly to a "distractor" if they were not engaged in any notable activity, as compared to normals. They were relatively undistractable when engaged in motivated behaviour such as drinking.

One final observation on this point was, alas, cut from the Douglas and Pribram (1969) distraction study by the editors. In that study hippocampectomized and control monkeys were actively engaged in performing a learned sequential response to two stimuli. Then, at unpredictable intervals, a distracting stimulus appeared simultaneously with the second stimulus of the sequence. In this case the distractor was a loud (but not painfully loud) buzzer. The sequential stimuli were visual pattern cues. The sudden onset of the buzzer produced startle responses in all animals of every group, with most literally hitting the low ceiling of their testing cage. At onset of the buzzer the normal animals (and those with amygdala lesions) failed to complete the sequence and instead turned around and oriented towards the buzzer. After a typical minute or two they turned around and resumed the sequential responding. They rapidly habituated to the buzzer, eventually behaving as if it were being ignored or unheard. In contrast, the hippocampectomized monkeys, though startled, completed the sequential response on the way up. Their interresponse latencies were even shorter, as a rule, than on their nondistraction trials. As in the Raphelson study above, the distractor appeared to have the effect of energizing ongoing behaviour rather than halting it. In any event it seems clear that, as expected, animals with hippocampal lesions are more difficult to distract than are normals, at least when engaged in goal-directed behaviour.

E. DIFFERENTIAL INHIBITION

Pavlov demonstrated that a differential conditioned reflex was importantly mediated by internal inhibition. For years this hindered our complete equation of hippocampal function and inhibition because it had been repeatedly demonstrated that hippocampectomized animals were normal in discrimination learning. But the problem turned out to be a classic error of confusing the name with the thing. Pavlov's procedure for discrimination training differed significantly from the one usually used in instrumental training, since he by necessity could present only one stimulus at a time. In our instrumental techniques the two stimuli were simultaneously present. Pavlov further compounded the difference by regularly training with only the rewarded stimulus and then gradually introducing the negative. Considering the wide generalization that occurs when only one stimulus is used, this procedure almost guaranteed that extinction would be involved. The closest instrumental analogies to the Pavlovian situation are successive discrimination and Go;No go problems. In successive discrimination the subject has the two crucial stimuli presented one at a time, as in Pavlov's case, and hippocampectomized rats do indeed have great difficulty in solving such a problem (Kimble, 1963). The Go; No go problem has a variety of possible procedures, and unfortunately I know of no case in which the one most like Pavlovian differentiation was used. With some possible versions of the Go;No go task one might, in fact, suspect that animals with hippocampal lesions might be superior to normals. An example would be a case in which the same stimulus is used on both trials, with Go and No go requirements alternating. It is conceivable in this situation that internal inhibition would be generated in normal animals who might view the No go trials as extinction. Means *et al.* (1970) used this technique and did in fact find the hippocampectomized rats to be superior to normal, although they "explained" the results differently, as is their privilege. There are other cases where seemingly slight changes in procedure produce vast differences. For example, it was mentioned previously that hippocampally lesioned monkeys are sharply superior to normals in acquiring a sequential response to two stimuli when these are presented in succession, one at a time. But they are very much inferior to normals when the two stimuli are simultaneously presented. Kimble and Pribram (1963) first claimed these results to indicate a loss of ability to learn sequences, but Kimble later admitted (personal communication) that the results did appear to support the "lack of inhibition" hypothesis. That is, all monkeys in all groups on that problem early developed a maladaptive tendency to respond to the second stimulus of the pair, the one immediately preceding the reward on successful trials. With further training the normals eventually ceased this fruitless behaviour, while the hippocampectomized monkeys did not. Thus, it would appear that, once again, animals with hippocampal lesions are superior or inferior to normals depending on whether the procedure makes inhibition a positive or negative factor in learning.

F. SLEEP AND TRAUMA

Pavlov made two other observations about internal inhibition which may appear to be anecdotal, but which are well documented. The first was that conditions in which internal inhibition was supposedly generated tended to produce sleep. So striking was the relation between internal inhibition and sleep that Pavlov went so far as to believe that sleep *was* a kind of internal inhibition. We now know, however, that sleep is a much more complicated phenomenon that Pavlov dreamed. His evidence merely shows that internal inhibition, in the absence of excitation, is an inducer of sleep. Thus, we might expect animals with hippocampal lesions to spend perhaps less time in sleep than normals. Two different experiments have now shown this to be the case (Jarrard, 1968; Kim et al., 1970).

Second, Pavlov noted that a traumatic experience could selectively abolish internal inhibition for days, with excitatory mechanisms still intact, as if a fuse had blown in the internal inhibition circuitry. We now know that the hippocampus is peculiarly susceptible to electrical seizures which are followed by prolonged "post-ictal" depression. Pavlov found his "blown fuse" in dogs which were barely rescued from the Petrograd flood. Douglas, et al (1970) attempted to do the same thing with the profound trauma of an electroconvulsive shock. Rats were tested at frequent intervals for spontaneous alternation for one week following a single ECS treatment. Roughly half of the group failed to alternate for up to a week after the experience, although all were excellent alternators before the ECS. Many other studies have also reported post-ECS behavioural changes identical to those seen after hippocampectomy (e.g. Vanderwolf, 1963).

IV. Behaviour Unaffected by Hippocampal Lesions

Our thesis demands, of course, that hippocampal lesions do not merely interfere with learning and behaviour in general, and the previous discussion has pointed out that it does not do so. The lesion has either no effect or a very mild one on many responses, and in other cases the lesioned animals are actually superior to normal. As a general rule, an animal with large hippocampal lesions is within the normal range on problems requiring an active excitatory response to a reinforced stimulus. In our very first experiment (unpublished), for example, we found a remarkably quick development of a leg lift response (excitatory, defensive) to a tone in dogs with hippocampal lesions. These animals tend to be superior to normal in cases where there are reasons for believing that inhibition detracts from performance. They are inferior to normal on precisely those tasks or responses believed by theorists or experimenters to involve inhibition as a positive factor.

V. Excitation and the Mediation of Reinforcement

We could almost define excitation as something the hippocampus does not do, but we can go further than that. As we shall see later, there is good reason to believe that excitation and an excitatory reaction are two different things. The closest term in modern psychology to "excitation" is "arousal". And arousal has two meanings, at the very least. The first is the general overall level of excitability or wakefulness. The second is a reaction to a stimulus. These are roughly equivalent to Sharpless and Jasper's (1956) concepts of tonic and phasic arousal. The growth of the magnitude of the excitatory reaction to a CS, as a function of reinforcement, would appear to be a function of another part of the limbic system, the amygdala. For example, Douglas and Pribram (1966) found amygdalectomized monkeys, after learning a discrimination problem, to fail to respond to the positive stimulus preferentially, when it was paired with novel stimuli. In contrast, they did tend to shy away from the negative cue, responding preferentially to a novel stimulus paired with the negative cue. Animals with amygdala lesions tend to fail miserably on a variety of excitatory tasks, and they do poorly on just about every avoidance task known to man (see review by Goddard, 1964). In the most direct study yet undertaken, Bagshaw and Coppock (1968) found that it was apparently impossible to establish a simple excitatory conditioned GSR reflex in amygdalectomized monkeys, although they did have a GSR response to the unconditioned stimulus. In contrast, animals with amygdala lesions tend to be normal or even superior on such inhibitory tasks as extinction (Douglas and Pribram, 1966), habituation (Douglas and Pribram, 1969), spontaneous alternation (Douglas et al., 1968) and many others.

VI. Association Learning

It is paradoxical that although Pavlov rarely used the term "association" his model is basically a stimulus-stimulus association theory. Stranger yet, his seemingly endless discussions of excitation and inhibition are unaccompanied by any explicit statement as to their relationship to the end result of conditioning: the formation of a "pathway" or associative bond. It is clear that he considers this pathway to be a physical entity, while excitation and inhibition are dynamic processes which are here today and gone tomorrow, so to speak. There are many ways in which excitation can be gauged for intensity, and one of these is the strength of the orienting reflex, as discussed by Pavlov. But some investigators have found that as training progresses to the point where behaviour becomes automatic, the orienting reflex drops out (see Sokolov, 1963). The orienting reflex is related to attention in about the same way as the GSR is related to emotionality. And who among us has not noticed that conscious attention, so necessary in the beginning stages of learning, disappears once a skill has been acquired? This suggests that associative bonds, once formed, may be independent of the very processes which gave them birth. This leads to the following set of expectations. First, it may be possible for associative bonds to be formed even without the help of excitation or inhibition. That is, the two dynamic processes may be merely aids to learning, and not learning itself. Second, once an associative bond has been formed, with the aid of the dynamic processes, excitation and inhibition may be superfluous as far as continued performance is concerned.

A study bearing directly on this point was performed by Pribram *et al.* (1969). They intensively investigated discrimination learning, reversal and memory in monkeys who had both amygdala and hippocampus removed prior to training. In brief, the differences between these and normal monkeys were as follows. When a normal monkey learns a discrimination problem there is usually an initial period of varying length in which success is at a chance level; this is terminated by an abrupt rise to very high levels of success (90% range). On a reversal problem this jump in success is more dramatic than on the original discrimination because it goes all the way from a very low point to a very high one. This behaviour in no way resembles the mythical gradually rising learning curve reported in ancient text books or demanded by early theorists. Several different theorists treat this fact as indicating that discrimination learning involves a process which might be called "hypothesis testing" or attention control. Until the subject sees the stimuli as differing along the relevant dimension his success is random, since his hypotheses are at right angles to the correct solution. In any event, the monkeys with combined hippocampal-amygdaloid lesions had the same sudden jump in performance seen in the normals; the difference was *where* the take-off point occurred. A normal monkey might have a "chance success" interval lasting for anywhere between ten and a hundred trials or so, but with our lesioned animals one thousand trials was typical. On the reversal problem the differences were again dramatic. The normal animals jumped quickly from 10 to 90% correct, while the lesioned subjects learned the reversal problem in two stages. First they drifted slowly to the 50% chance mark. Then they tended to stay at 50% for prolonged periods (the mid-reversal plateau). Finally, they "jumped up" to the 90% range with their slope being almost identical to that of original learning. The curves were consistent with the idea that they "gave up" on the original problem and then later acquired it as if it were a new problem they were solving for the first time. The behaviour of the lesioned animals suggested that they lacked mechanisms which are very helpful in learning, and which greatly enhance learning speed, but which are not actually required for association learning to occur. The same phenomena reported here have been observed in human retardates, and the explanation is similar. They lack mechanisms which allow the subject to "lock on" to reinforced stimuli or stimulus dimensions and to "shift off" nonreinforced cues or dimensions. In Pavlovian terms, these would be excitation and internal inhibition. It has been pointed out (Douglas, 1967) that the Pavlovian model can be translated one-to-one into an attention model, with increases in excitation being related to increases in attention probability and internal inhibition to decreases. Finally, it should be mentioned that our lesioned animals were tested for memory, using the savings method, after a one month lapse. The lesioned subjects were 95% correct on the 100 retraining trials, while the normals were about 90%. One would judge that this indicated rather phenomenal memory, as one might expect to be the case with association learning if it were a permanent change in the brain.

Several studies have now shown that once an animal has securely learned a problem he retains it after removal of either the amygdala or hippocampus. Douglas and Pribram (1966) found that the learning of a differential partial reinforcement problem was very difficult for hippocampectomized monkeys. But those learning that problem before the surgery retained it after removal of the hippocampus. Amygdalectomized rats have a great deal of difficulty in learning a shuttle box problem, but if they are well trained before the operation they continue to perform correctly afterwards (Thatcher and Kimble, 1966). All of this evidence suggests that association learning occurs outside the hippocampus and amygdala, and that these structures merely aid in the formation of associations. But perhaps "merely" is too weak a term.

VII. The Drug Parallel

The arguments used earlier to relate internal inhibition to the hippocampus could now be repeated almost point for point with the term "cholinergic system" substituted for "hippocampus". Carlton (1963) has done perhaps more than anyone else to call attention to the behavioural syndrome resulting from injection of the anticholinergic (antimuscarinic) drugs like atropine and especially the more centrally potent scopolamine. These drugs block the type of cholinergic synapse known as "muscarinic" while having little effect on "nicotinic" cholinergic synapses. Thus, in the periphery they block the parasympathetic system but not the sympathetic, and they do not paralyse the neuromuscular junction. Fortunately, the early investigators of these drugs used problems much like those employed by hippocampus investigators, and by the middle 1960s it was already apparent that scopolamine produced the now-familiar "hippocampal syndrome" in all its nuances. As merely a few of many possible examples, scopolamine injections produce exactly the same effects on one-way, two-way and passive avoidance as do hippocampal lesions (Suits and Isaacson, 1968; Meyers, 1965). The drug abolishes both habituation (Carlton, 1968) and spontaneous alternation (Douglas and Isaacson, 1966). But one of the more crucial experiments in this area was performed by Warburton (1969). He first trained hippocampally lesioned and control rats on a type of alternation problem sensitive both to hippocampal lesions and atropine injections (see Warburton, Chapter 17, this volume for details); atropine was then injected, and it interfered with performance in the control animals but had no effect on the group with large hippocampal lesions. It had a mild effect on rats with small hippocampal lesions. The significance of this study is that it demonstrates what many of us always intuitively believed to be true: that there are indeed alternate brain mechanisms for solving many problems. In this case the system mediated by cholinergic synapses was the superior one, but another noncholinergic system apparently could also do the job. We should point out that hippocampectomized animals as a general rule can *eventually* solve most problems on which they have deficits.

Carlton (1963 and later papers) has postulated that the cholinergic system is sensitive to nonreinforcement or errors. In other words, internal inhibition is cholinergically mediated. The cholinergic "system" is of course more extensive than the hippocampus. It would appear, however, that the hippocampus is a crucial link in the system. Certainly there is no brain structure more "cholinergic" than the hippocampus. Its two main cell types (and others as well) are activated by cholinergic, muscarinic synapses (see Lewis and Shute, 1967; Shute and Lewis, 1967). The hippocampus has a distinctive electrical rhythm known as theta, consisting of high amplitude waves between 4 and 7 cycles per second. These theta waves are paced by a cholinergic pathway which ascends in the lateral hypothalamus and synapses in the septal region. Theta waves are blocked by anti-cholinergic drugs and potentiated by drugs which potentiate cholinergic activity through interfering with cholinesterase (Stumpf, 1965). Various recent evidence has finally supported the old idea that when the hippocampus is actively generating theta waves it is "doing something". Thus, it is not without relevance that Wyrwicka (1964) recorded large theta-like waves in the "hunger centre" of the hypothalamus during the extinction (but not learning) of a food reinforced conditioned reflex. The hippocampus massively innervates the hypothalamus.

But while a great deal of work has been done using cholinergic blocking agents, surprisingly little of value has been discovered about the effects of the anticholinesterases like physostigmine. Perhaps one reason is that they are tricky to use. In low doses they enhance cholinergic transmission, but in high doses they block transmission, probably by maintained depolarization (see Russell, 1966). It is not easy to say how much is "too much", but my own recent research indicates that most studies in the literature employed vast overdoses. Thus, it is little wonder that some studies report similar effects for such oppositely acting drugs as scopolamine and physostigmine. Whitehouse (1966) is an exception in that he used doses below 0·1 mg/kg and found the drug to facilitate a type of learning sensitive to both hippocampal removal and atropine, successive discrimination. My work of the last two years shows that a dose of 0·1 mg/kg is just about right for the rat and just a little too much for the DBA strain mouse. In both species that dose significantly increased the rate of spontaneous alternation. I was amazed to discover that Warburton (see Chapter 17) had similar results on a task believed to require inhibition, and at about the same dose level. Thus, it would appear that inhibition can be manipulated at will, in either direction, through drug injection.

VIII. Development

For several years now I have been involved in the study of the development of inhibition (as measured by spontaneous alternation) in man and beast. Some of the preliminary results in a variety of animal species have been publicly presented (Douglas et al., 1968; Douglas and Peterson, 1969b), but the most important findings are still in preparation. Most animals have been found to alternate at a chance rate of 50%, or to have a perseverative tendency, in some cases for long periods, with a sudden increase to adult rates occurring at characteristic ages. In the rat, with well over 100 subjects intensively tested, the typical age of this jump is 25–30 days. In contrast, guinea pigs alternate at the adult rate as early as 11 days of age, and possibly sooner. In human children a dramatic appearance of alternation occurs at typically four years of age (data gathered by Ken Packhouz and my wife Dorothy Douglas). The data were interpreted as indicating that the hippocampus becomes functional in an adult manner at 25–30 days in the rat, before 11 days in the guinea pig (possibly at birth) and at four years in the human. Brunner (1969) used a different response (passive avoidance) as an index of hippocampal function and found this ability to increase suddenly at about a month of age in the rat.

Quite independently of our research, another group of investigators has been studying the development of the cholinergic system. Both the pro-excitatory drug amphetamine and the anti-inhibitory drug scopolamine produce increases in activity, though for different reasons, and they do so as a function of dosage. Campbell et al. (1969) found the amphetamine dose-response curve to be essentially adult in shape as early as 10 days of age in the rat. In contrast, the adult dose-response curve for scopolamine did not occur until the age of 25 days, although there may have been some effect at 20. In a later study Fibiger et al. (1970) went further and first primed the excitatory system with amphetamine and then attempted to antagonize it through the injection of cholinergic activators like pilocarpine. Once again, the pilocarpine antagonism did not fully occur until 25 days of age.

The relation between these findings and the development of the hippocampus is truly amazing. In many animals the hippocampus is poorly
developed at birth, and considerable cell division occurs postnatally. These
cells are located in the walls of the lateral ventricles, and in the rat there is
a big flare-up in mitosis at about 10 days of age (Altman and Das, 1965).
These cells migrate to a part of the hippocampus known as the dentate
gyrus and then either grow axons and dendrites (differentiate) or further
divide before doing so. The migration probably takes about five days,
since at that time the DNA in the hippocampus suddenly increases to
about 140% of its former value (Fish and Winick, 1969). Between two
weeks and one month of age in the rat there is roughly a six-fold increase
in differentiated dentate gyrus granule cells, and the increase is rather
sharp, levelling off at roughly 25–35 days of age. To say the least, this
time table is in agreement with the behavioural findings. But what about
the guinea pig, the precocious alternator? Altman and Das (1967) found
that in comparison to the rat, the guinea pig is born with the dentate gyrus
cells already comparatively differentiated, even though a small degree of
division seems to go on even in adulthood. In the case of human children,
of course, we know nothing, as the new methods of study are not suitable
for man. Behaviourally, however, many studies (e.g. Lynn, 1966) indicate
that internal inhibition either appears or is greatly strengthened at roughly
four years of age in children.

IX. The Model: Putting it all Together

Many plausible-sounding theories self destruct as soon as they are dia-
grammed. In this case the opposite seems to be the case. The relations
shown in Fig. 1 are actually much clearer than words alone could tell,
although they need further discussion. The boxes in Fig. 1 represent
anatomical structures or regions, while the arrows indicate functional
relations. If the figure looks familiar it is because it is taken from Lynn's
(1966) presentation of Sokolov's model. Behaviour-determining processes
are broken down into two major interacting components called the analysing system and the motivational system. These correspond roughly to
Sokolov's modelling and amplifying systems, respectively. The names were
changed because the correspondence is not exact.

In order to understand the diagram it is best to begin with the analysing
system and the way in which it receives information. The locus of the
analysing system is the neocortex plus the nonreticular nuclei of the thalamus. In addition, one subdivision of this system is localized in the amygdala
and another in the hippocampus, but these limbic components will be
discussed later. The analysing system receives two different kinds of
sensory input. The first is that which arrives by way of the "classical"

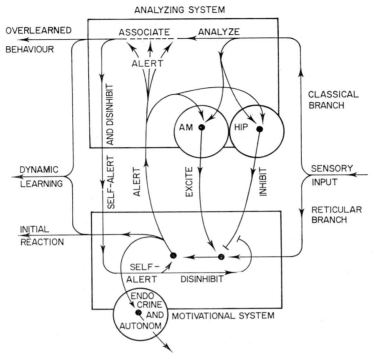

Fig. 1. Schematic neural model of orienting and conditioning.

sensory pathways which ultimately project to the so-called specific sensory projection regions like area 17. It is not yet clear whether the pulvinar circuit should be included here. The second kind of input to the analysing system is provided by collaterals from the ascending classical systems which synapse in the motivational system and are then projected upwards into the analysing system. The motivational system is localized in what will be called the reticular core brain. This is here defined as a combination of the brain stem, hypothalamus and reticular thalamus. This reticular core brain is viewed as having capacities far beyond those of the familiar "reticular activating system". It is a brain (however crude) in its own right, and it is just about all the brain that some animals possess. The motivational system reacts to its input by alerting (or not alerting) the analysing system. The significance of the two pathways is as follows. The classical input provides "intellectual" or cool information which is analysed for detail and pattern. The alerting input is a priority signal for such processing. We all know that conscious attention is severely limited. Relatively few of the estimated three million impulses per second which bombard our brain appear in consciousness. The job of the motivational system is to decide which signals should be attended to, among other things which will be discussed later. A conscious percept (attention) is the intersect of both kinds of input to the analysing system. Surprisingly, there is data which supports this idea. Libet, *et al.* (1967) actually recorded cortical sensory evoked potentials subdurally in conscious human subjects. The early or first components of such a sensory evoked potential are commonly believed to reflect the arrival of the input signal and its production of postsynaptic potentials at the reception site. The later components of the evoked potential are widely believed to represent an upward discharge from what is here called the reticular core brain. It was found that sensory evoked potentials could be clearly recorded even with stimuli below the threshold for conscious awareness. But significantly, the late components of the evoked potentials were absent or poorly developed.

The job of the analysing system (nonlimbic portion) is to analyse sensory input for detail and to form associative bonds. Note that the analysing system can "activate itself" by discharging downwards to the motivational system and receiving an "answer". This interaction is theoretically vital, because there are many alerting stimuli which can be analysed only by the higher parts of the brain. This pathway is postulated to be the one involved in disinhibition, dreaming, and other cases of self-arousal through internal symbolism. The limbic subdivision of the analysing system also receives the dual input, but the classical input is first analysed by the cortex. At any point in time the amygdala might receive a signal that a stimulus has appeared (classical system) and that it has produced an emotional reaction (from the motivational system) or, in other words, is associated with reinforcement. On receipt of this dual information the amygdala acts to modify the motivational system in such a way that in the future the reception of the signal will cause an even greater alerting of the analysing system. Similarly, the hippocampus relates a signal to the absence of an arousing event (nonreinforcement) and acts to block further activation of the motivational system by that signal.

According to Fig. 1, the initial reaction to a novel stimulus is primarily determined by the motivational system. When that stimulus has consequences, a dynamic learning phase goes into action, and this largely consists of modulation of the motivational system by the amygdala and hippocampus. As a result, certain stimuli are given high attention priority, become associated with others, and eventually automatic behaviour occurs. In the last phase the contribution of the motivational system is at a minimum.

The importance of Fig. 1 is that each box and arrow does have a physical (hypothetical) existence, and we can thus examine some relevant anatomical and physiological evidence. First, let us consider what happens when the reticular core brain (motivational system) is "turned on" by electrical stimulation. Stimulation of the core, especially the hypothalamus, produces a wide range of behaviour including threat, attack, flight, attention or orienting, mating and maternal acts, grooming, crouching, gnawing, nest building, eating, drinking, stalking and killing (see Roberts, 1970, for review). While a very small part of this behaviour may be automatic or robot-like, most of it simply cannot be explained in terms of motor responses. A rat stimulated in the "gnawing centre", for example, does not gnaw the air. Instead, he starts looking around for something to gnaw, and he will learn a maze in order to secure a gnawable object (Roberts, 1970). Even a naïve, lovable pussycat will stalk and kill rats like a veteran, with the *coup de grace* being a bite to the neck, provided that his hypothalamic "stalking centre" is stimulated. But he will stalk only in so far as a small live moving animal is present, and he will vary his behaviour in accordance with the circumstances. Even the most automatic-appearing component of the stalking attack, the bite to the neck, is not simply due to the initiation of a motor response. The cat will not bite the rat if the sensory component of the trigeminal nerve (sensory-face) is severed, even though the cat can and does move his jaws normally under other circumstances (see review by Flynn *et al.*, 1970). Thus, activation of various reticular core regions results in the initiation of what we might call emotional or motivated behaviour. At the same time it also results in desynchronization or activation of sensory and motor cortex (see Gellhorn, 1968). It is obvious, however, that this complex behaviour could not be directed by the motivational system *acting by itself*. In many cases the behaviour requires the highest forms of sensory analysis. The evidence suggests that the reticular core acts by causing the subject to be sensitized to certain specific stimuli and to preferentially attend to them. If these are not present, a perceptual set is generated. In addition, this motivated behaviour demands that the appropriate degree of energy be made available for the task, and that the subject have a motor set, or be prepared to engage in a subset of all possible acts. Motivated behaviour, of course, involves all of these facets and cannot be understood when any one of them is ignored. In terms of Pavlovian psychology, we are claiming that excitation is generated within the reticular core, and that it is related to attention, activation and motor sets simultaneously.

Next, we will consider that branch of sensory input which goes to the motivational system. It has been known to generations of neuroanatomists that all sensory systems send profuse collaterals to all parts of the reticular core brain. Feldman (1962) demonstrated that stimulation of the cat's leg (or nerve) resulted in a very short latency evoked potential in the same hypothalamic regions associated with the eliciting of motivated acts. Feldman went on to show that stimulation of the hippocampus prior to sensory or nerve stimulation could totally abolish this hypothalamic evoked potential. Adey *et al.* (1957) also demonstrated that stimulation of the hippocampal region greatly reduces transmission within the reticular core. It is no accident that exactly these relations are shown in Fig. 1, as they are partly based on this data.

Amygdala stimulation has not, unfortunately, been shown to enhance hypothalamic evoked potentials. But it has been shown to facilitate the kinds of *behaviour* elicited by hypothalamic stimulation, as if it were activating these regions, as in Fig. 1. Flynn *et al.* (1970) reported that the stalking response was facilitated by amygdala stimulation and suppressed by stimulation of the dorsal hippocampus. The multitude of fibre connections from the amygdala to the hypothalamus are almost certainly excitatory, because stimulation at various points within the amygdala results in much the same kinds of behaviour as is associated with hypothalamic stimulation, with attention, fear, flight and anger being notable examples (Ursin and Kaada, 1960).

While stimulation of the amygdala produces emotional dynamism, electrical or chemical stimulation of the hippocampus is more notable for its failure to produce consistent behavioural effects. I have personally stimulated the hippocampus of the waking unrestrained cat on hundreds of occasions. The most I ever saw was a yawn. Many others before and since have reported similar results. MacLean (1957) intensively activated the hippocampus by carbachol injections and by seizure-inducing electrical stimulation. The result was an apparent loss of emotional reactivity to all but the most intense pain stimuli. Since the animal hippocampus has hundreds of thousands of efferent connections with all parts of the reticular core (millions in man), results like this are hard to explain if these connections are not inhibitory in nature.

I would like to make clear at this point that my former theory (Douglas, 1967) that the hippocampus blocked sensory input in the *classical* pathways is no longer tenable, if it ever was. In six months of trying I could find no consistent change in the primary evoked potential as a result of hippocampal stimulation. There was some suggestion of an effect on the late components of the wave, but that would only support the present analysis were it to be supported by further research.

Finally, the results of several endocrine system studies decisively support the present model. The ACTH-adrenal steroid stress system is highly related to arousal and emotionality (excitation). This system can be activated by either amygdaloid or hypothalamic stimulation, and suppressed by hippocampal stimulation (see discussions in Gellhorn, 1968). Hippocampal stimulation can either reduce ACTH (and thus the adrenal steroids) or prevent the amygdala from producing an increase. Furthermore, excitatory conditioning increases and internal inhibition decreases the secretion of the excitatory hormone 17-hydroxycorticosterone from the adrenal cortex (Gellhorn, 1968).

X. The Nature of Internal Inhibition

According to the present model there are two kinds of behaviour which could conceivably be called "inhibitory", but they are mediated by different subsystems. The amygdaloid subdivision of the analysing system is activated equally well by "pain and pleasure". Each is reinforcing. Each is excitatory. But reward tends to produce what Lewin (1935) might call a positive valence, a tendency to gravitate towards the stimulus source. Punishment does just the opposite. Both, however, result in a direct control of behaviour by the stimulus. Nonreinforcement, on the other hand, activates the hippocampal circuitry to inhibit an excitatory reaction by the reticular core to sensory input. As a result, that stimulus *loses control* over behaviour except in a negative sense. The subject, so to speak, ignores the stimulus instead of avoiding it. Behaviourally, ignoring or avoiding look much the same, and this is where the problem comes in. The problem is compounded by the distinct possibility that one and the same event can be reacted to as if it were either simple nonreinforcement or severe punishment, depending on the circumstances. Those of us who have carefully observed animals during extinction know full well that the animal acts differently the first time the reward is withheld than he did early in learning when he made an error. After extensive experience I can make the general statement that animals do not make any notable emotional displays when making errors as they learn. But after prolonged training a monkey may actually "throw a fit" when placed on an extinction schedule. There is much more to extinction than simply "internal inhibition". Thus, I suggest that internal inhibition may act as a safety valve to rescue a subject from a "schizophrenic" amygdala which has received information which suggests incompatible courses of action. That is, the only solution to an irreconcilable approach-avoidance conflict is to leave the field. But this is prevented by the action of both reward and punishment in riveting attention onto the same stimulus. The ideal solution would be to have a system which, in such cases, blocks the excitatory effects of both reward and punishment and allows behaviour to be determined by other alternative stimuli. This, in a nut shell, is passive avoidance. It is also a good definition of repression, although in this case the motivational system cannot be activated even by the analysing system. In any event, the nature of internal inhibition, according to this extensive and intensive analysis, is *not* the suppression of a response at all. The response observed by the psychologist is not suppressed because it was not generated in the first place. True response suppression, as discussed by many at this conference, would be, so to speak, a battle raging within the amygdala. Two mutually exclusive tendencies would be cancelling each other out.

Last, I would like to thank Asratian (Chapter 15, this volume) for helping me out. His revelation that inhibition acts on the unconditioned reflex rather than the conditioned reflex fits in very well. The site of most unconditioned reflexes has long been conceded to be the reticular core.

Acknowledgements

I am grateful to the Graduate School and College of Arts and Sciences of the University of Washington for a generous grant that made it possible to attend the conference.

References

Ackil, J. E., Mellgren, R. L., Halgren, C. and Frommer, G. P. (1969). Effects of CS preexposure on avoidance learning in rats with hippocampal lesions. *Journal of Comparative and Physiological Psychology*, **69,** 739–747.

Adey, W. R., Segundo, J. P. and Livingston (1957). Cortical influences on intrinsic brain stem conduction in cat and monkey. *Journal of Neurophysiology*, **20,** 1–16.

Altman, J. and Das, G. D. (1965). Autoradiographic and histological evidence of postnatal hippocampal neurogenesis in rats, *Journal of Comparative Neurology*, **124,** 319–336.

Altman, J. and Das, G. D. (1967). Postnatal neurogenesis in the guinea pig. *Nature*, **214,** 1098–1101.

Bagshaw, M. H. and Coppock, H. W. (1968). Galvanic skin response conditioning deficit in amygdalectomized monkeys. *Experimental Neurology*, **20,** 188–196.

Brunner, R. L. (1969). Age differences in one-trial passive avoidance learning. *Psychonomic Science*, **14,** 134.

Carlton, P. (1963). Cholinergic mechanisms in the control of behavior by the brain. *Psychological Review*, **70,** 19–39.

Carlton, P. (1968). Brain acetycholine and habituation. In: P. B. Bradley and M. Fink (Eds.) *Anticholinergic Drugs and Brain Functions in Animals and Man.* Amsterdam: Elsevier, pp. 48–60.

Campbell, B. A., Lytle, L. D. and Fibiger, H. C. (1969). Ontogeny of adrenergic arousal and cholinergic inhibitory mechanisms in the rat. *Science*, **166,** 635–636.

Clark, C. V. H. and Isaacson, R. L. (1965). Effect of bilateral hippocampal ablation on DRL performance. *Journal of Comparative and Physiological Psychology*, **59,** 137–140.

Dennis, W. and Sollenberger, R. T. (1934), Negative adaptation in the maze exploration of rats. *Journal of Comparative Psychology*, **18,** 197–205.

Douglas, R. J. (1966). Cues for spontaneous alternation. *Journal of Comparative and Physiological Psychology*, **62,** 171–183.

Douglas, R. J. (1967). The hippocampus and behavior. *Psychological Bulletin*, **67**, 416–442.

Douglas, R. J. and Isaacson, R. L. (1966). Spontaneous alternation and scopolamine. *Psychonomic Science*, **4**, 283–284.

Douglas, R. J. and Peterson, J. J. (1969a). Is it true what they say about two-stage hippocampal lesions? Paper read at Western Psychological Association meeting, Vancouver, B.C.

Douglas, R. J. and Peterson, J. J. (1969b). The sudden development of spontaneous alternation in baby rats. Paper read at Western Psychological Association meeting, Vancouver, B.C.

Douglas, R. J. and Pribram, K. H. (1966). Learning and limbic lesions. *Neuropsychologia*, **4**, 197–220.

Douglas, R. J. and Pribram, K. H. (1969). Distraction and habituation in monkeys with limbic lesions. *Journal of Comparative and Physiological Psychology*, **69**, 473–480.

Douglas, R. J., Kowal, D. and Clark, G. (1968). Spontaneous alternation and the brain. Paper presented at Western Psychological Association meeting, San Diego.

Douglas, R. J., Barrett, T. W., Pribram, K. H. and Cerny, M.C. (1969). Limbic lesions and error reduction. *Journal of Comparative and Physiological Psychology*, **68**, 437–441.

Douglas, R. J., Pagano, R. R., Lovely, R. H. and Peterson, J. J. (1970). Proactive ECS effects, the adrenal system, and the hippocampus. Proceedings, 78th Annual Convention, American Psychological Association, 221–222.

Feldman, S. (1962). Neurophysiological mechanisms modifying afferent hypothalamo-hippocampal conduction. *Experimental Neurology*, **5**, 269–291.

Fibiger, H. C., Lytle, L. D. and Campbell, B. A. (1970). Cholinergic modulation of adrenergic arousal in the developing rat. *Journal of Comparative and Physiological Psychology*, **72**, 384–389.

Fish, I. and Winick, M. (1969). Cellular growth in various regions of the developing rat brain. *Pediatric Research*, **3**, 407–412.

Flynn, J. P., Vanegas, H., Foote, W. and Edwards, S. (1970). Neural mechanisms involved in a cat's attack on a rat. In: R. E. Whalen, R. F. Thompson. M. Verzeano and N. M. Weinberger (Eds.) *The Neural Control of Behavior*. New York: Academic Press, pp. 135–173.

Gellhorn, E. (Ed.) (1968). *Biological Foundations of Emotion*. Glenview, Ill.: Scott Foreman.

Glanzer, M. (1953). Stimulus satiation: An explanation of spontaneous alternation and related phenomena. *Psychological Review*, **60**, 257–268.

Goddard, G. V. (1964). Functions of the amygdala. *Psychological Bulletin*, **62**, 89–109.

Hendrickson, C. W. and Kimble, D. P. (1966). Hippocampal lesions and the orienting response: A progress report. *Ammon's Horn*, Fall, 71–81.

Isaacson, R. L. and Wickelgren, W. O. (1962). Hippocampal ablation and passive avoidance. *Science*, **138**, 1104–1106.

Isaacson, R. L., Douglas, R. J. and Moore, R. Y. (1961). The effect of radical hippocampal ablation on acquisition of avoidance response. *Journal of Comparative and Physiological Psychology*, **54**, 625–628.

Jarrard, L. E. (1968). Behavior of hippocampally lesioned rats in home cage and novel situations. *Physiology and Behavior*, **3**, 65–70.

Kim, C., Choi, H., Kim, J. K., Chang, H. K., Park, R. S. and Kang, I. Y. (1970).

General behavioral activity and its component patterns in hippocampectomized rats. *Brain Research,* **19,** 379–394.

Kimble, D. P. (1963). The effects of bilateral hippocampal lesions in rats. *Journal of Comparative and Physiological Psychology,* **56,** 273–283.

Kimble, D. P. (1968). The hippocampus and internal inhibition. *Psychological Bulletin,* **70,** 285–295.

Kimble, D. P., and Pribham, K. H. (1963). Hippocampectomy and behaviour sequences. *Science,* **139,** 824–825.

Kimble, D. P., Kirkby, R. J. and Stein, D. G. (1966). Response perseveration interpretation of passive avoidance deficits in hippocampectomized rats. *Journal of Comparative and Physiological Psychology,* **61,** 141–153.

Lewin, K. (1935). *A Dynamic Theory of Personality.* D. K. Adams and K. E. Zener (transl.) New York, McGraw-Hill.

Lewis, P. R. and Shute, C. C. D. (1967). The cholinergic limbic system: Projections to hippocampal formation, medial cortex, nuclei of the ascending cholinergic reticular system, and the subfornical organ and supra-optic crest. *Brain* **90,** 521–540.

Libet, B., Alberts, W. W., Wright E. W., Jr. and Feinstein, B. (1967). Responses of human somatosensory cortex to stimuli below threshold for conscious sensation. *Science,* **158,** 1597–1600.

Lynn, R. (1966). *Attention, Arousal and the Orienting Reflex.* London: Pergamon Press.

MacLean, P. D. (1957). Chemical and electrical stimulation of hippocampus in unrestrained animals. II. Behavioral findings. *Archives of Neurology and Psychiatry,* **78,** 128–142.

McCleary, R. A. (1966). Response-modulating functions of the limbic system: Initiation and suppression. In: E. Stellar and J. M. Sprague (Eds.) *Progress in Physiological Psychology.* New York: Academic Press, pp. 209–272.

Means, L. W., Walker, D. W. and Isaacson, R. L. (1970). Facilitated single-alternation go, no go acquisition following hippocampectomy in the rat. *Journal of Comparative and Physiological Psychology,* **72,** 278–285.

Meyers, B. (1965). Some effects of scopolamine on a passive avoidance response in rats. *Psychopharmacologia:* **8,** 111–119.

Pavlov, I. P. (1960). *Conditioned Reflexes.* New York: Dover; Pribram, K. H., Douglas, R. J. and Pribram, B. J. (1969). The nature of nonlimbic learning. *Journal of Comparative and Physiological Psychology,* **69,** 765–772.

Raphelson, A. C. Isaacson, R. L. and Douglas, R. J. (1965). The effect of distracting stimuli on the runway performance of limbic damaged rats. *Psychonomic Science,* **3,** 483–484.

Roberts, W. W. (1970). Hypothalamic mechanisms for motivational and species-typical behavior. In: R. E. Whalen, R. F. Thompson, M. Verzeano and N. M. Weinberger (Eds.) *The Neural Control of Behavior.* New York: Academic Press, pp. 175–206.

Russell, R. W. (1966). Biochemical substrates of behavior. In: R. W. Russell (Ed.) *Frontiers in Physiological Psychology.* New York: Academic Press, 185–246.

Schmaltz, L. and Isaacson, R. L. (1966). The effects of preliminary training conditions on DRL performance in the hippocampectomized rat. *Physiology and Behavior,* **1,** 175–182.

Sharpless, S. and Jasper, H. (1956). Habituation of the arousal reaction. *Brain,* **79,** 655–680.

Shute, C. C. D. and Lewis, P. R. (1967). The ascending cholinergic reticular system: Neocortical, olfactory and subcortical projections. *Brain*, 497–519.

Snyder, D. R. and Isaacson, R. L. (1965). The effects of large and small bilateral hippocampal lesions on two types of passive avoidance responses. *Psychological Reports*, **16**, 1277–1290.

Sokolov, Ye. N. (1963). *Perception and the Conditioned reflex*. New York: Macmillan.

Stumpf, Ch. (1965). Drug action on the electrical activity of the hippocampus. *International Review of Neurology*, **8**, 77–138.

Suits, E. and Isaacson, R. L. (1968). The effects of scopolamine hydrobromide on one-way and two-way avoidance learning in rats. *International Review of Neuropharmacology*, **7**, 441–446.

Thatcher, R. W. and Kimble, D. P. (1966). Effect of amygdaloid lesions on retention of an avoidance response in overtrained and non-overtrained rats. *Psychonomic Science*, **6**, 9–10.

Ursin, H. and Kaada, B. R. (1960). Functional localization within the amygdaloid complex in the cat. *Electroencephalography and Clinical Neurophysiology*, **12**, 1–20.

Vanderwolf, C. H. (1963). Improved shuttlebox performance following electroconvulsive shock. *Journal of Comparative and Physiological Psychology*, **56**, 983–986.

Warburton, D. M. (1969). Effects of atropine sulfate on single alternation in hippocampectomized rats. *Physiology and Behavior*, **4**, 641–644.

Whitehouse, J, M. (1966). The effects of physostigmine on discrimination learning. *Psychopharmacologia*, **9**, 183–188.

Wickelgren, W. O. and Isaacson, R. L. (1963). Effect of the introduction of an irrelevant stimulus on runway performance of the hippocampectomized rat. *Nature* **200**, 48–50.

Wyrwicka, W. (1964). Electrical activity of the hypothalamus during alimentary conditioning. *Electroencephalography and Clinical Neurophysiology*, **17**, 164–176.

Author Index

Numbers in *italic* type indicate pages where references are listed at the end of each chapter.

A

Ackil, J. E., 532, *550*
Adey, W. R., 516, *528*, 548, *550*
Ahlskog, J. E., 62, 64, 66, *70*, 474, *495*
Ain, B. R., 462, *493*
Ajmone-Marsan, C., 501, *527*
Akert, K., 362, *380*
Alberts, W. W., 546, *552*
Albin, R., 183, 187, 200, *204*
Aleksanian, A. M., 390, *395*
Allen, C. J., 491, *494*
Altman, J., 544, *550*
Amsel, A., 110, *117*, 198, 199, *203, 204*, 273, 275, 277, 278, 279, 281, 282, 285, 286, 287, 289, 294, 296, *295, 297, 298*, 401, 472, 473, 474, 481, 483, 489, 490, 491, *493*
Andersen, P., 426, *428*
Anderson, W. H., 12, *37*
Anger, D., 68, *69*, 443, *458*
Ángyár, L., 407, *429*
Annau, Z., 321, 334
Anokhin, P. K., 383, 389, *395*
Antunes–Rodrigues, J., 378, *379*
Askew, H. R., 62, 64, 66, *70*, 474, *495*
Asratian, E. A., 382, 383, 384, 387, *395*, 550
Azrin, N. H., 236, *249, 267*, 286

B

Bagshaw, M. H., 518, *525*, 539, *550*
Balvin, R. S., 6, 9, *37*
Banks, A., 439, *458*
Barker, D. J., 481, 490, *495*
Baron, A., 268, *269*
Barrett, T. W., 532, *551*

Baum, W. M., 42, 68, *69*
Beale, I., 15, 16
Beale, I. L., 44, 46, 47, 48, 49, 50, 51, 52, 53, 58, 59, 64, *69, 71*, 123, 125, 137, 138, 145, *150*, 157, 160, 172, *174*
Beckman, G. J., 518, *526*
Behrend, E. R., 154, 156, 157, 166, 168, 171, *174, 175*
Benzies, S., 518, *525*
Berger, B. D., 167, 172, *175*
Beritov, I. S., 361, *379*
Bernheim, J. W., 108, 118, 182, *203*
Besley, S., 6, 7, 9, 12, 13, 15, 30, 31, 32, *37*, 41, 44, 47, 65, *70, 96*, 100, 102, 103, 104, *118*, 224, *226*, 230, *249*, 310, *334*
Bignami, G., 432, *458*
Birch, D., 192, 193, *203*
Bishop, H. E., 156, *175*
Bitterman, M. E., 154, 155, 156, 157, 163, 164, 166, 167, 168, 170, 171, 172, *174, 175, 176*
Black, A. H., 253, 264, *270*
Bloomfield, T. M., 8, 16, *37*, 47, *70*, 86, *96*, 121, 150
Blough, D. S., 144, *150*
Boakes, R. A., 10, 76, 78, 79, 80, *96*, 355
Bolles, R. C., 22, 23, 24, *37*, 259, 260, 261, 263, 268, *269, 270*
Boneau, C. A., 44, 47, *70*, 102, *118*
Born, D. G., 372, *380*
Bower, G., 263, *270*, 303, *336*
Bower, G. H., 6, *39*, 182, *204*, 293, *298*
Brady, J. V., 236, *249*, 463, *493*
Bremer, F., 455, 456, *458*
Brethower, D. M., 94, *96*
Brimer, C. J., *37*, 94, 179, 207, 210, 211, 212, 213, 214, 219, *225, 226*, 253, 264, *270*

Broadbent, D. E., 449, *458*
Brown, K., 443, 444, 448, *458*
Brown, P. L., 12, 17, 24, *37*, 95, *96*, 103, 104, *118*, 275, *298*
Brown, W. L., 154, *175*
Brownstein, A. J., 43, *70*
Bruner, A., 236, *249*
Bruning, J. L., 482, *493*
Brunner, R. L., 543, *550*
Brunton, T. L., 362, *379*
Brutkowski, S., 350, *356*
Bull, J. A., 22, *38*, 318, *334*
Bullock, D. H., 154, 157, *174*, *175*
Burke, C. J., 302, 305, 334
Burstein, K. R., 44, 47, *70*, 102, *118*
Bush, J. A. III, 302, 305, *334*
Bush, R. R., 435, 437, *458*

C

Campbell, B. A., 427, *428*, 543, *550*, *551*
Candland, D. K., 154, 156, *174*
Caplan, M., 481, 483, *493*
Cardo, B., 453, *459*
Carlson, N. R., 462, 471, 482, *493*
Carlton, P., 541, 542, *550*
Carlton, P. L., 326, *334*
Carmona, A., 295, *298*
Case, T. J., 455, *458*
Catania, A. C., 43, *70*, 138, *150*, 198, *204*, 244, *250*
Cerny, M. V., 532, *551*
Chang, H. K., 517, *526*, 538, *551*
Chistivich, L. A., 383, *395*
Cho, C., 261, *270*
Choi, H., 517, *526*, 538, *551*
Chorazyna, H., 330, 334
Clark, C. V. H., 517, *525*, 534, *550*
Clark, F. C., 157, *174*
Clark, G., 533, 539, 543, *551*
Clark, R. L., 236, *249*
Clayton, K. N., 124, *151*
Clemente, C. D., 361, *380*, 405, *429*
Clody, D. E., 471, *493*
Cole, J. R., 462, *493*
Collins, N., 31, 33, *39*
Conrad, D. G., 236, *249*
Contrucci, J. J., 212, *226*, 231, *249*
Cook, L., 235, *249*
Coppock H. W., 539, *550*

Cortell, R., 375, *379*
Covian, M. R., 378, *379*
Cox, C. V., 407, *428*, *430*
Cumming, W. W., 236, *250*
Czopf, J., 407, *429*

D

Dabrowska, J., 352, *356*
Dafney, N., 516, *525*
Daly, H. B., 473, 492, *494*
Daly, H. D., 182, *204*
Daniel, R., 315, *334*
Das, G. D., 544, *550*
Davenport, J. W., 157, 161, *174*, 483, *494*
Davidova, E. K., 387, *395*
Davies, K., 198, 199, *204*
Davis, J. M., 30, *37*
Delgado, J. M. R., 369, *379*, 523, *525*
Dennis, W., 533, *550*
Deterline, W. A., 167, *174*
Diamond, F. R., 6, 9, *37*
Diamonds, S., 6, 9, *37*
Dickinson, A., 202, 401, 466, 484, *494*
Doane, B., 395, *396*
Domesick, V. B., 156, 168, *174*
Domjan, M., 317, *335*
Donhoffer, H., 523, *526*
Donin, Janet, A., 279, *298*
Donovick, P. J., 462, 470, 482, *494*, *495*
Doty, R. W., 519, *526*
Douglas, R. J., 122, 402, 450, 453, *459*, 462, 482, *495*, 501, 525, *526*, 530, 531, 532, 533, 535, 536, 538, 539, 540, 541, 543, 548, *550*, *551*, *552*
Duncan, P. M., 490, *494*
Dunham, P. J., 492, *494*
Dweck, C. S., 316, *334*

E

Eccles, J. C., 341, *356*, 361, *379*, 405, 426, *428*
Eccles, R. M., 361, *379*
Edwards, D. D., 74, *96*
Edwards, S., 547, 548, *551*
Egan, J. P., 443, *458*
Ellen, P., 462, *494*
Ellison, G. D., 321, *336*
Endörczi, E., 515, *526*

Erickson, C. K., 522, *526*
Erofeyeva, M. N., 390, *395*
Estes, W. K., 11, 13, 29, *37*, *270*, 302, 305, 334, 360, *379*

F

Fantino, E., 92, *96*, 138, *151*
Farthing, G. W., 6, 7, 9, 12, 13, 15, 16, 29, 30, 31, 32, *37*, 41, 44, 47, 65, *70*, *96*, 100, 102, 103, 104, 116, *118*, 224, *226*, 230, 231, *249*, 310, 334
Fein, G. G., 292, *299*
Feinstein, B., 546, *552*
Feldman, J., 375, *379*
Feldman, S., 516, *525*, 547, 548, *551*
Ferraro, D. P., 212, *227*, 236, *249*
Ferster, C. B., 104, *118*, 257, *270*
Fibiger, H. C., 543, *550*, *551*
Findley, J. D., 43, *70*, *151*
Fish, I., 544, *551*
Flanagan, B., 207, 212, *226*, 231, *249*
Flanigan, S., 523, *527*
Flynn, J. P., 523, *527*, 547, 548, *551*
Foote, W., 547, 548, *551*
Francis, J. G. F., 127, *151*
Frank, K., 361, *379*
Frankenhauser, M., 432, 439, *460*
Frommer, G. P., 532, *550*
Fry, W., 235, *249*
Funderbunk, W. H., 455, *458*
Fuortes, M. G. F., *361*, *379*
Fursikov, D. S., 383, *396*
Fuster, J. M., 455, *458*

G

Gagne, R. M., 207, *226*
Galanter, E., 437, 448, *458*
Galeano, C., 317, *335*
Garner, W. R., 6, *37*
Gasanov, U. G., 383, 387, 392, *396*
Gay, R. A., 182, 198, *204*
Gellhorn, E., 375, *379*, 513, *526*, 547, 548, 549, *551*
Gelman, R., 303, *336*
Gerbrandt, L. K., 36, *37*, 470, *494*
Gergen, J. A., 516, *526*
Gershuni, G. V., 392, *396*
Gilinskii, M. A., 456, *459*

Giurdzhian, A. A., 392, *396*
Glanzer, M., 532, 533, *551*
Glass, D. H., 182, *204*
Glickman, S. E., 517, *526*
Gluck, H., 362, *379*
Godbout, R. C., 8, 16, *39*
Goddard, G. V., 519, 520, *526* 539, *551*
Goldberg, L. J., 361, *380*
Goldrich, S. G., 519, *526*
Goldstein, D. A., 236, *250*
Gonzalez, R. C., 154, 156, 157, 166, 167, 171, 172, *174*, *175*
Goodfellow, E. F., 508, *526*
Gormezano, I., 291, *298*
Gotsick, J. E., 491, *494*
Gourevitch, V., 448, *458*
Grav, V., 157, *175*
Grastyán, E., 401, 407, 408, 410, 413, 414, 415, 416, 418, 419, 420, 421, 422, *429*, 455, *458*, 523, 524, *526*
Gray, J. A., 473, *494*
Green, D. M., 447, *458*
Green, R. H., 470, *494*
Greenberg, G. Z., 443, *458*
Greeno, J. G., 434, 438, *460*
Gregory, M., 449, *458*
Grossen, N. E., 22, 23, 24
Grossman, L., 454, *458*
Grossman, S. P., 453, 454, *458*, 470, 471, 482, *494*
Grusec, T., *96*, 108, *118*
Guerrero–Figueroa, R., 377, *379*
Guttman, N., 101, 114, *118*

H

Halgren, C., 532, *550*
Halliday, M. S., 10, 76, 78, 79, 80, *96*, 355
Hamilton, G. L., 505, 507, 508, *526*
Hamilton, L. W., 470, 471, 482, *494*
Hammond, L. J., 315, 318, 334
Hanson, H. M., 47, *70*, 108, 113, *118*
Harrison, R. H., 44, *70*, 102, 113, *118*
Harzem, P., 229, 230, *249*
Hearst, E., 6, 7, 9, 12, 13, 14, 15, 16, 29, 30, 31, 32, 33, *37*, *39*, 41, 42, 44, 47, 65, *70*, *96*, 100, 101, 102, 103, 104, 116, *118*, 121, 123, *151*, 224, *226*, 230, 231, 232, 245, 248, *249*, 255, 310, 334
Heath, R. G., 378, *379*

Hebb, D. O., 292, 293, *298*
Heise, G. A., 157, 161, 172, *175*, 433, 437, 438, 442, *459*
Heistad, G. T., 482, *495*
Hendrickson, C. W., 536, *551*
Hernández-Peon, R., 377, *379*
Heron, W. T., 207, *226*
Herrnstein, R. J., 42, 55, *70*, 74, *96*, 236, *249*, 268, *270*, 492, *495*
Hess, W. R., 411, 413, 414, 415, 416, 418, *428*, 498, 512, 513, *526*
Higgins, T., 517, *526*
Hilgard, E. R., 293, *298*, 389, *396*
Hineline, P. N., 268, 269, *270*
Hines, K. M., 491, *494*
Hinrich's J. V., 212, *226*, 231, *249*
Hodes, R., 378, *379*
Hodos, W., 236, *249*, 444, *459*
Hoffman, H. S., 23, *39*, 370, 371, *379*
Holdgate, V., 124, *151*, 154, *175*
Holmes, N. K., 164, *175*
Holmes, P. A., 154, *175*
Holz, W. C., 236, *249*, 269
Honig, W. K., 14, 15, 34, *37*, 43, 44, 47, 52, 53, 54, 55, 57, 58, 59, 64, 67, 68, *69*, *70*, *71*, 102, *118*, 123, 124, 137, 145, *151*
Hori, Y., 395, *396*
Horns, H. L., 207, *226*
Hostetter, G., 481, 490, *495*
Hothersall, D., 212, *226*, 231, *249*
House, B. J., 155, *176*
Hovland, C. I., 207, *226*
Hug, J. J., 491, *494*
Hull, C. L., 99, *118*, 155, *175*, 302, 303, 305, 306, 321, 326, 334, 360, *379*, 426, *429*, 461, *494*
Hunt, J. Mc V., 207, *226*
Hunter, W. S., 207, *226*

I

Il'yuchenok, R. Yu, 456, *459*
Isaacson, R. L., 122, *151*, 401, 402, 453, *459*, 462, 482, *495*, 501, 502, 505, 507, 517, *525*, *526*, *527*, 534, 535, 536, 537, 541, 550, *553*
Ison, J. R., 179, 182, 185, 186, 187, 188, 189, 190, 191, 192, 193, 195, 196, *203*, *204*, 482, *496*

J

Jackson, J. H., 362, *379*
Jackson, V., 74, *96*
Jarrard, L. E., 538, 551
Jasper, H., 539, 552
Jasper, H. H., 395, *396*
Jenkins, H. M., 12, 17, 20, 24, 25, *37*, 41, 44, 47, *70*, 95, *96*, 100, 101, 102, 103, 104, 106, 113, *118*, 146, *151*, 275, 279, 281, *298*, 360, *379*
Johnson, D. F., 12, 30, *37*
Johnson, H. C., 501, *528*
Jouvet, M., 405, 406, *429*

K

Kaada, B. R., 378, *380*, 470, *494*, 515, *528*, 548, *553*
Kakolewski, J. W., 407, *428*, 430
Kalish, H. I., 101, *118*
Kamn, L. J., 13, *38*, 307, 209, 212, 213, *225*, *226*, 253, 264, *270*, 291, *298*, 303, 304, 305, 308, 316, 321, 334
Kanai, T., 455, *459*
Kandel, E. R., 382, *396*
Kang, I. Y., 517, *526*, 538, *551*
Karmos, G., 523, *526*
Kasherininova, N. A., 383, *396*
Kekesi, F., 455, *458*
Kelleher, R. T., 235, *249*
Kellenyi, L., 523, *526*
Keller, C., 433, 437, 438, 442, *459*
Keller, F. S., 237, *250*
Kellicut, M. H., 462, 482, *495*
Kelsey, J. E., 470, 471, 482, *494*
Kemble, E. D., 518, *525*, *526*
Kesner, R. P., 519, *526*
Khavari, K. A., 157, 161, 172, *175*, 433, 437, 438, 442, *459*
Khodorov, G. I., 383, *396*
Kim, C., 517, 523, *526*, *527*, 538, *551*
Kim, J. K., 517, *526*, 538, *551*
Kimble, D. P., 122, *151*, 518, *525*, 530, 531, 534, 536, 537, 541, *552*
Kimble, G. A., 292, *298*
King, F. A., 470, *494*
Kinnard, M. A., 516, *526*
Kirk, K. L., 155, *175*
Kirkby, R. J., *552*

Klestchov, S. V., 321, *334*
Klüver, H., 514, *526*
Kogan, A. B., 362, *380*, 383, *396*
Kollros, J. J., 501, *528*
Kolta, P., 408, 410, *429*
Konorski, J., 6, 7, 15, 22, 30, 34, *38*, 93, 224, *226*, 273, 306, 309, 313, 317, 318, 319, 321, 331, 333, *334*, *336*,, 342, 343, 344, 346, 347, 348, 350, 352, 353, 355, 356, *356*, *357*, 363, 370, 377, *380*, 390, 392, *396*, 492
Kopa, A., 419, *429*
Kowal, D., 533, 539, 543, *551*
Kramer, T. J., 62, 64, 66, *70*, 230, 232, 236, *249*, 474, 483, *494*, *495*
Krane, R. V., 179, 185, 186, 187, 188, 189, 190, 191, 192, 193, 195, 196, *204*
Krasnogorski, N. I., *396*
Kratin, Y. G., 383, 392, *396*
Krechevsky, I., 154, *175*
Kremer, E. F., 13, *38*
Krnjevic, K., 456, *459*
Kulig, B. M., 462, *493*
Kupalov, P. S., 384, 389, *396*
Kveim, O., 470, *494*

L

Ladioray, G. I., 207, *227*
Lander, D., 15
Lander, D. G., 52, 53, 58, 59, 64, *69*
Laptev, I. I., 383, *396*
Laties, V. C., 236, *249*, *250*, 442, *459*
Laver, D. W., 291, *298*, 321, *335*
Laughlin, N., 433, 437, 438, 442, *459*
Lazarovitz, L., 263, *270*
Leibotwitz, S. F., 453, *459*
Leitenberg, H., 474, *494*
Lejeune, H., 231, 232, 233, 235, 237, 239, 240, *250*
Le Moal, M., 453, *459*
Lénárd, L., 420, 421, 422, *429*
Leonard, D. W., 183, 187, 200, *204*
Levine, M. S., 519, 524, *526*, *527*
Lewin, K., 549, *552*
Lewis, P. R., 449, 453, *460*, 542, *553*
Libet, B., 456, *459*, 546, *552*
Lidsky, A., 519, 520, 522, 523, 524, *527*
Linden, D. R., 254, 264, *270*
Lindsley, D. B., 455, *459*

Lissák, K., 455, *458*, 515, 523, *526*
Litner, J. S., 79, 254, 256, 258, 260, 264, 265, 267, 269, *270*, 317, 319, 332, *336*
Little, L., 155, *175*
Livesey, P., 519, *526*
Livingston, C. P., 548, *550*
Lloyd, D. P. C., 361, *380*, 404, *429*
Logan, F. A., 282, *298*
Lolordo, V. M., 254, 255, *270*, 313, 316, 317, 318, 331, 332, *335*, *336*
Loucks, R. B., 99, *118*
Lovejoy, E. P., 155, *175*
Loveland, D. H., 55, *70*
Lovely, R. H., 538, *551*
Lubar, J. F., 462, 482, *493*, *496*
Lubow, R. E., 27, 28, *38*, 326, 335
Ludvigson, H. W., 182, *204*
Lynn, R., 544, *552*
Lyons, J., 30, *38*, 104, *118*
Lytle, L. D., 543, *550*, *551*

M

Macar, F., 233, 236, 237, 242, 243, 244, *250*
MacDougall, J. M., 470, 471, 472, 481, *494*, *495*
McGaugh, J. L., 521, *527*
McGonigle, B., 124, *151*, 154, 155, *175*
Mackintosh, J., 161, *175*, 303, *336*
Mackinnon, J. R., 277, 282, *297*
Mackintosh, N. J., 29, *38*, 68, *70*, 124, *151*, 154, 155, 161, 171, *175*, 289, *299*, 329, *336*
MacLean, P. D., 516, 523, *526*, 548, *552*
Macphail, E. M., 122, 124, 128, 135, 140, 146, *151*
McCleary, R. A., 470, *494*, 533, 535, *552*
McLennan, H., 439, *459*
Madarasz, I., 523, *526*
Magni F., 361, *379*
Magoun, H. W., 405, *429*, 449, *460*
Maiorov, F. P., 392, *396*
Malmo, R. B., 378, *380*
Malott, R. M., 20, *39*
Malott, R. W., 236, *250*
Marquis, D. G., 293, *298*, 389, *396*
Marrissett, J. R., 518, *527*
Martin, J., 523, *526*

Masserman, J. H., 369, *380*
Matsumoto, H., 501, *527*
Maurissen, J., 235, 237, *250*
Means, L. W., 537, *552*
Mellgren, R. L., 532, *550*
Meyer, D. R., 261, *270*
Meyers, B., 541, *552*
Michelson, M. J., 431, 439, *459*
Migler, B., 20, *38*
Millenson, J. R., 20, *38*
Miller, J., 303, *335*
Miller, N. E., 183, *204*, 231, *250*, 369, *379*
Miller, N. W., 295, *298*
Miller, S., 352, *356*
Mills, J. A., 482, *496*
Milner, B., 499, *527*
Mishtovt, G. W., 383, *396*
Mitchell, J. C., 470, 471, 472, 481, *494*, *495*
Molnár, P., 401, 408, 410, 413, 414, 415, 416, 418, 420, 421, 422, *429*, 525
Moon, R. D., 462, *493*
Moore, A. U., 28, *38*, 326, *335*
Moore, R. Y., 453, *459*, 501, *526*, 535, *551*
Morgan, J. M., 472, *495*
Morrell, F., 501, *528*
Morton, A., 155, *175*
Moruzzi, G., 405, *429*
Moscovitch, A., 317, *335*
Mosteller, F., 302, 305, *334*
Mowrer, O. H., 268, *270*, 296, *298*
Muir, D., 15

N

Nakamura, Y., 361, *386*
Nakao, H., 369, *380*
Nauta, W. J. H., 449, *459*, 463, *493*, 513, 528
Neimer, W. T., 508, *526*
Neuringer, A. J., 74, 92, *96*
Nevin, J. A., 198, *204*
Noah, J. C., 22, *38*
Norman, D. A., 448, *460*
Norman, R. J., 482, *493*
North, A. J., 155, 157, *175*
Norton, T., 292, 293, *299*, 363, *380*

O

O'Flaherty, J. J., 378, *379*
Olton, D. S., 501, 502, 507, 508, 509, 527
Osborne, F. H., 491, 494
Oscar, M., 155, *176*
Ost, J. W., 291, *298*
Ost, J. W. P., 321, *335*
Overall, J. E., 155, *175*
Overmier, J. B., 22, 23, *38*, *39*, 291, *298*, 318, *334*

P

Pack, K., *38*
Pagano, R. R., 538, *551*
Palermo, D. S., 482, *495*
Palmer, J. A., 12, *39*, 44, *70*
Papez, J. W., 473, *495*
Park, R. S., 517, *526*, 538, *551*
Parmeggiani, P. L., 405, *429*
Patel, J. B., 522, *526*
Pavlov, I. P., 6, 7, 8, 12, 21, 22, 30, 34, 36, *38*, 93, *96*, 99, 100, 103, 110, *118*, 181, 183, 185, *204*, 205, 206, 212, 213, 216, 218, 219, 224, 225, *226*, 230, *250*, 274, 292, 306, 308, 313, 318, 320, 321, 326, 330, *335*, 359, 360, *380*, 381, 382, 383, 387, 389, 390, 392, 394, *396*, *397*, 403, 404, 405, *429*, 431, 457, *459*, 529, 530, 531, 534, 536, 537, 538, *552*
Peacock, S. M., 378, *379*
Pear, J. J., 104, *118*
Pennypacker, H. S., 44, 47, *70*, 102, *118*
Perelzweig, I. J., 383, 389, *397*
Perkins, C. C. Jr., 293, *298*
Peterson, J., 29, *38*
Peterson, J. J., 533, 538, 543, *551*
Phillis, J. W., 456, *459*
Pliskoff, S. S., 43, *70*
Poletti, C. E., 516, *527*
Pollack, I., 448, *460*
Pond, F. J., 519, 523, 524, *526*, *527*
Popp, R. J., Jr., 263, *270*
Porter, R. W., 516, *528*
Powell, E. W., 462, *494*
Powers, A. S., 154, *174*
Premack, D., 29, *38*, 110, *118*
Pressman, Y. M., 392, *397*

Pribram, K. H., 449, *460*, 518, 521, *525*, *527*, 531, 532, 536, 537, 539, 540, *551*, *552*
Prokasy, W. F., 291, *298*
Pumain, R., 456, *459*

R

Rabinovich, M. J., 382, 393, 395, *397*
Rachlin, H., 492, *495*
Rachlin, H. C., 42, 68, *69*
Raphelson, A. C., 462, 482, *495*, 536, *552*
Rashotte, M. E., 277, 279, 280, 282, 285, *297*, *298*
Rasmussen, E. W., 470, *494*
Razran, G. H., 207, *226*
Reid, L. S., 183, *204*
Reiss, S., 28, *38*, 326, 327, 329, *335*
Renaud, L., 456, *459*
Renshaw, B., 361, *380*, 404, *429*
Rescorla, R. A., 6, 7, 10, 11, 12, 13, 14, 15, 16, 17, 19, 20, 21, 22, 23, 24, 25, 26, 27, 28, 30, 34, 35, 36, *38*, 41, 65, *70*, 73, 74, *96*, *97*, 100, 101, 103, 104, *118*, 200, 224, 225, *226*, 230, 245, 248, *250*, 253, 254, 255, 256, 257, 268, 269, *270*, 273, 291, 296, *297*, *298*, *299*, 301, 302, 304, 305, 310, 313, 314, 315, 316, 318, 320, 324, 326, 328, 329, 331, 332, 333, *335*, 355, 360, 370, *380*, 532
Revusky, S. H., 236, *249*
Reynolds, G. S., 75, 94, *96*, *97*, 110, 113, *118*, 198, *204*, 236, 244, *250*, 466, *495*
Reynolds, M. D., 236, *249*
Rhines, R., 405, *429*
Ricci, G. F., 395, *396*
Richardson, J., 6, *38*
Richelle, M., 230, 233, 235, *250*
Rilling, G. M., 230, 232, *249*
Rilling, M., 62, 64, 66, *70*, 236, *249*, 483, *494*
Rilling, M. E., 474, *495*
Roberts, W. W., 369, *379*, 425, *429*, 547, *552*
Rodnick, E. H., 21, *39*
Roig, J. A., 317, *335*
Roitbak, A. I., 383, *397*
Ross, G. S., 236, *249*
Ross, L. E., 291, *299*

Ross, R. R., *298*
Roussel, J., 483, *493*
Rowland, V., 362, *379*
Rudenko, L. P., 384, 385, 386, 391, 392, *397*
Russell, R. W., 432, 439, 441, 452, *458*, *460*, 542, *552*

S

Schade, A. F., 156, *175*
Saavedra, M., 306, 325, *335*
Schaeffer, B., 303, *336*
Schaub, R. E., 213, *226*
Schlag, J., 230, *250*
Schlosberg, H., 292, *299*
Schmalz, L., 534, *552*
Schmalz, L. W., 501, 504, 506, 517, *527*
Schmeck, R. R., 482, *493*
Schmidt, R. P., 500, *527*
Schneirla, T. C., 406, 407, *429*
Schoel, W. M., 163, *176*
Schoenfeld, W. N., 236, *249*
Schulman, A. I., 443, *458*
Schusterman, R. J., 154, 155, *175*
Schwartzbaum, J. S., 462, 470, 482, *494*, *495*, 518, 519, 523, 524, *526*, *527*
Scoville, W. B., 499, 500, *528*
Scull, J., 198, 199, *204*
Sechenov, I. M., 361, *380*
Segundo, J. P., 317, *335*, 548, *550*
Selekman, W., 116, *118*
Seligman, M. E. P., 13, *39*
Senf, G. M., 183, *204*
Seraganian, D., 15
Seraganian, P., 54, 57, 59, 60, 67, *70*
Setterington, R. G., 156, *175*
Sevillano, M., 523, *525*
Sharpless, S., 539, *552*
Sheffield, P. D., 427, *428*
Sheffield, V. F., 482, *495*
Sherrington, C. S., 341, 342, *357*, 392, 394, *397*, 403, 407, *429*
Shettleworth, S. J., 198, *204*
Shute, C. C. D., 449, 453, *460*, 542, *553*
Sidman, M., 236, *249*, 267, 269, *270*
Siegel, A., 378, *380*, 523, *528*
Siegal, L., 236, *250*
Siegel, L. S., 292, *299*
Siegel, R. K., 55, *70*

Siegel, S., 34, *39*, 125, 131, *151*, 317, 321, 326, *335*, *336*
Silberberg, A., 138, *151*
Silver, A. I., 482, *493*
Simonov, P. V., 382, *397*
Singh, D., 207, 212, *226*, 231, *250*
Skinner, B. F., 16, 17, 19, 23, 24, 25, 34 36, *39*, 74, *97*, 99, 103, 104, *118*, *119*, 182, 198, *204*, 207, 216, 225, *226*, 257, *270*, 276, *299*
Skipin, G. V., 392, *397*
Skog, D., 378, *380*
Skucy, J. C., 74, *97*
Slotnick, B. M., 519, 520, 522, 523, *527*
Smith, S. G., 20, *39*
Snapper, A. S., 236, *249*
Snyder, D. R., 534, *553*
Sodetz, K. J., 472, *495*
Sokolov, E. N., 382, 390, *397*
Sokolov, Ye. N., 539, *553*
Sollenberger, R. T., 533, *550*
Solomon, R. L., 21, 22, 23, 24, *38*, 253, 255, 257, *270*, 291, *299*
Sommer-Smith, J. A., 317, *335*
Spehlmann, R., 456, *460*
Spence, K. W., 99, *118*, 121, *151*, 184, *204*, 277, 292, 294, *299*, 302, 321, *335*, 462, 472, *495*
Spencer, W. A., 382, *396*
Sperling, S. E., 192, 193, *203*
Spieth, T. M., 462, 482, *495*
Squier, L. H., 156, *176*
Squire, L. R., *553*
Staddon, J. E. R., 198, *204*, 230, 236, 237, *250*, 483, *495*
Starr, R., 263, *270*
Starzl, T. E., 449, *460*
Stein, D. G., *552*
Stein, N., 23, *39*
Sterman, M. B., 405, *429*
Sternberg, S. H., 435, *458*
Stevens, J. R., 523, *527*
Stinus, J., 453, *459*
Stitt, C., 23, *39*
Stone, G., 432, *460*
Stoupel, N., 455, *458*
Stretch, R. G. A., 155, *175*
Struchkov, M. I., 384, 385, *397*
Stuart, D. G., 516, *528*
Stubbs, A., 244, *250*

Stümpf, C., 453, *460*
Stumpf, Ch., 542, *553*
Suits, E., 535, 541, *553*
Surridge, C. T., 279, 286, *298*
Sutherland, N. S., 68, *70*, 127, *151*, 155, *176*, 289, *299*, 303, 329, *336*
Sutier, R. D., 316, *336*
Swanson, A. M., 122, *151*
Swets, J. A., 447, *458*
Switzer, S. A., 207, *226*
Szabo, I., 407, 408, 410, 413, 414, 415, 416, 418, 419, *429*
Szwejkowska, G., 309, 318, 319, 331, 333, *334*, *336*, 343, 344, 345, 346, 347, *357*, 370, *380*
Szerb, J. C., 455, *459*

T

Taylor, C. W., 449, *460*
Terrace, H. S., 12, 16, 20, 24, 30, 31, 32, *39*, 41, 62, 64, 66, *70*, 75, 76, 86, 93, 94, *97*, 103, 104, 105, 107, 108, 109, 110, 113, 114, *118*, 137, 145, *151*, 182, 198, 199, 202, 203, 204, 230, *250*, 294, *299*, 355, 360, 370, 383, 474, 492, 531
Thatcher, R. W., 541, *553*
Theios, J., 279, 281, *299*
Thomas, D. R., 50, *70*
Thomas, E., 292, 293, *299*, 321, *336*, 363, *380*, 491
Thomas, G. J., 481, 490, *495*
Thompson, C. I., 483, *494*
Thompson, J. B., 462, 482, *495*
Thompson, T., 482, *495*
Thorndike, E. L., 294, *299*
Thorpe, W. H., 382, *397*
Tolman, E. C., 293, 294, *299*
Toyohara, I., 395, *396*
Trabasso, T., 6, *39*, 303, *336*
Trapold, M. A., 23, *39*
Traupmann, K. L., 286, 287, 289, 290, 297, *299*
Treisman, A., 449, *460*
Trenholme, Irene A., 268, *269*

U

Ulrich, R. E., 236, *249*
Ursin, H., 515, *528*, 548, *553*
Ushakova, A. M., 384, *396*

V

Valenstein, E. S., 407, 425, *428*, *429*, *430*, *459*, 513, *528*
Vanderver, V., 124, *151*, 154, *175*
Vanderwolf, C. H., 538, *553*
Vangegas, H., 523, *528*, 547, 548, *551*
Van Hoesen, G. W., 470, 471, 472, 481, *494*, *495*
Vereczkey, L., 523, *526*
Verga, M. E., 392, *397*
Verhave, T., 267, *270*
Vogel, J. R., 326, *334*
Voskrensensky, L. N., 383, *397*

W

Wagner, A. R., 10, 15, 26, 28, *38*, 73, 94, 97, 200, 268, 273, 292, 293, *299*, 301, 302, 303, 304, 305, 306, 308, 311, 312, 313, 314, 315, 316, 318, 321, 324, 325, 326, 327, 329, 330, 331, *334*, *335*, *336*, 355, 363, *380*, 483, *495*, 532
Walker, A. E., 501, *528*
Walker, D. W., 537, *552*
Warburton, D. M., 401, 432, 434, 438, 439, 441, 442, 443, 444, 448, 452, *458*, *460*, 541, 542, 543
Ward, A. A., Jr., 501, *528*
Ward, J. S., 199, *203*, 277, *295*, 491, *493*
Warren, J. M., 156, *176*, 361, *380*
Watson, R. H. J., 432, 439, *460*
Webb, W. B., 207, 212, *226*, 231, *249*
Weimer, J., 183, 187, 200, *204*
Weisman, R. G., 12, *39*, 44, *70*, 75, 76, 86, 92, 93, *97*, 114, *118*, 179, 254, 255, 258, 260, 264, 265, 267, 269, *270*, 317, 319, 332, *336*
Weiss, B., 236, *249*, *250*, 442, *459*
Wendt, G. R., 24, *39*
Wenger, M. A., 207, *226*
Wesemann, A. F., 261, *270*
West, J. R., 74, *96*
Westbrook, F., 95, *97*

Whitehouse, J. M., 439, *460*, 542, *553*
Wickelgren, W. O., 534, 353, *551*, *553*
Wickens, C. D., 372, *380*
Wickens, D. D., 207, 212, *226*, 231, *249*, *250*, 372, *380*
Wickson, Susan, 207, 211, 212, *226*
Wilder, B. J., 500, 501, *528*
Wilkie, D. M., 104, *118*
Williams, D. R., 182, *203*
Wilson, A. S., 462, *494*
Wilson, M. P., 237, *250*
Wilson, W. A., 155, *176*, 518, *527*
Wilton, R. N., 8, 16, *39*, 198, *204*
Winick, M., 544, *551*
Winnick, W. A., 207, *226*
Winocur, G., 482, *496*
Winton, A. S. W., 44, 46, 47, 48, 49, 50, 51, *69*, *71*, 123, 125, 137, 138, 145, 150
Wodinsky, J., 154, 156, 170, *174*, *176*
Wolach, A. H., 212, *227*
Wolfe, J. B., 289, *299*
Wolfe, J. W., 482, *496*
Wong, P. T. P., 286, 287, 289, 290, *297*, *299*
Woodbury, C. B., 306, *336*
Woodward, W. T., 163, *176*
Wright, E. W., Jr., 546, *552*
Wyckoff, L. B., 155, *176*
Wyrwicka, W., 542, *553*

Y

Yamaguchi, H. I., 207, *227*
Yoshii, N., 395, *396*

Z

Zbrozyna, A. W., 317, *336*
Zeaman, D., 155, *176*
Zeiler, M. D., 74, *97*
Zentall, T., 31, 33, *39*
Zuckerman, E., 454, *460*

Subject Index

A

Advance procedure, 3, 41–69, 467
Active inhibition, 3, 19, 66, 111–117, 137
Amygdala, 515, 545, 548–549
  lesions, 517–518, 539, 541
  stimulation, 519–520
Ascending reticular pathways, 449–456, 545, 547–548
Attention, 14, 17, 25–26, 540
  as mechanism of internal inhibition, 431–456
  theories of compound stimuli, 303–304
  transfer in serial reversal, 155–156
Autonomic conditioning, 295, 371–375
  (*see also* Salivary conditioning)
Aversive properties of S⁻ (*see* Escape from S⁻)
Avoidance, 194–197, 253–269, 470–472, 501–508, 534–535
  hippocampal activity in, 501–508, 516, 522–523
  hippocampal lesions, 534–535
  as positive reinforcement learning, 267–269
  septal lesions, 470–472, 490

B

Backward conditioning, 10, 317
Behavioural contrast, 3, 16, 73–95, 110, 113–117, 139–150, 182–184, 296 355, 466
  relation to positive induction, 182–184, 198–199
  simultaneous discrimination, 139–150
Blocking, 68, 304, 309
By-products of discrimination learning, 3, 15, 66–67, 99–116, 232, 296

(*see also* Behavioural contrast; Escape from S⁻; Inhibitory generalization; Peak shift)

C

Choice, 15, 86–92, 167–172
  (*see also* Simultaneous discrimination)
Cholinergic effects, 401, 431–456, 541–544
Combined cue test, 14, 18, 34
  (*see also* Summation test)
Complex maze, 462, 531, 533
Compound stimuli, 301–333
Conceptual discrimination, 54–58
Concurrent schedules, 42–43, 86–92, 138–139
Conditional discrimination, 306, 384–387
Conditioned emotional response (CER)
  (*see* Conditioned suppression)
Conditioned excitation, 7, 13
Conditioned inhibition, 382–387
  definition, 6–11, 99–101
  discriminative conditioning, 311, 318–319, 536–537
  and inhibitory generalization, 17
  measurement, 11–17
  produced by negative correlation, 315–317
  produced by reinforcement, 321–325
  reinforcement specificity, 21–22, 347–348, 383–385
  response specificity, 21–25
Conditioned suppression, 11, 23, 211, 255, 291, 316, 322–326, 328–329, 490, 519

D

Disinhibition, 16, 94, 161, 180, 197, 205–224, 230–231, 243, 342–343, 360, 362, 426, 530

DRH schedules, 257
DRL schedules, 10, 75–76, 86, 92, 94, 180, 212, 215, 229–248, 257, 282, 471, 472, 481, 483, 517, 534
Drug effects, 16, 521
    (*see also* Cholinergic effects; Penicillin)

E

Epilepsy, 500–509
Errorless discrimination, 20, 30–31, 67, 93, 104–111, 137–138, 344–346, 355, 360, 370–371
Escape,
    from frustration, 473
    from S⁻, 15, 42, 62, 66, 110–111, 474–481
    from shock, 491
    (*see also* Advance procedure)
Experimental neurosis, 242, 346, 538
External inhibition, 8, 12, 103, 216–218, 342, 535–536
Extinction, 73
    below zero, 296, 330–331
    compound stimuli, 311–312
    following partial reinforcement, 275–290
    following simultaneous discrimination, 126–139
    hippocampal lesions, 531
    in isolation, 126–139, 330–331
    of inhibition, 331–333
    positive induction effects, 181–202
    reciprocal effects, 347–351
    septal lesions, 462
    (*see also* Multiple schedules)
Eye-blink conditioning, 291, 311–314, 326–327, 384–387, 390–391

F

Fear, 180, 253–269, 291, 296, 315–317, 320–325, 367–369, 419, 548
Fixed-interval (FI) schedules, 74, 92, 180, 229–237, 483–489
Fixed-ratio (FR) schedules, 158, 287–288, 433, 475, 483–489
Free reinforcement, 10, 66, 73–95, 104, 355–356

Frustration, 16, 112–115, 155, 273, 275–297, 401, 423, 472–474
    anticipation, 277–278
    conditioned responses to, 110, 277–286, 473
    energizing aspect, 148, 277–278, 473, 481–483
    partial reinforcement, 275–290, 474
    unconditioned responses to, 199, 277–278, 472–473

G

Generalization (*see* Inhibitory generalization; Positive generalization)
General inhibition, 23, 237–248, 361, 377–378

H

Hippocampus, 401–402, 449, 471, 545
    avoidance, 501–508
    cholinergic effects, 452–454
    electrical activity, 408–424, 473–474, 523–524
    lesions, 438, 462, 516–517, 530–543
    memory, 498–500
    relation to hypothalamus, 512–514
    stimulation, 522–523
Hypothalamus, 407, 449, 491, 515, 545
    relation to hippocampus, 512–515
    stimulation, 363–379, 408–422

I

Induction (*see* Negative induction; Positive induction)
Inhibition,
    attentional effects, 17, 25–30, 326–330, 431–456
    as counter-conditioning, 21–22, 66–67, 275–297
    as reduced excitation, 16–21, 276
    as antagonistic response, 94, 106–108, 111–112, 200–202, 352–353, 383, 403–428
    in simultaneous discrimination, 121–150
    relation to physiological usage, 9, 275–276, 359–363, 403–406